D0245701

From Fragmentation to Financial Integration in Europe

EDITORS

Charles Enoch, Luc Everaert,
Thierry Tressel, and Jianping Zhou

INTERNATIONAL MONETARY FUND

© 2014 International Monetary Fund

Cover design: IMF Multimedia Services Division

Cataloging-in-Publication Data
Joint Bank-Fund Library

From Fragmentation to Financial Integration in Europe. – Washington, D.C. : International Monetary Fund, ©2014.
      p. ; cm.

   Includes bibliographical references and index.
   ISBN 978-1-48438-766-5

1. Finance – European Union countries. 2. Financial crises – European Union countries. I. International Monetary Fund.

HG186.A2 E97 2013

Disclaimer: The views expressed in this book are those of the authors and should not be reported as or attributed to the International Monetary Fund, its Executive Board, or the governments of any of its member countries.

Please send orders to:
International Monetary Fund, Publication Services
P.O. Box 92780, Washington, DC 20090, U.S.A.
Tel.: (202) 623-7430   Fax: (202) 623-7201
E-mail: publications@imf.org
Internet: www.imfbookstore.org
www.elibrary.imf.org

Contents

Foreword

Since the global financial crisis first erupted in 2008, the IMF has been intensively involved with member countries, as well as in regional and multilateral fora, seeking to address the crisis and restore financial stability. Much of this has necessarily been "fire-fighting"—taking emergency action to contain the crisis. At the same time, we have also had an eye to the future, working with our members and partners to improve the architecture of the international financial system—one that is better able to avoid crises and to handle crises when they occur.

The global financial crisis did not originate in Europe, but it quickly spread there and has lingered there, exposing the fragilities and gaps in Europe's financial stability armor. In nearly all countries, the infrastructure for handling a financial crisis was inadequate or nonexistent, and the regional dimension in Europe has complicated crisis management even more.

During this period, much has been achieved in Europe, using both conventional and novel approaches. The European Commission (EC) and the European Central Bank (ECB)—working with the IMF—have contained the crisis in a number of countries. The ECB's innovative interventions have significantly reduced the "tail risks" from the financial system. Meanwhile, important steps have been taken to create a new financial sector management infrastructure, initially at a national level, but increasingly at the level of the 27-member European Union (EU), and particularly among the 17 members that currently make up the euro area.

Much, however, remains to be done. The vision of where the European partners wish to go is becoming increasingly clear, but the path taking us there is narrow, and in some parts not well defined. It is also not a path on which one wishes to linger. The sooner it takes to get to the destination, the sooner the financial system in Europe—and globally—will be safe.

This book draws together recent work that the IMF has been undertaking to map out the path to safety. For over a decade, the IMF has conducted exercises at the national level, under its Financial Sector Assessment Program (FSAP), assessing vulnerabilities in a country's financial system and providing recommendations on how to address them. For the first time in late 2012, we conducted such an analysis for the EU as a whole, recognizing the region-wide dimension of financial stability in Europe.

Given the ongoing crisis in the EU, this regional FSAP was particularly forward-looking, focusing substantially, although not exclusively, on the institutional infrastructure in the EU and, within it, the euro area. It thus provided an opportunity for the IMF to bring into the spotlight the importance of the ongoing architecture reforms in resolving this crisis.

This book covers the major themes that emerged from that exercise, adds significant related work, and looks forward to the challenges ahead. I hope it will make a useful contribution to the current discussions on these issues in Europe and to the future shape of Europe's financial architecture.

Christine Lagarde
Managing Director
International Monetary Fund

Foreword

The IMF has been conducting Financial Sector Assessment Programs (FSAPs) for our member states since 1999, and all the member states of the European Union (EU) have had this assessment at least once. It became clear, however, in the course of the more recent national FSAPs that the answers to the problems identified at the national level would in many cases require a supranational answer at the European level. EU member states have become highly interconnected, and in many areas are now covered by a common set of laws and regulations determined at the Union level—or for those countries using the euro, at the level of the common currency. Hence, any assessment at a national level needed to be complemented by one covering the EU, and the common institutions of the EU and the euro area, as a whole. This would serve also to complement the regional surveillance that the IMF has conducted for the euro area through its Article IV consultations over the past several years.

The first EU assessment took place against a background of uncertainty and fragility, with the crisis still not resolved in parts of the Union. Banks, in general, are stronger than at the outset of the crisis, and the EU institutional framework has evolved significantly, but some key underlying challenges remain. There remain pockets of bank weakness, and questions in areas where the financial situation remains opaque, while the effectiveness of transmission of monetary policy in the euro area has been impaired. Officials have been laboring over many years, but in some regards the work seems to have only just begun. The inherent but natural tensions in a union of sovereign states, as to the boundary between what is done at the center and what is done in the separate states, continue to complicate decision making.

As the crisis has continued, there have been several examples of difficulties in cross-border coordination and cooperation in the resolution of distressed international banks. Failing banks had to be resolved at a national level, often at cost to taxpayers of the country where the bank is headquartered. Lacking binding ex ante burden-sharing agreements, cross-country supervisory colleges did not alter the fact that supervisors were accountable to national authorities. As a result there has been a substantial reversal from the progressive integration of financial sectors in the EU member states that had been set in train by the EU's single market policy, and the "common passport" arrangement under which a bank license issued in one member state would be recognized in all other member states. As member states have sought to protect themselves, and in particular their taxpayers, from the financial cost of problems arising from cross-border activities, policies of "ring-fencing" were introduced across parts of the EU (as well as elsewhere in the world). This added to the market fragmentation forces unleashed by the crisis and contributed toward reversing many years of progress toward integrated financial markets in Europe and undermining the effectiveness of monetary policy for the currency union. A key concern of policymakers is to reverse this fragmentation.

In this regard, two fundamental changes in paradigm are underway. First, recognizing that EU's problems need, in many regards, to be resolved at a European level, regional institutions are being established and strengthened; a common regulatory framework is in the process of being put in place through an ambitious program of EU directives, regulations, and guidelines; and limited regional financial backstops are being established. Second, measures are being introduced to limit the need for public backstops, whether at a national or regional level, through strengthening banks' capital and liquidity positions, and increasing internal and sectoral sources of finance—the aim being to "bail-in" bank creditors rather than to "bail-out" the bank with taxpayers' money. Achieving both these changes in paradigm is challenging, especially in the midst of an ongoing crisis. Nevertheless, given the fundamental nature of these changes in paradigm, the progress made over the past few years, especially as regards establishing relevant new institutions, has been striking.

This book seeks to take this process further. An FSAP is a comprehensive look at a financial system, and the chapters in this book—reflecting that—cover a great deal of ground. The first chapter provides an overview of the issues central to securing a safer financial system for the EU. Part I of the book looks at issues relating to the crisis, both at the macro level—the pendulum of financial integration and fragmentation—and at a micro level—the institutional reforms that are taking place to address the crisis. Part II covers issues relating to the emerging financial sector management infrastructure, associated with both the prospective Single Supervisory Mechanism (SSM) and other elements of the banking union for the euro area, and the regulatory program under the auspices of the European Commission for the EU as a whole. Part III looks forward at some of the broader challenges.

I would like to extend my thanks to all those responsible for the creation of this book, the members of the FSAP team, others in the Monetary and Capital Markets Department, as well as colleagues in the European, Legal, and Research Departments of the IMF who provided comments and support, and all the counterparts in Brussels, Frankfurt, London, Luxembourg, and Paris who met with the team and offered their perspectives and insights. I hope that this volume provides a valuable resource for policymakers, academics, and private sector participants as we move forward in exiting from crisis and enter a new stage of European financial development.

José Viñals
Financial Counsellor and Director
Monetary and Capital Markets Department
International Monetary Fund

Acknowledgments

This work derives in large part from the Financial Sector Assessment Program (FSAP) exercise for the European Union that was conducted by the IMF in December 2012. The team for the FSAP comprised Charles Enoch (Chief), Luc Everaert (Deputy Chief), Myrvin Anthony, Ana Carvajal, Heiko Hesse, Nadege Jassaud, Elias Kazarian, Fabiana Melo, Rodolfo Wehrhahn, Froukelien Wendt, and Jianping Zhou (all from the Monetary and Capital Markets Department), Scott Roger (Office in Europe), Thierry Tressel (European Department), Alessandro Gullo and Barend Jansen (Legal Department), Luc Laeven (Research Department), and Daniel Hardy (expert). Contributions were also provided to the team by Jorge Chan-Lau and Dale Gray. Research assistance was provided by Gabriel Presciutti. On the banking union, the volume draws heavily on the staff notes on "A Banking Union for the Euro Area" (IMF Staff Discussion Notes No. 13/01). The staff worked under the guidance of José Viñals (Financial Counselor and Director of the Monetary and Capital Markets Department). Extensive collaboration was provided by other staff at IMF headquarters, including Giovanni Dell'Ariccia, Rishi Goyal, Matthew Jones, Petra Koeva Brooks, Martin Muhleisen Ceyla Pazarbasioglu, Mahmood Pradhan, Ratna Sahay, and Christopher Towe.

The team also extends its appreciation to Thomas Wieser, Head of the Economic and Financial Committee (EFC) of the European Union, as well as members of the EFC, and to many officials of the European Commission, European Central Bank, European Supervisory Authorities, European Stability Mechanism, and European Systemic Risk Board for their extensive discussions with the FSAP team. The team met also with academics, think tanks, and representatives of the private sector. The team is grateful also to Robert Specterman for successful organization of the complicated logistics of this exercise.

Excellent assistance was provided by Jacky Aluvi and Amelia de Lucio Ramos in producing this volume. Finally, we would like to acknowledge the support received from Joanne Johnson in the IMF's Communication Department, who coordinated the editing and production of this volume.

CHAPTER 1

Securing a Safer Financial System for Europe[1]

Charles Enoch, Luc Everaert, Thierry Tressel, and Jianping Zhou

The global financial crisis hit the European Union (EU) at a time when EU financial markets had moved a considerable way toward integration, and a European architecture to safeguard stability was being designed and was just beginning to be built. Since the start of the global financial crisis, it has become increasingly clear that resolution of the crisis, as well as maintaining stability thereafter, will depend upon the development and functioning of this architecture, and decisions made within this architecture, as well as those at a national level. Two somewhat contradictory forces are strengthening as the crisis continues: intensified progress toward a European framework, with new institutions established and old institutions given new powers; and retrenchment from integration as banks reassess risks in cross-border activities and de-lever from them, while governments and national supervisors—mindful of obligations to national taxpayers—seek ring-fencing and other constraints on cross-border activities to protect themselves from the costs that many of them have already incurred or will incur one way or another from the inability to handle cross-border considerations effectively. It is the restoration of confidence in financial stability in the EU—or, for a number of purposes, the euro area—as a whole, that will serve to mitigate and ultimately reverse this latter trend. Also, it is the emerging European architecture and its track record of operations as it comes into play that will be critical for establishing this confidence.

This volume derives from a study undertaken by IMF staff in late 2012 looking at EU institutions and the issues that they will need to address in this environment; it also draws upon analysis of comparable exercises at a national level. The next section summarizes the volume and elucidates what the various chapters will cover. The remaining sections of this chapter provide the overview and the key findings of the study.

---

[1] This chapter derives heavily from the Financial Sector Stability Assessment of the December 2012 EU Financial Sector Assessment Program (FSAP) and reflects also contributions from the rest of the FSAP team.

SUMMARY AND OVERVIEW

From Integration to Crisis Management

Before the global financial crisis, Europe had made considerable progress in integrating its financial system, although the institutions supporting integration and stability remained mostly at the national level. The Treaty of Rome in 1957 put Europe on a steady course toward a single market. It proved much easier to integrate goods markets than markets in services, including financial services, but the Single European Act (1986) provided momentum for also a single financial market, characterized by free flows of capital and free provision of financial services across borders. Integration was facilitated by far-reaching political measures in the EU to reduce regulatory obstacles to cross-border activity, promoting a single market in financial services, and more specifically by the creation of the euro in 1999 following the 1992 Maastricht Treaty (see Chapter 2). The creation of the euro and expectations of convergence resulted in a surge in capital inflows to the emerging economies of Europe and to the periphery of the euro area. Large banks and insurance companies from western Europe established strong local presence in the newly opened emerging economies of Europe.

The process of financial market integration came to a halt, and indeed began to be reversed, after the 2008 global financial crisis. Prior to the crisis, integration was strong, albeit uneven, across countries and markets, and macro-financial risks were not fully foreseen (Chapter 3). Integration in the euro area had gone farthest in wholesale funding markets and bond markets while retail lending markets remained mostly national. Large EU banks had maintained strong expansion abroad and had broadened the scope of their activities, becoming larger, more systemic, and complex to resolve. When the crisis hit, fragmentation forces first affected emerging Europe as some banks from western Europe reduced or withdrew their presence, weakened by losses on legacy assets and facing funding pressures aimed at curtailing liquidity lines to subsidiaries, and in some cases encouraged by their home country supervisors. The so-called Vienna initiative brought together the major banks with supervisors and policy makers from both "home" and "host" countries, and helped stabilize the foreign capital invested in emerging Europe, although, it did not resolve underlying problems. The reassessment of risks by banks and their supervisors, and the lack of an effective cross-border resolution mechanism, led to a resumed reduction of cross-border exposures. Within the euro area, similar and even stronger reversals have contributed to fragment the financial system and disrupt the transmission channels of monetary policy. The collapse of cross-border exposures was particularly severe in the wholesale funding market and sovereign bond markets; the amplification of the resultant adverse sovereign-bank links caused the most visible and extreme problems in the periphery of the euro area.

Restoring financial stability in the EU has been a major challenge. The initial policy response to the crisis in the EU was handicapped by the absence of robust national and EU-wide crisis management frameworks. Moreover, the initial conditions and the macroeconomic background have made resolving the crisis particularly difficult. In the low-growth environment, several EU countries are still struggling to regain competitiveness, fiscal sustainability, and sound private sector balance sheets. Their financial systems are facing funding pressures as a result of excessive leverage, risky business models, and an adverse feedback loop with sovereigns and the real economy (Chapters 4 and 8).

Much has been done to address these challenges. Banks have boosted their capital adequacy ratios, although partly through deleveraging. Unconventional monetary operations have enhanced liquidity and firewalls have been put in place (Chapter 5). New tools for addressing financial stability, including coordinated stress tests, have come into play. The newly established European Supervisory Authorities (ESAs) are making their marks. More specifically, the European authorities are strengthening bank stress testing procedures and their application (Chapter 6). Following the poor reception of the 2010 exercise, the 2011 solvency stress testing and recapitalization exercises were marked by extensive consistency checks, higher hurdle rates, and more transparency about methodology and data, for example, regarding sovereign exposures. The exercises succeeded in prompting banks to increase the quantity and quality of their capitalization, and they contributed to a reduction in uncertainty and an increase in the credibility of the process. Progress has been made with bank resolution and restructuring, especially in the context of EU rules on national government support to distressed banks, whereas 10 to 15 percent of the EU banking system is now under the State Aid framework and undergoing some forced restructuring (Chapter 7). Perhaps most significantly, market confidence was enhanced with the agreement that was reached in December 2012 to establish a Single Supervisory Mechanism (SSM) for the euro area, but open also to non-euro area members.

Underpinning Financial Stability

Nevertheless, financial stability has not been assured. Despite banks raising more than €200 billion as a result of the European Banking Authority (EBA) recapitalization exercise, confidence in European banks is not fully restored, as market concerns remain about the quality of bank assets. Recent IMF Financial Sector Assessment Program (FSAP) assessments of individual EU member states have noted remaining vulnerabilities to stresses and dislocations in wholesale funding markets; a loss of market confidence in sovereign debt; further downward movements in asset prices; and downward shocks to growth. These vulnerabilities are exacerbated by the high degree of concentration in the banking sector, regulatory and policy uncertainty, and the major gaps in the policy framework that still need to be filled.

A key priority, EU-wide, is to complete the framework for financial oversight needed to sustain a currency union and the single market for financial services. The crisis has shown that national decisions, even well-intended ones, have Union-wide repercussions on financial stability, and that there is a need for single frameworks for crisis management, deposit insurance, supervision, and resolution, with a common backstop for the banking system, especially for the monetary union. Recent measures taken by national authorities and central banks, together with a euro-area-wide backstop for sovereigns, have mitigated downside risks. Although progress has been made, the lack of a full embrace of a Union-wide approach to financial stability leaves the system vulnerable to shocks and generates incentives for national ring-fencing and fragmentation.

In the near term, more forceful action is warranted to cement recent gains in market confidence and end the crisis. The priorities are repairing bank balance sheets, including addressing impaired assets; fast and sustained progress toward the SSM and the banking union; and essential steps toward a stronger EU financial oversight framework. Governance arrangements need to be adapted to have an EU- (or banking union)-wide perspective and also evolve to meet the diverse needs of members of the euro area, SSM members not part of the euro area, and other members of the EU (Chapter 9). The effectiveness of the banking union will also hinge critically on strong legal underpinnings (Chapter 10).

It will be critical that the SSM delivers high-quality supervision as soon as it becomes effective (Chapter 11). Operational risk regarding the SSM needs to be guarded against by ensuring that the European Central Bank (ECB) builds supervisory expertise of the highest quality and has at its disposal resources commensurate to its supervisory tasks. The ECB's effectiveness as a supervisor needs to be safeguarded by giving it powers to maintain general oversight over all banks and to intervene when necessary in any bank, and ensuring information-sharing and cooperation within the SSM. The ECB's governance and its "will to act" need to be robust, including through ensuring that the SSM avoids "nationality dominance" and that a regional perspective is consistently maintained.

The SSM—while critically important—represents only one of a number of crucial steps that need to be taken to fill key gaps in the EU's financial oversight framework. The Single Resolution Mechanism (SRM) should become operational at around the same time as the SSM becomes effective (Chapter 12). This should be accompanied by agreement on a time-bound roadmap to set up a single resolution agency and common deposit guarantee scheme (DGS) with common backstops (Chapter 14). Eventually providing an explicit legal underpinning for financial stability arrangements of a fully fledged banking union would further strengthen the framework. Recently agreed guidelines for the ESM to directly recapitalize banks need to be finalized as soon as possible, so that it becomes operational as soon as the SSM is effective (Chapter 13).

Proposals by the European Commission (EC) to harmonize capital requirements, resolution, deposit guarantee scheme, and insurance supervision frameworks at the EU level need to be implemented promptly. Recent European Council agreement on the Bank Resolution and Recovery Directive is welcome, as it will introduce bail-in of bank creditors and depositor preference. In addition, more effective supervision and resolution arrangements need to be worked out for financial institutions crossing the borders between the SSM and the rest of the EU and beyond.

Meanwhile, the ESAs and the European Systemic Risk Board (ESRB) need further strengthening. Governance arrangements need to be adapted to avoid potential national biases (Chapter 15). The European Banking Authority (EBA) can play an important role in ensuring a level playing field between countries inside and outside the SSM (Chapter 16). It should be more assertive in cross-border colleges of supervisors and crisis management groups. Importantly, it should ensure that national authorities are undertaking careful and consistent analysis of the underlying quality of bank assets, to ensure the credibility of its stress tests (Chapter 17). The European Securities and Markets Authority (ESMA) has performed well during its first two years of operation, especially in connection with the single rulebook and credit rating agency (CRA) supervision. Going forward, it would need to step up its role in other areas, in particular on supervisory convergence (Chapter 18). Significant issues in insurance also require attention. Importantly, a weak economic environment, if it persists, can threaten the financial health of the life insurance and the pensions industries as they have already been adversely affected by exposures to banks and sovereigns, and they will need to cope with stricter Solvency II requirements (Chapter 19). The European supervisor on insurance and pension funds (EIOPA) has had intensive engagement in its oversight role of supervisory colleges, but much work remains to be done.

The ESRB, as the EU systemic risk watchdog, should play a more important role, and modalities for interaction with the SSM needs to be devised (Chapter 20). It usefully set out in its recommendations the macroprudential policy mandate, institutional arrangements, and more recently, a proposed macroprudential toolkit for EU member states. It needs also to analyze macroprudential effects on the cyclical downside and not just the upside, and ensure consistent application of macroprudential policies across the various parts of the financial sector and across the EU. The ECB's macroprudential tools should go beyond those identified in the EU's fourth capital requirements directive (CRD IV). For all these agencies, their heightened responsibilities would warrant increased resources.

Strong coordination across the various supranational agencies will be critical, so that decision-making can be smooth and policies consistent. Especially for crisis management, it would be desirable to establish a mechanism or a committee that brings a holistic perspective, integrating the crisis related work of the ESAs, the ESRB, the SSM, the forthcoming resolution agency, the EU Directorate-General for Competition (DG COMP), and the supranational support facilities.

Risks related to financial infrastructure seem to be manageable but care will be needed on this front too (Chapter 21). The EA's central bank payment system, TARGET2, functioned well in the crisis although it would be safer if enhanced by information-sharing with the ECB. The ECB's' capacity and competences over payments systems should be strengthened as it moves toward a risk-based oversight approach. Increasing reliance on Central Clearing Counterparties (CCPs) and Central Securities Depositories (CSDs) reduces overall risk to the financial sector; risks in the event of the failure of a CCP or CSD are substantial, however, and important work is in train to seek to address them.

Real estate boom-and-bust has seriously endangered financial stability in several European countries, for example Ireland and Spain. The experiences of these countries demonstrated that mortgage laws and practices could lead to different outcomes in terms of mortgage default and foreclosures, as well as influence the speed of resolving the mortgage crisis and recovering of the housing market. Delays in the foreclosure processes create room for moral hazard that lead to increases in default rates (Chapter 22).

Beyond the Crisis

Low growth or renewed recession in the EU makes emergence from the financial crisis and the construction of a framework for financial sector management much more difficult. Past financial crises have been resolved to a considerable extent by the resumption of strong growth, often external, that drove down debt ratios and enabled affected countries to emerge from austerity programs before austerity fatigue had set in too heavily. Earlier forecasts for growth in Europe are now regarded as having been overly optimistic, with some of the countries mostly affected by the crisis showing significant declines in output for several years ahead, and even the stronger economies not providing a powerful enough engine to lift the region as a whole.

The present environment makes even stronger the case for a number of the policies put forward in this volume. Most fundamentally, it reinforces the message about the need to reverse fragmentation and resume economic and financial integration. Given where we are, only a secure and credible EU financial management architecture can be expected to reverse this fragmentation and to provide for resumption in Europe's progress toward creating a genuine single market. This in turn would contribute toward stimulating growth both in the region and in the wider global economy.

The new financial architecture is being established against two basic paradigm shifts: first, that financial sector oversight in the EU can no longer be predominantly national; and second, that concern for financial sector stability will no longer be an argument justifying that the public sector (the "taxpayer") will pick up the pieces when things go wrong. But the new paradigms themselves pose challenges.

As important, the oversight architecture being put in place is designed to eliminate, or at any rate to minimize, bailout-related public sector expenditures. Several factors have driven the consensus away from using taxpayer money to resolve banking problems. The first is that most EU countries feel they have exhausted their fiscal space, and that protecting their banks would not be their greatest priority. Moral hazard is the second factor leading to a change in paradigm. Public sector support is seen as a "bail out" of the banks, which in turn implies that the private sector does not incur the costs of its own actions and may therefore not be deterred from undertaking such actions again. While the recent financial crisis was geographically and quantitatively different from previous ones, many of the largest banks played a repeat role in the crisis, having been involved earlier in other crises in other places. There is an increasing view that with bailouts lessons may not be fully learned, and that behavior leading to crisis may rapidly resume.

Proposals to "bail-in" creditors as an alternative to taxpayer bailouts have been in the center of policy debate, often with confusion. Bail-in, a statutory power to recapitalize a distressed systemically important financial institution by writing down or converting (or both) its unsecured debt while maintaining its legal entity, could be a useful additional tool to a resolution toolkit that could help restore a distressed financial institution to viability while reinforcing market discipline and minimizing counterparty risks associated with a disorderly liquidation. However, a clear and coherent legal framework for bail-in is essential. To safeguard financial stability, statutory bail-in mechanisms must be carefully designed to manage systemic risks, including counterparty risks, liquidity risks, and contagion risks (Chapter 23). More importantly, insolvent banks should be allowed to fail in an orderly fashion and with other resolution tools.

Proposals to separate banks' retail activities from those deemed more risky are no panacea. However, such separation could reduce cross-subsidization of the latter and could make resolvability easier (Chapter 24). These proposals are not substitutes for other enhancements in loss-absorption capacity, such as capital surcharges, bail-ins, ex ante deposit insurance funds, and common backstops, which should in any case be taken forward. Also, care must be taken to avoid regulatory arbitrage to the extent that EU or national proposals differ.

Taking forward the reform agenda set out in this book is urgent and critical for resolving the crisis, and it cannot wait until the economic environment has improved (Chapter 25). Indeed, as argued here, the environment may well not improve until the reform agenda is in place. Reversing the fragmentation in EU financial markets, enhancing disclosure of financial statements, and increasing transparency more generally, as well as building strong banks, are necessary and interrelated conditions to create for the best possible backdrop for taking forward the agenda to establish the new architecture for European financial oversight.

MAIN FINDINGS

The Regional Dimension for Financial Stability in Europe

The recent financial crisis has underscored the need for the EU to take a regional approach to financial stability. The regional dimension is important at two levels: first, the single currency area that binds many EU countries and second, the existence of an EU-wide single market for financial services. Together, these have left countries highly interconnected through substantial cross-border exposures and common money and capital markets.

Preserving financial stability in such an environment requires a supranational oversight framework. Its construction has been under way for more than a decade, supported by the Lamfalussy process and the follow up to the De Larosiere report, which established the ESAs and the ESRB. However, as flagged in the 2011 European Financial Stability Framework Exercise (EFFE), crisis management and resolution remains an important gap, and it was noted that the new ESAs and ESRB would face challenges to establish their credibility.

Progress has been made toward stronger pan-European approaches. A number of crisis management tools have been established beyond the national level, such as through the European Financial Stability Facility/European Stability Mechanism (EFSF/ESM). EU institutions, such as the DG COMP, have sought to incorporate financial stability considerations in their operations. Meanwhile, central banks engaged in unconventional policies to support macro-financial stability and buy time to address deep-rooted problems. IMF-supported programs were necessary to prevent deeper crises in parts of the Union. The regulatory reform agenda has accelerated and, most fundamentally, the Single Supervisory Mechanism is being established as an element toward the banking union.

The focus of this volume is on these supranational institutions. It assesses the effectiveness of the institutions and the possible contributions of the proposed institutional reforms to financial stability. It analyzes how the EU and European Economic and Monetary Union (EMU)-wide institutional setups can complement national financial stability frameworks and how financial stability risks can be further mitigated. It defers to national Financial Sector Assessment Programs for quantitative analysis to avoid duplication, but draws from them as well as from recent *Global Financial Stability Reports* (GFSRs) for its financial stability assessment, and from staff papers on the banking union for policy recommendations (Goyal and others, 2013).

SYSTEMIC RISK AND VULNERABILITIES ACROSS BORDERS

The current financial turbulence in Europe has multiple causes, with EU and EMU-wide policy frameworks playing an important role. Financial innovation, deregulation, and soft touch supervision were key factors that led to the global financial crisis. Europe was afflicted and probably hit harder than other parts of the world because of its traditional reliance on bank-based finance and high bank leverage (Figures 1.1 and 1.2).

EU and euro area institutional features and the absence of an EU-wide crisis manager amplified the crisis when it hit:

- *Single market in financial services.* The EU's objective to create a single market in financial services, including through passporting and cross-border branching, led to rapid financial integration and sharp increases in cross-border exposure (Figure 1.3).

- *National approach to supervision.* Countries continued their own supervisory approach and national financial systems varied in size and structure and relative to fiscal capacity (Figure 1.4).

- *Monetary union.* The elimination of currency risk and interest rate convergence contributed to rising cross-border lending, including to sovereigns. However, mechanisms to instill discipline through the Stability and Growth Pact and markets failed.

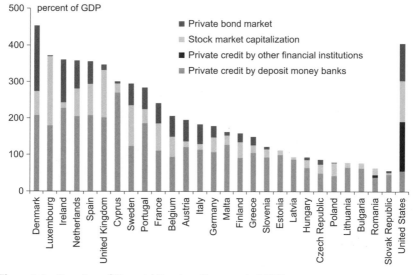

Figure 1.1 Overview of Financial Structure (in percent of GDP)

Source: World Bank Financial Structure database (2012).
Note: Data are for 2010, except private credit 2008 for Bulgaria, Czech Republic, Denmark, and Hungary.

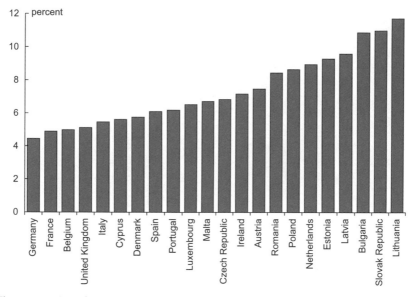

Figure 1.2 Capital-to-Asset Ratio (in percent)

Source: IMF, Financial Soundness Indicators.
Note: 2012:Q2, except for Bulgaria (2009), Spain, France (2010), Lithuania, the Slovak Republic (2012:Q1), and the United Kingdom (2011:Q4).

- *Commitment to euro adoption by the emerging market economies in the EU.*
  Financial liberalization upon joining the EU led to very large investments in western European banks, while expectations of euro adoption fostered foreign currency borrowing. Together with deep integration came credit

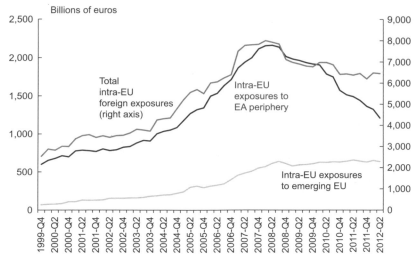

Figure 1.3   Total Intra-EU Foreign Exposure (in billions of euros)

Source: Bank for International Settlements (BIS) consolidated banking statistics, immediate risk basis.
Note: Ireland and Finland not included due to breaks in data reporting.

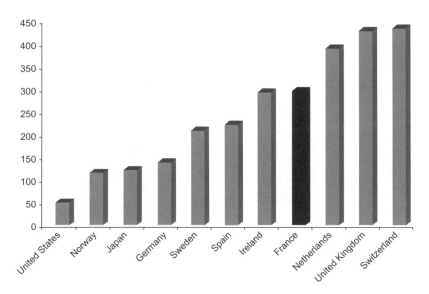

Figure 1.4   Selected Advanced Economies—Assets of Four Largest Banks/GDP (in percent)

Sources: Bloomberg, L.P.; and IMF staff calculations.

booms, especially in countries pegging their currencies to the euro (Figures 1.5 and 1.6).

EU-wide institutions, still in their infancy, lacked the power to respond to the contagion within the Union. Initial policy responses by national and EU authorities sometimes led to adverse policy spillovers (Figure 1.7). Examples include the

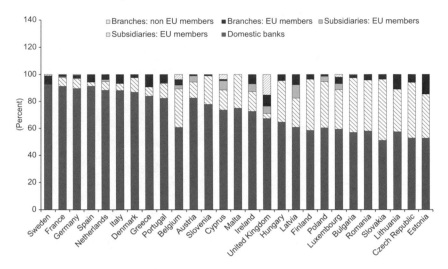

Figure 1.5 Market Shares of Foreign Banks in EU Member States (2011, in percent)

Sources: European Central Bank, Financial Structure database (2011); and Monetary Financial Institutions database.

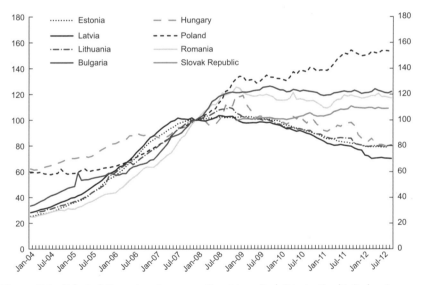

Figure 1.6 Selected Emerging European Countries—Real Private Credit (Index January 2008 = 100)

Sources: Bloomberg, L.P.; and IMF staff calculations.

guaranteeing of all liabilities of the Irish banking system and the decision to break up some troubled cross-border institutions along national lines. As a result, central banks, in particular the ECB, were forced to step in with unconventional measures, to buy time to address underlying problems (Table 1.1).

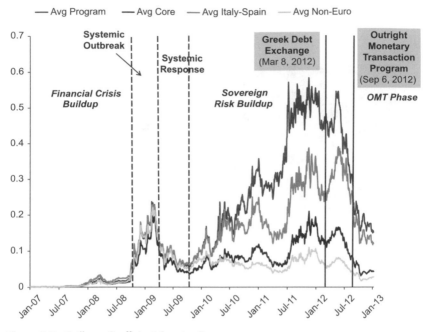

Figure 1.7 Spillover Coefficient Country Groups

Sources: Bloomberg, L.P.; and IMF staff calculations.

Chart Technical Explanation

The Spillover Coefficient (SC) is estimated in order to quantify the role that contagion plays in driving sovereign spreads. The SC characterizes the probability of distress of a country conditional on other countries becoming distressed. The SC embeds sovereigns' distress dependence, and how such dependence changes along different periods of the economic cycle, reflecting that dependence increases in periods of distress.

For each country A_i, the SC is computed using the formula: $SC(A_i) = \sum P(A_i/A_j) \cdot P(A_j)$ for all $j \neq i$, which is essentially the weighted sum of the probability of distress of country A_i given a default in each of the other countries in the sample. This measure of distress dependence is appropriately weighed by the probability of each of these events to occur.

The probability of sovereign distress in country A_i given a default by country A_j, referred to here as the probability of A_i given A_j, denoted by $P(A_i/A_j)$, is obtained in three steps: (1) the marginal probabilities of default for countries A_i and A_j, $P(A_i)$ and $P(A_j)$, respectively, are extracted from the individual credit default swap (CDS) spreads for these countries; (2) then, the joint probability of default of A_i and A_j, $P(A_i, A_j)$, is obtained using the consistent information multivariate density optimizing (CIMDO) methodology, which embeds sovereigns' distress dependence, and its changes at different points of the economic cycle.[1] (3) Finally, the conditional probability of default $P(A_i/A_j)$ is obtained by using the Bayes' law: $P(A_i/A_j) = P(A_i, A_j) / P(A_j)$.

[1]The CIMDO methodology is used to estimate the multivariate empirical distribution (CIMDO distribution) that characterizes the probabilities of distress of each of the sovereigns under analysis, their distress dependence, and how such dependence changes along the economic cycle.

The absence of a robust cross-border crisis management framework in the EU contributed to negative sovereign-banking loops and financial fragmentation. Where sovereigns ran into trouble, the banking system suffered as the value of sovereign backstops fell and funding costs rose. In countries where banking systems had to be supported, the sovereign weakened, in turn reducing the value of its banking system support. In both cases, the real economy suffered, further fueling the adverse loop (Figure 1.8). This situation led to a reversal of cross-border capital flows and a reduction of cross-border holdings, especially affecting

TABLE 1.1

ECB: Unconventional Measures 2007 To Date

Decision date	Measure
October 8, 2008	Fixed rate, full allotment tenders adopted for weekly main refinancing operations, for as long as needed.
	Reduction of the corridor between standing facilities to 100 basis points, for as long as needed.
October 15, 2008	Expansion of eligible collateral through end–2009.
	Enhance longer term refinancing operations through end–Q1:2009.
	Provision of U.S. dollar liquidity through foreign exchange swaps.
December 18, 2008	Increase of corridor between standing facilities to 200 basis points.
February 5, 2009	Fixed rate, full allotment tenders to continue for as long as needed on all main, special term, supplementary, and regular longer-term refinancing operations.
	Supplementary and special term refinancing operations to continue for as long as needed.
May 7, 2009	One year long-term refinancing operations introduced.
	Covered bond purchase program announced.
March 4, 2010	Return to variable rate tender for three-month long-term refinancing.
May 10, 2010	Securities Markets Program introduced to intervene in the euro area public and private debt securities markets.
	Fixed rate, full allotment tenders adopted and extended for regular three-month long-term refinancing.
August 4, 2011	Supplementary longer-term refinancing operation with a maturity of approximately six months, fixed rate and full allotment introduced and subsequently extended.
October 6, 2011	Two longer-term refinancing operations introduced—one with a maturity of approximately 12 months in October 2011, and another with a maturity of approximately 13 months in December 2011.
	New covered bond purchase program launched.
December 8, 2011	Further nonstandard measures introduced, notably: (1) to conduct two longer-term refinancing operations with a maturity of approximately three years; (2) to increase the availability of collateral; (3) to reduce the reserve ratio to 1 percent; and (4) for the time being to discontinue the fine-tuning operations carried out on the last day of each maintenance period.
February 9, 2012	Further collateral easing by approving specific national eligibility criteria and risk control measures for the temporary acceptance in a number of countries of additional credit claims as collateral in Eurosystem credit operations.
September 6, 2012	Outright Monetary Transactions introduced to purchase sovereign bonds in the euro area in secondary markets.

Sources: European Central Bank and IMF staff.

the euro area periphery; this reversal was only stemmed with the introduction by the ECB of its Outright Monetary Transactions program (Figure 1.9).

Recent financial sector assessments at the national level illustrate that financial stability remains tenuous. Risks include the continued threat of stresses and dislocations in wholesale funding markets; deteriorating or high sustained sovereign risk; and further downward movements in asset prices. Macroeconomic risks are associated with a global recession and protracted slow growth in Europe. Regulatory uncertainty and high concentration in the banking sector in some countries could amplify vulnerabilities (see Chapter 6).

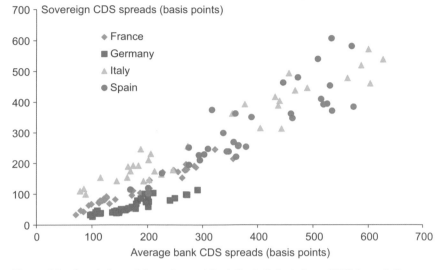

Figure 1.8 Correlations of Sovereign and Bank Credit Default Swap (CDS) Spreads (January 2010–October 2012)

Sources: Bloomberg, L.P.; and Dealogic.

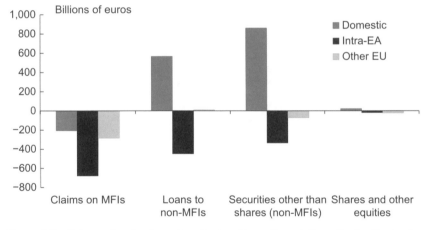

Figure 1.9 Deleveraging by Euro Area Banks—Domestic and Cross-Border (September 2008–September 2012)

Sources: European Central Bank, Consolidated Banking Statistics; and IMF, International Financial Statistics database.
Note: MFIs = monetary financial institutions. Domestic claims on MFIs are adjusted to exclude claims on the Eurosystem.

Policy initiatives have helped ease funding pressures, but fragilities and challenges remain. Aggregate capital ratios have increased, but differ considerably between stronger and weaker banks. Banks now face the consequences of the economic slowdown on asset quality, while longer-term market and regulatory forces add to the pressure. Together with weak demand, credit growth has become anemic across the region.

Fragilities stem from four intertwined vulnerabilities:

- *Low growth.* Reflecting deep recessions in the euro area periphery, real activity in the euro area is projected to decline slightly in 2013 while slowing in most other EU countries. Low growth will put bank profitability at risk, removing an important source of capital growth. Solvency in the insurance sector is under pressure from low returns and the stagnant economy (Figure 1.10).

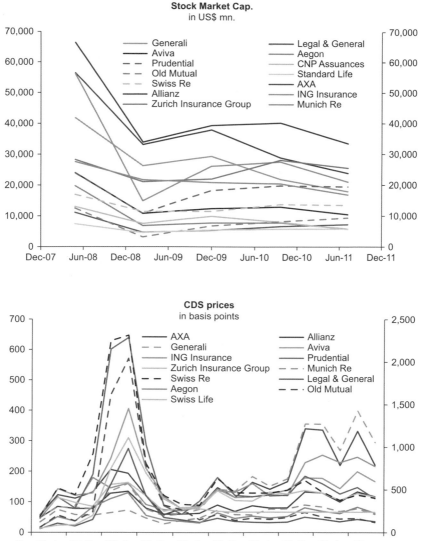

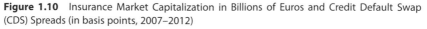

Figure 1.10 Insurance Market Capitalization in Billions of Euros and Credit Default Swap (CDS) Spreads (in basis points, 2007–2012)

Source: Bloomberg, L.P.

- *Fiscal vulnerabilities.* Lackluster growth will hamper efforts to restore fiscal sustainability where needed. Weak confidence in the fiscal sustainability of many euro area members—and fiscal crises in some—has severely undermined banks given their large exposures to sovereigns.

- *Funding pressure.* Market funding remains a challenge with wholesale markets segmenting along national borders, and many banks remaining reliant on central bank support. The eventual withdrawal of central bank support operations will be challenging for many banks.

- *Deleveraging.* Since 2008, EU banks have deleveraged considerably, mainly across borders, including outside the EU. Bank deleveraging can be explained by structural and cyclical forces (see IMF, 2012a and 2012b). These include adjustment of business models to new regulatory and economic environments; pressures to build capital; reduction in reliance on unstable market funding; and strained financial conditions and weak demand for credit. Tight lending conditions risk weakening growth and the scope for repairing balance sheets.

OVERCOMING THE CRISIS—THE SUPRANATIONAL DIMENSION

Moving banks and sovereigns jointly to safety is essential. This should be accomplished by policy combinations that strengthen banks without weakening public sector balance sheets or vice versa. The first set of policies involves raising private capital. The second set involves policies, such as bail-ins, that minimize the potential burden on the taxpayer from too-important-to-fail institutions. If national capacity is insufficient, support from supranational entities should be deployed in the form of direct support for banks and asset management companies (capital and guarantees); common backstops and safety nets (deposit guarantee schemes, and resolution funds); borrowing from official sources; or further fiscal integration. Many of these elements will be facilitated for those countries that join the prospective banking union.

Good progress has been made but gaps and challenges remain:

- *Bank recapitalization.* Banks have raised considerable new capital, both in the context of the European Banking Authority recapitalization exercise and national efforts, but pockets of weak banks remain.

- *Banking system restructuring.* During 2007–2012, the number of credit institutions fell by 5 percent: 20 banks were resolved, or are in the process of resolution, and 60 banks have undergone deep restructuring. However, many banks are still excessively dependent on wholesale funding, while others remain exposed to illiquid or impaired assets.

- *Burden sharing with creditors.* Recourse to bail-in may be more difficult during periods of stress, and only a handful of banks have so far made progress in raising liabilities subject to bail-in.

- *National sovereign support.* Financial system support from sovereigns has been large, which has sometimes triggered an adverse loop between banks and some sovereigns.

- *Sovereign adjustment.* Virtually all EU countries have embarked on fiscal adjustment and other reforms to strengthen the sovereign.

- *Supranational support.* The EFSF and ESM have provided support to sovereigns in funding difficulties. The eurogroup has reached agreement on the main features of the operational framework of the ESM direct recapitalization instrument but the operational framework must be finalized as soon as possible.

- *Resolution in systemic situation.* Common fiscal and monetary backstops are essential, alongside bail-ins and resolvability, to cope in an effective and orderly way.

More forceful steps to overcome the crisis can and should be undertaken in three areas:

- *Bank balance sheet repair.* Progress toward strong capital buffers needs to be secured. Greater disclosure requirements, especially of impaired assets, would buttress credibility in the improvement in banks' condition. The forthcoming asset quality review of euro area banks, required ahead of the start of the SSM, provides an opportunity to resolve the uncertainty about bank balance sheets and improve the prospects for attracting private capital to weak banks. It is also critical to establish the ECB's credibility as a supervisor.

- *Fast and sustained progress toward an effective SSM and banking union.* This will anchor financial stability and ongoing crisis management, and allow the ESM to directly recapitalize banks, thereby weakening the bank-sovereign link. Interests of member states not in the euro area—both those that join the SSM and those that do not—will need to be protected.

- *Further steps toward a stronger EU financial oversight framework.* Finalization of the capital requirements directive and regulation is welcome. With respect to capital requirements directives and regulations (CRD IV/CRR), full consistency with Basel III is essential. Swift adoption of the resolution and deposit guarantee scheme directives, as well as strong coordination across various institutions, are important to achieve policy consistency, including with national policies.

With weaknesses in national resolution regimes and without an EU-wide common resolution framework, implementation of the resolution directive is essential. Some enhancements are necessary: to allow for strong early intervention powers; clarification on mechanisms to constrain discretion in bail-ins is needed to ensure predictable and consistent application across countries; introduction of depositor preference in the Council agreement is welcome. Meanwhile, national legal frameworks need to be modified to facilitate borrower restructuring and accelerate collateral repossession to free up management resources, capital, and funding to support viable projects and fuel economic activity.

With the European Central Bank taking on supervision for a large subset of EU members, safeguards for non-SSM members need to be built into governance arrangements for the other pan-European institutions. Coordination across the various supranational agencies will be critical, so that decision-making can be smooth and policies consistent. Especially for crisis management, establishing a mechanism or a committee that brings in a holistic perspective, integrating the crisis related work of the ESAs, the ESRB, the SSM, the forthcoming resolution authority, DG COMP, and the supranational support facilities would be desirable. Within the euro area, such enhanced coordination would be essential.

In addition, a statutory mechanism can be considered to provide clarity, powers, responsibility, and accountability during systemic situations. Such systemic risk exception would lend clarity and credibility to the bank resolution process. Formal vetting procedures would limit moral hazard and protect resolution funds.[2]

BANKING UNION—IMPLEMENTATION AND RISK MITIGATION

The proposed roadmap to a banking union represents a critical way forward. The banking union's effectiveness will require that the ultimate financial stability framework includes all elements, such as the SSM, the single resolution mechanism based on a single resolution authority, and the common financial safety net, underpinned with a strong legal basis. Meanwhile, risks to the design of the SSM and the ongoing transition to a banking union need to be mitigated.

Single Supervisory Mechanism

The Basel Core Principles provide a basis for defining key elements for an effective SSM. These include (1) operational independence; (2) clarity of objectives and mandates; (3) legal protection of supervisors; (4) transparent processes, sound governance, and adequate resources; and (5) accountability. The EU Council agreement by and large is in line with these prerequisites, but clarity is required, including on resources and responsibilities within the SSM.

The December 12, 2012, agreement on the establishment of the SSM and announced roadmap toward a banking union is appropriately ambitious. It also correctly calls for giving the utmost priority to the adoption of a harmonized regulatory set-up (the CRR/CRD IV), and to reaching agreement on the draft directive for bank recovery and resolution and harmonization of deposit guarantee schemes.

---

[2] This is discussed further in Goyal and others, 2013, Box 4.

A proposal for a single resolution mechanism has been put forth by the European Commission on July 10, 2013.

Establishing the SSM under the existing EU Treaty has implications for its governance and powers. Given the Treaty requirement that all ECB decisions must be made by the Governing Council that comprises only member states in the euro area, a newly created Supervisory Board, comprising representatives from all EMU countries and any other EU member states that join the SSM, will undertake the planning and execution of the supervisory tasks conferred on the ECB, including the proposal to the Governing Council of draft decisions. The Governing Council of the ECB, which comprises the governors of euro area national central banks and the members of the ECB Executive Board, formally has the ultimate decision-making power for any tasks carried out by the ECB, including supervision.

Risks arising from these governance arrangements will need to be guarded against:

- Decisions by the Supervisory Board may not be fully independent from national interests. The ECB functions in a nationality-blind manner, but it will be harder to ignore national interests when taking supervisory decisions, particularly at the outset.

- As the Governing Council of the ECB will be in charge of both supervisory and monetary policy decisions, the ECB will need to establish a comprehensive framework for transparency and accountability for the SSM and Chinese walls between supervision and monetary policy at an operational level. Nonetheless, the setup should still permit synergies between the two functions, for instance from data sharing. Accountability needs to be further safeguarded through appearances of the ECB leadership before the European Parliament, and where relevant also before national parliaments.

- As non-EMU countries cannot vote on the Governing Council, credibility in the maintenance of a level playing field for such countries that join the SSM will need to be achieved through the operation of the envisaged special arrangements.

The ECB is to take direct supervisory responsibility for the largest 150 banks and for the effectiveness of the SSM, but will have authority to directly supervise any bank it deems necessary. The mandate appears pragmatic, given the resource and other challenges that will be faced by the ECB, and it will be important that the metrics for identifying the 150 banks are clear and capture the importance of a bank in cross-border activities, and in domestic and EU significance. However, the crisis has illustrated that problems can emerge also from amongst the smaller banks, especially when confidence is fragile. According to the EU Council Agreement, the ECB retains the responsibility and scope for oversight over the rest of the banking sector and has power to quickly exert direct supervisory authority over any bank, or group of banks, if it deems it necessary. To ensure consistent supervision and safeguard against forebearance, the national supervisory authorities, which will continue to supervise most banks in the countries covered by the SSM, are required to share information and cooperate among each other and with the ECB.

Transition risks will need to be managed. Initially, the ECB will need to rely on cross-country teams supplied by national authorities and led by an ECB supervisor. It will be critical to avoid mistakes during this start-up period, since these could cause a loss in credibility that would take much time and effort to reverse. The bank asset quality review undertaken by the ECB with national authorities and coordinated with the EBA will be critical to establish the credibility of the ECB as a supervisor, avoid early difficulties, and get a better understanding of the condition of the banks. The ECB has scope to postpone the date when the SSM becomes effective if the bank feels it is not ready. However, this may have knock-on effects; thus every effort is needed to ensure that the ECB has its necessary resources in place by the SSM's October 2014 postulated starting date.

Resolution

It is essential that an SRM for the countries participating in the SSM be established around the same time that the SSM becomes effective. As banks are too interconnected to be effectively supervised at a national level, national resolution regimes would have difficulty, even under harmonized arrangements, in handling the bigger banks of the EU or cross-border contagion. Moreover, incentives among national resolution authorities for least-cost and rapid action to address problems could remain limited; also, coordination difficulties, especially for large cross-border banks, may undermine effectiveness. In addition, there is the danger that—absent a single resolution mechanism—national authorities could be left to bear the fiscal implications of decisions made by the ECB, which would perpetuate bank-sovereign links and create potential conflict (and deadlock) among national authorities in cross-border resolution. As crisis tensions abate, it is important that the implicit sovereign bank guarantees in place for the last several years be effectively removed through a reaffirmation and implementation of the principle that institutions with solvency problems must be resolved. To be fully aligned with best practices, the resolution authority should seek to achieve least-cost resolution of financial institutions without disrupting financial stability. It should protect insured depositors and ensure that shareholders and unsecured, uninsured creditors absorb losses. The SRM will need a mandate to intervene before insolvency using well-defined quantitative and qualitative triggers. It will need strong powers and a range of tools to restructure banks' assets and liabilities (for example, bail-in subordinated and senior unsecured creditors; transfer assets and liabilities with "purchase and assumption;" and separate bad assets by setting up asset management vehicles); override shareholder rights; establish bridge banks to maintain essential financial services; and close insolvent banks. Coordination with the SSM should be ensured, particularly when early intervention measures are triggered by the SSM.

The SRM will need to coordinate closely with other EU institutions. Coordination with the SSM could be through regular formal meetings with the Chair of the supervisory board of the ECB. Alternatively, the SSM Chair of the supervisory board could serve on the board of the SRM, together with national representatives and representatives of other EU bodies. Coordination with DG COMP will also be important, as unless and until all EU member states participate in the SRM, its interventions may be subject to State Aid rules. Finally, as most large euro area banks have presence outside the BU perimeter, there will need to be coordination between banking union resolution authority and those in the remaining EU states and possibly beyond.

As with the SSM, use of the existing treaty framework determines the structure and operations of the SRM. The SRM will use the framework of the resolution directive, rely in the first place on financing from national authorities, have powers such a bail-ins to reduce likely exposures, and have the ESM as financing backstop. In time, a single dedicated resolution authority should be created. This authority should have backstop financing, including through a single resolution fund. It will need to coordinate closely with the national resolution agencies in the member states outside the banking union, as well as countries outside the EU.

Legal Basis

Due care has been given to underpinning the proposed BU with an as strong as possible legal basis under the current treaties. Article 127(6) of the Treaty on the Functioning of the European Union allows the conferral of specific supervisory tasks to the ECB, and is now being used to establish the SSM. Certain elements of an effective safety net such as an SRM can be designed through secondary legislation on the basis of the current treaty.

In the medium term, providing an explicit legal underpinning for financial stability arrangements in the treaties could further enhance the legal robustness and transparency of those arrangements. It could be useful to enshrine directly in the treaty, similarly to the approach followed for other EU competences, such as monetary union, competition, and agriculture: (1) explicit financial stability objectives; (2) the key institutional set-up of supervision and the financial safety net; and (3) the necessary powers. This would ensure that a single resolution authority could stand institutionally at par with the Commission and the ECB, thus facilitating collaboration and mutual checks and balances. Also, a treaty could explicitly provide for the desired allocation of responsibilities between SSM countries and the broader EU. It would also mitigate legal risks that core aspects of the banking union are challenged before the European Court of Justice.

STRENGTHENING THE FINANCIAL STABILITY FRAMEWORK

The EU's financial oversight framework will necessarily remain complex. It will need to address the needs of three groups of countries with very different economic and financial governance arrangements: members of the monetary union that will automatically be members of the banking union, non-euro area countries that opt in to the banking union but retain their own monetary policy frameworks, and EU countries that remain outside the banking union. These three groups will retain different degrees of national autonomy, while adhering to (and benefiting from) a single market in financial services.

Ring-fencing of domestic banking from foreign operations has been part of the crisis response. This response, while understandable given policymaker's account-ability to national taxpayers, has itself contributed to instability, leading to initiatives to prevent disorderly cross-border deleveraging and minimize negative externalities from self-interested national moves (e.g., the Vienna initiative). The benefit of capital and liquidity withdrawal and ring-fencing may be more apparent than real, with adverse feedback effects on the initiator of such measures. If risk is properly assessed and there are no policy distortions, capital will flow to where it is most productive. Especially at a time when growth in the EU is anemic, which itself poses a risk to financial stability, restricting such potential flows can exacerbate the problems the policy is designed to avoid. Restoring the single market in financial services could thus enhance financial stability.

To restore safe functioning of the single market, a continued strengthening of its financial oversight framework is essential. With the non-banking part of the single market functioning comparatively well, measures need to focus on banking, but further strengthening of other parts will be important too. Further measures should be guided by an explicit EU-wide financial stability objective so that actions from national and supranational entities are consistent. Priorities discussed below are: remaining regulatory reforms; strengthening and adapting institutions (ESAs and DG COMP); implementing macroprudential policy; addressing structural issues; and securing safe market infrastructure.

Regulatory Reforms

Banking and Deposit Guarantees

Implementing the directive to harmonize deposit guarantee schemes will be a first step toward an EU-wide financial safety net. National deposit guarantee schemes should be aligned not only in terms of quantities (through minimum coverage limits), but also in terms of prices, with premiums adjusted for risk as far as practicable. The length of time to payout should be shortened, likely requiring additional efforts from those member states with the least developed structures. To safeguard depositor confidence and efficient resolution, prefunding of national DGS will be necessary, but may need to be combined with a common backstop should national deposit schemes run out of funds. Agreement is needed on the amount of targeted prefunding and on mutual borrowing agreements across national DGSs. The former can be established on the basis of international practices and phased in over time to modulate pressures on the industry, with transitional arrangements to take account of varying initial conditions.

Insurance

Timely implementation of Solvency II Directive would help reduce vulnerabilities in the insurance sector. The Directive codifies and harmonizes the EU insurance regulations and its implementation is now scheduled for January 2014, but there remain disagreements, mainly around extending the long-term guarantees package. The delay implies that important aspects of supervision, including valuation, disclosure, and risk management, would remain noncompliant with the International Association of Insurance Supervisors principles (see national FSAPs) in several EU member states, preventing the urgently needed proper assessment of the risks in this sector in the present low-interest-rate environment.

Under the market-consistent valuation of liabilities required under Solvency II, use of a low interest rate discount curve for the valuation of liabilities will be necessary in the current environment. Such a methodology would likely lead to the solvency positions of insurers being seen as weaker than hitherto presented. Indeed, the situation may throw into question insurance and pensions companies' traditional business models, suggesting that significant refocusing or restructuring may ultimately be called for.

Securities

The approval of the Second Markets in Financial Instruments Directive (MiFID2) and reforms to the Market Abuse Directive will be key to fostering market resilience and integrity. Although the text still needs refinement, MiFID2 addresses the main concerns brought by market fragmentation and technological innovation.

Consumer and investor protection issues should get sufficient priority. In particular, approval of Packaged Retail Investment Products and reforms to MiFID and the Second Insurance Mediation Directive (IMD2) to ensure cross-sector harmonization in regard to investment-like products are important.

Addressing risks from shadow banking should continue to be a priority. Provisions to encourage work on reducing reliance on ratings are part of the Third Credit Rating Agency Directive, and the implementation of the Alternative Investment Fund Managers Directive should bring further transparency to the hedge fund industry. Two areas where further work is warranted vis-à-vis the Financial Stability Board agenda are (1) money market funds and exchange traded funds; and (2) securities lending and repos. Regarding the former, the European Securities and Markets Authority has issued guidelines—including in connection to their use of securities lending and repos—which should be the starting point for the reforms to be incorporated in the Undertakings for Collective Investment in Transferable Securities Directive. Feedback from the consultation of the EU green paper should provide further input as to other areas where additional work is warranted.

European Supervisory Agencies

The ESAs have undertaken significant work in the two years of their existence, but there is scope to do more in areas including supervisory convergence, risk identification, and consumer protection. The ESAs are performing a critical role for the single market. They are preparing the single rulebooks and are contributing to the implementation of new directives and regulations. But among other elements in their remits are fostering supervisory convergence (through creation of centers of expertise, and peer reviews), risk identification, and investor protection. To fulfill these, they need additional resources and better governance arrangements.

The upcoming review of the ESAs should be an opportunity to sharpen mandates and strengthen governance arrangements. Governance arrangements should be reviewed with the aim of promoting a more supranational orientation of decision making. Providing voting rights to the Chairs of the ESAs, moving fully to a full-time board, or delegating more decisions to the management board should be considered.

Data transparency is a significant handicap to effective supervision and market discipline. Lack of direct, easy access to institution-specific data creates inefficiencies, poses reputational risks, and should be replaced by a mechanism allowing joint but still direct and straightforward access. Since the ESAs need to go through national supervisory authorities (NSAs) to obtain detailed supervisory data, delays and bureaucratic costs arise, which affect work on real-time analysis of risks and crisis-related work. In particular, requiring a vote from the NSAs to provide data for particular studies for an ESA might undermine the timeliness of the ESA's work.

Banking

The European Banking Authority (EBA) had high visibility from the moment of its creation. It has significant achievements in its first two years of existence, but the pace and prioritization of its activities have been dictated by the crisis. EBA played a crucial role in securing bank recapitalization, but despite a high level of transparency, the June 2011 stress tests failed to signal some subsequent bank failures. The recapitalization exercise in June 2012 was more effective and led to substantial infusions of capital into EU banks, although some banks enhanced their capital positions through risk-weight optimization. Despite its limited resources and cumbersome governance structure, EBA has made significant progress in the area of rule making, but it needs additional resources and independence and to seek synergies with ESRB, such as on cross-sector risk assessment.

EBA should continue to prioritize strengthening transparency and the reliability of data. The 2011 stress test exercise showed the value brought by disclosure of detailed information. But now EBA should strive to enhance the quality assurance process; coordinate an asset quality review; standardize nonperforming loan definitions, loan classifications, and provisioning rules; and promote the timely disclosure of granular asset quality information. EBA should accelerate convergence on Pillar 2 practices (common methodologies for risk assessment) and raise supervisors' awareness on asset quality issues, in particular by issuing guidance for supervisors on best practices for the conduct of asset quality reviews (Box 1.1).

Box 1.1 Lessons and Recommendations for European Banking Authority Stress Testing

It is important that full transparency about banks' data be obtained, preferably through an asset quality review. A high degree of transparency, including on reference date data and on sensitivity to differences in data definitions, would strengthen confidence; conversely, further failures of banks after passing a stress test would substantially damage the credibility of the process.

In light of these considerations, the following are recommended:

- Moving to standardize definitions of nonperforming loans, loan classifications, provisioning, etc. while initiating a review of input asset quality data.[a] This review would complement an enhanced system of consistency checks built into the stress testing procedures. Acknowledgment of the concerns, and quantification of possible effects through sensitivity analysis, would be worthwhile.

- Continuing to publish a wide range of detailed information on banks.

- Incorporating as far as possible banks' funding and capitalization plans in the 2013 stress test projections, including the effects of the phase out of the Long-Term Refinancing Operations. Further efforts could be made to assess the sensitivity of results to likely changes in balance sheet composition.

- Ensuring the consistency and quality of tests run by national supervisory authorities and the Single Supervisory Mechanism with its own, and running tests on hitherto relatively neglected topics such as structural issues and funding vulnerabilities. Developing furthering liquidity stress testing, and running stress tests and related simulations to incorporate longer-term and cross-sector factors (for example, using contingent claims analysis) that relate to structural issues are needed.

---

[a] The definitions should be as consistent as possible while recognizing real differences, for example, in loss given default rates across countries and across time.

The creation of the SSM will bring a new dimension and urgency to EBA's supervisory convergence role. The ECB will need to implement supervisory procedures and guidance for the operation of the SSM in the established timeframe, which may front run some parts of the envisaged European Supervisory Handbook. While this is unavoidable, it is important that EBA work closely with the new supervisor so that the SSM can build its procedures on best available practice.

EBA will have a key role to play in supervisory colleges after the establishment of the SSM. Most large EU banks have activities inside and outside the SSM perimeter. EBA should be assertive in the colleges in ensuring a level playing field, and that practices do not diverge across the two areas. It can have a major role also in the EU's relationships with the outside world.

In the area of consumer protection, EBA has EU-wide responsibility. More staff and building of knowledge are needed. Support may be drawn from the other ESAs, which have been more proactive, issuing guidelines, and reports on good practices and consumer trends.

Insurance

The European supervisor on insurance and pension funds (EIOPA) can point to some significant achievements. In contributing to a common supervisory culture, a soft approach has been taken, based on peer reviews, training, and frequent engagement in the colleges of supervisors. In anticipation of the introduction of Solvency II, EIOPA has been developing regulations and designing technical standards, guidelines, and recommendations. Its work on Solvency II equivalence certification has concluded on three countries, and transitional Equivalence measures for several countries are being evaluated. The mutual recognition work with the United States continues. EIOPA has created a common EU voice in insurance and pension matters on selected international topics.

Challenges ahead will require EIOPA's realignment, particularly if weaknesses in the industry become apparent. Solvency II is scheduled to be implemented in 2014 and revised legislation for occupational pensions should be soon in force. Shifting from developing technical standards toward monitoring, implementing, and enforcement will be necessary. EIOPA will need to prevent delays in Solvency II implementation that could result in regulatory arbitrage. EIOPA's human resources framework as well as its operational processes will need to be realigned to the new challenges.

EIOPA's engagement in its oversight role of supervisory colleges has been intense, but much remains to be done. In 2012, colleges of supervisors having at least one actual meeting or teleconference were organized for 69 groups. Important issues such as crisis preparedness were introduced and some aspects tested, confidentiality agreement templates were developed, and best practices on group supervision presented. However, work is needed to ensure a harmonized level of group supervision in the EU once the Level 3 legislation is in force. Also, EIOPA's engagement in colleges should go beyond the EU and encompass larger international groups active in Europe, as well as take a leading role in the supervision of the largest EU groups.

EIOPA has been proactive in consumer protection. Promoting transparency, simplicity, and fairness in the market for consumer financial products and services across the internal market is a stated objective. EIOPA is engaged in the revision of IMD2 and working with ESMA on MiFID2, where EIOPA is in a position to highlight the particular aspects of insurance products and insurance distribution practices.

The approval of internal models is a crucial step in evaluating capital levels, and resources need to be allocated to this effort. The level of expertise and amount of work required is imposing severe strain on the NSAs. EIOPA has agreed a work process for the NSAs and insurers. Consideration should be given to centralizing aspects of the approval of internal models, so as to make best use of limited highly-qualified resources.

EIOPA's stress tests under a Solvency II regime should focus on EU-wide vulnerabilities and interlinkages. To date, EIOPA's main effort has been to quantify the effect on assets of single factor shocks and traditional insurance factors such as mortality, lapse, and market exposures. EIOPA's stress tests should complement national stress testing activity with a special focus on identifying EU-wide risks, spillovers to and from other sectors, and medium-term resilience related to, for instance, low profitability in some business lines, and to coordinate with EBA and the ESRB in assessing risks related to bancassurance.

Securities Markets

Within its resource envelope, ESMA has performed well during its first two years of operation, especially in connection with the single rulebook and credit rating agencies supervision. Technical standards, opinions, and advice to the EC were developed. ESMA has built up its expertise on credit rating agencies and has worked on the development of a risk framework to anchor its supervisory program. Results are more modest in connection with other functions.

As it acknowledged, ESMA needs to step up its role in other areas, in particular on supervisory convergence. It has set up strategic directions for each area, and in many cases has identified concrete actions.

- *Supervisory convergence.* Reengineering and strengthening peer reviews is essential. Reviews can be made more rigorous by increased onsite work, and their outcomes enhanced by linking reports to the development of best practices and/or guidelines, implementation of which can be monitored; if necessary, for instance for breach of law, stronger actions should be taken. In this context, it is important that the national supervisory authorities take the necessary steps to ensure the enforceability of ESMA's opinions and guidelines in their respective jurisdictions.
- *Risk identification and crisis management.* Projects under way will allow ESMA to make a qualitative jump in its contribution to financial stability and crisis management. To this end, besides needing timely and granular data, ESMA should coordinate simulation exercises amongst the national supervisors, setting out common assumptions to ensure comparability of results.
- *Investor protection.* ESMA's emphasis on product monitoring is warranted. Effective monitoring of financial innovation should also improve financial stability.
- *ESMA is encouraged to acquire skills that enable validation of the complex risk models of CCPs, including for the clearing of OTC derivatives.* As the accuracy of these models is essential to safeguard CCPs in extreme market circumstances, the independency of the review of these models should receive attention.

DG COMP

Competition and State aid policy has served as the de facto coordinating mechanism in bank restructuring during the crisis, as it is the only binding EU framework available for this purpose. The EU DG COMP has the exclusive mandate and power to ensure that State aid is compatible with the treaty, and that State aid provision is accepted in exchange for strict conditionality. Member states have provided aid through capital injections, guarantees, and asset purchases. Compensatory measures required by DG COMP have included divestments, penalty interest rates, management removals, dividend suspensions, and burden-sharing (shareholder dilutions, and, lately, bail-in of subordinated debt).

Interventions by DG COMP have been instrumental in imposing restructuring on banks but have on occasion heightened macro-financial concerns. In particular, there have been concerns about the speed of decision making and insufficient transparency, and the impact of compensatory measures on financial stability and economic growth. Since DG COMP could only act in response to national state aid proposals, decisions were taken case-by-case on an individual basis even in the presence of system-wide problems.

State aid management is evolving to respond more flexibly to the crisis, but faces fundamental challenges. DG COMP is assigned a difficult task in mitigating competitive distortions, preserving financial stability, and limiting the costs to the taxpayers while ensuring the long-term viability of the institutions that receive state aid. The design of intervention strategies, therefore, sometimes involves significant trade-offs. Procedures have been accelerated, and sector-wide implications have been taken into account. The ongoing Spanish arrangement, for example, takes a broader approach. The Commission's powers regarding the resolution of banks have been strengthened further, since ESM support to bank recapitalization is now conditional upon the Commission's approval of those banks' restructuring plans. The new mechanism has given DG COMP greater influence in the restructuring and resolution of banks receiving state aid and led to a significant acceleration in the approval process. For instance, it took less than six months to approve the restructuring plans of eight Spanish banks, consistent with the timelines of the European program of assistance to Spain. Stronger coordination with other institutions is desirable with a view to achieving the Commission's objective of "restoring financial stability, ensuring lending to the real economy, and dealing with systemic risk of possible insolvency."

DG COMP's practices in systemic cases can be further enhanced to ensure consistency with a country's macro-financial framework. Phasing and composition of bank restructuring is critical to mitigate adverse macroeconomic effects. DG COMP seeks to set the right incentives to make the best use of state aid and withdraw from state protection as soon as possible. A pricing policy has been established based on recommendations of the ECB that seeks to limit moral hazard by ensuring a sufficient degree of burden sharing, although at a level which is still below the remuneration that would, in the absence of state aid, be requested by the market. However, increased transparency in pricing and proposed deleveraging would give added credibility to DG COMP's efforts, which sometimes appear to be ad hoc. An examination, for instance with the IMF and ECB, of its policy for determining the remuneration of instruments used for capital support would be appropriate, to ensure on the one hand that it is not double-hitting a fragile institution and on the other not simply delaying the institution's demise, and thereby undermining financial stability going forward. Similarly, it would be helpful to look again at the methodology for determining the required degree of bank deleveraging.

DG COMP's role will change as a dedicated resolution framework for the banking union is developed. The challenge will be to find a balance to foster a more integrated approach between the Commission as the guardian of competition and institutions that, concomitant with the banking union, will be charged with overseeing bank resolution and safeguarding financial stability at the EU level. One option would be to foster a permanent coordination mechanism between DG COMP and financial stability authorities to deal efficiently with the competition and State aid aspects of future resolution cases. Moreover, as most large euro area banks have presence outside the likely banking union perimeter, there is likely to be an important role in coordinating between the banking union resolution authority and those in the remaining EU member states using the framework of the prospective resolution directive.

Macroprudential Policies and the ESRB

The role of macroprudential supervision is to identify and reduce risks to financial stability. Macroprudential policy relies on instruments to: (1) limit the buildup of financial imbalances; (2) address market failures to assess risk externalities among financial institutions; and (3) dampen the procyclicality of the financial system. It can apply both at the peak of a cycle "taking away the punchbowl," as well as at the trough, to ensure that procyclicality on the downside does not prevent a revival of growth after a downturn.

Currently, national authorities in the EU are responsible for macroprudential oversight, although adequate frameworks are still lacking in some countries. Coordination and internalization of cross-border spillovers is achieved at the EU level by the ESRB through a (non-binding) "act or explain" mechanism for member countries in response to its warnings and recommendations. In December 2011, the ESRB issued recommendations on the macroprudential mandates of national authorities. As national authorities establish institutional arrangements, guidance for establishing common macroprudential toolkits is being developed. Some harmonization of tools is required to facilitate coordination and reciprocity of those policies with cross-border effects, but flexibility must be allowed to tailor responses to local conditions.

The coordination of national macroprudential policies is especially important in the EU, given its highly integrated markets, as well as constraints on the use of monetary policy in the EMU. National authorities may not have power over all lending within their territory, including by foreign bank branches. The use of macroprudential instruments over a particular activity could be referred by national authorities to the ESRB for approval so that all EU banks regardless of origin are covered. Such coordination is important to minimize negative spillover effects of national policies, reduce the possibility of regulatory arbitrage, and foster policy effectiveness. The last is particularly relevant for emerging European economies with a high degree of cross-border banking activities and direct cross-border lending. The ESRB has announced its intention to establish coordination procedures when considered appropriate.

The ESRB currently lacks binding legal authority, so relies on "soft" power. It is also handicapped by its very limited resources and burdensome governance structure. Nevertheless, it has established itself as an important body. Its first warning, over foreign currency lending in emerging European economies, was effective, although the ESRB will achieve further credibility once it issues warnings to major "core" economies and obtains a positive response. Further work on the downside of the cycle, looking, for instance, at the aggregate effects of deleveraging or of asset sales, would be particularly relevant at the present juncture.[3]

Within the countries of the SSM, the ECB will have a role in macroprudential policy, as well as the national authorities, as it takes on its microprudential responsibilities. There are synergies with microprudential policies; also, the ECB already has good understanding of European financial markets, and its deep knowledge of the monetary transmission mechanism will be helpful in assessing the transmission mechanism of macroprudential policies. Moreover, a key challenge for macroprudential supervision will be to design and calibrate macroprudential instruments and implement them against political interference. The established independence of the ECB would help in this regard; the national macroprudential authorities also need adequate independence. Since the monetary union prevents participating member states at different points of the cycle from having divergent monetary policies, macroprudential instruments may be particularly important for these countries. The ECB should cooperate closely with national authorities to benefit from their local knowledge, as well as with the ESRB in the oversight of non-EMU countries and the non-bank financial sector. It should be responsible for a wide range of instruments going beyond those included in CRD IV/CRR.

The ESRB will continue to have an important role and will continue to be responsible for macroprudential oversight over the financial sector at the EU level. While the ECB only has authority over banks, the ESRB covers the entire financial system, including insurance and occupational pensions, as well as market infrastructure and financial markets and products. The ESRB would be well suited for effective identification, analysis, and monitoring of EU-wide systemic risks, and for assessing the array of instruments potentially available to address them. The ESRB should interact with the ECB on macroprudential toolkits when the ECB takes on macroprudential responsibilities, as it does with national agencies. It must be able to exercise its powers and issue the same kind of recommendation to the ECB as it does to any national central bank or bank supervisor; this would require a substantial revision to the ESRB legal framework, a

---

[3] Recommendations on money market funds and bank funding were approved by the ESRB General Board in February 2013.

detachment from the ECB "umbrella," and a clear delineation with the mandate of the latter.

Structural Reforms

High-level working groups chaired respectively by John Vickers of Oxford University and Governor Erkki Liikanen of the Bank of Finland assessed the need for additional banking reforms. These could be targeted at individual banks to reduce the probability and impact of failure, ensure the continuation of vital economic functions in the event of failure, and better protect vulnerable retail clients. One conclusion was that the experience of the crisis showed that no one type of bank performed systematically better than the others, and no one type did systematically worse.

The Liikanen group recommended the mandatory separation of the investment banking business. This type of business was deemed riskiest, and that separation would limit danger of contagion to core functions such as deposit-taking and payments and hence reduce taxpayers' contingent liabilities. It would also limit the scope for cross-subsidization, improve the scope for effective monitoring and risk management, and facilitate resolution. This proposal is in the spirit of others elsewhere, including the Volcker Rule in the United States and the Vickers group's recommendations for ring-fencing of retail banking.[4] More recently, the French authorities proposed that banks separate the same businesses that are prohibited by the Volcker rule, albeit banks would be allowed to run these businesses in a separate subsidiary.

The Liikanen proposal allows the preservation of the universal banking model, characteristic of much of Europe. It mandates that businesses be placed in a stand-alone subsidiary including proprietary trading, market making, and investments in hedge funds and private equity funds. The trading subsidiary and the subsidiary housing deposits and payments would need to meet capital and other regulatory requirements on a stand-alone basis. The report argues that any increased costs from the removal of synergies between the two may simply reflect the withdrawal of the hidden taxpayer subsidy for the implicit saving of the institution.

Proposed measures to enhance resolvability are welcome. The Liikanen group argues for enhancing the bank resolution regime, developing a comprehensive system of bail-ins, applying more robust weights in the determination of minimum capital, more consistent treatment of internal risk models, and governance

---

[4] Among the differences of the Vickers proposal from Liikanen are: Vickers pushes almost all investment banking activities out of the deposit bank, whereas Liikanen allows the deposit bank to retain underwriting and client facing hedging services; Vickers would apply to almost all banks, whereas Liikanen would apply only to the largest banking groups; Vickers applies the ring-fencing only to the U.K. business, whereas Liikanen would apply to all affiliates of an EU banking group. Both the Vickers and the Liikanen proposals differ from the Volcker proposal for the United States in that retail and investment banking would be allowed to remain within the same legal entity.

reforms. It recommends higher loss absorbency requirement for the trading subsidiaries engaging in separated businesses via a leverage ratio.

However, separation of banking activities would not have helped address some of the most serious problems of the crisis. Lehman Brothers, for example, was not a retail deposit-taking institution. Also, many banking sector difficulties derived from the "plain vanilla" side of banks, most particularly lending for residential real estate. Now the sovereign-bank linkage is causing difficulties, particularly for those banks that invested in their countries' government bonds, notionally the most conservative of strategies. Most importantly, from the perspectives of ease of resolution and minimizing contingent fiscal liabilities, separation may not work as intended because trading subsidiaries may remain systemically important, especially since they will house market-making operations of the largest banks.

Consistency with structural reform proposals in comparable jurisdictions, at least insofar as application to internationally active banks is concerned, is important.

- There is a danger that the major international banks may optimize across different structural constraints by moving operations, changing corporate structures, and redesigning products in ways that could weaken policy effectiveness. This would put further pressure on cross-border supervision and resolution.

- It will be important to manage differences across the proposals so that they do not result in mutually inconsistent structural constraints on internationally active banks.

- A level playing field will need to be developed vis-à-vis banks from outside the EU that are competing within the EU.[5]

Financial Market Infrastructure

Regulation

The adoption of the European Market Infrastructure Regulation (EMIR) and the legislative work on the draft Central Securities Depositories (CSD) Regulation are important for the creation of a single market for CCPs and CSDs. The regulations significantly reduce sources of risks related to the cross-border offering of clearing and settlement services, and they provide for a level playing field, enhancing fair and efficient competition between CCPs and CSDs. The intention of the Commission to further centralize supervisory responsibilities in the medium term is appropriate.

Measures are needed to ensure that recovery and resolution plans for CCPs and CSDs will work across borders in case of large market disruptions. With national competent authorities bearing the primary supervisory responsibilities,

---

[5] Further discussion of this topic will be provided in a forthcoming IMF paper, "Making Banks Safer: What Role Can Structural Measures Play?"

the framework does not provide safeguards to ensure that the national interest may sometimes prevail over the general interest to have safe and efficient CCPs and CSDs. The active participation of ESMA in the CCP colleges should contribute significantly to supervisory consistency and oversight. Access rights of CCPs and CSDs for other markets and infrastructures should be further developed in line with international standards. The establishment of a comprehensive framework for cooperation between national supervisors of CSDs is needed too, given the increased cross-border nature of CSDs. The supervision and oversight of the two international CSDs in the EU should be enhanced, in cooperation with the ECB in its responsibility for financial stability and by participation in the SSM, as competitive pressures may encourage competition on risk management frameworks.

Regulatory risks arise due to differences in the legal and regulatory frameworks in the EU, the United States, and elsewhere to handle the mandatory clearing obligation for standardized derivative contracts. Globally operating OTC derivative CCPs face regulatory uncertainty and inefficiencies. Regulators should continue ongoing joint work to give priority to the identification and mitigation of conflicts, inconsistencies, and gaps between EMIR and other non-EU frameworks through bilateral and multilateral coordination. The EU has drafted flexible arrangements for the identification and recognition of third-country CCPs that limit the risks of conflicts of laws by ensuring that foreign CCPs remain subject to their home regulation.

EU crisis management procedures for financial market infrastructures should be further developed and tested. A notification regime should be in place that allows for immediate information-sharing between all relevant authorities, CCPs, CSDs, and other systems and market participants. Central monitoring of potential market-wide disruptions should be enforced, for example in relation to the quality of collateral kept by CCPs and international CSDs.

Euroclear's Soundness and Efficiency

Euroclear Bank is a securities settlement system that contributes to the safety and efficiency of global markets for government bonds and other international securities but also concentrates systemic risk. It is one of the largest securities settlement systems worldwide with a daily average settlement value of around €1.1 trillion, providing settlement services for securities from 44 markets in 53 currencies. In particular, Euroclear Bank services the largest global banks with triparty repo arrangements to secure their interbank financing.

Important risk measures have been taken to reduce systemic risk, but some of the risk management frameworks need to be further improved to fully observe the recently adopted international standards.[6] Euroclear Bank should in particular prepare measures to be operationally ready for the implementation of its recovery

---

[6] Committee on Payment and Settlement Systems (CPSS) and the Technical Committee of the International Organization of Securities Commissions (IOSCO) Principles for Financial Market Infrastructures.

plans and plans for the orderly winding down of its operations. In addition, it should upgrade some risk management policies and practices to reduce its (potential unsecured) credit exposures to participants and other linked securities settlement systems. It has recently made important improvements to its collateral and its liquidity management frameworks.

Euroclear Bank is subject to effective regulation, supervision, and oversight of the National Bank of Belgium and the Financial Services and Markets Authority, but cooperation with the Luxembourg authorities should be improved. The legal framework provides the Belgian authorities with sufficient powers to obtain timely information and induce change. However, as Euroclear Bank is in competition with the Luxembourg-based Clearstream Banking Luxembourg—which offers similar settlement and banking services—close cooperation with the Luxembourg authorities is needed to avoid any competition on risk management frameworks. As both entities are highly relevant for the global financial stability, the Belgian and Luxembourg authorities should evolve from the existing cooperation toward a cooperative framework that would allow them to take common decisions and implement these simultaneously in both entities. The plans to include Euroclear Bank on the list of eligible banks for the SSM may further contribute to a level playing field.

The national securities depositories of Belgium, France, and the Netherlands, which share a common information technology platform provided by the Euroclear Group, are subject to effective regulation, supervision, and oversight of the Belgian, Dutch, and French authorities, despite the fact that the legal frameworks differ substantially between the three countries. The cooperation between the different authorities is effective and contributes to the financial stability in Belgium, France, and the Netherlands. Crisis management frameworks are in place that are regularly tested and updated.

TARGET2's Soundness and Efficiency

TARGET2 displays a high level of observance of international standards. The system has a sound, coherent, and transparent legal basis. It has developed an adequate risk management framework to address financial and operational risks. As a real-time gross settlement system, credit risk is minimized. Liquidity risk is mitigated by participants having access to central bank intraday liquidity based on adequate collateral and the liquidity saving mechanism offered by the system. TARGET2 business continuity arrangements are well developed and comprehensive, covering operational as well as communication network aspects.

Nevertheless, TARGET2 crisis management and risk communication procedures can be enhanced by giving the ECB direct access to information on participants' liquidity as well as collateral positions. For most large participants, liquidity positions are maintained in several countries, and national central banks can only monitor positions maintained on their own account systems. Furthermore, the collateralization process and securities holding are decentralized. Centralizing the monitoring of participants' liquidity and, where possible, collateral positions at the level of the ECB is crucial in order to allow the

Eurosystem to maintain financial stability across the euro area by acting quickly and effectively in the event of financial distress.

Eurosystem's Oversight Framework for Payments

The ECB's oversight capacity should be strengthened. The ECB is in the process of moving from a rule-based to risk-based and forward-looking oversight approach. In particular, it is developing more dynamic oversight tools such as interdependencies analysis, stress testing, and an early warning system. The ECB oversight team has the responsibility to define the Eurosystem's strategy and policy, develop rules and guidance, coordinate the Eurosystem, and contribute to international forums. In addition, the ECB will soon participate in several EMIR colleges for CCPs. In order to implement the new risk-based approach credibly, the ECB needs access to confidential bank-by-bank data which is within the remit of the NCBs and to strengthen the capacity and the skill of its staff. ECB oversight staff should be significantly increased, and their work organized in cluster modules, focusing on overseeing individual entities as well as on specific risks across entities. They need the right skills and continuity in running critical areas, such as interdependencies and stress testing.

REFERENCES

Goyal, Rishi, and others, 2013, "A Banking Union for the Euro Area," IMF Staff Discussion Note 13/01 (Washington: International Monetary Fund).

International Monetary Fund, 2012a, *Global Financial Stability Report: The Quest for Lasting Stability*, World Economic and Financial Surveys (Washington, April).

————, 2012b, *Global Financial Stability Report: Restoring Confidence and Progressing on Reforms*, World Economic and Financial Surveys (Washington, October).

PART I

From Integration to Crisis Management

CHAPTER 2

Institutional Setup for the Single Market and Economic and Monetary Union

JIANPING ZHOU

The 1957 Treaty of Rome established the European Economic Community, ultimately putting a much wider group of European countries on a path toward the European Union (EU), where goods, services, people, and capital could move freely. This chapter presents a brief background history of the developments of European institutions underpinning the single market and the framework as it was on the eve of the global financial crisis.

THE DEVELOPMENT OF EUROPEAN INSTITUTIONS, 1957–2007

The European Parliament, the Council of the EU (the Council), and the European Commission (the Commission) (Figure 2.1) are the three key political institutions that hold executive and legislative power to implement policies related to the single market. The Council sets the EU's overall policy direction and reform agenda. All three institutions are involved in the EU legislation process: the Parliament represents the EU's citizens and is now directly elected by them; the Council represents the governments of individual member states; and the Commission represents the interests of the Union as a whole.

The European Parliament is one of the EU's main law-making institutions, along with the Council. Its main roles include debating and passing EU budget and other laws (together with the Council) and ensuring that other EU institutions, particularly the Commission, are working democratically. Until 1979, the members of the Parliament were appointed by each of the Member States' national parliaments, but since then they have been directly elected.[1] Over the years, the powers of the European Parliament had been expanded and

---

[1] The first direct elections of members of the European Parliament took place in 1979, in 9 member states with a turnout of 63 percent. Currently the Parliament consists of 785 members from 27 member states, a result of a total of 5 waves of enlargement. It works with 23 official languages, representing the interests of the EU citizens.

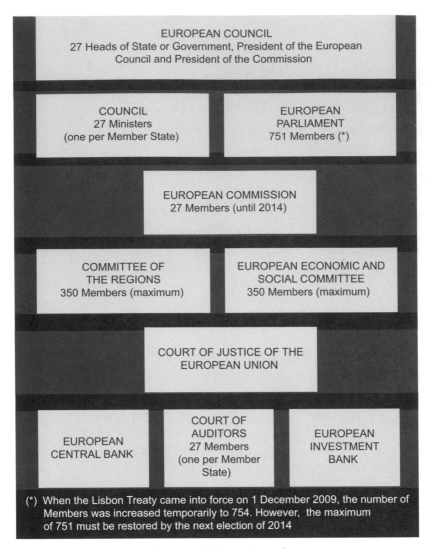

Figure 2.1 An Overview of the European Union Institutions[1]

Source: EU-Lex.
[1] According to the Treaty on the Functioning of the European Union.

strengthened.[2] In particular, the Maastricht Treaty (1992) introduced the co-decision procedure in certain areas of legislation and extended the cooperation procedure to others. It gave Parliament the power of final approval over the membership of the Commission, which was an important step forward in establishing

---

[2] For example, the first extension of Parliament's budgetary powers, under the Treaty of Luxembourg (1970), extended Parliament's budgetary powers, while a second treaty in 1975 on the same subject further strengthened these powers.

Parliament's political control over the European executive. The 2009 Lisbon Treaty brought together various policy areas (including the budget) under the co-decision procedure, further increasing the power of the Parliament.

The Council (informally known as the EU Council) is where national ministers from individual EU member states meet to adopt EU laws and coordinate policies.[3] More specifically, it passes EU laws proposed by the Commission (together with the Parliament), coordinates the broad economic policies of the EU member countries, and signs agreements between the EU and other non-EU countries. The Council brings together the heads of state of individual EU countries, with its presidency rotating among the 28 member states every six months. Decisions of the Council are taken by qualified majority as a general rule. Two types of majorities are needed to support the passage of a proposed law: a majority of countries (at least 15) and a majority of the total EU population (the countries in favor must represent at least 65 percent of the EU population).[4]

The Commission is the executive arm of the Union. Although it is composed of one commissioner from each member state, it represents and upholds the interests of the Union as a whole and is designed to be independent of national interests. The Commission is responsible for drafting all laws of the EU. It also manages the day-to-day business of implementing EU policies and spending EU funds. The Commission president is nominated by the Council. The appointment of all commissioners, including the president, is subject to the approval of the Parliament. As "guardian of the Treaties," the Commission monitors the member states' compliance with EU laws (Box 2.1).

While the fundamental decision-making procedure has not changed since the creation of the EU, the relative decision-making powers of the three institutions has evolved. For example, the Treaty of Amsterdam (1997) extended the co-decision procedure to 32 legal bases and reformed the procedure, putting Parliament as co-legislator on an equal footing with the Council. The Nice Treaty (2000) extended the co-decision procedure further to 37 legal bases.

The journey toward a single financial market has proven to be much harder than for a single market for goods. While the Treaty of Rome in 1957 set out to be a road map and created institutions to create a common market where goods, services, people, and capital could move freely, capital and banking markets were highly fragmented through the late 1980s.

In response, the European Economic Community members signed the Single European Act in Luxembourg in 1986 that resulted in significant institutional reforms. The Act represented the first major revision of the Treaty of Rome. It set the objective of establishing a single market by December 31, 1992. To achieve this objective, a more collaborative legislative process known as the Cooperation

---

[3] The Council of the EU is different from the European Council, which sets the EU's general policy direction and priorities but has no powers to pass laws. The European Council was established informally in 1974 as a forum for discussion between EU leaders, but has rapidly become the most influential EU institution that sets the political and economic agenda for the Union. Decisions of the European Council are generally based on consensus, unless the treaties provide otherwise.

[4] In 2014, a system of "double majority voting" will be introduced.

Box 2.1 Timeline of European Financial Integration Policies

1957	Treaty of Rome
1983	EC White Paper on Financial Integration (COM (83)207)
1986	Single European Act
1992	Maastricht Treaty on the European Union
1999	Establishment of the Monetary Union
2002	Introduction of the single currency, euro
2010	Establishment of the European Micro- and Macro-prudential Supervisory Authorities

Banking sector integration

1973	Directive (73/183/EEC) on the freedom of Establishment for Credit Institutions
1977	First Banking Directive (77/780/EEC)
1989	Second Banking Directive (89/646/EEC): Single Passport for Banks
2012	EC proposal for a regulation for a creation of a Single Supervision Mechanism (SSM)
2013	EC proposal for a Directive for establishing a framework for the recovery and resolution of credit institutions and investment firms (COM (2012)280/3)

Financial Services

1999	Financial Services Action Plan (FSAP)
2005	The completion of an integrated market for financial services
2005	EC White Paper on Financial Service Policy 2005-10 (COM (2005)629)

Insurance Sector integration

1964	Directive (64/225/EEC) on the Freedom of Establishment in Reinsurance
1976	Directive (76/580/EEC) on the Freedom of Establishment in Direct Insurance
1979	Coordinating Directive (79/267/EEC) on Direct Life Insurance

Capital Market integration

1979	Directive (79/279/EEC) Coordinating the Conditions for the Admission of Securities to Official Stock Exchanges
1980	Directive (80/390/EEC) Coordinating the Requirements for the Admission of Securities to Official Stick Exchange
1988	Directive (88/361/EEC) on the Free Movement of Capital

Procedure or the Article 252 Procedure was adopted, and qualified majority voting was extended to new areas. These reforms granted the Parliament formal legislative power. Under the procedure, the Council could, with support of the Parliament, adopt the Commission's legislative proposals by a qualified majority. It could also overrule a rejection by the Parliament by adopting a proposal unanimously.

The eventual integration of banking, money, and capital markets took place after the introduction of the Maastricht Treaty in 1992 and the introduction of a single currency in 1999. The debate on an economic and monetary union (EMU) was fully re-launched at the Hannover Summit in June 1988. The 1989 report by the Delors Committee set out a plan to introduce EMU in three stages, with the creation of a set of new EU institutions that further underpinned the single market:[5]

- The European Monetary Institute was established in 1994 as the forerunner of the European Central Bank (ECB), with the task of strengthening monetary cooperation between the member states and their national banks (the second stage of EMU).

- The ECB replaced the European Monetary Institute on June 1, 1998, under the Treaty of Maastricht and began to exercise its full powers with the introduction of the single currency, the euro, on January 1, 1999 (the third stage of EMU) for those members of the EU that met specified "convergence criteria" and that did have an "opt-out" waiver. It sets and implements the monetary policy for the euro area and safeguards price stability in the area.

- The ECB works with the central banks of all EU countries; together they form the European System of Central Banks. The ECB manages the foreign reserves of the euro area and ensures the smooth operation of the financial market infrastructure under the TARGET2 payments system and the technical platform for settlement of securities in Europe (TARGET2 Securities).

Over the years, efforts were made to achieve an integrated market for financial services within the national-based EU supervisory framework. Following the 2000 Lamfalussy Report, a four-level EU regulatory process (the Lamfalussy process) was set up to speed up the adoption of EU financial service directives (see Figure 2.1). It provided a framework and mechanism for timely decision making, based on the technical expertise of the "level 3 committees" (the Committee on European Banking Supervisors, the Committee of European Securities Regulators, and the Committee of European Insurance and Occupational Pensions Supervisors), open consultation, and political accountability. The Lamfalussy process aimed to foster the convergence of national supervisory practices, reach agreement on interpretations and applications of EU directives with non-binding guidelines, and foster greater trust among national supervisors. However, largely due to the lack of binding legal powers, the level 3 committees were unable to fulfill these tasks.[6] For example, no agreement was reached with regard to a common supervisory reporting framework, common standards for clearing and settlements, or unified registration and supervision of credit rating agencies at the EU level.

FINANCIAL STABILITY FRAMEWORK ON THE EVE OF THE GLOBAL FINANCIAL CRISIS

Despite the rapid financial integration prior to the 2008 global financial crisis, financial stability arrangements in Europe were (and remain) strongly based on national financial stability frameworks.[7] To monitor cross-border financial

---

[5] The committee of the central bank governors of the 12 member states was chaired by the president of the European Commission at that time, Jacques Delors.

[6] High-Level Group on Financial Supervision (2009).

[7] Decressin, Faruqee, and Fonteyne (2007).

institutions and cross-border risks, arrangements were put into place to govern cooperation, information exchange, and a specific home-host division of labor between the national supervisors in line with the 1983 agreement known as the Basel Concordat. Home countries are responsible for regulating and supervising their banks' foreign branches and performing consolidated supervision of cross-border banking groups; the supervision of their foreign subsidiaries, however, is the responsibility of the banks' host countries. National supervisory powers are constrained by the "single European passport" under which banks licensed to operate in one European country automatically can operate in any other European country. Also, the effectiveness of the cross-border supervision under this arrangement has been undermined by the lack of an effective bank resolution framework, both at the national and at the EU level. The lack of ex ante, as well as ex post, burden-sharing arrangements among EU countries hindered cross-border resolution as banks failed during the crisis, and it remains one of the key policy challenges today.

At the onset of the 2008 crisis, the regulatory framework in Europe lacked cohesiveness. EU members maintained considerable flexibility in the interpretation and enforcement of common EU directives, leading to wide divergences in national regulations. This lack of harmonization at the EU level reflected mainly a well-identified problem with the EU's four-level regulatory approach under the so-called Lamfalussy process (Figure 2.2): EU directives (levels 1 and 2) have often left member states with a substantial range of options; this made it difficult for level 3 committees to compare regulatory practices, conduct peer reviews, and enforce national compliance of EU common directives (level 4) with the EU legal framework. The resources available to the level 3 committees also severely limited their capacity to act and affected their performances.

The lack of a harmonized set of core regulatory rules hampered the efficient functioning of the single market. Different national rules and regulations resulted in competitive distortions and encouraged regulatory arbitrage. In particular, for cross-border financial groups such regulatory differences went against efficient group approaches toward risk management and capital allocation, and made the resolution of cross-border financial institutions even more difficult.[8] According to the De Larosiere report, "the European Institutions and the level 3 committees should equip the EU financial sector with a set of consistent core rules. Future legislations should be based, whenever possible, on regulations (which are of direct application). When directive are used, the co-legislator should strive to achieve maximum harmonization of the core issues."

The increasingly integrated financial market in the EU also posed a great challenge for financial supervision that relied on close collaboration between home and host country supervisors. Integration implies contagion risks, and a level playing field would be difficult to ensure when rules and supervisory practices differ substantially at the national level. Supervision in Europe was (and remains) largely based on national, home state supervision but with a more complex

---

[8] High-Level Group on Financial Supervision (2009), page 27.

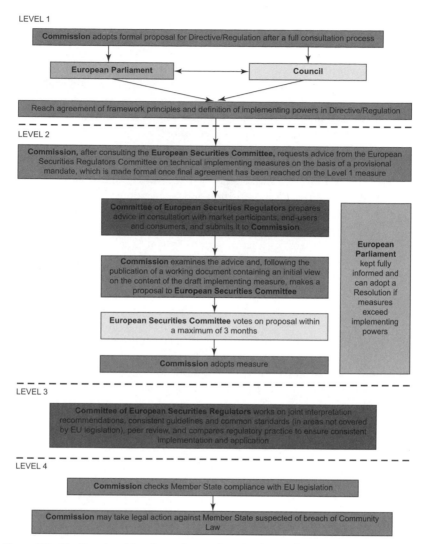

Figure 2.2 The Four-Level Regulatory Approach under the Lamfalussy Process

Source: European Commission (2004).

home-host division of supervisory responsibilities for cross-border financial institutions. While the subsidiaries of foreign firms are regulated by the host countries, the branches are regulated by the home country of the foreign firms, but EU law provides various safeguards for the host country to, for example, protect its depositors. In the area of investment services, host countries retain significant control over the foreign branches, including the rights to examine branch agreements, control branch liquidity, and access relevant information. This has resulted multiple reporting lines and complex mechanisms of home-host cooperation between home and host supervisors.

The home-host collaboration was largely ineffective within the EU institutional setting. The EU law did not offer host supervisors sufficient means to challenge the home country supervision of a group. Host supervisors also lacked incentives to contribute to the resolution of a distressed cross-border institution when it involved sharing a substantial financial burden. A binding mediation mechanism arbitrating between home and host supervisors was lacking. When a national supervisor failed to act promptly, there was no mechanism in place at the EU level allowing for a timely collaborative action.[9]

The crisis also revealed the lack of consistent crisis management and bank resolution tools across the single market. Due to the lack of crisis management framework at the EU level, the resolution of a distressed cross-border financial institution requires intensive coordination and cooperation of national resolution authorities. However, difficulties arose, not only because of the lack of burden-sharing arrangements but also because of different crisis management and resolution tools (and the lack of them), company and insolvency laws, creditor rankings, and depositor protection. These differences presented significant obstacles to a timely resolution and/or an orderly liquidation of cross-border financial institutions.

The organization of deposit guarantee schemes (DGSs) in the EU member states prior to the crisis has proven to be another major weakness in the EU banking regulatory framework that remains to be addressed. DGS is an important element of a financial safety net that helps prevent bank runs and cement confidence in the financial system. The significant variations in terms of DGS coverage and funding across EU member states were evidently inconsistent with the objective of a well-functioning single market, as the banks of the EU countries with the more protective regimes and stronger government backstops are more likely to attract deposits, at possibly lower rates. The De Larosiere Report supports harmonized and pre-funded DGSs in the EU countries.[10] However, the idea of a pooled EU DGS fund did not gain wide support, even from the De Larosiere Group.

Finally, but not least importantly, there was a lack of adequate macroprudential supervision at both the EU and national levels at the onset of the crisis. The EU lacked institutions charged with the tasks to systematically and effectively identify and monitor systemic risks and take policy actions when necessary; this was a weakness revealed in the supervisory frameworks of many countries around the world at that time. When macroprudential risks (such as those associated with rising and unsustainable macroeconomic imbalances) were spotted, no EU institution, including the ECB, had the explicit and formal financial stability mandate to take timely policy actions. Such mandate would be necessary for accessing all relevant information from national supervisors.

---

[9] High-Level Group on Financial Supervision (2009), page 35.
[10] Funded by the private sector and topped up by the states only in exceptional cases.

De Larosiere Report and a European System of Financial Supervision (2009–2011)

In response to the crisis, a European System of Financial Supervision was introduced after publication of the Commission's 2009 Larosiere Report. Three European Supervisory Authorities were created in 2010, replacing the existing Committees of Supervisors: a European Banking Authority replaced the former Committee of European Banking Supervisors; a European Insurance and Occupational Pensions Authority succeeded the Committee of European Insurance and Occupational Pensions Supervisors; and a European Securities and Markets Authority succeeded the Committee of European Securities Regulators. The new EU financial supervisory architecture also included the macroprudential dimension with the establishment of a European Systemic Risk Board.

The performance of these new EU institutions will be assessed in detail in this book.

REFERENCES

Acharya, Viral, 2009, "Some Steps in the Right Direction; A Critical Assessment of the de Larosiere Report," VOX, March 4. http://www.voxeu.org/article/critical-assessment-de-larosiere-report.

European Central Bank, 2012, "Financial Integration in Europe," Frankfurt, April.

European Commission, 2004, "The Application of the Lamfalussy Process to EU Securities Markets Legislation," Commission Staff Working Document.

High-Level Group on Financial Supervision in the EU, chaired by Jacques de Larosière, 2009, *Report*, Brussels, February 25, http://ec.europa.eu/internal_market/finances/docs/de_larosiere_report_en.pdf.

Decressin, Jorg, Hamid Faruqee, and Wim Fonteyne, eds., 2007, *Integrating Europe's Financial Markets,* (Washington: International Monetary Fund).

CHAPTER 3

European Union Financial Integration before the Crisis[1]

Luc Laeven and Thierry Tressel

During the past decades, financial markets in the European Union (EU) integrated at a rapid pace. The integration of financial systems was facilitated by far-reaching political measures by the EU to reduce regulatory obstacles to cross-border activity, promoting a single market in financial services, including by the creation of the euro, which removed exchange rate risks, and through the European Central Bank (ECB) collateral policy, which created a large pool of substitutable assets that could be used for refinancing operations.

The process of integration was strong but uneven. Large banks and insurance companies from advanced Europe established strong local presence in the newly opened markets of emerging Europe. In Western Europe, the creation of the euro and expectations of convergence resulted in a surge in capital inflows from Western to emerging Europe. The process of financial market integration was strong (as also evidenced by the convergence of interest rates) but uneven across countries and markets, and macro-financial (notably sovereign) risks were mispriced. Integration in the euro area went farther in wholesale funding markets and bond markets while retail lending markets remained mostly national. Large EU banks continued their strong expansion abroad and broadened the scope of their activities, becoming larger, more systemic, and more complex to resolve.

This integration took place against the backdrop of financial systems that remained mostly bank-based. With the exception of the United Kingdom, stock and bond markets played a small role in financing the economy. Centers for financial services remained few, including the United Kingdom and smaller economies (Ireland, Luxembourg, and so on). Many countries appeared "overbanked," either in number of institutions or in volume of bank assets.

[1] An earlier version of this chapter appeared partly as a Technical Note prepared by Luc Laeven and Thierry Tressel on "Financial Integration and Fragmentation in the European Union" (European Union: Publication of Financial Sector Assessment Program Documentation), IMF Country Report No. 13, March 2013. The authors thank Charles Enoch, Luc Everaert, Daniel Hardy, Jianping Zhou, and European authorities (especially the European Commission and the European Central Bank) for comments and Lindsay Mollineaux for excellent research assistance.

Financial integration reduced macroeconomic volatility, but in an uneven manner. Banking integration within the euro area led to reduced fluctuations in output growth since at least 1999, although the effect was uneven across countries and substantially weakened during the most recent period. Moreover, evidence suggested that macroeconomic risks went largely ignored.

PATTERNS OF FINANCIAL INTEGRATION

Financial integration in the EU increased markedly after the inception of the euro, supported by the single passport and common market. From the inception of the euro to the start of the financial crisis in 2008, the integration of EU banking systems progressed at a fast pace, as reflected in the rapid growth of foreign exposures of EU banks to residents from other EU countries. Between the start of 2000 and the first quarter of 2008, total intra-EU foreign exposures to nonresidents grew by €5.5 trillion (about 215 percent).[2] About 40 percent of this deepening of financial integration was accounted for by the combined increased foreign exposures to the euro area periphery from the "core" of the euro area and the United Kingdom (by about €1.6 trillion; Figure 3.1), as well as to emerging EU countries from advanced EU countries (by about €540 billion; Figure 3.2).[3]

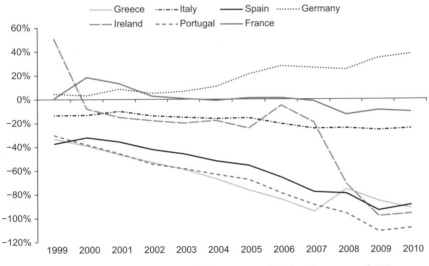

Figure 3.1   Net Financial Asset Positions of the Euro Area Periphery in percent of GDP

Source: IMF, International Financial Statistics database.

---

[2] Valuation effects arising from exchange rate movements are corrected for under the assumption that all claims are in euros.

[3] The euro area periphery includes Greece, Ireland, Italy, Spain, and Portugal. Emerging EU countries include Bulgaria, the Czech Republic, Estonia, Hungary, Latvia, Lithuania, Poland, Romania, the Slovak Republic, and Slovenia.

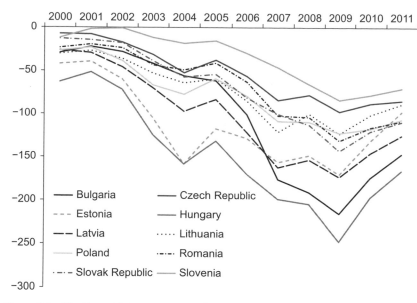

Figure 3.2 Net Financial Asset Positions of Emerging European Union countries in Percent of GDP

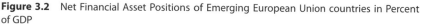

Source: IMF, International Financial Statistics and World Economic Outlook databases.

These capital flows from the "core" euro area and the United Kingdom to the periphery of the euro area and to emerging EU countries helped sustain large external imbalances.[4] In the euro area, current account balances of Greece, Ireland, Italy, and Spain worsened significantly during the first decade of European Monetary Union, while Portugal's deficit remained at the very high levels it had reached early in the decade. As a result of the increasing recourse to external financing, net external liabilities of these countries rose sharply, reaching levels close to or above 100 percent of GDP by the end of 2010 in Greece, Ireland, Portugal, and Spain.[5] During this period, Germany and a number of other countries in Northern Europe progressively built large current account surpluses, with the current account for the euro area as a whole remaining in broad balance throughout the period. Meanwhile, emerging European countries also experienced sharp deteriorations of their net foreign asset positions.

Financial integration was accompanied by a strong reduction of spreads across EU countries:

- *Sovereign bond markets.* The compression of sovereign bond yields in the euro area reached a maximum at the onset of the 2008 financial crisis, when the spreads between German bunds and bond yields of Greece reached 20 basis points only (Figure 3.3).

---

[4] See for example Chen, Milesi-Ferretti, and Tressel (2012).
[5] Italy's net financial assets deteriorated moderately as a share of GDP, but were among the five largest in absolute terms at the onset of the crisis.

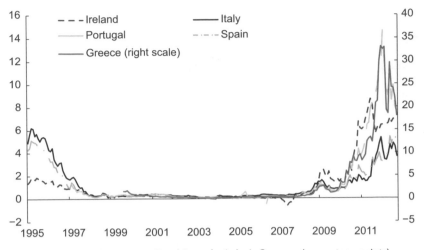

Figure 3.3   10-Year Government Bond Spreads vis-à-vis Germany (percentage points)

Sources: Bloomberg, L.P.; and IMF staff calculations.

- *Interbank markets.* There was also a strong convergence of funding costs in wholesale funding markets in the euro area. From the inception of the euro to 2007, the dispersion of rates on unsecured and secured (repo) lending to banks also collapsed. By 2007, the standard deviation of repo rates or unsecured rates (at one-month maturity) had fallen to between 0.5 and 0.7. Furthermore, until the start of the crisis, there was little differentiation of bank credit default swap (CDS) spreads across countries (Figure 3.4).

- *Retail markets.* The convergence of funding costs for banks and sovereigns spilled over to retail local markets across member states: (1) *deposit rates* strongly converged across the euro area; and (2) *loan rates* also converged significantly across member states.

Yet, integration was uneven across markets and geographies, with remaining fragmentation, notably in several domestic banking markets. Integration went farther in markets such as interbank markets and sovereign bond markets, and was more limited in retail deposit and loan markets, or equity markets:

- Evidence from euro area banks' geographical allocation of assets shows that the degree of cross-border integration varied across markets (Appendix 3.1):

  1. *Interbank markets.* Interbank markets were significantly integrated across borders according to the ECB's monetary financial institution (MFI) statistics. On the eve of the crisis, almost 40 percent of euro area banks' interbank claims were vis-à-vis nondomestic banks in the EU.

  2. *Bond markets.* Bond markets were the most integrated, with cross-border holdings accounting for 54 percent of total holdings of EU bonds by euro area banks at the end of 2007.

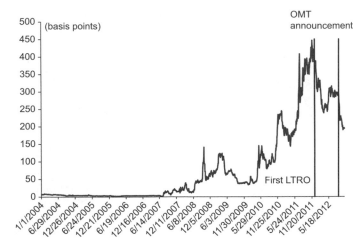

Figure 3.4 Dispersion of 5-Year Credit Default Swap Premiums of Commercial Banks in the Euro Area

Source: European Central Bank.
Note: LTRO = Long-Term Refinancing Operations; OMT = Outright Monetary Transactions.

3. *Loan markets.* Cross-border integration of loan markets remained limited. According to the ECB MFI data, cross-border loans were only a very small fraction of total loans to nonbanks. At the end of 2007, about 85 percent of loans supplied by euro area domestic credit institutions were to domestic residents, 12 percent to residents of other euro area countries, and 3 percent to residents of other EU countries.

4. *Equity markets.* Euro area banks had, to some extent, contributed to the integration of equity markets across the EU. At end 2007, about 25 percent of equity holdings of euro area banks were in other EU countries.

- *Intra-EU interbank markets are very large.* Evidence suggests that interbank markets are very large in the EU. Before the start of the crisis, claims of euro area banks on other banks in the EU amounted to about 70 percent of EU gross domestic product (GDP), among which about 30 percent of EU GDP were cross-border claims (Figure 3.5). At the end of 2011, the interbank market remained large, in spite of a substantial contraction, and the same ratios were, respectively, 66 percent and 22 percent of EU GDP.

- *EU foreign banks dominate emerging Europe's retail banking markets but have a more limited presence in euro area countries.* Foreign-owned banks account for a very significant share of domestic deposits and loans in emerging EU countries (Figure 3.6), and have remarkably remained stable since the start of the crisis in 2008, partly owing to the Vienna initiative. Deposits held in foreign-owned banks range from 45 percent in Latvia to about 90 percent in Estonia, and are typically much smaller in more mature EU countries,

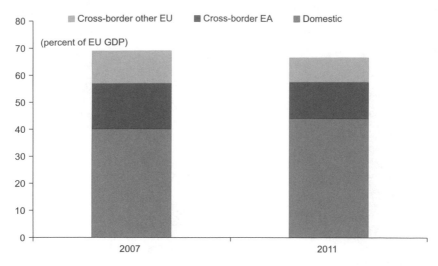

Figure 3.5 Interbank Claims of Euro Area (EA) Monetary Financial Institutions on Other Banks in the EU

Sources: European Central Bank, Monetary Financial Institutions database; and IMF, International Financial Statistics and World Economic Outlook databases.

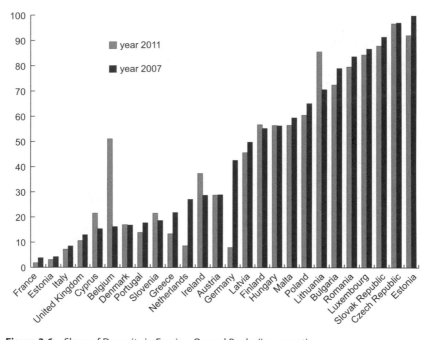

Figure 3.6 Share of Deposits in Foreign-Owned Banks (in percent)

Source: European Central Bank, Consolidated EU Banking Statistics.

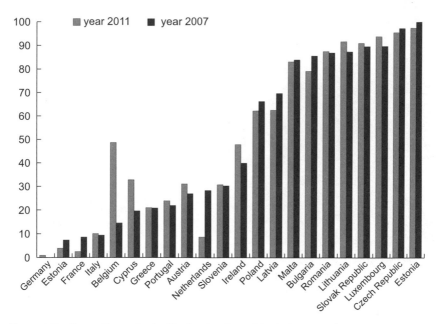

Figure 3.7 Share of Loans Booked by Foreign-Owned Banks (in percent)
Source: European Central Bank, Consolidated EU Banking statistics.

suggesting a much more limited integration of retail markets in these countries. Note, for example, that only about 10 percent of U.K. deposits are held within foreign banks, in spite of a much larger share of foreign banks in total bank assets booked in the United Kingdom. Data on loan shares provides a similar picture, suggesting a much higher local retail presence of foreign banks in emerging European countries than in more mature EU countries (Figure 3.7).

- *The dichotomy of foreign bank presence between emerging Europe and euro area countries may be related to "overbanking" in more advanced EU countries. Domestic retail banking is typically large in percent of GDP in more advanced EU countries, and remains instead more limited in emerging Europe.* While the penetration by foreign banks in emerging Europe was also a consequence of the banking crises that took place during the transition of the 1990s, differences of profitability and of "saturation" of domestic retail markets may also be a possible explanation for the limited retail presence of foreign banks in most advanced EU countries.

BANKING STRUCTURES IN THE EUROPEAN UNION

The financial integration took place in the context of a "bank-based" financial system. The EU financial systems are mostly bank-based, as stock and bond markets provide a relatively modest share of the financing to the private sector in most

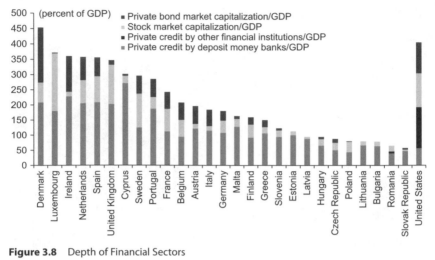

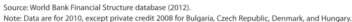

Figure 3.8 Depth of Financial Sectors

Source: World Bank Financial Structure database (2012).
Note: Data are for 2010, except private credit 2008 for Bulgaria, Czech Republic, Denmark, and Hungary.

countries (Figure 3.8). Total bank assets account for 283 percent of GDP in the EU, compared to about 65 percent of GDP in the United States. Large banks dominate EU banking systems, but medium-sized banks also play significant roles (Table 3.1). Even so, medium-sized banks, and to some extent small banks, remain an important component of the EU banking system. Indeed, as of end 2011, medium-sized banks and small banks accounted for 63 percent and 9 percent, respectively, of EU GDP.[6]

However, the structure of banking systems varies significantly across countries. Countries such as Austria, Germany, and Poland have very large numbers of small credit institutions. The banking systems of countries such as Austria or Germany have traditionally comprised three pillars of (1) private commercial banks, (2) public sector banks, and (3) large numbers of local cooperative banks

TABLE 3.1

Distribution of Banking Assets by Bank Size		
	Euros (billions)	% EU GDP
Large	26,780	211
Medium	8,040	63
Small	1,082	9
Total	35,902	283

Sources: European Central Bank; and IMF, World Economic Outlook database.

---

[6] In the ECB Consolidated Banking Statistics, the size thresholds are defined in relative terms. A bank is large if its assets account for more than 0.5 percent of total EU banking assets, and it is medium sized if its assets account for more than 0.0005 percent of total EU banking assets. On the basis of 2011 data, the two thresholds are, respectively, €180 billion for large banks and €180 million for medium-sized banks.

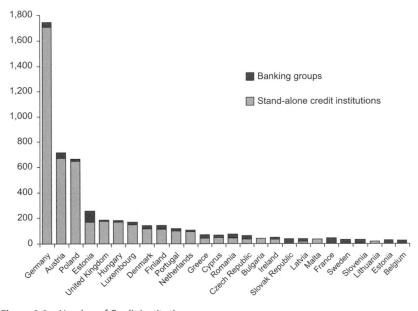

Figure 3.9   Number of Credit Institutions

Sources: European Central Bank, Consolidated Banking Statistics 2011.
Note: For France, data on stand-alone credit institutions are for 2007.

organized as a network. In Germany, private commercial banks accounted for 36 percent of total bank assets, public sector savings banks—Sparkassen and their associated Landesbanken—for 31 percent of total bank assets, and Volksbanken (cooperative banks) for 11 percent of total bank assets.[7] At the other end of the spectrum, countries such as France or Sweden have very small numbers of stand-alone credit institutions (Figure 3.9).

The process of financial integration was to a significant extent the outcome of the cross-border expansion of large EU banks. The main EU banking systems are dominated by a set of global systemically important banks (G-SIBs). These European G-SIBs have grown in size and importance and are highly interconnected with the rest of the global financial system. Their assets more than tripled since 2000, amounting to US$27 trillion in 2010 (Figure 3.10). As key players in global derivatives and cross-border interbank markets (see below section on funding), they are also among the most interconnected G-SIBs. European G-SIBs tend to be larger and more leveraged than their peers.[8]

---

[7] Germany FSAP Technical Note Banking Sector Structure (July 2011).

[8] In part, this is because European banks tend to follow the universal banking model, which combines a range of retail, corporate, and investment banking activities under one roof. There are some accounting differences that would make the balance sheets of the international financial reporting standards (IFRS)-reporting banks appear more "inflated" than the balance sheets of banks reporting under the U.S. generally accepted accounting principles (GAAP), e.g., netting of derivative and other trading items is only rarely possible under IFRS, but netting is applied whenever counterparty netting agreements are in place under U.S. GAAP.

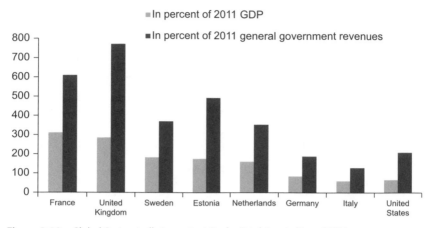

Figure 3.10   Global Systemically Important Banks: Total Assets (June 2012)

Sources: Bankscope; Financial Stability Board; and IMF, World Economic Outlook database.

In particular, they are very large relative to home country GDP, and in many EU countries, their size may dwarf the capacity of the home government to raise revenues.

Across EU countries, the distribution of bank assets is broadly aligned with economic size. Larger economies (France, Germany, Italy, Spain, and the United Kingdom) tend to have larger banking systems. However, because of its role as the main financial center of the EU, the United Kingdom accounts for a much larger share of assets of banks residing in the EU than its share of EU GDP. In contrast, Germany, Italy, or Spain each accounts for a smaller share of EU bank assets than its share of EU GDP (Figure 3.11).

Despite an increase in banking integration since inception of the euro, banking integration in the euro area still lags behind that in the United States, where banking integration increased rapidly following interstate deregulation in the 1980s. While cross-border banking activity has grown rapidly in the euro area, the integration of local banking markets remains low on average. Indeed, the non-local share of the banking system in the United States (as measured by the share of the banking system held by banks from other U.S. states) is a multiple of the non-local share of the banking system in the euro area (as measured by the share of the banking system held by banks from much other euro area countries). The non-local shares are computed using information from the Federal Reserve on out-of-state deposits[9] held by U.S. bank holding companies, and data from the ECB on financial assets held by financial institutions residing in other euro area countries (Figure 3.12).[10]

---

[9] Using deposits has the advantage that they are a better proxy than assets for residency-based activity of banks, as banks can book assets out of state where loans are made. This is less the case for deposits that remain mostly a local affair.

[10] For the comparison with the United States, as well as for any time that conclusions are drawn on the basis of the ECB cross-border data, a caveat is in order given the way that the data are reported for

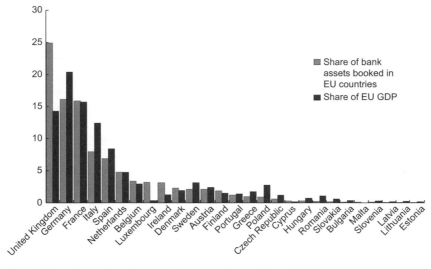

Figure 3.11   Share of Total Bank Assets Booked in the EU (end 2011)

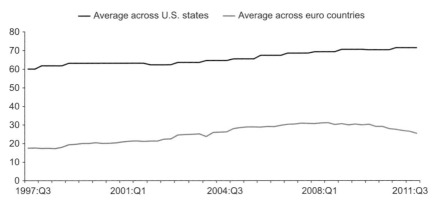

Figure 3.12   Non-local Share of Banking System in the United States and Euro Area (1997–2011)

Note: For the United States, share is the fraction of deposits in a state owned by a holding company that has deposits in other states. For the euro countries, share is the fraction of financial instruments invested within a country by financial institutions residing in other euro countries. Data are in percentages.

the EU. Specifically, such data are reported by residency rather than by nationality of the ultimate owner, and therefore miss any dynamics related to the resident subsidiaries of foreign banks. These resident subsidiaries may not have cut back as much on local loans as the direct cross-border loan numbers would suggest, and there are a few examples of core EU banks acquiring these foreign banks since the crisis, even as the Bank for International Settlements (BIS) claims show a decrease in foreign claims in the aggregate.

However, as a result of the integration process, cross-border credit by nonresident banks plays a non-negligible role in several countries with financial centers. Private credit by nonresident banks accounts for a significant portion of bank credit to the real economy in many EU countries, most likely a consequence of the process of financial integration within the EU (more on this below). This contrasts with the experience of a large country such as the United States, where credit by nonresident banks remains relatively small. At the end of 2010, 22 EU countries had loans from nonresidents exceeding 50 percent of GDP (Figure 3.13). Credit by nonresident banks is particularly large in financial centers (Ireland and the United Kingdom), small countries (Cyprus, Malta), in several core euro area countries (e.g., France), and in the Baltics (Estonia, Latvia).

FINANCIAL CENTERS

Financial markets in the EU are concentrated, with financial centers in London and elsewhere playing an important role. U.K.-based banks account for a disproportionate share of EU banking assets (about a quarter of the total) and the London-based capital markets and financial institutions account for a substantial share of global finance, including equity issuance, syndicated loan markets, foreign exchange trading, and Eurobond issuance, among others (Figure 3.14). Indeed, the U.K. financial system plays a central role not only within the EU financial system, but also globally, linking many EU financial systems to the rest

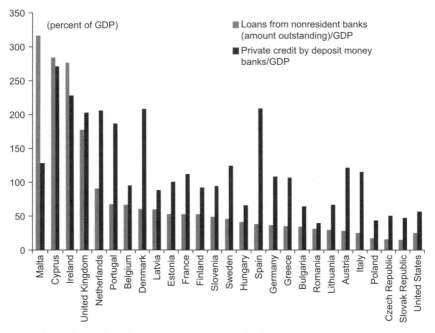

Figure 3.13 Loans from Resident and Nonresident Banks

Source: World Bank Financial Structure database (2012). Data are for 2010.

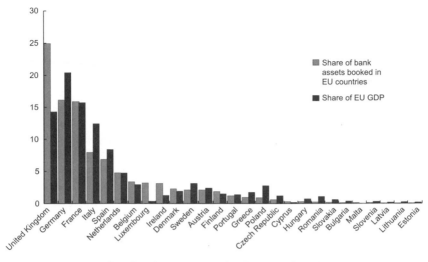

Figure 3.14a   Share of Total Bank Assets Booked in the EU (end 2011)

Sources: European Central Bank; IMF, World Economic Outlook database.

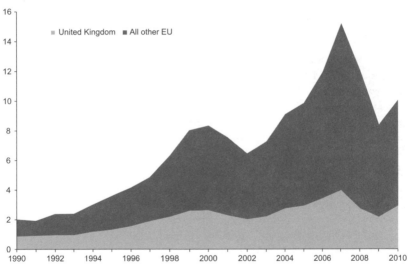

Figure 3.14b   Stock Market Capitalization in the U.K. and Rest of the EU, 1990–2010 (in trillions of U.S. dollars)

Source: World Bank, Financial Structure Database.

of the world. In addition, the asset management industry in the EU is spread over a number of financial centers, with after London also Amsterdam, Dublin, Frankfurt, Luxembourg, and Paris playing significant roles (in addition to off-shore centers).[11] The emergence and growth of these financial centers rests not

---

[11] For a description of small EU off-shore centers, see also Milesi-Ferretti and Lane (2010).

exclusively on the importance of comparative advantage and economic clusters but is also due to tax considerations and differences in regulatory requirements.

Even prior to the crisis, there was a discussion on the role of financial centers in the context of a single market, and whether the concentrated nature of financial markets in the EU posed concerns for competition. Mergers and acquisitions have been closely watched under EU rules to ensure that consumer welfare does not suffer from industry consolidation, and some efforts have been made to harmonize taxes and regulatory requirements across jurisdictions, although more progress toward harmonization would benefit the single market for financial services. From a competition perspective, there is also growing concern that financial restructuring in light of current banking problems will result in further industry consolidation.

SMOOTHING OF ECONOMIC CYCLES

In theory, banking integration could cause higher or lower economic volatility, depending on the prevalence of national versus regional shocks and the degree of product and labor market integration. A large literature has investigated the link between integration of banking markets and the amplitude of business cycles. In a seminal paper, Morgan, Rime, and Strahan (2004) analyze how integration of banks through ownership links and physical presence across U.S. states has affected economic volatility within U.S. states. They find that annual fluctuation in state-level economic growth falls and converges as banks become more integrated (through ownership links) with banks in other states, suggesting that banking integration across U.S. states has made state business cycles smaller and more alike. However, recent work by Kalemli-Ozcan, Papaioannou, and Peydro (forthcoming) finds a strong negative effect of banking integration on the synchronization of economic cycles for a broader set of advanced economies, including in the EU. This difference arises in large part from measuring banking integration using time-varying, country-pair data on bilateral banking flows from the BIS International Locational Banking Statistics. In this section, we combine the insights and approaches in these two papers by analyzing the impact of banking integration on economic fluctuations using time-varying, country-pair data on both bank ownership links and cross-border banking flows.

Regression analysis shows that banking integration within the euro area has led to reduced fluctuations in output growth since at least 1999, although the effect is uneven across countries and substantially weakened during the recent crisis period (see Box 3.1). This suggests that the amplitude of economy cycles across the euro area was reduced after euro adoption, in part due to increased financial integration, thus benefiting the real economy. However, this effect comes primarily from integration through foreign bank presence (inward banking integration), not from cross-border banking flows, even though the latter grew much more rapidly during the run-up to the recent crisis. At the same time, outward banking integration (that is, banking assets held in other states) appears to have increased economic fluctuations at home, suggesting that economies with international banks are

Box 3.1   Economic Fluctuations and Local and Cross-Border Banking Integration in Euro Area Countries

	Fluctuations in Real GDP Growth			
	(1) Local Banking Integration		(2) Cross-Border Banking Integration	
Variables	(A) 1999q1–2012q1	(B) 1999q1–2007q4	(A) 1999q1–2012q1	(B) 1999q1–2007q4
Interstate asset ratio	−2.276	−12.79***		
	(3.882)	(4.867)		
Other states asset ratio	1.850**	3.406***		
	(0.886)	(0.950)		
Total Bank for International Settlements claims/ GDP			−0.0398	−0.717
			(0.303)	(0.753)
Country fixed effects	x	x	x	x
Time fixed effects	x	x	x	x
Observations	612	419	317	130
Adjusted R-squared	0.393	0.424	0.399	0.400

Robust standard errors in parentheses *** $p < 0.01$, ** $p < 0.05$, * $p < 0.1$, clustered by country
Countries included in regression: Austria, Belgium, Germany, Spain, Finland, France, Greece, Ireland, Italy, Netherlands, and Portugal
Notes: Dependent variable is the residual of ln(GDP, t/GDP, t-1) when regressed on country and time FE. IAR denotes Interstate asset ratio, computed as banking assets in country i held by monetary financial institutions (MFIs) from all other Euro countries divided by total banking assets in country i held by domestic and all other Euro countries. OSAR denotes Other states asset ratio (OSAR), computed as banking assets held by MFIs from country i in countries other than country i (including outside euro area) divided by banking assets held by MFIs from country i in country i. IAR and OSAR variables are constructed using quarterly cross-border banking data from the ECB. Cross-border claims are from BIS on a quarterly, bilateral basis. Total BIS claims denote the sum of claims by home country banks on other countries and claims by foreign banks on the home country. Exchange rate for construction of BIS Claims/GDP variable is from the European Central Bank (ECB), using last daily exchange rate of the quarter. Population is at the country level. Regressions include a constant term and control for the labor shares of major industries, as in Morgan, Rime, and Strahan (1994) (coefficients not reported). Sector data is from Eurostat. 1998–2012, quarterly. GDP denotes real GDP. Nominal GDP data are from the ECB and chain-linked.

vulnerable to shocks from abroad. Additionally, the positive effect of banking integration operates primarily through output, not income growth. Importantly, these benefits from financial integration obtain even though the effect is substantially weakened (or even reversed) during the recent crisis period. Overall, the results are rather weak, suggesting that the benefits of financial integration in term of smoothing of economic cycles have not accrued to all economies.

But it has also contributed to a mispricing of risks. Although sovereign bond spreads prior to euro adoption were strongly correlated with indicators of macroeconomic vulnerability such as current account and government debt ratios, during the run-up to the crisis, sovereign risks within the euro area were seriously mispriced; there was virtually no correlation between sovereign spreads of individual member states (relative to Germany) and their current account or government debt ratios (Figure 3.15). Since the sovereign debt crisis in the euro zone, such macro factors have again become priced (Figure 3.16).

These patterns are confirmed in regression analysis of sovereign CDS spreads (relative to Germany) for EU member states (see Box 3.2). These regressions

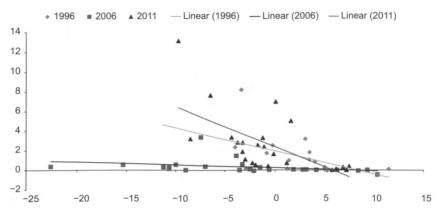

Figure 3.15 Sovereign Bond Spreads on German Bonds against Current Account/GDP

Sources: Bloomberg L.P.; IMF, World Economic Outlook database; and authors' calculations.

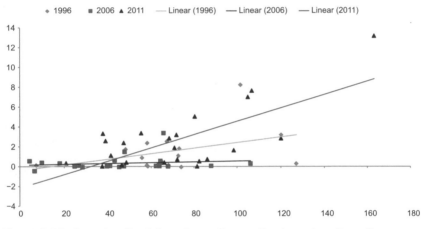

Figure 3.16 Sovereign Bond Spreads on German Bonds against Gross Government Debt/GDP

Sources: Bloomberg L.P.; IMF, World Economic Outlook database; and authors' calculations.

related sovereign CDS spreads to measures of government indebtedness while controlling for other measures of macroeconomic vulnerability, including current account deficits, household debt, and house prices. While government indebtedness (as measured by the ratio of gross government debt to GDP) has been strongly reflected in CDS spreads since the start of the crisis in 2008, this was not the case during the run-up to the crisis.

CONCLUSION

The process of financial integration was very strong before the crisis, both within the euro area and between Western Europe and emerging European countries.

Box 3.2   Sovereign Spreads and Indicators of Macroeconomic Vulnerability (2004–2011)

Dependent variable is average of sovereign CDS spread relative to German CDS during year	(1) Full Period: 2004–2011	(2) Precrisis: 2004–2007	(3) Crisis Period: 2008–2011
Gross debt of government/GDP	8.626*	0.0714	11.80*
	(1.958)	(0.275)	(1.983)
Current account/GDP	19.99	−2.065***	17.66
	(1.529)	(−4.437)	(1.068)
Gross debt-to-income ratio of households	−0.623	−0.274***	−2.687
	(−0.416)	(−4.271)	(−0.386)
Housing price index	4.634	−0.223*	6.503
	(1.026)	(−1.911)	(1.059)
Year fixed effects	×	×	×
Country fixed effects	×	×	×
Observations	81	36	45
Adjusted R-squared	0.603	0.682	0.594

Sources: Bloomberg, L.P.; IMF, International Financial Statistics database; and Eurostat.
Notes: Countries included in regression: Austria, Belgium, Estonia, Finland, France, Ireland, Italy, Netherlands, Portugal, Slovak Republic, Slovenia, and Spain. All regressions include a constant term (not reported). Robust t-statistics in parentheses. *** $p < 0.01$, ** $p < 0.05$, * $p < 0.1$. CDS = credit default swap.

The financial integration within the euro area took place mostly in wholesale bank funding markets and sovereign bond markets, while retail markets remained mostly national. In emerging Europe, a large presence of foreign banks built up over time, which relied on internal capital markets within groups to fund their expanding activities in host countries. The integration was underpinned by strong beliefs that capital receiving countries would converge fast toward the per capita income levels of the more developed countries—a belief that was to some extent verified for central European countries, but much less for the periphery of the euro area, where gaps with the relatively more developed countries did not in general diminish.

The integration lacked a macroprudential perspective. The large and sustained capital inflows sowed the seeds of the subsequent reversal of capital flows. Large current account deficits and growing net foreign asset liabilities were allowed to accumulate unchecked, while the risks associated with balance sheet vulnerabilities and asset price bubbles were not priced in. Although some countries, particularly in emerging Europe, took regulatory actions, the mere size of external liabilities made the size of the shock associated with the reversal of capital flows particularly large.

REFERENCES

Chen, R., G. M. Milesi-Ferretti, and T. Tressel, 2012, "External Imbalances in the Euro Area," IMF Working Paper 12/236 (Washington: International Monetary Fund).

Kalemli-Ozcan, Sebnem, Elias Papaioannou, and Jose-Luis Peydro, forthcoming, "Financial Regulation, Globalization and Synchronization of Economic Activity," *Journal of Finance*.

Milesi-Ferretti, G. M., and Lane, P. R., 2010, "Cross-Border Investment in Small International Financial Centers," IMF Working Paper 10/38 (Washington: International Monetary Fund).

Morgan, Donald P., Bertrand Rime, and Philip E. Strahan, 2004, "Bank Integration and State Business Cycles," *Quarterly Journal of Economics* Volume 119, No. 4, pp. 1555–84.

APPENDIX 3.1. EURO AREA MONETARY FINANCIAL INSTITUTIONS: SHARE OF CROSS-BORDER HOLDINGS OF FINANCIAL ASSETS

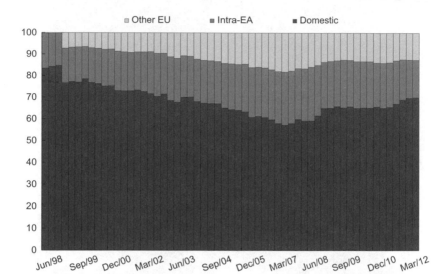

Figure A3.1 Interbank Assets of Euro Area (EA) Banks

Source: European Central Bank.

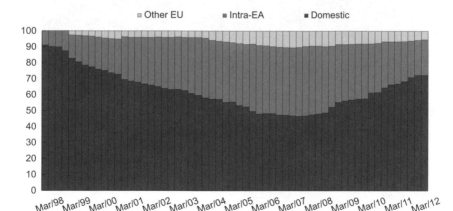

Figure A3.2 Securities Other than Shares Held by Euro Area (EA) Banks

Source: European Central Bank.

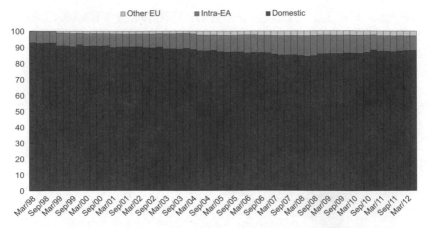

Figure A3.3   Loans to Non-Monetary Financial Institutions by Euro Area (EA) Banks

Source: European Central Bank.

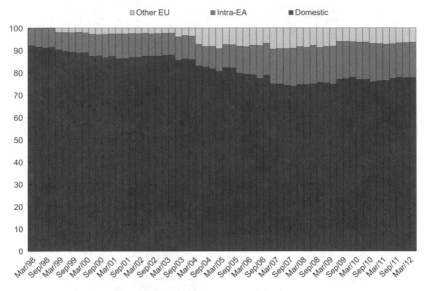

Figure A3.4   Shares and Equities Held by Euro Area (EA) Banks

Source: European Central Bank.

CHAPTER 4

Financial, Sovereign, and Macro Risk in the European Union: Contingent Claims Approach

DALE GRAY

One of the key features of the recent global and euro area financial crises is the role of interconnectedness across financial institutions, sectors of the economy, and across borders. A Contingent Claims Analysis (CCA) framework lends itself to analyzing such interconnections and the transmission of risk within and outside the EU. Such a framework was used for two applications. First was a CCA-network model to estimate the connectedness between 63 banks, 39 insurers, and 17 sovereigns, most of which are in the EU (but some from the United States and Japan are also included). This model shows how interconnectedness evolved during the different stages of the financial crisis that began in 2008 and the more recent sovereign-financial crisis in the EU. The second application is a model framework for the analysis of interactions among banking sector risk, sovereign risk, corporate sector risk, real economic activity, and credit growth for 15 European countries and the United States. Key to the framework is that sovereign credit spreads, banking system credit risk, corporate sector credit risk, economic growth, and credit variables are combined in a fully endogenous setting. This framework permits an analysis of the impact and spillovers of shocks, and helps identify policies that help mitigate banking system, sovereign credit risk, and recession risk.

INTRODUCTION

Contingent Claims Analysis (CCA) indicators capture the nonlinearity of changes in bank assets, equity capital, bank credit spreads, and default probabilities that are derived from forward-looking equity market information, in conjunction with balance sheet data. It captures the expected losses, spreads, and default probability for sovereigns.

The first application is a CCA-network network model to estimate the connectedness between 63 banks, 39 insurers, and 17 sovereigns, most of which are in the EU (the United States and Japan are also included). It has the advantage of using forward-looking CCA risk indicators and network connectedness measures (Granger causality and degrees of connectedness) during different stages of the financial crisis that began in 2008, and the more recent sovereign-financial sector crisis in the EU that began in 2010. The data used is monthly data from 2002 to March 2012.[1]

The second application is a CCA global vector autoregression (GVAR) model framework for 16 countries. For each country, there is banking system CCA risk indicator, sovereign risk indicator, corporate sector risk indicator, economic growth, and credit to the private sector. The data is based on a monthly sample covering the period from January 2002 to December 2012 (132 observations). After estimation, the model is used to conduct scenario simulations, involving multiple shocks to selected sovereigns and banking systems. Input shocks and output responses for the banking systems, corporate sectors, and sovereigns can be transformed into credit spreads and interpreted as changes in bank funding costs, sovereign credit spreads, and corporate sector funding costs. Both positive and negative shock scenarios are illustrated. Such output responses could be input to banking/sovereign submodules, which are used to compute aggregate loss estimates and changes in bank capital.[2]

INTERACTIONS BETWEEN FINANCIAL INSTITUTIONS AND SOVEREIGNS

There are numerous channels of interaction between the sovereign and the banks. As shown in Figure 4.1, the mark-to-market fall in the value of sovereign bonds held by banks reduces bank assets. This can increase bank-funding costs, and if the sovereign is distressed enough, the value of official support (guarantees) will be eroded. These have knock-on effects, as shown. An adverse feedback loop ties sovereigns' stresses to banking-sector challenges. In some situations, this vicious cycle can spiral out of control, resulting in the inability of the government to provide sufficient guarantees to banks and leading to a systemic financial crisis and a sovereign debt crisis. In such cases, the relationship of expected losses (ELs) of sovereigns, ELs of banking systems, and gross domestic product (GDP) are interrelated in a way subject to costly destabilization processes. If funds for a banking sector recapitalization come from increased sovereign borrowing, this increases sovereign risk.

Negative-feedback effects could arise in a situation where the financial system is outsized compared to the government. Thus, distress in the financial system triggers a large increase in government financial guarantees/contingent liabilities. Potential costs to the government, due to the guarantees, can lead to a rise in sovereign spreads. Bank's spreads depend on retained risk, which is lower given

---

[1] This is joint work with several academics at MIT (Robert Merton and Andrew Lo), University of Massachusetts (Mila Getmansky), and University of Venice (Monica Billio and Loriana Pelizzon), and results have been published in Merton and others, 2013 and in Billio and others, forthcoming.

[2] This is joint work with the European Central Bank (ECB). The details of this model and results can be found in the forthcoming IMF Working Paper (Gray and others, forthcoming).

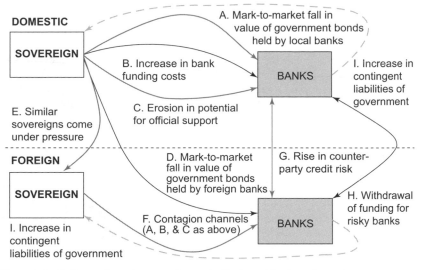

Figure 4.1 Spillovers from the Sovereign to the Banks and Banks to Sovereign

Source: International Monetary Fund (2010).

the application of government guarantees, and also on the creditworthiness of the sovereign (as a result of fiscal sustainability and debt service burden), as investors view the bank's and the sovereign's risks as intertwined. Concern that the government balance sheet will not be strong enough for it to make good on guarantees could lead to deposit withdrawals or a cutoff of credit to the financial sector, thereby triggering a destructive feedback loop in which both bank and sovereign spreads increase. In some situations, this vicious cycle can spiral out of control, resulting in the inability of the government to provide sufficient guarantees to banks, and leading to a systemic financial crisis and a sovereign debt crisis (see Gray, Merton, and Bodie, 2007; Gray, Jobst, and Malone 2010; Gray and Jobst 2011; and Jobst and Gray 2013 for more on financial, sovereign, and macroeconomic/macro-financial interactions).

CONTINGENT CLAIMS ANALYSIS FOR FINANCIAL INSTITUTIONS AND SOVEREIGNS

CCA originated with the Merton model, and it provides a methodology to combine balance sheet information with widely used finance and risk management tools to construct marked-to-market balance sheets that better reflect underlying risk (see Merton, 1973, 1974; and Gray, Merton, and Bodie, 2008). It can be used to derive a set of risk indicators for individual firms and financial institutions, which can serve as risk indicators and barometers of vulnerability, and in particular, to calculate default probabilities. An estimate of the market value of assets and asset volatility is needed, but the market value of assets is not directly observable, because many of the assets on the balance sheet of a financial institution are not traded. CCA imputes the value and volatility of assets indirectly, using the market value of equity from stock price data, equity volatility (from equity data and/or equity options), and the book value of short- and long-term obligations. This is then used to calculate risk indicators, such as the probability of default, credit spreads, or other risk indicators.

CCA balance sheets are risk-adjusted balance sheets. On the CCA balance sheet, the total market value of assets, A, at any time, t, is equal to the sum of its equity market value, E, and its risky debt, D, maturing at time, T. The asset value is stochastic and may fall below the value of outstanding liabilities. Equity and debt derive their values from the uncertain assets. As pointed out by Merton (1973), equity value is the value of an implicit call option on the assets, with an exercise price equal to default barrier, B. The value of risky debt is equal to default-free debt, minus the present value of expected loss due to default. The firm's outstanding liabilities constitute the bankruptcy level. The expected loss due to default can be calculated as the value of an implicit put option on the assets, A, with an exercise price equal to the default-free value of debt, B, over time horizon, t, risk-free rate, r, and asset volatility σ_A. The implicit put option value will be called the expected loss value, ELV.

Risky debt = default-free debt – expected loss due to default

$$D(t) = Be^{-rT} - ELV \tag{1}$$

Equity values are consensus views of market participants and thus provide forward-looking information. The value of assets is not directly observable, but it can be implied using CCA. The calibration of the model for banks and firms uses the value of equity, the volatility of equity, and the distress barrier as inputs into two equations in order to calculate the implied asset value and implied asset volatility.[3] The implied asset value and volatility can then be used with the other parameters to calculate risk indicators, such as the spreads, the implicit put option, default probabilities, and other risk indicators. There are a variety of techniques that can be used to calibrate the CCA parameters.

From the CCA model, the credit spread, s, can be written as:

$$s = \frac{\ln(B/D)}{T} - r = -\frac{1}{T}\ln\left(1 - \frac{ELV}{Be^{-rt}}\right) \tag{2}$$

where the $D = Be^{-yT}$ risky debt and B = the default barrier, T is the time horizon and r is the risk-free rate. The expected loss ratio[4] (defined as EL) is the expected loss value per unit of default-free debt and it is equal to:

---

[3] See Merton (1974, 1977, 1992); Gray, Merton, and Bodie (2008); Gray and Malone (2008); and Gray and Walsh (2008).
[4] The expected loss ratio can be shown to also equal to the risk neutral default probability times loss given default.

$$1 - \exp(-sT) = \frac{ELV}{Be^{-rt}} \equiv EL \tag{3}$$

In principle, there are a variety of CCA calibration techniques that could be used to calculate CCA parameters for individual banks, insurance companies, and firms. For the calibration of implied assets and volatility in the original Merton model, the following inputs are used: market capitalization value and volatility, default barrier estimates from promised payments on debt, the risk free rate, and a time horizon.[5] After the calibration, the expected loss value, ELV (i.e. implicit put option value), and the expected loss ratio (EL) which in turn are used to calculate credit spreads; the credit spread from the CCA model derived from equity and balance sheet information is called the "fair value spread."

Strong evidence supports the claim that implicit and explicit government backing for banks depresses bank credit default swap (CDS) spreads to levels below where they would be in the absence of government support. Bank creditors are the beneficiaries of implicit and explicit government guarantees, but equity holders are not. CCA, which uses bank equity market information together with balance sheet data, can estimate credit risk indicators and infer a fair value CDS spread (FVCDS) for financial institutions. The FVCDS is an estimate of the spread without implicit or explicit government support, thus disentangling its effect. Several studies have shown that for banks during the crisis in 2008–2009, the CCA-based fair value spreads are higher than the observed market CDS spreads in many cases (see Gray, Merton, and Bodie, 2008; Gapen, 2009; Moody's Analytics, 2010; Gray and Jobst, 2011; and Schweikhard and Tsemelidakis, 2012). The observed CDS spreads of banks are lower than fair value spreads because of the effect of implicit and explicit government guarantees on observed CDS, especially in times of crisis; thus, the bank CDS is distorted. Also, it is observed that for banks in countries with very high sovereign spreads, the observed CDS is frequently higher than the fair value spreads.

A database from Moody's CreditEdge provides a long time series of risk indicators, calculated in a consistent manner, which can be used to calculate what Moody's CreditEdge refers to as the FVCDS. This FVCDS is a good proxy for the fair value spread we need, so we can use it to obtain the individual bank expected loss ratio, EL_b, insurer expected loss ratio, EL_b, and corporate expected loss ratio, EL_c. These expected loss ratios have a five-year horizon ($T = 5$), monthly frequency, and are reported in basis points.

For countries in the euro area periphery (Greece, Ireland, Italy, Portugal, and Spain), Figure 4.2 shows the average bank FVCDS was higher than average observed bank CDS, and higher than the average observed sovereign CDS spread during the 2008–2009 crisis period. However, from mid-2010 to 2012, both the observed bank and sovereign CDS spreads are higher than the bank FVCDS.

---

[5] Models could be used that incorporate not just the volatility of the asset return process but higher moments as well (e.g., jump diffusion, Gram-Charlier, or some other process as described in Backus and others, 2004, and Jobst and Gray, 2013).

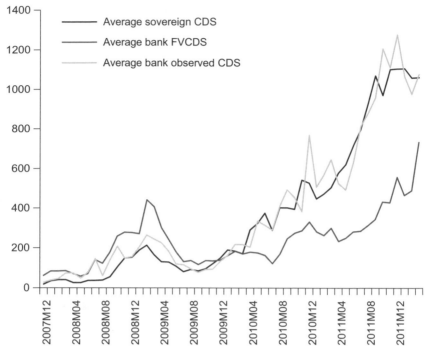

Figure 4.2 Eurozone Periphery Average Sovereign CDS, Bank CDS, and Bank FVCDS (*Basis points, average 5-year spreads*).

Sources: Bloomberg, L.P.; Moody's Analytics; and IMF staff estimates.
Note: CDS = credit default swaps; FVCDS = fair value CDS.

The FVCDS and its associated expected loss ratio EL_b are not distorted in a major way by the effect of government guarantees (situations where FVCDS > CDS in the 2008 to 2009 period), or from spillovers from high sovereign spreads (situations where CDS > FVCDS seen in the 2010 onward in Figure 4.2). Our aim is to try to measure a bank's pure "stand alone" risk, minimizing distortions caused by implicit and explicit guarantees or sovereign spillovers, so we will use a measure of fair value spreads for each financial institution and the associated EL.

The relationships between bank expected default frequency (EDF), the FVCDS, EL, and the ratio of market capitalization to assets are nonlinear, as shown in Box 4.1. In the center of Figure 4.3, the areas within the respective dotted lines show a "safe zone" where the relationships are less nonlinear and an even safer "investment grade" zone. Various negative or positive shocks—and combinations of policies—can push a bank out of, or into, the safe zone/investment grade zone.

The smaller rectangle in the center of Figure 4.3 is the safest zone, "investment grade" zone and above: CCACR 3 percent and above, EL of 1000 basis points or less, spreads less than 200 basis points, and EDF of less than 0.5 percent. The slightly larger "safe" zone, just below investment grade, in Figure 4.3 is where EDFs are less than 1.5 percent, spreads are 400 basis points or less, EL is less than 2000 basis points, and CCACR is above 2.5 percent.

Box 4.1 Relationships between Contingent Claims Analysis Capital Ratio, Expected Default Frequency, Fair-Value Credit Default Swap Spreads, and Expected Loss Ratio for a Typical Bank

It is useful to understand the nonlinear relationships between the ratio of market capital to assets, the CCA capital ratio (CCACR), the expected default frequency (EDF), the spread (FVCDS spread), and the expected loss ratio (shown in the graphs as a fraction), as illustrated in Figure 4.3. This is the typical pattern for a bank which has experienced periods of distress and nondistress. It is compiled from a data sample covering approximately three years that is taken from the CreditEdgePlus database (Moody's). If the CCACR is high, 0.8 to 0.9 (8 or 9 percent), EDF is very low, the EL is low (around 0.05, or 500 basis points), credit spreads are low (around 100 basis points). In distress periods, when the CCACR falls from 0.3 to 0.1, the EDF is very high (6 to 7 percent), spreads are 700 to 900 basis points, and the EL is 0.3 to 0.4 (equal to 3000 to 4000 basis points). Once the capital ratio starts moving below 3 percent, the EDF increases over 1 percent, spreads go over the 250 basis points "threshold" and EL is higher than 1000 basis points there is increasing risk of negative shocks leading to sharply higher spreads and EDFs. The dynamics are nonlinear.

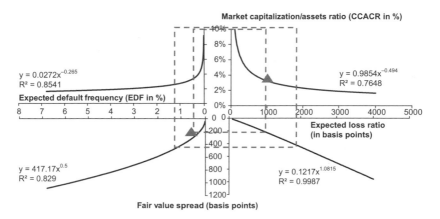

Figure 4.3 Relationships between Contingent Claims Analysis Capital Ratio (CCACR), Expected Default Frequency (EDF), fair-value credit default swap (FVCDS), and Expected Loss Ratio for a Typical Bank

Sources: Moody's CreditEdge data; and author's estimates.

The relationship between Moody's ratings, one-year EDFs, and fair-value spreads is shown in Figure 4.4. Investment grade is defined as ratings BBB- and higher. Spreads of 400 basis points or less corresponds to EDFs of about 1.5 to 2 percent and ratings of B or higher. The sharp increase in spreads and EDFs at rating below B shows significant non linearity. The comparison of ratings spreads and EDFs is shown in Figure 4.4. Once the rating becomes sub-investment grade, the spreads and default probabilities increase sharply as ratings decline further.

One can think of the "safe zone" as a target zone that one would like to reach using combinations of policies (capital injections, increasing the level and lowering asset volatility, and risk transfer policies described in more detail later).

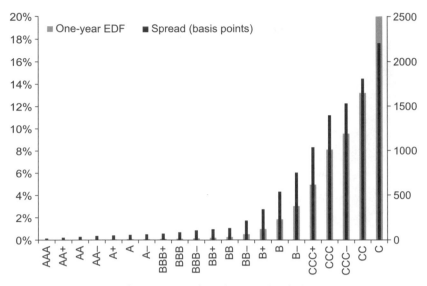

Figure 4.4 Comparison of Ratings, Spreads, and Expected Default Frequencies (EDFs)
Sources: Gray and others (forthcoming); Moody's CreditEdge data; and author's estimates.

For the EU banks in the Moody's CreditEdge database, Table 4.1 give the statistics by size range—assets (market value of assets), market capitalization, EDF, FVCDS, CDS value, and the sensitivity value of percent change in market cap, divided by the percent change in assets (derived from scenario analysis). Insurance companies are also shown.

For the sovereigns, we do not have equity values, so we use actual market sovereign CDS spreads, because we assume there is no one guaranteeing their debt and CDS should reflect the sovereign credit risk (see Merton and others, 2013).[6] Recent analysis of sovereign CDS (IMF, 2013) shows the sovereign CDS market is not prone to speculative excesses, nor does it lead to higher sovereign funding costs, and this market does not appear to be more prone to high volatility than other financial markets. The CDS expected loss ratio for a sovereign is a function of the time horizon and the sovereign CDS.

CCA-NETWORK MODELS

The CCA-network model uses inputs from the individual CCA risk indicators in a network model using connectedness measures. The model uses ELs from 63 individual banks, insurers, and 17 sovereigns, including 13 EU countries, plus

---

[6] If the ESM or another entity outside of a certain country were to explicitly guarantee sovereign debt then it might be possible to measure the effect on the sovereign CDS. The potential ECB Outright Monetary Transactions (OMT) purchases of sovereign debt in the euro area is not a guarantee but rather more like rollover financing and thus sovereigns risk would decrease and the sovereign CDS would be expected to decline.

TABLE 4.1

EU Banks—Contingent Claims Analysis Statistics for 136 Banks in EU Countries

Bank size range (millions of euros)	Number	Assets (millions of euros)	Market capitalization (millions of euros)	Market capitalization to assets (percent)	Debt (DB) (millions of euros)	EDF one-year, (percent)	FVCDS (basis points)	CDS (basis points)	Percent change in market capitalization/percent assets ratio
1,000,000 to 2,000,000	8	11,798,600	451,246	3.82	10,163,067	1.24	640	181	12.2
500,000 to 1,000,000	5	3,243,830	137,600	4.24	2,783,083	1.06	604	203	11.2
100,000 to 500,000	19	3,983,896	241,279	6.06	3,313,135	1.38	606	300	10.7
0 to 100,000	104	1,540,592	73,418	4.77	1,333,491	3.60	643	619	13.5
Totals/Averages	**136**	**20,566,919**	**903,543**	**4.72**	**17,592,775**	**1.82**	**623**	**326**	**12**
Insurance Companies	**59**	**5,963,580**	**374,575**	**6.28**		**3.0**	**539**	**445**	**8.9**

Sources: Moody's Credit Edge; and author's estimates.

Note: Debt is default barrier, CDS if available, otherwise FVCDS is used for an average. A shock in percent of assets multiplied by sensitivity value gives change in market capitalization. CDS = credit default swaps; EDF = expected default frequency; FVCDS = fair value credit default swap

Japan, Norway, Switzerland, and the United States (ELs calculated as described in the previous section.

To estimate feedback effects of credit quantitatively, Granger causality tests take the EL of entity X at time, t, and relate it to the EL of entity Y at time, $t +$ 1. If, for example, entity X is a sovereign, the sovereign credit measure EL is related to the EL credit measure of entity Y—perhaps a domestic bank (or insurer) or another sovereign's bank (or insurer)—in the next period (month). Then, the model is estimated in the other direction. If something happens to the credit of domestic bank Y, how does it affect sovereign X's credit? Equation 4 presents the formal Granger causality test.

$$X_t = \sum_{j=1}^{m} a_j X_{t-j} + \sum_{j=1}^{m} b_j Y_{t-j} + \epsilon_t$$

$$Y_t = \sum_{j=1}^{m} c_j X_{t-j} + \sum_{j=1}^{m} d_j Y_{t-j} + \eta_t$$

(4)

If the set of b_j coefficients is statistically significant, then Y influences or "Granger-causes" X. Similarly, if the set of c_j coefficients is significant, then X influences or "Granger-causes" Y. If both sets of coefficients are significant, then there is mutual influence between Y and X. Of course, Y and X can be any pair of entities. It is important to understand that, in addition to assessing general connectedness between two entities, we are assessing the direction of the connectedness; for example, it may be that Y influences X, but X does not influence Y.[7] The degree of connectedness between banks (BAN), sovereigns in euro area periphery countries (SOV-PER), sovereigns in euro area non-periphery countries (SOV-NPER), and insurers (INS) for different periods during the crisis are shown in Table 4.2.[8]

The degree of interconnectedness between banks, insurers, and sovereigns varies with the stages of the crisis. The numbers in Table 4.2 are percent of causal connections out of the total number of possible connections that were significant at 99 percent or higher confidence level. Interconnections are not symmetric; sovereigns seem to affect banks and insurers (and other sovereigns) more than the reverse. Interconnections were low before the crisis, but increased sharply during the global financial crisis. From September 2005 to August 2008, the non-periphery sovereigns were affecting other sovereigns and insurers, and periphery sovereigns were affecting non-periphery sovereigns, banks, and insurers. During the European sovereign debt crisis and Greek credit event (April 2009 to March 2012), the periphery sovereigns, in particular, were having a big impact on each other and on banks and insurers.

By integrating network models using CCA risk indicators between sovereigns and selected types of financial institutions (banks and insurers together), we can

---

[7] For more information on this type of analysis, see Billo and others (2012) and Merton and others (2013).
[8] Sovereigns in the periphery include Greece, Ireland, Italy, Portugal, and Spain.

TABLE 4.2

		TO		
	BAN	SOV-PER	SOV-NPER	INS
		Jul04–Jun07		
BAN	3.90%	0.94%	0.54%	1.93%
SOV-PER	1.88%	0.00%	3.33%	3.59%
SOV-NPER	4.71%	6.67%	6.82%	5.13%
INS	7.02%	5.13%	6.20%	5.87%
		Sep05–Aug08		
BAN	13.51%	4.06%	7.94%	17.50%
SOV-PER	26.88%	0.00%	43.33%	46.67%
SOV-NPER	13.77%	23.33%	34.09%	33.33%
INS	7.36%	0.51%	5.77%	17.34%
		Apr09–Mar12		
BAN	9.14%	7.81%	2.86%	6.21%
SOV-PER	21.88%	25.00%	13.33%	22.05%
SOV-NPER	9.18%	8.33%	6.82%	9.83%
INS	9.81%	2.56%	1.07%	8.30%

Degree of Interconnectedness between Banks, Insurers, and Sovereigns: Various Stages of the Financial Crisis *(percent significant 99 percent level or higher)*

FROM

Source: Billio and others (forthcoming).

Note: BAN = banks; SOV-PER = sovereigns in euro area periphery countries; SOV-NPER = sovereigns in non-euro area periphery countries; INS = insurers.

gauge how, when, and how strongly sovereign risks are transmitted to financial institutions and vice versa.[4] Figure 4.5 shows the percentage of significant connections to sovereigns from financial firms (banks and insurers), and from financial firms to sovereigns from January 2001 through March 2012. An examination of results shows that from 2003 to 2005 the proportion of significant connections to sovereigns from financial institutions was greater, whereas the reverse

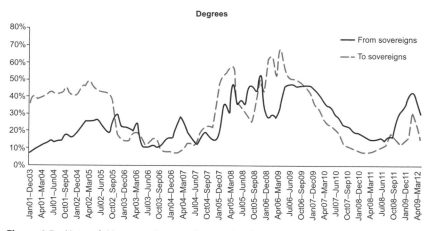

Figure 4.5 Network Measures: Degrees from and to Sovereigns

Source: Merton and others (2013); reproduced in IMF (2013).

Note: The x-axis captures 36-month rolling windows from January 2001 through March 2012.

(connections from sovereigns to institutions) was dominant from mid-2009 to 2012 (right-hand side of Figure 4.5).

CCA-Global VAR Model

To analyze the interactions between banking, sovereign, and corporate risks and real economic activity, an integrated macroeconomic systemic risk model framework was built, drawing on the advantages of forward-looking CCA risk indicators for the banking systems in each country, forward-looking CCA risk indicators for sovereigns, and a GVAR model to combine the banking, the sovereign, and the macro sphere. Key to the framework is that sovereign credit spreads, banking system credit risk, corporate sector credit risk, economic growth, and credit variables are combined in a fully endogenous setting.

Individual banks' and nonfinancial corporations' risk indicators that belong to country j were aggregated by computing a weighted average of the expected loss ratios of major banks in the country (weighted respectively by bank or corporate asset size, i.e. the market value of assets). The banking system expected loss ratio is $EL_{bs,j}$, and the corporate sector expected loss ratio is $EL_{cs,j}$ in country j.

After estimating and calibrating the global model, it was used to conduct shock scenarios, particularly to bank or sovereign risk (for a full description of the model, see Gray and others, forthcoming). The goal is to use this framework to help analyze the impact and spillover of shocks, and to help identify policies that mitigate banking system, sovereign credit risk and recession risk—policies that include bank capital increases, purchase of sovereign debt, and potential guarantees.[9]

The model is used to conduct scenario simulations, involving multiple shocks to selected sovereigns and banking systems. Input shocks and output responses for the banking systems, corporate sectors, and sovereigns can be transformed into credit spreads and interpreted as changes in bank funding costs and sovereign credit spreads. The output responses are inputs to banking/sovereign submodules, which are used to compute aggregate loss estimates and changes in bank capital.

Taking Italy as an illustration, one can clearly note how the banking sector expected loss ratio (here at a five-year horizon) spiked when real activity dropped sharply in the course of 2008–09 (Figure 4.6). More recently, banking, sovereign, and corporate risk indicators increased significantly, and while sovereign risk indicators fell back below their peaks, financial institutions' indicators continue to show stresses. Similar indicators for all countries are shown in Appendix 4.1.

---

[9] The CCA-GVAR model variables are real GDP, credit to the private sector, sovereign EL, national banking system EL, and corporate sector EL. The sample of data has a monthly frequency and ranges from January 2002 to December 2012 (132 observations). The sample covers 16 countries (13 EU countries plus Norway, Switzerland, and the United States). GDP is interpolated from quarterly to monthly by means of a quadratic match sum conversion method. With five endogenous model variables and 16 countries, the global model has 80 equations in total. All variables are modeled in first (i.e., monthly) differences of logarithmic levels. The first differences of the variables are stationary at conventional levels of significance for all countries.

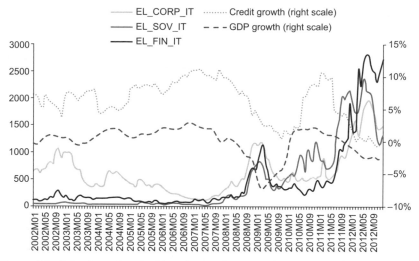

Figure 4.6 Italy: Sovereign, Banking System, Corporate Sector Expected Loss, Real GDP Growth, and Credit Growth

Sources: Eurostat; Gray and others (forthcoming); Moody's; and author's estimates.

SHOCK SCENARIO ANALYSIS

To illustrate the linkages among sovereigns, the financial sectors, the corporate sectors, GDP growth, and credit growth, the global model was subject to four different shock scenarios: negative and positive shocks to banks and sovereigns, respectively, of Italy and Spain. Two indicators are reported: the shock profile on impact and the largest cumulative shock for a two-period horizon (see Gray and others, forthcoming, for details). It is important to note that the starting point of the model simulations was December 2012.[10] All expected loss values are converted in fair value spread equivalents for ease of comparison.

Shock Scenario One—Adverse Shock to Sovereigns in Italy and Spain

The adverse shocks to the sovereign EL, with marginal shock probabilities set to 5 percent (resulting in a joint probability of 0.7 percent), let the ELs for the two countries increase by about 250–260 basis points on impact of the scenario. Responses are pronounced for other euro area periphery countries, such as Ireland and Portugal.

---

[10] Since all variables are modeled in first differences of logarithmic levels, the simulated raw model responses, including those for ELs for banks, sovereigns, and the corporate sectors are to be understood as logarithmic percentage point deviations. ELs in are transformed back to absolute EL basis point changes by chaining the relative changes implied by the scenario to end-sample (December 2012) EL ratios.

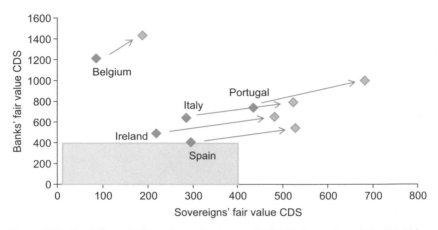

Figure 4.7 Shock Scenario One—Sovereigns' versus Banks' Maximum Cumulative Fair-Value Spread Responses

Source: Gray and others (forthcoming).
Note: CDS = credit default swaps.

Spillovers to banking system ELs are notable for Greece, Ireland, Italy, Portugal, and Spain. The corporate sector EL shock profile on impact shows smaller effects, yet suggests a rather similar ranking of countries, with Greece, Ireland, Portugal, and Spain, attaining the highest ranks with respect to corporate sector EL deviations.

With respect to GDP and credit, impact rankings suggest strong effects for Greece, Ireland, and Spain, with their GDPs falling by between –0.6 percent (Spain) and –1.4 percent (Greece) in the first month of the simulation horizon. Credit to the private sector for the first five most strongly affected countries would be contracting by –0.5 percent (Greece) and –1.4 percent (Italy) in the first month.

Turning to the maximum cumulative deviations, the same set of euro area periphery countries attain the highest ranks (Figure 4.7). For Ireland and Portugal, the simulated sovereign fair value CDS responses equal about 250 basis points. The Italian and Spanish banking systems have cumulative maximum responses ranging around 140 basis points. Corporate sector responses appear moderate. Maximum deviations for GDP and credit can again be observed for several euro area periphery countries. Overall, the scenario thus implies sizable adverse responses for risk across sovereigns, banks, and the corporate sector. Real activity and credit contract markedly.

Shock Scenario Two—Adverse Shock to Banking Systems in Italy and Spain

The adverse shocks to banking systems in Italy and Spain, with marginal probabilities set to 5 percent (resulting in a joint probability of 0.8 percent), imply shock sizes to the bank EL ratios for the two countries of 665 and 275 basis

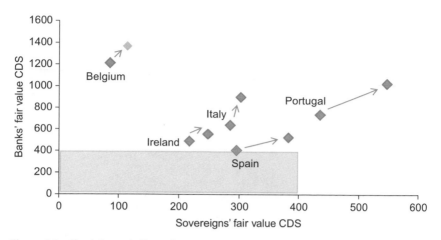

Figure 4.8 Shock Scenario Two—Sovereigns' versus Banks' Maximum Cumulative Fair-Value Spread Responses

Source: Gray and others (forthcoming).
Note: CDS = credit default swaps.

points, respectively. With regard to the corporate sector ELs, responses are large in France, Greece, Italy, and Portugal. Most adverse cumulative deviations are again summarized for a smaller subset of strongly affected countries in Figure 4.8.

In comparison to the sovereign shock scenario one, it can be seen that responses are now more pronounced along the bank EL dimension, and relatively less along the sovereign dimension. Corporate sector responses are high for Portugal. Scenario two results imply a cumulative contraction of GDPs up to –0.5 percent for Italy, and let credit to private sector contract by close to –2.5 percent for Spain.

Shock Scenario Three—Positive Shock to Sovereigns in Italy and Spain

The positive shocks to the sovereigns, with marginal shock probabilities set to 5 percent (resulting in a joint probability of 1.6 percent), mean the ELs for Italy and Spain fall by about 290–352 basis points on impact of the scenario.

Turning to cumulative responses to assess how much deviation the scenario implies for along the horizon, Figure 4.9 scatters sovereign and bank fair value spread deviations for a small subset of countries.

For the countries shown in Figure 4.9, all sovereign and banking system fair value spreads would move back into the "safe zone," comprising less than 400 basis points for banking systems and sovereigns. For the sovereigns, fair value spreads would fall by between –70 basis points for Belgium and –310 basis points for Portugal. For the banking systems, the cumulative deviations range between –500 and –900 basis points for Italy and Belgium, respectively. The simulated corporate sector responses for the median of the countries range

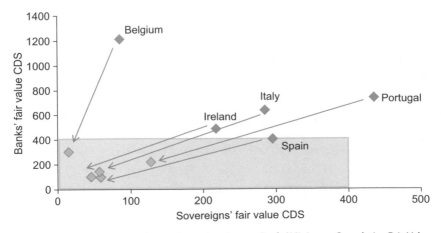

Figure 4.9 Shock Scenario Three—Sovereigns' versus Banks' Minimum Cumulative Fair-Value Spread Responses

Source: Gray and others (forthcoming).
Note: CDS = credit default swaps.

between –65 basis points for Belgium and –400 basis points for Greece. With respect to GDP and credit growth, the scenario implied relative strong positive cumulative reactions for all countries. Cumulative credit growth rises in Belgium, Greece, Ireland, Italy, and Spain.

Shock Scenario Four—Positive Shock to Banking Systems in Italy and Spain

The positive shocks to the banking systems, with marginal shock probabilities set to 5 percent (resulting in a joint probability of 0.8 percent) let the ELs for banks in Italy and Spain fall by about 1,700–580 basis points on impact of the scenario. Italy's end-sample EL ratio would fall by over 50 percent. The scenario therefore envisages a sizable positive impulse to the two banking systems.

Real GDP responses on impact are somewhat less pronounced when compared to scenario three, with the most positive response being recorded for Spain's GDP that would rise by +0.9 percent upon arrival of the shock. Credit growth responses, on the other hand, are somewhat more pronounced on average compared to scenario three, with credit in Spain for instance growing by 2.7 percent. Figure 4.10 presents the most positive cumulative responses along the simulation horizon again for the subsample of countries for which responses are most pronounced.

Despite the banking systems (in Italy and Spain) having been the shock origins in scenario four, it is Belgium's and Portugal's sovereigns that move back into the safe zone that is delineated by the 400 basis point threshold for the fair value spread. Their banking system fair value spreads remain at elevated levels, at 770 basis points for Belgium and 550 basis points for Portugal. To the extent that scenarios three and four are comparable in terms of severity in a probabilistic

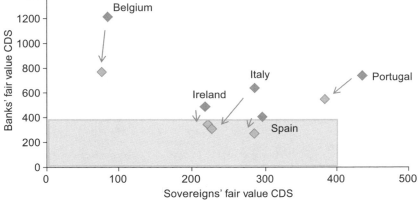

Figure 4.10 Shock Scenario Four—Sovereigns' versus Banks' Minimum Cumulative Fair-Value Spread Responses

Source: Gray and others (forthcoming).
Note: CDS = credit default swaps.

sense (1 percent marginal shock probabilities), the simulation results suggest that positive impulses to sovereign risk have more potential to compress jointly banks' and sovereigns' risk, as measured by their fair value credit spreads.

Refinements and Extensions

The framework developed here may be a tool to assess the combinations of policies that reduce risk for banking systems and sovereigns while increasing real GDP growth. Going forward, there are several extensions and refinements to the framework described above. One is to consider alternative thresholds/criteria for defining the boundaries of the "low risk zone." This framework could be adapted for conditional/unconditional forecasting of CCA-GVAR model variables. Also, additional fiscal variables and sovereign debt analysis could be included.

One of the benefits of CCA is its ability to compare different types of risk mitigation policies, both on balance sheet changes and risk transfer-type instruments and policies, as shown in Table 4.3. Ways to mitigate risk (lower the EL and reduce spreads) are to increase bank capital or debt to equity conversion (bail-in). Guarantees on bank debt or toxic ring-fenced asset guarantees will lower spreads and reduce risk. For sovereigns, ways to mitigate risk include increasing debt maturity, having debt roll-over backstops from supra national organizations, and credible long-term fiscal policies. Sovereign debt purchases or explicit guarantees by a public entity (ECB, the European Stability Mechanism, or other entity) help lower sovereign spreads. Other policies such as Outright Monetary Transactions (OMT) purchases, or potential for OMT purchases of sovereign debt, can lower sovereign spreads, lower risk, and have positive growth impacts.

TABLE 4.3

Risk Mitigation Policies

On-balance sheet adjustment policies to mitigate risk to:		Risk transfer-type instruments and policies to mitigate risk to:		
Banks	**Sovereign**	**Banks**	**Sovereign**	**Firms**
Increase market capital	Increase regulatory capital; increase solvency ratio	Reduce or increase maturity of debt	Guarantees on bank senior debt; asset protection guarantees	Guarantees or insurance or selling CDS protection on sovereign debt	Incentives for banks to lend to firms
Increase assets and lower asset risk	Macroprudential policies that affect credit growth	Raise assets and lower asset risk	EU-wide deposit insurance	Debt purchases by banks (e.g., LTRO) Debt purchases by public entity (SMP/OMT, EFSF/ESM, other)	Corporate debt (or equity) across the board purchases by government or central bank
Debt equity conversion/bail-in	Extending debt maturity or restructuring	EU-wide bank resolution	Mutualize, socialize existing and/or new sovereign debt	

Source: authors' compilation.
Note: CDS = credit default swaps; EFSF/ESM = European Financial Stability Facility/European Stability Mechanism; LTRO = long-term refinancing operation; OMT = Outright Monetary Transactions; SMP = Securities Market Program.

CONCLUSIONS

CCA indicators capture the nonlinearity of changes in bank assets, capital, and bank credit spreads that are derived from forward-looking equity market information in conjunction with balance sheet data, and the expected losses for sovereigns. It can be used for simulation and stress testing or can be used in Network models of interconnectedness, or used in VAR and global VAR models to capture risk transmission between sectors and macro variables within and across countries. The CCA-GVAR model successfully integrates forward-looking banking system, sovereign, and corporate risk indicators in a GVAR with real GDP growth and credit levels in a 16-country framework which is fully endogenous. It is a stable global model which provides meaningful responses in terms of directions and magnitude. CCA framework allows a range of policy options to be modeled, and their risk mitigation impact to be quantified.

APPENDIX 4.1. CONTINGENT CLAIMS ANALYSIS-GLOBAL VECTOR AUTOREGRESSION: EXPECTED LOSS, GDP, AND CREDIT INDICATORS FOR 16 COUNTRIES

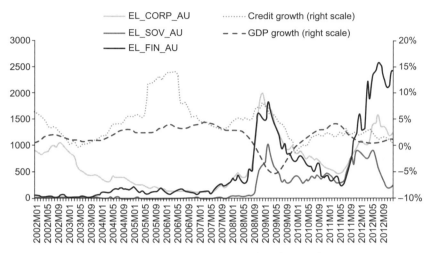

Figure A4.1   Austria: Risk Indicators, GDP Growth, and Credit Growth

Sources: Eurostat; Moody's CreditEdge; and author's estimates.

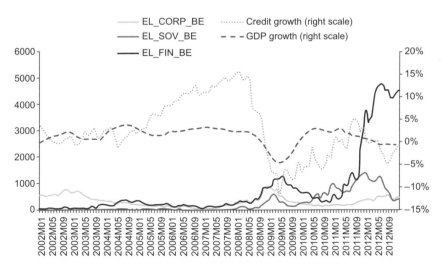

Figure A4.2   Belgium: Risk Indicators, GDP Growth, and Credit Growth

Sources: Eurostat; Moody's CreditEdge; and author's estimates.

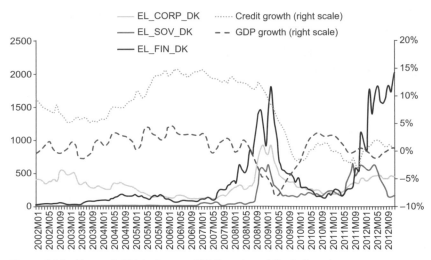

Figure A4.3   Denmark: Risk Indicators, GDP Growth, and Credit Growth

Sources: Eurostat; Moody's CreditEdge; and author's estimates.

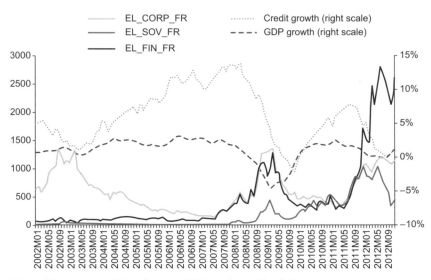

Figure A4.4   France: Risk Indicators, GDP Growth, and Credit Growth

Sources: Eurostat; Moody's CreditEdge; and author's estimates.

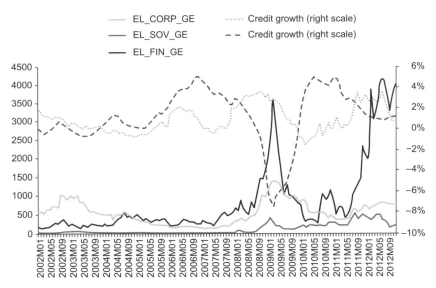

Figure A4.5 Germany: Risk Indicators, GDP Growth, and Credit Growth

Sources: Eurostat; Moody's CreditEdge; and author's estimates.

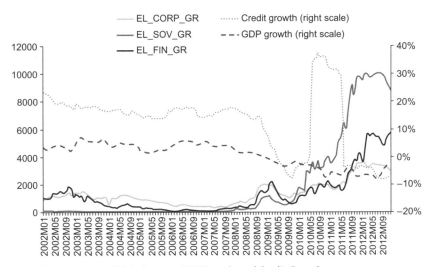

Figure A4.6 Greece: Risk Indicators, GDP Growth, and Credit Growth

Sources: Eurostat; Moody's CreditEdge; and author's estimates.

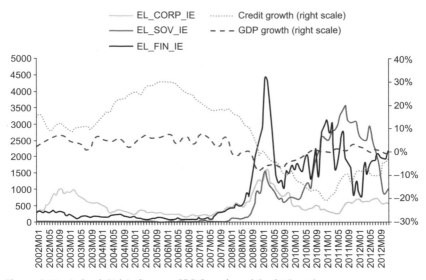

Figure A4.7 Ireland: Risk Indicators, GDP Growth, and Credit Growth

Sources: Eurostat; Moody's CreditEdge; and author's estimates.

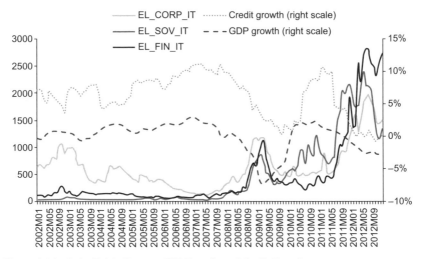

Figure A4.8 Italy: Risk Indicators, GDP Growth, and Credit Growth

Sources: Eurostat; Moody's CreditEdge; and author's estimates.

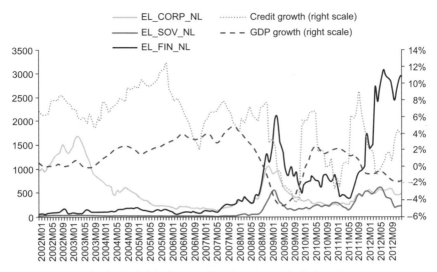

Figure A4.9 Netherlands: Risk Indicators, GDP Growth and Credit Growth

Sources: Eurostat; Moody's CreditEdge; and author's estimates.

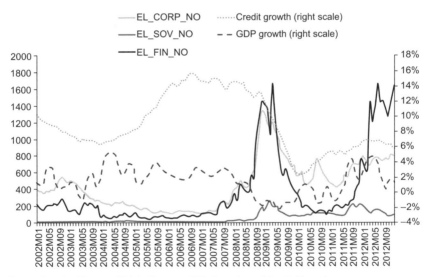

Figure A4.10 Norway: Risk Indicators, GDP Growth, and Credit Growth

Sources: Eurostat; Moody's CreditEdge; and author's estimates.

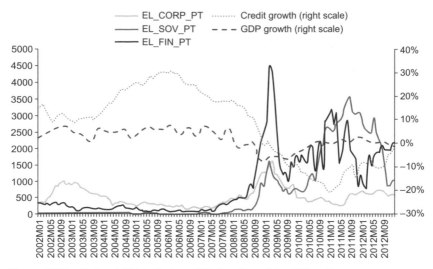

Figure A4.11   Portugal: Risk Indicators, GDP Growth, and Credit Growth

Sources: Eurostat; Moody's CreditEdge; and author's estimates.

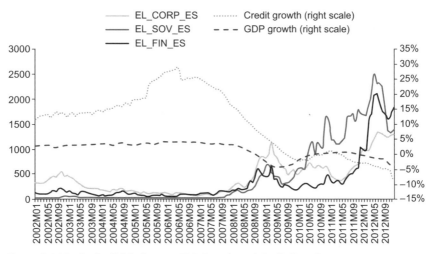

Figure A4.12   Spain: Risk Indicators, GDP Growth, and Credit Growth

Sources: Eurostat; Moody's CreditEdge; and author's estimates.

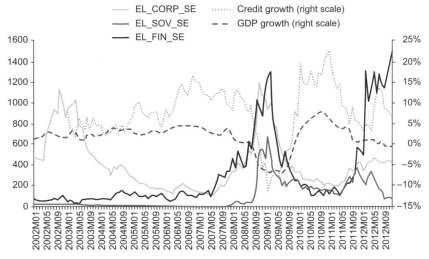

Figure A4.13 Sweden: Risk Indicators, GDP Growth, and Credit Growth

Sources: Eurostat; Moody's CreditEdge; and author's estimates.

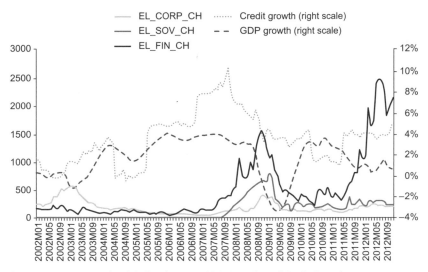

Figure A4.14 Switzerland: Risk Indicators, GDP Growth, and Credit Growth

Sources: Eurostat; Moody's CreditEdge; and author's estimates.

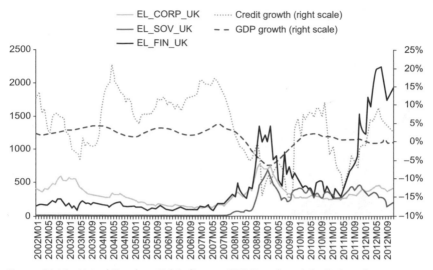

Figure A4.15   United Kingdom: Risk Indicators, GDP Growth, and Credit Growth

Sources: Eurostat; Moody's CreditEdge; and author's estimates.

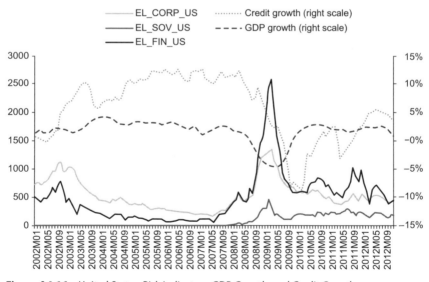

Figure A4.16   United States: Risk Indicators, GDP Growth, and Credit Growth

Sources: Eurostat; Moody's CreditEdge; and author's estimates.

REFERENCES

Backus, David, Silvereio Foresi, and Liuren Wu, 2004, "Accounting for Biases in Black-Scholes," Working Paper, New York University, Goldman Sachs Group, and Baruch College.

Billio, M., M. Getmansky, D. Gray, A. Lo, R. C. Merton, and L. Pelizzon, forthcoming, "Sovereign, Bank, and Insurance Credit Spreads: Connectedness and System Networks" MIT Working Paper.

Billio, M., M. Getmansky, A. Lo, and L. Pelizzon, 2012, "Econometric Measures of Connectedness and Systemic Risk in the Finance and Insurance Sectors," *Journal of Financial Economics* Volume 104, 535–59.

Bohn, J., 2000, "An Empirical Assessment of a Simple Contingent Claims Model for the Valuation of Risky Debt," *Journal of Risk Finance* Volume 1, 55–77.

Chen, Q., D. Gray, P. N'Diaye, and H. Oura, 2010, "International Transmission of Bank and Corporate Distress," IMF Working Paper No. 10/124 (Washington: International Monetary Fund).

Crouhy, M., D. Galai, and R. Mark, 2000, *Risk Management* (New York: McGraw Hill).

Chudik, A., and M. Fratzscher, 2011, "Identifying the Global Transmission of the 2007–2009 Financial Crisis in a GVAR Model," *European Economic Review* Volume 55, No. 3, 325–339.

Davidson, R., and J. G. MacKinnon, 2005, "Bootstrap Methods in Eeconometrics," Chapter 23 in *Palgrave Handbook of Econometrics: Volume 1 Theoretical Econometrics,* ed. K. Patterson and T.C. Mills (Basingstoke, UK: Palgrave Macmillan).

Dees, S., F. Di Mauro, M. H. Pesaran, and L. . Smith, 2007, "Exploring the International Linkages of the Euro Aarea: A Gobal VAR Analysis," *Journal of Applied Econometrics* Volume 22, 1–38.

Dwyer, D., and I. Korablev, 2007, "Power and Level Validation of Moody's KMV EDF™. Credit Measures in North America, Europe, and Asia," Moody's Analytics White Paper.

Draghi, M., F. Giavazzi, R. C. Merton, 2003, "Transparency, Risk Management and International Financial Fragility" NBER Working Paper 9806, June. (Earlier version presented at the Fourth Geneva Conference on the World Economy: Financial Markets: Shock Absorbers or Shock Creators? May 2002.)

Dwyer, D., Z. Li, S. Qu, H. Russell and J. Zhang, 2010, "CDS-implied EDF™ Credit Measures and Fair-value Spreads," Moody's Analytics White Paper.

Eickmeier, S. and T. Ng, 2011, "How Do Credit Supply Shocks Propagate Internationally? A GVAR Approach," Bundesbank Discussion Paper No. 27/2011.

Gapen M. T., D. F Gray, C. H. Lim, and Y. Xiao, 2005, "Measuring and Analyzing Sovereign Risk with Contingent Claims," *IMF Staff Papers*, Volume 55.

Garcia, C., D. Gray, L. Luna, and J. Restrepo, 2011, "Incorporating Financial Sector into Monetary Policy Models: Application to Chile," IMF Working Paper No. 11/228 (Washington: International Monetary Fund).

Gray, D., M. Gross, J. Paredes, and M. Sydow, forthcoming, "Modeling Banking, Sovereign, and Macro Risk in a CCA Global VAR," IMF Working Paper (Washington: International Monetary Fund).

Gray, D., and A. Jobst, 2011, "Modeling Systemic Financial Sector and Sovereign Risk," *Sveriges Riksbank Economic Review,* September.

Gray, D. F., A. A. Jobst, and S. Malone, 2010, "Quantifying Systemic Risk and Reconceptualizing the Role of Finance for Economic Growth," *Journal of Investment Management,* Volume 8, No. 2, 90–110.

Gray, D., and S. Malone, 2008, *Macrofinancial Risk Analysis* (New York: Wiley).

Gray, D. and S. Malone, 2012, "Sovereign and Financial Sector Risk: Measurement and Interactions," *Annual Review of Financial Economics,* Volume 4, No. 9.

Gray, D. F., R. C. Merton, and Z. Bodie, 2002, "A New Framework for Analyzing and Managing Macrofinancial Risks," C.V. Starr Conference on Finance and Macroeconomics. October 2, 2002, New York University.

————, 2007, "Contingent Claims Approach to Measuring and Managing Sovereign Credit Risk," *Journal of Investment Management* Volume 5, No. 4, 5–28.

————, 2008, "A New Framework for Measuring and Managing Macrofinancial Risk and Financial Stability," Harvard Business School Working Paper No. 09-015.

Gray, D. and J. Walsh, 2008, "Factor Model for Stress-testing with a Contingent Claims Model of the Chilean Banking System." IMF Working Paper No. 08/89 (Washington: International Monetary Fund).

Gross, M. 2013, "Estimating GVAR weight matrices," ECB Working Paper No. 1523 (Frankfurt: European Central Bank).

International Monetary Fund, 2010, *Global Financial Stability Report: Sovereigns, Funding, and Systemic Liquidity* (Washington; October).

————, 2013, *Global Financial Stability Report: Old Risks, New Challenges*, World Economic and Financial Surveys (Washington; April), Chapter 2.

Jobst, A., and D. Gray, 2013, "Systemic Contingent Claims Analysis—Estimating Market—Implied Systemic Risk," IMF Working Paper No. 13/54 (Washington: International Monetary Fund).

Korablev, Irina, and S. Qu, 2009, "Validating the Public EDF Model Performance during the Credit Crisis," Moody's Analytics White Paper.

Merton, R. C., 1973, "Theory of Rational Option Pricing," *Bell Journal of Economics and Management Science* Volume 4 (spring), 141–83 (Chapter 8 in *Continuous-Time Finance*).

————, 1974, "On the Pricing of Corporate Debt: The Risk Structure of Interest Rates," *Journal of Finance* Volume 29 (May), 449–70. (Chapter 12 in *Continuous-Time Finance*).

————, 1977, "An Analytic Derivation of the Cost of Loan Guarantees and Deposit Insurance: An Application of Modern Option Pricing Theory." *Journal of Banking and Finance* Volume 1 (June), 3–11 (Chapter 19 in *Continuous-Time Finance*).

————, 1992, *Continuous-Time Finance, rev. ed* (Oxford, U.K.: Basil Blackwell).

Merton, R. C., M. Billio, M. Getmansky, D. Gray, A. W. Lo, and L. Pelizzon, 2013, "On a New Approach for Analyzing and Managing Macrofinancial Risks," *Financial Analysts Journal* Volume 69, No. 2.

Moody's Analytics, 2011, "Quantifying the Value of Implicit Government Guarantees for Large Financial Institutions," Moody's Analytics Quantitative Research Group, January.

Pesaran, M. H., T. Schuermann, and L.V. Smith, 2009, "Forecasting Economic and Financial Variables with Global VARs," *International Journal of Forecasting* 25 (4): 642–75.

Pesaran, M. H., T. Schuermann, B.-J. Treutler, and S. M. Weiner, 2006, "Macroeconomic Dynamics and Credit Risk: A Global Perspective," *Journal of Money, Credit, and Banking* Volume 38, No. 5, 1211–61.

Pesaran, M. H., T. Schuermann, and S. M. Weiner, 2004, "Modeling Regional Interdependencies Using a Global Error-Correcting Macroeconometric Model," *Journal of Business & Economic Statistics* Volume 22, No. 2.

Pesaran, M. H., L. V. Smith, and R. P. Smith, 2007, "What If the UK or Sweden Had Joined the Euro in 1999? An Empirical Evaluation Using a Global VAR," *International Journal of Finance & Economics* Volume 12, No. 1, 55–87.

Schweikhard, F. A., and Z. Tsesmelidakis, 2012, "The Impact of Government Interventions on CDS and Equity Markets," Paper presented at Preliminary Program of the Allied Social Science Associations, Chicago (January).

CHAPTER 5

Crisis Management

LUC EVERAERT, HEIKO HESSE, AND NADEGE JASSAUD

Managing a financial crisis is a challenge even if the crisis has no cross-border dimensions. By its very nature, a financial crisis is unexpected and an indication that prevention failed. Diagnosis and a viable solution need to be arrived at in real time, under limited information, and with suboptimal policy coordination frameworks. Often, multiple combinations of interventions are possible and resolving a financial crisis involves public guarantees or funding, the approval of which is subject to a democratic process. Consequently, crisis management is seldom smooth, mistakes are made that need to be corrected along the way, and adverse consequences for the real economy are rarely avoided.

Global financial integration, the single market in financial services in the European Union (EU), and the economic and monetary union (EMU) add increasing layers of cross-border complexity to managing a financial crisis in various parts of Europe. The global financial crisis may have been triggered by the subprime mortgage problem in the United States, but it quickly exposed home-grown weaknesses in Europe, in particular the excessive leverage of different sectors of the economy in a number of countries. Tied through cross-border exposure, cross-border ownership, international wholesale funding, or a common currency, most countries in Europe became engulfed in the financial crisis in one way or another. Unfortunately, when the crisis hit, the cross-border framework for crisis management was still in its infancy.

To draw lessons for the design of a robust crisis management framework in the EU, it is useful to briefly review how the global financial crisis turned into a full-fledged crisis in the EU and in EMU more particularly, how the cross-border dimension played out, and how policymakers responded in the various defining moments of the crisis.

FROM CALIFORNIA TO CYPRUS

Initially, from Europe's perspective the financial crisis had a foreign label and a degree of remoteness to it. Derivatives involving mortgages in the United States, with California being among the most affected, turned out to be illiquid, causing difficulties for highly leveraged financing vehicles. Some of these products were held in Europe, and BNP Paribas was one of the first firms to suspend payouts of three of its investment funds in August 2007, citing (in a press statement) that it had "no way of valuing the collaterized debt obligations (CDOs)" that were in them. But the crisis quickly took hold in Europe. A few months after BNP Paribas' decision, it turned out that Northern Rock's business model, based on securitization of its mortgage portfolios, could no longer be funded. The market for securitized products had dried up.

At this early stage, the financial crisis was treated essentially with national measures, and coordination was limited to central banks providing foreign currency swaps and ensuring interbank liquidity. In 2008, Northern Rock was "temporarily nationalized" and HBOS rescued in the United Kingdom, while in the United States Bear Stearns was taken over by JP Morgan Chase, Fannie Mae and Freddie Mac were bailed out by the government, and in mid-September, Lehman Brothers was allowed to file for bankruptcy. A few weeks later, the Irish government decided to underwrite the entire liability side of its banking system, while Iceland's biggest banks collapsed, leaving foreign depositors adrift. In the United Kingdom, the rescue package was extended to cover Lloyds TSB. In the Benelux, Fortis was partly nationalized and broken up along national lines while Dexia was bailed out. The common denominators underlying problems in these banks were high leverage, wholesale funding, and exposure to impaired or difficult-to-value assets.

As the financial crisis took a broader economic toll and plunged the global economy into recession, it spread well beyond the financial sector in several countries. In emerging Europe, the Baltics, which were highly overleveraged, were very hard hit, while Hungary and Romania experienced difficulties as a result of the global crisis. For Hungary, Latvia, and Romania, external financial assistance became necessary in 2008 to support their adjustment.

The crisis next headed south and west. Greece, revealing a massive hole in its public finances, had to be bailed out in May 2010, followed by Ireland in November 2010, when contingent liabilities from its banking sector bailout became too heavy for the government to carry. Portugal followed in April 2011 as its economic recession revealed competitiveness problems and markets doubted the sovereign's ability to continue to finance large deficits and rollover public debt. Finally, Cyprus succumbed to the turmoil, partly as a result of its close links to Greece—which entered into a large sovereign debt restructuring—but also because of a home-grown real estate bubble and an oversized banking system which the sovereign would not be able to support. Italy and Spain suffered severely from contagion, in the case of Spain exacerbated by a deflating real estate bubble, requiring the European Central Bank (ECB) to take extraordinary measures—Long-Term Refinancing Operations (LTROs) and Outright Monetary Transactions (OMT)—to preserve liquidity for banks and sovereigns.

CROSSING BORDERS

While one could argue that policy mistakes by national authorities were the root cause of the financial crisis, such an argument ignores the limitations of national policy action in an interconnected world. Global integration of trade and finance are generally accepted as beneficial to global growth and development. However, together with the benefits, risks also travel across borders and policy actions in any given country have implications abroad.

In the EU, the setting up of the single market in financial services promoted financial integration. The single market concept postulates that within the EU and even the European Economic Area, the financial system is fully unified, as if it were a single domestic system. All financial services are free to cross borders without obstacles and banks can set up branches anywhere they like under the so-called single passport regime: a bank licensed in any EU country is allowed to operate throughout the entire EU. This even applies to banks that are originally from outside the EU: so a Chinese bank incorporated and licensed in Luxembourg can establish a branch in Poland and sell mortgages to residents of Italy out of that branch. As a result of these institutional arrangements, cross-border exposure rapidly grew through 2007 (Figure 5.1) and cross-border ownership of banking institutions took on significant proportions, especially in emerging Europe (Figure 5.2).

The strong integration of capital markets and the existence of financial centers further tied the region together. Equity markets operated seamlessly across borders, linking the liability side of the banking and insurance companies closely together. Many transactions went through financial centers, with London providing a diversity of services to the continent, and Dublin and Luxembourg becoming hubs for investment funds.

In the EMU, financial integration went even further because of the use of the single currency. Here, financial institutions across borders became connected through the euro interbank market, while sovereigns and corporate funded themselves in euro area capital markets in which there was very limited national distinction. Indeed, from a regulatory perspective, sovereigns were considered risk-free with zero risk weights for bank capital, while the Stability and Growth Pact and the no bailout clause of the Maastricht treaty were meant to secure fiscal

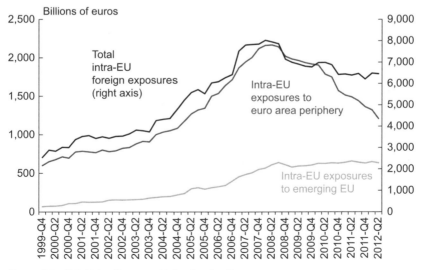

Figure 5.1 Total Intra-European Union Foreign Exposure

Source: Bank for International Settlements, consolidated banking statistics, immediate risk basis.
Note: Ireland and Finland not included due to breaks in data reporting.

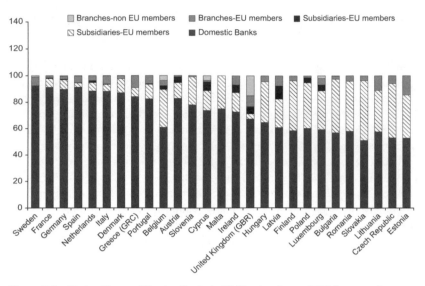

Figure 5.2 Market Shares of Foreign Banks in EU Member States, 2011 (*In percent*)

Source: European Central Bank, Structural Financial database and Monetary Financial Institution (MFI) database.

discipline. The resulting interest rate convergence was associated with very large cross-border flows of capital inside the euro area, to a large extent intermediated through the banking system and involving the buildup of sizeable current account imbalances in the euro area (Figure 5.3).

The prospective adoption of the euro by emerging European economies that are members of the EU lead to an important convergence play. When eastern European countries joined the EU, western European banks invested massively in those

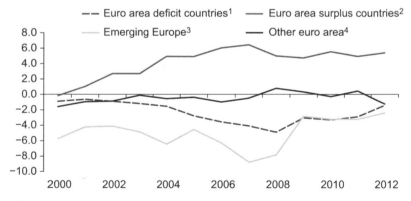

Figure 5.3 EU: Current Account Balances (*In percent of GDP for each subgroup*)

Sources: *World Economic Outlook*, IMF (2012).
[1] Countries with current account deficits before the crisis: Cyprus, Estonia, France, Greece, Ireland, Italy, Malta, Portugal, Slovakia, Slovenia, and Spain.
[2] Austria, Belgium, Finland, Germany, Luxembourg, and the Netherlands.
[3] Bulgaria, Czech Republic, Hungary, Latvia, Lithuania, Poland, and Romania.
[4] Denmark, Sweden, and the United Kingdom.

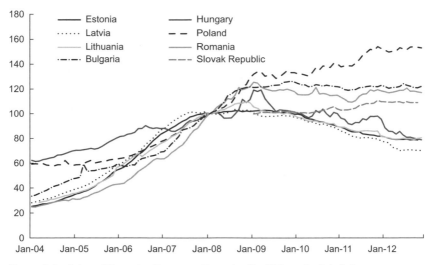

Figure 5.4   Selected Emerging European Countries (*Real Private Credit Index*)

Source: IMF, International Financial Statistics database, and staff calculations.

countries and provided funding to their subsidiaries and branches there. Conversely, profits from rapid expansion in emerging Europe underpinned the profitability of the parent groups. With expectation of euro adoption, a lot of borrowing took place in foreign exchange, leading to credit booms, especially in countries which were already pegged to the euro (Figure 5.4 on credit in emerging Europe).

Hence, on the eve of the financial crisis, the financial systems of EU countries were closely intertwined, but their supervision was not and the institutional framework to deal with a systemic crisis was virtually inexistent. Despite unbridled cross-border banking and EU and euro area-wide capital markets, countries had adopted their own supervisory approaches, leading to large divergences in the size and structure of national financial systems. Cross-border coordination was largely limited to the encouragement to jointly supervise cross-border banking groups by means of Memoranda of Understanding and the beginnings of harmonization of regulation and supervision through the various EU-wide committees (e.g., the Committee of European Banking Supervisors).

In these circumstances, managing the crisis has proven very difficult. The crisis was initially perceived as localized and treated with national solutions. However, even national crisis management frameworks were insufficient to deal with it effectively. Many EU countries had to substantially modify their crisis management and resolution regimes to address banking problems. The need for coordination of such regimes in a single market for financial services has been duly recognized, leading to the EU directive on resolution, which should support a better cross-border response to future crises.

Many of the decisions taken by national and EU authorities, while wellintentioned, led to significant adverse policy spillovers. The break-up of Fortis along national lines ended the usefulness of the Memorandum of Understanding process for handling cross-border institutions, thus creating uncertainty about how problems in other cross-border institutions could be resolved efficiently.

The guaranteeing of all liabilities of the Irish banking system by the Irish sovereign unleveled the playing field in the single market for financial services as creditors and depositors of banks in other countries suddenly ended up comparatively less protected. On the one hand this attracted depositors to the Irish banks at the expense of mostly U.K. institutions, and on the other it caused difficulties in resolving the institutions as no bail-in of investors was deemed possible.

The proposal launched by the European Commission to bail-in unsecured creditors on the heels of a bail-out of these creditors, in the context of Ireland's rescue, caused market jitters. There was no doubt that the Commission proposal was well intended: in the long run it is necessary to ensure that financial institutions are resolvable at the lowest cost to the taxpayer, a position that is now embraced throughout the world and embedded in the Financial Stability Board's principles for effective resolution. However, launching such proposals in the middle of a crisis may not have been the most opportune time as it aggravated the funding difficulties of the banking system.

The handling of the Greek crisis also contributed to the turbulence. The authorities' position on sovereign debt shifted considerably. On April 15, 2010, Olli Rehn, the Economic and Monetary Affairs Commissioner, told a conference in Brussels: "There will be no default." However, in May 2011, the commissioner suggested that a voluntary debt reprofiling could be considered. And in July 2011 came a clear statement from European leaders that a haircut would be necessary. In addition, some leaders indicated that euro area exit would be Greece's choice.

At this point, contagion was spreading rapidly throughout the euro area, threatening other sovereigns with financing difficulties. Spain and Italy had to embark on significant adjustment programs, triggering discussions about their financing needs and the capability of the European Financial Stability Facility and subsequent European Stability Mechanism (ESM) to meet funding needs should they arise. Policy reversals on how to handle the crisis in Cyprus, and the difference in approach compared to the other programs, once more added to uncertainty.

POLICY DECISIONS TO MANAGE THE CRISIS

In these circumstances, financial market turbulence has been difficult to address. Central banks, and in particular the European Central Bank, had no choice but to step in with unconventional measures to buy time and to guard against tail risks. The decision-making process on these measures was also drawn out, and tail risks were not removed until the outright monetary transactions (OMT) were introduced (Table 5.1).

Liquidity support provided by central banks has been extraordinary, especially in the euro area and the United Kingdom. In the euro area, the ECB

TABLE 5.1

European Central Bank: Unconventional Measures 2007–2012

Decision date	Measure
October 8, 2008	**Fixed rate, full allotment tenders** adopted for weekly main refinancing operations, for as long as needed. **Reduction of the corridor** between standing facilities to 100 basis points, for as long as needed.
October 15, 2008	**Expansion of eligible collateral** through end–2009. **Enhance longer-term refinancing operations** through end–Q1 2009. **Provision of U.S. dollar liquidity** through foreign exchange swaps.
December 18, 2008	**Increase of corridor** between standing facilities to 200 basis points.
February 5, 2009	**Fixed rate, full allotment tenders** to continue for as long as needed on all main, special term, supplementary, and regular longer-term refinancing operations. **Supplementary and special term refinancing operations** to continue for as long as needed.
May 7, 2009	**One year long-term refinancing operations** introduced. **Covered bond purchase program** announced.
March 4, 2010	Return to variable rate tender for three-month long-term refinancing.
May 10, 2010	**Securities Markets Program** introduced to intervene in the euro area public and private debt securities markets. **Fixed rate, full allotment tenders** adopted for regular three-month long-term refinancing, extended through today.
August 4, 2011	**Supplementary longer-term refinancing** operation with a maturity of approximately six months, fixed rate and full allotment introduced—subsequently extended through today.
October 6, 2011	**Two longer-term refinancing operations** introduced—one with a maturity of approximately 12 months in October 2011, and another with a maturity of approximately 13 months in December 2011. **New covered bond purchase program** launched.
December 8, 2011	Further nonstandard measures introduced, notably: (1) to conduct **two longer-term refinancing operations with a maturity of approximately three years**; (2) **to increase the availability of collateral**; (3) to **reduce the reserve ratio to 1 percent**; and (4) for the time being to **discontinue the fine-tuning operations** carried out on the last day of each maintenance period.
February 9, 2012	**Further collateral easing** by approving specific national eligibility criteria and risk control measures for the temporary acceptance in a number of countries of additional credit claims as collateral in Eurosystem credit operations.
September 6, 2012	**Outright Monetary Transactions (OMTs)** introduced to purchase sovereign bonds in the euro area in secondary markets.

provided enhanced support by (1) broadening the scope of eligible assets for central bank funding and setting up full allotment liquidity facilities for banks; (2) undertaking refinancing operations at fixed and historically low rates; (3) extending the maturity of central bank funding to a historical high via the Long-Term Refinancing Operations; and (4) actively purchasing assets (Figure 5.5). National central banks have also granted Emergency Liquidity Assistance in crisis situations. In the United Kingdom, the Bank of England set up an Asset Purchase Facility, for example, to buy high-quality assets, with cumulative assets purchased net of sales and redemptions totaling £360 billion (as of September 2012). However, while central banks can provide liquidity, they cannot address the underlying real problems or the need to restructure banks and resolve fiscal problems.

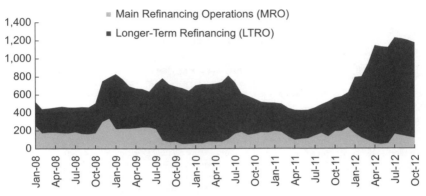

Figure 5.5 European Central Bank Monetary Financing Operations vis-à-vis Euro Area Banks (*In billions of euros*)

Source: Bloomberg, L.P.

Hence, moving banks and sovereigns jointly to sustainability was and still is the key challenge to decisively end Europe's crisis. Meeting this challenge is essential to restore confidence and a functioning financial system, which is in turn indispensible for growth and fiscal sustainability. The right combination of policies that strengthen banks and public sector balance sheets should do the trick:

- Strengthen market capitalization of banks: raising regulatory capital, solvency ratios, asset quality, and economic growth; eliminating nonviable banks and supporting consolidation.
- Increase bank liabilities available for bail-in.
- Provide sovereign guarantees to bank creditors or through asset protection schemes, provided there is fiscal room.
- Reduce sovereign debt and deficits and engage in asset-liability management exercises to improve sovereign sustainability.
- Provide support from supranational entities: direct support for banks and asset management companies (capital and guarantees); common safety nets (deposit guarantees and resolution funds); and further fiscal integration (e.g., through joint debt issuance).

Each of these policies on its own has its limits, however. In the middle of a crisis, it is difficult to raise bank capital from private sources or raise debt subject to bail-in. Pushing too hard on deficit reduction could jeopardize growth in such a way that consolidation fails. Sovereign debt restructuring could undermine the banking system. Charging high fees for bank support from sovereigns, where those very sovereigns are the source of the banking system difficulties, further weakens the financial system. And public sector backstops are only effective if fiscal capacity and room are available.

Against this framework, good progress has been made along many dimensions but gaps still remain to be closed.

TABLE 5.2

Public Interventions in the EU Banking Sector: 2008–2011 *(In billions of euros, unless indicated otherwise)*				
	Used Amounts		Approved Amounts	
		% of GDP		% of GDP
Capital injections	288	2.4	598	4.9
Guarantees on bank liabilities	1,112	9.1	3,290	26.8
Relief of impaired assets	121	1.0	421	3.4
Liquidity and bank funding support	87	0.7	198	1.6
Total	1,608	13.1	4,506	36.7

Source: European Commission (2011).
Note: Figures do not include the amounts owing to Long-Term Refinancing Operations (LTROs); including LTROs, the amount committed to banks stands at 23 percent of EU GDP.

- *Bank recapitalizaton*: Banks have raised a considerable amount of new capital, especially in the context of the European Banking Authority recapitalization exercise and national efforts. However, some EU banks have used the recalibration of risk weights to release capital, and there are still concerns about the underlying quality of bank assets.

- *Banking system restructuring* (see Chapter 7 for details). Over the past five years (2007–2012), the number of credit institutions has decreased by 5 percent. Under the State Aid regime, 20 banks were liquidated, or are in the process of liquidation, of which five are in Denmark; four in Spain; two each in Ireland, Luxembourg, and the United Kingdom; and one in Finland, Germany, Greece and Portugal. Meanwhile 60 banks have undergone deep restructuring as part of the State Aid process.

- *Burden sharing with creditors.* Some burden-sharing with private investors was achieved via partial nationalization and with some bail-in on subordinated debt in Denmark, Greece, Portugal, and Spain, and broader bail-in in Cyprus. But many market participants express concern that this approach may not be adequate to resolve underlying balance sheet problems.

- *National sovereign support:* During the crisis, EU governments have committed unprecedented support for backstopping the financial sector with taxpayer money. Over the period September 2008 to December 2011, member states committed a total of nearly €4.5 trillion, that is, 37 percent of the EU gross domestic product (GDP).[1] The amount of taxpayer money effectively used (mainly via capital injections, State guarantees issued on bank liabilities, etc.) amounted to €1.7 trillion, or 13 percent of EU GDP (Table 5.2). Guarantees and liquidity measures account for €1.2 trillion or 9.8 percent of EU GDP. The remainder of the state aid used refers to recapitalization and impaired assets measures. Out of the 76 top EU banking groups, 19 had a major or even a 100 percent government stake at end-2012.

---

[1] Estimated at €4.9 trillion or 39 percent of EU GDP in October 2012.

- *Sovereign adjustment.* Virtually all countries in the EU have embarked on fiscal adjustment and other reforms that should strengthen the sovereign. In some cases, there are concerns that the pace of adjustment could jeopardize growth.

- *Supranational support.* The European Financial Stability Facility and—more recently—the ESM have provided support to sovereigns with funding difficulties. IMF support has been called upon in the context of adjustment programs in the EA periphery and in some emerging European economies. A decision has been taken to allow the ESM to directly recapitalize banks, but it is contingent on the effective functioning of the single supervisory mechanism.

To end the crisis durably and handle future ones, it would be helpful to adopt a unified approach to crisis management. Ideally, actions by national authorities, central banks, and pan-European institutions should be centrally coordinated. This would allow the adoption of consistent and balanced solutions that bring banks and sovereigns jointly to safety. A unified approach would be able to take into account all externalities, feedback loops, and cross-border contagion effects. Absent a political consensus on such an approach, the crisis is likely to linger and measures such as extended liquidity support to banks and sovereigns may need to remain in place, even though they blunt incentives to restructure and adjust. Solutions that may be economically optimal, such as cross-border consolidation of institutions, will remain out of reach.

REFERENCES

European Commission, 2011, "Public Finances in EMU," *European Economy* Volume 3.

International Monetary Fund, 2012, *World Economic Outlook: Coping with High Debt and Sluggish Growth,* World Economic and Financial Surveys (Washington, October).

CHAPTER 6

Risks and Vulnerabilities

JORGE CHAN-LAU, LUC EVERAERT, DANIEL C. HARDY,
HEIKO HESSE, AND NADEGE JASSAUD

The incompleteness of European Union (EU)-wide and Economic and Monetary Union (EMU) policy frameworks played an important role in the recent financial turbulence in Europe. It exacerbated the impact of financial innovation, deregulation, and soft touch supervision were key factors that led to the global financial crisis. Europe was also afflicted and was probably hit harder than other parts of the world because of its traditional reliance on bank-based finance and its high bank leverage (Figures 6.1 and 6.2).

SOURCE OF VULNERABILITIES

Fragilities stem from four intertwined vulnerabilities:

- *Low growth.* Real activity in the euro area and the United Kingdom is projected to decline slightly in 2013 while slowing in most other EU countries. The deep recessions in the southern periphery have spilled over to the rest of the euro area and affected the emerging economies in the EU. Medium-term growth prospects are highly uncertain but modest at best. This implies that banks' nonperforming loans are likely to rise and that their profitability will be under pressure, thus removing an important source of capital growth. For the insurance sector, low growth, and the likely accompanying low returns on assets, will put pressure on solvency. Solvency levels have also been decreasing as a result of the poor investment climate and the stagnant economy, which resulted in higher claims.

- *Fiscal vulnerabilities.* Lackluster medium-term growth will hamper efforts to restore fiscal sustainability. Weak confidence in the fiscal sustainability of many euro area members—and fiscal crises in some—has severely undermined financial sector balance sheets of banks, insurance companies, and pension funds, given their large exposures to euro area sovereigns. This is reflected, for example, in the share price and credit default swap spread observed across the insurance industry.

- *Funding pressure.* Market funding remains a challenge, especially for periphery banks, though pressures have eased somewhat following the European Central Bank's (ECB) Outright Monetary Transactions (OMT) announcement. Wholesale funding markets have segmented along national borders, and the Eurosystem has served the role of buffer by intermediating funds between surplus countries and countries experiencing a funding gap—as

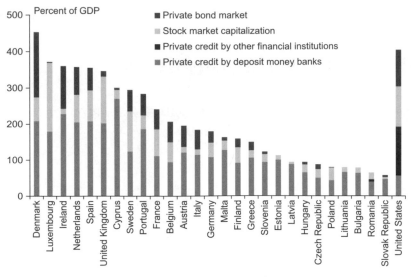

Figure 6.1 Overview of Financial Structure *(in percent of GDP)*

Source: World Bank Financial Structure database (2012).
Note: Data are for 2010, except private credit; and 2008 for Bulgaria, the Czech Republic, Denmark, and Hungary.

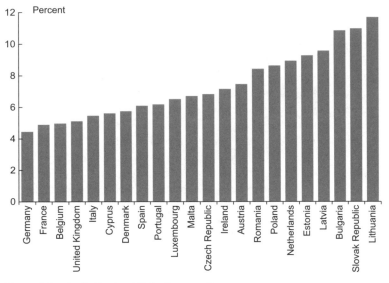

Figure 6.2 Capital-to-Asset Ratio *(in percent)*

Source: IMF, Financial Soundness Indicators.
Note: 2012:Q2, except Bulgaria (2009); Spain; France (2010); Latvia; Slovak Republic (2012:Q1); and the United Kingdom (2011:Q4).

reflected in the TARGET2 imbalances. Many banks are still heavily reliant on ECB funding, with challenges on asset encumbrance and collateral eligibility due to, for instance, rating downgrades, valuation effects on their collateral, and overall loss of market confidence. The phasing out of unconventional central bank operations will also be challenging for many banks.

In the absence of further easing of market funding conditions, banks may be compelled to shed further noncore activities or reduce credit supply.

- *Deleveraging.* Since the start of the crisis in 2008, European banks have deleveraged considerably, mainly across borders. Total intra-EU exposure to non-residents of the country of the bank has declined by €1.5 trillion, among which €950 billion was accounted for by the reduction of exposures to residents in the euro area periphery. Within the euro area, the decline in cross-border claims of euro area monetary financial institutions amounted to almost €500 billion since the onset of the crisis. EU banks have also been running down their activities outside the EU.[1] Bank deleveraging can be explained by a combination of structural and cyclical forces (IMF, 2012e, 2012f): adjustment of business models to the new regulatory and economic environment, pressures to build capitalization, reduction in reliance on unstable market funding, and strained financial conditions and weak demand for credit.

These vulnerabilities are prone to fuel adverse feedback loops. In countries where sovereigns ran into trouble, the banking system suffered severely as the value of sovereign backstops fell and funding costs rose. In countries where banking systems had to be supported massively, the sovereign weakened, in turn reducing the value of its support to the banking system. In both cases, the real economy suffered, further fueling the adverse loop. The underlying difficulties often arise from other sectors in the economy. Excessive household leverage often leads to a boom-and-bust cycle in residential real estate. In some countries, a corporate debt overhang threatens the financial system and constitutes a contingent liability for the sovereign through the banking system.

Against this background and despite substantial reform progress, our analysis suggests that the EU banking system remains fragile. Based on a sample of large financial institutions, soundness indicators show resilience in European emerging economies though with concerns about liquidity, comparatively better performance in non-euro area advanced EU economies, and very mixed results in the euro area. Across indicators, capitalization and earnings show improvement, but there remains a great deal of dispersion between stronger and weaker banks (Figure 6.3), while asset quality remains mixed (Figure 6.4).[2]

Market pressures on EU banks have eased in recent months, bank bond issuance has picked up, and customer deposit levels have stabilized. Credit default swap spreads have come down from high levels, though they still remain elevated for banks in the euro area periphery (Figure 6.5). The cost of issuance, therefore, still remains too high to economically support lending in these economies. The combination of bank balance sheet pressures—as well as weak demand—has led to a fall in credit growth in many economies in the region (Figure 6.6). Small- and medium-sized enterprises (SMEs) are unable to obtain sufficient credit in some economies in the region (Figure 6.7) and interest rates on SME loans are diverging between the core and noncore euro area (Figure 6.8).

---

[1] Estimates from the Bank for International Settlements (BIS) suggest that French and German banks, for example, cut their U.S. dollar asset activities (including in trade finance and project financing) by $270 and $100 billion, respectively, in the year up to the second quarter of 2012

[2] Partly because banks outside this large-bank sample have proven a source of trouble, these observations need to be interpreted with care.

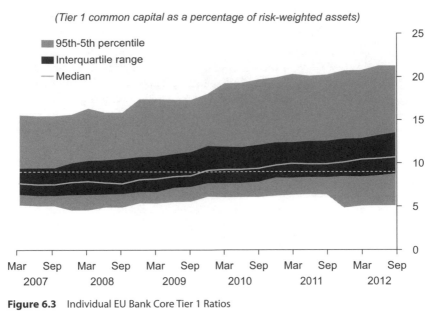

(Tier 1 common capital as a percentage of risk-weighted assets)

Figure 6.3 Individual EU Bank Core Tier 1 Ratios

Sources: SNL Financial; and IMF staff calculations.
Note: Based on consolidated data from a sample of about 220 EU banks.

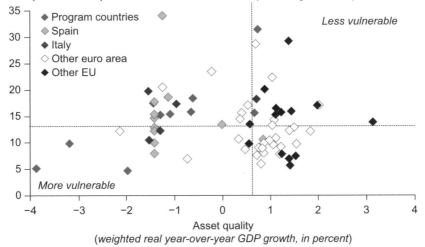

Bank buffers
(core Tier 1 capital and loan loss reserves as a percentage of loans)

Figure 6.4 Individual EU Bank Buffers

Sources: Bank for International Settlements (BIS); the European Banking Authority (EBA); SNL Financial; and IMF staff estimates.
Note: The asset quality indicator is a weighted average of real GDP forecasts for 2012 and 2013, weighted by a bank's exposure to each economy. The exposures are taken from data published by the EBA and updated using BIS consolidated banking data.

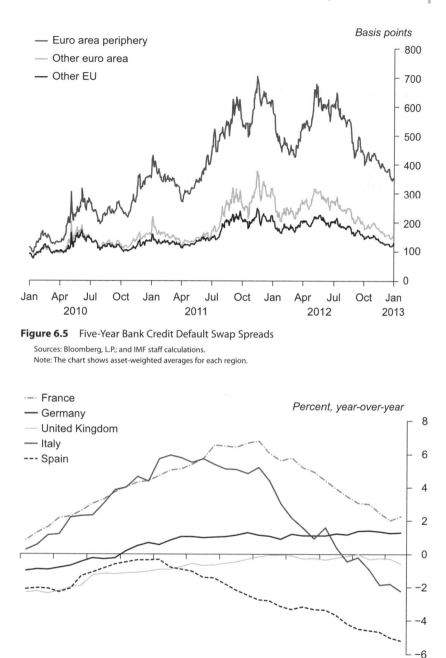

Figure 6.5 Five-Year Bank Credit Default Swap Spreads

Sources: Bloomberg, L.P.; and IMF staff calculations.
Note: The chart shows asset-weighted averages for each region.

Figure 6.6 Bank Lending in Selected EU Countries

Sources: Bank of England; Haver Analytics; and IMF staff calculations.
Note: Adjusted for securitizations.

Percent of respondents

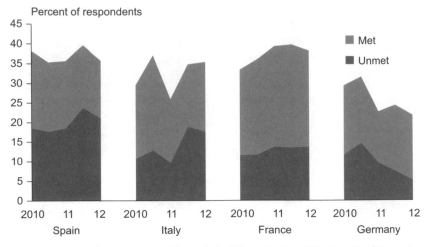

Figure 6.7 Met and Unmet Demand for Bank Credit from Small- and Medium-Sized Enterprises

Source: European Central Bank Survey on the Access to Finance of SMEs; and IMF staff calculations.
Note: Unmet demand is the percentage of respondents that applied for a loan and did not get all or most of the loan.

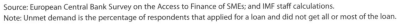

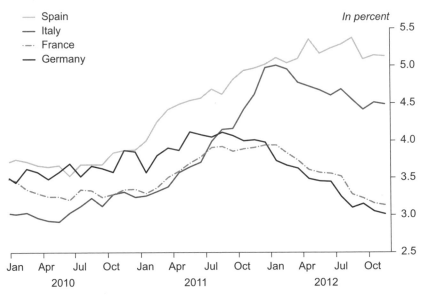

Figure 6.8 Interest Rate on New Loans to Small- and Medium-Sized Enterprises

Source: European Central Bank, monetary and financial statistics.
Note: Chart shows the interest rate on new loans to nonfinancial corporations up to and including €1 million in value.

FINDINGS FROM NATIONAL FINANCIAL SECTOR ASSESSMENTS

The overstatement of asset quality has been one major cause of the banking crisis experienced by some EU countries. Medium-term financial and macroeconomic risks, common across the region, could further impair asset quality and damage banking sector balance sheets. Stress tests, however, suggest that capital buffers appear broadly adequate. Against liquidity shocks, the availability of official facilities help protect the banking system, but central banks in smaller countries may face difficulties shoring up foreign currency shortages, especially in U.S. dollars. Safeguarding against tail risk scenarios requires continuing building up capital and liquidity buffers to meet the Basel III targets. Enhancing financial sector oversight and macroprudential supervision will also help reduce balance sheet risks.

The experience of EU crisis countries underscores the importance of an adequate assessment of asset quality in banks' balance sheets. In Greece and Portugal, domestic banks suffered substantial losses mainly from their domestic sovereign debt holdings. In Ireland and Spain, losses in the banking system were triggered by the burst of domestic real estate bubbles. Capital buffers and provision regimes, including dynamic provisions, as in the case of Spain, were not designed to withstand the massive losses entailed by the downgrade of risk-free assets to junk status and the large downward price corrections when asset price bubbles burst. Markets concerns about banks' creditworthiness also led to funding shortages, reducing their ability to continue funding their domestic economies and sovereigns.

Recent Financial Sector Assessment Programs (FSAPs) in EU countries highlight a number of common financial and macroeconomic risks across the region.[3] These risks emerged in the aftermath of the global financial crisis and the sovereign debt crisis in the euro area (as demonstrated in the tables in Appendix 6.1). The main financial risks are stresses and dislocations in wholesale funding markets that could lead to adverse liquidity and refinancing conditions; deteriorating or sustained high sovereign risk if the euro area crisis intensifies; and a major further downward correction of asset prices. The main macroeconomic risks are associated with the scenarios of a global double-dip recession and a protracted slow growth in Europe. Uncertainty about the regulatory environment and the burden it may place on banks and financial institutions is also viewed as a source of risk in jurisdictions hosting systemic banking systems and financial institutions. In several EU countries, the high degree of concentration in the banking sector creates too-big-to-fail problems that could amplify the country's vulnerability were the risks to materialize.

These risks could materialize in further deterioration of asset quality in banks' balance sheets, a contraction of credit to the real economy, and rising stress in funding markets. Rising sovereign risk could affect banks still holding substantial claims on sovereigns and corporates from countries in recession, raising their funding costs and encouraging further deleveraging that could shrink credit supply in the banks' home and host jurisdictions. Given the strong trade and financial linkages within the EU, adverse global macroeconomic scenarios characterized by slow and/or negative growth and rising unemployment would lead to higher non-performing loans (NPLs) and declining profits, reducing the scope for bank recapitalization without further deleveraging. Banks in the region that rely heavily

---

[3]The assessment is based on a review of EU countries' FSAPs conducted in 2011–12, including the Czech Republic, France, Germany, Luxembourg, the Netherlands, Slovenia, Spain, Sweden, and the United Kingdom.

on market funding would face liquidity problems in the face of declining capital buffers, increasing impaired assets, and a weak earnings outlook. While official measures adopted by the ECB have helped to restore some normalcy to funding markets, central banks in smaller countries may face difficulties providing liquidity in foreign currency. Finally, the recent FSAPs in EU countries note that these risks contribute to reinforcing the bank–sovereign linkage, with weaknesses in the banking sector contributing to increased sovereign risk, and vice versa.

Notwithstanding these risks, FSAP stress tests suggest that capital buffers in EU countries appear mostly adequate to withstand severe macroeconomic shocks, but there are some caveats. The resilience of the banking sector to macroeconomic shocks follows from efforts to repair balance sheets in the banking system, including the divestment of noncore assets. These efforts contributed to an earnings recovery for some large internationally diversified banks. However, impaired assets from the past remain a problem in many EU countries, and there are concerns in some cases that reported NPLs and provisions could understate losses. Outside the crisis countries, comprehensive asset quality reviews have not been conducted, with the exception of Spain. Absent such reviews, the loss estimates may not reflect the underlying quality of the banks' balance sheets. Banking, by nature, builds up on leverage, which magnifies asset losses. Even though capital buffers relative to assets will increase under Basel III, assessing asset quality is a must.

FSAP recommendations point toward the need to continue building up buffers and strengthening financial sector oversight and macroprudential supervision. The need for larger and better quality buffers has been highlighted by recent experience, with Basel III providing the roadmap and timelines. FSAP recommendations related to financial sector oversight and macroprudential supervision aimed mainly at improving the legal framework, enhancing the review, supervisory and crisis management processes, and improving the quality of the data used to monitor and measure risks. The proposed banking union could help anchor oversight and supervision within a macroprudential perspective emphasizing the proper assessment of asset quality.

FINDINGS FROM EU-WIDE STRESS TESTS

The stress test exercises conducted by the European authorities, first by the Committee of European Bank Supervisors (CEBS) and subsequently by the European Banking Authority (EBA), succeeded in prompting banks to increase the quantity and quality of their capitalization, and contributed to a reduction in uncertainty and an increase in the credibility of the process. However, despite banks raising more than €200 billion as a result of the recapitalization exercise, confidence in European banks is not fully restored, in part because the market suspects some banks of having been insufficiently transparent—including as part of the stress testing exercises—about their losses and exposures to problem sectors. Most major banks now seem comparatively well capitalized, but funding remains problematic, for example, because of reliance on official funding and asset encumbrance in some banks. The sector also faces deep structural challenges relating to low profitability and growth and the longer-term impact of regulatory changes.

Stress testing has become an essential and very prominent tool in the analysis of financial sector stability and development of financial sector policy. Starting with the 2010 test led by the CEBS, and reinforced by the 2011 test and the bank recapitalization exercise led by the EBA, the output of EU-wide stress tests has been viewed as essential information on the health of the system. Moreover, the reliability of the results and the efficiency with which they were generated (especially the recapitalization exercise) have greatly influenced the credibility of the European and national authorities involved.

The 2010 CEBS-led stress testing exercise, which can be viewed as the start of EU-wide stress testing and which was initiated near the start of the financial crisis, was relatively poorly received. The stress scenario was regarded as too mild in the circumstances, and there was little assurance that banks had not been able to incorporate an optimistic bias into the results. Limited information disclosure did little to relieve the intense uncertainty prevalent at that time. The sample of banks included some that quickly proved to pose systemic risks in certain countries.

In the 2011 EBA-led exercise, the final estimated capital shortfall was modest. This result was largely the product of many banks—especially those with relatively weak capital buffers—preemptively increasing their capitalization and what with hindsight appears to be unduly optimistic baseline and stress scenarios, including with regard to the treatment of sovereign risk. Three main quality control mechanisms were: the banks' own controls; those by National Supervisory Authorities (NSAs), for example, supervisory judgment; and the quality assurance process led by EBA. For the latter, EBA formed a Quality Assurance Task Force with members seconded from NSAs, the ECB, and the European Systemic Risk Board, who challenged their peers in other NSAs on the consistency of the banks' bottom-up assumptions, methodologies and results. Compared to the 2010 stress test, EBA improved its off-site review by checking bank input data for errors, ensuring the correct adoption and application of the stress testing methodologies, and using statistical benchmarks (mainly cross-sectional) for probabilities of default, loss given default, and default rates by counterparties, country and sector.

For the 2011 stress test, EBA's board of supervisors decided not to include market risk haircuts to the banks' sovereign exposures in the banking book, but did publish relevant data. Only the banks' sovereign holdings in the trading book would be subject to mark-to-market. Given the intensification of the euro area sovereign debt crisis, this assumption was debatable and criticized, but the enhanced disclosure and transparency of the banks' sovereign exposures allowed market analysts to calculate their own sovereign haircuts and eventually the capital shortfall of banks in the sample.

The subsequent recapitalization exercise contained some elements common to stress testing. Importantly, all sovereign securities' holdings were subject to mark-to-market. Most banks have met the 9 percent core Tier 1 capital requirement; the exceptions are banks in unusual circumstances where action is being taken, especially where governments apply. One important implication of this achievement is that banks already more or less have the capital necessary to meet requirements under Basel III or the EU's Capital Adequacy Directive IV, even were the requirements to be applied in full or imposed through market discipline.

APPENDIX 6.1. RISKS AND VULNERABILITIES IN EU COUNTRIES IDENTIFIED BY RECENT FINANCIAL SECTOR ASSESSMENT PROGRAMS (FSAPS)

TABLE 6A.1

Systemic EU Countries: France, Germany, and Luxembourg

Main Source of Risk	France (FSAP Completion Date: July 2012)	Germany (FSAP Completion Date: July 2011)	Luxembourg (FSAP Completion Date: May 2011)
		Vulnerabilities	
Stresses and dislocations in wholesale funding markets; adverse liquidity and refinancing conditions.	• Likelihood: medium; impact: high. • Bank refinancing needs in 2013–14 are significant and heavily reliant on wholesale funding. • Domestic interbank market frozen as of end-October 2012. • Vulnerable to systemic liquidity shocks owing to cross-border interbank exposures and derivatives positions.	• Likelihood: medium; impact: medium. • Some banks may face distressed U.S. dollar funding conditions. • Certain banks rely heavily on market funding including through interbank borrowing, securitization, and covered bond issuance. • Landesbanken seem to be more vulnerable than other banks; retail banks exhibit more resilience.	• Likelihood: medium; impact: medium to high. • Liquidity pressures on local bank subsidiaries could materialize if parent bank is under severe stress; the failure of the parent bank would likely lead to the failure of the subsidiary.
• Deteriorating or sustained high sovereign risk; intensification of the euro area crisis.	• Likelihood: medium; impact: medium to high. • Large exposure of SIFIs to periphery countries in Europe could translate into losses from deteriorating loan quality and sovereign bond values. • Bank deleveraging may lower returns and profitability. • Downgrade of own sovereign could negatively impact banks' ratings, funding costs, and ability to support derivatives operations.	• Likelihood: medium; impact: medium to high. • Financial institutions' holdings of foreign sovereign, sovereign-linked, and subnational government claims are substantial.	• Likelihood: high; impact: high. • GIIPS exposures amount to half of the aggregate bank capital in the jurisdiction. • GIIPS-related losses of parent groups could lead to additional losses through indirect exposures arising from solvency and liquidity pressures. These exposures are difficult to quantify though.
Declining or sharp downward correction to asset prices.	• Likelihood: medium; impact: medium to low.	• N.A.	• Likelihood: low to medium; impact: medium (domestically), high (globally).

	• LTV ratios are high but the risks to banks from a downward house price correction appear limited owing to households' comparatively low debt levels and sound lending standards. • A housing price correction could still have an indirect impact on banks through its impact on real GDP.		• Turbulence in bond and asset markets could lead to large scale fund redemptions; damaging the domestic and European fund industry. • Run on funds could depress asset market prices further, forcing fund sponsors, depository and custodian banks to provide liquidity. • Linkages to domestic banks appear limited; similarly, the direct impact on European bank funding through fire sale of assets is also limited. • Likelihood: medium; impact: medium to high. • Strong capital buffers make banks resilience as long as the parent bank does not fail.
Double-dip recession.	• Likelihood: medium; impact: high • Bank asset quality would be affected; NPLs likely to rise; lower earnings from lower interest margins and higher provisioning needs. • Increased financial distress and heightened risk aversion could dampen growth by widening spreads and reduced credit supply.	• Likelihood: low; impact: medium. • Credit quality deterioration. • Reduced bank profitability from an inversion of the yield curve. • Non-bank financial institutions affected by market losses on securities; losses in pension funds and insurance companies from the impact of low rates on long-term liabilities. • A short recession is unlikely to generate systemic risk.	• N.A.
Slow growth in Europe; low interest rate environment	• N.A.	• Likelihood: medium; impact: high. • Reduced profitability and ability to meet higher capital requirements. • Losses in pension funds and insurance companies from the impact of low rates on long-term liabilities.	• N.A.
Regulatory uncertainty and regulatory burden.	• N.A.	• Likelihood: high; impact: low. • Money market banks and large financial groups will be the most affected, having to increase core capital and decrease leverage.	• Likelihood: low; impact: high.

Sources: IMF (2011a, 2011c, 2012d).

Note: GIIPS: Greece, Ireland, Italy, Portugal, and Spain; LTV: loan-to-value; N.A.: not available; NPL: nonperforming loan; SIFI: systemically important financial institutions.

TABLE 6A.2

Systemic EU Countries: The Netherlands, Spain, and Sweden

Main Source of Risk	The Netherlands (FSAP Completion Date: March 2011)	Spain (FSAP Completion Date: May 2012)	Sweden (FSAP Completion Date: July 2011)
		Vulnerabilities	
Stresses and dislocations in wholesale funding markets; adverse liquidity and refinancing conditions.	• Likelihood: medium; impact: medium. • Banks reliant on interbank borrowing, securitization and covered bond issuance would be the most affected. • Increased competition for retail deposits could squeeze profitability further; "safe haven" concerns could reduce the returns for banks with funding surpluses.	• Likelihood: medium to high; impact: high. • Substantial bank refinancing needs in 2012–13. • Despite comfortable buffers of ECB instruments that could be used as repo collateral, worsening market conditions could impose higher haircuts to banks' collateral. • Refinancing difficulties could prevent an orderly deleveraging in the banking sector.	• Likelihood: medium; impact: high. • Banks could face refinancing risks, including higher funding rates. • The central bank has limited ability to offset foreign currency liquidity shortages.
Deteriorating or sustained high sovereign risk; intensification of the euro area crisis.	• Likelihood: medium; impact: low. • Banks appear less exposed to GIIPS countries than are some in neighboring countries. • Spillovers from the periphery to the core raise concerns.	• Likelihood: high; impact: high. • Limited direct exposure of the banking system to periphery countries, but exposure to domestic sovereign is high, amounting to 150 percent of core Tier 1 capital. • Trading book and mark-to-market value of the available for sale book only minimally affected by valuation haircuts.	• N.A.
Declining or sharp downward correction to asset prices.	• Likelihood: medium; impact: high. • Banks are heavily exposed to the residential housing market; falling prices and lending arrears would have a negative impact on banks' balance sheets.	• Likelihood: high; impact: high. • Since real estate exposures are large, recapitalization needs will further increase. • About one out of four banks in the stress test sample would face severe capital losses.	• Likelihood: medium; impact: high. • Falling housing prices would lead to direct losses in the banking system and indirect losses from weaker economic growth and higher unemployment.

Double-dip recession in advanced economies.	• Likelihood: medium; impact: medium. • Bank solvency affected by high and/or rising unemployment rates; sharp housing price corrections; rising NPLs from firms and households. • Difficulties of foreign subsidiaries would impact parent banks negatively.	• N.A.	• Likelihood: medium; impact: medium. • Bank asset quality would be adversely affected through various transmission channels including increased unemployment, deteriorating corporate earnings, and a sharp correction in real estate prices.
Slow growth in Europe; low interest rate environment.	• Likelihood: medium; impact: medium to high. • Impact considerations largely in line with the realization of the double-dip recession risk. • Scenario not included in stress test.	• Impact similar to second bullet item above but scenario not included in stress test.	• N.A.
Regulatory uncertainty and regulatory burden.	• N.A.	• N.A.	• Likelihood: medium; impact: high. • Banks need to extend their funding maturity to comply with new liquidity regulations, leading to higher lending rates, reduced lending and/or lower bank profitability.

Sources: IMF (2011b, 2011d, 2012c).

Note: FSAP: Financial Sector Assessment Program; GIIPS: Greece, Ireland, Italy, Portugal, and Spain; N.A.: not available; NPL: nonperforming loan.

TABLE 6A.3

Systemic (the United Kingdom) and Nonsystemic (the Czech Republic and Slovenia) EU Countries

Main Source of Risk	Systemic	Nonsystemic	
	United Kingdom (FSAP Completion Date: May 2011)	**Czech Republic** (FSAP Completion Date: February 2011)	**Slovenia** (FSAP Completion Date: October 2012)
		Vulnerabilities	
Stresses and dislocations in wholesale funding markets; adverse liquidity and refinancing conditions.	• Likelihood: medium and rising; impact: high. • Stable funding in the banking sector beyond six months is inadequate.	• Likelihood: medium; impact: high. • Mainly associated with the failure of a foreign parent bank. • Upstreaming capital and/or liquidity to parent may limit the operational scope of the subsidiaries. • Reputational risk would pressure liquidity and funding costs; and encourage deleveraging.	• LTROs have contributed to alleviate banks' funding pressures but the loan-to-deposit ratio for the system is high. • Foreign-owned banks are more reliant on wholesale funding than domestic banks.
Deteriorating or sustained high sovereign risk; intensification of the euro area crisis.	• Likelihood: medium and rising; impact: low. • Extreme tail risk losses in the banking sector could amount to about 6 percent of 2010 GDP. • Rising sovereign risk could expose banks to funding disruptions.	• N.A.	• Impact: low. • GIIPS exposures are small.
Declining or sharp downward correction to asset prices.	• Likelihood: medium; impact: medium. • Commercial real estate loans account for a substantial share of corporate loans, putting banks at risk if CRE prices decline sharply. • Housing loans to low-income households are more sensitive to housing price declines and real interest rate shocks. • Lender forbearance practices could be masking increased risks in housing and CRE markets. • Two large U.K. banks have very large exposures to Asia, which has experienced rapid asset price increases on the back of strong capital inflows.	• See fourth bullet item below on housing prices and commercial real estate prices.	• Housing and commercial real estate prices have remained relatively stable since the price correction experienced in 2008; however, the inventory of foreclosed properties and NPLs in the sector has increased. • Further declines in CRE and housing prices are likely to accelerate foreclosures and NPLs in the banking sector, resulting in impairments. • Protracted bankruptcy procedures suggest increased foreclosures would affect prices only after a substantial lag of about 2–3 years.

Double-dip recession in advanced economies.	• Likelihood: medium; impact: medium. • Major banks would be able to absorb losses, with extreme tail risk losses amounting to about 2½ percent of 2010 GDP.	• Likelihood: medium; impact: medium to high. • Unfavorable export markets; slower domestic growth; drop in asset prices; reversal of capital flows. • Negative effects on banks' asset quality leading to a substantial drop in capitalization. • Heavy concentration of bank loans in commercial real estate and mortgages makes banks especially sensitive to a severe macroeconomic shock.	• Likelihood: high; impact: high. • Negative impact through trade and financial channels. • Further recapitalization needs required for the largest domestic bank.
Slow growth in Europe; low interest rate environment.	• Likelihood: medium; impact: low. • The insurance sector exhibits resilience to low interest rates; extreme tail risk losses in the banking system could be as high as 5 percent of 2010 GDP.	• Likelihood: high; impact: medium. • Negative impact on economy through main trading partners, especially Germany; asset quality and income deterioration in the banking sector. • Higher funding costs resulting from competition for deposits and the adoption of Basel III to a certain degree. • Higher exchange rate volatility could amplify stress conditions.	• N.A.
Regulatory uncertainty and regulatory burden.	• Likelihood: medium; impact: medium. • Basel III could have a significant impact on banks; core Tier 1 capital reduced by half for six largest banks under new definition; new liquidity requirements will affect short-term wholesale funding practices; SIFIs profitability adversely affected. • Solvency II, which becomes effective January 1, 2013, could encourage search for yield among insurers.	• N.A.	• N.A.

Sources: IMF (2011e, 2012a, 2012b).
Note: CRE: commercial real estate; GIIPS: Greece, Ireland, Italy, Portugal and Spain; LTROs: long-term refinancing operations; N.A.: not applicable; NPL: nonperforming loan; SIFIs: systemically important financial institutions.

REFERENCES

International Monetary Fund, 2011a, "Luxembourg: Publication of Financial System Stability Assessment," IMF Country Report No. 11/148 (Washington, June), http://www.imf.org/external/pubs/ft/scr/2011/cr11148.pdf.

—————, 2011b, "Kingdom of the Netherlands: Publication of Financial System Stability Assessment," IMF Country Report No. 11/144 (Washington, June), http://www.imf.org/external/pubs/ft/scr/2011/cr11144.pdf.

—————, 2011c, "Germany: Publication of Financial System Stability Assessment," IMF Country Report No. 11/169 (Washington, July), http://www.imf.org/external/pubs/ft/scr/2011/cr11169.pdf.

—————, 2011d, "Sweden: Publication of Financial System Stability Assessment," IMF Country Report No. 11/172 (Washington, July), http://www.imf.org/external/pubs/ft/scr/2011/cr11172.pdf.

—————, 2011e, "United Kingdom: Publication of Financial System Stability Assessment, IMF Country Report No. 11/222 (Washington, July 2011), http://www.imf.org/external/pubs/ft/scr/2011/cr11222.pdf.

—————, 2012a, "Czech Republic: Publication of Financial System Stability Assessment Update," IMF Country Report No. 12/177 (Washington, July), http://www.imf.org/external/pubs/ft/scr/2012/cr12177.pdf.

—————, 2012b, "Slovenia: Publication of Financial System Stability Assessment," IMF Country Report No. 12/325 (Washington, June), http://www.imf.org/external/pubs/ft/scr/2012/cr12325.pdf.

—————, 2012c, "Spain: Publication of Financial System Stability Assessment," IMF Country Report No. 12/137 (Washington, June), http://www.imf.org/external/pubs/ft/scr/2012/cr12137.pdf.

—————, 2012d, "France: Publication of Financial System Stability Assessment," IMF Country Report No. 12/341 (Washington, December), http://www.imf.org/external/pubs/ft/scr/2012/cr12341.pdf.

—————, 2012e, *Global Financial Stability Report: The Quest for Lasting Stability*, World Economic and Financial Surveys (Washington, April), http://www.imf.org/External/Pubs/FT/GFSR/2012/01/index.htm.

—————, 2012f, *Global Financial Stability Report: Restoring Confidence and Progressing on Reforms*, World Economic and Financial Surveys (Washington, October), http://www.imf.org/External/Pubs/FT/GFSR/2012/02/index.htm.

CHAPTER 7

Progress with Bank Resolution and Restructuring in the European Union

Luc Everaert, Heiko Hesse, and Nadege Jassaud

Restructuring of the banking system in the European Union (EU) is under way, but further progress is necessary, and the planned asset quality review provides a good opportunity. The level of Tier 1 capital ratios of EU banks has been substantially increased, thanks to government backstops and the recapitalization exercise coordinated by the European Banking Authority (EBA).[1] But systemwide, capital ratios have been met partly by deleveraging or recalibrations of the risk weights on activities. Consolidation in the banking sector has been slow, with banks rarely merged or closed.[2] Nonperforming loans (NPLs) are building up in banks' balance sheets, and dependence on central bank liquidity remains high, especially for banks in peripheral countries. Despite the EBA recapitalization exercise having led to €200 billion of new capital or reduction of capital needs by European banks, fresh capital is difficult to attract in an environment where prospects for profitability are uncertain.

To expedite bank restructuring, it will be essential to adjust policies along several dimensions (see part II of this book for details). As is being coordinated by the EU resolution directive, bank resolution tools need to be strengthened to give national authorities all tools necessary to find the least-cost solution to bank restructuring and resolution. Restructuring of NPLs should be facilitated. The legal framework should be adapted to remove obstacles to restructuring and to allow maximum asset recovery. In several EU countries, such as Italy, Greece, and in Eastern Europe, bankruptcy reforms lag behind in that, for instance, current practice does not allow the seizure of collateral in a reasonable timeframe. Banks should also manage more actively their NPLs, facilitating the expansion of a market for distressed assets. Disclosure should be significantly enhanced and harmonized by the EBA to restore market confidence. In particular, interpretable metrics regarding the quality of banks' assets, in terms of NPLs, collateral, probability of defaults, and loan recovery rates, are key for assessing the strength of banks and restoring confidence in the banking system.

---

[1] Ten percent in June 2012 against 7 percent in December 2008; 57 EU banks (EBA).
[2] While banks were rarely closed, some have downsized by closing branches, selling or closing business lines, and significantly reducing their staff levels in some cases.

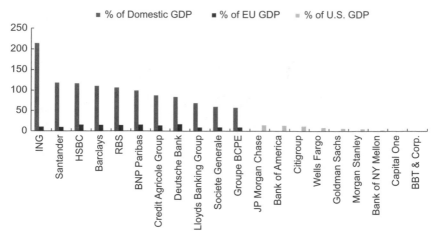

Figure 7.1 Assets of EU and U.S. Banking Groups (*2011, in percent of GDP*)
Sources: Total assets data from SNL Financial; GDP data from Eurostat, EU Commission.

Before the onset of the crisis, relatively favorable conditions—and, in some economies, asset price and credit bubbles—masked underlying vulnerabilities. Many financial systems in Europe were bank-dominated, complex, and very large in proportion to domestic gross domestic product (GDP). Global assets of the five largest banks were typically more than 300 percent of their home country's GDP (Figure 7.1).[3] Credit and asset price bubbles (Reinhart and Rogoff, 2009; Laeven and Valencia, 2008) built up in several jurisdictions, with sharp increases in leverage for households, also reflected in many countries in a substantial increase in house prices. While risks were building up, the overall resilience of banks improved little. From 2000 to 2007, solvency ratios increased by only 0.2 percent.[4] Return on equity was high, about 17 percent in 2007 for European banks. Leverage of many large financial institutions also increased, reflecting a reliance on short-term wholesale funding that was not generally considered a concern.

DIRECT SUPPORT, RECAPITALIZATION, AND RESOLUTION

The initial response to the crisis consisted of unprecedented broad public support for the financial system out of concern to safeguard financial stability (see Chapter 5 for details). It took the form of guarantees of different elements of the liability side of the banking system, direct government recapitalization, liquidity

---

[3] Total bank assets account for 283 percent of GDP in the EU, compared to about 65 percent of GDP in the United States.

[4] From 10.7 percent to 10.9 percent (sample of the largest 90 EU banks included in the 2011 EBA stress test), Bloomberg.

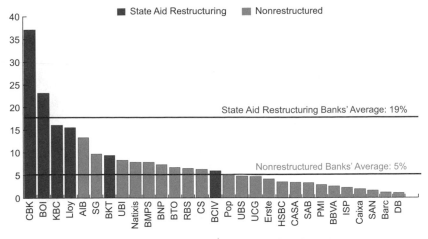

Figure 7.2 Deleveraging/Restructuring Plans[1] (*In percent of total assets*)

Source: Morgan Stanley.
[1] Banks under formal EU State Aid program as of September 2012.

provision by central banks, and forbearance by supervisors. While these interventions protected against tail risks and provided time to take the necessary adjustment measures, they also had the potential to contribute to delays in restructuring.

To promote restructuring of banks receiving public assistance, direct government support measures were normally complemented by action to restructure the affected banks, in part thanks to EU rules on state aid. According to the Directorate-General for Competition (DG COMP), 10–15 percent of the EU banking system is now under the State Aid framework and undergoing some forced restructuring. Based on a sample of 30 EU large institutions, banks under EU State Aid rules have been (in the process of) deleveraging, with reductions of up to 19 percent of their total assets, according to Morgan Stanley research, while other banks that did not fall under DG COMP state rules deleveraged much less (Figure 7.2). Indeed, the state aid framework does not include proactive intervention in banks, but is applied only once banks receive aid. For those who did not, restructuring had to rely on national measures or private initiatives.

Competition and state aid policy has served de facto as the main coordinating mechanism in bank restructuring during the crisis, as it is the only binding EU framework available for this purpose.[5] DG COMP has the exclusive mandate and power to ensure that state aid is compatible with the Treaty on the Functioning

---

[5] The Treaty on the Functioning of the European Union contains strict limitations on state aid to avoid distorting competition and the internal market. According to the Article 107 of the treaty, no state aid should be granted in any form which distorts or threatens competition. However, state aid can be exceptionally allowed under paragraph 3 of Article 107 in cases of serious disturbances to the economy.

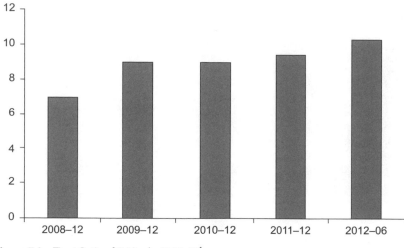

Figure 7.3 Tier 1 Ratio of EU Banks 2008–12[1]

Source: European Banking Authority.
Note: Sample consists of 57 banks and excludes hybrid instruments.
[1] Tier 1 ratio, excluding hybrid instruments, is used as a proxy for core Tier 1 ratio.

of the EU, and that state aid provision is accepted in exchange for strict conditionality. Compensatory measures required by DG COMP have included divestments, penalty interest rates, management removals, dividend suspensions, and burden-sharing (shareholder dilutions and bail-in of subordinated debt). According to DG Comp, 60 EU banks—accounting for 10–15 percent of the EU banking assets—underwent a deep restructuring. Under the state aid regime, 20 banks were resolved.

Direct government support to banks went in parallel with supervisory actions on banks to recapitalize. Led by the EBA, stress testing and recapitalization exercises resulted in banks increasing the quantity and quality of their capital. After the 2010 Committee of European Banking Supervisors and 2011 EBA EU-wide stress tests,[6] the EBA conducted a recapitalization exercise.[7] Capital plans submitted by banks have led to €200 billion of new capital or reduction of capital needs, for an aggregate capital shortfall of €115 billion, at end–June 2012. Tier 1 ratios[8] are now exceeding 10 percent, against 7 percent in December 2008 (Figure 7.3).

Publication of EBA stress test results allowed for enhanced transparency, but remaining data gaps impede market discipline. Enhanced transparency was

[6] The second EBA stress test (2011) that included 90 banks examined the resilience of the European banks against a single adverse macroeconomic scenario, using a core Tier 1 (CT1) capital threshold of 5 percent.

[7] The EBA recapitalization exercise recommended a higher core Tier 1 capital (CTI) target of 9 percent by end-June 2012 after establishing a sovereign buffer against banks' holdings of government securities based on a market-implied valuation of those holdings as of September 2011.

[8] The Tier 1 excluding hybrid instruments so that it gives a proxy of the core Tier 1 ratio in EBA definition.

achieved with the disclosure of over 3,000 data points by EU banks. However, consistent public data across banks are missing on many fronts, including the funding side (collateral encumbrance, ECB funding, liquidity coverage ratios), derivatives portfolio and other off-balance-sheet activities, risk-weighted assets, and probabilities of default.

In reaction to the crisis, a number of countries modified their approach to bank resolution. The United Kingdom created a special resolution regime and Germany adopted a restructuring law, both of which granted the authorities the power to utilize various resolution tools. Now both countries can sell failing businesses, that is, to transfer all or part of the business to a private sector purchaser, and or to create a bridge bank. The German Bank Reorganization Act (January 2011) also provides for an asset separation tool (the power to transfer all or part of a business to an entity, even if not a bank, in which the restructuring fund owns shares) and the possibility to bail-in senior unsecured creditors through a court-led proceeding on the initiative of the bank.

Several EU countries, including Greece, Italy, and Portugal, are involved in bankruptcy/insolvency law reform, including by introducing fast-track restructuring tools and an out-of-court restructuring process. For instance, repossession of the collateral backing a retail mortgage may take several years in Italy versus a few months in Scandinavia and United Kingdom. The asset recovery process remains prolonged in many emerging economies in Eastern Europe countries.[9]

ASSET QUALITY AND ASSET QUALITY REVIEWS

Asset quality has held significant surprises in the course of the financial crisis and continues to cause concern. NPLs have jumped from 2.6 percent of total loans in December 2007 to 8.4 percent of total loans in June 2012 (Figure 7.4), outpacing loan growth in the EU (over the same reference period, loans have decreased by 3 percent and NPLs increased by almost 150 percent, that is, by €308 billion in absolute terms). European banks have also seen much larger NPL increases than the largest U.S. banks (Figure 7.5). This trend has not yet shown signs of reversal, reflecting the continued deterioration of the macroeconomic situation and the slow pace of restructuring.

Banks at the periphery of the euro area have been particularly hurt by this asset quality deterioration. There is a large dispersion in NPLs across European banks with those in the periphery countries Greece, Ireland, Italy, Portugal, and Spain witnessing the largest increases (Figure 7.6). For instance, the NPL ratio for Italy and Spain increased from 5 and 3.4 percent in early

---

[9]The European Banking Coordination "Vienna" Initiative (2012) in a working group focused on NPL issues in central, eastern, and southeastern Europe. Recommendations, among others, focused on establishing a conducive legal framework for NPL resolution and removing tax impediments and regulatory obstacles, as well as enabling out-of-court settlements.

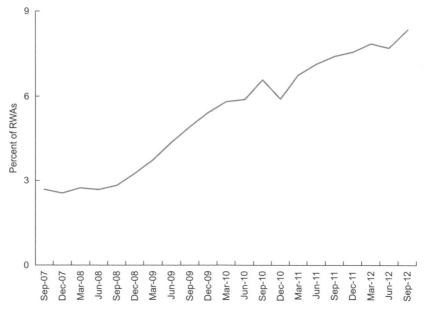

Figure 7.4 Nonperforming Loan (NPL) Ratio of EU Banks (*NPLs to Total Loans*)

Sources: Bloomberg, L.P. and European Banking Authority.
Note: Ninety banks in sample. RWAs = risk-weighted assets.

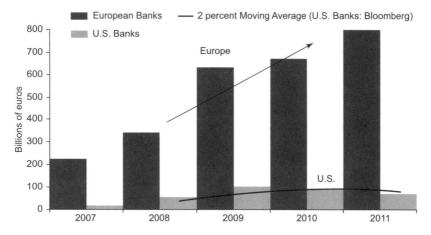

Figure 7.5 Trends in Nonperforming Loans: Europe versus the United States (*in billions of euros*)

Source: Bloomberg, L.P.

2008 to 13 and 9.6 percent in June 2012, respectively. Ireland stands out with average NPLs close to 30 percent for our sample of banks followed by Hungary and Greece. However, definitions in this area are not harmonized and impair comparability across the EU.[10]

---

[10] Across European countries, there can be large differences in NPL definitions, making asset quality assessment across countries and banks difficult.

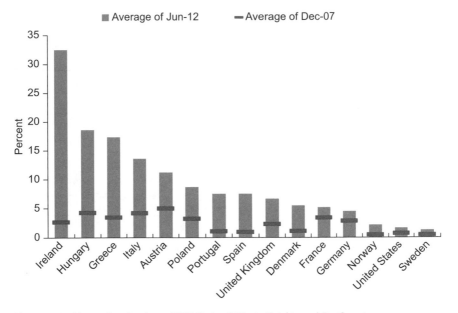

Figure 7.6 Nonperforming Loan (NPL) Ratios (NPLs to Total Loans) Per Country

Sources: Bloomberg, L.P. and European Banking Authority.

The deepening financial crisis in Europe and larger-than-expected loan losses in some countries have heightened market skepticism about the soundness of banks in general. These concerns have sometimes resulted in entire banking systems being tarred with the same brush, including healthy ones that will need to shoulder the burden of restarting credit to the real economy.

In some of the countries subject to high financial stress, the authorities have embraced independent third-party diagnostics of asset quality, supplementing the EBA-led stress testing and recapitalization exercises, to regain market confidence in the system. Countries under/near financial assistance (Cyprus, Greece, Ireland, Portugal, and Spain) have carried out independent asset quality reviews to regain market confidence (Table 7.1). Self-assessments are usually difficult in a crisis environment because supervisors may be under political pressures to hide losses. The independent reviews have generally uncovered valuation problems that other supervisory exercises did not detect. In general, the reviews have paid off as several of the crisis countries have made progress toward restoring market credibility.

ASSET MANAGEMENT COMPANIES

One way to address impaired assets is through asset management companies (AMCs). In previous financial crises, such AMCs have proven effective in

TABLE 7.1

Asset Quality Reviews Conducted in EU Countries: 2008–12

Ireland	Greece	Portugal	Cyprus	Spain
Jan–Mar 2011	Aug–Dec 2011	Jul–Nov 2011	Sept–Dec 2012	May–Jun 2012
In December 2010, as part of the EU/IMF program, BlackRock Solutions was engaged to perform a loan diagnosis of over €275 billion across the five largest Irish banks. The diagnosis had five building blocks: • an asset quality review to assess the quality of aggregate and individual loan portfolios and the monitoring processes employed; • a distressed credit operations review to assess the operational capability and effectiveness of distressed loan portfolio management in the banks including arrears management and workout practices in curing NPLs and reducing loan losses; • a data integrity validation exercise to assess the reliability of banks' data; • a loan loss forecast under base and stress scenarios; and • a public communication. Under the loan loss forecast, BlackRock estimated future losses with forecasted financial statements through end-2013 (three-year horizon) as well as baseline losses.	As part of the 2nd Memorandum of Economic and Financial Policies, BlackRock was engaged to perform a loan diagnosis over all Greek banks. Individual results were communicated to banks but no disclosure has been made to the public.	Under the EU/IMF program, the supervisor led detailed asset quality reviews of the eight largest national banking groups' loan portfolios and regulatory capital (RWA) calculations. Those eight largest banking groups account for more than 80 percent of the banking system's total assets. This "Special Inspection Program" (SIP) was carried out with support from external parties, Ernst & Young, PWC, and Oliver Wyman. The SIP had three different work streams: • the valuation of the credit portfolio, • a credit risk capital requirements calculation, and • a stress test conducted (by Olivier and Wyman). The results of the W1 and W2 were made public in December 2011. The results of the W3 were not disclosed.	An asset quality review of the Cypriot banks will be conducted, including a stress test exercise. The Central Bank of Cyprus appointed the investment companies Pimco and Deloitte to conduct the asset quality review of on 22 institutions, which is a mix of EU subsidiaries, cooperative credit institutions, and domestic banks. The participating banks account for 73 percent of the Cyprus banking system. The stress test will have a three-year horizon from mid-2012 to mid-2015.	Olivier and Wyman and Roland Berger were assigned to assess the resilience of the main Spanish banking groups (14 which hold 88 percent of the market asset share). Cumulative credit losses for the top-down stress test with a three-year horizon are €250–270 billion in the adverse scenario and €170–190 billion in the base scenario. The estimated capital needs range from €51–62 billion and €16–25 billion in the adverse and base scenario, respectively, and the capital buffer requirement of €37 billion for a core Tier 1 threshold of 7 percent. The second part of the assessment with four domestic auditors was completed at the end of September.

Source: Authors' compilation.

Note: NPL = nonperforming loan; RWA = risk-weighted asset.

addressing restructuring.[11] The EU experience with asset management companies is at an early stage. A number of AMCs were established in the context of the crisis, including in Belgium, Denmark, Ireland, Spain, and the United Kingdom. AMCs are being set up in Cyprus and Slovenia, and AMCs were considered but ruled out in Iceland. It is too early to assess this experience fully but some observations can already be made.

While there is no single optimal solution in setting up AMCs, fair asset valuation, operational independence, appropriately structured incentives, and commercial orientation are key design features (Table 7.2). The experience in Ireland with setting up the National Asset Management Agency (NAMA) in late 2009 is that lack of a universally accepted methodology for the valuation of assets led to a protracted process whereby bank book values were repeatedly discounted, prolonging uncertainty, delaying normalization of bank funding, and undermining the credibility of the process.[12]

Funding of an AMC is a key design feature. The AMC must have sufficient funds to perform its intended functions, with the operating budget separate from funding for asset takeover. In past crises, funding came from either the proceeds of government bond issues or the AMC's own bond issuance backed by the government, with losses absorbed by the budget as private investor participation is unlikely to materialize in the early stages.[13] There are a few precedents for central bank funding of AMCs, most involving protection against potential losses. A number of central banks in Central and Eastern European transition economies were engaged in funding AMCs or bad banks; the losses incurred were covered by the national budget or over time via seignorage. The Swiss National Bank (SNB) supported in 2008 the transfer of illiquid securities and other troubled assets of UBS to a special purpose vehicle—the Swiss Stabilization Fund—controlled and mainly funded by the SNB.[14] Protections were provided to the SNB in the form of loan overcollateralization and warrants for UBS shares, to cover any losses on liquidation of assets. The broad recovery of secondary market asset valuations in 2010 allowed the fund to dispose of assets with sales mostly above their intrinsic

---

[11] Examples include the U.S. Resolution Trust Corporation and the Thai Financial Sector Restructuring Agency; U.S. Maiden Lane LLCs established by the Federal Reserve to resolve Bear Sterns and AIG, and Sweden's Securum; the Korea Asset Management Institution and the Malaysian Danaharta. Centralized AMCs, often with broad mandates, were also widely used during the 1990s transition in Central and Eastern Europe, for example, in the Czech Republic, Georgia, Hungary, Kazakhstan, Lithuania, Macedonia, Slovakia, and Ukraine.

[12] NAMA had acquired assets with a nominal average discount of over 50 percent. The process lasted for over a year and required detailed asset-by-asset valuation. The alternative, nationalization combined with a creation of a "good bank" has been used in Latvia for resolving Parex bank in 2008–2010.

[13] For instance, in Ireland banks received government-guaranteed securities in return for assets transferred to the Irish National Asset Management Agency (NAMA).

[14] Assets were transferred to the fund at market prices and thus, on average, with a discount to notional value. Asset transfer from UBS was financed by a 90 percent loan from SNB, backed by a security interest in all the fund's assets, and 10 percent financing contribution from UBS. Management of assets was outsourced to UBS and UBS was given an option to repurchase the fund.

TABLE 7.2

Asset Management Companies—Challenges and Key Design Features

Costs and Benefits	Key Design Features	EU Crisis Countries
AMCs allow consolidation of scarce workout skills and resources in one agency, and the application of uniform workout procedures: • help securitization because of the larger pool of assets; • provide greater leverage over debtors (especially if AMCs are granted special powers of loan recovery); • prevent fire sales or destabilizing spillover effects, as banks deleverage; and • allow the good banks to focus on their core business. However, asset purchases by an AMC do not raise banks' net worth unless the operation is done at above-market prices, which should be avoided. Asset purchases, thus, do not solve a problem of lack of capital in the banking sector. The overall cost may be higher than expected, depending on the legal and operational environment for loan recovery and the likelihood of being subject to political pressure.	• Governance: operational independence is necessary to assure the effective operation of an AMC. • Structured incentives: the AMC should not become a "warehouse" of NPLs and have incentives to ensure effective and efficient asset management and asset disposals. • Commercial orientation: assets should be purchased at a price as close to a fair market value as possible to minimize losses (possibly considering some form of profit-sharing arrangement).[1] Funding shall be adequate. The AMC must have sufficient funds to perform its intended functions, with the operating budget separate from funding for asset takeover. In past crises, funding came from either the proceeds of government bond issues or the AMC's own bond issuance backed by the government. A key advantage of using a company without a banking license (an AMC) instead of a bank is that AMCs do not need to meet regulatory capital and liquidity requirements, thereby reducing their overall costs.	Ireland: the National Asset Management Agency (NAMA) was set up in December 2009, to help Irish banks divest of bad loans (Irish commercial property) and in turn receive government-backed securities as collateral against ECB funding. NAMA aimed to achieve this task by: • Acquiring bad loans from the five participating banks, • Working proactively on a business plan for acquiring and disposing of bad loans, and • Protecting and enhancing to the maximum possible level, the value of these assets. Spain: the legislation enacted in August 2012 established the Asset Management Company for assets arising from bank restructuring (Sareb) and empowers the Fund for the Orderly Restructuring of the Banking Sector (FROB) to instruct distressed banks to transfer problematic assets to it. Mid–December 2012, Sareb increased its capital to allow its main private participants (banks) to become shareholders.

Sources: Ingves and Hoelscher (2005); Enoch, Garcia, and Sundarajan, (2001); and Bank of Ireland, FROB websites.
Note: AMC = asset management company; ECB = European Central Bank; NPL = nonperforming loan.
[1] The Malaysian Danaharta, for example, purchased impaired loans at an average discount of 55 percent, while banks that sold assets retained the right to receive 80 percent of any recoveries in excess of acquisition costs that the AMC was able to realize.

values. In the euro area, in most cases, funding for AMCs has been provided by the sovereign which in some cases has been expensive and had to be supported with official financing from external sources.

Finally, the size of the impaired assets under management of AMCs is quite large compared to the economy. Working through these assets quickly to allow asset prices to find their new equilibrium and attract new private investment will be important. While there are tradeoffs between speed and financial stability, an excessively drawn out process of asset disposal by AMCs may dampen the outlook. For example, SABER has a portfolio of about €50 billion in assets, which it intends to sell off at a very slow pace of a few billion euros per year.

HOW FAR HAS BANK RESTRUCTURING COME?

Most EU banking systems appear well-capitalized, but pockets of vulnerability remain, and leverage is still high. The average Tier 1 capital ratio now exceeds 9 percent. Individual bank capital Core Tier 1 capital buffers—consistent with Basel III norms—also appear to be strong as of June 2012, even after accounting for buffers for specific sovereign exposures requested for the EBA recapitalization exercise. According to the benchmark considered, only four banks in the EBA sample appeared to have Core Tier 1 ratio below 9 percent after sovereign buffers.

Still, in spite of generally solid regulatory capital ratios, many EU banking systems, in particular where large universal banks account for a significant share of assets, remain highly leveraged, in particular in Belgium, France, Italy, and the United Kingdom (Figure 7.7). Concerns have been expressed about the consistency of the Basel risk weights across firms. During the last EBA recapitalization exercise, 30 percent of the shortfall that banks were required to make up was met through reduction in risk-weighted assets (RWAs), of which €10 billion came through RWA "recalibrations" (validation, roll out, or changes to parameters of internal models). Such recalibrations of RWAs are expected to continue, contributing to opacity in bank capital computations. The recent Bank of England Financial Stability Report (November 2012) showed that banks' RWAs calculations for the same hypothetical portfolio can be vastly different, with the most prudent banks calculating over twice the needed capital as do the most aggressive banks.

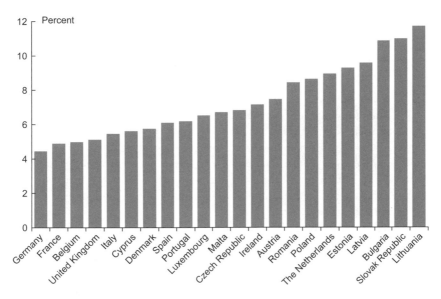

Figure 7.7 EU Large Banks Capital-to-Asset Ratio

Source: IMF Financial Soundness Indicators.
Note: 2012:Q2, except Bulgaria (2009); Spain; France (2010); Latvia; Slovak Republic (2012:Q1); and the United Kingdom (2011:Q4).

Funding remains a large challenge, especially for banks in the euro area periphery. Many such banks are heavily reliant on ECB funding, with challenges on asset encumbrance and collateral eligibility due to, for instance, rating downgrades, valuation effects on their collateral, and overall loss of market confidence. Banks in Greece and Ireland have also substantially used emergency liquidity assistance. Following the announcement of the Outright Monetary Transactions program by the ECB, funding conditions have somewhat eased for banks in the periphery countries, and some have been able to issue debt in primary markets; and bank credit default swap spreads in the periphery have been easing. However, wholesale funding remains prohibitively expensive for the euro area periphery banks to sustainably support lending in the current environment.

Many large EU banks are structurally reliant on wholesale financing while the interbank funding markets are heavily concentrated on both the demand and supply side. This reliance on potentially volatile funding turned out to be a significant vulnerability during the euro area financial crisis. Several banks failed partly as a result of weak wholesale funding models and risk management (Dexia, HRE, and LBBW). Several key euro area systemically important financial institutions remain largely dependent on wholesale or derivative funding. For example, the funding of BNP Paribas is about 70 percent wholesale and derivative funding. Most of the demand for interbank funding in the EU originates from large banks in France, Germany, Italy, Spain, and the United Kingdom. Similarly, the source of interbank funds is also very concentrated, as funding from within the EU account for more than two thirds of total interbank funding.

Many European cross-border banks have significant overseas activities funded in U.S. dollars. A significant part of this funding has remained short-term, contributing in creating structural funding gaps (for example, the gap between long-term assets and long-term funding in U.S. dollars) in balance sheets, including among euro area banks. These funding gaps remained significant at the end of quarter two of 2012, in spite of heavy reductions in U.S. dollar assets of French and German banks.[15]

EU banks liquidity buffers remain low. Indicators of liquidity such as the ratio of liquid assets to short-term liabilities, however, suggest that many European banks are lacking sufficient liquidity buffers. In aggregate, liquid assets exceed short-term liabilities of the banking system only in Germany, the Netherlands, Portugal, and Romania. Moreover, the level of collateral pledged in the Eurosystem may have reduced available collateral funding going forward, in particular in countries under stress.

Profitability is generally low, and there is significant heterogeneity across and within countries. Return on assets remains generally low across EU banking systems, with significant variations across EU countries (Figure 7.8). The highest profitability, observed in emerging European countries, partly reflects higher interest margins in some of these countries. Return on equity has declined since

---

[15] Estimates from Bank for International Settlements data suggest that French and German banks have reduced their gross U.S. dollar assets by respectively US$270 billion and US$100 billion between 2011:Q2 and 2012:Q2.

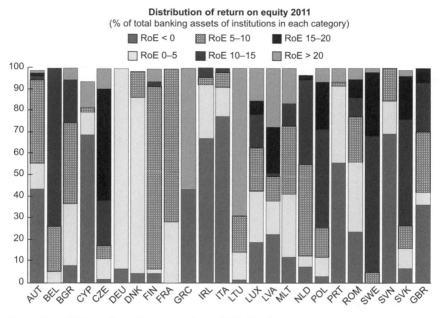

Figure 7.8 EU Large Banks: Return on Equity (RoE) Distribution

Source: Financial Stability Committee, European Central Bank.
Note: AUT = Austria; BEL = Belgium; BGR = Bulgaria; CYP = Cyprus; CZE = Czech Republic; DEU = Germany; DNK = Denmark; FIN = Finland; FRA = France; GRC = Greece; IRL = Ireland; ITA = Italy; LTU = Lithuania; LUX = Luxembourg; LVA = Latvia; MLT = Malta; NLD = Netherlands; POL = Poland; PRT = Portugal; ROM = Romania; SWE = Sweden; SVN = Slovenia; SVK = Slovak Republic; GBR = United Kingdom.

the crisis, and large proportions of domestic banking systems are not profitable in peripheral EA countries, Austria, and the United Kingdom.

CHALLENGES AHEAD

An environment of very low interest rates, quantitative monetary injections, tolerated forbearance, and government backstops has helped avoid very abrupt restructuring and an intense credit crunch, but the underlying pressures remain. The policies in place are not by themselves a solution, and must be combined with sound macroeconomic policies and comprehensive restructuring strategies. The inevitable exit from these policies will constitute a major challenge to the EU's banking system.

The weak outlook constitutes a threat even to healthy financial institutions. The economic environment in much of the EU remains weak. The recession in most of the periphery has been spilling into other EU economies (see IMF, *World Economic Outlook*, October 2012). Activity in the EA is expected to contract by 0.3 percent in 2013 (*World Economic Outlook* Update, July 2013). This reflects delays in the transmission of lower sovereign spreads and improved bank liquidity to private sector borrowing conditions, and still high uncertainty about the ultimate resolution of the crisis despite recent progress. Credit conditions are still tight in some EU countries, especially those in the periphery and the emerging economies in the EU, which threatens the economic recovery.

Over the medium-term, the absorption of the many changes to the regulatory environment, the remaining uncertainty over some of the parameters of these reforms, and the need to make large financial institutions resolvable will undoubtedly further affect the structure of the EU's banking system (see Part III for more discussion).

REFERENCES

Bank for International Settlement, 2013, "Summary Description of the LCR," Basel Committee on Banking Supervision, January 6, 2013, Basel.

Bank of England, 2012, "Financial Stability Report" (November 2012).

Center for European Policy Studies, 2010, "Bank State Aid in the Financial Crisis, Fragmentation or Level Playing Field (October).

Claessens, Stijn, Ceyla Pazarbasioglu, Luc Laeven, Marc Dobler, Fabian Valencia, Oana Nedelescu, and Katharine Seal, 2011, "Crisis Management and Resolution: Early Lessons from the Financial Crisis," IMF Staff Discussion Note No. 11/05 (Washington: International Monetary Fund).

Cuñat, Vicente and Luis Garicano, 2010, "Did Good Cajas Extend Bad Loans? Governance, Human Capital and Loan Portfolios," Foundation for the Study of Applied Economics Fedea Working paper 2010-8.

Directorate-General for Competition, 2011, "The Effects of Temporary State Aid Rules Adopted in the Context of the Financial and Economic Crisis," Autumn 2011.

Enoch, Charles, Gillian Garcia, and V. Sundarajan, 2001, "Recapitalizing Banks with Public Funds," *IMF Staff Paper,* Vol. 48, No.1.

European Banking Authority, 2012, "Results of the Basel III Monitoring Exercise Based on Data as of 31 December 2011," September 2012.

European Banking Coordination "Vienna" Initiative (2012) "Working Group on NPLs in Central, Eastern and Southeastern Europe" (March).

EU Parliament report, 2011, "State Aid, Crisis Rules for the Financial Sector and the Real Economy."

Goyal, Rishi, Petya Koeva Brooks, Mahmood Pradhan, Thierry Tressel, Giovanni Dell'Ariccia, Ross Leckow, Ceyla Pazarbasioglu, and an IMF Staff Team, 2013, "A Banking Union for the Euro Area," IMF Staff Discussion Note No. 13/01 (Washington: International Monetary Fund).

Haldane, Andy, 2011, Capital Discipline, January 2011, BIS central bankers speeches, based on a speech given at the American Economic Association, Denver, Colorado, January 9, 2011.

Hoelscher, David S., and Marc Quintyn, 2003, *Managing Systemic Crisis*, IMF Occasional Paper No. 224 (Washington: International Monetary Fund).

Ingves, Stefan, and David S. Hoelscher, 2005, "The Resolution of Systemic Banking System Crises," in *Systemic Financial Crises: Resolving Large Bank Insolvencies,* edited by Douglas Darrell Evanoff and George G. Kaufman (Hackensack, NJ: World Scientific Publishing).

International Monetary Fund, 2010, "Crisis Management and Resolution for a European Banking System."

———, 2011, "European Financial Stability Framework Exercise (EFFE)."

———, 2012a, *Global Financial Stability Report: The Quest for Lasting Stability,* World Economic and Financial Surveys (Washington, April).

———, 2012b, *Global Financial Stability Report: Restoring Confidence and Progressing on Reforms*, World Economic and Financial Surveys (Washington: October).

———, 2012c, *World Economic Outlook: Coping with High Debt and Sluggish Growth*, World Economic and Financial Surveys (Washington, October).

———, 2013a, *World Economic Outlook Update*, January (Washington).

————, 2013b, "European Financial Sector Assessment Program: Technical Note on Stress Testing of Banks" (Washington, February).

————, 2013c. "European Financial Sector Assessment Program: Technical Note on Financial Integration and De-integration in the EU (Washington, February).

————, 2013d, "European Financial Sector Assessment Program: Technical Note on European Banking Authority" (Washington, February).

————, 2013e, "European Financial Sector Assessment Program: Financial System Stability Assessment (FSSA)" (Washington, February).

Financial Stability Board, 2011, "Key Attributes of Effective Resolution Regimes for Financial Institutions."

JP Morgan, 2012, "Deleveraging Versus Growth Financials Sector Outlook 2013," November 2012.

Laeven, Luc, and Fabián Valencia, 2012, "Systemic Banking Crises Database: An Update," IMF Working Paper 12/163 (Washington: International Monetary Fund).

CHAPTER 8

Fragmentation of the Financial System

LUC LAEVEN AND THIERRY TRESSEL

In the European Union (EU), the integration of financial markets came to a halt in 2008 following the failure of Lehman Brothers (Figure 8.1). Fragmentation forces first affected emerging European countries as some banks from advanced EU countries, weakened by losses on legacy assets and facing funding pressures, aimed at curtailing liquidity lines to subsidiaries. The Vienna initiative achieved coordination and helped stabilize the foreign capital invested in some countries in emerging Europe, though it did not resolve underlying problems, while the creation of the European Supervisory Authorities and the European Systemic Risk Board (ESRB) improved policy coordination. Growing concerns about sovereign risk in the euro area and the lack of adequate buffers reignited deleveraging forces, this time affecting mostly the periphery of the euro area, while high dependence of euro area banks on wholesale funding made them highly vulnerable to funding shocks originating from money markets funds and other creditors. Overall, total intra-EU exposure to nonresidents has declined by €1.5 trillion through quarter two of 2012, among which €950 billion accounted for by the reduction of exposures to the euro area periphery.

Uncoordinated actions resulted in a simultaneous reduction of cross-border exposures, in particular within the euro area, thereby contributing to fragment the financial system and disrupt the transmission channels of monetary policy. The collapse of cross-border exposures was particularly severe in the wholesale funding market and sovereign bond markets, and amplified adverse sovereign–bank links in the periphery of the euro area.

Substantial policy measures have been taken since the start of the crisis to stabilize financial systems and resolve the crisis and important steps toward the creation of a banking union for euro area countries have been taken to provide a common safety net and safeguard the single market. The EU also continued its regulatory effort to harmonize rules and remove barriers to cross-border financial

An earlier version of this chapter appeared as a Technical Note on "Financial Integration and Fragmentation in the European Union" (European Union: Publication of Financial Sector Assessment Program Documentation), IMF Country Report No. 13, March 2013. The authors thank Charles Enoch, Luc Everaert, Daniel Hardy, Jianping Zhou, and European authorities (especially the European Commission and European Central Bank) for comments and Lindsay Mollineaux for excellent research assistance.

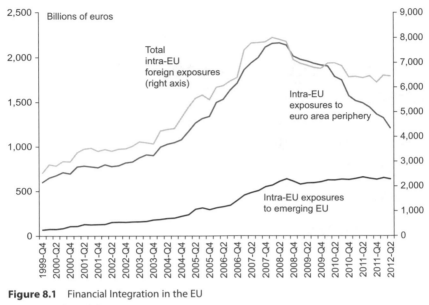

Figure 8.1 Financial Integration in the EU

Source: Authors' calculations.
Note: Ireland and Finland not included due to breaks in data reporting.
Bank for International Settlements consolidated banking statistics, immediate risk basis.

transactions. The crisis and fragmentation of financial systems of the EU, however, and the deleterious effects on stability of the contamination of risk between banks and sovereign have raised important questions about the future of the EU financial structure. Restoring the solvability of banks is a necessity, but it must be achieved in a way that will preserve the single market for financial services and restore financial integration. Furthermore, while some degree of macroprudential flexibility at the national level is desirable to ensure early identification of national risks, it is essential to create a more integrated approach to systemic risk identification and macroprudential policy actions at the European level through the ESRB and the European Central Bank (ECB) to prevent uncoordinated actions that may further damage the single market for financial services.

FRAGMENTATION AND DELEVERAGING DURING THE CRISIS

Integration came to a halt during the financial crisis, raising concerns of de-integration of the euro area financial system:

- *Sharp reversals of capital flows in the periphery of the euro area.* The Eurosystem and official creditors stepped in to cushion the shock of the capital flow reversal. In particular, net reliance on ECB funding has segmented along national lines, and the Eurosystem has intermediated funds from surplus countries' banks to banks in the periphery of the euro area, resulting in an indirect mutualization of liabilities through the so-called "TARGET2 imbalances" (Figure 8.2).

- *Sharp increase in counterparty risks in euro area funding markets, on the back of sovereign risk concerns.* Sudden changes in the availability of wholesale funding in secured and unsecured markets in the second half of 2011 amplified the crisis that spread to the core of the euro area financial system (Figure 8.3).

- *Euro area banks experienced severe funding pressures starting in mid-2011, on the back of concerns about sovereign risks.* Part of the funding shock originated from U.S. money market funds (MMFs), which sharply reduced their exposures to French and other euro area banks. Between June 2011 and December 2011, the 10 largest U.S. MMFs reduced their exposures to French banks by about US$100 billion (Figure 8.4).

- *Significant divergence of retail deposit markets also occurred.* Retail deposit markets have exhibited divergent trends in the core and in the periphery since 2010 (for Greece, where deposit flight has been substantial) or mid-2011 (for Spain, where some firms have shifted deposits).[1] However, the deposit base stabilized in the periphery after the summer of 2012, including in IMF program countries, perhaps a consequence of the outright monetary transactions (OMT) announcement (Figure 8.5).

Evidence from the Monetary and Financial Institution (MFI) data confirms that the deleveraging by euro area banks was a key driver of the sharp fragmentation of the EU financial system. Since the onset of the crisis in 2008, euro area banks as a whole have sharply reduced their cross-border exposures within the euro area and from other EU countries, while broadly preserving or increasing their domestic exposures. In other words, a very strong process of re-nationalization of euro area banking systems has taken place during the past years. In absolute terms, intra-euro area cross-border positions of euro area banks have fallen by about €1.5 trillion, while their cross-border exposures to other EU countries have on aggregate fallen by €370 billion. During the same period, the domestic positions of euro area banks (excluding claims on the Eurosystem) have increased by about €1.2 trillion.

Specifically, as shown in Figure 8.6, the following fragmentation took place in various financial markets as a result of euro area banks deleveraging:

- *Interbank markets.* Cross-border claims of euro area banks on MFIs located in other euro area countries and in other EU countries have collapsed by respectively €670 billion and €285 billion, or 42 percent and 23 percent, since the onset of the crisis in September 2008. In the meantime, domestic claims on other banks have fallen by €206 billion (or 3 percent).

---

[1] Part of the drop in deposits was driven by a temporary shift from bank deposits to commercial paper ("pagares").

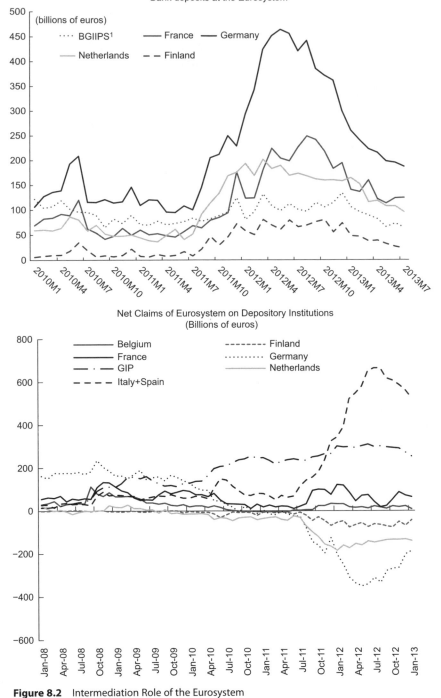

Figure 8.2 Intermediation Role of the Eurosystem

[1]BGIIPS: Belgium, Ireland, Italy, Portugal, and Spain. GIP: Greece, Ireland, Portugal

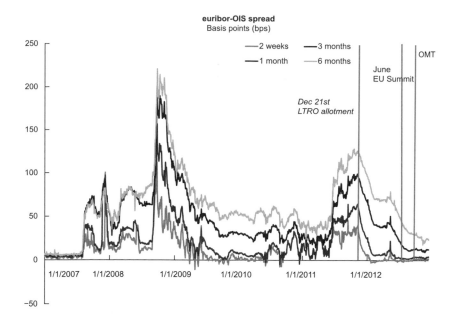

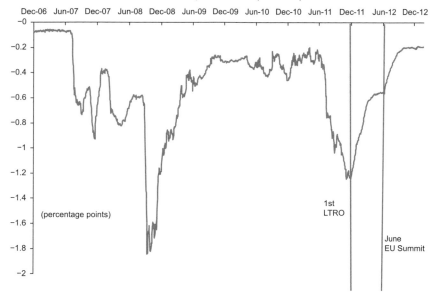

Figure 8.3 Funding Markets and Counterparty Risk

Source: Thomson Reuters Datastream.
Note: LTRO = long-term refinancing operation; OMT = outright monetary transactions.

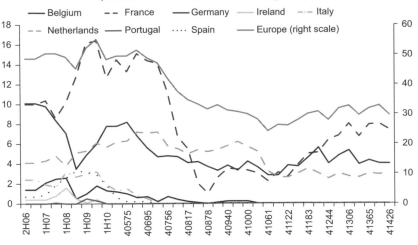
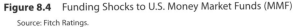

Figure 8.4 Funding Shocks to U.S. Money Market Funds (MMF)

Source: Fitch Ratings.

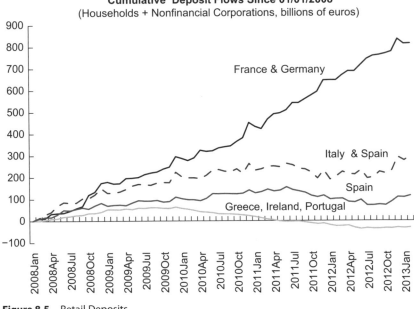

Figure 8.5 Retail Deposits

Source: European Central Bank (ECB)

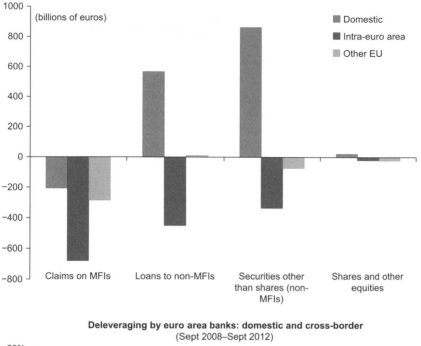

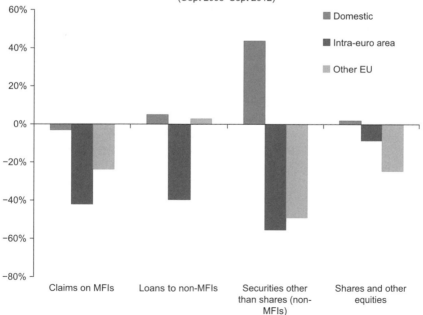

Figure 8.6 Euro Area Bank Domestic and Cross-Border Deleveraging

Sources: European Central Bank, Consolidated Banking Statistics; and IFS, International Financial Statistics database.
Note: Domestic claims on MFIs are adjusted to exclude claims on the Eurosystem. MFIs = monetary and financial institutions.

- *Loans to the private sector.* Evidence of domestic bias has also been very strong for loans to the nonbank private sector. Considering all euro area banks as a whole, loans to the domestic nonbank private sector have increased by €570 billion (or 5 percent) but cross-border loans have fallen by €450 billion (or 40 percent) vis-à-vis other euro area (and have been broadly stable vis-à-vis other EU countries).[2]

- *Securities other than shares.* Home bias in bond markets has, perhaps, been the strongest. Indeed, domestic exposures of euro area banks have strongly increased by €860 billion (or 43 percent) since the 2008 crisis, while cross-border exposures vis-à-vis other euro area countries have fallen by 55 percent (about €340 billion), and by 50 percent (about €70 billion) vis-à-vis other EU countries.

- *Shares.* Cross-border equity markets have been the most stable since the start of the crisis, but have also been subject to home bias. While domestic exposures have slightly increased (by 2 percent); cross-border exposures vis-à-vis euro area countries and other EU countries have fallen by 8 percent and 23 percent, respectively, since September 2008.

The financial fragmentation process and the associated decline in cross-border lending are a consequence of several factors, including a broader deleveraging process triggered by the global financial crisis, increased fragmentation within the euro area as a result of a repricing of risks, capital and funding shortages, and structural developments, including the new Basel III rules at banks. Bank deleveraging can be explained by combinations of both structural and cyclical forces (Figure 8.7).[3] Structural forces include the need to adjust banks' business models to the new regulatory and economic environment (and often reflected in business plans announced by banks), the need to further strengthen capitalization, and the necessity to reduce reliance on less stable (short-term, wholesale) sources of funding. But bank deleveraging has also been the outcome of cyclical factors such as financial conditions in sovereign and bank funding markets (where the ECB long-term refinancing operation [LTRO] liquidity provision helped cushion the funding shocks, and the OMT stabilized sovereign debt markets, with positive knock-down effects on bank access to wholesale markets), the state of the economy, which affects banks' retained earnings, and forces of financial fragmentation and financial repression in the euro area. Moreover, the stronger reduction recorded in cross-border claims on distressed economies in the euro area periphery illustrates the increasing fragmentation between those euro area economies that are distressed and those that are not. Interbank lending from

---

[2] The reported figures are changes in position, hence include asset write-downs.
[3] See the IMF's *Global Financial Stability Report: Restoring Confidence and Progressing on Reforms* (October 2012), and *Global Financial Stability Report: The Quest for Lasting Stability* (April 2012).

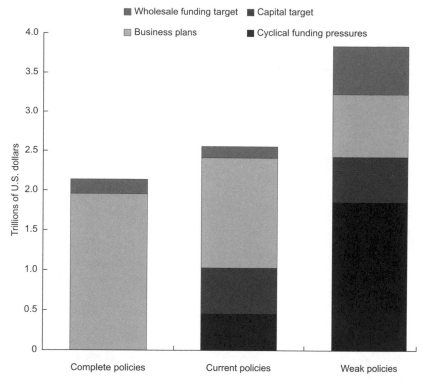

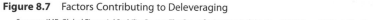

Figure 8.7 Factors Contributing to Deleveraging

Sources: IMF, *Global Financial Stability Report: The Quest for Lasting Stability* (April 2012), and IMF staff estimates.

banks resident in countries less affected by the sovereign debt crisis to banks in the distressed countries has fallen substantially.[4]

EU banks also withdrew from overseas markets and U.S. dollar activities (Figure 8.8). Many European cross-border banks have significant overseas activities funded in U.S. dollars. A significant part of this funding has remained short term, contributing to creating structural funding gaps (e.g., a gap between long-term assets and long-term funding in U.S. dollars) in balance sheets, including among euro area banks. These funding gaps remained significant at the end of 2012:Q2, in spite of heavy reductions in U.S. dollar assets of French and German banks.[5]

---

[4] Special feature in the European Central Bank's December 2012 *Financial Stability Review*.

[5] Estimates based on data from the Bank for International Settlements suggest that French and German banks reduced their gross U.S. dollar assets by US$270 billion and US$100 billion, respectively, between 2011:Q2 and 2012:Q2.

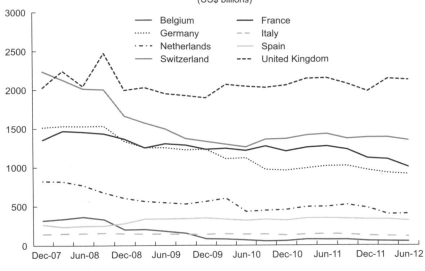

Figure 8.8 U.S. Dollar Activities of European Banks

Source: Bank for International Settlements (preliminary data for 2012:Q2).

DETERMINANTS OF CROSS-BORDER LEVERAGING AND DELEVERAGING

To assess the determinants of the cross-border leveraging and deleveraging in the EU, a panel regression analysis of the evolution of foreign claims of international banks is performed. We estimate standard panel regressions to explain the determinants of the quarterly percent changes in bilateral bank exposures between EU home and host countries (where host countries include euro area countries, excluding Luxembourg, and other EU countries) and all Bank for International Settlements (BIS) reporting countries are included as home countries.

$$y_{ijt} = a + \beta \cdot \frac{FC_{ijt-1}}{GDP_{jt-1}} + \delta \cdot \frac{FC_{.jt-1}}{GDP_{jt-1}} + \varphi \cdot DXrate_{jt} + \phi \cdot X_{jt-1} + f_i + g_j + \varepsilon_{ijt}$$

where FC_{ijt} is the total foreign claims of reporting banks of country i on country j, FC_{jt} is the total claims of BIS reporting countries on country j,

$$y_{ijt} = \frac{\left(FC_{ijt} - FC_{ijt-1}\right)}{GDP_{jt-1}}$$

is the change in bilateral foreign claims, scaled by GDP of the previous period, $DXrate_{jt}$ is the percent change in the U.S. dollar exchange rate during the period, and X_{jt} is a set of additional control variables. Regressions contain home country (f_i) and host country (g_j) fixed effects to account for unobservable time invariant factors. The sample period covers 2005:Q1 to 2012:Q2. We also consider three subperiods: the precrisis period (2005:Q1 to 2008:Q3); the period following the Lehman collapse and global repercussion (2008:Q4 to 2009:Q4); and the euro area crisis period (2010:Q1 to 2012:Q2). We rely on various data sources: quarterly BIS consolidated banking statistics (ultimate risk basis); World Economic Outlook and Balance of Payments–International Investment Positions quarterly data of the IMF; ECB banking system structure data; and Bloomberg.[6]

Explanatory variables aim to capture various potential determinants of foreign bank activities. The exposure to country j of banks from country j captures whether there is momentum in the bilateral capital flows of country i's banks to country j: a positive coefficient would imply that banks with a larger initial exposure are increasing their exposure at a faster pace than other banks, and therefore that there is a tendency in increasing concentrations of bilateral exposures. A negative coefficient would instead imply either that there is a correction mechanism stabilizing bilateral exposures at some level (if flows are positive) or that banks with a greater initial exposure are withdrawing faster than others (if flows are negative. Total claims of BIS reporting banks on country j is a measure of gross external liabilities to banks, and therefore a measure of external vulnerability to capital outflows. Additional control variables include (1) the share of country j in country's banks' foreign assets (as an indicator of portfolio composition); (2) the net international investment postion (IIP) in percent of GDP, as an indicator of potential external imbalances; (3) gross external liabilities of the government in percent of GDP; and (4) gross external liabilities of resident banks in percent of GDP. We also include quarterly indicators of macroeconomic performance, such as annual real GDP growth and inflation rate.

Regression analysis of the evolution of foreign claims of international banks, summarized in Table 8.1, offers the following insights:

- *Before the start of the financial crisis:* Bilateral bank exposures to EU countries showed signs of momentum and increasing concentration of bilateral exposures as banks with greater initial exposures tended to increase exposures at a faster pace than other banks. Bilateral exposures were, however, growing at a slower pace in countries that had the largest gross liabilities to foreign banks—a finding consistent with the hypothesis that bank capital flows took into account potential gross external vulnerabilities. However, bilateral bank exposures were growing *faster* in countries with the largest *net* IIP liabilities. This finding implies that a key indicator of external imbalances was not only ignored by bank bilateral capital inflows; instead it had the oppo-

---

[6] The sample includes the following countries. BIS reporting countries: Austria, Belgium, Finland, France, Germany, Greece, Ireland, Italy, the Netherlands, Spain, Portugal, Sweden, and the United Kingdom. Host countries: Austria, Belgium, Bulgaria, Denmark, Estonia, Finland, France, Germany, Greece, Hungary, Ireland, Italy, Latvia, Lithuania, Netherlands, Portugal, Romania, the Slovak Republic, Slovenia, Spain, Sweden, and the United Kingdom.

TABLE 8.1

Determinants of Leveraging and Deleveraging						
	(1)	**(2)**	**(3)**	**(4)**	**(5)**	**(6)**
	Precrisis		**Lehman**		**Euro area crisis**	
$FC(ij)/GDP(j)$, $t-1$	0.0449***	0.0457***	−0.0247*	−0.0165	−0.0333***	−0.0232***
	0.000	0.000	(0.069)	(0.300)	0.000	(0.004)
$FC(j)/GDP(j)$, $t-1$	−0.0214***	−0.0019**	−0.0472***	−0.0011	−0.0126***	−0.0004
	0.000	(0.014)	(0.001)	(0.520)	(0.002)	(0.444)
$FC(ij)/FC(i)$, $t-1$	−0.024	−0.0288	0.0747	−0.0185	0.1232***	0.0553**
	(0.657)	(0.360)	(0.412)	(0.797)	(0.002)	(0.033)
$Drate$ (j), t	−0.1234**	−0.0720**	−0.1275***	−0.0758*	−0.0483***	−0.0457***
	(0.018)	(0.033)	0.000	(0.097)	0.000	(0.001)
Real GDP growth (j), $t-1$	0.1612*	0.0989**	0.3464***	0.0766	0.0453	0.0792***
	(0.098)	(0.026)	(0.001)	(0.136)	(0.246)	(0.008)
Inflation (j), $t-1$	0.0119	0.0081	−0.4339**	0.0041	0.006	0.0093
	(0.857)	(0.839)	(0.011)	(0.925)	(0.383)	(0.130)
Net IIP$(j)/GDP(j)$, $t-1$		−0.0013*		0.0001		0.0013*
		(0.085)		(0.953)		(0.099)
Home and host fixed effects	yes	no	yes	no	yes	no
Observations	2,933	2,298	1,497	1,217	3,331	2,934
R-squared	0.18	0.16	0.14	0.05	0.15	0.1
Robust p-values in parentheses		*** $p < 0.01$, ** $p < 0.05$, * $p < 0.1$				

Sources: Bank for International Settlements (BIS), Consolidated Banking Statistics on ultimate risk basis; IMF, International Financial Statistics and World Economic Outlook databases.

Note: The sample includes the following BIS reporting countries: Austria, Belgium, Finland, France, Germany, Greece, Ireland, Italy, the Netherlands, Spain, Portugal, Sweden, and the United Kingdom. Host countries: Austria, Belgium, Bulgaria, Denmark, Estonia, Finland, France, Germany, Greece, Hungary, Ireland, Italy, Latvia, Lithuania, Netherlands, Portugal, Romania, the Slovak Republic, Slovenia, Spain, Sweden, and the United Kingdom.

site effect on these flows than what prudent behavior would have implied, as bilateral bank inflows where stronger in countries with larger net foreign liabilities, suggesting a mispricing of risks. There was no indication of significant portfolio reallocation among foreign exposures of EU banks.

- *The failure of Lehman Brothers and its aftermath.* There was a reversal of bilateral bank exposures in the EU. Bilateral bank capital flows declined faster where bilateral exposures where the largest. Hence, the observed correction in bilateral flows was consistent with prudent behavior. However, other factors did not seem to influence bank capital flows significantly, in particular there was no indication of a stronger reversal in countries with the largest net foreign liabilities.

- *Euro area crisis.* During the period 2010–2012:Q2, the reversal of bilateral exposures responded to the previous quarter's bilateral exposure in a stronger way than during the period 2008:Q3–2009:Q4. There is, however, evidence that portfolio allocation mattered. In particular, the reversal of bank capital flows was weaker in host countries where EU banks had a larger share of their foreign activities. Moreover, bilateral bank capital flows were correlated with net foreign asset positions, consistent with the hypothesis of a

TABLE 8.2

Foreign Ownership and Exposures to Emerging Europe		
	Precrisis	**Crisis**
Log (Foreign)	−1.6355	4.8095***
EE dummy	6.6518**	5.7968***

Source: Authors' calculations.
Note: *** $p < 0.01$, ** $p < 0.05$, * $p < 0.1$.

correction mechanism as banks withdrew more from countries with initially larger external imbalances.

Next, we assess whether the patterns of cross-border leveraging and deleveraging of EU banks differed between emerging Europe and euro area countries. We perform cross-sectional regression over the periods 2005:Q1–2008:Q3 (precrisis) and 2008:Q4–2012:Q2 (postcrisis) of cumulative change in bilateral foreign claims of EU banks between home country i and host country j on a set of control variables defined at the beginning of the period (hence 2005:Q1 for the precrisis period, and 2008:Q4 for the postcrisis period). The variable of interest is an indicator variable EE for emerging European countries and/or log FGN defined as the log of the share of foreign banks in total banking assets:[7]

$$y_{ij} = a + \beta \cdot EE + \delta \cdot Foreign + \phi \cdot DXrate_j + \varphi \cdot X_{j0} + f_i + \varepsilon_{ij}$$

Control variables include the following: (1) the initial bilateral claims of country i on country j in percent of GDP; (2) the initial total claims of foreign banks on country j in percent of GDP; (3) the share of country j in the foreign portfolio of banks from country j; (4) the initial net foreign asset position in percent of GDP; (5) the initial gross public-debt-to-GDP ratio; (6) the initial current account balance-to-GDP ratio; and (7) the cumulative percent change in the bilateral exchange rate vis-à-vis the U.S. dollar.

There is little evidence that, before the crisis, the cumulative increase in foreign liabilities of emerging European countries was significantly larger than for euro area countries, after controlling for the factors cited in Table 8.1. After the crisis, it appears that foreign exposures to emerging European countries also turned more stable than the foreign exposures to other countries (notably countries in the euro area periphery) after accounting for the set of indicators above cited. Furthermore, when including the foreign ownership variable, we find that while this variable is insignificant during the precrisis period, it turns strongly and positively significant during the crisis period. From estimated coefficients, we find that a one standard deviation increase in foreign share is associated with foreign liabilities to foreign banks that are higher by 2 percentage points of initial GDP over 2½ years (Table 8.2). R-squared vary between 0.26 and 0.5, implying that our empirical specification explains a large share of the cross-sectional variation in the cumulative change of bilateral exposures of foreign banks.

---

[7] This variable is constructed as of end-2007.

The pattern of capital flows before and after the crisis suggests that the type of financial integration matters in a crisis. Before the crisis, emerging European countries (with a large domestic presence of foreign banks, and large cross-border intragroup capital flows) experienced a significantly faster buildup of liabilities to foreign banks than other EU countries. However, after the crisis erupted in 2008 and capital flows started to reverse within the EU, emerging European countries experienced a slower reversal of capital flows on average, after accounting for various determinants and home country factors. This finding is consistent with the hypothesis that the Vienna initiative played an important role in stabilizing capital flows between some countries in emerging Europe and the rest of the EU. Furthermore, it seems that a larger initial foreign bank presence was indeed a stabilizing factor, perhaps as these banks were more likely to consider these countries as home markets. This suggests that the type of financial integration (local presence, potentially partially funded by intragroup flows, as opposed to cross-border flows between unrelated lenders and borrowers) matters in a crisis. Foreign bank presence can a stabilizing factor when the vulnerability is home grown, but this presence can also contribute in accumulating vulnerabilities.

We further make use of our empirical approach to estimate the extent to which the sovereign-bank nexus in the EU contributes in explaining the sudden stops in capital flows. Assessing such links is important. Financial fragmentation and the reversals of capital flows within the euro area and possibly the broader EU contribute to amplifying the crisis, disrupting the transmission channels of monetary policy in the euro area and causing contagions and spillovers through financial markets. Using bilateral exposures, we are able to control for all unobserved home factor effects that may have impacted capital flows during the crisis.

For this purpose, we re-estimate the panel regression, but focusing on the post–Lehman crisis period. To empirically test a link between sovereign and banking fragilities and the evolution of bilateral foreign exposures of EU banks, we add as explanatory variables sovereign credit default swap (CDS) spreads and bank CDS spreads averaged on a quarterly basis.[8] The period of observation is 2010:Q1–2012:Q2.[9] Specifically, we estimate the following regression, where control variables include (1) the initial bilateral claims of country i on country j in percent of GDP; (2) the initial total claims of foreign banks on country j in percent of GDP; (3) the share of country j in the foreign portfolio of banks from country j; and (4) the percent quarterly change vis-à-vis the U.S. dollar. In contrast to specification (1), we do not include host country fixed effects to ensure that identification also accounts for cross-sectional differences in sovereign or bank stress. Finally, building on the results of specification (2), we also include in some specifications, interaction terms between sovereign or bank CDS spreads

---

[8] Weekly bank CDS spreads for the sample of EBA banks are averaged per country and quarter.

[9] In addition to the set of control variables defined above, we also add in some robustness tests the sectoral composition of foreign claims (public sector, banks, nonbank private sector), for which data are publicly available from 2010:Q4 onward.

TABLE 8.3

Banking Stress and Deleveraging				
	(1)	(2)	(3)	(4)
Bank CDS spread	−0.0008***	−0.0040***		
Bank CDS spread * Foreign		0.0001**		
Sovereign CDS spread			−0.0003***	−0.0013
Sovereign CDS spread * Foreign				0.0001
Observations	2,192	2,192	3,044	2,868
R^2	0.15	0.15	0.13	0.13

Source: Authors' calculations.
Note: CDS = credit default swaps. *** $p < 0.01$, ** $p < 0.05$, * $p < 0.1$.

with the foreign ownership variable described above. The period of observation is 2009:Q3 to 2012:Q2.

$$\begin{cases} y_{ijt} = a + \mu \cdot sovCDS_{jt} + \lambda \cdot sovCDS_{jt} * Foreign_j + \varphi \cdot X'_{jt-1} + f_i + \varepsilon_{ijt} \\ y_{ijt} = a + \mu \cdot bankCDS_{jt} + \lambda \cdot bankCDS_{jt} * Foreign_j + \varphi \cdot X'_{jt-1} + f_i + \varepsilon_{ijt} \end{cases}$$

Bilateral changes in foreign bank exposures to a particular EU country are significantly and negatively correlated with bank CDS spreads (Table 8.3, column 1). According to our estimates, a one standard deviation increase in bank CDS spread is associated with a 0.28 percent of GDP average decrease in bilateral exposure of EU banks. Similarly, a one standard deviation increase in sovereign CDS spread is associated with a decrease in bilateral exposure of EU banks by 0.3 percent of host country GDP (column 3). Furthermore, there is evidence that the impact of bank CDS spreads on bilateral exposures of EU banks is muted when foreign banks have a larger presence in the domestic market (column 2). According to our estimates, the impact of a one standard deviation increase in bank CDS spreads translates into a 1.1 percent of GDP decrease in foreign banks bilateral exposures to that country if domestic bank presence is at the lowest level (about 9 percent of total bank assets), but translates into a 0.18 *increase* in foreign bank exposures if domestic presence is that the sample maximum of about 45 percent of bank assets (Figure 8.9).

REAL EFFECTS OF FINANCIAL FRAGMENTATION

The fragmentation of the euro area financial system contributed to intensifying downward spirals between sovereigns, banks, and the real economy.[10] The sudden stop of capital flows affecting euro area periphery countries reinforced the intertwining of sovereign–bank balance sheet risks as investors withdrew simultaneously from sovereign bond markets and interbank markets, and

---

[10] This section focused on euro area countries where de-integration is a fundamental issue as it disrupts the transmission of monetary policy impulse.

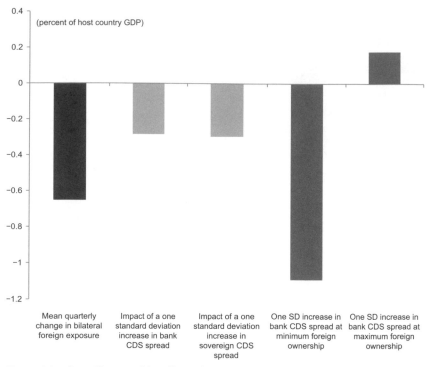

Figure 8.9 Quantification of the Effects of Banking Stress

Source: IMF staff.

Note: CDS = credit default swap; SD = standard deviation.

contributed to impairing the transmission mechanism of monetary policy across borders in the euro area (Figure 8.10, panel a). Furthermore, stressed banking systems curtailed the supply of credit through banks raising interest rates on loans, further disrupting the transmission channels of monetary policy (Figure 8.10, panel b). Sovereign–bank linkages were also strengthened in the periphery, as a side effect of the three-year LTROs, which allows funding the purchase of domestic sovereign bonds by local banks (Figure 8.11).

The fragmentation of the euro area financial system and the associated sovereign–bank nexus have disrupted the transmission channels and countercyclical role of monetary policy. High sovereign stress in the periphery has disrupted the traditional interest channel of monetary policy, while banking stress has impaired the bank lending channels. As a result, as lending conditions tightened in countries experiencing stronger downturns and interest rates diverged across countries, monetary policy has become procyclical across euro area countries. Bank funding costs in the periphery have increased as the cross-border interbank market is fragmented and banks in the periphery have to offer higher deposit rates to attract funds. With banks struggling to build capital buffers, credit risk remains high because of the weakening economic outlook. Thus, despite the recent easing in the ECB's policy rate, lending rates in banking systems under stress have edged upwards (Figure 8.12), and monetary impulses from the policy rate are not transmitted to the real economy.

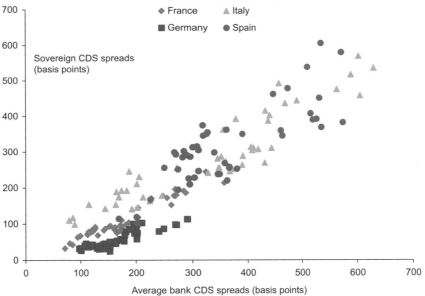

Figure 8.10a Intertwined Bank–Sovereign Stress

Source: Bloomberg, L.P.
Note: CDS = credit default swaps.

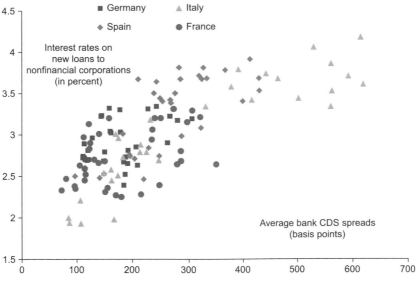

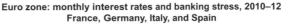

Figure 8.10b Banking Stress and the Real Economy

Source: Bloomberg, L.P.
Note: CDS = credit default swaps.

Average monthly change in bank exposures to the domestic sovereign

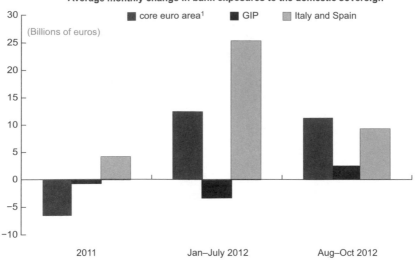

Figure 8.11   Exposures to the Domestic Sovereign

Source: IMF, International Financial Statistics database.
[1] Core euro area includes Austria, Belgium, Finland, France, Germany, and the Netherlands. GIP: Greece, Ireland, Portugal.

Euro Area Corporate Lending Rates
(loans greater than 1 mm, percent)

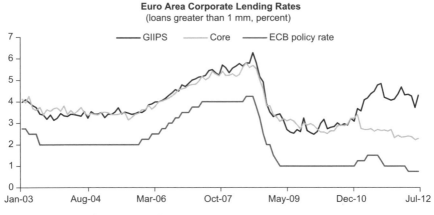

Figure 8.12   Retail Lending Conditions

Note: Unweighted average; Monetary and Financial Institution lending to corporations over €1 million, 1–5 years. Belgium and Portugal reflect rates on all maturities. ECB = European Central Bank.
Core: Germany, France, Belgium, Netherlands. GIIPS: Germany, Italy, Ireland, Portugal, Spain.

The deleveraging process raises concerns about a credit crunch that would particularly affect the small- and medium-sized enterprises (SMEs). SMEs in the euro area periphery are particularly hard hit by the deleveraging process, as deposit outflows and capital shortages at banks limit the availability and raise the cost of bank loans. Data from the European Commission and European Central Bank Survey on the Access to Finance of SMEs show that the availability of external finance from banks has decreased since 2009, while the demand for external finance has increased

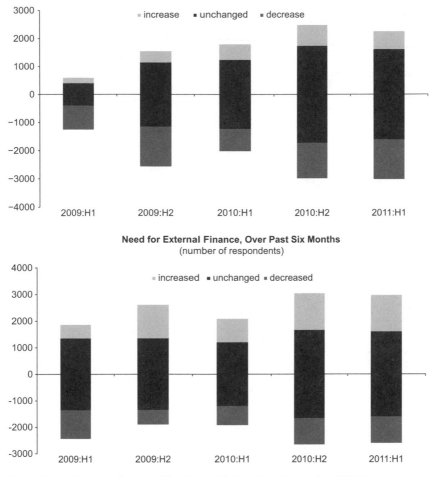

Figure 8.13 Access to Finance of Small- and Medium-Sized Enterprises (SMEs)

Source: European Central Bank, Survey on the Access to Finance of SMEs in the euro area.

(Figure 8.13). However, there is much cross-country variation, with the availability of external finance having deteriorated markedly since 2009 in Greece and Ireland and having remained fairly stable in countries like Finland and Germany. Regression analysis suggests that the deterioration in the supply of credit to SMEs is partly driven by the financial disintegration process, as measured by the decline in cross-border BIS claims (Table 8.4).

However, demand factors play an important role in the lack of borrowing by SMEs. Indeed, limited access to finance is not reported by most firms to be their main challenge (Figure 8.14). Limited demand for products is the most common obstacle according to this SME survey, indicating that demand for finance has reduced as well. Furthermore, regression analysis shows that the demand for credit is closely associated with declines in GDP, while the availability of credit is not.

TABLE 8.4

Access to Finance, Domestic Financial Activity, and Cross-Border Banking, 2009:H1–2012:H1

VARIABLES	Availability index	Need for finance index	Turnover index
Change in total BIS claims/GDP	0.00293**	−0.000951	−0.000761
	(2.903)	(−1.138)	(−0.672)
Change in logarithm of GDP	0.502	−1.237**	4.141***
	0.475)	(−2.629)	(7.134)
Change in DFA/GDP	−0.00399*	0.000465	0.00213
	(−2.182)	(0.453)	(1.237)
Constant	−0.209***	−0.314***	0.198***
	(−4.966)	(−8.750)	(5.892)
Country and survey fixed effects	x	x	x
Firm characteristics	x	x	x
Observations	23,064	26,405	34,269
R^2	0.057	0.029	0.125

Sources: Bank for International Settlements (BIS); and European Central Bank, Survey on the Access to Finance of SMEs in the euro area.

Note: Dependent variables are from the European Commission and European Central Bank (ECB) Survey on the Access to Finance of SMEs. Each index is calculated from responses where the variable of interest has increased, decreased, or remained unchanged over the past six months. These responses are coded 1, −1, and 0, respectively. The need for finance index is based on the change in need for external finance in the form of bank loans. The availability index is based on the change of the availability of bank loans for the individual firm. The turnover index is based on changes in the turnover of the firm. Total BIS claims is the sum of BIS claims on other countries and BIS claims by other countries from the BIS Consolidated Banking Statistics. DFA is the sum of all financial instruments invested in the country by resident financial institutions as defined by the ECB cross-border statistics. Regressions are estimated using ordinary least squares. Statistical significance levels are denoted as follows: *** $p < 0.01$, ** $p < 0.05$, * $p < 0.1$. Robust t-statistics or z-statistics in parentheses, clustered at the country level. Firm-specific control variables included are dummy variables for whether the firm is small/medium, public/private, new/old, and in trade/other industries. Country and survey specific fixed effects are included in all regressions. BIS = Bank for International Settlements; DFA = domestic financial activity; ECB = European Central Bank; SMEs = small-and medium-sized enterprises.

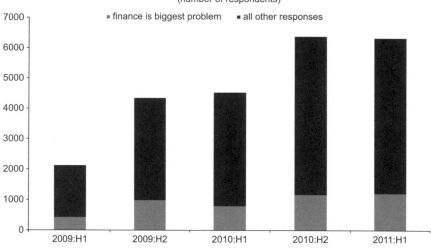

Figure 8.14   Constraints on Access to Finance

Source: European Central Bank, Survey on the Access to Finance of SMEs in the euro area.

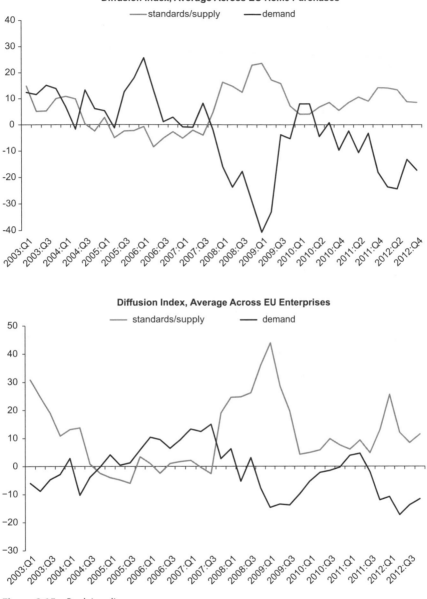

Figure 8.15 Bank Lending

Source: European Central Bank, Bank Lending Survey.

Demand factors also play an important role in the lack of borrowing by corporations and households. Lending standards for corporations and households are stable but credit demand conditions remain weak, suggesting that the reduced lending activity is primarily demand driven (Figure 8.15). Data from the ECB bank lending survey show that lending standards for corporations and households have stabilized, while credit demand, especially for corporations continues to fall (both measured using the diffusion index).[11] But, as lending standards and credit demand conditions are driven by common factors, such as economic conditions, it is difficult to infer a causal interpretation based on lending survey data (in the absence of exogenous shifts in the supply of credit).

To disentangle whether changes in lending standards or credit demand conditions are driving loan growth, regression analysis of bank lending survey responses is used. To gauge the importance of supply-side constraints for credit growth, regressions of loan growth are estimated where demand is purged from supply factors, and vice versa. These regressions use ECB bank lending survey responses to changes in lending standards and credit demand conditions as proxies for changes in supply and demand factors, respectively. These regressions are estimated separately for lending to firms and households. Purging demand from supply factors, and vice versa, allows for an estimate of upper and lower bounds of the effect of supply-side factors on credit growth. While this approach is subject to criticism, primarily because it assumes that the loan survey responses are accurate and exogenous, it offers some guidance on the relative importance of supply and demand factors.

Regressions are first estimated using data on the bank lending survey for corporations. The basic regression model is:

$$\Delta L_t = a_t + \Delta S_t + \Delta D_t + \varepsilon_t,$$

where the dependent variable is the growth rate of loans to nonfinancial corporations in a given quarter. ΔS denotes the change in the supply of credit to corporate, measured as the change in lending standards over the past three months on loans or credit lines to enterprises.[12] Higher numbers denote a relaxation in standards, which are taken to be equivalent to an increase in supply. ΔD denotes the demand for credit from corporate, measured as the change in demand for loans or credit lines to enterprises over the past three months. Higher numbers denote an increase in demand.

---

[11] It should be noted that the number of banks responding to the Bank Lending Survey in each quarter in some EU countries is very small.

[12] The change in lending standards variable is based on the survey question: "Over the past three months, how have your bank's credit standards as applied to the approval of loans or credit lines to enterprises changed?," and the change in demand variable is derived from the survey question: "Over the past three months, how has the demand for loans or credit lines to enterprises changed at your bank, apart from normal seasonal fluctuations?" The survey responses on lending standards and credit demand conditions are effectively lagged one period in the regression analysis. For example, the results reported in the April 2012 bank lending survey relate to changes during the first quarter of 2012 and expectations of changes in the second quarter of 2012. This ECB Bank Lending Survey was conducted between March 23 and April 5, 2012.

TABLE 8.5

EU: Supply and Demand of Loans to Nonfinancial Companies 2006:Q1–2012:Q3				
Dependent variable: Growth rate of loans to nonfinancial companies	(1)	(2)	(3)	(4)
Supply to corporations	–0.0135		–0.0277	
	(–0.630)		(–1.258)	
Demand from corporations		0.110***		0.108***
		(3.798)		(3.804)
Demand from corporations - residual			0.116***	
			(3.580)	
Supply to corporations - residual				0.0181
				(0.710)
Constant	9.849***	8.863**	9.057**	8.995**
	(2.606)	(2.477)	(2.530)	(2.513)
Quarter fixed effects	x	x	x	x
Observations	222	222	222	222
Adjusted R-squared	0.502	0.529	0.528	0.528

Source: European Central Bank, Bank Lending Survey.
Note: Robust t-statistics in parentheses. *** $p < 0.01$, ** $p < 0.05$, * $p < 0.1$.
Countries in the sample are Austria, Cyprus, Estonia, Germany, Italy, Luxembourg, Malta, the Netherlands, Portugal, Slovenia, and Spain.

To purge demand factors from supply factors and obtain a *lower-bound* estimate of the effect of supply-side factors on credit growth, the regression model is adjusted as

$$\Delta L_t = a_t + \Delta \hat{S}_t + \Delta D_t + \varepsilon_t,$$

where $\hat{S}_t$ denotes the residual of a country-specific ordinary least square (OLS) regression of S on D for corporations.

To purge supply factors from demand factors and obtain an *upper-bound* estimate of the effect of supply-side factors on credit growth, the regression model is adjusted as

$$\Delta L_t = a_t + \Delta S_t + \Delta \hat{D}_t + \varepsilon_t,$$

where $\hat{D}_t$ denotes the residual of a country-specific OLS regression of D on S for corporations.

Regressions are estimated using ordinary least squares (OLS) and include quarterly fixed effects (Table 8.5). The sample consists of quarterly loan growth and survey data from March 2006 to September 2012 for a sample of EU countries. The regression in column (3) gives an upper bound of the effect of supply on loan growth because it removes supply factors from demand and therefore attaches maximum weight to supply factors, while the regression in column (4) gives a lower bound on the effect of supply on loan growth because it removes demand factors from supply and therefore attaches maximum weight to demand factors.

The economic effect of demand-side factors for lending to corporations is substantial. Based on the estimates reported in column (4) of Table 8.5, a one standard deviation increase in demand from corporations implies an increase in

TABLE 8.6

Supply and Demand of Household Loans for Home Purchase 2006:Q1–2012:Q3				
Dependent variable: Growth rate of household loans for home purchase	(1)	(2)	(3)	(4)
Supply to households	−0.0384*		−0.0507**	
	(−1.965)		(−2.595)	
Demand from households		0.0811***		0.0811***
		(4.439)		(4.480)
Demand from households - residual			0.0967***	
			(3.893)	
Supply to households - residual				0.0388
				(1.352)
Constant	12.97***	10.93***	10.39***	10.74***
	(4.205)	(3.555)	(3.399)	(3.516)
Quarter fixed effects	x	x	x	x
Observations	249	249	249	249
Adjusted R-squared	0.116	0.171	0.172	0.172

Source: European Central Bank, Bank Lending Survey.
Note: Robust t-statistics in parentheses. *** $p < 0.01$, ** $p < 0.05$, * $p < 0.1$.
Countries in the sample are Austria, Cyprus, Estonia, Germany, Italy, Luxembourg, Malta, the Netherlands, Portugal, Slovenia, and Spain.

loan growth of nonfinancial companies of 1.7 percentage points. This is substantial, given that it amounts to about one-fifth the standard deviation in loan growth of nonfinancial companies.

Similar regressions are estimated using bank lending survey responses on lending to households (Table 8.6). The dependent variable in these regressions is the growth rate of loans to households for house purchase in a given quarter. Supply to households is the change in lending standards over the past three months on loans to households for house purchase, with higher numbers denoting a relaxation in standards (an increase in supply). Demand from households is the change in demand for loans to households for house purchase over the past three months, with higher numbers denoting an increase in demand. Otherwise, the regressions are similar to those for corporations.

The economic effect of demand-side factors for lending to households is also substantial. Based on results in column (4), a one standard deviation increase in demand from households implies an increase in household loan growth for house purchase of 2.1 percentage points. This is substantial, given that it amounts to about one-fourth the standard deviation in loan growth of household loans for home purchase.

Regressions indicate that supply factors play a more important role in lending to households than in lending to corporations. Moreover, demand factors play a similar role in lending to households and lending to firms. Importantly, these results are for the corporate sector as a whole and may not prove a firm basis for inference of the relevance of supply factors for lending to SMEs.

Overall, the evidence suggests that the real effects of financial disintegration and deleveraging are mitigated by policy responses and sharp declines in aggregate demand, although there are pockets of vulnerabilities and signs of credit supply shocks. They also suggest that increased financial integration would be beneficial to credit conditions in individual member states.

POLICY OPTIONS TO RESTORE FINANCIAL INTEGRATION

The ongoing financial crisis has shown that it is essential that the EU regulatory and supranational institutional environment be strengthened to ensure that policies for the stability of the financial system are consistent with the single financial market. Two questions in particular have been raised:

- How to stop the deleveraging and fragmentation process to restore the single financial market?
- How to ensure that financial integration and stability of the financial system are supported by an adequate financial architecture?

Policy action should be coordinated to level the playing field and counter market forces that contribute to the deleveraging process and fragmentation of the financial system. Uncoordinated actions have resulted in a simultaneous reduction of cross-border exposures, in particular within the euro area, thereby contributing to fragmenting the financial system further and disrupting the transmission channels of monetary policy. The collapse of cross-border exposures has been particularly severe in the wholesale funding market and sovereign bond markets, and amplified adverse sovereign–bank links in the periphery of the euro area. While some policies have been coordinated (notable monetary policy and competition policy), other policies have been less so (such as supervision and financial safety nets) and have contributed to ring-fencing behavior, causing adverse cross-border externalities. A coordination of policies at the EU level will counter market forces that contribute to a fragmentation of the financial system and help repair the single market.

The establishment of a banking union with common supervision, resolution authority, and financial safety net would go a long way to provide the necessary underpinnings to a stable and integrated financial market. A banking union would substantially reduce the tail risk that an individual member state will not be able to honor the financial safety net provided in support of its financial sector, and it would help delink banks and sovereign risk. It would also bring about higher quality of supervision and help solve coordination problems in the resolution of cross-border banks within the union. Although the banking union is more urgent and essential for euro area countries, other EU countries would also benefit from joining the union. With the prospect of some member states, notably the United Kingdom, which plays a dominant role in the provision of international financial services, having expressed a desire not to join the banking union, questions are raised about unintended consequences of the establishment of a union for the single market. In particular, the creation of a single supervisory mechanism (SSM)—as recently announced—should not conflict with the role of existing EU regulatory agencies, such as the European Banking Authority (EBA), to avoid unintended consequences for the single market between the "ins" and the "outs." For example, ECB decisions to issue its own supervision guidelines should be accompanied by efforts led by the EBA to harmonize supervision practices among the ins and the outs.

The possibility of European Stability Mechanism (ESM) direct recapitalizations would help speed up addressing solvency issues. It is primordial that solvency issues are addressed to restore proper financial intermediation and supply of credit to the real economy. Having in place the possibility of direct ESM recapitalization of banks would relieve contingent liabilities from the balance sheet of weak sovereign, thereby weakening incentives for forbearance and helping create some fiscal space.

The merits of limits on size and activities of financial institutions are being actively debated (for example, Vickers and Liikanen reports). Current initiatives aim to address the problems associated with size can be addressed through improving supervision and resolvability (including cross-border and bail-in arrangements) and the establishment of a banking union (which will weaken sovereign–bank linkages and ensure a more systemic and coordinated approach to supervision). However, too-big-to-fail considerations will remain. These can in principle be partially addressed through regulation or taxation. More generally, the introduction of financial sector taxes can address externalities associated with systemic risk created by the financial sector. However, the political reality of bank failures will remain complicated, including between countries that are part of the banking union and others. Importantly, regulatory and taxation initiatives to address systemic risk have to be closely coordinated among EU member states to ensure they do not distort the single market and that they enable a level playing field.

In this light, it should be stressed that the protection of financial centers out of national interests, or indeed the implementation of restrictive measures against a financial center, would be against the principle of a single market. In this context, the flexibility provided by the Capital Requirement Regulation (CRR) and Capital Requirement Directive IV (CRD IV) should, in practice, be used only for macroprudential purposes and not as a tool to protect specific national approaches which might impede integration of banking systems. In this regard, the ESRB should play a forceful role in coordinating the use of macroprudential instruments among member states, while efforts to establish a "single rule book" should be furthered.

The increasing focus on improving the resolvability of banks and limiting use of taxpayer money throughout the EU can help to reduce the risks associated with bank size. The EU Directive for the recovery and resolution of credit institutions will limit the use for bank bailouts in the future by ensuring preparedness, providing strong powers for early intervention and resolution of credit institutions in the EU. The possibility of statutory bail-ins and the establishment of resolution funds would provide first lines of defense to address individual bank failures and may help contain deleveraging pressures out of countries experiencing bank failures. It is also critical that the SSM is complemented by a single resolution mechanism involving a central resolution authority with strong intervention and resolution powers, and with common backstops.

FINANCIAL INTEGRATION GOING FORWARD

Going forward, the answer is more and better, not less, financial integration. The evidence presented shows that there can be large benefits from financial integration, including ensuring a smooth transmission of monetary impulses. However, integration must be realized in a way that does not pose serious risks to financial stability, and must be accompanied by reforms to complete the financial architecture of the monetary union and of the broader EU.

Policy action thus far has mitigated the deleveraging process but more is needed to address underlying weaknesses. In the absence of major policy action in the areas of monetary and fiscal policy, as well as government recapitalization of banks and the Vienna Initiative, deleveraging would have been more severe and damaging, with substantial associated fire sales.

The integrity of rules and institutions for the EU's single financial market has been maintained. The EU has continued to develop its regulatory framework designed to promote market integration so as to further dismantle regulatory hurdles to cross-border financial transactions, reduce scope for regulatory arbitrage, and ensure a consistent implementation and application of the EU financial market framework.

However, to ensure the functioning of the single market for financial services, increased financial integration will need to be supported by a credible financial safety net, higher supervisory quality, and strong resolution tools. This requires progress toward banking union;[13] the centralization and strengthening of supervisory and resolution frameworks, and the harmonization of depositor guarantee schemes (more details can be found in a separate technical note on depositor guarantee schemes), as well as a strengthening of capital requirements under CRR/CRD IV (more on this in Chapter 18) and constraints on the provision of liquidity support to ailing financial institutions.[14] It has become clear now that, in spite of the "no-bail-out clause" of the Treaty, imbalances do matter in a monetary union.

---

[13] For a motivation and characterization of the elements of the banking union, see R. Goyal, P. Koeva-Brooks, M. Pradhan, T. Tressel, G. Dell'Ariccia, C. Pazarbasioglu, and an IMF staff team, 2013, "A Banking Union for the Euro Area," IMF Staff Discussion Note No. 13/1 (Washington: International Monetary Fund).

[14] The recent decision to establish the SSM under the auspices of the ECB is a welcome step in this direction, but more is needed, as also highlighted by the blueprint issued by the European Commission.

PART II

Underpinning Financial Stability in the Economic and Monetary Union and the European Union

CHAPTER 9

Banking Union and Single Market: Consistent Setup and Risk Mitigation

THIERRY TRESSEL

The fiscal and financial crisis in the euro area has exposed critical gaps in the architecture of stability in the region.[1] In the years preceding the crisis, large capital flows within the euro area fueled the buildup of sovereign and private sector imbalances. The subsequent deterioration of balance sheets and reversal of flows has forced very sharp economic contractions and financial market fragmentation (Figure 9.1). Borrowing costs of sovereigns and national private sectors have diverged widely and persistently, cuts in monetary policy rates have had limited or no effects in several economies, and adverse sovereign–bank–real economy dynamics have been prevalent across the region (Figures 9.2 and 9.3). The monetary union, in short, is malfunctioning.

Important measures—for near-term crisis management and longer-term architecture—have been undertaken. Adjustment programs are being implemented and progress is being made to unwind fiscal and external imbalances that developed over years. Regional firewalls—the European Financial Stability Facility and European Stability Mechanism (ESM)—have been created and strengthened to smooth adjustment. The framework for fiscal and economic governance has been enhanced through the "Six Pack" and the Treaty on Stability, Coordination and Governance. The European Central Bank (ECB) has provided substantial liquidity to banks, stepped in to address market strains through government bond purchases, announced its framework for Outright Monetary Transactions, and given forward guidance. The Eurosystem has recycled part of the capital flight from the periphery to the core through the "TARGET2" payments balances.

As part of this comprehensive policy response, the role of a banking union for the euro area is twofold. As part of crisis management, it can reduce fragmentation of European banking markets. Direct bank recapitalization by the ESM can help restore the health of bank balance sheets and remove tail risks and potential contingent liabilities affecting sovereigns under stress. A precondition for direct

---

[1] This chapter draws on the February 2013 IMF Staff Discussion Note "A Banking Union for the Euro Area (Goyal and others, 2013)." The contribution by the authors of the Staff Discussion Note is gratefully acknowledged.

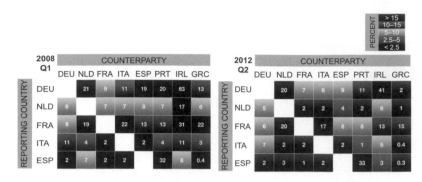

Figure 9.1 Financial Market Integration and Fragmentation

Sources: Bank for International Settlements (BIS); and IMF staff calculations.
Note: Shows BIS cross-border bank claims (in percent of reporting country's GDP). DEU = Germany; ESP = Spain; FRA = France; GRC = Greece; IRL = Ireland; ITA = Italy; NLD = the Netherlands; PRT = Portugal.

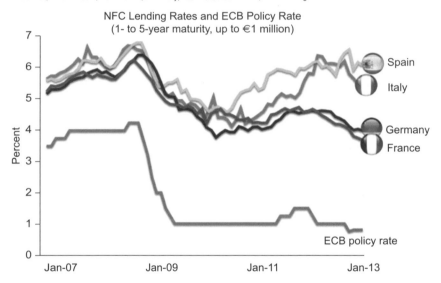

Figure 9.2 Diverging Funding Costs in the Region Do Not Reflect Falling Policy Rates

Source: European Central Bank.
Note: ECB = European Central Bank; NFC = nonfinancial corporations.

recapitalization of banks by the ESM is the creation of an effective single supervisory mechanism (SSM), which was called for by euro area leaders in June 2012. In steady state, an integrated architecture for financial stability in the euro area would bring a uniformly high standard of enforcement, remove national distortions, and mitigate the buildup of risk concentrations that compromises systemic stability. By moving responsibility for potential financial support—and the associated banking supervision—to a shared level, it would reduce financial fragmentation and weaken the vicious loop in many countries of rising sovereign and bank borrowing costs.

The European Commission (EC) presented a plan on September 12, 2012, on the elements of a new SSM that could begin operating in 2013. It called for

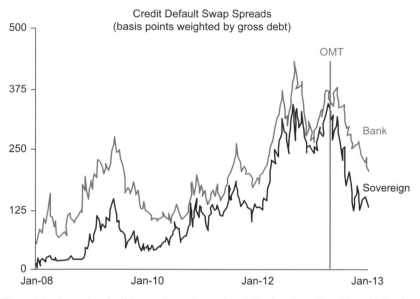

Figure 9.3 Sovereign–Bank Loops: Sovereign and Bank Funding Costs Have Moved in Tandem

Sources: Bloomberg, L.P.; and the European Central Bank.
Note: OMT = Outright Monetary Transactions.

adoption by end-2012 of European Union (EU) legislative proposals establishing a harmonized regulatory setup, harmonized national resolution regimes for credit institutions, and standards across national deposit insurance schemes. On December 13–14, 2012, the European Council agreed that the SSM would come into operation in March 2014 or one year after the SSM legislation enters into force, whichever is later, and put out a roadmap toward the banking union. A compromise agreement between the Council, the European Parliament, and the EC on the SSM regulation and on the modifications of the European Banking Authority (EBA) regulation was reached on March 19, 2013. Once the SSM legislation is adopted, ESM direct recapitalization could occur, with the ECB supervising the bank in need of assistance. The Council noted that adoption of a harmonized regulatory set up transposing Basel III in the EU (Fourth Capital Requirement Regulation and Directive (CRR/CRDIV)) is "of the utmost priority," and called for the adoption of the draft Directive for bank recovery and resolution (BRRD) and for harmonization of deposit guarantee schemes (DGS) by June 2013. It affirmed that a Single Resolution Mechanism (SRM) based on a common resolution authority with adequate powers and tools is required. This mechanism would be based on financial sector contributions and backstop arrangements that recoup taxpayer support over the medium term. The CRR/CRDIV was adopted by the Council of the European Union on June 20, 2013, and the new rules will apply from January 1, 2014. The euro-group reached an agreement on the main features of the operational framework for ESM direct recapitalization on June 20, 2013, while finalization has been linked to adoption of the BRRD and of the DGS Directive. On June 27–28, 2013, the European

TABLE 9.1

Progress on the Banking Union and the Single Rule Book					
	Single Supervisory Mechanism	Single Resolution Mechanism	Capital Requirement Regulation & Directive IV	Bank Recovery & Resolution Directive	Deposit Guarantee Scheme Directive
European Commission Proposal	September 12, 2012	July 10, 2013	July 20, 2011	June 6, 2012	July 12, 2010
Decision at Council	December 13–14, 2012		May 15, 2012	June 27, 2013	
Tri-partite Agreement Council/EP/EC	March 19, 2013		March 27, 2013		
Adoption Council	Expected September 2013	Expected end current EP term	June 20, 2013	Expected end-2013	Expected end-2013
Transposition to national legislation as required/New rules apply	One year after entry into force of regula- tion / ECB declares SSM effective		January 1, 2014	Expected end-2014	

Note: EC = European Commission; ECB = European Central Bank; EP = European Parliament; SSM = single supervisory mechanism.

Council reached agreement on the BRRD. Progress on the various elements of the banking union are summarized in Table 9.1. Last, on July 10, 2013, the EC published a draft proposal of a regulation establishing a Single Resolution Mechanism.

While agreement has been reached on the SSM and on the main features of the operational framework for ESM direct recapitalization, there remain differences of views on the modalities of the other elements of a banking union. These differences partly reflect concerns over the potential mutualization of liabilities and asymmetric cost sharing across members, as well as on the desirability of separating near-term crisis resolution, such as needed fiscal solutions and backstops for bank recapitalization, from longer-term architecture issues. They also reflect the complexities and difficulties of setting up a banking union in a relatively compressed period of time, and striking the right balance between allowing national flexibility and ensuring predictability and consistency of rules across EU member states without unsettling markets during crisis resolution.

HOW WILL A BANKING UNION HELP?

The EU single market for financial services supported by national stability frameworks worked too well in the run-up to the crisis. Before the crisis, the common currency and single market promoted financial integration and interconnections in the EU. Banks and financial institutions operated with ease across countries; credit went where it was in demand; portfolios became increasingly more diversified. The interbank market functioned smoothly, monetary and retail interest rate conditions were relatively uniform across the euro zone. There were side effects, such as large capital flows within the euro area and the associated buildup of sovereign and private sector imbalances. By and large, a hybrid financial architecture based on a single currency and common market, as well as nationally based financial safety nets, bank supervision, and regulation, seemed to serve the euro zone well.

The crisis laid bare the deep tensions inherent in this institutional design. Private borrowing costs rose with those of sovereigns, imparting procyclicality (costs rose as conditions deteriorated and capital flew out) and impairing monetary transmission (as rate cuts had limited or no effect in countries that needed them the most). This amplified financial fragmentation (Figure 9.1) and volatility, and thus exacerbated the economic downturn. This adverse dynamic resulted from the inability to control local interest rate conditions in the economic and monetary union, interacting with an architecture that strengthened the links between a country's banking and real sectors and the health of its public finances. In hindsight, it is evident that, in good times, banks grew in many places to a scale that overwhelmed national supervisory capacities, while in bad times, they overwhelmed national fiscal resources. It is also clear that, in the existing architecture, if a sovereign's finances are sound, then its backstop for its banks is credible. But if they are weak, then its banks are perceived as vulnerable and, therefore, face higher funding costs, which exacerbates the downturn (Figures 9.2 and 9.3).

The crisis also brought to the forefront a tension in the national approach to supervision. Nation-bound regulators may unduly favor a country's banking system and economy and may not internalize cross-border spillovers, which lie beyond their mandates. This national approach to supervision can be very damaging as the single currency requires an integrated financial system to function effectively. In good times, they may not take into account how their actions contribute to the buildup of excesses and imbalances in other countries. In bad times, they may encourage uncoordinated reductions of cross-border activities by their banks, exacerbating financial fragmentation and the disruption of monetary policy. Moreover, delays in resolving stresses—potentially as a result of closeness between national regulators and their banks—only exacerbate the eventual cost. But because a bank's distress may have adverse significant cross-border externalities in an integrated financial market, other countries may have no choice but to support those whose banking systems run into trouble.

WOULD A BANKING UNION HAVE PREVENTED THIS CRISIS?

The banking union would not have halted the sovereign debt crisis in some countries such as Greece. But a well-functioning banking union could have substantially weakened the adverse sovereign–bank-growth spirals, maintained depositor confidence, and attenuated the liquidity and funding freezes that followed and affected simultaneously banks and their sovereigns. The credibility of safety nets would not have been dependent on the sovereign's strength; and significant bailouts would not have resulted in loss of market access by the sovereign (as happened in Ireland). As a result, the rate cuts of the ECB would more likely have fed through to lower borrowing costs for the private sector in countries with the deepest downturns. A strong banking union would also have limited the concentrated exposures of banks to certain risks. For example, euro area-wide supervisors would arguably not have allowed size, structure, and concentration risks to grow as they did in countries such as Cyprus, Ireland, or Spain—or for general banking weaknesses to have accumulated in some other places. That said, as the United States and other recent experiences suggest, supervision would have had to strive to be of a high standard. Merely reorganizing supervisory structures would not of itself have addressed the buildup of systemic risk or the too-big-to-fail problem. Effective single supervision would have to take a broader perspective, and would need to counterbalance any tendency of common safety nets to allow imbalances to grow even larger.

A banking union will not solve all the euro zone's problems but it can help speed the process of repairing banks. Having common resources deployed through the ESM will help recapitalize and repair banks where the sovereign is weak by removing future contingent liabilities from the sovereign balance sheet. Having a credible, deep-pocket shareholder such as the ESM will also provide assurance to creditors that an investor would stand ready to shoulder future unexpected losses. This would contribute to generating a virtuous cycle of lower funding costs for both the sovereign and the banks. To align incentives, proper governance and control must be in place. Common supervision at the ECB will mitigate regulatory ring-fencing and ensure timely intervention in banks.[2] Having a SRM aligned with international best practices would also help ensure least cost and swift resolution while protecting financial stability. All in all, these actions will reduce fragmentation of financial markets, help repair monetary transmission, and stimulate the provision of credit to sound borrowers, thereby facilitating the economic recovery in the euro area.

THE EU PROPOSAL FOR A BANKING UNION

EU Agreements

The September 12, 2012, EC proposal and December 13–14, 2012, EU Council agreement covered the design of an SSM, the passage of three draft EU legislations, and the role of the EBA. According to the agreement, the ECB would start carrying out supervisory tasks in March 2014 or one year after the SSM legislation takes effect, whichever is later. Banks receiving or requesting public financial assistance would be targeted first; at the ESM's request and as a precondition for direct recapitalization, the ECB could begin directly supervising these banks, regardless of the starting date of the SSM. The Council further called for adoption of the CRR/CRD IV as of the utmost priority, and for adoption by June 2013 of draft EU legislations harmonizing and strengthening national resolution regimes and DGS, thus creating a "single rule book."[3] The

---

[2] Agarwal and others (2012) show that, in the United States, federal regulators are significantly less lenient than state regulators (although the United States also has federal backstops in place).

[3] Agreement between the Council and the EU Parliament on the CRR/CRD IV was reached on March 27, 2013, and the new rules were adopted June 20, 2013.

powers of the EBA were confirmed as the regulatory and supervisory standard-setter and the mediator of cross-border supervision and resolution issues arising in the EU.

A tripartite agreement between the Council, the European Parliament, and the EC on the SSM regulation and on the changes to the EBA regulation was reached on March 19, 2013. The euro-group reached an agreement on the main features of the operational framework for ESM direct recapitalization on June 20, 2013, and on the way forward-linking finalization of the operational framework to finalizing the BRRD and the DGS Directive with the European Parliament, which makes final agreement uncertain. On June 27–28, 2013, the European Council reached agreement on the BRRD (including on features of bail-ins of bank creditors and depositor preference), with the aim of reaching agreement with the Parliament and adoption by end-2013, and also called for adoption of the DGS Directive by end-2013. It also reiterated that, to break the adverse cycles between banks and sovereigns, the ESM should have the possibility to recapitalize banks directly when the SSM is effective, and that Council agreement on the EC proposal for an SRM should be reached by the end of the year with a view of adoption by end of the parliamentary cycle. The Council also noted the importance of the balance sheet assessment comprising an asset quality review and a stress test to be conducted in the transition toward the SSM. Agreement on the SSM regulation was reached at the European Parliament on September 12, 2013, after transparency and accountability requirements were strengthened, and at the Council on October 15, 2013. The regulation entered into force following its publication in the official journal of the EU on October 29, 2013, and the ECB will fully assume its supervisory tasks 12 months later or when the ECB declares itself ready. On October 23, 2013, the ECB announced key features of the comprehensive assessment of the banking system, which will be concluded prior to assuming supervisory tasks in November 2014.

The EC published its proposal for an SRM on July 10, 2013. The SRM proposal goes in the right direction of establishing a strong central resolution authority and a single resolution fund, essential elements of a banking union that would reduce fragmentation and mitigate sovereign–bank links. It provides for strong centralized powers (at the EC and at a new Single Resolution Board) to achieve swift and least-cost resolution while protecting stability and internalizing cross-border effects. There are, however, issues to be resolved and clarified, such as: the scope of the EC powers and associated risks; the division of responsibilities between the EC and the SRB; the governance of the SRB; the operational independence of the SRM; and the lack of a common fiscal backstop (apart from ESM and the single resolution fund). There is also a risk that the legal basis for the SRM may be challenged before the European Court of Justice. Given explicit opposition to the proposal by some member states, the discussions are likely to be complex and difficult. The legal foundations of the EC proposal for the SRM have been scrutinized by the European Council Legal Service (CLS). CLS agreed that Article 114 of the Treaty on the Functioning of the European Union may be a suitable legal basis for the establishment of the SRM subject to certain conditions. However, the SRM proposal encountered legal objections over the envisaged delegation of powers to the Board. CLS argued that the powers delegated to the SRB in the EC proposal need to be further detailed to be compatible with the EU treaties and the Meroni doctrine. Separately, the EC announced a new state aid regime for banks that appropriately affirms financial stability and minimal fiscal costs as overarching objectives, but the regime also introduces rigidities such as giving the EC an ex ante veto right on restructuring plans, and requiring bail-ins of shareholders and of junior unsecured creditors as a precondition for state aid (see Chapter 12).

Supervision

The SSM regulation specifies a clear mandate for bank safety and soundness to the ECB and its accountability to the EP and the euro-group. The ECB would directly supervise banks accounting for about 80 percent of euro area banking assets, including banks with over €30 billion in assets or 20 percent of national GDP or if otherwise deemed systemic (for example, given cross-border reach). At least the three largest banks in each member state would be directly supervised, with the ECB retaining the power to bring any bank under its supervision if deemed necessary. At the ECB, a supervisory board and a steering committee are being created to prepare and implement decisions and give voice to non-euro area members that opt in (as the Governing Council remains ultimately responsible).

Operational Details

The SSM regulation appropriately confers broad investigatory and supervisory powers on the ECB, which is responsible for the effective and consistent functioning of the SSM (although national authorities are also responsible for the banks remaining under their direct supervision). The challenges of effective implementation must not be underestimated. Operational arrangements now need to be specified—these must make incentives compatible between national authorities and the ECB, ensure an adequate division of labor, and provide for appropriate information sharing within the SSM to underpin effective supervisory decision-making. The ECB is to adopt a detailed framework for the practical modalities of supervisory cooperation within the SSM. The governance set-up is complex but must seek to promote, not hinder, timely decision-making. Moreover, to be effective, it is essential to appropriately and urgently staff the ECB. The SSM regulation provided both national authorities and the ECB with powers to make use of macroprudential instruments specified in the relevant EU Directives, although accountability must be clarified. In practice, close cooperation will be critical to ensure coherence and effectiveness of measures.

Resolution and Safety Nets

An SRM is an indispensable supplement of effective supervision, ideally centered on a single resolution authority, deposit insurance, and common backstops. The

Council recognized the importance of an SRM with adequate powers and tools, and the EC subsequently published a draft regulation for an SRM. This mechanism is to be based on financial sector contributions and backstop arrangements that recoup taxpayer support over the medium term, and could ensure that an SRM is established around the time the Single Supervisory Mechanism is declared effective. Though the immediate priority is to strengthen and harmonize national regimes, funds raised over time from financial institutions could cover individual small-to-medium-size bank failures. Common backstops are essential to handle systemic failures. A time-bound roadmap to common safety nets—needed for depositor confidence and to break sovereign bank links—would limit the risks of an incomplete banking union.

DESIGN OF THE BANKING UNION

Steady-State Analysis

This section presents considerations for a banking union in the longer run, but highlights where some issues are particularly important in the near term. Transition and crisis management issues are elaborated on further in the section below on "Transition in Crisis Time."

High-Level Principles to Design a Banking Union

To complete the monetary union and provide effective stability architecture, the banking union must have all three elements in place. Progress is required on all elements now; under the well-known economic principle that effective control and resources must go hand-in-hand. Aligning incentives is important for the steady-state, but also in the near term as elements of the banking union are put into place. The governance of and steps toward the banking union must provide the right incentives and promote timely decision making that would help repair banking systems swiftly and at a least cost, lest national interests prevail and effectiveness is compromised.

- A Single Supervisory Mechanism without an SRM and common safety nets will do little to break the vicious circle between banks and sovereigns or to stabilize the euro area. Moreover, lack of a credible resolution framework would hamper the effectiveness of the SSM, and impede timely decision making by leaving national authorities to deal with the fiscal consequences of others' supervisory decisions. This would open the door to conflicts with potential reputational consequences for the ECB.

- Bank recapitalization, as well as resolution mechanisms, would lack credibility without the assurance of fiscal backstops and burden-sharing arrangements.

- Conversely, common safety nets and backstops without effective supervision and resolution would break sovereign–bank links, but would risk distorting incentives, reinforcing tendencies for regulatory forbearance, and shifting losses to the euro area level.

What Is the Necessary Country Coverage?

A banking union is necessary for the euro area, given how destabilizing financial fragmentation and sovereign–bank links are in a monetary union. In short, a monetary union is not viable if financial markets are not integrated, and a banking union would provide the stability architecture supporting integration. An EU banking union would also be desirable given the single market for financial services and the deep financial interconnections among EU countries. But this raises more complex issues, not least the interaction of multiple central banks, lenders of last resort, and exchange rates. Potentially different access to backstops or safety nets, such as the ESM that is a euro area intergovernmental institution, adds to the complexities. It is, therefore, prudent to proceed first with a euro area banking union, albeit with an option to "opt in" for non-euro area EU members and with adequate governance safeguards for those who wish to stay out.

What Should Be the Institutional Coverage?

All banks should be included, regardless of size, complexity, and cross-border reach. Banks that are systemic at a global level or for the euro area as a whole should be included in the banking union, given the spillovers that they generate. But banks systemic at the national level could also become significant for the euro area if they destabilize their sovereign, and should therefore also be included. However, larger numbers of small banks with correlated exposures can threaten systemic stability (for example, Spanish cajas), especially when policy buffers are low. Hence, banks of a variety of size, complexity, cross-border relevance, and business models may become systemic for the euro area and require the need for common solutions and backstops. The ultimate goal should therefore be to include *all* banks, not just systemic or vulnerable ones. This approach would also allow for complete and evenhanded treatment and limit the scope for regulatory arbitrage or capture.

DESIGN OF A SINGLE SUPERVISORY MECHANISM

What Is the Role of the Single Supervisory Mechanism?

The SSM would facilitate a more systemic approach to tracking the buildup of risk concentrations, and contribute to achieving a comprehensive macroprudential oversight of the euro area. It would coordinate supervisory actions across countries, and ensure consistent application of prudential norms. It would foster convergence of best practices across members, partly alleviate concerns of regulatory capture at the local level, and promote integration of the single market for financial services. In concrete terms, higher standards of supervision in place before the crisis might have meant a swifter identification of an unsustainable build-up of risk (for example, in Ireland or Spain) and a more timely and effective intervention to diffuse such risk (for example, by applying higher capital buffers or restricting excessive concentrations).

Why Is the Single Supervisory Mechanism Centered on the ECB?

Conferring supervisory tasks and responsibilities upon the ECB is reasonable under the current Treaty on the Functioning of the European Union, given its financial stability expertise and the existing institutional frameworks in the euro area. The ECB has access to supervisory skill sets as most Eurosystem national central banks are also national supervisors. Involving the ECB would give it access to supervisory information in support of its monetary policy and lender-of-last resort duties. Having banking oversight and monetary policy under one roof could potentially lead to difficult trade-offs between the two, for example, when monetary policy decisions impact bank solvency, or when the need to safeguard financial stability may call for liquidity provision to insolvent banks, but it will also allow to exploit synergies between the two functions. It will also help ensure that microprudential regulation does not overlook systemic considerations. As a creditor, the ECB may also face conflicts of interest when, as a supervisor, it is required to withdraw a license and trigger resolution, resulting in losses to its own claims. These trade-offs call for appropriate checks and balances, such as transparency in the decisions taken and implemented by the supervisory board.

Guidance for effective supervision is provided the Basel Core Principles (or "Core Principles for Effective Supervision"). According to these Principles, a number of preconditions and prerequisites will have to be met at the euro area level. Some of the preconditions are beyond reach in the immediate future, but they are essential for the effectiveness of the new system in the longer term.

- Preconditions for sound banking include: (1) the implementation of coherent and sustainable macroeconomic policies; (2) a clear framework for financial stability policy; (3) an effective crisis management and resolution framework to deal with bank failures and minimize disruptions; (4) an adequate safety net to deal with a confidence crisis while minimizing distortions; (5) a well-developed public infrastructure; and (6) effective market discipline.

- Prerequisites to establish a sound basis for the SSM include: (1) operational independence; (2) clear objectives and mandates; (3) legal protection of supervisors; (4) transparent processes, sound governance, and adequate resources; and (5) accountability. The EC proposal and EU Council agreement by and large meet these prerequisites (see below). But clarity and strengthening is required on resources, and aspects of the governance mechanism and legal robustness, for example, on the specifics of the delegation mechanism.

Effective supervision will also require designing an effective delegation mechanism involving interactions between supranational and national institutional layers. Designing a system involving many countries is a complex undertaking. Given that the euro area has over 6,000 banks (a similar order of magnitude as in the United States, see Figure 9.4), an appropriate division of labor will be needed

	# of banks
U.S. FDIC INSURED	7246
# OF BANKS REGULATED BY:	
FEDERAL RESERVE	6027
OF WHICH ASSETS > US$ 100 BIL	26
FEDERAL DEPOSIT INSURANCE CORPORATION (FDIC)	4551
OFFICE OF THE COMPTROLLER OF THE CURRENCY (OCC)	2036
NATIONAL CREDIT UNION ADMINISTRATION (NCUA)	7094
EA CREDIT INSTITUTIONS	6180
OF WHICH ASSETS > €100 BIL	> 30

Figure 9.4 Banks under Supervision

Sources: European Central Bank; Federal Reserve; Federal Deposit Insurance Corporation; and National Credit Union Administration.

between the center and the national agencies, as no single new body could supervise all banks with full effect in the near future. Thus, some degree of delegation is necessary. Full centralization is neither practical nor desirable, as supervisory knowledge and resources remain at the national levels. Full decentralization in which the center merely validates decisions is not desirable either, particularly when common resources are at stake (for example, ESM direct recapitalization of banks or future common backstops).

How Should Delegation Be Designed Within the Single Supervisory Mechanism?

Supervisors at the national level and at the ECB must have clear responsibilities and the powers necessary to perform their tasks. Having formal responsibility but no real enforcement power (as could occur at the ECB level) would carry serious risks, while having the power but no clear responsibility or accountability (as could occur at the national level) could lead to misaligned incentives and distorted outcomes. A mechanism of monitoring and clarity over tasks and responsibilities, thus, becomes important. The goal should be to create a coherent and consistent supervisory mechanism with adequate information flow and final significant decisions taken at the center.

To ensure incentives are compatible, the degree of delegation should be clarified. It would depend on the ECB's supervisory classification of risks for each bank, and factors such as the importance of local knowledge and know-how, the systemic dimension of banks and/or tasks, and the amount of discretion required in decision making. For example, institutions with systemic implications should be subject to more intrusive supervision from the center, as should functions that are more subject to discretion, capture by the industry, or influence by politics. Consolidated supervision of financial groups would involve interagency coordination to oversee nonbank financial institutions as well.

In sum, the ECB will need to rely partly on the competencies and resources at the national level, with clarity on the allocation of tasks and powers as well as strong oversight and accountability to ensure incentive compatibility and contain risks of slippages. At the same time, the ECB must be adequately resourced to ensure that it has the capacity to perform key and strategic tasks itself while being able to supervise systemically important banks and those that require or may potentially require public support.

The ECB must have powers to perform effective macroprudential oversight. Given its financial stability expertise, the ECB is well placed to ensure information-sharing, home-host coordination, and internalization of cross-border externalities. Hence a shift in macroprudential mandates, powers, and tools is appropriate, away from member states and toward the ECB. The ECB should be given binding powers to use macroprudential instruments if it deems necessary. At the same time, the framework should involve national authorities and be sufficiently flexible to tailor solutions to local conditions. In particular, national authorities should also be able to make use of macroprudential tools in response to local conditions within the parameters and guidelines set by the ECB.

DESIGN OF A SINGLE RESOLUTION MECHANISM

What Is the Role of a Single Resolution Mechanism?

Without a strong SRM complementing the Single Supervisory Mechanism, the credibility and effectiveness of the banking union would be jeopardized. Leaving resolution responsibilities at the national level while supervision is centralized carries significant risks, such as perpetuating bank–sovereign links and creating potential conflict (and deadlock) among national authorities in cross-border resolution. A single resolution authority, as presumptive receiver of failed banks, can facilitate timely resolution, including of banks that operate across borders. It provides a mechanism to internalize home-host concerns and reach agreement on least-cost resolution and burden-sharing when common backstops are needed, and is therefore important to ensure effectiveness of the SSM. It can thus help to avoid the protracted and costly resolutions that occurred, for instance, in the cases of Fortis and of Dexia (Box 9.1). A single authority is also necessary to align incentives for least-cost resolution—since a common backstop in the context of a decentralized mechanism would provide incentives to shift residual losses from national taxpayers to those in the euro area. Pooling bank resolution capacity in a single body would achieve economies of scale, avoid incoherence and duplication, align incentives, and

---

Box 9.1   Resolutions of Fortis and Dexia

Fortis. In the aftermath of the Lehman collapse, an agreement was reached on September 28, 2008, to save the troubled Fortis group with taxpayer support from Belgium, Luxembourg, and the Netherlands. The agreement, however, fell apart soon thereafter as liquidity pressures mounted. Subsequently, the Belgian parent company sold the shares of the Dutch parts of Fortis to the Netherlands' government, whereas Belgium and Luxembourg sought a common solution for their parts of Fortis, eventually agreeing to sell the banking arm to BNP Paribas. This break-up along national lines constitutes a setback to financial integration in the Benelux and was likely more costly than a first-best joint solution for the group.

   Dexia. Dexia failed in 2011 after losing access to wholesale funding and it faced increased collateral demands on interest rate derivatives. The resulting break-up was segmented along national interests. On October 10, it was announced that the Belgian operations would be purchased by the Belgian government; foreign subsidiaries in Canada, Italy, Luxembourg, Spain, and Turkey would be put up for sale; and parts of the French operations would be purchased by two French public sector banks. The remaining troubled assets, including a €95 billion bond portfolio, would remain in a bank in runoff (Dexia SA) that would receive funding guarantees of up to €85 billion provided severally (but not jointly) by the governments of Belgium, France, and Luxembourg, along with recapitalization of €5.5 billion. At end-2012, the EC approved the resolution plan for Dexia group.

---

accumulate expertise including for preparation and implementation of recovery and resolution plans for systemic institutions.

Characteristics of a Single Resolution Mechanism

The SRM should comply with emerging best practices as laid out in the Financial Stability Board's "Key Attributes of Effective Resolution Regimes for Financial Institutions." The SRM should seek to resolve financial institutions without disrupting financial stability. It should minimize costs to taxpayers, protect insured depositors, and ensure that shareholders and unsecured, uninsured creditors absorb losses. There are prerequisites and preconditions of effective resolution:

- Preconditions for effective bank resolution include: (1) a well-established framework for financial stability; (2) an effective system of supervision, regulation, and oversight of financial institutions; (3) effective safety nets and protection schemes; (4) a robust accounting, auditing, and disclosure regime; and (5) a well-developed legal framework.

- Prerequisites for a strong authority include: (1) operational independence consistent with the statutory responsibilities; (2) transparent processes; (3) legal protection; (4) sound governance, rigorous evaluation and accountability mechanisms; and (5) adequate resources.

- The SRM should be centered on a single resolution authority. A single resolution authority would be based on supranational legislation, but any treaty change would require time. A single authority would need a mandate, alongside the supervisor, to develop resolution and recovery plans well ahead of, and intervene before, insolvency using well-defined quantitative and qualitative triggers. They would need strong powers to take early intervention measures (for example, to require capital conservation measures or restrictions on activities), restructure banks' assets and liabilities (for example, apply a "bail-in tool" to subordinated and senior unsecured creditors, transfer assets and liabilities—"purchase and assumption"—to a sound acquirer, and separate bad assets by setting up an asset management vehicle), override shareholder rights (subject to them being no worse off), establish bridge banks to maintain essential financial services, and close banks.

Burden Sharing

The SRM should provide clear and specific burden-sharing mechanisms. As resolution involves sensitive choices over the distribution of losses, clear ex ante burden-sharing mechanisms would be necessary to realize least cost resolution. The resolution mechanism should specify clear exit strategies that maximize the value of participations acquired and prohibit national preference.

- *Hierarchy*. Respecting the hierarchy of creditor claims, the resolution authority should be able to haircut or extinguish unsecured liabilities, starting with equity and potentially extending to senior unsecured debt (that would be bailed-in), according to a clear creditor priority list. This would reduce uncertainty in the capital structure and any eventual resort to taxpayer funding. Given their explicit taxpayer backing, insured depositors would need to be given clear priority among unsecured and secured bank liabilities, to maximize recovery of deposit payouts from failed banks in resolution. Hence, depositor preference provisions should be included in EU legislation such as the recovery and resolution directive.

- *Contributions from the industry*. A resolution fund, partly funded ex ante by contributions from the industry, should be used first to finance resolution after unsecured claimants have been extinguished. Insofar as private sector contributions and loss allocation across uninsured and unsecured claimants would be insufficient in a systemic crisis, a common backstop, adequately designed, would also need to be tapped.

- *A systemic risk exception*. A systemic risk exception for the banking union could be considered for systemic events to override the least cost requirements. This approach would adapt the U.S. statutory "risk exception" and would provide clarity and credibility to the bank resolution process. To address moral hazard concern, a high bar would be needed to invoke the exception.

Institutional Considerations

Given the complex fiscal decisions involved and the need for checks and balances, the resolution authority should be set up independently of, but on par with, the ECB supervisory mechanism and should manage the resolution and deposit insurance fund. Collaboration and information sharing between the two is essential. For instance, consideration could be given to the creation of a committee comprising the head of the supervisory function of the ECB and the chairman of the resolution authority. Alternatively, the ECB head of supervision could serve on the board of the resolution authority, together with national representatives and representatives of other EU bodies.

COMMON SAFETY NETS

Why a Common Deposit Insurance and Resolution Fund?

By pooling risk, a deposit insurance and resolution fund will not only help countries avoid disruptions that may overwhelm their individual capacities but will also form a key pillar in the incentive compatibility of banking union. If a weak sovereign is perceived not to be able to honor its safety net obligations, losses of confidence can quickly follow, triggering capital flight and deposit outflows. A pooled mechanism with credible backstops would be more effective in protecting confidence and in diversifying risks across banks. Without common safety nets and backstops, the banking union would remain an incomplete and risky construct that fails to delink the funding costs of weak sovereigns from that of their banks. It would also risk jeopardizing the credibility of the ECB and the SSM by leaving the system vulnerable to financial fragility.

What Could Be the Size of the Fund?

The resolution and deposit insurance fund could be relatively small and cover some individual bank failures, with fiscal and central bank backing to be used in the event of a systemic crisis. The fund could, in practice, cover both resolution and deposit insurance—if the ranking of claimants is clear and adequate, the objectives of the two functions would be aligned. While there is no well-established good practice, the typical target size of resolution *and* deposit insurance funds could range from about 1 to 2 percent of total liabilities (excluding equity) in large systems, where the aim is to cover two to three mid-sized banks and four to six small banks.

Why Centralize Lender-of-Last-Resort Functions at the ECB?

The lender-of-last-resort makes liquidity support available to solvent yet illiquid banks. Centralizing all lender-of-last-resort functions at the ECB would in the steady state eliminate bank–sovereign linkages present in the current Emergency Liquidity Assistance (ELA) scheme (that were described in Box 9.1). This would require changes to the ECB's collateral policy, as by definition euro area banks that tap ELA cannot access Eurosystem liquidity owing to collateral constraints. Until such time as all banks are brought under the ECB's supervisory oversight, ELA would be sourced through both the ECB (for banks brought under its purview) as well as national central banks (NCB) (for banks that remain under national supervision, albeit with adjustments made to the national ELA limits).

EUROPEAN STABILITY MECHANISM DIRECT RECAPITALIZATION

Purpose

Mobilizing the ESM direct bank recapitalization tool in a forceful and timely manner is critical to developing a path out of the current crisis and would complement other measures such as the ECB's Outright Monetary Transactions. Recapitalization of frail, domestically systemic banks in the euro area, including some migration to the ESM of existing public support to such banks, can help break the vicious circle between banks and sovereigns, reduce financial fragmentation, repair monetary transmission, prepare for banking union, and thus help complete the economic and monetary union. To be sure, failing nonsystemic banks should be resolved at least cost to national resolution funds and taxpayers. Equally, systemic banks benefiting from ESM support will need effective supervision and reform to be returned to full viability and private ownership, with state aid rules mandating formal restructuring plans. In some cases, the sovereign itself may need an adjustment program, providing an enabling environment for asset price recovery.

Approach

The mobilization of the ESM direct recapitalization tool should ensure frail, domestically systemic banks have adequate capital, access to funding at reasonable cost, and positive profits—in short, a viable business model. To this end, asset valuations are critical, as are the roles of shareholders, creditors, and the domestic sovereign in bearing costs.

- *Purpose.* In principle, there would be significant advantages to breaking the vicious bank–sovereign circle if all capital needed to ensure that a systemic bank was adequately capitalized was ultimately provided by a central fiscal authority. This would especially be the case if the scenario were to play out in a small jurisdiction, and even more so if it also had to internalize spillovers to others (that might result, for example, if external creditors did not share in losses, for fear of triggering wider problems). More generally, pooling risk would provide protection ex ante to all, as any country could in theory find itself in a similar position in the future.

- *Principles.* In practice, although the Treaty establishing the ESM provides for the possibility of losses, such losses are not expected in its financial operations, including bank recapitalization. As a bank investor, the expectation is that the ESM must be careful to take balanced risk positions. It likely could not provide capital that a patient investor would not expect to recover over time. Thus, capital needed to bring a systemic bank out of insolvency (that is, to bring it from negative to nonnegative equity) would in the first instance need to be provided by shareholders and creditors, and then by the national government, with any remaining shortfall covered by the ESM. Fortunately, there are unlikely to be large, insolvent banks currently in most economies.

- A balanced approach allowing the possibility of risk sharing would prudently internalize the benefits of ESM capital support by looking ahead over a time horizon sufficiently long to realize the benefits. As a patient, deep-pocket investor, the ESM should take a long-term perspective in its investment decisions, cognizant that gross upfront crisis outlays tend to dwarf ultimate costs net of recoveries/capital gains and, in many instances, generate positive financial returns. In other words, while the ESM would not take on expected losses, it would shoulder the risk of *unexpected losses going forward*. This approach is in line with efficient risk sharing, wherein the patient investor bears the residual risk.

- *Asset valuation*. The implications for asset valuation, which determine the size of recapitalization needs as well as the investors' up/downside risk, are twofold. First, asset values should be neither too high (which would imply mutualization through the back door) nor too low (in which case, the private sector could simply buy the assets, and there would be limited benefit to having an official investor). Second, because the ESM is a patient investor willing to give the banks the necessary time to restructure, assets should be priced at values that give due consideration of the positive effect of recapitalization on asset values. This includes not just the direct positive effect of recapitalization (including more favorable funding costs) and recovery but also the removal of tail risk events (see next bullet).

- *Safeguards*. There should be safeguards for the ESM (for example, built into the sales contract) against domestic policies that could directly harm the viability or profitability of the recipient banks (for example, onerous taxes ex post or stiff resolution levies). But ESM investments should not benefit from loss protection provided by the sovereign. Such approaches would preserve sovereign–bank links, undermining the purpose of ESM direct recapitalization.

- *Exit strategy*. There should be incentives for an early ESM exit and private investor entry. The timing would be built around the EU-approved restructuring plans. Mandatory sunset clauses should be avoided as they could affect negotiating power ahead of the deadline.

- *Adequate resources*. Direct equity injections into banks could absorb significant amounts of ESM capital. It would be important to ensure that the ESM has adequate capital to not only allay any investor concerns about ESM credit quality, and thereby limit any rating implications, but also play its potential role of a common backstop for bank recapitalization.

Legacy Assets

This term has been very controversial, reflecting concerns that creditor countries could be expected to put capital into nonviable banks. This is not what is being suggested above. Rather, losses on impaired "legacy" assets should be recognized through upfront provisioning and proper (long-term/postcrisis) valuation. It is not recommended that all impaired assets be segregated from the bank prior to ESM direct recapitalization and placed into recovery vehicles ultimately backed by the national taxpayer; such an approach would greatly reduce the effectiveness of the tool in addressing bank–sovereign links. Rather, bank health should be restored with shareholders, including the sovereign, bearing the expected loss of past excesses by being subjected to an independent valuation exercise consistent with the shared commitment to restore full viability after the restructuring period.

Further Support

To further support balance sheet clean-up, certain classes of legacy assets could be transferred to asset run-off vehicles such as asset management companies (AMCs) under ESM ownership. Expected losses would remain with the sovereign, given the terms of the foregoing recapitalization. But to limit further contingent fiscal liabilities and harness efficiencies, consideration could be given to allowing the ESM to set up and own AMCs. Possible roles for the ECB in supporting AMC operations could also be considered (although concerns regarding the prohibition on monetary financing may also be raised). ECB funding, if possible under its statute, would help smooth over time the warehousing and disposal of hard-to-value and hard-to-sell assets. An alternative would be for the ECB to support AMC operations indirectly by accepting ESM-guaranteed AMC bonds issued to banks in Eurosystem refinancing operations.

TRANSITION IN CRISIS TIME: HOW DO WE GET THERE?

In an ideal world, the transition to a banking union would be gradual. After all, there was a decade between the European Council decisions to realize the monetary union in 1989 and the launch of the euro in 1999. Most likely, it would start with harmonizing supervision, resolution, and safety nets across countries—a process that may take some years before EU Directives are agreed upon and fully adopted at the national levels. This would be followed by gradual development of new common institutions, including fiscal backstops and burden-sharing arrangements. Finally, the process would culminate with the transfer of powers and responsibilities to a full banking union, with an SSM, a single resolution authority, a common resolution and deposit insurance fund, and common backstops.

But times are far from tranquil, and rapid action is needed. Repairing the financial sector, ending fragmentation, and reestablishing a properly functioning monetary policy transmission mechanism are key elements of any crisis resolution strategy. From that standpoint, the decision by euro area leaders to allow the ESM to recapitalize banks directly once a SSM involving the ECB is effective is the right one. In the context of private and public sector deleveraging, raising resources domestically to recapitalize banks is challenging (and impossible in some jurisdictions). At the same time, closing domestic systemic banks continues to pose a risk of uncontrollable consequences. Shared support for recapitalization would facilitate financial and economic stabilization at the national level, and thus for the monetary union as a whole, although it raises questions about burden-sharing and moral hazard. Hence, the transfer of financial responsibilities to the center needs to be balanced by the transfer of supervisory power. In that context, the decision to subordinate ESM direct recapitalization to the establishment of an effective single-supervision mechanism within the ECB is a sensible one.

How to Sequence the Banking Union?

All the elements—an SSM, single resolution with common backstops, and common safety nets—are necessary for a successful banking union. Missing elements would result in an incoherent banking union and, at worst, an architecture that is inferior to the current national-based one. Therefore, ideally, progress would be made on each of the elements. Given the need to resolve outstanding differences of views on the details and timing, however, it may not be possible to make progress on all the elements now. However, a well-defined timetable at the outset would remove uncertainty, bolster confidence in the political willingness to build a robust financial stability architecture, and anchor execution. In this respect, the timeline agreed upon by the EU Council is commendable, although agreement on the third component (common safety net) is still missing. But above all, agreement upon and adoption of the single rule book in national laws (the CRD IV/ CRR, the recovery and resolution directive, and the deposit insurance directive) must proceed urgently to ensure robust environments are in place at the country level as the SSM is rolled out.

Finally, although working under the existing treaty framework is the swiftest way to start, strengthening the legal framework over time would minimize implementation and litigation risks (Box 9.2).

How Should the ECB Be Judged as Having Become Effective?

Following the finalization of the agreement on the SSM regulation, the ECB will take full supervisory responsibilities one year after the SSM regulation enters into force, or when the ECB declares itself ready, whichever comes later. An approach based on the Basel Core Principles would take years to achieve as it would demand completeness of the banking union. Instead, the more modest and pragmatic approach adopted by the EU Council at their December 2012 meeting is appropriate. A phased roll-out of the SSM could seek to make it "effective" for troubled systemic banks during the transition. The forthcoming balance sheet assessment (or asset quality review) of euro area banks together with an agreed strategy on how to address capital shortfalls and to restructure failed banks. It will increase transparency about the condition of European banks and provide the ECB with a consistent view of the banks it will supervise under the SSM. It will be critical to establish the ECB's credibility as a supervisor and prevent procyclical deleveraging. The emphasis should be on establishing a strong SSM in which the

Box 9.2　Legal Considerations

Legal basis of the banking union. Under Article 127(6) of the Treaty on the Functioning of the European Union (TFEU), the ECB is able to take on specific supervisory tasks without treaty change, upon a unanimous decision of the European Council and after consultation with the European Parliament and the ECB. The EU Council agreement vests in the ECB exclusive authority for a wide range of supervisory tasks. While Article 127(6) provides a legal basis, it has been interpreted expansively in order to establish the SSM. The draft SSM regulation carefully attempts to specify the ECB remit, but litigation risks may in principle not be excluded, as any financial institution confronted with a supervisory decision by the ECB could bring a case before the European Court of Justice on grounds of lack of competence. In the medium term, providing an explicit legal underpinning for financial stability arrangements in the Treaty would further strengthen their legal soundness. This would allow to anchor financial stability as a key objective under the Treaty and to define roles and powers of all the safety net players, including a fully fledged resolution authority with a common backstop.

Shared competences and responsibilities. Under Article 127(6) and the regulation that is based upon it, supervision will remain a shared competence between the ECB and member states. The ECB will be responsible for certain supervisory measures, while member states retain their powers with respect to any aspect that is not covered by the draft SSM Regulation (for example, anti-money-laundering, consumer protection, and some macroprudential tools). For the tasks conferred to it, the ECB would take the final decisions vis-à-vis "significant" banks, while the national competent authorities (NCAs) will assist the ECB with the preparation and implementation of such decisions, pursuant to the ECB's instructions. For other banks, NCAs will formally take supervisory decisions, but still under ECB instructions. The ECB will be responsible for the effective and consistent functioning of the SSM, and both the ECB and the NCAs will be subject to a duty of cooperation. The overall division of tasks and responsibilities will need to be clarified, to remove any remaining uncertainties as to who, as a legal matter, will be ultimately accountable for supervisory decisions.

ECB Governance. The Governing Council is the ultimate decision-making body of the ECB, as enshrined in the Treaty, including for any supervisory tasks conferred upon the ECB under Article 127(6). Several challenges may arise from this setup. First, as the Supervisory Board can only prepare the supervisory decisions to be taken by the Governing Council, it is only the latter that will formally be responsible for supervision, in addition to monetary policy. Therefore, the separation of monetary and supervisory responsibilities can only be implemented at an operational level, as the legal mandate of the ECB, pursued by the Governing Council as the ultimate decision making body, remains unaltered. Second, the existence of multiple layers of governance arrangements, coupled with the impossibility to delegate decisions to the Supervisory Board, may create a burdensome process; legal risks may arise from the need to align the practice of daily supervision with the legal requirements dictated under the Treaty and the SSM regulation. Lastly, as non-euro area SSM participants cannot be represented on the Governing Council of the euro area, taking part in the SSM decision making process would require alternative arrangements to have their voices heard, such as through the supervisory board, with mediation channels to resolve differences.

EU banking laws. The EU's banking laws feature significant weaknesses on both form and substance. On form, the current approach based on directives implemented in national laws must swiftly be replaced by a directly applicable single rule book. On substance, current weaknesses in EU banking law will also have to be remedied, e.g., weak fit and proper criteria and the absence of restrictions on related party lending.

Legal actions at the national level. Whether the EU Regulation conferring on the ECB supervisory tasks also requires legal changes at the national level is unclear. However, legal amendments of national legislation seem to be inevitable to provide legal clarity to ensure a smooth functioning of the SSM. Absent a single, directly applicable rule book, such amendments of the domestic legislation may also be necessary to improve national supervisory regimes.

ECB has formal powers, the decision-making processes, and the capability to perform essential supervisory tasks in an intrusive delegated monitoring model. A well-functioning information and evaluation infrastructure must be established quickly so that the ECB can serve as a central supervisor. The ECB must be able to request and receive all necessary information, conduct off-site diligence, field on-site inspections while relying on cross-country teams, and pursue further action on any bank in the euro area. The ECB would need to put in place adequate resources and organizational capacity to commence selected supervisory tasks, which will be a complex and demanding exercise. Based on information to be provided by national authorities on their banks' supervisory histories and risk profiles, the ECB could then start offsite stocktaking of the banks under its supervision to prioritize institutions in need of deeper diagnostics based on risk.

The Single Resolution Mechanism

It is essential that the European Council commit to a firm timeline for implementing an SRM, including burden-sharing arrangements, on the basis of the EC proposal. When agreements on adequate resolution (and deposit insurance) funding and backstops are in place, the single resolution authority could begin operating. Meanwhile, resolutions would be handled by the national authorities under strengthened regimes (and, as needed, support from the sovereign with borrowing from the ESM). During the interim period, the SSM would work with national resolution authorities to resolve or restructure weak institutions, until a single resolution authority with common backstops is established. To facilitate the process, there may be merit to establishing a temporary body or creating urgently an EU agency tasked with the coordination of bank crisis management and resolution among national authorities and the ECB. Agreeing on clear principles about the hierarchy of claimants and reducing expectation of bailouts would also help contain the fiscal costs of future resolutions, including by allowing the possibility of bailing-in uninsured creditors. But, to be sure, a strong SRM, is critical to minimize risks to the credibility of the SSM and to ensure timely and least cost resolution while protecting financial stability. It should become operational at around the time when the ECB takes full responsibility for the SSM in 2014 to enhance the ECB's effectiveness as a supervisor.

Common Safety Nets

Steps should also be taken toward common safety nets to remove stability risks and help delink sovereigns and banks. A reinsurance scheme, for instance, could be created from national DGS, funded at the euro area level through industry levies and contributions from member states. It would pool risk and weaken sovereign–bank links. Ex ante agreement on the shares of national and supranational funding in depositor payouts would limit moral hazard. Over time, the fund would build administrative capacity and could be a step toward a permanent euro area scheme and resolution fund.

THE BANKING UNION AND NON-EURO AREA EU MEMBER STATES

Non-euro area EU member states will benefit indirectly from a euro area banking union. A banking union is necessary for the euro area. It should be recognized upfront that, by enhancing stability and removing financial market fragmentation, a well-functioning euro area banking union generates positive spillovers and enhances the functioning of the EU single market for financial services as a whole. Therefore, other EU member states have a legitimate interest in ensuring that the new system is set up properly. A single euro area supervisory mechanism can also solve coordination problems related to the supervision of cross-border banks.

A euro area banking union raises a number of complex issues for the "outs." To ensure the integrity of the single market for financial services, the system must be balanced between the interests of the "outs" and decisions taken by the SSM. Specifically, decision making in the EBA and supervisory colleges where the SSM would be represented by the ECB must ensure integrity of the single market, including on issues such as the fiscal consequences of decisions on banks with cross-border operations. It is also important that the interests of those who wish to join the banking union but keep their own currency be represented, within the constraints of the EU Treaty under which they would not have a voice in the ECB Governing Council. The banking union should also be made more attractive to join, for instance, by facilitating access to backstops and safety nets, albeit with commensurate contributions.

The role of the EU bodies should be reaffirmed when the banking union is established. Strengthening EU bodies will enhance the effectiveness of the banking union and reinforce the EU architecture. The EBA provides an avenue not only for protecting the interests of the "outs" but also for coordinating action and harmonizing rules (such a regulation and supervision) within the EU. In this regard, the EC proposal and EU Council agreement confirming the role of the EBA as the mediator of cross-border supervision and resolution issues and as the regulatory and supervisory standard-setter in the EU is helpful. Non-euro area EU members should retain an adequate voice within the EBA. The European agreement modified voting procedures within the EBA Board with double-majority voting to balance the interests of the "outs." It will be important that the EBA be an effective and credible force in the single financial market, including limit concerns about regulatory arbitrage. Likewise, the European Systemic Risk Board's role as the main macroprudential oversight body in the EU for banks and non-banks would need to be strengthened further. It should cooperate closely with the ECB, once the ECB takes on greater macroprudential responsibilities, but should also acquire independence.

Non-euro area countries are provided voice in the SSM. The SSM regulation agreed upon by the EU lawmakers provides a welcome opt-in for non-euro area EU countries, through representation and procedures on the supervisory board (since these members cannot be represented on the ECB's Governing Council). Draft decisions prepared by the supervisory board are deemed adopted, unless the

Governing Council objects within 10 days in normal times or two days in stressful ones. A mediation panel and a steering committee would also be created. These structures seek to aid decision-making and resolve disagreements and to reinforce cooperation between the ECB and national authorities. But it will also be important to ensure that the complexity of the setup does not undermine effective and prompt supervisory decision making.

Further steps will be needed to incentivize opt-ins and stabilize their participation in the banking union. Over time, some EU countries may want to be part of the banking union even if they do not join the euro area. A strong banking union that offers risk sharing (while avoiding the mutualization of legacy issues) and ensures least-cost bank resolution could be an attractive proposition for non-euro area countries as well. Moving supervision to the ECB could improve supervisory quality in some countries, reduce compliance costs for cross-border banks, limit scope for regulatory arbitrage, eliminate host-home coordination issues, and increase the congruence between the market for financial services and the underlying prudential framework. A single resolution authority and common safety nets, with backstops, would provide further benefits in terms of risk-sharing, when these are in place. But there are also drawbacks and complications, including the interaction of multiple central banks (with implications for the lender-of-last-resort function and the conduct of macroprudential policies), difficulties in ensuring adequate participation of the "opt-ins" in SSM decisions, a loss of sovereignty, and potentially less flexibility to deal with country specificities. These costs are likely to be less, especially for those whose currencies are pegged to the euro, or have high levels of foreign currency liabilities, or have a sizable presence of euro area banks in their financial systems. If these members adopt the euro at the same time as they join the banking union, the benefits would likely outweigh the costs, just as it does for euro area members currently.

REFERENCES

Agarwal, Sumit, Davind Lucca, Amit Seru, and Francesco Trebbi, 2012, "Inconsistent Regulators: Evidence from Banking," NBER Working Paper No. 17736 (Cambridge, MA: National Bureau of Economic Research).

Goyal, Rishi, Petya Koeva Brooks, Mahmood Pradhan, and others, 2013, "A Banking Union for the Euro Area," IMF Staff Discussion Note No. 13/1 (Washington: International Monetary Fund).

CHAPTER 10

Legal Underpinnings of an EU Banking Union

BAREND JANSEN, ALESSANDRO GULLO, AND NIKITA AGGARWAL

As we have discussed in earlier chapters of this book, fast and sustained progress toward a banking union is needed to anchor financial stability in the euro area.[1] The journey toward a banking union will be incremental and measures that have been taken to respond to the crisis in the short to medium term should be welcomed: crucial progress has been made to strengthen the framework for financial oversight. This chapter has a forward-looking approach, focusing, beyond the crisis and as the banking union will evolve over time, on the legal architecture that will be needed to support it.[2]

Crucial progress has been made to restore financial stability in the European Union (EU), including through establishing European Supervisory Authorities, setting up firewall mechanisms such as the European Stability Mechanism (ESM), and reaching an agreement in the EU Council to create a single supervisory mechanism (SSM), as well as on the EU bank recovery and resolution directive (BRRD). Other important contributions have been made, such as the EU Commission proposal for a Single Resolution Mechanism (SRM), that is envisaged to be established shortly after the SSM enters into force. This chapter seeks to look beyond the crisis and the necessary reforms that are being undertaken, by focusing on the legal underpinnings that would be needed in the longer term to support financial stability in the euro area and in those non-euro area members that would opt into the banking union, with positive spillovers to other EU member states.[3]

---

[1] The authors are grateful to Wouter Bossu, Atilla Arda, and Christophe Waerzeggers for their contributions to this chapter. Information provided in this chapter is as of July 3, 2013.

[2] See also IMF (2013); Goyal and others (2013); the 2012 and 2013 Staff Reports for the Article IV Consultation with the Euro Area; and Fonteyne and others (2010). See also related speeches by Fund management: "Completing the Task: Financial Sector Reform for Stability and Growth," address to the Annual Leaders' Dialogue Hosted by Süddeutsche Zeitung, by Christine Lagarde, June 8, 2012, http://www.imf.org/external/np/speeches/2012/060812a.htm; "Reviving Growth in Europe," by Nemat Shafik, Brussels Economic Forum, Brussels, May 31, 2012, http://www.imf.org/external/np/speeches/2012/053112.htm.

[3] Useful reference can be made to the SSM draft regulation, which includes a mechanism for opt-in through close cooperation with non-euro area member states. An alternative legal mechanism for joining the banking union could envisage the automatic buy-in of EU member states, save for those that wish to opt out when the fundamental features of the banking union are defined.

Thus, taking as a given that swift progress on the key elements of the banking union—in particular an SSM, an SRM, and a common backstop—is crucial for the resolution of the crisis, we describe the legal mechanisms and foundations that would strengthen the banking union over time and possible legal approaches that can be taken in its design. We discuss both what, in our view, can be achieved under the existing EU Treaties,[4] as well as the components of this architecture that would likely require Treaty change to strengthen their basis over time. As the evolution of the banking union will entail further transfer of powers and possibly competences from member states to the EU level, the essential elements of the banking union should be solidly anchored in the Treaties. This would ensure that all aspects of the banking union are comprehensively enshrined in EU law, similarly to the approach followed for other EU exclusive competences such as monetary union, competition and fisheries.

To this end, we assume, for the purposes of our analysis in this chapter, that there would be no obstacles to Treaty change in the long term, where this may be needed to build a more robust banking union. It is important to note that the discussion of a possible Treaty change should be viewed in the context of broader, more fundamental changes in the design of the EU, encompassing deeper fiscal integration and enhanced governance to underpin fiscal risk sharing, which would necessarily take place over a longer time horizon.

In this respect, depending on the specific features of the relevant changes, amendments to the Treaties may be made according to one of the two legal procedures provided under Article 48 of the TEU. The "ordinary revision" procedure must be used for any amendment that would increase or decrease the EU's competences and requires ratification by all member states "in accordance with their respective constitutional requirements." The "simplified revision" procedure can only be used for revisions to Part 3 of the TFEU (*inter alia*, this includes the provisions on economic and monetary policy), and cannot be used to increase the EU's competences; this requires approval by national parliaments in accordance with their respective constitutional requirements. Although the precise requirements of such "approval" are not specifically defined, some member states have elected to apply lighter approval requirements to amendments adopted under the simplified revision procedure.

This chapter is divided into sections on general legal considerations, as well as specific legal considerations relating to each of the components of the banking union.

GENERAL LEGAL CONSIDERATIONS

As discussed in Chapter 9, the essential elements of a banking union are: (1) an integrated supervisory framework, both from the standpoint of the underlying institutional arrangements (including the ECB as single supervisor) and of the

---

[4] The principal treaties governing the EU are the Treaty on European Union (TEU or the "Maastricht Treaty") and the Treaty on the Functioning of the European Union (TFEU) (and together with the TEU, "Treaties").

substantive law applicable in supervision; (2) an integrated resolution framework, based on a strong, centralized resolution authority with powers and tools aligned with international best practices; (3) a single, centralized deposit insurance and resolution fund, funded ex ante by the industry with an effective common fiscal backstop; and (4) a centralized "lender-of-last-resort" function at the level of the ECB for euro area member states. Among other core objectives of the banking union outlined in earlier chapters, these features seek to enhance financial stability by breaking the adverse link between banks and sovereigns, ensuring a systemic approach to supervision in the euro area and, to the maximum extent possible, enhancing the functioning of the EU single market in financial services. The fulfillment of these objectives must be based on sound and clear legal grounds, informed by the following overarching legal considerations:

- *First,* establishing an explicit, financial stability objective for the EU under the Treaties would underpin in the legal robustness of financial stability arrangements in the euro area, the member states that take part in the banking union, and in the EU as a whole. Such an objective could be inserted in Article 3 TEU. An explicit financial stability objective would further enhance the financial stability powers and tasks that are assigned to EU institutions and bodies, inform their actions in a crisis, and allow for coordination and conflict resolution mechanisms to be established among themselves and between the financial stability authorities of member states that are not part of the banking union, as well as third countries.[5] For instance, in a crisis this would ensure that the objective of restoring financial stability can more adequately be balanced against the objective of the EU to enhance competition in the financial sector.

- *Second,* as the banking union moves forward, there may be a greater centralization of competences and the further transfer of legal powers to the EU level. The Treaties set out an exhaustive list of the areas in which the EU has "exclusive competence" to legislate and adopt legally binding acts, which includes monetary policy.[6] On the other hand, areas of "shared competence" between member states and the EU include the common market and the free movement of services such as financial services (Articles 3 and 4 TFEU). Under the legal principle of conferral enshrined in the Treaties, competences not conferred upon the EU under the Treaties remain with the member states, and the EU must pursue its objectives by means commensurate with such competences.[7] Within areas of shared competences, both the EU and member states may legislate and adopt legally binding acts. The Treaties may

---

[5] For a related discussion on these aspects, see "Implementing Macroprudential Policy – Selected Legal Issues," IMF Board Paper, 2013.

[6] The EU has exclusive competences in the following areas only: (1) customs union; (2) competition rules for the functioning of the internal market; (3) euro area monetary policy; (4) conservation of marine biological resources under the common fisheries policy; and (5) common commercial policy (Article 3, TFEU).

[7] See Articles 3, 4, and 5 TEU.

set out the explicit powers of the EU, or provide for the further transfer of powers by member states to the EU—EU powers may also be implied from the explicit provisions of the Treaties. Indeed, under Article 127(6) TFEU, certain supervisory powers will be transferred by member states to the SSM.[8]

The use of powers in the areas of shared competences is governed by the legal principle of subsidiarity as a result of which the EU may only act "if and in so far as the objectives of the proposed action cannot be sufficiently achieved by EU member states, but can rather, by reason of the scale or effects of the proposed action, be better achieved at the EU level."[9] In the context of the evolution of the banking union over time, certain transfers of powers by member states to operationally autonomous EU-level bodies or EU institutions would need to be supported by an explicit Treaty basis, if such powers cannot be implied, for the latter to be able to take directly binding decisions with respect to entities within their scope. This includes, for example, the power to take final and directly binding decisions on third parties in the area of bank resolution. If, over time and as the banking union evolves, a decision were to be taken to give the EU exclusive competence for the banking sector for those member states participating in the banking union, so as to fully underpin in the Treaties the integrated framework of the banking union and similar to monetary policy, a Treaty change would be needed.

- *Third,* the democratic legitimacy of this enhanced EU decision-making framework must continue to be supported by robust transparency and accountability mechanisms, enshrined in EU law, including active scrutiny by the EU Parliament and a coherent system of checks and balances that avoids excessive concentration of legal powers in any one body.

- *Fourth,* a robust banking union requires a single, fully integrated legal framework encompassing all relevant areas of substantive law. Given the highly interconnected nature of EU financial markets, the legal framework for financial services can no longer operate effectively (and be backstopped financially) on a partially harmonized yet ultimately national basis. To create a level playing field and minimize the scope for divergence between member states participating in the banking union, the legal framework should be driven primarily by directly applicable EU regulations rather than directives.

- *Fifth,* it is important that all agencies making up the banking union are integrated into a coherent and comprehensive legal framework. In addition to an explicit, Treaty-based objective to contribute to financial stability, as discussed above, this framework should include legal obligations

---

[8] The SSM draft regulation is based on the premise that EU and member states will continue to share competences for financial services—however, with enhanced powers for the EU institutions (in this specific case, the ECB). EU institutions include the European Parliament; the European Council; the Council; the Commission; the European Court of Justice, the ECB; and the European Court of Auditors.

[9] See Article 5 TEU.

for information exchange, cooperation, prior consultation, and conflict resolution mechanisms between all relevant players. Cross-representation in the respective governance structures of the relevant agencies should also continue to play a positive role in this respect. In turn, building upon an explicit financial stability objective under the Treaties, this framework will need to coordinate with the relevant agencies in member states that are not part of the banking union, yet remain part of the EU single market, as well as with the existing framework for coordination under the European System of Financial Supervisors.

AN INTEGRATED SUPERVISORY FRAMEWORK

Legal and Institutional Arrangements for Centralized Supervision

Following the decision of the Eurogroup in June 2012 and the legislative proposal from the Commission in September 2012, the EU Council agreed in December 2012 on the design of the SSM.[10] This provides for the ECB to be tasked with carrying out certain supervisory tasks for the euro area and those EU members that opt into the SSM.[11] The agreement on the SSM, vesting supervisory responsibilities in the ECB, is a critically important step in moving toward an integrated financial oversight framework for the euro area.

The SSM is designed as a "hub and spoke" model under which the ECB and member states continue to share competences for financial supervision and regulation, on the basis of Article 127(6) TFEU under which the ECB can assume "specific tasks" relating to prudential supervision. The SSM, while centralizing a significant number of powers at the ECB level, hinges on a delicate division of responsibilities and shared competences between the ECB and national supervisors—hence the set-up of a "mechanism" which does not amount to the creation of a single supervisory authority and legally differs from the European System of Central Banks (ESCB) that is based upon the EU's exclusive competence in the area of monetary policy. For instance, national supervisors retain powers for a number of supervisory activities and will be formally in charge of taking supervisory decisions for "nonsignificant banks" (albeit upon ECB instructions).[12]

---

[10] Since the date of writing this chapter, the legislative package to set up the SSM has come into force, on October 29, 2013, following publication in the Official Journal (Council Regulation No. 1024/2013 of October 15, 2013 and Regulation of the Council and Parliament No. 1022/2013 of October 22, 2013).

[11] For a full description of the SSM, see Chapter 11.

[12] It should be noted that the existing European System of Financial Supervisors is based on a soft federal model; it facilitates the *coordination* of national supervisors and provides for certain dispute resolution mechanisms to eliminate national divergences in the application of EU law. However, there is no centralization of supervisory powers, which remain at the national level.

Over time, the legal design of the ECB supervisory framework could be further tailored to the requirements of common supervision and could address asymmetries between euro area and other EU member states. Under Article 14.3 of the ECB Statute, national central banks are an integral part of the ESCB, acting in accordance with the guidelines and instructions of the ECB. The SSM draws, and benefits, from such set-up, and the associated powers conferred to the ECB. However, the existing design of the ESCB may not permit the diversity of financial supervisory arrangements in EU member states to be fully reflected. Specifically, in countries with a "twin peaks" model of financial supervision, the heads of the national banking supervisors, not being central bank governors, cannot sit in the ECB Governing Council even where supervisory decisions alone are concerned.

In the medium term, a revision of the ECB's mandate through Treaty change may be warranted to reflect the specificities of its supervisory tasks, by inserting a chapter on supervision in the TFEU, alongside monetary policy, and including supervisory provisions in the ECB Statute. These provisions could also allow autonomous governance arrangements for supervision to be enshrined in the Treaties, with final and binding decision-making powers in the area of supervision that do not rely upon the ECB's Governing Council as the ultimate decision-making body. In this context, clarity could also be provided with respect to the interaction between the ECB's monetary mandate in the monetary union and its supervisory mandate in the banking union, while preserving robust mechanisms to exploit synergies and reconcile possible conflicts between the two mandates.[13]

A possible ultimate step may be the transfer of exclusive responsibilities for supervision to the EU level, with the ECB delegating certain powers and tasks to national supervisory authorities for the purposes of implementing supervisory measures, similar to the division of responsibilities in the area of monetary policy. This would be in line with the creation of a single resolution authority, discussed below.

Additional legal considerations are relevant for the design of the ECB's supervisory mandate. In particular, while certain features proposed by Fund staff may not require Treaty change (for example, having a stronger representation of independent experts or executives in the governing bodies), the implementation of certain other measures would appear to require a revision to the Treaties. This applies to the possible full representation of opt-in member states in the ECB and to possible leaner governance arrangements involving a higher degree of delegated responsibilities to internal decision-making bodies (see Chapter 11).

Single Supervisory Legal Regime

Under the SSM, the ECB will continue to rely on the existing supervisory legal frameworks and enforcement regimes, which are either unharmonized or, even when they are harmonized, are still subject to a significant degree of national discretion. This is the case, for instance, for nonpecuniary administrative

---

[13] See further Chapter 11 and Veron (2012).

sanctions, which are issued, upon ECB instruction, under national laws. As a result, while supervision will be more centralized, the substantive laws will still be subject to significant variation, depending on different national legal traditions, interpretations, and scope of discretion (see Ferran and Babis, 2013).

Achieving a more robust banking union calls at a minimum for continued progress in the efforts to harmonize financial legislation, including banking laws, across *all* EU member states, not only within the banking union, through the transposition of relevant legal instruments into national laws based on Article 114 of the TFEU. One approach to achieving greater harmonization, which would not require a Treaty change, would be based on adopting directly applicable EU regulations rather than directives, possibly complemented by the use of Article 127(6) TFEU in conjunction with Article 34 of the ESCB Statute to issue ECB Regulations that would further harmonize banking rules.[14] This would lead to the creation of an all-encompassing "Single Rulebook" that includes but is broader than the harmonization of certain prudential standards currently envisaged under CRR/CRDIV.

COMMON FINANCIAL SAFETY NETS

Single Resolution Authority

As of July 2013, the Commission has issued a proposal for an SRM for the banking union. This would establish a "resolution board," comprised of representatives from national resolution authorities, the ECB, and the Commission, that would make a recommendation to the Commission to decide on a bank resolution. The recent Commission proposal on the establishment of an SRM, based on Article 114 of the TFEU, gives directly binding powers to the Commission, while the resolution board is in charge of a number of preparatory and implementation tasks. In the memo accompanying the proposal, the Commission explains that only an EU institution (such as the Commission) and not an agency (such as, for instance, the European Banking Authority) can assume these powers. The Council legal services issued an opinion (14547/13 of October 7, 2013) stating that powers can be delegated to the resolution board as long as it will not have a wide margin of discretion within the meaning of the so-called Meroni case law. The draft BRRD, which would harmonize resolution laws in EU member states, was proposed by the Commission in June 2012 and is currently passing through the EU legislative process: the EU Council has agreed on a general approach and has called on the Council Presidency to start negotiations with the European Parliament with the aim of adopting the BRRD before the end of 2013. A draft EU directive that would further harmonize deposit insurance schemes is also under consideration. These measures are welcome progress in the journey toward establishing the banking union.

---

[14] The latter would need to be coordinated with the role of the European Banking Authority as an EU-wide standard setter.

In principle, elements of an effective safety net can be designed on the basis of the current Treaties, notably Article 114 TFEU. This may include a harmonized legal framework for resolution, and measures to further coordinate national resolution authorities. Article 114 permits the EU to take measures for the harmonization of national laws, regulations or administrative actions which have as their object the establishment and functioning of the internal market. Measures taken pursuant to Article 114 must aim therefore to remove obstacles for the functioning of the internal market due to divergence of national rules and practices. Article 114 TFEU has been used to establish agencies, including EU supervisory agencies such as the European Banking Authority, as well as directly applicable EU financial services rules. Indeed, the proposed BRRD is based on Article 114.[15]

Other legal approaches may also be examined to set up an effective safety net under the current Treaties. One possibility would be to consider the application of Article 352 TFEU, which permits action by the EU to attain the objectives of the Treaties where the latter have not provided the necessary powers. Although broadly worded, the scope of action under Article 352 is carefully circumscribed by the Treaties and jurisprudence of the Court of Justice of the European Union (CJEU). Another option arises under Article 20 TEU, by which nine or more EU member states may establish enhanced cooperation between themselves in areas of shared competence of the EU to further the objectives of the Union, protect its interests, and reinforce its integration process. The feasibility of this legal avenue would depend on the extent to which enhanced cooperation does not undermine the internal market or economic, social, and territorial cohesion of the EU.

In the longer term, a Single Resolution Authority (SRA) for the banking union could be established as a supranational EU institution, which, unlike the proposed resolution board, would be operationally independent from the executive arm of the EU. Such an institution would also need adequate accountability and a strong central governance structure (see Chapter 12). As envisaged for the ECB's supervisory mandate, legal mechanisms, enshrined in the Treaty, for coordination with EU member states not participating in the banking union and therefore not joining the SRA could be established. The SRA would be subject to checks and balances, as well as adequate mechanisms for coordination and information sharing with the ECB *qua* supervisor, enshrined in the EU legal framework. The resolution framework would need to be administrative instead of court driven, with the possibility for ex post judicial review by the CJEU on the legality of the SRA's decisions.

A strong and autonomous SRA along these lines would need to exercise broad and discretionary powers directly binding on third parties, with ultimate

---

[15] Since the date of writing this chapter, two legal opinions have been issued by the Council legal services and the ECJ Advocate General, respectively, relating to the interpretation of Article 114 TFEU. The Council opinion, relating to the SRM (14547/13 of October 7, 2013) is broadly supportive of the use of Article 114 as the legal basis for the SRM and a resolution fund, provided that adequate safeguards for national budgetary sovereignty are introduced. The AG opinion, relating to EU short-selling rates (Case 270/12, September 12, 2013), casts doubt on the use of Article 114 to replace national decision making with EU-level decision making.

decision-making authority on the distribution of costs in a bank failure. To the extent that such powers cannot be exercised by the SRA on the basis of Article 114, or other existing provisions of the Treaties, they may require an explicit basis to be established in the Treaties. Whether the existing Treaties provide such a basis is a matter for determination by the CJEU. However, it is important for the legitimacy of such binding powers that they are underpinned by a sound legal basis under the Treaties, as well as in order to mitigate litigation risks; moreover, this would ensure a consistent legal approach toward supervisory, monetary and resolution powers under the Treaties.

The tasks of the SRA would also have to be coherently integrated into the overall EU institutional architecture; in particular, the interaction with the Commission as guardian of state aid rules merits careful consideration.[16] In principle, the SRA should be able to take resolution decisions that affect financial stability, while the Commission's remit, focused on the longer-term goal of competition, would concern single market issues when state aid is involved. In any event, clear roles and responsibilities, and conflict resolution mechanisms to speedily resolve any possible divergences, would be essential.

Single Resolution Legal Regime

As noted at the outset, a fully harmonized legal framework for resolution in the EU should be primarily regulation-based in order to minimize variations between member states. This framework may be achieved within the scope of Article 114 TFEU, on the grounds that diverging national bank resolution rules are deemed to constitute an obstacle to the internal market. As noted, Article 114 is the legal basis for the proposed BRRD.[17] However, a regulation-driven framework would entail going beyond the BRRD. The envisaged resolution framework in a more robust banking union would best be supported by an explicit basis in the Treaties, to provide a strong financial stability objective for the EU and to establish an autonomous SRA.

In the implementation of the resolution framework in a more robust banking union, possible asymmetries may still result from the decision of certain EU member states not to join the banking union. These may be mitigated through legally binding ex ante burden-sharing agreements to allocate the net costs of resolution among EU member states. Forms of cooperation may be enhanced through progress on resolution planning and resolvability assessments, governing orderly resolution in a manner that can preserve, to the maximum extent possible, financial stability in the EU. Lastly, a financial stability objective under the Treaties would inform the action of key players, including central banks, the SRA, and national resolution authorities, in response to a crisis.

---

[16] For a discussion on the role of the Commission in resolution, see also Dewatripont and others (2010).

[17] See Chapter 12 for further discussion of the existing proposal, and the requirements for an effective resolution regime reflecting emerging international best practice.

Single Deposit Insurance Scheme and Resolution Fund

In order to effectively break the bank–sovereign nexus, and to level the playing field between member states, the existing arrangements for resolution and deposit insurance funding, which continue to be predominantly nationally based, would in a more robust banking union be replaced by a supranational EU deposit insurance and resolution fund, with a common fiscal backstop.[18] The deposit insurance fund could be combined with the resolution fund, as a "European Deposit Insurance and Resolution Fund" (EDIRF), and managed by the SRA, acting as both the deposit insurance and resolution authority.

A framework combining such privately financed arrangements with certain forms of common fiscal backstop discussed below will likely require an explicit legal basis in the Treaties. The framework for privately financed resolution should be developed through regulations rather than directives in order to minimize the scope for variation between member states. The legal framework should also set out a clear legal mandate for the SRA to act as deposit insurance agency, which should be clearly distinguished from its function as resolution authority and subject to tailored legal constraints.[19]

Crucial legal issues arise in relation to the design of the funding mechanism for a common safety net, in particular: (1) mechanisms for raising funds ex ante and ex post; and (2) the common fiscal backstop to provide funding in a systemic crisis.

Ex Ante and Ex Post Funding

The traditional mechanisms for funding deposit insurance at the national level give rise to new legal considerations when applied at the EU level. In particular, in order to apply a levy on scheme members for the purposes of both ex ante and ex post funding, the EDIRF would need to be empowered with fund-raising powers vis-à-vis financial institutions, either directly or indirectly.

The EU does not appear to have direct taxation authority. It could however harmonize national turnover taxes, excise duties, and other forms of indirect taxation of the industry pursuant to Article 113 TFEU, and channel some of the revenue to the EU budget pursuant to Article 311 TFEU, as the EU did with VAT and as it intends to do with the financial transactions tax. A similar mechanism could be designed to fund the EDIRF. The question arises as to whether, under the current Treaty, Article 114 provides a sound legal basis for the enactment of a directly applicable EU regulation, under which national deposit guarantee schemes would be required to channel premiums paid by the industry to the EDIRF. Premiums would in turn be pooled and used to finance the resolution of EU banks, in the interest of financial stability. The argument in favor of using Article 114 hinges on the goal of harmonizing national resolution and deposit insurance regimes, in view of preserving the cohesion of the single market, of which financial stability is viewed as a precondition.

---

[18] See Chapter 12 for additional discussion.
[19] See further Chapter 12.

Common Fiscal Backstop

In order to break the sovereign–bank nexus and in view of the objectives of banking union, the EDIRF should be supported by a common government backstop that is not reliant upon the fiscal capacity of individual member states, subject to adequate safeguards to mitigate moral hazard.[20] As discussed in Chapter 12, the most feasible legal design for a common backstop appears to be an ECB liquidity line to the SRA, backed by fiscal resources (which could be provided through the ESM or a form of tax levied at the euro area level); this could be combined with the issuance of SRA bonds. The SRA would ultimately be guaranteed by a fiscal backstop from member states.

The design of the fiscal backstop may take various legal forms and would need to be carefully assessed in light of Article 125 TFEU, the "no bailout" rule. Based on the ECJ's judgment in *Pringle v Ireland*,[21] Article 125 would currently prevent member states from assuming the obligations of other member states in the sense of a "joint and several" guarantee;[22] however, it would not be breached by a "multiple and several" guarantee from member states (for example, under the ESM). Thus, it is possible to imagine a guarantee for the purposes of the common fiscal backstop that operates in a manner similar to the ESM, whereby the commitments of each member state are limited by a pre-agreed contribution key. Under this arrangement, the backstop would function as a loan from member states, to be repaid ex post by the beneficiary member state including through levies on the industry.

Centralized Lender-of-Last-Resort

The logic of an optimal banking union necessarily entails centralized lender-of-last-resort responsibilities at the euro area level. Under the current approach, member states are exposed to potential losses arising through the provision of emergency liquidity assistance by national central banks. In order to sever the sovereign-bank nexus, emergency liquidity assistance lending within the euro area should shift from national central banks to the ECB, in order to transfer emergency liquidity assistance risk to the euro system as a whole. This raises various legal issues:

- From a strictly legal perspective, it could be argued that the ECB could provide emergency liquidity assistance under the current Treaty based on Article 18 of the ESCB Statute in case this is required to safeguard monetary stability within the euro area. A special emergency liquidity assistance collateral regime would probably also have to be put in place as the relevant banks under such circumstances are not likely to be in a position to borrow on regular terms from the ECB.

---

[20] See further Chapter 12.

[21] *Thomas Pringle v Government of Ireland* Case C-370/12 [2012] ECR I-000.

[22] Under a "joint and several," or unlimited, guarantee, each member state would be individually liable for the total guaranteed amount. By contrast, under a "multiple and several," or limited, guarantee, each member state would be liable only for its share of the total guarantee commitments, as specified.

- However, under the current Treaties the ECB cannot provide emergency liquidity assistance on financial stability grounds only. Also for that reason a financial stability anchor in the Treaties, and possibly in the ESCB Statute, is recommended.

- Still, the question arises as to the possible losses for the emergency liquidity assistance provided by the ECB. The current arrangements for loss-sharing within the ESCB are strictly designed for monetary purposes and losses of the ECB are finally allocated to the national central banks of the euro area in proportion to their paid-up shares in the capital of the ECB. Alternative legal mechanisms, such as an additional, precommitted fiscal backstop, would need to be established in the ESCB Statute.

CONCLUSIONS

Taking as a given that swift progress on the core elements of the banking union is crucial for the resolution of the crisis, this chapter has adopted a forward-looking approach, focusing, beyond the crisis, on the legal mechanisms and foundations that would strengthen the banking union over time and possible legal approaches that can be taken in its design.

We have identified certain overarching legal considerations that should inform the journey toward a more robust banking union, namely: an explicit, financial stability objective for the EU under the Treaties; greater centralization of legal powers and possibly competences at the EU level; a single, fully integrated legal framework encompassing all relevant areas of substantive law; and integration of all agencies making up the banking union into a coherent and comprehensive legal framework.

Acknowledging the significant progress made by current legislative proposals, we have also identified specific legal considerations relating to each component of the banking union in the longer term. Over time, the ECB supervisory mandate could be more specifically tailored to the requirements of common supervision, with corresponding governance arrangements legally separate from its monetary function. Resolution powers would be centralized in a supranational and autonomous EU institution acting as a single resolution authority. Banking legislation, including resolution laws, would be further harmonized through the adoption of directly applicable regulations under an all-encompassing Single Rulebook. Deposit insurance and resolution could be funded through fees on the industry at the EU level, and in a systemic crisis, a fiscal backstop from member states, possibly structured along the lines of the ESM. The centralization of lender-of-last-resort functions at the ECB would require a clear EU financial stability objective.

In some cases, these considerations entail the transfer of powers and possibly competences from member states to the EU. Although the full spectrum of this transfer would likely require Treaty change in the longer term, such changes would necessarily take place as part of a broader, more fundamental shift in the design of the EU over time, involving deeper fiscal and political integration between member states.

REFERENCES

Dewatripont, Mathias, Gregory Nguyen, Peter Praet, and André Sapir, 2010, "The Role of State Aid Control in Improving Bank Resolution in Europe," Bruegel Policy Contribution 2010/04 (Brussels).

Ferran, E., and V. Babis, 2013, "The European Single Supervisory Mechanism," University of Cambridge Faculty of Law Legal Studies (March).

Fonteyne, Wim, Wouter Bossu, Luis Cortavarria, Alessandro Giustiniani, Alessandro Gullo, Daniel C. L. Hardy, and Sean Kerr, 2010, "Crisis Management and Resolution for a European Banking System," IMF Working Paper 10/70 (Washington: International Monetary Fund).

Goyal, Rishi, and others, 2013, "A Banking Union for the Euro Area," IMF Staff Discussion Note No. 13/1 (Washington: International Monetary Fund).

International Monetary Fund, 2013, "European Union: Financial System Stability Assessment," IMF Staff Country Report No. 13/75 (Washington).

Veron, N, 2012, *Europe's Single Supervisory Mechanism and the Long Journey towards Banking Union* (Washington: Peterson Institute for International Economics.

CHAPTER 11

The Single Supervisory Mechanism

THIERRY TRESSEL

While the single market for financial services created dense interconnections of cross-border banking activities and obligations, the supervisory architecture remained mostly national before the 2008 crisis. Minimum harmonization of regulations and supervisory principles in the European Union (EU) was guided by the internationally agreed standards set by the Basel Committee on Banking Supervision in its Core Principles for Effective Banking Supervision, and implemented through EU directives. Supervisory handbooks and practices varied across the euro area countries, reflecting among other things different market structures, underlying laws, taxes, and accounting rules. The European Banking Authority, established at the start of 2011 following a recommendation of the De Larosiere High Level Group, was set up as a cooperative body to enable EU bank supervisors to coordinate the supervision of cross-border banks in the European Union; it contributed to harmonizing the regulatory and supervisory standard settings of the European Union, but it lacked power to enforce decisions.

The crisis uncovered a clear drawback of having a national approach to supervision in an integrated financial system. National authorities may unduly favor their own national banking system and economy, regardless of outward spillovers that lie beyond their mandates. In good times, national authorities may not be stringent or capable enough to limit the buildup of excesses. In bad times, they may encourage reductions in cross-border activities by their banks and the ring-fencing of liquidity, exacerbating financial fragmentation. Delays in resolving stresses would only exacerbate the eventual cost of crisis resolution. And because a bank's distress can have adverse cross-border externalities, other countries may have no choice but to support those whose banking systems run into trouble.

The establishment of the Single Supervisory Mechanism (SSM), which is a precondition for the possibility of direct recapitalization of banks by the European Stability Mechanism (ESM), will help correct some of these above-mentioned cross-border distortions for the countries belonging to the banking union. It will also bring about uniformly high standards of supervision. The next section of this paper describes the regulation agreed by the European Union to establish the SSM.

This chapter draws on the European Union Financial Sector Assessment Program (IMF, 2013), Goyal and others (2013), and the accompanying technical background note on the single supervisory mechanism. The contributions of the various authors are gratefully acknowledged.

That is followed by a discussion of the principles for setting up the SSM. The next-to-last section identifies the main risks in the transition toward the banking union, and the final section discusses risk mitigation measures.

THE SINGLE SUPERVISORY MECHANISM REGULATION

Initial Proposal

The European Commission published a draft regulation on September 12, 2012, conferring supervisory tasks on the European Central Bank (ECB) as part of a roadmap toward establishing a banking union. The tripartite agreement on the SSM regulation was reached on March 19, 2013, and the roadmap agreed upon by the EU Council in December 2012 was reaffirmed. The legislation is based on Article 127(6) of the European System of Central Banks/ECB statute and provides a clear mandate and broad powers to the ECB to perform supervision of all euro area banks. While the ECB may start carrying out supervisory tasks on any institution from adoption of the SSM regulation on September 10, 2013, the draft regulation proposes that banks receiving or requesting public financial assistance would be targeted first. Systemically important banks were to be subject to ECB supervisory activities from July 2013, and from January 2014 all other credit institutions were.[1] Agreement on the SSM regulation by the European Parliament (EP) was reached on September 12, 2013, after transparency and accountability requirements were strengthened, and at the Council on October 15, 2013.

Main Elements

The regulation, which provides clear tasks and strong supervisory powers to the ECB, covers all credit institutions authorized in the euro area. The main elements are the following.

Risk-Based Approach

The transition is rapid, sequenced in a pragmatic manner, with a focus first on banks requiring public support, then on systemic banks. The SSM will come into operation one year after the legislation enters into force or when the ECB considers itself ready, whichever is later, after a comprehensive assessment of euro area banks is completed. The December 2012 EU Council agreement provided

---

[1] These dates have subsequently been pushed back. The October 18–19, 2012, European Council meeting called for agreeing on the legislative framework by the start of 2013, with the effective operation of the SSM in the course of 2013. The draft of the regulation, agreed upon by EU leaders on December 13, 2012, calls for entry into force of the SSM regulation on March 1, 2013, while the Council conclusions postpone the adoption of the other EU draft legislation. The SSM regulation was adopted by the European Parliament on September 12, 2013, after transparency and accountability requirements were strengthened, and by the Council on October 15, 2013. The regulation was published in the Official Journal of the EU on October 29, 2013, and the ECB will be declared effective one year later or when the ECB declares itself ready.

that when the ESM requests the ECB to take over direct supervision of a credit institution as precondition for direct recapitalization, the ECB may immediately assume its supervisory duties concerning this bank, regardless of the starting date of the SSM. On October 23, 2013, the ECB announced key features of the comprehensive assessment of the banking system, which will be concluded prior to assuming supervisory tasks in November 2014.

Coverage

The SSM would cover all credit institutions established in participating countries, although most tasks related to the supervision of those institutions considered "less significant" would normally be carried out by the national authorities. The criteria under which banks would be under the direct supervision of the ECB include size, importance to the economy of the European Union or of a member state, and significance of cross-border activities.[2] The ECB appropriately retains the power to bring any bank under its direct supervision, if it deems necessary.

Mandate

The ECB is provided with a clear mandate for bank safety and soundness and financial stability.

Tasks and Powers

The ECB is provided with broad powers that are available to competent supervisory authorities under EU legislation. Broad investigatory and supervisory powers include enforcing compliance with prudential norms regarding its own funds, large exposure limits, liquidity requirements, leverage, disclosure requirements, licensing and withdrawal of authorization, assessing mergers and acquisitions, performing on-site inspections, requesting all necessary information, carrying out stress tests and assessment for public recapitalization, imposing macroprudential (capital and liquidity) buffers, conducting consolidated supervision and supervision of financial holding companies, carrying out early intervention tasks in relation to the listed prudential requirements, and assessing governance and internal capital adequacy processes.

Operational arrangements now need to be specified. These must ensure an adequate division of labor between national authorities and the ECB, make incentives compatible, and provide for appropriate information sharing within the SSM to underpin effective supervisory decision making at the supervisory board. The ECB is to adopt a detailed framework for the practical modalities of supervisory cooperation within the SSM.

---

[2] Under the criteria specified in Article 5(4) of the Council agreement of the regulation, banks accounting for about 80 percent of euro area banking assets would be under the direct supervision of the ECB. A bank would be under the direct supervision of the ECB if any one of the following conditions were met: (1) assets exceeded €30 billion; (2) the ratio of total assets to GDP of the home member state exceeded 20 percent; or (3) national competent authorities considered the institution to be significant. An institution could also be considered as significant by the ECB if it had significant cross-border assets or liabilities, relied upon ESM financial assistance, or was among the three largest institutions in the home member state (to ensure direct supervision of banks of smaller countries).

Other EU Countries and Institutions

Nonparticipating member states will be able to enter into close cooperation with the ECB, under the condition that the national authority will abide by ECB guidelines and requests and provide all necessary information that the ECB may require. The ECB is tasked to coordinate and express a common position of euro area national supervisors at the Board of Supervisors and with the management of the European Banking Authority for issues relating to the supervisory tasks conferred on the ECB.

Governance

A Supervisory Board (aided by a Steering Committee) will be created to achieve appropriate governance and facilitate timely supervisory decision making by, or subject to the oversight and responsibility of, the Governing Council. The council agreement strengthened the governance arrangements relative to the European Commission proposal, reflecting concerns related to the separation between monetary policy and supervision (to minimize conflicts of interest between the two functions) and to ensure that non-euro area countries have a voice in the SSM (since non-euro area "opt-ins" cannot be represented on the ECB's Governing Council). Strict differentiation between monetary policy and supervision will apply, including by strengthening the power of the supervisory board with a complex voting procedure that ensures representation of the non-euro area members.

Draft decisions of the Supervisory Board will follow a "silent procedure," that is, they will be deemed adopted unless the Governing Council objects within a short period (10 days in normal times, and two days in stressful times). A mediation panel and a Steering Committee are to be created to help resolve disagreements and aid decisions. In practice, it will be important to balance the representation of national interests and public officials from the ECB in the governance structure of the SSM. It will also be important to ensure that the complexity of the set-up does not undermine effective and prompt supervisory decision making.

Accountability

The Governing Council, and in particular the chair of the supervisory board, is accountable to the Eurogroup and the European Parliament, among other things through an annual report on the execution of the ECB's supervisory tasks and the transparency of its supervisory budget. The European Parliament added transparency and accountability requirements stipulated in an Inter-institutional Agreement between the ECB and the EP. These will include, in particular, providing the ECON committee of the EP with comprehensive and meaningful records of the proceedings of the Supervisory Board to enable an understanding of the discussions, including an annotated list of decisions. Moreover, the ECB is subject to internal and external audits, also by the European Union Court of Auditors, and judicial scrutiny by the European Union Court of Justice. Both the ECB and the national authorities are responsible for the banks under their direct supervision, although the ECB is responsible for the effective and consistent functioning of the SSM.

Role of National Authorities

National authorities will prepare and implement ECB acts under the oversight of the ECB, perform day-to-day supervision activities, and directly supervise banks not classified as "significant." They will remain exclusively responsible for consumer protection and anti-money laundering tasks, receiving notifications from credit institutions related to the right of establishment, supervising the activities of the branches of third countries' credit institutions, and supervising payments services.

Macroprudential Policies

The ECB will be able to impose capital buffers, such as a countercyclical capital buffer, in addition to capital requirements and any other measures aimed at addressing systemic or macroprudential risks as specified in EU acts, such as the legislative package that yielded the Fourth Capital Requirement Directive and Capital Requirement Regulation. The Council agreement provided both national authorities and the ECB with powers to make use of macroprudential instruments, in close collaboration with each other, and included specific reporting to national parliaments to strengthen accountability. But the ECB powers are limited to those specified in the relevant EU directives. Either party that takes such a step needs to inform and hear the other party ahead of time. In practice, cooperation will be critical to ensure the coherence and effectiveness of measures.

Resources

Supervision could be financed partly by risk-based levies on credit institutions.

Assessment

There are many positive aspects to the regulation, which mentions all the elements necessary to make the SSM effective. Among these elements is the allowance that the ESM can request the ECB to take over direct supervision of a credit institution as a precondition for direct recapitalization, regardless of the starting date of the SSM— direct bank recapitalization by the ESM is critical for stabilization in the near term.[3] This ambitious though risk-based approach will require rapidly putting into place the resources and frameworks needed for effectiveness. The proposal specifies a clear mandate and accountability of the ECB and appropriately confers upon it broad investigatory and supervisory powers. Moreover, the proposed fast adoption (by June 2013) of the draft directives on regulation—the Deposit Guarantee Schemes and Bank Recovery and Resolution—was a welcome step.[4] The call for a single resolution mechanism is welcome, including the need for appropriate and explicit backstops.[5]

---

[3] The requirement for the SSM to be in place before direct recapitalization by the ESM is permitted was initially set out in the statement of euro area leaders at the European Union Summit of June 2012.

[4] The target was met for the Fourth Capital Requirement Directive and the Capital Requirement Regulation, and agreement on the BRRD was also reached at the Council in June 2013, with the view of having adoption of both the BRRD and Deposit Guarantee Schemes Directive at the European Parliament by end-2013.

[5] The European Council's conclusions of June 27–28, 2013, reiterated the importance of an SRM to ensure effectiveness of the SSM.

Greater Clarity Needed

However, further clarity is needed on a number of matters, including how the delegation of supervisory tasks and the associated control will be realized in practice. Greater clarity is also needed concerning macroprudential oversight, the powers to assume national discretion as defined in the Capital Requirement Regulation, the allocation of powers to intervene and to enforce administrative sanctions and trigger resolutions (alongside a single resolution authority to be established), home-host supervisory arrangements for non-EU banks, and the interaction with the European Banking Authority. While Article 127(6) ESCB/ECB Statute allows the European Union to confer some supervisory tasks on the ECB, strengthening the legal basis of the new framework with a view to minimizing litigation risk may require changes to the Treaty on the Functioning of the European Union—hereafter the EU Treaty—over time.[6]

The regulation could risk becoming an incomplete framework. While it sketches a process for swiftly implementing an SSM, it lacks a roadmap for reaching a common safety net, which will be essential for depositor confidence and to weaken the sovereign–bank links.

Moreover, greater clarity in the agreement would be useful to specify how and when a single resolution authority (essential to complement the SSM) could be established, as it would be conditional on the adoption of the directives on deposit guarantee schemes (DGS Directive) and bank recovery and resolution (BRRD). In that respect, the European Commission proposal for an SRM, published on July 10, 2013, is a welcome step forward, but there are areas of concern and hurdles are significant (see Chapter 12).

Clarity is also needed to know whether the implementation of an SSM would require changes in national legislation, including banking laws.

PRINCIPLES FOR THE DESIGN OF A SINGLE SUPERVISORY MECHANISM

Cross-Country Lessons

In federations such as the United States and Canada, banking supervision, safety nets, and resolution are all established at the federal or central level.[7] Different models of organization may be chosen, whether delegation or full centralization.

---

[6] In particular, the legality of the legal instrument establishing the SSM and its decisions could be challenged before the European Union Court of Justice by EU institutions (including the European Parliament), member states, and any private person or entity affected by SSM decisions. See Chapter 10 for a detailed discussion of legal considerations.

[7] For example, there is more than one banking supervisory agency in the United States. While the Federal Reserve has a range of supervisory responsibilities, including supervising bank holding companies, and must coordinate with the Financial Stability Oversight Council for systemic issues, it shares supervisory and regulatory responsibilities for domestic banking institutions with the Office of the Comptroller of the Currency (OCC), the Federal Deposit Insurance Corporation (FDIC), and the Office of Thrift Supervision (OTS) at the federal level, and with the banking departments of the various states.

The Board of Governors of the U.S. Federal Reserve, for example, delegates supervisory tasks to regional reserve banks, with strong internal governance mechanisms, while the Federal Deposit Insurance Corporation (FDIC), a supervisory and resolution authority in the United States, operates as a fully centralized body. The experience of the United States and Canada demonstrates that supervision and resolution functions can be centralized in a monetary union. It also suggests the clear benefits of having in place mechanisms to ensure effective coordination and information flows between sister agencies (including between regulators and the resolution agency), the benefits of creating overlaps rather than living with gaps, the need for strong corrective action mechanisms and early intervention, and the value of having horizontal checks and balances between sister supervisory bodies.

International Standards

The "Core Principles for Effective Supervision" or Basel Core Principles (BCPs)[8] issued by the Basel Committee on Banking Supervision are the accepted minimum standards for sound practices in prudential bank regulation and supervision. These principles provide guidance for designing and assessing the new SSM for the euro area.

Other Considerations

Designing an effective supervisory mechanism for the euro area has added complications. The ECB will be formally accountable for supervision but will have to rely on competencies and resources at the national level. This is not just because of resource constraints in the near term, but also differences in legal, accounting and tax frameworks, as well as differing local language, business and supervisory cultures, and local knowledge and relationships that are important to assess bank activities. In such an environment, the center will need to delegate, but also monitor supervisory operations to contain reputational risks. The design of this interaction between the center and national authorities, of the decentralization and delegation of tasks, and the allocation of powers between the two levels will play a key role in achieving effective supervision.

Preconditions and Prerequisites

Preconditions

According to the BCPs, a number of preconditions for sound banking supervision must be met in the longer term. A clear framework for financial stability policy must be in place, one that includes the provision of strong macroprudential oversight and, for the sake of crisis management and resolution, the provision of ways to deal effectively with bank failure and minimize disruptions. An appropriate common safety net is essential to deal with risks to confidence in the financial

---

[8] See "Core Principles for Effective Banking Supervision," dated September 2012, available at the website of the Bank for International Settlements, at https://www.bis.org/publ/bcbs230.htm.

system and contagion to sound banks while minimizing distortions.[9] Some preconditions are beyond the jurisdiction of supervisors, and some elements are not yet in place at the euro area level. For example, resolution regimes (and safety nets) remain national, and in most countries they need to be strengthened to be aligned with the Financial Stability Board's "Key Attributes for Effective Resolution."[10]

Prerequisites

A set of prerequisites is essential to establish a sound basis for the SSM. The supervisory mechanism should have operational independence consistent with its statutory responsibilities, legal protection for its supervisors, transparent processes, sound governance, and adequate resources, and it should be accountable for the discharge of its duties. Among these, the following considerations are noteworthy.

- *Objectives and mandates.* As supervisor, the ECB should ensure the safety and soundness of credit institutions, while adopting a systemic approach to financial stability that helps preserve the integrity of the single market for financial services. Under the EU Treaty, the primary objective of the ECB is price stability, and its secondary objective is to support the general economic policy objectives of the European Union, such as a high level of employment and sustainable and non-inflationary growth. Involving the ECB in supervision will give it access to supervisory information in support of its monetary policy and lender-of-last-resort functions and will also provide the ECB with more information to separate illiquid from insolvent banks. Housing both supervision and monetary policy under one roof can also lead to difficult choices when monetary policy decisions impact the soundness of important banks. Therefore, a revision of ECB objectives through EU Treaty changes may be warranted to provide greater clarity with respect to the interaction between the ECB's monetary mandate in the monetary union and its supervisory mandate in the banking union. It may also be warranted to explicitly specify that the ECB's supervisory mandate includes financial stability and macroprudential oversight.

- *Operational independence and legal protection.* Operational independence regarding the ECB's supervisory mandate derives legally from the ECB/ESCB statutes. But bringing supervision under the umbrella of the ECB creates risks to the ECB's independence (and hard-won reputation), given the added potential for political interference. Modifications to the Treaties should be considered to safeguard the ECB's independence in its supervisory mandate as well and to strengthen legal protections for supervisors.

- *Governance.* The Governing Council is the decision-making body of the ECB, and is responsible for supervisory tasks according to Article 127(6) of the EU Treaty. Sound governance will be crucial to ensure early identification

---

[9] The BCP preconditions for effective supervision also include the implementation of coherent and sustainable macroeconomic policies and a well-developed public infrastructure and effective market discipline.
[10] "Key Attributes of Effective Resolution Regimes for Financial Institutions", Financial Stability Board, October 2011. See: http://www.financialstabilityboard.org/.

of risks and timely and effective decision making in the interest of the whole banking union (and not of individual countries). Because supervisory decisions have distributive implications, the decision making body may have to adopt a mechanism that protects effective and timely decision-making (e.g., to ensure the "will to act").

- A one-member-one-vote rule would ensure that regional interests are better accounted for and would provide a balance to large countries' influence. On the other hand, allocating voting rights based on economic size would align countries' rights with the relative importance of their economies. A balance between the two could be considered (perhaps a uniform set of basic votes, combined with voting rights relative to economic size). Consideration should be given to providing voting rights to non-euro area members that join the supervisory mechanism.

- Robust firewalls between monetary policy and supervision would protect the independence and credibility of each function of the ECB, ensure the confidentiality of supervisory information, and help limit potential conflicts of interest while ensuring that synergies between the two functions are exploited. (Conflicts of interest may arise when interest rate policies impact weak banks, or when the lender-of-last-resort function safeguards financial stability but risks lending to insolvent banks). In the United Kingdom, for example, the supervisory function is being established as a subsidiary of the central bank.

- One way to ensure swift decision making based on delegation is to establish a Supervisory Board within the ECB, assisted by a Steering Committee and a Supervisory Department, which could be given supervisory tasks and related decisions (as under the European Union regulation establishing the SSM). Under this model, which was agreed to by the European Union Council in December 2012, monetary policy and supervision decisions would be reconciled at the Governing Council. Alternatively, a separate body from the Governing Council could be established to provide stronger firewalls and ensure full representation of non-euro area countries. However, establishing a separate body in this way could make coordination and synergies more complex to achieve, could be legally complex to establish, and would require a change to the EU Treaty.

- Additional considerations relate to the delegation of supervisory tasks to national authorities and the need to establish clear chains of command and adequate incentives.

- *Accountability*. Independence must be complemented with accountability to European citizens. Pursuant to the EU Treaty, the ECB's standard monetary policy reporting is addressed to the European Parliament, the European Union Council, the European Commission, and the European Council. Given the fiscal implications of supervision, stronger (such as more frequent) reporting to the European Parliament and to the euro-group could be envisaged for the supervisory function. The EU regulation establishing the SSM also added accountability to national parliaments.

- *Resources*. Any supervisor needs secure and adequate funding. Pragmatism will need to govern decisions related to funding and implementation, both in the near term and in the steady state, but the resources obtained should allow the ECB to build adequate capacity while protecting it from influence by national authorities or the industries. In particular, the ECB will need to establish highly trained and independent staff at the center, including but not only from national authorities, to be able to directly supervise a subset of banks (including globally systemic banks). In this regard, the challenge of developing the requisite competence at the ECB and building credibility in supervision should not be underestimated. At the same time, national supervisors must retain sufficient resources to perform their tasks. Funding models could consider combinations of industry levies (based on the size and the risk profile of supervised banks) and central bank support (seigniorage) that balance these considerations, provided that budgetary transfers from the ECB's monetary policy leg (seigniorage income) to its supervisory leg do not hamper the execution of its monetary mandate.

Bank Coverage

The SSM will cover all of the roughly 6,000 credit institutions licensed in the eurozone, although only some 130 "significant" banks (accounting for about 85 percent of total bank assets) will be under the direct supervision of the ECB. The following are among the key reasons why this is so.

Sovereign–Bank Links

The motivations for forming the banking union include weakening, or severing, sovereign–bank links and limiting the buildup of systemic risk. Large and cross-border banks should be included. But, as the experience of Spain and others has demonstrated, small banks with correlated risks can represent a major fiscal risk to the sovereign and a systemic risk to the euro area. Covering only "systemic" banks (with the difficult decision of demarcating systemic from nonsystemic banks), while potentially easier to implement technically and politically, would only partially address these risks.

Competitive Distortions

A banking union covering only a subset of euro area banks would have implications for the level playing field and could encourage regulatory arbitrage between centrally and nationally supervised banks.

Uneven Distribution of Costs and Benefits

Because banking size and activities differ greatly across euro area countries, a partial banking union that covered only a subset of large banks would benefit some countries more than others and would therefore have implications for the distribution of costs and benefits of the banking union across countries.

BCP Principles, Tasks, and Powers

Principles

To ensure effective supervision, bank supervisors should have clear responsibilities and objectives for each authority involved in supervision (following BCP No. 1). To the extent that the ECB will be a supervisor in its own right, it will have to comply with the BCPs. Assessing the SSM will also require discerning how effective it is to have a supranational setup sharing some responsibilities with national authorities and delegating some of the tasks. The effectiveness of the SSM, which will be the responsibility of the ECB to ensure, will depend, among other things, on the functions delegated, the capacity constraints, and the accountability and control mechanisms used.

Tasks

The ECB should have clear responsibilities over the life cycle of banks to fulfill its safety and soundness mandate. This implies that the ECB should be tasked with authorizing banks; assessing and authorizing mergers and acquisitions; ensuring compliance with prudential requirements; imposing additional buffers (including countercyclical and systemic buffers); applying requirements regarding internal bank governance and processes; imposing all measures determined necessary to address, early on, banks' unsafe and unsound practices; carrying out stress tests; conducting consolidated supervision; and taking on tasks related to home-host arrangements for cross-border banks. The EU regulation establishing the SSM broadly confers these tasks on the ECB.

Powers

To carry out its tasks effectively, possibly including the solo supervision of a set of banks (without delegation to national authorities), the ECB should have adequate formal powers to do all of the following:

- Enforce minimum prudential standards and any restrictions prescribed by the supervisory review, including increasing the prudential requirements for individual banks and banking groups based on their risk profile and systemic importance (BCP No. 1 and No. 16).

- Request information and have full access to banks' boards, management, and staff records, and perform general investigations and onsite inspections (BCP No. 1 and No. 10).

- Require all necessary early corrective actions to address unsafe and unsound practices or activities that could pose risks to banks or to the banking system, and prevent banks from breaching standards (BCP No. 11).

- Ring-fence banks from the actions of parent companies, subsidiaries, parallel-owned banking structures, and other related entities in matters that could impair the safety and soundness of a bank or the banking system (BCP No. 11).

- Take measures and sanctions in line with the gravity of the situation, including revoking licenses (BCP No. 11).
- Determine supervisory plans (BCP No. 8).
- Review, reject, and impose conditions on transfers of ownership and major acquisitions (BCP No. 7).
- Perform consolidated supervision, including application of prudential standards for an entire group (BCP No. 12).
- Withdraw licenses and collaborate with relevant authorities in deciding when and how to effect orderly resolution (BCP No. 11).
- Identify and assess the buildup of risks, trends, and concentrations within and across the system, in coordination with other relevant authorities, and address proactively any serious threat to the stability of the banking system (BCPs No. 8 and No. 9). (See below on macroprudential responsibilities.)

Formal versus Real Powers

Distinguishing formal from real power is important. Because supervisory incentives are skewed at the national level, it is essential that the ECB has real powers (requiring adequate resources) and does not simply validate (and take responsibility for) decisions proposed by national authorities. A prerequisite is to confer formal supervisory powers on the ECB, and ensure monitoring of supervisory tasks during a transitional phase, since real powers may continue to reside partly with the national authority until supervisory decision-making and capacity are in place at the ECB. Having a mechanism for the effective delegation and monitoring of supervisory tasks is also important in the steady state when a common backstop is in place.

Ensuring Real Powers

To ensure that national incentives are aligned with those of the center, and that the center has real powers in the conduct of supervision, further arrangements could be considered. For instance, the ECB could be provided with the ability to immediately conduct peer reviews and joint inspections, including lead supervisors from other countries or the ECB, with cross-country teams. The ECB could use a range of metrics, including solvency and liquidity stress tests, to discern which banks warrant particularly close attention or review by the ECB.

Design of a Delegated Supervisory Mechanism

"Hub and Spokes" Model

Since all banks are to be included in the SSM, a division of labor between the center and national authorities is necessary, while all information should be shared among supervisory bodies of the SSM. Both of the two extreme models of the division of labor—full centralization and full decentralization—are neither practical nor desirable. A centralized system is not an option, given that supervisory knowledge and resources remain at the national levels. A decentralized mechanism, in which the center validates the decisions taken locally, is not desirable either, particularly when common backstops are fully in place at the euro area level, since consistency cannot be assured in the quality of the local implementation of supervisory practices. Conferring formal responsibilities on the ECB without adequate enforcement power could result in weak supervision and put the ECB's reputation at risk.

Steady-State Framework

Common risk-based supervision in a supranational setting. A common analytical approach should be agreed to and applied to the SSM, comprising the ECB and national supervisory bodies. A risk-based framework would attribute a risk classification to each banking organization within the euro area. Based on this methodology, the ECB would develop a protocol for supervision and establish the frequency, level, and type of supervisory action to be conducted. The level of centralization and intrusiveness and the mix of multinational members in supervisory teams would be made proportionate to the supervisory assessment of risk. The model would also define a nonrigid perimeter of institutions subject to supplementary intense scrutiny by the ECB, allowing a fluid response to emerging information.

Principles. The framework should create a coherent and consistent supervisory mechanism with final decisions taken at the center. To promote incentive compatibility in the delegated supervisory mechanism, the extent to which the tasks or the supervision of a set of banks is divided between national authorities and the center could be derived from a set of principles, such as these:

1. *The systemic dimension.* The center will have a comparative advantage in adopting a systemic approach to supervision and internalizing cross-border externalities inherent to the supervision of systemically important financial institutions (SIFIs).

2. *Local knowledge and know-how.* National supervisors may have better specific knowledge about individual banks, and could therefore be more effective in supervising smaller banks.

3. *Risks of regulatory capture.* National supervisors may be more likely to favor national banks, which would create distortions that can have financial stability consequences for the region.

4. *Discretion in decision making.* The degree of delegation must decrease with the degree of discretion associated with specific tasks.

5. *Consistency of delegation.* When tasks are delegated, *the consistency of approach* among national authorities and between the national authority and the center is essential.

Bank classifications. An initial framework would classify each bank on the basis of size, interconnections, complexity, cross-border orientation, and whether the bank requires common funding, as follows.

- Group I: Global systemically important financial institutions, banks identified as systemic for the euro area, and banks requiring (or nearly requiring) direct recapitalization by the ESM.

- Group II: Banks of intermediate size, simple but potentially systemic for their sovereign (either individually or as a group).

- Group III: Very small banks unlikely to be systemic or to require access to a common backstop.

Delegation by group. The degree of delegation of day-to-day supervision by the ECB would vary by group. Group I banks would be under the direct and intrusive supervision of the ECB, which would maintain an on-site supervisory presence, with a mix of international supervisors in teams led by an ECB supervisor. Group II could be supervised mainly by national authorities, which would maintain an on-site presence, with supervision performed by teams of mixed nationalities appointed and compensated by their home countries (e.g., for governance purposes), and off-site monitoring by the ECB and the local supervisor. Day-to-day supervision of Group III banks would be fully delegated to the national authority, but the ECB would be entitled and ready to request participation equivalent to the other groups at any time (e.g., if a group of banks became systemic because of correlated exposures). For all groups, off-site monitoring should be carried out by the ECB and the local supervisor. The SSM regulation defines two categories of banks—"significant" banks, which are brought under the direction supervision of the ECB, and "nonsignificant" banks, which remain under the supervision of national authorities—which provides a system of delegation by groups of banks.

Delegation by task. Tasks that are more difficult to standardize, that require more intrusion and discretionary decisions, or that are more critical for the system as a whole or are more subject to political interference would be less conducive to delegation. National authorities could perform day-to-day assessments of banks' soundness and carry out some examinations (provided they are consistency with the allocation of tasks by groups of banks). The assessment and monitoring of internal risk models could be performed locally, under general guidance from the ECB. But supervisory reviews, licensing, corrective actions, inspections, and decisions about imposing higher individual or macroprudential buffers and about sanctioning and initiating resolutions should be less amenable to delegation. Also undertaken by the center or by supervisors of mixed nationalities would be approvals for the use of advanced approaches, approvals of certain capital instruments, model validations, and thematic/horizontal inspections. The ECB should be closely involved in stress tests to identify pockets of vulnerability among euro area banks and in performing (or requesting from national authorities) intrusive examinations, approving mergers and acquisitions, and initiating early corrective actions, if needed.

Escalation of decision making. Supervisory responses should be escalated appropriately. Preliminary recommendations to address problems detected during supervision would need to be left behind by each inspection team, regardless of their level of risk. For banks with a higher risk classification, such as I and II above, review by the center would be required. For less systemic banks, the national level would implement corrective action and only elevate the issue to the center if concerns had not been addressed by the institution in the established timeframe. As a first step in escalation, inspection reports could be shared with different teams for a peer review.

Two-dimensional delegation. The allocation of tasks within the supervisory mechanism between the ECB and the national authorities could be based on a flexible approach, combining delegation by bank category and by task, with tasks escalating to the center as institutions become more systemic and tasks become more critical to financial stability and subject to greater discretion.

Transitional Stages

Steps toward the steady-state supervisory mechanism include these three stages:

First stage. In a first, urgent phase of the transition, the ECB must be provided with the full legal powers and protections needed to perform its supervisory tasks, including the powers to impose a complete range of corrective actions and initiate resolution. An embryo off-site supervisory structure and a decision-making body must be created at the ECB; standardized templates of information should be developed and supervisory data should be shared; outstanding legal uncertainties must be clarified (e.g., regarding the respective responsibilities of the ECB and national authorities). The centralized analysis should be used to create the first thresholds for centralized supervisory actions, and the classification of banks should be established. A balance sheet assessment of the most important euro area banks must be performed before the SSM becomes effective; it will be key to establishing the credibility of the ECB.

Second stage. In a second stage, the ECB should develop a consistent risk-based supervisory approach, establishing protocols that would specify, for example, the frequency, level, and type of supervisory action, the levels of centralization and intrusiveness, and the mix of multinational members in supervisory teams. It should also establish the characteristics of supervisory processes that will prevail in the steady state. The development of common protocols for corrective action should, ideally, be front-loaded, including protocols for the minimum actions by supervisors. Common timeframes for banks to address detected deficiencies and common settings for the escalation of corrective actions and sanctions should also, ideally, be established up-front.

Third stage. In a third stage, systemically important banks and, more generally, banks higher in the supervisory risk matrix would be brought under the direct supervision of the ECB, and common protocols and design of the system of delegation would be finalized.[11] When the ECB started supervising systemically

---

[11] Note that the draft regulation published by the Council of the European Union stipulates that the ECB may also start, from the date of entry into force of the SSM regulation, directly supervising a bank if the ESM unanimously requests the ECB to take over the direct supervision of this bank (Article 27(3)).

important banks, international teams would start to perform risk assessments of each institution and develop supervisory plans for them. These plans would identify the areas that would need to involve mixed-nationality teams and would estimate the work force and skills needed at headquarters and at the national level. The ECB would decide the most suitable approach for the banks, including whether there was the need for a permanent presence, for intensive diagnostic on-site inspections before a regular cycle of on-site programs could be restored, or for the use of mixed-teams only for the supervisory review process and authorization for advanced approaches.

Macroprudential Oversight Within the Single Supervisory Mechanism

The Case for Centralization

The ECB should be given the responsibility and powers to perform macroprudential oversight in the euro area and involving national authorities.

Benefits. The ECB should act as a macroprudential oversight institution for euro area countries, with binding powers to use macroprudential instruments if it deems that necessary. The high degree of financial integration calls for a coherent approach to macroprudential policies, one that internalizes cross-border externalities and addresses information and home-host coordination problems when using macroprudential tools. Note, however, that the centralization of decision making does not imply a homogeneity of policies across countries. Policies would still need to be adapted flexibly to macrofinancial developments in particular countries or asset markets, and they would need to be applied to all financial institutions active in these countries or markets.

Costs and limitations. There are costs to building capacity for designing macroprudential policies tailored to specific country conditions. But given the ECB's established expertise in financial stability, these costs might not be high. There could be an overlap with the role of the European Systemic Risk Board that would require some coordination. There could also be a risk that taking on macroprudential responsibilities could subject the ECB to political pressures or disagreements with national authorities, adding rigidities to the framework. Because the ECB mandate does not include insurance firms or securities markets, it would need to collaborate with competent authorities whenever such institutions were involved.

The Case for a Mixed Model

A pragmatic approach, as provided under the SSM regulation, may be a mixed model that would involve both the ECB and national authorities to ensure effective macroprudential oversight of the euro area, as implied in the legislative proposal for a SSM. In particular, the ECB could be conferred power to impose a systemic or countercyclical capital buffer if national authorities did not act, thus countering the lack of "will to act." Other tools not included in the Fourth Capital Requirement Directive/Capital Requirement Regulation, such as limits on debt-to-income and loan-to-value ratios, could also be provided to the ECB when a common macroprudential toolkit was in place. Thus, the ECB would be provided a macroprudential mandate for the euro area as a whole and for individual countries.

Alternatively, if national authorities retained *some* macroprudential policies, as foreseen in the Council agreement, the use of tools might have to be coordinated and validated by the ECB, and mechanisms might need to be designed to resolve conflicts of interest that could arise between national authorities and the ECB (e.g., the ECB could be more prone to act than national authorities, who may be subject to political pressures).

THE RISKS OF PROCEEDING WITH A SINGLE SUPERVISORY MECHANISM IN A TIME OF CRISIS

This section identifies the main risks in the transition toward the banking union.

European Union Features that Constrain the Single Supervisory Mechanism

A range of risks can be ascribed to the design features of the European Union that constrain the construction of the SSM. Following are five of them.

The European Union Setup

The European Union can act only in those areas where it has exclusive or shared competencies, or can support the actions of the member states, as provided under the Treaty. When competencies are shared with EU member states (such as the single market for financial services), under the principle of subsidiarity the European Union may act only insofar as its objectives can be better achieved at the European Union level than at the member state level.

Legal Contours of the SSM

Regarding the supervisory sphere, Article 127 (6) of the EU Treaty provides that specific supervisory tasks may be conferred upon the ECB and therefore presumes the continued existence of "competent authorities of member states." This implies a division of responsibilities between the ECB and national competent authorities and, consequently, constraints on the design of the SSM.

Governance

The governance arrangements of the ECB are not designed for a supervisory function, and country coverage is restricted to euro area member states. The Governing Council is the ultimate decision-making body of the ECB, as enshrined in the EU Treaty, including for any supervisory tasks conferred upon the ECB under Article 127 (6). The governance structure of the ECB hinges on its monetary mandate, since the Governing Council comprises the governors of the national central banks and the members of the Executive Board; heads of other national supervisory agencies cannot be part of the Governing Council. Given such predetermined design, a number of constraints, as well as legal, reputational, and implementation risks, may arise from the assumption by the ECB of supervisory tasks.

Legal Responsibility

Any ECB internal body established for a supervisory task, as foreseen under the draft SSM regulations, cannot have decision-making powers, which are ultimately vested with the Governing Council. Any delegation of activities to a supervisory board—composed of national and ECB representatives—cannot override such a setup.

Delegated Decision Making

The Governing Council will have to process a wealth of information on short deadlines. While being accountable for all supervisory decisions, the Governing Council will scarcely have the capacity to analyze each case brought to its attention. Rather, the Governing Council will validate the decisions prepared by the Supervisory Board, following a "silent procedure," that is, the decisions will be deemed adopted unless the Governing Council objects within a short period (10 days in normal times, and two days in stressful times). The following risks are of potential concern.

- There is a risk that, within the supervisory board or Governing Council, decision makers may not be fully independent from national interests.

- There is a risk of conflicts of interest between the monetary policy function and the supervisory function. Given that the ECB Governing Council must pursue its primary objective of price stability, it may take decisions that from a supervisory perspective are not optimal.

- Member states that are not part of the euro area but join the SSM cannot be represented in the Governing Council, which will nonetheless take decisions affecting them. This may open the door to conflicts and accountability problems within the SSM. At the same time, if such states have the possibility to opt out of decisions taken by the Governing Council, the level playing field of the single market may be tilted.

Transitional Risks

Bringing all euro area banks under the supervision of the ECB is a major task and entails many practical difficulties and risks. A swift transition to covering all banks would reduce the risk of an entrenchment of regulatory forbearance between the time the decision to create an SSM was announced and the actual transfer of supervisory responsibilities. An effective SSM would also make it possible to start direct ESM recapitalization of banks; on the other hand, there is a possibility that specific banks in need of direct recapitalization by the ESM could be brought under the SSM before it is generally effective. Unless supervisory capacity at the center is established quickly and incentives at the national and central levels are well aligned, there would be risks of information loss, supervisory drift, and regulatory forbearance. However, the challenge of putting in place an effective capacity at the center should not be underestimated, making it worthwhile to emphasize the urgency of efforts to plan for and ensure success under a realistic but ambitious timeline.

Taking on responsibilities in the crisis carries its own risks. By definition, in a crisis banks are likely to be weak and credibility in institutions is likely to be low. While it would be desirable for the ECB to conduct a relicensing exercise before taking responsibility for a bank, this will not be possible. Thus, the ECB may have to take early action against problem banks while its own expertise is not yet fully established and its credibility in supervision is not yet assured.

Risks in the Division of Responsibilities between the Center and the National Authorities

Serious risks could derive from the division of responsibilities between the ECB and the national authorities, particularly during the transition.

Banks under Direct ECB Supervision

To ensure stability, it is essential that the ECB be able to identify risks at an early stage, including for banks that will not be under its direct supervision. The regulation of the SSM specifies a set of criteria to identify which banks are "significant" for the euro area and should therefore be directly supervised by the ECB, and which banks should remain under the direct supervision of national authorities. These criteria relate to the importance of cross-border activities, domestic and EU significance, and size. Moreover, the ECB will be able to designate as "significant" and bring under its direct oversight institutions (or groups of institutions) that could jeopardize the stability of the euro area financial system—for instance through their impact on the balance sheet of the respective sovereign. The SSM regulation safeguards the capacity of the ECB to investigate all credit institutions and bring them under its direct oversight at any time. Nevertheless, at least during the transition stage, the process of taking over credit institutions from national authorities may be lengthy and unwieldy and could therefore allow risks to build up.

Identification of Macroprudential Risks

The ECB will have to be able to identify pockets of growing systemic risks and take action at an early stage. A purely microsupervisory approach is insufficient when banks are interconnected or take correlated exposures and also when localized macroeconomic conditions affect a specific region or a specific type of institution. Thus, the microprudential analysis will need to be complemented with a macroprudential approach to risk assessment.

Incentives under Decentralized Supervision

National authorities may be biased toward favoring the national banking system. Risk-based supervision will always rely, to some extent, on supervisory judgment, and the ECB may rely on such qualitative assessment by national authorities. Yet national authorities may tend to be too optimistic about their respective banks, thus increasing the risk of supervisory slippage at the SSM level. The accountability mechanisms could reinforce these incentives to the extent that the ECB would be responsible for the effective and consistent functioning of the SSM and for the supervision of "significant banks," while the National Competent Authorities under the instruction of the ECB would be responsible for the direct supervision of all other banks. The risk could be compounded during the transition due to the very limited resources available to the ECB, including resources to control actions at the national level. As a result, the ECB's ability to reach its own supervisory judgment on the soundness of institutions' risk management could be put at risk during the transition.

National Supervisory Practices, Frameworks, and Enforcement

In practice, the ECB will need to operate with recourse to the national supervisors for ongoing supervision, especially on-site supervision. Moreover, in order to apply nonpecuniary administrative sanctions—different from the remedial measures provided under the draft SSM regulation—the ECB will need to instruct national authorities, which will implement the sanctioning actions according to national laws. Recent Financial Sector Assessment Programs in EU countries have identified supervisory laws and practices—and especially enforcement practices—that differ from country to country and diverge from international best practices and standards. Thus, ensuring uniformity of treatment may be difficult.

National Resolution Regimes

The ECB will be given powers to withdraw a license, but until an SRM based on a strong single resolution authority is established, the SSM may have to operate with multiple regimes and authorities. This will entail additional operational complexity because the ECB, local supervisors, resolution agencies, and DGSs will have to interact both in the preparation and validation of recovery and resolution plans for SIFIs and in decisions leading to the possible withdrawal of bank licenses. Lack of a credible resolution framework could also impede timely decision making by leaving national authorities to deal with the fiscal consequences of others' supervisory decisions.

Operational Risks

Perhaps most immediately, the authorities need to be alert to operational risks. Establishing a critical new authority over the euro area and beyond without providing sufficient resources, both financial and human, would be self-defeating and would jeopardize the entire exercise.

Capacity, Expertise, and Resources of the ECB

Currently, the ECB has impressive human capital to conduct monetary policy and monitor financial stability in the euro area, but it has no supervisory expertise.

Overall supervisory resources in the euro area are fixed in the near term; it will take time to build supervisory resources, skills, and expertise at the center without depleting the local level of its own needed experts. Although the dates for being operationally ready have been reasonably set in the SSM regulation, there is a risk that the ECB may be pressured to operate as a single supervisor before it is adequately resourced.

Data Management and Information Sharing

To operate, the ECB system and staff must be able to receive, store, and analyze large amounts of confidential information, and they must also be able to translate these analyses into supervisory operations and decisions. Establishing systems and internal mechanisms to handle these tasks will be demanding.

MITIGATION OF RISKS

As the SSM is put into effect, comprehensive risk mitigation should be a central complement. Following are measures to mitigate risks related to the establishment of the SSM under EU Treaty constraints.

Addressing Risks While Establishing the Single Supervisory Mechanism

Harmonized Legislation

Agreement to and adoption of harmonized legislation should proceed swiftly, as should its transposition into national laws. From this perspective, it is important not only to adopt the Capital Requirement Regulation/Fourth Capital Requirement Directive, but to build a uniform single supervisory rule-book in the European Union. The rule-book should go beyond the necessary harmonization prompted by the Capital Requirement Regulation/ Fourth Capital Requirement Directive, the BRRD, and the deposit insurance directive. The European Banking Authority can play a positive role here in ensuring that supervisory practices are harmonized.

Effective Governance

A steering committee, supporting the work of the Supervisory Board, will play a useful role in the chain of supervisory tasks that could avoid cumbersome processes at the higher level. The establishment of internal and external monitoring mechanisms or "watchdogs" would also enhance checks and balances, contribute to better scrutiny, and incentivize the effectiveness of the ECB supervision. Effectiveness could also be enhanced by a more significant representation of permanent, full-time officials or independent experts at the Supervisory Board who are not linked to national interests. In time, the governance structure could be buttressed by measures that would require a treaty change—for instance, allowing non-euro area countries to have representation in the Governing Council when deciding supervisory matters.

Accountability Mechanisms

Additional accountability mechanisms, such as the possibility of reporting to national parliaments in addition to the European Parliament, are provided in the SSM regulation. However, the respective responsibilities of the ECB and the NCAs should be clarified to help make the system of decentralization incentives compatible, given the ECB's ultimate responsibility for ensuring the effectiveness of the SSM.

Addressing Risks during Transition

Risk Mapping Exercise

The ECB should receive from the national supervisors the risk assessments and local risk classifications of the local banks as soon as possible. Based on this information, the ECB would map banking risks and target supervisory actions accordingly—for instance, by requiring national supervisors to undertake additional due diligence on specific portfolios and capital planning, or by providing information on the availability of additional shareholder resources.

Asset Quality Assessment

The ECB must undertake an asset quality assessment or review for a set of banks as they are brought under the SSM. The exercise, which would need to be conducted with the involvement of the national supervisors and third parties, should follow harmonized guidance on how such assessments must be conducted, as issued by European Banking Authority, in coordination with efforts to review and harmonize data and relevant definitions (e.g., of nonperforming loans, provisioning rules, and risk weights). Such an asset quality review is critical to establish the credibility of the ECB as a supervisor. To ensure success, it should be based on a forward looking framework that incorporates risks to growth and is clearly communicated in advance of the exercise; it should cover all banks that will come under the direct supervision of the ECB.

Moreover, independent third-party involvement (preferably from the private sector), along with the ECB, the European Banking Authority for the stress tests, and national authorities, would be essential to ensure full credibility and transparency of the exercise. In the absence of such involvement, prospects for raising private capital would be jeopardized. There should be an agreed strategy on how to address capital shortfalls to avoid creating uncertainty and procyclical deleveraging. This would encourage a realistic write-down of assets and full recognition of losses, which would encourage private capital. Absent such a strategy, there is a high risk that the asset quality review (which will be followed by stress tests) would be counterproductive: if banks shed assets to preemptively build buffers, this could reinforce fragmentation rather than resolve it. The incentives to conduct a thorough and credible exercise could be distorted, whereas a clear plan would encourage a realistic write-down of assets and recognition of losses, which would help attract private capital. In the event that both private capital and fiscal space were limited, clarity about a common backstop would be critical to avoid reigniting adverse bank–sovereign links and to improve the incentives to recognize losses. The ECB announced the methodology for the comprehensive assessment of euro area banks on October 23, 2013. The exercise is expected to start in November 2013 and be completed in time for the SSM's inauguration in January 2015 (see Box 11.1 for a description of the methodology of the comprehensive assessment).

Box 11.1 The SSM Comprehensive Assessment[1]

The SSM assessment is broad and comprehensive in methodological and institutional coverage. About 130 credit institutions comprising 85 percent of euro area bank assets will be assessed. The assessment consists of three elements: (1) a supervisory risk assessment to review key risks quantitatively and qualitatively; (2) an asset quality review (AQR) of key risk exposures; and (3) a stress test to assess banks' resilience to forward-looking stress scenarios.

- *The supervisory assessment* examines key risks in a forward- and backward-looking manner, including risks relating to liquidity, leverage, and funding. This enables assessment of a bank's intrinsic risk profile, its position in relation to its peers, and its vulnerability to a number of exogenous factors. The risk assessment methodology will in the future be a new supervisory tool of the SSM.

- *The AQR* performs a comprehensive review of bank assets, including important elements such as restructured loans, collateral valuation, and provisions. It focuses on balance sheet items that are more risky or nontransparent. It is broad in scope, covering credit exposures—including nonperforming and restructured loans—and market exposures. It includes corporate, retail, interbank, and sovereign exposures (although the latter will continue to carry a zero risk weight); on- and off-balance-sheet positions; and both domestic and foreign exposures. While internal risk models will not be assessed, the exercise results in adjustments of risk weights.

- *The stress test* will build on and complement the AQR by providing a forward-looking view of shock-absorption capacity under stress. It will be conducted in collaboration with the European Banking Authority (EBA), with the methodology and scenarios to be agreed upon in due course.

The announcement clarifies several important details of the exercise:

- *Harmonized definitions* will be used for nonperforming exposures and forbearance, in line with recent guidance from the EBA.

- *Portfolio choice and sampling will be risk based.* National authorities will propose, at the bank level, the portfolios to be assessed. The European Central Bank (ECB) will "review and challenge" these proposals before making selections. It will be important for the ECB to ensure that there is methodological consistency across countries and banks in this regard, and high-risk and nontransparent segments will be subject to higher sampling rates. A broad range of credit and market exposures, both domestic and foreign, will be included, although the review will concentrate on those elements of individual bank balance sheets that are believed to be the most risky. The exercise will be subject to minimum coverage criteria at both the country and bank levels, although those are yet to be specified.

- *The minimum capital requirement* for the AQR is set at 8 percent of Common Equity Tier 1, which will be stricter than regulatory requirements. The capital definition of

---

[1] Details of the methodology announced on October 23, 2013, can be found at: http://www.ecb.europa. eu/ssm/html/index.en.html.

(continued)

Box 11.1 (*Concluded*)

January 1, 2014 will apply for the AQR, whereas the definition that is valid at the end of the horizon will be used for the stress test—a difference being the phasing in of capital deductions for deferred tax assets and holdings in financial companies envisaged under the fourth Capital Requirements Directive (CRD IV).

- *Independent third-party involvement* has been confirmed. Oliver Wyman will support the ECB, providing independent advice on methodology, while assisting in design and implementation.
- *Disclosure* of the outcomes, at the country and bank levels, will conclude the exercise by end-October 2014, and will include recommended follow-up supervisory measures.

Several important aspects of the assessment remain to be agreed upon:

- *Backstops.* Use of the European Supervisory Mechanism's (ESM's) direct recapitalization remains the first-best option to keep adverse bank–sovereign feedback loops at bay for countries that do not have fiscal space. National backstops—possibly via ESM sovereign loans—need to be established and communicated well in advance of the completion of the AQR, in line with the June 2013 European Council June agreement to establish national backstops ahead of the assessment.
- *Bail-ins.* Agreement and clarity on an appropriate strategy for bailing-in private creditors while ensuring financial stability is essential. The revised state aid rules specify that, as a requirement for state aid to be granted, and to the extent that these measures do not endanger financial stability, "Hybrid capital and subordinated debt holders must contribute to reducing the capital shortfall to the maximum extent" while exceptions to this rules are possible to address financial stability concerns and "proportionality" considerations.
- *Recapitalization.* Formulation and communication of details of the approach for follow-up and corrective actions, including a timeline for recapitalizations, will be critical. Filling capital gaps should be accompanied by a realistic write-down of assets, full recognition of losses and restructuring of nonviable bank businesses.

ESM Recapitalization

Reaching final agreement on the possibility of ESM recapitalization of banks is of the utmost importance. The possibility of direct recapitalization of banks would provide incentives to make progress in addressing solvency issues in countries by relieving pressures on weak sovereigns. The interpretation given to the ESM Treaty is that it is flexible enough to enable the ESM to recapitalize banks directly—subject to political agreement and unanimous consent of the ESM membership. Indeed, under Article 19 of the ESM Treaty, the Board of Governors may also review and change the range of financial assistance instruments that can be made available by the ESM. The Board of Directors may adopt guidelines for implementing financial assistance through recapitalization or loans.

Ultimately, the breadth of the investment decisions that can be made by the ESM rests upon the decision of its member states, in due consideration of the risks and potential upsides or downsides inherent in such investments. It will be important to agree on and clarify the investment mandate of the ESM as well as the specifics of ESM recapitalization, including the definition of legacy assets, the pricing of assets, the role of bail-ins, the principle for access, and the design of instruments. Moreover, if the ESM were to inject ordinary equity into banks, governance arrangements and ownership policies would need to be carefully elaborated. Possible conflicts arising from concurrent significant stakes in competing institutions would need to be dealt with, and disclosure requirements would need to be strengthened.

Lastly, it would be important to ensure that the ESM had adequate capital, not only to allay any investor concerns about ESM credit quality, with resulting rating implications, but also so it could leverage its capital to play the role of a common backstop for bank recapitalization. The Eurogroup agreement of June 20, 2013, on the "ESM direct bank recapitalization instrument" is an important step forward and provides the main features of the operational framework, including conditions for access, time of entry, burden sharing, valuation, conditionality, and governance. Nevertheless, the recapitalization instrument will require further clarification and detailed features, in particular regarding the timing (since the final agreement has been linked to the adoption of the BRRD and the DGS Directive), conditionality, burden sharing, size, and conditions for access (see Chapter 13 for greater details).

Addressing Risks Related to the European Central Bank

Measures to mitigate risks related to operations and the division of responsibilities between the ECB and the National Competent Authorities include the following.

Build Capacity and Expertise at the ECB

The ECB should be able to intervene in a timely manner in any bank, as deemed necessary, and it should be able to bring any bank under its direct supervision. The off-site supervisory structure should be established as soon as possible at the ECB. Specialist expertise should be hired externally and also obtained by second-ments from national authorities. Cross-country teams led by an ECB supervisor should be in place as soon as possible for the most systemic or fragile banks (including those requiring ESM direct recapitalization). Funding of the ECB's supervisory activities should be derived not only from transfers from the national supervisory authorities, but also from additional revenues, in part to minimize potential adverse effects on national supervisory resources.

Specify the Roles of National Authorities and the ECB

It will be important to specify the respective roles of national authorities and the ECB and how cooperative action under the SSM will be performed. The SSM hinges on a division of labor between the ECB and the national authorities. Clear, precise, and transparent rules defining such divisions of labor and the attribution of tasks given by the ECB to the national authorities will be important to prevent overlaps, gaps, or conflicts. For this purpose, the ECB should, as soon as possible, prepare a supervisory manual and clarify any outstanding legal uncertainties.

Define Steps Toward a Single Resolution Authority

EU authorities should define and agree on steps toward a single resolution authority and common backstops, and establish an SRM around the time the SSM is declared effective. It will reduce the risks of an incomplete framework and ensure that national interests do not prevail over that of the European Union. Pending the establishment of an EU-wide resolution framework, it is welcome that the prompt update of national resolution regimes has been agreed to be a priority. In the meantime, it is essential that an SRM be established for the countries participating in the SSM around the time that the SSM becomes effective. Leaving resolution at the national level while supervision was being centralized would carry significant risks, such as perpetuating bank–sovereign links and creating potential conflicts (and deadlocks) among national authorities. An SRM based on a strong centralized resolution authority would allow for swift decisions on burden sharing while ensuring stability and least-cost resolution.

An effective common fiscal backstop, combining a credit line to the ESM as a bridge to a more permanent solution and a single resolution fund backed by industry resources, would weaken sovereign-bank links. The European Commission proposal for an SRM, described in Chapter 12, is an important step forward, as it would provide the possibility for a strong central resolution authority backed by a single resolution fund, which are desirable characteristics, in time for the start of the SSM. However, the proposal itself would need to be strengthened along several dimensions and may be subject to legal challenges.

Develop the ECB's Macroprudential Powers

The ECB should identify systemic risks, take early actions, and use macroprudential instruments when deemed necessary, in coordination with national authorities and the European Systemic Risk Board.

REFERENCES

Goyal, Rishi, and others, 2013, "A Banking Union for the Euro Area," IMF Staff Discussion Note No. 13/1 (Washington: International Monetary Fund).

International Monetary Fund, 2013, "European Union: Financial System Stability Assessment," IMF Staff Country Report No. 13/75 (Washington).

CHAPTER 12

The Single Resolution Mechanism

THIERRY TRESSEL

Establishing a Single Resolution Mechanism (SRM) is an essential step toward the banking union. The absence of an SRM based on a common resolution authority would hamper the effectiveness of the Single Supervisory Mechanism (SSM) and impede timely decision making by leaving national authorities to deal with the fiscal consequences of supervisory decisions made at the center. It would also create the potential for reputational risks to the European Central Bank (ECB) whenever national authorities had a different perspective from that of the ECB, since it would create potential conflicts (and deadlocks) between national authorities and the ECB.

It is desirable to move quickly beyond the harmonized national regimes and set up an SRM, ideally one with common backstops and safety nets. The SRM should include at least the countries participating in the SSM and should be established by the time the SSM becomes effective. Just as banks nowadays are too interconnected to be effectively supervised at a national level, so national resolution regimes would have difficulty, even under harmonized arrangements, handling the bigger banks of the European Union (EU). There would be limited incentives among national resolution authorities to take rapid and least-cost action to address problems. Coordination difficulties for large cross-border banks, in the absence of common backstops, could undermine effectiveness. Incentives could also be skewed for smaller banks, since authorities could shift losses to the center. The recent European Commission proposal is a step forward in this regard and could ensure that an SRM is in place at the time the SSM is effective. However, crucial issues remain to be resolved and clarified.

To be fully aligned with best practices, the common resolution authority should seek to achieve least-cost resolution of financial institutions without disrupting financial stability.[1] It should protect and give preference to insured depositors and ensure that shareholders and unsecured, uninsured creditors absorb losses. The SRM will need a mandate, alongside the SSM, to develop

---

This chapter draws on the February 2013 IMF Staff Discussion Note "A Banking Union for the Euro Area" (Goyal and others, 2013), and its accompanying technical background note, and on the European Union Financial Sector Assessment Program. The contributions by the authors of the background note are gratefully acknowledged.
[1] The Financial Stability Board Key Attributes of Effective Resolution Regimes for Financial Institutions. Available at the website of the Financial Stability Board, at http://www.financialstabilityboard.org/.

resolution and recovery plans and intervene before insolvency using well-defined quantitative and qualitative triggers. It will need strong powers and a range of tools to take early intervention measures and restructure banks' assets and liabilities (for example, by the bail-in of subordinated and senior unsecured creditors, the transfer of assets and liabilities with "purchase and assumption," and the separation of bad assets by setting up asset management vehicles), override shareholder rights, establish bridge banks to maintain essential financial services, and close insolvent banks. The SRM should specify burden-sharing arrangements with access to a common backstop for systemic failures, while the resolution of small and medium-sized banks could be funded by a common resolution fund, ideally one merged with a common deposit guarantee scheme (DGS).

This chapter first presents an overview of the European Union's approach to bank resolution and restructuring. It then discusses the design of the SRM, before characterizing more specifically the common resolution authority. Following that, it discusses the risks in the transition toward the SRM. The next section is devoted to resolution funding and common backstops.

BANK RESOLUTION AND RESTRUCTURING IN THE EUROPEAN UNION

Resolution Frameworks in the European Union

Need for Resolution Tools

National Financial Sector Assessment Programs (FSAPs) had found that several EU countries lacked domestic resolution tools.[2] In reaction to the financial crisis, the United Kingdom created a special resolution regime under the Banking Act of 2009. This was a major step forward in U.K. legislation and has been in many respects the model for the current proposed resolution framework in the European Union. It applies to commercial banks and other deposit-taking institutions and includes powers to transfer assets and liabilities, establish bridge banks, and take over control of a bank while ensuring that shareholders are appropriately compensated. However, it does not provide the possibility of applying a bail-in tool to wind-down or recapitalize failing banks.

The U.K. Independent Commission on Banking has proposed creating a resolution fund and adding the power to bail-in creditors to the other resolution powers. Germany has adopted a restructuring law, which granted the authorities the power to utilize various resolution tools (see Box 12.1). Now both countries can sell failing businesses, that is, to transfer all or part of a failing business to a private sector purchaser or to create a bridge bank. The German Bank Reorganization Act (January 2011) also provides for an asset separation tool (the power to transfer all or part of a business to an entity, even if not a bank, in which

---

[2] See, for example, FSAPs on the Kingdom of the Netherlands, Germany, the United Kingdom, Spain, and Luxembourg, available at http://www.imf.org/external/index.htm.

Box 12.1 Resolution Framework in Germany

Upgraded framework. A new bank restructuring law came into force in 2011. It introduces broad powers and instruments to facilitate the resolution of systemic banks, including the ability to transfer the banking business to another institution, stronger remedial powers, reorganization procedures involving the courts, the appointment of a special administrator to take over the management of a bank, and measures to improve own funds' adequacy and liquidity. The law provides the basis for the restructuring fund, administered by the Federal Agency for Financial Market Stabilization (FMSA). While the authorities are engaging with the large banks regarding the preparation of resolution plans, there is no specific requirement in the law for establishing resolution plans ("living wills"). Individual small banks are subject to corporate insolvency proceedings (i.e., bank liquidation).

European progress. The new law reflects many aspects of stronger bank resolution frameworks currently under discussion at the European level. The authorities decided to move forward with legislative reform (the U.K. authorities are taking the lead in Europe with their introduction of an SRR in 2009) and are aware that some adjustments to the law might be needed once agreement has been reached at the European level.

Agencies. BaFin—Bundesanstalt für Finanzdienstleistungsaufsicht (Federal Financial Supervisory Authority)—is granted the lead in formulating resolution strategies. Several other agencies are also involved. The FMSA is tasked with providing resources to facilitate the resolution process and therefore becomes a key player. The Bundesbank will need to assess implications on overall financial stability, especially when granted a stronger role in macroprudential supervision. Finally, the BMF—Bundesministerium der Finanzen (Federal Ministry of Finance)—is understood to have a central role in systemic cases even though no direct responsibility is assigned in bank resolution (the BMF is represented on the FMSA's steering committee and oversees the operations of BaFin). Crisis management coordination will be a task of the Financial Stability Committee that will be established under the framework for macroprudential oversight.

Resolution fund. The new restructuring fund provides additional resources for bank resolution. The restructuring fund has a target size of €70 billion and is administered by the FMSA under the general oversight of the BMF. The restructuring fund is meant to facilitate the resolution of systemically relevant banks through the establishment of bridge banks, providing guarantees (up to €100 billion or 20 times the size of the restructuring fund), capital injections, and other support measures. The restructuring fund is financed ex ante by a bank levy, but expected receipts in the range of €650 million to €1.3 billion per year are low relative to the target size and the potential costs of the failure of a systemically relevant bank. With limited amounts of resources built up so far, existing contingency funding arrangements remain important.

Levy. The bank levy will be higher for banks that engage in activities creating systemic risk (based on size and interconnectedness). The levy is being collected in addition to contributions to the various deposit insurance schemes to cover the costs of operating the restructuring fund and financing the support measures, and it is calculated according to government regulations. Subject to an overall ceiling linked to a bank's annual profit (over a multiyear period), the levy has been set at 2 basis points of bank liabilities (excluding deposits and capital) up to €10 billion, 3 basis points from €10 billion up to €100 billion, 4 basis points from €100 billion up to €200 billion, 5 basis points from €200 billion up to €300 billion, and 4–6 basis points in excess of €300 billion. Small banks (for example, cooperative banks) will benefit from this staggered structure of the levy. An additional element of the levy, based on the nominal value of off-balance-sheet derivatives, covers interconnectedness.

the restructuring fund owns shares) and the possibility to bail-in senior unsecured creditors through a court-led proceeding on the initiative of the bank.

In Ireland, a new resolution regime was passed into law in October 2011. It covers all credit institutions and enables the Central Bank of Ireland to seek a court order for a range of measures to facilitate effective and efficient resolution, subject to a set of intervention conditions including financial stability concerns. The central bank would be able to take over management of a firm, transfer assets and liabilities, create a bridge bank, and override shareholders' rights subject to appropriate compensation. The new regime would also provide for the preparation of recovery and resolution plans, and resources would be provided by a resolution fund administered by the Central Bank of Ireland and financed by a levy on credit institutions.

Resolution Directive to Be Adopted

A new European Union resolution directive is soon to be adopted. The European Commission has taken steps to harmonize and strengthen domestic resolution regimes in line with international best practices. This should help avoid regulatory arbitrage and make orderly resolution effective and efficient for cross-border banks. In June 2012, the European Commission issued a draft Bank Recovery and Resolution Directive (BRRD) for a harmonized crisis management and resolution framework in all EU countries. The Irish presidency made the adoption of the resolution framework a top priority and planned to adopt it during the first part of 2013 as a precondition to ensure effectiveness of the SSM. The new national resolution regimes would endow EU countries with strong early intervention powers and resolution tools. The transposition of the BRRD into national laws should be accelerated relative to the current deadlines (January 2015 and January 2018 for bail-ins) as part of the announced roadmap toward a Banking Union. The European Parliament published its position on May 21, 2013, and the European Council reached an agreement on the BRRD on June 27–28, 2013, and called for adoption by the European Parliament by end-2013.

New International Standards

Council agreement on the BRRD marks a big step forward (Box 12.2). The Financial Stability Board has developed new international standards for resolution (Key Attributes) that were endorsed by the G-20 leaders in 2011, and the BRRD is well aligned with the Financial Stability Board standards. These standards specify essential features that should be part of the resolution framework at both the national and international levels for Global Systemically Important Financial Institutions. The key objective is to make resolution feasible without severe systemic disruption and without exposing taxpayers to loss.[3] The BRRD

---

[3] In recognition of the impending legislative proposals, the EBA has been active in developing methods for the recovery and resolution of failing banks, such as in its efforts for recovery plans, including the development of templates.

Box 12.2 Proposed Bank Recovery and Resolution Directive: Risks and Areas for Enhancements

- The resolution of banks is undermined by the absence of a more effective EU-wide framework to fund resolution. Binding mediation powers for the European Banking Authority and mutual borrowing arrangements between national funds face inherent constraints (in particular, the European Banking Authority cannot impinge on the fiscal responsibilities of EU member states).

- Adoption of the European Union's Bank Recovery and Resolution Directive (BRRD) will substantially enhance the range of tools available to resolution agencies in the European Union. But the scope of the directive should be widened to include systemic insurance companies and financial market infrastructures. It is a welcome development that all banks should be subject to the regime, without the possibility of ordinary corporate insolvency proceedings.

- The breadth and timing of the triggers for resolution should be enhanced by providing the authority with sufficient flexibility to determine the nonviability of the financial institution (including breaches of liquidity requirements and other serious regulatory failings, not just capital/asset shortfalls). There should be provision for mandatory intervention in the event that a specified solvency trigger is crossed.

- The June 28, 2013, Council agreement sets out a detailed framework for imposing losses in resolution to be introduced by 2018, including a requirement for shareholders and unsecured creditors to absorb losses up to 8 percent of total liabilities (including own funds) before other funding arrangements can be tapped. Some liabilities are excluded from bail-in *a priori* (for example, insured deposits, trade creditors and short-term interbank loans). Other liabilities can be excluded in "extraordinary circumstances," after European Commission approval, where conditions are met. These conditions would require further clarification, and the role of the European Commission in approving exclusions must be supported by a rules-based framework to avoid delays and uncertainties in resolution.

- It is a welcome development that tiered depositor preference has been agreed upon in the Council version of June 28, 2013. The provisions rank the deposits of individuals and SMEs (as well as liabilities owed to the EIB) above those of other uninsured creditors, such as bondholders and large corporate depositors. Insured deposits (with the right of subrogation for the DGS) would rank above uninsured deposits.

- The BRRD affords less flexibility for using certain resolution powers than the Key Attributes. For instance, it does not permit exercising the mandatory recapitalization power and the asset separation tool on a stand-alone basis. Also, departures from *pari passu* treatment should not be prevented where necessary on grounds of financial stability or to maximize value for creditors as a whole.

- The revised state aid rules published on July 10, 2013, which may require bail-ins of unsecured uninsured creditors, should ensure clear and consistent bail-in regimes across countries. The introduction of bail-in powers sooner than 2018 would be necessary to access direct recapitalization by the European Stability Mechanism (ESM), but it should not create uncertainty.

Note: Depositor preference is not drawn from the Key Attributes best practices.

offers principles for early intervention and resolution of cross-border banks, such as on liquidity provision within cross-border groups, and establishes resolution colleges to develop nonbinding mechanisms for crisis planning and resolution (with the European Banking Authority in a mediating role).

However, the absence of a binding ex ante agreement on burden sharing would leave the key coordination problem in resolving cross-border banks unsolved (e.g., Fortis, Dexia) and put into question the capacity to achieve least-cost resolution. Fast transposition of the BRRD at the national level is highly desirable. It would set the stage for further legislation, including EU Treaty change, to create an integrated resolution regime in the European Union. Such an integrated regime could result in the creation of a fully centralized and autonomous European Resolution Authority backing the SRM (see below).

Legal Hurdles to Borrower Restructuring

Legal hurdles to borrower restructuring must be lifted. The legal framework should facilitate the restructuring of nonperforming loans and maximize asset recovery. In several EU countries, including Italy, Greece, and Portugal, the IMF is involved in bankruptcy/insolvency law reform, including by introducing fast-track restructuring tools and out-of-court restructuring process. For instance, repossession of the collateral backing a retail mortgage may take several years in Italy versus a few months in Scandinavia and the United Kingdom. The asset recovery process is also very prolonged in many emerging economies in the European Union.[4] Sometimes in those jurisdictions, the issue is implementation, with banks being unable to enforce collateral. This can weigh heavily on the value of the bank, making its collateral worth less and leaving nonperforming loans on their balance sheets. An efficient framework for handling nonperforming loans is key to rehabilitate viable borrowers and provide the exit of nonviable borrowers.

Active Management of Nonperforming Loans

There is a need for active management of nonperforming loans. In principle, nonperforming loans can be (1) retained and managed by banks themselves at appropriately written-down values, while the banks receive financial assistance from the government for recapitalization; (2) relocated or sold to one or more decentralized "bad banks," loan recovery companies, or asset management companies (AMCs) that specialize in the management of impaired assets; or (3) sold to a centralized AMC set up for public policy purposes (possibly when the size of nonperforming loans reaches systemic proportions).

Government Support and State Aid Rules for Financial Sector Action

The Role of State Aid Policy

Competition and state aid policy has in practice served as the main coordinating mechanism in bank restructuring during the crisis, being the only binding EU

---

[4] See the European Banking Coordination "Vienna" Initiative (2012) in a working group focused on nonperforming loan issues in central, eastern, and southeastern Europe. Recommendations, among others, focused on establishing a conducive legal framework for nonperforming loan resolution, removing tax impediments and regulatory obstacles, and enabling out-of-court settlements.

framework available for this purpose.[5] The European Commission Directorate General for Competition (hereafter, DG Competition) has the exclusive mandate and power to ensure that state aid is compatible with the treaty, and that state aid provision is accepted in exchange for strict conditionality. Member states have provided aid through capital injections, guarantees, and asset purchases. Compensatory measures required by DG Competition have included divestments, penalty interest rates, management removals, dividend suspensions, and burden sharing (shareholder dilutions and bail-in of subordinated debt).[6]

Unintended Consequences of State Intervention

Interventions by DG Competition have been instrumental in imposing restructuring on banks but have on occasion heightened macro-financial concerns. In particular, there have been concerns about the speed of decision making and insufficient transparency, and the impact of compensatory measures on financial stability and economic growth. State aid decisions have involved relatively long timeframes, and rules not well understood by markets have at times exacerbated uncertainties. Since DG Competition could only act in response to national state aid proposals, decisions were taken case by case even in the presence of system-wide problems. The case-by-case approach has occasionally led to concerns about excessive private sector deleveraging and undesirable macro-financial outcomes.

Evolving Flexibility in Management

State aid management is evolving to respond more flexibly to the crisis, but it faces fundamental challenges. DG Competition has been assigned difficult tasks in mitigating competitive distortions while yet preserving financial stability and limiting the costs to taxpayers while ensuring the long-term viability of the institutions receiving state aid. The design of intervention strategies therefore sometimes involves significant tradeoffs. Procedures have been accelerated, and sectorwide implications have been taken into account.

The ongoing Spanish arrangement, for example, takes a broader approach. The European Commission's powers regarding the resolution of banks have been strengthened further, since European Stability Mechanism (ESM) support to bank recapitalization is now conditional upon the European Commission's approval of those banks' restructuring plans. The new mechanism has given DG Competition greater influence in the restructuring and resolution of banks receiving state aid, and it has led to a significant acceleration in the approval process. For instance, it took less than six months to approve the restructuring plans for eight Spanish banks, consistent with the timelines of the European program of assistance to Spain.

---

[5] The Treaty on Functioning of the European Union contains strict limitations on state aid to avoid distorting competition and the internal market. According to the Article 107 of the treaty, no state aid should be granted in any form which distorts or threatens competition. However, state aid can be exceptionally allowed under paragraph 3 of Article 107 in cases of serious disturbances to the economy.

[6] The European Commission framework for state aid in the financial sector was described in a set of six communications issued from 2008 onwards. For more details, see: http://ec.europa.eu/competition/state_aid/legislation/temporary.html.

Stronger coordination with other institutions is desirable, with a view to achieving the European Commission's objective of "restoring financial stability, ensuring lending to the real economy, and dealing with systemic risk of possible insolvency."

Where the Directorate General for Competition Can Be Improved

DG Competition's practices in systemic cases can be further enhanced to ensure consistency with a country's macro-financial framework.[7] The phasing and composition of bank restructuring are critical to mitigate adverse macroeconomic effects. DG Competition seeks to set the right incentives to make the best use of state aid and withdraw from state protection as soon as possible. A pricing policy has been established based on the ECB's recommendations, which seeks to limit moral hazard by ensuring a sufficient degree of burden sharing at a level that is still below the remuneration that the market would request in the absence of state aid. However, increased transparency in pricing and proposed deleveraging would give added credibility to DG Competition's efforts, which sometimes appear to be ad hoc. An examination of its policy for determining the remuneration of instruments used for capital support would be appropriate. Similarly, it would be helpful to review the methodology for determining the required degree of bank deleveraging.

The New State Aid Rules

The new state aid rules, which apply as of August 1, 2013, provide a new framework for state aid to the financial sector. The new rules introduce a potentially more effective framework focused on minimizing costs to the state and on ensuring financial stability. The framework is also relatively restrictive, however, as it gives a prominent role to the European Commission and requires burden sharing prior to the granting of state aid. Banks will have to present a viable restructuring plan, including burden-sharing measures to be approved ex ante by the European Commission before being able to receive state aid. Burden sharing will require shareholders and subordinated junior debt-holders to incur losses either through write-downs or conversion into equity before recapitalization with public funds could take place, but is subject to exceptions such as when their implementation could endanger financial stability or lead to disproportionate results. Bail-ins of senior unsecured creditors and uninsured depositors will not be mandatory. Thus, the rules require that a legal framework for statutory bail-ins be in place before aid is granted, and this implicitly brings forward part of the statutory bail-in requirement of the BRRD from 2018. State aid requirements would need to be justified in the restructuring or liquidation plans based on an asset quality review or a stress test.

Issues Raised by the New Regime

The new regime, while appropriately affirming financial stability and least cost as the main objectives, also raises some issues. Giving the European Commission an

---

[7] As announced in the European Council conclusions of June 28, 2013, the European Commission has adopted revised state aid rules for the financial sector in the summer of 2013 to ensure a level playing field in resolution decisions involving public support.

ex ante veto right on restructuring plans and the provision of aid could introduce delays and uncertainties, and it would grant resolution powers to the European Commission that would interfere with those of the SRM. The advancement of part of the BRRD bail-in provisions could create uncertainty by opening the door to uneven treatments during the transition. Lastly, the requirement to bail-in junior debt prior to state aid would mean that, short of voluntary liabilities management exercises, only banks under resolution could receive state aid, a situation that could destabilize weak banking systems.

The European Commission Proposal for a Single Resolution Mechanism

The Blueprint

The European Commission blueprint for the Banking Union of November 27, 2012, stated that a proposal for a SRM would be put forward in the months following the adoption of the SSM. The EU Council agreements of December 2012, March 2013, and June 2013 reaffirmed that an SRM with adequate powers and tools is required to make the SSM more effective and welcomed a European Commission proposal for an SRM. On July 10, 2013, the European Commission took a welcome step toward a more complete Banking Union by issuing an important proposal for an SRM.[8]

The draft European Commission regulation for an SRM provides for a central resolution authority backed by a single resolution fund, which are desirable characteristics. When the ECB or national authorities signal the need to trigger the resolution of a bank participating in the SSM, a Single Resolution Board (SRB)—consisting of members appointed by the Council, national authorities, the European Commission, and the ECB—would recommend to the European Commission certain key resolution decisions, such as placing an entity under resolution and determining the framework for the use of the resolution tools and funding arrangements. Such decisions would then be formally taken by the European Commission, which could also act on its own initiative. The SRB and national authorities would then be in charge of the implementation process, with the former being able to override the latter. The SRB would also have control over a single resolution fund financed by industry contributions.

Assessment of the Proposal

The proposal goes in the right direction of establishing a strong central resolution authority and a single resolution fund, essential elements of a Banking Union that would reduce fragmentation and mitigate sovereign–bank links (Box 12.3). It provides for strong centralized powers (at the European Commission and at the new SRB) to achieve swift and least-cost resolution while protecting stability and internalizing cross-border effects.

---

[8] The proposal can be found at: http://ec.europa.eu/internal_market/finances/banking-union/index_en.htm.

Box 12.3 The European Commission Proposal for a Single Resolution Mechanism: An Early Assessment

The SRM proposal of July 10, 2013, contains important positive elements. Being established under the existing Treaties, the SRM could be established by the time the SSM becomes effective.

- *Strong powers.* In principle, the SRM draft regulation would enable the European Commission and the SRB to make swift decisions to achieve least-cost resolution, while ensuring stability at the system level and internalizing cross-border effects. The SRM would have a broad range of powers to plan resolutions, assess resolvability, and prepare and adopt key resolution decisions, including with respect to the use of tools and funding arrangements. The SRB would also have investigatory and sanctioning powers and the powers to oversee and assess implementation by national authorities; it would be able to directly address executive orders to a specific bank to ensure implementation.

Funding. A single resolution fund would pool contributions from all banks participating in the SRM, thus weakening sovereign–bank links. Such pooled contributions would be more effective in funding resolutions than funds levied solely at the national level. A single resolution fund would be able to borrow from the ESM in extraordinary circumstances and under strict conditions, after extensive use of burden-sharing powers. DGS would remain at the national level.

However, **crucial aspects of the SRM proposal could raise concerns:**

- *Legal risks.* The SRM is based on Article 114, Treaty on the Functioning of the European Union, which may not allow a transfer of national powers to the European Union. As the SRM proposal entails the transfer of directly binding resolution powers from member states to the European Commission, there is a legal risk that it might not be considered lawful by the Court of Justice of the European Union.[1] The proposal gives substantial discretion to the European Commission in the decision-making process. This could create uncertainties regarding the allocation of responsibilities within the SRM, cause conflicts of interest, and hinder its operational independence:

  - For legal reasons, the European Commission has the final say, but the proposal also allows it to initiate action on its own initiative and overrule the SRB. This could create uncertainty regarding accountability.

  - A lack of clarity on the precise scope of the European Commission's powers and its division of labor with the SRB in the decision-making process may create tensions with national authorities that have to implement its decisions. In this respect, the new European Commission state aid powers could create conflicts with the SRM. To contain such risks, a procedure should be designed to constrain the Commission's discretion and more decision-making powers should be given to the SRB.

  - The strong powers given to the European Commission could impede the operational independence of the SRB, given the Commission's multiple objectives. For example, emphasis on state aid carries the risk that DG Competition would be extensively involved in resolution decisions, which could create conflicts with the SRB. To contain such risks, the SRB should be strongly independent from the European Commission.

---

[1] The EU FSAP established that "Certain elements of an effective safety net such as an SRM can be designed through secondary legislation on the basis on the current treaty" while "in the medium term, providing an explicit legal underpinning for financial stability arrangements in the treaties could further enhance the legal robustness and transparency of those arrangements."

> ### Box 12.3 *(Concluded)*
>
> - *Lack of ex ante agreements on burden sharing and backstops could affect decision making.* The SRB would not be able to specify how fiscal costs would be handled by national authorities. This could create deadlocks in the decision-making process.
> - *Governance of the SRB.* Executive sessions of the board regarding specific banks would involve only home and host national authorities. It would be important to ensure that spillovers on others and the supranational interests are well internalized.

However, there are legal and operational issues to be resolved and clarified, such as the legal risk that the SRM could be found to exceed the scope of the European Commission powers under the existing Treaties by the European Court of Justice; the scope of the European Commission powers and associated risks and conflicts of interest; the division of responsibilities between the European Commission and the SRB; the governance of the SRB; the operational independence of the SRM; and the lack of a common fiscal backstop and of ex ante burden-sharing agreements (apart from the ESM). The legal foundations of the EC proposal for the SRM have been scrutinized by the European Council Legal Service (CLS). In two opinions, the service addressed the questions of whether Article 114 of the Treaty on the Functioning of the European Union (TFEU) is the suitable legal basis for the proposal and whether the delegation of powers to the Single Resolution Board envisaged in the proposal is compatible with the EU Treaties and the general principles of EU law. CLS opinions are not binding, yet they play an important role in policy debates. CLS agreed that Article 114 of the TFEU may be a suitable legal basis for the establishment of the SRM subject to certain conditions. Specifically, the SRM proposal responds to a genuine need of uniform application of the rules on resolution that could not be achieved through other methods of harmonization. The Single Resolution Fund could be established provided that it is deemed to be indispensable for the efficient operations of the SRM and an adequate mechanism to safeguard the budgetary sovereignty of Member States is introduced. However, the SRM proposal encountered legal objections over the envisaged delegation of powers to the Board. CLS argued that the powers delegated to the SRB in the EC proposal need to be further detailed to be compatible with the EU treaties and the Meroni doctrine. The service expressed reservations about a number of competencies such as the drafting of certain aspects of the resolution plan, determining the investment strategy of the Single Resolution Fund, and others. In principle CLS argued that it is necessary to exclude that a wide margin of discretion is entrusted to the Board unless an institution of the Union vested with executive competences is involved in the exercise of SRB powers.

Alternatives Proposed

The European Commission SRM proposal is preferable to alternatives that would merely coordinate resolution mechanisms between national authorities. For example, under the French-German proposal of May 29, 2013, national authorities would lack the right incentives to act timely and in the least costly way, especially on cross-border banks.

DESIGN OF THE SINGLE RESOLUTION MECHANISM

Standards

International Standards

The powers of a Single Resolution Mechanism (SRM) based on a central resolution authority for the Banking Union should be in line with the emerging best practices laid out in the Financial Stability Board's "Key Attributes of Effective Resolution Regimes for Financial Institutions." Its objective should be to make the resolution of financial institutions feasible without systemic disruption while minimizing costs to taxpayers. Burden-sharing mechanisms should ensure that, wherever possible, shareholders and unsecured and uninsured creditors absorb losses in a manner that respects the hierarchy of claims in liquidation. Furthermore, the single resolution authority should comply with preconditions and prerequisites for effective resolution as set out by the Financial Stability Board.

Specific Considerations

In addition to complying with international best practices, the single resolution authority should be designed to address concerns arising from the euro area's multicountry setting. Having a single, fully centralized, supranational resolution authority would set the right incentives, correct externalities and resolve coordination issues, provide a mechanism for swift decision making, and avoid duplication at national levels. It would also ensure that individual countries are not forced to internalize all the resolution costs and the spillovers to others at enormous cost to themselves. Moreover issues related to burden-sharing, governance, accountability, and interaction with the SSM need to be addressed. Legal difficulties would also arise (for example, the need for a change to the Treaty on the Functioning of the European Union—hereafter the EU Treaty—to establish a new EU institution and an insolvency regime that supersedes national regimes).[9]

In contrast to supervision, complete centralization of tasks is easier to achieve in the steady state, as the experience of the United States demonstrates, and there would be no need to design a mechanism delegating some tasks to the national level. However, in the short run, it may remain necessary to delegate some tasks, and this will raise two issues: monitoring the delegated tasks and interacting with the SSM. Addressing the need for a common backstop also becomes essential, since a resolution framework requires adequate backing to be effective, in particular to deal with systemic crises.

Preconditions and Prerequisites

Preconditions

Emerging best practices include a set of preconditions to ensure effective resolution: (1) a well-established framework for financial stability, surveillance, and policy formulation; (2) an effective system for the supervision, regulation, and

---

[9] See Chapter 10 for a detailed discussion.

oversight of financial institutions; (3) effective protection schemes for depositors, insurance policy holders, and other customers; (4) a robust accounting, auditing, and disclosure regime; and (5) a well-developed legal framework and judicial system. In the context of the banking union, these preconditions have implications for EU legal regimes and for the existence of an effective and credible SSM and deposit insurance scheme for all banks in the banking union.

Prerequisites

To establish a sound basis for effective resolution, a resolution authority with a common fiscal backstop should be operationally independent, consistent with its statutory responsibilities; have transparent processes, legal protections, sound governance, and adequate resources; and be subject to rigorous evaluation and accountability mechanisms. Some considerations are particularly relevant in the supranational context of the banking union.

- *Objectives and mandate.* A common resolution authority for the euro area should seek to maximize recovery value in resolution and minimize the overall cost of resolution and losses to creditors. Establishing a strong and autonomous resolution authority will ensure that home-host concerns are internalized within the euro area, but the cost and stability impact on other jurisdictions (in the European Union or outside) will have to be taken into account. The resolution authority should pursue financial stability and ensure continuity of systemically important financial services and functions while protecting depositors and other claimants protected by insurance schemes and arrangements.

- *Operational independence and legal protection.* EU Treaty changes that would establish a strong and autonomous resolution authority should provide for an appropriate level of operational autonomy. Complementary EU Treaty revisions should be considered to ensure legal protection of officials for their actions and decisions in the exercise of resolution powers.

- *Accountability.* Independence must be complemented with accountability. Resolution is an intrusive process with fiscal implications; it involves difficult and complex decisions about burden sharing and the distribution of costs between various claimants and taxpayers. In the context of the banking union, it would potentially involve choices about the distribution of losses between taxpayers of different countries, and it may impact ownership and competitive conditions both domestically and for the entire eurozone. These considerations call for particular attention to designing even more rigorous accountability mechanisms and evaluating resolution measures in the context of a banking union. The transparency of the single resolution authority would be essential, as would strong accountability and reporting to eurozone finance ministers (Eurogroup/EU Council) and European citizens (European Parliament). If national authorities retain the prime responsibility for the resolution of a subset of banks (an option not to be favored), an accountability mechanism operating at two levels (with national authorities also accountable to the national parliament and to the ministry of finance) will need to be in place.

- *Sound governance*. Sound governance will be crucial to ensure early action and effective resolution decisions in the interest of the banking union as a whole. Specifically, conflicts of interest may arise for cross-border systemically important financial institutions during the preparation of recovery and resolution plans or during early intervention and resolution, since ownership structures remain national while assets and liabilities cross borders. A single resolution authority should provide the mechanism to remove these impediments to effective resolution, but its effectiveness and timeliness will depend on its governance, decision-making structure, and access to fiscal resources. It would have to prevent undue political interference and long negotiations that could hold up its decisions.

For example, one possible model could be to rely on a two-tier governance structure to balance effective decision making with the need for oversight. An executive board could be tasked with making decisions affecting specific financial institutions in the interest of the banking union. A resolution council, including national representatives from all countries participating in the SRM, could be tasked with the oversight of decisions made by the executive board and with decisions on broader policy matters, such as those related to burden-sharing mechanisms and fiscal backstops. The voting mechanism should ensure that resolution decisions would not be blocked, and it would guarantee the "will to act." Effective resolution also requires cooperating and exchanging information with the SSM as well as having checks and balances.

- *Resources and competencies*. The resources allocated to the central resolution authority should be sufficient to build capacity at the center while protecting it from undue influence by national authorities and the industry. Given the importance of global systemically important banks in the euro area financial system, the central authority will need to hire independent staff with the expertise and capacity to implement preventative, early intervention and resolution measures with respect to large and complex financial institutions. In the interim period, pragmatism would call for relying on national resources and expertise. But to avoid duplication of resources at the national levels, swift centralization of resources and expertise would be essential to ensure that capacity is built for the resolution of these financial institutions.

- *Funding*. To be effective, the central resolution authority will require access to common funding and a fiscal backstop (this is discussed in more detail under "Risks to the Single Resolution Mechanism," below).

Scope

Coverage

Consistent with the scope of the SSM, the common resolution mechanism should include all the banks licensed in the eurozone. No bank should remain under nonbank national insolvency proceedings. Consideration should be given to extending the scope of the resolution authority to other financial institutions such as holding companies, nonregulated operational entities within a financial group or conglomerate, and branches of foreign banks (other EU and non-EU banks). Covering these institutions would be important insofar as they could be systemic and therefore would need to be dealt with using adequate tools when they failed. Extending the coverage of the SSM to these institutions, if that turns out to be possible, would ensure consistency and help contain risks of failure.

Powers and Tools

Preparation and Prevention

The central resolution authority should be able to ensure preparation and prevention, in close cooperation with the SSM, and should have powers to

- *review and validate the recovery plans of systemic banks.* This task should be performed in close cooperation with the SSM, which should also be involved in the process.
- *prepare resolution plans for systemic banks.* Critically, these plans would include details on the application of resolution tools and ways to ensure the continuity of critical functions; the ECB, as the center of the SSM, should be closely involved.
- *take investigatory actions* to ensure preparedness of the resolution authority, including requests for information and on-site inspections.
- *require actions to remove impediments to resolvability* to ensure that the available tools can allow resolutions to be performed in a way that does not compromise critical functions, threaten financial stability, or involve undue costs to taxpayers. These could include changes to a firm's business practices, structure, or organization to reduce complexity and other potential costs.
- *be involved in decisions related to intra-group support agreements, alongside the ECB.*

Early intervention

Powers to take early intervention measures should also be provided to the resolution authority, which alongside the SSM should be able to

- require capital conservation measures;
- impose restrictions on activities, including implementation of measures set out in the recovery plan; and
- trigger resolution.

Resolution powers and tools, which consist partly in taking control of the failed institutions, should include the possibility to

- take over control of a firm, including by nominating a special manager and removing the senior management and directors;
- transfer assets and liabilities ("Purchase & Assumption" agreement) to a sound acquirer;

- set up a bridge bank, taking over good assets or services to ensure continuity of essential services;

- separate bad assets by setting up an asset management vehicle (a "bad bank"), in conjunction with other measures;

- apply a bail-in tool, involving the SSM, to recapitalize or wind down the bank with shareholders wiped out or diluted and creditors' claims reduced, wiped out, or converted to shares; and

- override shareholders' rights regarding any decision needed in resolution, subject to the condition that shareholders should not be worse off than they would be under liquidation of the firm.

Coordination with Other Institutions

Coordination with the Single Supervisory Mechanism

Decisions to trigger early intervention or resolution will be highly sensitive and have distributional consequences that may bring conflicting interests among member states to the fore. In that respect, providing powers to the resolution authority that overlap with some powers of the SSM may contribute to a strong and robust financial stability framework for the euro area. For example, the resolution authority would also have investigatory powers, be able to trigger early intervention, require prompt corrective actions and be able to initiate resolution (for example, by withdrawing deposit insurance).

Coordination with the Directorate General for Competition

The Directorate General for Competition (DG Comp) will remain the EU agency with approval over state aid and competition policy. Therefore, it will continue to play a central role in the restructuring of banks in the European Union, but its role will change as a dedicated resolution framework for the banking union is developed. The challenge will be to find a balance to foster a more integrated approach between the European Commission as the guardian of competition and the SRM and the SSM and also to establish a permanent coordination between the three institutions. For banks outside the banking union perimeter, DG Comp may also play a coordinating role between the banking union's resolution authority and those in the remaining EU member states based on the BRRD framework.

ESTABLISHING AN EFFECTIVE CENTRAL RESOLUTION AUTHORITY

Steady-State Considerations

Central Resolution Authority

A fully centralized euro area resolution authority should be able, in the steady state, to handle the resolution of failed euro area banks with possible delegation of some tasks to internal offices located across member states. It should have powers and tools, mandates, independence, governance, and accountability to ensure effective resolution in line with international best practices and the BRRD, but with reinforced mechanisms or rules to ensure its effectiveness in a multicountry setting.

- *Positives.* This centralized approach is the best solution to internalize cross-border effects and solve coordination failures, help build solid resolution expertise for systemic institutions, provide flexibility to intervene and allocate resources where needed, and avoid national duplications. It would ensure that the ECB would interact at par with a strong supranational institution that would complement its functions and mandates. A strong resolution authority would contribute to ensuring effective supervision, provided there is clear coordination and information sharing between the two institutions. Conversely, a strong supervisory mechanism would also contribute in establishing the credibility of the resolution authority and in making it robust. In short, the two institutions would reinforce, complement, and balance each other. The central resolution authority would also provide mechanisms for clear ex ante burden-sharing arrangements, provided an adequate fiscal backstop is also in place.

- *Obstacles.* For an effective central resolution authority to be credible, agreement is needed on a common resolution and fiscal backstops, and including a loss-sharing mechanism involving taxpayers. Also, any EU Treaty change to create a strong supranational resolution authority would require time. Such authority should also be able to apply a single resolution regime, overriding national insolvency laws.

Burden Sharing

Clear and workable burden-sharing arrangements, including between participating member states and the common backstop, are essential for an effective resolution mechanism. In line with international best practices, the euro area resolution authority would have power to override shareholders' rights and impose losses according to clear ex ante rankings of claimants that would respect the hierarchy of claims but have some flexibility to depart from the pari passu principle. A "bail-in" mechanism haircutting or converting senior unsecured creditors would provide a tool for burden sharing. Meanwhile, depositor preference should be included in the framework to further protect depositors and the funding provided by the deposit insurance scheme (see "Resolution Funds and Deposit Insurance," below).

Next, pooled contributions from the euro area industry would be needed to finance the costs of normal resolution. Pooled contributions from euro area taxpayers (which would follow specific ex ante rules) would be needed only insofar as private sector contributions and allocation of losses among uninsured claimants are insufficient to cover the costs of resolution, subject to a systemic exemption. In addition to more standard burden-sharing rules that apply to any resolution authority, the single resolution authority should also be provided with a clear mechanism for decision making (see the discussion on governance under "Design of a Single Resolution Mechanism," above) and a combination of ex ante burden-sharing rules across member states, which could be based on capital keys similar to the capital contributions at the ECB.

Funding

A euro area resolution fund would finance the costs associated with bank resolution. Such a fund would build resources from risk-based contributions levied on all countries. The contribution base would, ideally, not only be total deposits but also include other liabilities, possibly adjusting for risk taking and externalities. A good benchmark would be to build a fund targeted to cover the net fiscal costs of up to a large or a few medium-sized bank failures. Adequate common fiscal backstops, which would be particularly important for systemic events, would also be crucial for the effectiveness of the resolution authority (see section "Common Safety Nets and Backstops"). A transition period would reduce the immediate impact on banks and, meanwhile, other costs could be recouped ex post from banks, although this may create moral hazard.

Institutional considerations

Since resolution involves sensitive decisions over distribution of losses, given the need for checks and balances an independent body should be established that would operate alongside the ECB supervisor. To ensure effectiveness, this resolution authority should be an EU institution established "at par" with the ECB, even if there could be merit in a transitional arrangement, such as the creation of a temporary EU agency. At the same time, governance arrangements would need to ensure close cooperation between the SSM and the resolution authority. These arrangements would be complemented by joint technical committees and working groups.

Transition

Scope

A possible approach would be to bring all euro area banks under a central resolution authority as they are brought under the supervision of the ECB.

- *Positives.* Bringing banks under a single resolution authority in parallel with the transition toward the SSM would ensure a more consistent treatment of resolution in the euro area and would greatly simplify the operational complexity of the supervisory tasks awaiting the ECB. Having a unique resolution authority in charge would be particularly relevant for banks being restructured and in need of, or nearly in need of, public support.

- *Temporary body.* To facilitate the process, there may be merit to establishing a temporary body or urgently creating an EU agency tasked with the coordination of bank crisis management and resolution among national authorities and the ECB. Such an agency could be linked to the ESM, with accountability to the Eurogroup. The experience of the Swedish Bank Authority in the 1990s and the U.S. Treasury unit set up to restructure AIG provide examples of the usefulness of temporary bodies.

- **Risks.** Time would be needed to build resources and capacity at the center. In the event of a delayed transition, the ECB would become tasked with supervising systemic banks, including complex ones, and would have to interact with multiple competent national authorities, including with respect to early intervention and corrective actions. The need for consistency among preparedness measures and mechanisms to deal with cross-border considerations and systemic banks also suggests that a delayed transition would be inefficient and result in duplication of tasks. A slow and delayed transition toward an SRM would also create the risk of an incomplete framework if political support weakened over time.

- **Speed.** There are two main strategies:

  A "big-bang" approach. A "big-bang" approach envisages a rapid move toward the establishment of a central resolution authority and supranational insolvency regime. This is the preferred approach, but it may be constrained by political realities and practical considerations.

  - *Pros.* This rapid approach would help ensure a smooth transition to the SSM by moving supervision and resolution in tandem. Building resources at the center may take time, but the temporary body mentioned above could be the stepping stone to a permanent framework. This approach would build cross-border expertise in early intervention, supervision, and recovery and resolution planning for systemic institutions.

  - *Cons.* Securing an EU Treaty change could be daunting in the near term. It would also require establishing pan-euro-area insolvency laws (requiring regulations) and the involvement of courts (the European Court of Justice) to supersede national regimes. The temporary body or EU agency, which may require its own treaty or could possibly be established under Article 352 of the EU Treaty, could remain active during the interim.

  A gradual approach. A gradual approach would consist of three steps. First, national regimes would be harmonized and strengthened, as prescribed in the BRRD. Harmonized national resolution funds would be set up, allowing cross-border borrowing arrangements. Second, an EU body, similar to the European Banking Authority, could be established by an EU regulation and tasked with the coordination of resolution in the euro area. It would play a coordinating role in ensuring a single approach to resolution. In the long term, a supranational central authority could be established.

  - *Pros.* This approach would ensure that no disruptions in resolution structure would happen during the transition. It would guarantee full compatibility across national regimes between national and federal bodies and between "ins" and "outs." It would not require changes in national laws beyond those needed to harmonize and ensure robustness of resolution regimes.

  - *Cons.* Until a federal agency is created, the SSM would have to interact with multiple national authorities, which could be unwieldy and constrain effectiveness. It could create incentive problems within the SSM insofar as national authorities would refrain from sharing with the ECB information that might result in a decision to trigger a resolution (one that might have to be financed by domestic taxpayers). The national approach to resolution funding would achieve little risk diversification and would therefore be inferior to a centralized approach. A long transition toward the most robust solution would increase the risks of a stalled process and an incomplete framework. A harmonization of frameworks could itself take time, since transposition into national law would be required in each EU country.

RISKS TO THE SINGLE RESOLUTION MECHANISM

Risks associated with an SRM include stalled reforms, the consequences for cost or risk sharing from the euro area crisis, and dealing with too-big-to-fail institutions.

Stalled Reforms

The main transitional risk in a gradual approach is that of a stalled reform process. This risk should be addressed by having a clear roadmap that would be time-bound and would indicate the main steps and key deliverables, including agreement toward a common safety net. This could occur at an early stage, for example while harmonizing national resolution regimes, or it could occur at an intermediate stage while agreeing on an SRM for the banking union.

Harmonization Stage

A fully harmonized system of rules with resolution authority remaining at the national level and coexisting with a common ESM backstop would create incentives to shift the costs of resolution to the euro area taxpayer. It could create an unwieldy system in which the SSM would have to interact with many national authorities during crisis time, but also during the steady state to be able to supervise the euro area systemic banks. The framework would achieve little to weaken the link between sovereign and bank funding costs. Lastly, the transposition of the BRRD into national laws would still leave the door open to different interpretations and, therefore, to different practices.

Centralization Stage

The banking union could transition to a framework with a resolution authority akin to the European Banking Authority (for example, an EU agency) tasked with the coordination and mediation of resolutions that would remain nationally based. Depending on the actual powers of this body, the framework may have to progress in the direction of centralizing bank resolution and internalizing cross-border externalities arising in the resolution of cross-border banks or in the use of a common backstop. However, there is a risk that the agency would lack adequate binding powers, and also a risk that it could be subjected to fiscal safeguards preventing infringements of member states' sovereignty, which would impede effectiveness.

Need for Burden Sharing and Adequate Fiscal Backstop

To be fully effective, the single resolution authority must be accompanied with burden-sharing rules and, at a minimum, provide a mechanism for swift decision making. Adequate common fiscal backstops are also required to ensure the effectiveness of a centralized resolution authority.

Precedent

Divergent interests during the transition may have consequences for the future, since the way legacy is addressed during this crisis will create a precedent for the future. The costs of existing bad bank debt should be left as much as possible to those that have been primarily responsible for them, that is, the creditors and national supervisors. But as government solvency is endangered and systemic risk rises, direct recapitalization by the ESM becomes necessary. Creditors may insist on control but resist enhancing backstops for fear that imperfect control would result in a "transfer union." Debtors may insist on the need to delink banks from sovereigns as a condition for transferring control to the center. An incomplete solution might result in an unstable Banking Union, in either of two alternative scenarios:

- *ESM direct recapitalization but no central resolution.* Some form of a common backstop, albeit imperfect (such as the announced mechanism of direct ESM recapitalization) would give strong incentives to national resolution authorities to shift the costs away from national creditors and onto the euro area taxpayers.

- *Central resolution but no adequate common fiscal backstop.* Centralizing resolution decisions without an adequate common fiscal backstop and lasting solution for burden sharing would not help address the sovereign–bank links and would not be conducive to information sharing. The fiscal consequences of decisions made at the center would fall entirely on national taxpayers and could generate political risks while jeopardizing the credibility and effectiveness of a single resolution authority.

Too-Big-to-Fail banks

Global systemically important banks' complexity, cross-border dimensions, and systemic roles place a high value on quickly establishing a robust supranational resolution authority, with powers and tools aligned with the Financial Stability Board's Key Attributes and with adequate common fiscal backstops. In contrast, national approaches to resolution and fiscal resources would become inadequate to resolving a systemic institution. The need to ensure preparedness and to remove impediments to resolvability suggests a key benefit to pulling scarce resources together and building shared knowledge and capacity at the center, as well as the benefit of the single resolution authority.

Legal Considerations

In time, a change in the EU Treaty would be necessary to establish a strong and autonomous resolution authority. The accompanying supranational insolvency regime would also have to override national insolvency laws. However, certain elements of an effective safety net such as an SRM could be designed through secondary legislation on the basis of the current EU Treaty.

COMMON SAFETY NETS AND BACKSTOPS

Essentials

Backstops and common insurance mechanisms form essential elements of the banking union. Absent backstops and safety nets, the banking union would be unable to delink or weaken the link between sovereigns and banks. It would possibly be unstable and risky and could jeopardize the credibility of the ECB; and the SRM would be ineffective and noncredible. Setting up backstops and common insurance mechanisms requires a transfer of control to the center, and must follow only after some preconditions have been met.

Common Fiscal Backstops

Adequate common backstops are essential to dealing with systemic crises, since prefunding by DGS and/or resolution funds would likely not suffice to deal with the gross fiscal costs of a crisis. Common backstops are therefore needed to create a framework that is robust and breaks sovereign–bank links in tail events. During the transition, direct recapitalization by the ESM will make it possible to break the link between banks and sovereigns when solvency concerns about the latter arise. To the extent that DGS and resolution funds will only progressively accumulate contributions from the industry, agreements on fiscal backstops and burden sharing may even be more important during the transitional phase.

Deposit Insurance

As noted, common deposit insurance is needed for stability reasons. A pooled mechanism would be more effective in protecting confidence (subject to an adequate fiscal backstop) and in diversifying risks across large numbers of banks. But the need for a common DGS also follows logically once an SSM and a single resolution authority are in place. To the extent that a resolution authority would require common funding from the industry, postponing the centralization of DGS makes little sense. Additional national DGS could be allowed to complement the euro area DGS.

Resolution Funds and Deposit Insurance

European Commission Proposal

The EU Council aims at a swift adoption of the DGS Directive and the BRRD by the European Parliament and transposition into national laws.

- **Resolution funding.** Financing arrangements funded with contributions from banks and investment firms that are in proportion to their liabilities risk profile and systemic importance must be established at the national level. Contributions will be raised from banks (on total liabilities, excluding own funds) at least annually to reach a target funding level of at least 1 percent of covered deposits after 10 years. If the ex ante funds are insufficient to deal with the resolution of an institution, further contributions will be raised (ex post). Mutual borrowing arrangements across schemes are allowed, subject to safeguards designed to protect creditor resolution funds. Funding already available in DGS could be used for resolution, in which case contributions for resolution would be based on total liabilities, excluding own funds and insured deposits. But the DGS would rank pari passu with unsecured creditors in insolvency proceedings for the amount of covered deposits. Finally, alternative funding means, such as borrowing from the central bank, should be enabled.

- **_Deposit insurance_**. The DGS Directive paves the way for harmonizing national DGS in payouts speed, coverage, and funding. In particular, it sets a 75 percent share of ex ante financing and a target coverage ratio of 1.5 percent of eligible deposits after 10 years, permitting ex post financing of up to 0.5 percent of covered deposits. Borrowing arrangements across national schemes are permitted, allowing up to 0.5 percent of eligible deposits of the borrower, and must be repaid within five years, with the claim ranking first in liquidation proceedings. After 10 years, the size will be recalibrated on the basis of covered deposits (instead of eligible deposits). Bank contributions to national DGS reflect risk, based on core indicators such as capital adequacy, asset quality, profitability, and liquidity. DGS can also be used for resolution funding, provided that the primary function of the DGS is not impeded.

Alternative Preferred Approach

The following describes an alternative to creating a pan-euro-area DGS and resolution fund:

- _Scope_. All euro area banks should be covered by the resolution fund and by the deposit insurance scheme for consistency with the SSM and the single resolution authority. Covering only a subset of banks could be destabilizing by inducing reallocations of deposits between the national segment and the euro area segment, and it could create distortions to competition within the single market, but additional schemes could be allowed to top-up the pan-European scheme. Given different sizes of banking systems across euro area countries, the coverage would be skewed toward the largest financial systems in the core of the euro area.

- _Funding_.
  - _Resolution fund_. The resolution fund should be prefunded through ex ante risk-based premiums (reflecting at least capitalization, profitability, liquidity, and asset quality) and should also be adjusted for the systemic importance of an institution. Use of funds could be complemented by arrangements to recoup losses through ex post levies on the industry. To the extent that ex post levies are procyclical and induce moral hazard, their share in the industry funding should be limited. The resolution fund

should also have access to common backstops; this which would be particularly important during the transition when the fund has insufficient reserves and for systemic events. The tax rate should be chosen to smooth the cyclical burdens on the industry while building a target prefunding ratio within 10 years. The tax base should include all liabilities (including wholesale funds) excluding capital.

- *Deposit insurance.* To a significant extent, the DGS should be prefunded through ex ante risk-based premiums levied on the industry and should be complemented, if needed, by ex post levies on the industry. The tax base should be the total eligible deposits. The tax rate should be chosen to minimize the cyclical burdens on the industry while ensuring that the deposit insurance fund reaches its target level within 10 years. As above, it should be risk-based and reflect the systemic importance of a bank. The prefunded element of the DGS should, in steady state, maintain a ratio of about 1.5 percent of total eligible deposits (hence, the total fund size would be about €100 billion). This would allow covering deposit payments for two or three medium-sized bank failures, but having a backstop available would be critical.

- *National DGS.* Specific national schemes could be allowed to continue to operate in addition to the pan euro area deposit insurance, provided they are aligned with the EU Directives.

Merging Resolution and Deposit Insurance Funds

A single integrated fund for resolution and deposit insurance would have benefits. There are synergies between DGS and resolution funding, as both contribute to stabilizing financial systems. There are economies of scale that derive from jointly administering the funds. Objectives do not conflict when the ranking of claimants is clear and adequate, provided insured depositors are protected. Furthermore, separating funds does not preclude the fungibility of fiscal outlays during banking crises. Nevertheless, DGS and resolution funds have different objectives. The former must ensure that eligible depositors are reimbursed up to the coverage limit, while the latter must ensure that failed banks can be wound up and cover all resolution costs while minimizing losses of value and contagion risks.

Mixed Model

There has also been discussion about creating a common resolution fund, administered by the single resolution authority, while harmonizing deposit insurance schemes but allowing them to remain at the national level. Such a model would go some way toward enhancing the effectiveness of the SSM while providing common financing for resolution, although without common backstops its impact would be limited. Under this model, it would be essential that national deposit insurance funds were available to contribute to resolution, up to the amount available for payout. Even so, the disadvantages would include less efficient risk pooling, which would not effectively decouple sovereigns and banks;

TABLE 12.1

Financial Sector Support 2008–11 (percent of 2011 GPD)	
Belgium	7.0
Ireland	41.2
Germany	12.2
Greece	6.1
Netherlands	14.1
Spain[1]	19.5
United Kingdom	6.8
United States	5.3

Source: IMF, *Fiscal Monitor*; Spain Financial Sector Assessment Program; and staff estimates.
[1] Includes actual use of debt guarantees. Asset purchases and capitial support from the Fund for Orderly Bank Restructuring as of March 2012 and the European Stability Mechanism/European Financial Stability Facility (EFSF) loan announced on June 9th.

complexities in cost allocation and implementation in the case of cross-border failures, requiring close coordination between national DGS and the single resolution authority; and duplication of costs and administrative resources, since both funds would be assessed on the same banks.

Desired Size

While there is no well-established good practice, the typical target size of deposit insurance and resolution funds could range from about 1 to 2 percent of insured deposits in large systems (as in the European Commission proposal or the United States) to 4 to 5 percent in smaller systems, where the aim is to cover two to five midsize bank failures or four to six small bank failures. Part of the gross outlays would be recouped from asset sales during resolution and from ex post contributions from the industry (see Table 12.1, which illustrates the size of financial sector support during the recent crisis).

Legal Concerns

A single resolution fund would require having a supranational resolution framework in place. This would require establishing a euro area insolvency regime, which may require an EU Treaty change. Treaty change would be required if a Euro Area Deposit Insurance and Resolution Fund is "joint and several." The no-bail-out clause of Article 125 prohibits the European Union, euro area, or member states from being liable for or assuming the liabilities of another state or of its public bodies. However, voluntary loans to other member states (as envisaged in the BRRD), or multiple several-guarantees arrangements (as under the ESM) would not appear to be in contradiction with the current EU Treaty.

Fiscal Backstops and Burden-Sharing Arrangements

Decision Making

At a minimum, clear rules for decision making should be put in place to ensure that resolution decisions can be taken promptly. These should include some ex ante agreed burden-sharing rules to ensure an orderly process—a clear hierarchy of claims (including bail-ins of unsecured senior creditors) and some ex ante rules for allocating fiscal costs across member states. To minimize moral hazard and conflicts of interest, rules allocating fiscal burdens across countries would be especially important insofar as some banks would remain under the supervision of national authorities while more systemic ones come under the direct responsibility of the ECB. The governance of the single authority should also leave some room for discretion to allow for swift decision making ("over a weekend") in emergency situations. Least-cost resolution and the allocation of losses should also weigh in stability concerns.

Pecking Order

The probability and severity of banking crises is minimized by effective supervision and ambitiously high capital requirements. But when crises occur, burden sharing should follow this order (subject to a systemic exemption):

1. haircutting shareholders
2. junior creditors
3. bailing-in senior unsecured creditors
4. bailing-in resolution and deposit insurance funds, and
5. taxpayer contributions.

(See the section below on "Layers of Backstops" for a discussion of rules that could govern the allocation of losses between the national sovereign and a common fiscal backstop.)[10]

Insured depositors should come last in the ordering of losses, and there should be depositor preference (for example, the deposit insurance fund should be senior to other claimants). In most crises, the hierarchy of losses would not conflict with stability concerns and would support market discipline ex ante. However, in systemic crises, taxpayer funding would become inevitable. Since 2008, according to the European Commission, over €4.5 trillion has been used to rescue banks in the European Union (including liquidity provision measures and asset guarantees by governments).

Plan for Tail Events

A common fiscal backstop and agreements on burden sharing would help ensure that banking crises do not endanger the solvency of the sovereign. Historical evidence shows that one-fourth of banking crises had gross fiscal costs in excess of 16 percent of gross domestic product (GDP), although net costs are invariably lower, as values of distressed assets recover. In the steady state, private sector resources will not suffice to cover the gross costs of systemic crises, but fiscal costs cannot be left entirely on national taxpayers.

---

[10] Secured claims should be secured up to the value of the collateral, and the remainder would be unsecured and treated as such.

Layers of Backstops

A series of common backstops, including elements of a fiscal union, must therefore be created at the euro area level to prevent downward spirals between sovereigns and the banks in tail scenarios. The following is one type of scheme that could be considered:

- *Common resolution fund/DGS.* A euro area fund of the kind described above would provide a first buffer to weaken the link between sovereigns and bank failures. It would cover a proportion of each banking crisis that would depend on its level of agreed prefunding. Ex post levies on the banking sector may also help reduce fiscal contributions in the medium term, although achieving full fiscal neutrality may be difficult in the case of systemic crises.

- *ESM direct recapitalization.* In extreme circumstances, if all ESM resources were used for directly recapitalizing banks and served as a loss-sharing mechanism (i.e., investing in going-concern banks with negative equity), ESM's eventual size would be able to cover crises requiring up to about 5 percent of euro area GDP in fiscal outlays. Its capital keys would provide an ex ante burden-sharing agreement, while its governance would facilitate swift decision making. In practice, a fraction of the resources would likely be available for bank recapitalization (and the rest for sovereign support).

- *Earmarked contingent euro area taxation.* A more ambitious approach would be to grant a eurozone institution (under the Eurogroup) with limited taxing power that could be relied upon to back blanket guarantees during systemic events.

- *ECB line of credit.* Temporary ECB lines of credit to the resolution authority, guaranteed by the common fiscal backstop, may be essential to finance a bank resolution in an emergency, contingent on a fiscal backstop being in place to cover the eventual net fiscal costs of the banking crisis.[11] A similar set-up is used, for example, in the United States, where the Federal Reserve was involved in financing the asset management company that dealt with AIG's and Bear Sterns' toxic assets. In Switzerland, the Swiss National Bank funded the Swiss Stabilization Fund to deal with UBS's legacy assets.

Cofinancing by the National Sovereign

If there are residual imperfections in the SSM, the presence of a common backstop could create incentive problems, reinforce regulatory forbearance, and unduly shift the costs of bank failures to euro area taxpayers. To mitigate this risk, consideration could be given to involving national taxpayers. For instance, the ex ante burden-sharing arrangements designed by the single resolution authority

---

[11] The possibility of such central bank lines of credit are envisaged in the European Commission draft Directive for bank recovery and resolution.

could specify the share of losses borne by national taxpayers (on top of loss-sharing rules associated with a common backstop), conditional on sovereign solvency being protected and on strong national fiscal rules. This is not unlike standard insurance with deductibles and copayments. However, the need to delink banks and sovereigns could constrain the usefulness of such arrangements. Allowing cofinancing also raises difficult questions. For example, after a bank is recapitalized by the sovereign, would the sovereign's shares be diluted should the situation worsen and require additional recapitalization by the common backstop? Several ex ante burden-sharing approaches could be considered:

- *Fixed amount of loss to national taxpayer.* Losses would be allocated to national taxpayers up to an ex ante defined maximum that could be expressed in percent of GDP. The threshold would balance the needs to align incentives and to attenuate the sovereign–bank nexus. Above the threshold, losses would be allocated to the common backstop. This approach could suffice in the steady state, but it might also be dynamically inefficient when the threshold limit was about to be breached.

- *Cofinancing starting with the first euro.* National taxpayers would contribute a minimum ex ante agreed share of the gross fiscal costs of each bank failure. While cumbersome, this approach would help align incentives, regardless of the size of the banking crisis.

- *Liquidity backstops.* Under the current set-up, national authorities would bear the risks of resolution but would be eligible for ESM loans. This approach might only marginally weaken the link from the banks to the sovereign, and may therefore not be desirable.

Transition

Harmonized National Resolution Funds and DGS

The European Commission approach could be a stepping stone toward the creation of a single pan-euro-area scheme in the long term. However, since risk sharing would take place at the national level, it would achieve little risk diversification in the interim, in particular in countries with smaller, less diversified banking systems. It also would not delink banks from sovereigns. The degree of harmonization of national funds achieved through a directive may not suffice to merge national resolution funds into a single euro area fund.

- ***Transitioning heterogeneous banks into the resolution fund.*** A slow transition to a single fund by gradually extending coverage to a larger sample of banks, for example in conjunction with the extension of the SSM, could be problematic. In countries with weak sovereigns, such an approach may create liquidity pressures for the banks remaining under the national DGS. A rapid phasing-in of a resolution fund might raise concerns about the cyclical effects of bank levies, if the transitioning period is too short.

- ***Euro area "reinsurance scheme".*** A reinsurance scheme for national DGS could also be created, funded at the euro area level through levies on the industry (although this too could suffer from the problem of procyclicality) and/or annual contributions from member states. Ex ante agreement on the degree of national funding and supranational funding in depositor payouts would prevent moral hazard. Over time, the reinsurance fund would build administrative capacity and could become a step toward the creation of a permanent euro area DGS and resolution fund.

Fiscal Backing

As noted, resolution funds and DGS require explicit fiscal backing, complemented at times by liquidity lines from the central bank, to cover the gross costs of systemic crises. Thus, agreement on backstops is required to transition to a euro area resolution fund.

CONCLUSION

Establishing a strong and autonomous resolution authority is key to enhancing the effectiveness of the single supervisory mechanism. To be effective, a centralized resolution authority requires clear rules for burden sharing and adequate common backstops to break sovereign–bank links. A pan-euro-area resolution fund should be built over time from risk-based industry contributions. It should be complemented by a fiscal backstop that could be provided by the ESM or, over the longer term, by earmarked pan-euro-area taxes, as well as a liquidity line from the ECB. Establishing a strong and fully independent single resolution authority at par with the ECB may, however, require an EU Treaty change.

In the near term, a single resolution mechanism, such as proposed by the European Commission, is a welcome step in the right direction and would ensure that an SRM is in place by the time the SSM becomes effective. It would allow for swift decisions on burden-sharing arrangements and ensure least-cost resolution, even if there remain areas of concern. Without a strong SRM complementing the SSM, the credibility and effectiveness of the banking union would be jeopardized. To effectively break bank–sovereign links, the SRM would have to have access to an effective common fiscal backstop, ultimately backed by a combination of ex ante and ex post industry levies from a single resolution fund. A credit line to the ESM could be a bridge to a more permanent solution.

Centralizing DGS would enhance credibility and risk diversification. In the long term, a single deposit insurance and resolution fund could be created by merging the resolution fund and national DGS.

Although it has not been a focus of this chapter, addressing transitional risks will be important. A temporary body or EU agency, which would be an embryonic resolution authority under the European Commission SRM proposal, could be created to help deal with the resolution of failed banks. Designing appropriate cofinancing arrangements, for example clear ex ante burden-sharing arrangements with room for discretion, may be useful to fully align the incentives of national authorities with the common good, although due consideration should be given to how burden-sharing arrangements might impact sovereign–bank links.

It will also be important to avoid a stalled reform process. Lacking a single resolution authority would weaken the effectiveness of the SSM. Centralized resolution without agreement on burden-sharing rules and on adequate fiscal backstops would lead to an ineffective and noncredible resolution authority. To address transitional risks, a clear and time-bound roadmap for the remaining elements of the banking union, demonstrating a shared understanding of the end point by all member states, should be announced, with strict deadlines and key deliverables at each step of the reform process.

REFERENCE

Goyal, Rishi, Petya Koeva Brooks, Mahmood Pradhan, and others, 2013, "A Banking Union for the Euro Area," IMF Staff Discussion Note No. 13/1 (Washington: International Monetary Fund).

CHAPTER 13

Bank Recapitalization

THIERRY TRESSEL

INTRODUCTION

A Potential Turning Point in the Euro Area Crisis

On June 29, 2012, euro area leaders correctly identified the vicious circle linking banks and sovereigns as a core problem with the monetary union and called for the establishment of an effective single supervisory mechanism (SSM) and common backstop for bank capital. On June 20, 2013, the Eurogroup reached agreement on the main features and way forward for the European Stability Mechanism (ESM) direct recapitalization instrument. This is an important step forward with many positive elements.

However, finalization of the operational framework has been linked to adoption of the Bank Recovery and Resolution Directive (BRRD) and the Deposit Guarantee Schemes (DGS) Directive, which may create uncertainty in the recapitalization instrument's start date. Mobilizing this recapitalization tool in a timely manner is critical to developing a path out of the current crisis. In this regard, it is of critical importance that ESM direct recapitalization of banks, including migration to ESM of existing public support to banks, is not subjected to overly burdensome preconditions, even if the ESM recapitalization would require unanimity in the ESM Board of Governors and approval by national parliaments in some jurisdictions (e.g., Germany). ESM investment decisions should take a long-term perspective, cognizant that gross upfront crisis outlays tend to dwarf ultimate costs net of recoveries/capital gains and, in many instances, generate positive financial returns.

Direct Recapitalization

The ESM's timely and effective direct recapitalization of domestically systemic banks in the euro area could play a key role not only in breaking the vicious circle linking banks and sovereigns but also in repairing monetary transmission and preparing for banking union, and it could therefore help complete the economic and monetary union. As a patient, deep-pocket investor, the ESM can maximize the financial stability benefits of, and long-run returns on, its investment.

This chapter draws on the February 2013 IMF Staff Discussion Note, "A Banking Union for the Euro Area" (Goyal and others, 2013), and on the accompanying technical background note on bank recapitalization. The contribution of the various authors of those notes is gratefully acknowledged.

The ESM would need to stand ready to take material losses in a downside scenario, but it would be unlikely to actually incur those losses, because the investment would also improve the funding environment for banks and minimize the risk of an adverse scenario occurring.

This chapter is structured as follows. The next section provides general principles for the design of a solution to delink sovereigns from weak banks, relying on the ESM. This is followed by a discussion of implementation issues and, finally, concluding remarks.

DESIGNING AN EFFECTIVE SOLUTION

Purpose

The ESM Board of Governors would appear to be authorized to develop a direct bank recapitalization instrument that is effective in breaking the sovereign-bank vicious circle. Creating such an instrument is consistent with the ESM's purpose:

> to mobilize funding and provide stability support under strict conditionality, appropriate to the financial assistance instrument chosen, to the benefit of ESM members which are experiencing, or are threatened by, severe financing problems, if indispensable to safeguard the financial stability of the euro area as a whole and of its member states.[1]

Member states ultimately decide on the scope of action that is allowed under the current ESM Treaty; in this regard, it appears that the current ESM Treaty may leave sufficient flexibility to accommodate related financial operations, such as ESM participation in or ownership of an asset management company (AMC).

The Eurogroup Agreement on the ESM Direct Recapitalization Framework

The June 20, 2013, agreement on the main features of the ESM direct recapitalization framework is an important and positive step forward (see Box 12.1 for a description). It includes conditions for access, time of entry, burden sharing, valuation, conditionality, and governance. Importantly, there is no *a priori* exclusion of legacy assets, and there could be retroactive application of the instrument on a case-by-case basis and by mutual agreement. Valuation would be based on the real economic value of the assets based on market data and on realistic and prudent assumptions of future cash flows and stress tests. Conditionality would be either institution-specific or more general and would be attached to the Memorandum of Understanding (MoU).

---

[1] Article 3 of the Treaty Establishing the European Stability Mechanism, available at: www.europeancouncil.europa.eu/media/582311/05-tesm2.en12.pdf.

Nevertheless, several issues appear to remain:

- *Timing.* The timing of the final agreement on the ESM direct recapitalization is still uncertain, since it is linked to the legislative processes of the BRRD and the DSG Directive.

- *Conditionality and burden sharing.* State aid conditionality would be a prerequisite for ESM direct recapitalization, which could raise issues about the use of bail-ins under the European Commission rules published on July 10, 2013. The role of bail-ins in ensuring burden sharing with the private sector has been usefully clarified in the BRRD, but the revised state aid rules introducing the early enactment of the bail-in provisions for junior debt could create uncertainty, while the move to give the European Commission an ex ante veto right on restructuring plans could introduce delays. If its early activation is required for ESM direct recapitalization, the new regime should be applied consistently across countries and with due regard to any adverse consequences for financial stability, especially in the event of the resolution of large systemic institutions.

- *Size and access.* Although it is difficult to prejudge the eventual needs, the limit for ESM resources available for direct recapitalization has been set at €60 billion (subject to review by the ESM Board). When needed, ESM direct recapitalization should be available on a timely basis, so that the ESM can be seen as an effective and credible common backstop.

What an Effective Instrument Requires

Interrelated goals. The mobilization of the ESM direct recapitalization instrument should ensure that systemic banks have adequate capital; it should also sever the link to the sovereign so banks are no longer a source of contingent fiscal liabilities.

Confidence effect. Achieving these goals will enhance market confidence in the credit standing of both the sovereign and the banks, including by reducing the extent to which exposure to the sovereign impairs market confidence in the banks. Nonetheless, the ESM recapitalization tool is not a panacea. Failing non-systemic banks should be resolved at least cost to national deposit insurance funds and taxpayers. Equally, systemic banks benefiting from ESM support will need effective supervision and sustained reform before they can be fully returned to private ownership, with state aid rules mandating formal restructuring plans. The sovereign itself will also need an adjustment program.

The European Stability Mechanism's Ownership of Banks

Source of strength. In a business where confidence is important, capital support for banks by the ESM would reassure creditors that, in the event of a negative surprise, potential future capital needs could be met. This virtuous dynamic is codified in U.S. banking statutes as the "source of strength" doctrine, asserting that the financial strength of a bank is inextricably wedded to the financial strength of its owner, thus justifying supervision of banks' holding companies. Confidence derived from ESM capital support, in turn, would feed into lower funding costs, restore profitability, and build capital over time. This much-needed stimulation to lending and growth in the periphery would help facilitate needed fiscal adjustment, while also helping return capital from the periphery to the core. Positive effects would be further amplified where ESM equity investments would have a significant immediate impact on sovereign credit standing. For all these reasons, a large equity participation in a bank by the ESM is quite distinct from a share transaction in the market, as it changes prospects for banks and for the economy by weakening the link between sovereigns and banks.

The ESM as a patient, deep-pocket investor. Although the Treaty establishing the ESM appropriately provides for the possibility of losses, it is clear that such losses should not be expected in its financial operations, including bank recapitalization—the expectation is that the ESM as bank investor must be careful to take balanced risk positions. Taken to the extreme, however, if the ESM were to restrict its investments to sanitized banks valued at depressed market prices—terms no more beneficial than those available from the private sector—it would likely fail to achieve the policy goals of the instrument. Therefore, a balanced approach is needed, one that prudently internalizes the benefits of ESM capital support by looking ahead over a time horizon sufficiently long to realize the benefits. As initial outlays rise to a threshold where banking stability and sovereign debt sustainability can improve decisively, so too does the likelihood of durable economic recovery underpinning a positive return on investment.

Risk sharing. As a patient, deep-pocket investor, the ESM provides assurance to creditors that, in the event of a negative surprise, potential future capital needs could be met. In other words, while the ESM would not take on expected losses, it would shoulder the risk of unexpected losses going forward. This approach is in line with efficient risk sharing, wherein the patient investor bears the residual risk. In this regard, it should be noted that, conditional upon the ESM standing ready to take material losses in a downside scenario, it would be unlikely to actually incur those losses, because the investment would minimize the risk of the adverse scenario occurring.

Broad Issues in Applying the Instrument

Which countries should be eligible? In view of moral hazard considerations and the need to husband finite ESM resources, the direct bank recapitalization instrument should only be applied where there is a paucity of private capital—including capital from burden sharing with creditors, as appropriate—and where use of national taxpayer capital would threaten sovereign market access or significantly undermine the terms on which the sovereign has such access.

What types of institutions should qualify? At this time, the instrument appears to be limited to domestically systemic banks. In principle, however, the AMCs and resolution corporations used to restructure such banks by warehousing certain segregated assets should also be eligible. When such vehicles remain under national ownership, the sovereign is exposed to residual uncertainty regarding the value of their assets, potentially leaving intact the most important part of the bank-sovereign link.

What extent of capital shortfall should be covered? ESM bank capital holdings should eventually be marketable. Given the mandate of the ESM as discussed above, capital that a patient, forward-looking investor could not expect to recover over time could not be furnished. Thus, capital needed to bring a systemic bank out of insolvency would in the first instance need to be provided by shareholders and creditors, and then by the national government, with any remaining shortfall covered by the ESM. In principle, however, there would be significant advantages to breaking the vicious circle if all the capital needed to ensure that a systemic bank was adequately capitalized were ultimately provided by a central fiscal authority, especially if the scenario were to play out in a small jurisdiction.

How should bank equity be valued? Current depressed market valuations of bank equity would not be appropriate, since they reflect downside risks stemming from bank-sovereign links. An historical-cost approach to valuing bank equity could be considered where the analysis underlying bank recapitalization has been conducted in coordination with relevant European authorities. Even here, however, stress tests designed to calibrate prudent equity buffers for a downside scenario do not provide balanced valuations of bank equity. This is so because they deliberately take a conservative view on economic variables and potential credit losses and factor in net income over a time horizon of, at most, a few years. Instead, the assessment should be based on internalizing the benefits of the investment (e.g., for funding costs), factoring in reasonable baseline projections rather than a stress scenario and using, for instance, a real long-term economic value approach that takes into account underlying profitability under stable macroeconomic conditions.

Should banks first have a balance sheet restructuring? A flexible approach is needed, recognizing that distressed asset workouts are a core function of banking. In most cases, where banks are best suited to manage in-house their own distressed assets, such assets should be retained on balance sheet at valuations that make prudent allowance for lifetime credit losses in a baseline scenario. Nonetheless, a separate legal vehicle may offer advantages in resolving certain asset classes, such as larger, more idiosyncratic loans with valuation uncertainty, while enabling banks to focus on improving their performance in their ongoing core businesses. Ideally, if a vehicle is used, it should also fall under ESM ownership; otherwise, effectiveness in breaking bank-sovereign links is diminished. Indeed, the ESM may choose to segregate the assets of banks under its control into separate but affiliated entities that would nonetheless be captured by a consolidated supervision of the banking group as a whole.

What types of risk-sharing arrangements are appropriate? To minimize contingent fiscal liabilities, a clean break would usually be best, with the sovereign providing no downside risk protection and correspondingly receiving no claim on a future upside, except if it retains a minority equity stake. Nevertheless, simple option structures can help facilitate transactions where there are large valuation uncertainties.

IMPLEMENTATION ISSUES

Direct Recapitalization by the ESM

Elements. The ability of the ESM to support bank restructuring hinges on several elements:

- *Mandate.* The ESM can directly recapitalize banks, based on diagnostics performed by (or under the leadership of) the SSM led by the European Central Bank (ECB). As noted in the euro area summit statement of June 29, 2012, this would require a "regular decision," albeit one that requires unanimity in the ESM Board of Governors and, in some jurisdictions, approval from national parliaments.[2]

- *Transparency, governance, and accountability.* The strategic approach of the ESM would need to be communicated clearly to ensure investor understanding and acceptance, enhance confidence, and secure broad public buy-in. Elements that would help in this respect include a transparent investment strategy and governance mechanism and an incentive structure in which the public sector shares any upside.

- *Principles for access.* The modalities for ESM investment should provide incentives for banks to seek private sources of capital first, in particular by diluting existing shareholders. National authorities would then be expected to cover at least any negative equity that might remain subject to the need to ensure sustainable public debt dynamics, as noted above, and an exit from the crisis.

- *Role of bail-in.* Holders of capital instruments (such as subordinated debt and preferred shares), in both going and gone concerns, should be subject to burden sharing to reduce the fiscal costs of bank resolution. For banks undergoing resolution, losses could be imposed on remaining creditors in line with the seniority of claims, including senior unsecured bond holders, if the systemic consequences could be contained. Insured depositors, which in most of Europe rank *pari passu* with senior creditors, would need to be protected and given preference to avoid contagion.

- *Operations.* The ESM would need to build capacity to manage its equity stakes in banks, including, as warranted, the exercise of ownership rights. Alternatively, a special vehicle could be established with a mandate to manage the ESM's investments at arm's length, as the U.K. Financial Institution does. In any event, the management of the ESM's investment should be at an arms-length from the political process and follow strictly commercial principles. The ESM could forgo annual dividend income on its holdings, however, as this would help reduce the funding costs of these banks and increase their prospects for returning to profitability. At the same time, the

---

[2] The June 29, 2012, statement of euro area leaders can be found at: http://www.european-council .europa.eu/home-page/highlights/euro-area-summit-statement.

beneficiary economies must not implement policies that could harm the profitability or viability of the recipient banks (e.g., through onerous taxes or ex post resolution levies).

- *Design of instruments.* Capital instruments utilized for ESM recapitalization should allow for transparency and flexibility. Recapitalizations should be effected through the acquisition of ordinary shares—resulting in dilution of existing shareholders. For banks that have already been nationalized by member states, debt-equity swaps should be considered, with the member states transferring the equity stakes in banks to the ESM with a corresponding reduction in their debt.

- *No first-loss guarantees.* ESM investments should not benefit from loss protection provided by the sovereign. Such approaches would preserve sovereign-bank links, undermining the purpose of ESM direct recapitalization. But there should be safeguards for the ESM (e.g., built into the sales contract) against domestic policies that could directly harm the viability or profitability of the recipient banks (e.g., onerous taxes ex post or stiff resolution levies).

- *Exit strategy.* There should be incentives for an early ESM exit and private investor entry. The timing would be built around the European Union-approved restructuring plans. Mandatory sunset clauses should be avoided, as they could affect negotiating power ahead of the deadline.

- *Adequate resources.* Direct equity injections into banks could absorb significant amounts of ESM capital. It would be important to ensure that the ESM has adequate capital not only to allay any investor concerns about ESM credit quality, and thereby limit any rating implications, but also to play its potential role as a common backstop for bank recapitalization.

Supporting a Work-out of Impaired Assets

Clean up. Resolving impaired assets in the euro area banking system is a necessary supplement to the roll-out of the banking union. While banks are in the business of collecting on delinquent loans, and thus must have the expertise, unresolved nonperforming assets can deepen the severity and duration of a systemic crisis, as they tie up bank managerial and financial resources and inhibit a recovery in lending. This is particularly the case with non-marketable assets and when secondary markets become illiquid. A clear segregation between impaired and performing assets would remove doubts about the quality of banks' balance sheets and thus contribute to restoring confidence in the euro area banking sector.

Legacy assets. This term has been very controversial, reflecting concerns that creditor countries could be expected to put capital into nonviable banks. This is not what is being suggested above. Rather, losses on impaired "legacy" assets should be recognized through upfront provisioning and proper (long-term/post-crisis) valuation. It is not recommended that all impaired assets be segregated from a bank prior to ESM direct recapitalization and placed into recovery vehicles

> ### Box 13.1 The Irish and Spanish Asset Management Companies (AMCs)
>
> *Ireland.* The National Asset Management Agency was set up in December 2009 to help Irish banks divest of bad loans (Irish commercial property) and in turn receive government-backed securities as collateral against European Central Bank (ECB) funding. The agency aimed to achieve this task by acquiring bad loans from the five participating banks, working pro-actively on a business plan for acquiring and disposing of bad loans, protecting and enhancing to the maximum amount possible the value of these assets. The agency had acquired assets at an average discount of over 50 percent. The process lasted for over a year and required detailed asset-by-asset valuation. The European Commission communication, however, allows for an alternative where valuation of assets appears particularly complex, including the creation of a "good bank" whereby the state purchases the good assets rather than the bad ones. Nationalization combined with the creation of a "good bank" was used in Latvia for the resolving of Parex bank in 2008–10.
>
> *Spain.* Legislation enacted in Spain in August 2012 established the AMC for assets arising from bank restructuring (SAREB), empowering the Fund for the Orderly Restructuring of the Banking Sector to instruct distressed banks to transfer problematic assets to it. In mid-December 2012, SAREB increased its capital to allow its main private participants (banks) to become shareholders.

ultimately backed by the national taxpayer; such an approach would greatly reduce the effectiveness of the tool in addressing bank-sovereign links. Rather, bank health should be restored with shareholders, including the sovereign, bearing the expected loss of past excesses by being subjected to an independent valuation exercise consistent with the shared commitment to restore full viability after the restructuring period.

Asset management companies (AMCs). AMCs have been used in the past in systemic crises and as a part of a wider package of measures to facilitate (1) resolution of insolvent and nonviable financial institutions; (2) restructuring of distressed but viable financial institutions; and (3) privatization of government-owned and government-intervened banks. Examples of (1) include the U.S. Resolution Trust Corporation and the Thai Financial Sector Restructuring Agency. Examples of (2) include the U.S. Maiden Lane LLCs established by the Federal Reserve to resolve Bear Stearns and AIG and Sweden's Securum. Combinations of (1) and (2) include the Korea Asset Management Institution and the Malaysian Danaharta. An example of (3) is the French Consortium de Realization. The Indonesian Bank Restructuring Agency combined all three elements. Centralized AMCs, often with broad mandates, were also widely used during the 1990s transition in central and eastern Europe, for example in the Czech Republic, Georgia, Hungary, Kazakhstan, Lithuania, Macedonia, Slovakia and Ukraine. In the current crisis, a number of AMCs have been established in the European Union, including in Belgium, Denmark, Ireland, Spain, and the United Kingdom; there have also been discussions concerning possible AMCs in Cyprus and Slovenia (Box 13.1).

Advantages and disadvantages. Centralized AMCs can remove balance sheet uncertainty by acquiring assets of unknown (or difficult to quantify) value; allow the consolidation of scarce workout skills and resources in one agency and the application of uniform workout procedures; help securitization by generating a larger pool of assets; provide greater leverage over debtors if AMCs are granted special powers of loan recovery; prevent fire sales or destabilizing spillover effects as banks deleverage; and allow the "cleaned up" banks to focus on their core business.

Such considerations need to be balanced against potential disadvantages. These include the loss of banks' specialized information about their borrowers; the AMCs' limited ability (relative to the bank) to provide additional financing to support restructuring of nonperforming loans; and the risk of a deterioration in asset values following transfer to an AMC if the assets are not actively managed. It may also be difficult to insulate public agencies such as centralized AMCs from political interference. Finally, centralized AMCs may raise concerns about asset warehousing and can extend their own lifespans by open-ended transfer arrangements that, ultimately, can also undermine credit discipline in banks.

Lessons. The experience with AMCs has been mixed and has helped identify common prerequisites and design features that can contribute to an AMC's success:

- *Prerequisites.* An insolvency framework that supports rehabilitation of viable firms, liquidation of nonviable firms, and out-of-court debt recovery and realization of collateral; a neutral tax framework; and robust financial regulation, supervision, and a bank resolution framework.

- *Design features.* Strong leadership and operational independence; accountability, transparency and strong governance; adequate funding; strong legal basis; appropriately structured incentives (including forms that enable AMC owners to benefit from future increases in the value of bank assets); and a commercial orientation.

Transfer price. Assets for transfer to the AMC need to be properly priced (Box 13.2). The general rule is that assets should be purchased at a price as close to a fair market value as possible based upon expected recovery, cash flow projections, and appraisal of collateral. But pricing nonperforming and illiquid or complex assets can be difficult, time consuming, and subjective, especially in the midst of a financial crisis—one reason why in the United States the Troubled Asset Relief Program was ultimately not used to purchase mortgage-related assets. The U.S. Treasury decided to conduct a second round of capital injections into financial institutions instead, stating that the original plan of purchasing troubled assets would take time to implement and would not be sufficient given the severity of the problem. When a large number of assets is involved, the transfer can take place at an initial price with the explicit agreement that the final price of the transaction be established after the value of the assets has been estimated or the assets have been sold. Some form of profit-sharing arrangement may be utilized to make transactions more palatable for banks, but these should not remove the full update for the government sponsoring the centralized AMC. The Malaysian Danaharta, for example, purchased impaired loans at an average discount of 55 percent, while banks that sold assets retained the right to receive 80 percent of any recoveries in excess of the acquisition costs that the AMC was able to realize.

Box 13.2   Key Considerations for Asset Management Companies (AMCs)

The transfer price at which impaired assets are removed from restructured banks' balance sheets is a key parameter with broad implications.

- The lower the transfer price, the larger the losses imposed on restructured banks: to the extent that the banks remain viable, this increases the need for capital injections. Transfer prices have a direct impact on whether or not there is "negative capital" to be filled in.
- Low transfer prices also limit the size and therefore the capital/funding requirements of the AMC, limiting the extent of fiscal costs to be incurred over time and perhaps even providing some potential upside as bad assets are liquidated and spur the interest of private-equity investors.
- There is therefore a trade-off between crystallizing large capital needs and setting up a large AMC that would also need to be capitalized and funded.
- The European Commission typically applies the principle that transfers should take place at the "real (long-term) economic value," which for impaired assets would typically be closer to the market value than to the historical value.

Long-term funding of asset run-off vehicles is critical to ensure that recovery values are not impaired by fire-sales.

- If the AMC has a banking license, it could in principle access Eurosystem refinancing directly. However, the bad assets are unlikely to be eligible for collateral under European Central Bank (ECB) operations, and emergency liquidity assistance is not an appropriate vehicle for long-term refinancing purposes. Even if the AMC is capitalized with government bonds, the ECB may challenge the eligibility of the entity itself as a monetary policy counterparty, or it may challenge the appropriateness of Eurosystem refinancing on the basis of the monetary financing prohibition.
- There are precedents for central bank funding of AMCs, most involving the protection of central banks' balance sheets against potential losses. However, even if the ECB were to provide funding, the risks on its balance sheet should be protected by a fiscal guarantee, for instance, from the ESM (which may require amendments to the ESM Treaty).
- A non-bank AMC can be funded by issuance of government guaranteed bonds that can be placed directly in the market or with the restructured banks as payment for the assets that are transferred. It is critical that such securities be eligible for Eurosystem refinancing (e.g., as per the Spanish MoU).

Private investors should be invited in AMCs, albeit with proper risk sharing arrangements, to maximize recovery values.

Competition policies. EU competition policies complicate asset pricing in the European context.[3] The European Commission requires a clear ex ante identification of the magnitude of a bank's asset-related problems and a viability review, with assets valued at market prices whenever possible. Since the current market value can be quite distant from the book value, the European Commission's approach allows for a transfer value reflecting a "long-term economic value" of the assets, on the basis of underlying cash flows and broader time horizons. In the

---

[3] Guidance to member states is provided by, among other sources, the European Commission (2009).

experience of setting up Ireland's national asset management agency in late 2009, lack of a universally accepted methodology for this valuation led to a protracted process whereby bank book values were repeatedly discounted, prolonging uncertainty and delaying normalization of bank funding. In the case of Spain, this process was more rapid, with transfer prices set conservatively, based on haircuts in line with the adverse stress test scenario.

AMC funding. Funding of AMCs is another key design feature. The AMC must have sufficient funds to perform its intended functions, with the operating budget separate from funding for asset takeover. In past crises, funding came from either the proceeds of government bond issues or the AMC's own bond issuance backed by the government, with losses absorbed by the budget since private investor participation is unlikely to materialize in the early stages. For instance, in Ireland, banks received government-guaranteed securities in return for assets transferred to the Irish national asset management agency. A key advantage of using a company without a banking license (an AMC) instead of a "bad bank" is that AMCs do not need to meet regulatory capital and liquidity requirements, thereby reducing their overall costs.

Sovereign–bank loops. In the current euro area context, funding by governments reinforces the sovereign–bank links and complicates AMC design. To the extent that AMC debt funding bears on public debt, there is an incentive to minimize the size of these vehicles and therefore the scope of the assets that are segregated. This raises a question about possible alternative sources of equity and liquidity for the AMC, and specifically of the potential roles of the ECB and ESM in these areas. In particular, to limit further contingent fiscal liabilities and harness efficiencies, consideration could be given to allowing the ESM to set up and own AMCs.

Potential Role of the European Central Bank

Direct support. The ECB is subject to a number of legal protections to safeguard its balance sheet, but it could have a role in funding AMCs. The European System of Central Banks Statute limits its credit operations counterparties to "credit institutions and other market participants, with lending based on adequate collateral." Hence, the statute may provide a leeway to fund non-banks. That said, funding the acquisition of bad assets or the resolution of bad banks remains a fiscal responsibility. Therefore, were the ECB to provide such funding, the risks to its balance sheet should be protected by a guarantee from euro area member states such as could potentially be extended by the ESM (Box 13.3).

Indirect support. An alternative route would be for the ECB to support AMC operations indirectly, subject to the prohibition of monetary financing. In particular, the ECB could accept government-guaranteed AMC bonds issued to banks in exchange for their assets as collateral for Eurosystem financing operations and for a range of safeguards, such as an observer status in the AMC governing committee(s) and special access to the AMC internal information. Bond

Box 13.3 Central Bank Funding of Asset Management Companies (AMCs)

There are precedents for central bank funding of AMCs, most involving protection against potential losses:

- In the United States, the "bad bank" of Continental Illinois was owned by the former shareholders of the bank and funded with liabilities to the Federal Reserve, fully guaranteed by the Federal Deposit Insurance Corporation (FDIC), which owned the good bank.

- A number of central banks in Central and Eastern European transition economies were engaged in funding AMCs or bad banks; the losses incurred were covered by the national budget or, over time, by seigniorage.

- The Swiss National Bank (SNB) supported in 2008 the transfer of illiquid securities and other troubled assets of UBS to a special purpose vehicle—the Swiss Stabilization Fund—controlled and mainly funded by the SNB. Assets were transferred to the fund at market prices and thus, on average, with a discount to notional value. Asset transfer from UBS was financed by a 90 percent loan from SNB, backed by a security interest in all the fund's assets, and a 10 percent financing contribution from UBS. The management of assets was outsourced to UBS, which was given an option to repurchase the fund. Protection was provided to the SNB in the form of loan overcollateralization and warrants for UBS shares, to cover any losses on liquidation of assets. The broad recovery of secondary market asset valuations in 2010 allowed the fund to dispose of assets with sales mostly above their intrinsic values.

characteristics will be important in determining acceptance by the ECB as repo collateral, including interest rate, maturity, and marketability.

Central banks accept collateral of a high credit quality that is liquefiable in secondary markets, which helps manage the risks associated with implementing monetary policy. They also typically accept government and quasi-government securities as collateral, subject to not being a direct party to monetary financing of the fiscal deficit.

Conversely, central banks would not typically accept nonmarketable securities (for example, special-purpose government bonds that may not be on-sold in the market). Open market purchases of bonds and the general acceptance of a class of securities as collateral from all counterparties are the acceptable ways central banks acquire government securities.[4] Hence, the mechanism through which the central bank acquires government securities is important in determining their acceptability by the central bank. A side deal in which the central bank agrees to purchase or accept a particular class of nonmarketable securities that have been directly issued to just a few banks would not generally be an acceptable practice.

---

[4] In the case of the ECB, various "opinions" discuss this matter. See, for example, CON/2010/2 in which the ECB indicated that "the prohibition of monetary financing prohibits the direct purchase of public sector debt, but such purchases in the secondary market are allowed, in principle, as long as such secondary market purchases are not used to circumvent the objective of Article 123 of the Treaty." Also see recital 7 of Council Regulation (EC) 3603/93.

Box 13.4 Eurogroup Agreement on the European Stability Mechanism (ESM) Direct Recapitalization Instrument: Main Features*

Objective: ESM direct recapitalization of banks will aim at preserving financial stability of the euro area as a whole and of its member states by delinking the sovereign from the financial sector.

Timing: The instrument will be ready as soon as the Bank Recovery and Resolution Directive (BRRD) and the Deposit Guarantee Schemes Directive are finalized with the European Parliament; it would be ready by mid-2014 for the Single Supervisory Mechanism Balance Sheet Assessment and European Banking Authority stress test.

Conditions for access: Four criteria must be met for accessing the new instrument, which are consistent with the objective of weakening the sovereign–bank links where they create risks to the sovereign's balance sheet:

- The sovereign is unable to recapitalize banks without endangering fiscal sustainability or high risk of losing market access in absence of ESM financing.
- There is a high risk to the financial stability of the euro area as a whole or of its member states.
- The bank is or will be in breach of prudential capital requirements but it must be viable, and private capital is not available.
- The institution is systemic for the euro area or for the member state.

Limit: An ex ante limit of €60 billion is set but the limit can be reviewed by the Board of the ESM.

ESM financial structure/instrument: Direct recapitalization of banks will be performed by a fully owned subsidiary of the ESM, against the acquisition of common equity shares. The ECB/supervisor will determine the appropriate capital requirement.

Valuation: Valuation of assets under the guidance of the ESM is based on the real economic value of the assets, based on market data, and realistic and prudent assumptions of future cash flows and stress tests, with the support of experts and in collaboration with the ECB and the European Commission. There is no exclusion of "legacy assets."

Burden sharing: Recapitalization is subject to a clear pecking order, relying first on private capital, including a write-down of shareholders and of creditors in line with state aid rules and with the BRRD. A scheme determining the respective contributions of the ESM and of the sovereign may remain to be further clarified:

- First part: The sovereign will recapitalize first up to the Basel III Common Equity Tier 1 capital minimum of 4.5 percent of risk-weighted assets.
- Second part: Above that threshold, the sovereign will contribute 20 percent in the first two years of entry into force of the instrument, and 10 percent afterwards.
- The contribution of the sovereign cannot be less than the second part.
- The contribution of the sovereign can be suspended by mutual agreement if the fiscal condition of the sovereign does not allow such contribution, including given implications for market access

Legacy: There could be retroactive application of the instrument, on a case-by-case basis and by mutual agreement.

Conditionality: State aid conditionality will be a prerequisite for ESM direct recapitalization. Additional institution-specific conditionality can be established by the ESM, in liaison with the ECB and the European Commission. More general conditionality can also be attached to the memorandum of understanding.

(continued)

> ### Box 13.4 (*Concluded*)
>
> **Governance:** Decisions regarding conditionality and the exercise of ownership rights will be made by the governing bodies of the ESM, and the degree of intrusiveness will be addressed on a case by case basis, in line with the European Commission Merger Regulation. The ESM will have access to all relevant information.
>
> **Review:** The instrument guidelines will be reviewed after two years of the instrument's entry into force, including the burden sharing scheme.
>
> _____
>
> *Based on the Eurogroup document, "ESM direct bank recapitalization instrument—Main features of the operational framework and way forward," Luxembourg, June 20, 2013. Available online at http://www. eurozone.europa.eu/media/436873/20130621-ESM-direct-recaps-main-features.pdf.

Potential Role of the European Stability Mechanism

Broadened mandate. Consideration could be given to broadening the ESM mandate, allowing it to own or lend support to AMCs. The main argument supporting this would be that the risk of losses on impaired assets for creditor member states (via the ESM) is likely to be much lower because of the retention of the long-term value of assets transferred to the AMC. In such circumstances, the transfer of conservatively valued assets from the banks' balance sheets to an ESM-owned AMC would be beneficial for all banking union participants (although, as noted, it would also increase the capitalization needs of banks).

Governance and accountability. There may be potential conflicts of interest between the various capacities in which the ESM is envisaged to operate. For example, the ESM could end up acting both as a (co-)owner of banks following an equity injection and as a purchaser through an AMC. Safeguards could entail: (1) clear and transparent evaluation criteria on asset prices, guided by the ECB's diagnostics; (2) clear rules on the interaction with the ECB in its capacity as single supervisor, as well as with resolution authorities; and (3) if needed, a potential revision of ESM governance and decision-making arrangements (which would require modifying the ESM Treaty).

CONCLUSIONS

Effectiveness. Banks benefiting from ESM participation will need time to reorder their operations and restructure their distressed loans. With moral hazard addressed through appropriate burden sharing, conditionality, and supervision, the ESM can act as the quintessential patient investor, taking a forward-looking approach to its equity holdings and internalizing the benefits of its ownership for the medium- to long-term outlook. Such an approach to ESM direct bank recapitalization would maximize effectiveness in breaking the vicious circle that links banks and sovereigns. By safeguarding the financial stability of the euro area as a whole, this approach would serve the common interest.

Urgency. With a large international body of experience showing that delays almost always ramp up the costs of crisis resolution, time is of the essence (see, for example, Laeven and Valencia, 2012). Some euro area member states continue to face severe stresses in both sovereign and bank funding markets, with broad ramifications for the currency union. Others may be poised at a decision point between durably restored market access and potentially prolonged dependence on official financing. In no case would a delay in applying the ESM direct bank recapitalization instrument improve the ultimate outcomes. The sooner the ESM can move, the sooner current market dislocations in both the periphery and the core can be resolved, for the benefit of all.

Specifically, it is of the utmost importance to have the ESM backstop in place ahead of the SSM balance sheet assessment to motivate national authorities and to address capital shortfalls where fiscal space is insufficient. If needed, the flexibility in the framework should be used to the fullest to prevent a flare-up of negative sovereign–bank loops and of procyclical effects in the context of the balance sheet assessment exercise. The ESM could also provide a line of credit to the SRM before a more long-term fiscal backstop is in place.

REFERENCES

European Commission, 2009, "Communication from the Commission on the Treatment of Impaired Assets in the Community Banking Sector." www.ec.europa.eu/competition/state_aid/legislation/impaired_assets.pdf.

Goyal, Rishi, Petya Koeva Brooks, Mahmood Pradhan, and others, 2013, "A Banking Union for the Euro Area," IMF Staff Discussion Note No. 13/1 (Washington: International Monetary Fund).

Laeven, Luc, and Fabian Valencia, 2012, "Systemic Banking Crises Database: An Update," IMF Working Paper No. 12/163 (Washington: International Monetary Fund).

CHAPTER 14

Deposit Insurance in the European Union

LUC LAEVEN

OVERVIEW OF EXISTING DEPOSIT INSURANCE ARRANGEMENTS

Deposit insurance in the European Union (EU) is provided by a variety of national deposit guarantee schemes (DGS). These schemes vary greatly in their coverage, contributions, fund sizes, and organizational set-up. Some countries, such as Austria and Germany, have more than one scheme.[1] (See Appendix Table A14.1 for a broad overview of existing statutory deposit insurance arrangements in the European Union.[2])

Most schemes have access to limited prepaid funds in relation to the total amount of deposits covered, reflecting the current lack of common EU funding standards (Figure 14.1). Many national DGS have limited prefunding or rely on ex post funding mechanisms. Some countries, such as Austria, Italy, and the United Kingdom, rely exclusively on ex post funding.[3]

In some cases, mandatory schemes are supplemented by voluntary schemes, and some schemes provide more than deposit protection. For example, the complex voluntary DGS for commercial banks in Germany provides insurance of up to 30 percent of bank capital per depositor, essentially offering unlimited coverage for most depositors.[4] The system linking German savings banks (and similarly that for cooperative banks) provides an "institutional guarantee," which implies mutualization of liabilities among participating banks. Under current arrangements, resources from the private DGSs and mutual protection schemes of various categories of banks could be committed to finance the restructuring of banks on a going-concern basis.

An earlier version of this chapter appeared as a Technical Note on "Deposit Insurance" (European Union: Publication of Financial Sector Assessment Program Documentation), IMF Country Report No. 13/66, March 2013.
[1] The German private scheme for commercial banks, with coverage of 30 percent of bank capital per depositor, offers essentially unlimited coverage for most depositors.
[2] The table only reflects statutory schemes, not voluntary or contractual schemes.
[3] In 2011, the Netherlands adopted a regulation to transform its ex post DGS into an ex ante funded scheme with risk-based contributions. The new regulatory framework will come into effect on July 1, 2013.
[4] This is to be gradually reduced to 8.75 percent over a span of 10 years, starting in 2015.

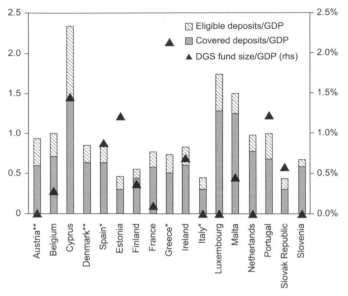

Figure 14.1 Ratio of Insured Deposits and Deposit Guarantee Scheme (DGS) Fund Size to GDP, 2011

Source: European Central Bank; European commission (2010); and IMF staff calculations.
Note: Eligible deposits is the sum of household and corporate deposits held by monetary and financial institutions. Covered deposits applies the coverage ratio of the European Commission to the amount of eligible deposits.
*DGS or IMF staff information at end-2011.
**Banking associations top up the mandatory scheme; hence, coverage ratio is lower bound.

HARMONIZATION

A process of harmonization of DGSs started in 1994 with the European Union Directive on Deposit Guarantee Schemes (DGS Directive). The DGS Directive was significantly amended following the failure of Lehman Brothers, and in 2010 the European Commission proposed a comprehensive reform of DGS in the European Union. The ongoing harmonization process is guided by the principle of creating a level playing field, with a focus on coverage limits and preference for ex ante funding. Harmonization of the coverage levels is limited to statutory DGS. However, other protection schemes in member states (e.g., on a voluntary or contractual basis) are allowed to offer additional deposit protection; this is outside the scope of the directive, except for some requirements concerning the information that needs to be given to depositors about the actual protection offered to them under the alternative scheme.

The recent financial crisis has led to a substantial increase in coverage and harmonization along some dimensions. After the 2008 financial crisis, and in particular the failure of Lehman Brothers, several EU member states announced in rapid succession increases in deposit insurance limits or blanket guarantees to forestall the possibility of a run (see Appendix Tables A14.2 and A14.3).[5] The

---

[5] These tables are indicative of the range of approaches taken and cannot capture all aspects.

European Union then moved quickly to harmonize minimum levels of deposit insurance coverage and maximum payout periods, as embodied in the 2009/14/ EC Directive. This increased the level of coverage to €50,000 by mid-2009 and to €100,000 per depositor per bank by end-2010, by which time the maximum payout period was shortened to 20 working days.

Since then, EU draft legislation has proposed further steps to harmonize national DGS, including their funding and mutual borrowing. Directive 2009/14/EC imposed the obligation to explore further elements of DGS harmonization but set no timeline for its implementation. In 2010, EU draft legislation proposed to harmonize the coverage and funding arrangements of national DGS and to clarify responsibilities. Specifically, the draft legislation proposed a harmonization of the scope of coverage (type of deposits), the introduction of common standards on financing (where the lack of common standards has allowed for diverging models of ex ante and ex post funding schemes), a target fund size of 1.5 percent of eligible deposits (eventually to be set in terms of covered deposits, i.e., eligible deposits not exceeding the coverage level), the introduction of risk-based contributions, shorter payout periods (limited to seven working days), a clarification of responsibilities to improve insurance payments for cross-border banks, and limited cross-border borrowing arrangements between various national DGS.[6] Moreover, in order to facilitate the payout process in cross-border situations, the European Commission has proposed that the host country DGS act as a single point of contact for depositors at branches in another member state (including paying out those depositors on behalf of the home country DGS, which would subsequently reimburse the host DGS).

Further harmonization of EU deposit guarantee schemes has been suspended pending the adoption of EU bank resolution arrangements through a new directive. The draft DGS Directive of July 2010 has been under discussion by the co-legislators (European Council and Parliament) since 2010, but a decision has not been made. In 2011, co-legislators failed to reach a compromise agreement, mainly over disagreements between member states over the potential use of DGS funds for resolution purposes in the context of the proposed BRRD.

In the absence of progress, the European Parliament voted in a plenary sitting on February 16, 2012, and endorsed the report adopted in May 2011. Since this plenary vote, there were no further discussions in the European Council until the adoption of the European Commission's legislative proposal on the BRRD in June 2012. The proposed BRRD framework establishes "financing arrangements" for bank resolution, requiring a target pre-funding of 1 percent of guaranteed deposits within 10 years. It characterizes the possibility of borrowing arrangements between resolution funds across countries, while also allowing for the use of DGS funds for resolution purposes in case this provides for an optimal protection of depositors. In July 2012, member states expressed their willingness to

---

[6] Such mutual borrowing arrangements would mean that if the financial capacity of one DGS became depleted, it could borrow money from other schemes.

pursue the DGS negotiations in parallel with those on the BRRD. The latter is currently under discussion in the council.

A key element of the European Commission's proposal on DGS is the harmonization of DGS funding to ensure that DGSs are credible and able to fulfill their obligations to protect depositors. However, there has been disagreement about the proposed size of funding (1.5 percent of eligible deposits, according to the commission's original proposal) and the proposed timeframe under which such funds need to be built up (10 years, according to the commission's original proposal), especially given that existing schemes in many member states are currently underfunded. Additionally, impact assessments conducted by the European Commission[7] indicate that building up these funds over the proposed timeframe will significantly reduce the profitability of an already weakened banking sector in several member states, especially when combined with the increased amount of deposit coverage.[8] Moreover, one member state has indicated no desire to move to an ex ante scheme with prefunding from the industry. There has also been disagreement about dealing with payouts in cross-border bank failures, including the possibility of mutual borrowing arrangements across national DGSs.

These developments should be seen in light of the recent discussion on the banking union. Proposed regulations establishing the Single Supervisory Mechanism (SSM) are currently under consideration with a view to their entering into force in 2013.[9] Although a pan-European Union DGS was originally proposed as one of the banking union elements, presently the SSM and the establishment of the pan-European Union bank resolution fund are being given a clear priority, with DGS harmonization considered an objective to be pursued at a later stage.

PRINCIPLES AND BEST PRACTICES FOR DEPOSIT GUARANTEE SCHEMES

The main purposes of deposit insurance are to provide a safety net for smaller depositors and to enhance financial stability. As an element of a country's overall financial safety net—which in addition to deposit insurance includes bank supervision, provision of emergency liquidity, and a bank resolution and insolvency framework—deposit insurance protects depositors from loss of deposit values up

---

[7] Details on the European Commission's impact assessments can be found at http://ec.europa.eu/internal_market/bank/docs/guarantee/20100712_ia_en.pdf.

[8] One possibility would be for the European Union to provide upfront funding to national DGSs, for example through the ESM, and then levy the charges on banks to be paid back over a period of time. This would serve to increase the credibility of a funded scheme without the additional burden on an already weakened banking system. This is akin to the U.S. Federal Deposit Insurance Corporation's (FDIC) credit lines from the Treasury that can be drawn upon in case funds are depleted and that eventually would be repaid by industry.

[9] For details of the December 14, 2012 agreement by the European Council on the establishment of the SSM, see http://www.consilium.europa.eu/uedocs/cms_data/docs/pressdata/en/ecofin/134265.pdf and http://www.consilium.europa.eu/uedocs/cms_data/docs/pressdata/en/ec/134353.pdf.

to a pre-specified level in the event of bank failure. It also strengthens overall financial sector stability by removing retail depositors' incentives for bank runs based on fear or uncertainty about the condition of their banks and thus should limit financial contagion.

There is an important distinction between the function of guaranteeing (small) depositors and financing bank resolution.[10] In many countries, including the United States, the functions are combined in one agency, but the mandates and constraints differ. This chapter focuses on DGS narrowly defined. (For more detailed treatments on best practices and principles of deposit insurance, see BCBS and IADI, 2009; Demirgüç-Kunt, Kane, and Laeven, 2008; Blinder and Wescott, 2001; and Garcia, 2000.)

The role of the deposit insurance agency varies widely, both within the European Union and worldwide. In some countries, the deposit insurer has broad responsibility to monitor the banking system and participate in the insolvency proceedings. In others, the insurer is limited to depositor payout and asset resolution or else to depositor payout only (see Appendix Table A14.1). The variation in their roles reflects differences in public policy objectives, institutional strengths, the legal framework, and resource availability. This variation need not be a weakness, so long as the safety net is well designed and agencies are well coordinated. Yet within the European Union's single market, a level playing field and the possibility of cross-border contagion require that safety nets be harmonized and safety net agencies coordinated not only within but also across member states. Under the proposed recast of the DGS Directive, the core deposit payout activities of the DGS would be further harmonized, while the possible involvement of DGS in the financing or administrating bank resolution would be harmonized through the proposed BRR.

Establishing a Credible Framework

For deposit insurance to be credible, it should offer appropriate coverage, ensure timely payouts, and be supported by adequate funding and backstops.

Appropriate Coverage

In determining coverage, authorities can review the banking system's distribution of deposits and determine an appropriate threshold for coverage (for example, a coverage level that fully protects 80 percent of depositors and 20 percent of deposits). In practice, coverage levels per depositor average about twice the value of per capita GDP, but there is a wide range around that average. From this perspective, the coverage limit of €100,000 might be regarded as high for a number of European Union member states with relatively low levels of economic and financial development (see also Nenovsky and Dimitrova, 2008). However, from

---

[10] For example, a DGS typically has a primary legal mandate to protect depositors, and secondly to minimize its own costs. Fulfilling those mandates may be inconsistent with minimizing overall costs, maintaining financial services and the credit supply, and promoting systemic stability.

the perspective of ensuring a level playing field within the single market, it is critically important that coverage levels and conditions be aligned, to limit incentives for depositors to place savings in the system with the most generous DGS.[11] Coverage levels can thus be viewed as being broadly appropriate.

Timely Payouts

Payouts need to be timely to reduce the possibility of disruptions to the payments system and prevent panics and bank runs. This means that the deposit insurer must have adequate information to be able to respond immediately in the event of a failure. In some jurisdictions, payouts occur within 48 hours of a failure. In jurisdictions where banks are subject to corporate bankruptcy law (as opposed to special bank insolvency regimes), shareholder appeals and strong creditors' rights can impose significant delays on depositor reimbursement. The principle of depositor preference—that is, giving insured depositors and the DGS priority rights over the estate of a failed bank—is currently missing in a number of national bank resolution regimes in the European Union. Depositor preference could increase recovery by the deposit insurer and might facilitate quick depositor payout, thus reducing the eventual costs of providing deposit insurance, and could enhance resolution by facilitating the transfer of the deposits to another institution.

However, depositor preference, by increasing the potential loss exposure of unsecured creditors other than depositors, may increase the funding costs of banks and could cause large shifts in unsecured funding when a bank faces distress that would need to be carefully managed (Marino and Bennett, 1999). More generally, convergence across EU member states in the treatment and ranking of depositor and other creditor claims in case of bank insolvency could promote cross-border cooperation and improve the predictability of cross-border resolution outcomes.

Adequate Funding

Systems can be funded by either ex post or ex ante funds. Ex ante funds are built up over time with bank contributions, and ex post funds rely on extraordinary charges on all banks in the event of a failure. Ex ante funding may strengthen private sector confidence and enhance financial stability, provided that risk is being correctly priced. Ex post funding may induce banks to monitor each others' activities, increasing market discipline, but it may also have procyclical effects—that is, charges are increased when other banks' balance sheets may be under pressure. Moreover, ex post funds will be levied on surviving banks, not the failed institutions, and can therefore be regarded as unfair. The European Commission's proposal therefore calls for the prefunding of deposit insurance. Government

---

[11] There is always healthy competition between insured and non-insured savings vehicles. What is not desirable in this context is regulatory competition. Moreover, while imposing the same coverage limit across member states levels the playing field for competition purposes, it may differentially affect market discipline at the member state level.

back-up funding is a prerequisite to any credible deposit insurance system. The role of such government funding is to allow for the intertemporal smoothing of the fund in the case of a shortfall of funds while money is being recovered from surviving banks.

Backstops

Financial safety nets need to be backstopped with fiscal resources to lend credibility to the system and deal with systemic crisis events. The current system of national DGSs within the European Union lacks a fully credible backstop for systemic risks, given the absence of mutual borrowing arrangements should individual DGSs run out of funds and concerns about the ability of individual member states to backstop their national DGSs in the event of a systemic crisis, reinforcing sovereign–bank linkages.

Clear Mandate

The deposit insurance agency should operate with a clear mandate and within an appropriate legal framework to be effective. The mandate must be unambiguous, preferably spelled out in the law. The role of the deposit insurer must be well established so that its role in the broader framework of problem-bank resolution is clearly understood. Also, its relationship with other agencies in this framework must be explicit, with means of communication and information sharing laid out in regulation or law.[12] The deposit insurance system must be informed immediately when a potential insolvency is identified so it can prepare for deposit payouts. Awareness of the deposit insurance system's existence as well as the terms and scope of its coverage are critical to effectively stabilize depositor fears. Public outreach activities must be extensive and frequent (FSB, 2008).

Limiting Moral Hazard

To limit moral hazard, the scope and coverage of deposit insurance needs to be limited, premiums need to properly reflect risk as far as practicable, and deposit insurance needs to be complemented with strong supervision and capital regulation.

Limited Scope and Coverage

Deposit insurance risks displacing market discipline (Demirgüç-Kunt and Huizinga, 2004). Coverage levels must be sufficient to prevent destabilizing deposit runs but not so extensive as to eliminate all market discipline. Specifically, deposit insurance should relieve only small depositors of the burden of monitoring their banks. The scope should also exclude interbank deposits and "insider" deposits (i.e., those of bank managers, owners, and connected persons) to further

---

[12] A recent French legislative draft proposes a comprehensive resolution regime with a Resolution Authority and the DGS fund in charge of both deposit insurance and resolution.

limit moral hazard. More generally, shareholders and uninsured creditors of failed banks must not be protected.

Risk-Adjusted Insurance Premiums

Banks should pay a fee commensurate to their relative risk of failure—that is, a higher premium for higher insurance risk. With correct risk pricing, the benefits of increased risk-taking can be taxed away, which helps to restore an element of market discipline. While appropriately assigning bank risk is not straightforward, efforts should be made to adjust premiums for risk, for example by assigning banks to risk "buckets" and charging different premiums for banks in each bucket. Currently, most EU DGSs do not adjust premiums for risk across banks,[13] and most levy premiums that do not adequately reflect the average risk in the system (that is, they are not actuarially fairly priced). Therefore, the burden may fall disproportionately on smaller and other deposit-rich banks. The proposed recast of the DGS Directive would alter this situation by introducing contributions that consist of both non-risk and risk-based elements.[14]

Strong Supervision

Deposit insurance therefore should be supported by strong supervision and least-cost resolution to contain its cost. Strong supervision, particularly when combined with adequate capital requirements, limits unsafe and unsound banking practices. This reduces the probability of failure, thereby protecting the deposit insurance funds and enhancing stability.

Mandatory Membership

National deposit guarantee schemes should be mandatory, not voluntary. This is not only to provide a level playing field, but also to avoid adverse selection and reduce the average cost of deposit insurance by expanding the insurance pool. The bigger the insurance pool, the more likely it is that actuarial calculations will hold so that the pool is better able to handle risks. This also calls for the merger of existing funds that operate in the same jurisdiction.[15] By expanding the insurance pool and reducing the concentration of insured deposits, a combined fund would have a lower probability of insolvency than either fund would have separately. Of course, separate funds, such as those in place for savings banks in Germany, can have specific benefits, such as the value of peer monitoring, but these benefits need to be weighed carefully against the opportunity cost of not merging these funds with national funds. In most cases, this would suggest that funds will need to be merged with national funds. Indeed, the U.S. experience in merging the Bank Insurance Fund and the Savings Association Insurance Fund into a new

---

[13] Exceptions include Finland, France, Greece, Hungary, Italy, Portugal, Romania, and Sweden.

[14] Risk-adjusted premiums are also consistent with the Basel Committee on Banking Supervision (BCBS) and International Association of Deposit Insurers (IADI)'s "Core Principles for Effective Deposit Insurance Systems."

[15] The proposed DGS Directive would permit but does not require such mergers of funds.

fund, the Deposit Insurance Fund, under the Federal Deposit Insurance Reform Act of 2005, has broadly been seen as having reduced the average cost of deposit insurance by expanding the insurance pool.[16]

CONCLUDING REMARKS

The harmonization of deposit guarantee schemes across the European Union is important to support the financial integration and the functioning of the internal market. The current system—with substantial differences in coverage, pricing, and funding arrangements across national DGSs—implies that there is no level playing field (sometimes even within countries) and encourages regulatory arbitrage (Huizinga, 2008; Huizinga and Nicodeme, 2003). A specific example is the differential treatment within the European Union of deposits in foreign bank branches and subsidiaries, with deposits in foreign branches being covered by the home-country deposit protection scheme of the bank (with the option to join the host-country deposit protection scheme if its coverage is higher or broader in scope) and deposits in foreign subsidiaries being covered by the host-country deposit protection scheme.

To ensure a level playing field for cross-border retail banking, national deposit insurance schemes should be aligned not only in terms of quantities (through coverage limits), but also in terms of prices, with fairly priced premiums that are adjusted for risk as far as possible. A number of schemes currently are not only severely underfunded (i.e., the buildup of ex ante funding is below target levels or, alternatively, insufficient to cover insured deposits in two or three mid-sized banks in the country) but also underpriced (i.e., premiums are lower than their actuarially fair premiums[17]). This means that, over time, premiums will have to be raised and brought more in line with the risks of individual banks.

Moreover, the scope of deposit insurance should be aligned, being limited mainly to household and SME deposits. The coverage level of €100,000 is broadly appropriate for most member states, given their level of economic and financial development. Differential coverage would be undesirable given the objective of harmonizing deposit guarantee schemes. Voluntary and contractual schemes outside of national schemes, such as those existing for savings banks in Germany, will at a minimum need to be harmonized over time in terms of coverage and pricing, but eventually they would benefit from pooling risks with

---

[16] See Attachment A of the FDIC Options Paper of August 2000, available at: http://www.fdic.gov/ deposit/insurance/initiative/OptionPaper.html. There can also be important adverse selection problems when banks are allowed to choose which fund they belong to, particularly if the choice of fund is associated with a different set of regulations or different regulators. This seems particularly important when the banks in different funds are very similar, so that there is an opportunity for regulatory arbitrage. U.S. experience during the savings and loan (S&L) crisis, where weaker S&Ls stayed in the FSLIC while stronger banks joined the FDIC, supports this view.

[17] Average premiums are low compared to both the cost of deposit insurance as implied by banks' credit ratings and the market valuation of banks' equity. For an overview of techniques to estimate actuarially fair premiums, see Laeven (2008).

national or cross-border schemes.[18] Resolution frameworks also need to be enhanced and harmonized by giving insured depositors and the DGS priority rights over the estate of a failed bank.

In the context of the banking union, steps should be taken toward a common funding of deposit insurance.[19] A common safety net is a critical element of a banking union, as it ensures that funds are readily available to resolve individual bank failures[20] and cover payouts to depositors in the event of failures, without endangering sovereigns or monetary stability. To this end, what matters is common funding, not the operational centralization of deposit insurance. Within the context of a common safety net, common or linked deposit insurance could, for instance, be designed as a reinsurance scheme, created from national deposit guarantee schemes and funded at the banking union level through industry levies and contributions from member states. It would pool risk and weaken sovereign-bank links. Over time, the fund would build administrative capacity and could be a step toward a permanent banking union scheme and resolution fund.

Until the common safety nets are established, funding arrangements should ensure that bank failures can be resolved in an orderly and credible fashion, including rapid deposit payouts. To restore depositor confidence and complete the banking union, prefunding will be necessary, combined with loss-sharing agreements for dealing with cross-border deposit payouts and a common, credible backstop should national deposit guarantee schemes run out of funds. The size of the DGS fund should be sufficiently large to cover depositor payouts and associated costs in the event of bank failures in most cases.[21] However, government backstops are needed in case of systemic crises.[22] As such, prefunded schemes (in the steady state) could operate with funds that are fairly small in size though substantially bigger than those currently in most member states. In such cases, funds should be raised over time from the financial sector to reach the target size, and contributions should be risk-based. Together with a least-cost resolution mechanism and common backstops for systemic banking crises, the available funds should be sufficient to ensure that bank failures are dealt with in an orderly fashion, while containing associated fiscal burdens and welfare costs.

---

[18] Such harmonization of voluntary schemes is currently not envisioned under existing European Commission proposals.

[19] As also reflected in the December 14, 2012, agreement by the European Council, the SSM and the establishment of the pan-EU bank resolution fund are currently given a clear priority, with the common funding of DGS considered as an objective to be pursued at a later stage.

[20] Potentially including funds for deposit transfers and purchase and assumption transactions.

[21] A large fund would result in an excessive buildup of sterile funds that were not available to support bank lending and therefore could negatively affect credit supply and the economy at large.

[22] Taxpayer costs associated with such backstops can be recouped over time from the financial sector. Any positive externalities for the real economy associated with the existence of deposit insurance could justify a government subsidy.

APPENDIX 14.1

TABLE A14.1

Characteristics of EU Deposit Guarantee Schemes, 2012

	Austria	Belgium	Cyprus	Estonia	Finland	France	Germany	Greece	Ireland	Italy	Luxembourg	Malta	Netherlands	Portugal	Slovakia	Slovenia	Spain	Bulgaria	Czech Republic	Denmark	Hungary	Latvia	Lithuania	Poland	Romania	Sweden	United Kingdom
Type of Deposit Insurance Scheme																											
explicit	x	x	x	x	x	x	x	x	x	x	x	x	x	x	x	x	x	x	x	x	x	x	x	x	x	x	x
legally separate	x	x	x	x	x	x	x	x	x	x	x	x	x	x	x	x	x	x	x	x	x	x	x	x	x	x	x
within central bank																x											
within banking supervision agency									x				x									x					
within Ministry of Finance																										x[1]	
Participation and Coverage																											
domestic banks	x	x	x	x	x	x	x	x	x	x	x	x	x	x	x	x	x	x	x	x	x	x	x	x	x	x	x
local subsidiaries of foreign banks	x	x	x	x	x	x	x	x	x	x	x	x	x	x	x	x	x	x	x	x	x	x	x	x	x	x	x
local branches of foreign banks	x	x	x	x	x	x	x	x	x	x	x	x	x	x	x	x	x	x	x	x	x	x	x	x	x	x	x
foreign currency deposits	x	x	x	x	x	x	x	x	x	x	x	x	x	x	x	x	x	x	x		x		x	x	x	x	x
interbank deposits																				x							
Payouts to Depositors																											
per depositor per institution	x	x	x	x	x	x	x	x	x	x	x	x	x	x	x	x	x	x	x	x	x	x	x	x	x	x	x
Funding																											
ex ante fund		x	x	x	x	x	x	x	x			x			x		x	x	x	x	x	x	x	x	x	x	x
ex post scheme	x									x	x		x[2]	x		x											
funded by government															x												
funded privately	x	x			x	x	x	x	x	x	x	x	x[3]			x[4]	x	x	x	x	x			x	x	x	x
funded jointly			x	x										x[5]	x		x					x	x		x		
guarantee from government in case of a shortfall of funds[6]	x					x	x	x	x		x	x		x		x	x	x	x	x	x			x	x	x	x
Contributions and Assessment Base																											
risk-adjusted premiums	x				x	x	x			x				x							x	x				x	
assessment base																											
covered deposits	x														x				x			x				x	
eligible deposits		x				x	x	x		x	x	x	x	x	x	x	x	x	x	x	x		x	x	x		x
total deposits		x	x	x	x				x																		

Sources: European Commission; International Association for Deposit Insurers; Financial Stability Board; and national deposit insurance agencies.

Notes: Table excludes voluntary and contractual schemes other than the national statutory scheme.

[1] Swedish National Debt Office.

[2] In 2011, the Netherlands adopted a regulation to transform its ex post deposit guarantee scheme (DGS) into an ex ante funded scheme with risk-based contributions, to come into effect on July 1, 2013.

[3] The Dutch Central Bank administers the scheme and pays out the depositors. The costs of the scheme are transferred (including the administrative costs) ex post to the members of the DGS, subject to an annual cap of 5% of own funds of each member.

[4] In case of a bank failure, the Bank of Slovenia temporarily assumes the obligation to pay the guaranteed deposits and then calls on other banks to contribute funds needed for the paying out of insured deposits. To ensure banks have sufficient liquid assets to contribute such funds, all banks are required to invest a minimum of 2.5% of insured deposits in debt securities that are eligible for the collateralization of Eurosystem receivables as defined by Bank of Slovenia.

[5] Initial contribution to the DGS fund provided by Banco de Portugal.

[6] In the case of a shortfall of funds, the DGS can issue bonds/receive loans guaranteed by the government.

TABLE A14.2

Changes in EU Deposit Guarantee Schemes in Response to the Recent Crisis

	Austria	Belgium	Cyprus	Estonia	Finland	France	Germany	Greece	Ireland	Italy	Luxembourg	Malta	Netherlands	Portugal	Slovakia	Slovenia	Spain	Bulgaria	Czech Republic	Denmark	Hungary	Latvia	Lithuania	Poland	Romania	Sweden	United Kingdom
Experienced a Banking Crisis Between 2007 and 2012[1]	x	x	x			x	x	x	x	x	x		x	x		x	x		x	x	x	x	x			x	x
Increase in Deposit Protection since 2008																											
increase in DGS coverage limit	x	x	x	x	x	x	x	x	x	x	x	x	x	x	x	x	x	x	x	x	x	x	x	x	x	x	x
government guarantee on deposits	x		x	x			x[2]	x	x[3]						x	x			x	x	x		x	x			
Government Guarantees on Non-Deposit Liabilities since 2008																											
None			x	x	x					x		x			x	x		x	x		x		x	x	x		
Partial	x	x				x	x	x			x		x	x			x					x				x	x
Unlimited									x[4]											x[5]							

Sources: European Commission; Laeven and Valencia (2012); and national deposit insurance agencies.

[1] Banking crisis dates for the period 2007–2011 according to Laeven and Valencia (2012). Cyprus is added to this list as of 2012.

[2] Covering only private savings accounts.

[3] The government guaranteed insured deposits up to the existing coverage limit in full should the insurance fund run out of funds.

[4] Limited to almost all liabilities of seven major Irish financial institutions.

[5] Excluding subordinated debt.

TABLE A14.3

Evolution of Coverage and Fund Size under EU Deposit Guarantee Schemes Since 2006

Country	Coverage limit, in euros, 2006	Deposit guarantee, 2008	Coverage limit, in euros, 2010
Austria	20,000[1]	x	100,000
Belgium	EUR 20,000		100,000
Cyprus	20,000, 10% coinsurance		100,000
Estonia	20,000, 10% coinsurance		100,000
Finland	25,000		100,000
France	70,000		100,000
Germany	20,000, 10% of coinsurance	x	100,000
Greece	20,000	x[2]	100,000
Ireland	20,000, 10% coinsurance	x	100,000
Italy	103,291		100,000
Luxembourg	20,000		100,000
Malta	20,000, 10% coinsurance		100,000
Netherlands	20,000		100,000
Portugal	25,000		100,000
Slovakia	20,000, 10% coinsurance	x	100,000
Slovenia	21,300	x	100,000
Spain	20,000		100,000
Bulgaria	12,782		99,324 (196,000 Bulgarian lev)
Czech Republic	25,000, 10% coinsurance		100,000
Denmark	40,000	x	100,000
Hungary	23,800, 10% coinsurance above first 4,000	x	100,000
Latvia	15,000		100,000
Lithuania	14,481		100,000
Poland	22,500, 10% coinsurance above first 1,000		100,000
Romania	15,000		100,000
Sweden	27,654		100,000
United Kingdom	52,222, 10% coinsurance above first 2,978		98,077 (85,000 pounds sterling)

Sources: European Commission; Laeven and Valencia (2012); and national deposit insurance agencies.
[1] 10% coinsurance for non-private persons.
[2] Political announcement to cover also deposits of legal persons.

REFERENCES

Basel Committee on Banking Supervision (BCBS) and International Association of Deposit Insurers (IADI), 2009, "Core Principles for Effective Deposit Insurance Systems," available at: https://www.bis.org/publ/bcbs156.pdf

Blinder, Alan S., and Robert F. Wescott, 2001, "Reform of Deposit Insurance: A Report to the FDIC," unpublished, FDIC and Princeton University. http://www.fdic.gov/deposit/insurance/initiative/reform.html.

Demirgüç-Kunt, Asli, and Harry Huizinga, 2004, "Market Discipline and Deposit Insurance," *Journal of Monetary Economics*, Vol. 51, No. 2, pp. 375-99.

Demirgüç-Kunt, Asli, Edward Kane, and Luc Laeven, eds., 2008, *Deposit Insurance around the World: Issues of Design and Implementation* (Cambridge, MA: MIT Press).

European Commission, 2010, "Review of Directive 94/19/EC on Deposit Guarantee Schemes," Report from the Commission to the European Parliament and to the Council.

Financial Stability Board, 2008, "Thematic Review on Deposit Insurance Systems," available at www.financialstabilityboard.org/publications/r_120208.pdf.

Garcia, Gillian G. H., 2000, "Deposit Insurance: Actual and Good Practices," IMF Occasional Paper No. 197 (Washington: International Monetary Fund).

Huizinga, Harry, 2008, "The EU Deposit Insurance Directive: Does One Size Fit All?" in *Deposit Insurance around the World: Issues of Design and Implementation*, ed. by Asli Demirgüç-Kunt, Edward Kane, and Luc Laeven (Cambridge, MA: MIT Press).

Huizinga, Harry, and Gaetan Nicodeme, 2003, "Deposit Insurance and International Bank Deposits," Discussion Paper No. 3244 (London: Center for Economic Policy Research).

International Monetary Fund, 2013, "Technical Note on Deposit Insurance ," IMF Country Report No. 13/66, March 2013. Available at www.imf.org/external/pubs/ft/scr/2013/cr1366.pdf.

Laeven, Luc, 2008, "Pricing of Deposit Insurance," Chapter 3 in *Deposit Insurance Around the World: Issues of Design and Implementation*, ed. by A. Demirgüç-Kunt, E. Kane, and L. Laeven (Cambridge, MA: MIT Press).

Laeven, Luc, and Fabian Valencia, 2012, "Systemic Banking Crises Database: An Update," IMF Working Paper No. 12/163. (Washington: International Monetary Fund). www.imf.org/external/pubs/ft/wp/2012/wp12163.pdf.

Marino, J. A., and Rosalind L. Bennett, 1999, "The Consequences of National Depositor Preference," *FDIC Banking Review*, Vol. 12, pp. 19-38.

Nenovsky, Nikolai, and Kalina Dimitrova, 2008, "Deposit Overinsurance in EU Accession Countries," in *Deposit Insurance Around the World: Issue of Design and Implementation*, ed. by A. Demirgüç-Kunt, E. Kane, and L. Laeven (Cambridge, MA: MIT Press).

Governance and Transparency of EU-Wide Institutions

SCOTT ROGER

The prospective introduction of the Single Supervisory Mechanism (SSM) and the experience to date with the European Supervisory Authorities (ESAs) raise some important transparency and accountability issues. So far as the SSM is concerned, the key issues are how this may affect the appropriate transparency arrangements for monetary policy and what arrangements should be put in place for the SSM. For the ESAs, the issue is how transparency, accountability, and governance arrangements might be strengthened, based on the experience since their establishment in 2011.

By and large, the levels of transparency and accountability in the areas identified in the IMF "Code of Good Practices on Transparency in Monetary and Financial Policies" are high; indeed, in many cases practices at the European level help in defining best practice. Consequently, an in-depth analysis of current practices would find relatively few areas in which standards may be notably below best practice.

More relevant is a forward-looking approach to the issues of transparency and accountability of monetary and financial policies at the European supranational level. In this regard, there are two main areas in which issues arise, either currently or in prospect. The first concerns the appropriate transparency and accountability arrangements for monetary and supervisory policies undertaken by the European Central Bank (ECB) when it takes responsibility for supranational banking supervision for the euro area and possibly other countries. The second concerns the transparency and accountability arrangements for the four ESAs established in 2011 and whether they should be modified in the comprehensive review of the ESAs initiated in April 2013.[1]

ISSUES FOR THE EUROPEAN CENTRAL BANK'S MONETARY AND FINANCIAL POLICIES

The ECB's transparency and accountability arrangements for monetary policy have traditionally met a high standard. The ECB's mandate is set out clearly in

---

[1] See Review of the European System of Financial Supervision (ESFS) 2013. http://ec.europa.eu/internal_market/finances/committees/.

European Union (EU) legislation. The ECB provides considerable information on its governance and decision-making structures. It reports clearly and promptly on its regular monetary policy decisions, complementing these with detailed monetary policy reports on a quarterly basis and published research on monetary policy issues, as well as speeches and other forms of public outreach by senior staff. The ECB also provides considerable information on its financial position, data and data requirements, and operations, and maintains a high-quality internet website. High ethical standards are required, and members of the ECB Governing Council are subject to a careful external approval procedure.

Nonetheless, it is apparent that the public perception of the ECB's policy objectives and the challenges of monetary policy communications have come under strain over the course of the financial crisis. These problems are by no means unique to the ECB, but they may be more challenging because of the particular features of the European financial crisis. More specifically, the range of measures taken to address the fragmentation of the monetary transmission mechanism and to help alleviate sovereign debt crises have led to ongoing concerns and criticism that the ECB is pursuing multiple objectives, potentially at the expense of the price stability objective.

Questions about the ECB's commitment to the price stability objective and potential trade-offs with other objectives are certain to increase when the ECB becomes host to the SSM in 2013.[2] Regarding current plans, a Supervisory Board within the ECB, largely composed of participating national-level supervisors, will have responsibility for formulating supervision policy, but final policy decisions will be made by the ECB Governing Council, which also decides on monetary policy. Many central banks have both monetary policy and banking supervision under the same roof. Typically, there is a defined degree of information sharing between the monetary policy and supervisory sides of the bank, but policy decisions are made by separate policy committees.[3] For example, the forthcoming reassumption of supervisory policy at the Bank of England is planned to involve the creation of a prudential regulatory authority as a separate entity within the bank; this new authority will have independent decision-making authority but will be accountable to the court of the bank and to Parliament.[4] The ECB does not appear to have the legal authority to delegate such decision making.

Both the challenges posed by the financial crisis in Europe and the ECB's forthcoming assumption of responsibility for supranational banking supervision pose reputational risks to the ECB's policy credibility. Uncertainty surrounding the formulation of both monetary and supervisory policies will also affect financial market pricing and volatility. Even small increases in risk premiums on a euro

---

[2] This note takes the ECB assumption of bank supervisory responsibilities as given. It does not consider the question of whether, over the longer term, those responsibilities should be undertaken by a separate institution.

[3] Although there is also overlap in the membership of the committees.

[4] See Bank of England and Financial Services Authority (FSA), (May 2011), "The Bank of England, Prudential Regulation Authority: Our Approach to Banking Supervision," http://www.fsa.gov.uk/pubs/speeches/boe_pra.pdf.

area level would have cumulative large costs. This suggests that the ECB should consider additional steps or measures to enhance the transparency of monetary policy and also to ensure that its formulation of supervisory policies meets high standards of transparency.

Monetary Policy

For monetary policy, perhaps the key requirement is to be more transparent about the inevitable trade-offs involved in policy decisions as well as the uncertainties associated with evaluating the trade-offs. In this regard, two kinds of measures could be considered.

The first measure is to begin providing timely minutes of Governing Council meetings on monetary policy decisions.[5] These could provide a more effective presentation than the Monetary Policy Report provides concerning the key trade-offs seen by the council and the associated risk assessments involved in coming to policy decisions. Minutes of this discussion would present the array of views and properly reflect the range of uncertainties involved as well as differences in assessments. Reporting need not identify the views of particular individuals, although this should be considered. Publishing the minutes of the Governing Council's decisions on monetary policy would have two critical benefits in terms of ECB credibility. First, it would demonstrate the extent to which monetary policy decisions are made independent of supervisory policy considerations. Second, it would facilitate presenting the range of views of council members and show how consensus was reached in a clearer and perhaps less confrontational way than currently occurs through the press.

A second measure that could help clarify where policy trade-offs occur—and how they could be resolved in a manner consistent with price stability—is to be more explicit in the publication of ECB projections for key variables. The main drawbacks to publishing these projections appear to be, first, that some observers may mistake them for unconditional forecasts, and second, the publication of point forecasts can give a misleading impression of forecast accuracy. However, the experience of central banks that do publish projections suggests that these concerns may be overblown.

The benefit of publishing projections, especially with alternative scenarios, is that they can be very useful in clarifying both the intertemporal trade-offs or consistencies of different policy concerns and the consequences of alternative policy choices for key variables. Of course, such projections have to be used with care. They are first and foremost vehicles for clarifying the policy issues and risks faced by policymakers, and they are also how the ECB staff understands key elements of monetary and financial transmission and interaction. As such, the presentation of projections needs to be kept simple and focused on the central issues;

---

[5] Article 10.4 of the European System of Central Banks (ESCB) Statute provides that "The proceedings of the meetings shall be confidential. The Governing Council may decide to make the outcome of its deliberations public." The Governing Council therefore has the authority to publish minutes of meetings.

it should not become bogged down in details that may be misleading or give a false sense of precision.

Recommendations

- The ECB should begin to publish timely minutes of meetings to decide on monetary policy settings.
- The ECB should begin to publish more medium-term details on its macroeconomic projections and alternative scenarios.

ISSUES FOR PRUDENTIAL SUPERVISION IN THE BANKING UNION

The ECB will need to establish a comprehensive framework for transparency and accountability for the SSM. A particular challenge is that the ECB's supervision will be subject to only limited accountability to an independent or outside authority, beyond the ECB's general obligation to report to the European Parliament and the Eurogroup.[6] This is especially awkward insofar as ECB decisions on supervision could well have important budgetary implications for SSM participants. Although there is no very neat solution to this, various measures could be taken to enhance transparency and strengthen accountability. To enhance accountability, the ECB could make regular presentations on supervisory matters to the European Parliament and also, on occasion, to national parliaments.

To increase transparency (as well as policy consistency), the Supervisory Board should set out as clearly as possible the principles and kinds of indicators or information it would generally use in coming to policy recommendations in different areas and publish them.[7] In addition to providing a useful guide to consistent policy formulation over time, the published principles could then also serve as benchmarks for policy evaluation. In this role, the guidelines would help the Supervisory Board in communicating the standard considerations entering its judgments and distinguishing these from the special considerations that inevitably need to be taken into account.

The ECB should publish regular reports on its supervisory work. At a minimum, this should include regular (perhaps semiannual) reports on the evolution of risks and vulnerabilities in the financial system under its supervision, and of its actions to monitor and address those risks and vulnerabilities. Press notices of official decisions should also be published.

---

[6] At the Economic and Financial Affairs Council (ECOFIN) meeting in December 2012, measures were agreed, based on European Commission proposals (13683/12). These spell out the ECB's proposed reporting obligations regarding its supervisory responsibilities. While clarifying reporting requirements for supervisory activities of the ECB, the measures do not overcome the limited accountability that is inherent in the Governing Council's decision-making autonomy.

[7] The guidelines would need to be based on the supervisory rulebook being developed by the European Banking Authority, but could be more specific to the particular needs of the ECB.

An additional measure that could be considered is to establish a panel of external experts to provide periodic reviews of the ECB's performance and practices with regard to the SSM function.[8] These experts would need to be independent both of the ECB and of participating national supervisors. They could include former supervisors, ex-bankers, and academics. The group could publish independent reports on the performance of the SSM, as well as provide expert feedback and suggestions as to how to improve the functioning of the SSM. This could be especially helpful in the early phases of the SSM's operations.

The ECB will also need to clarify the organization and other relationships between its macroprudential or financial stability activities and its microprudential or supervisory activities. At this point, it is not quite clear where macroprudential policy will fit—whether as part of the SSM function, or as an element distinct from monetary and microprudential supervision, as at the Bank of England and the U.S. Federal Reserve. Whatever institutional arrangements are selected, however, the operational links between the macroprudential and microprudential functions will need to be made as transparent as possible, since they involve using an overlapping set of policy instruments. In this connection, it would be helpful to agree on a clear distinction in macroprudential responsibilities between the ECB and the European Systemic Risk Board, which has an EU-wide mandate and as such may have to offer recommendations on all areas of ECB activity.

Recommendations

- The Supervisory Board of the SSM should develop and publish a set of guidelines that it will follow in formulating policy recommendations.

- The ECB should consider establishing an external panel of experts to provide independent oversight over the SSM. The panel should publish regular reports as well as provide direct feedback to the Supervisory Board.

- The ECB should clarify and make transparent the working relationships between the macroprudential and microprudential areas of its mandate as well as its relationship with the European Systemic Risk Board.

ISSUES FOR THE EUROPEAN SUPERVISORY AUTHORITIES

As supranational institutions, the ESAs are unusual in comparison with national-level regulatory and supervisory bodies, particularly with regard to their mandates, governance, and accountability arrangements. Although ESAs have achieved a great deal since they were established, some aspects of their design and operation inhibit transparency and effective accountability.

---

[8] This would go beyond the proposed annual reporting requirements of the ECB on supervision to the European Parliament, the European Council, the European Commission, and the Eurogroup.

The mandates of the ESAs are broad and imprecise, making transparency and accountability difficult. Each ESA has responsibilities in the areas of sectoral regulation, the promotion of convergence in supervision, the promotion of market and financial product transparency, consumer protection, and the provision of advice to other EU institutions. The ESAs, especially the European Banking Authority, also have financial stability roles in their mandates, while the European Securities and Markets Authority also has direct supervision responsibilities. The breadth and imprecision of these mandates creates some overlaps between them, as well as between the European Banking Authority and the proposed SSM. The Joint Committee, bringing together the ESAs and the European Systemic Risk Board, provides a very useful venue for coordinating activities and minimizing overlaps. Nonetheless, having multiple objectives inevitably requires trade-offs to be made between them when they conflict. Moreover, with limited budgets, difficult choices have to be made in prioritizing objectives. Although the ESAs are generally quite transparent about stating their work programs and decisions, it is very difficult for them to be clear about how decisions were reached and what trade-offs were involved.

The ongoing review of the ESAs offers an opportunity to sharpen the focus of their mandates, facilitating greater transparency and accountability. The mandate of the European Banking Authority in particular should be reassessed, with a view to reducing the overlaps between the European Systemic Risk Board and ECB with respect to financial stability assessment, including stress testing. For the other ESAs, especially as they move into more supervisory roles, it will be important to ensure that their powers vis-à-vis national level supervisors are clear, and that their respective responsibilities are well delineated. Crucially, it will be essential that the ESAs be able to act as truly supranational agencies, with direct and easy access to information and data from entities that they supervise, rather than having to work through national authorities.

Governance arrangements for the ESAs should be reviewed, with the aim of strengthening operational independence and effective accountability. The current governance arrangements for each of the ESAs include a Board of Supervisors made up of representatives from EU member state institutions, responsible for policy decisions, and a management board responsible for the operation of the ESA.

The ESAs have formal accountability to the European Commission, the European Parliament, and the European Council, but it is less clear that there is good effective accountability. Essentially this is because it is difficult to make large groups like the Boards of Supervisors accountable in any very meaningful sense. This is especially the case when the participants are actually representatives of their respective institutions rather than participants in their own right.[9] As a consequence, there is little motivation other than peer pressure within the boards for members to act as executives of supranational institutions rather than as

---

[9] Board members are meant to act in the overall interests of Europe, but that injunction is inconsistent with the fact that they are each nominated by their respective national authority.

representatives of national interests. To help overcome this problem, it might be helpful for published minutes of the ESAs to be more explicit regarding differences of view between participants, as well as between ESA staff and their respective Boards of Supervisors.

Modifying the composition of ESA Boards of Supervisors, as well as voting arrangements, should also be considered to strengthen the supranational orientation of decision making. At a minimum, each ESA's chair should have a vote on an *ex officio* basis. Additionally, consideration could be given to adding some voting members nominated on a pan-European rather than national basis, and have these members appointed for a relatively lengthy period so as to maximize their autonomy. Such a change would also help prevent the creation of coalitions that might block action or favor some countries over others. Further, ESA staff could be given responsibility for preparing proposed decisions on the issues coming before the Boards, in order to help focus discussion on a European perspective.

Governance reforms should also be aimed at increasing the responsibility and accountability of management boards. This would help to overcome the domination of national interests in decisions by the Boards of Supervisors. It would also facilitate more rapid decision making than is generally possible in such sizeable groups. The delegation of decision-making responsibility and corresponding accountability to management boards may be more appropriate in some areas than in others. For example, in areas where a high degree of consensus is desirable, it may be sensible for the Board of Supervisors to retain responsibility. However, in other areas, such as supervision, where an agreed set of rules is to be applied and where speedy action is needed, it may be more appropriate for the management board to have full responsibility and be accountable to the Board of Supervisors. With this sort of shift in the role of the management board, the effective accountability of the institutions would be more clearly focused on a small set of decision makers and executives. This type of arrangement would also be more transparent in the sense that these institutions, which are meant to be largely autonomous supranational institutions, would have a higher degree of autonomy in practice.

Funding arrangements for the ESAs should also be reconsidered. The financial arrangements of institutions are not normally a transparency issue, except insofar as the financial arrangements and position should be made public. However, in the case of the ESAs, it is evident that their budgetary positions and scope to manage their resources are so constrained that their ability to carry out important parts of their mandates is compromised. This amounts to a lack of transparency. In effect, external budget and staffing constraints are causing decisions on policy priorities to be transferred to the European Commission from the ESAs in a nontransparent manner, which is inconsistent with the original mandates given to the institutions. To remedy this problem, the ESAs need to be given significantly greater responsibility for managing their own resources and budgets, with appropriate accountability required by the management of the ESAs.

Recommendations

- The mandates of the ESAs should be reviewed with a view to reducing overlaps with others ESAs, the European Systemic Risk Board, and the ECB.

- The decision-making responsibility of ESA management should be strengthened, including by introducing more Europe-wide representation on the Boards of Supervisors.

- ESA funding arrangements should be modified to give them greater responsibility and autonomy in staff and budget management.

CHAPTER 16

European Union Banking Regulatory Framework and Authorities: An Overview

Nadege Jassaud and Fabiana Melo

This chapter provides an overview of the European Union (EU) banking regulatory framework and institutions. It reviews the European Banking Authority's (EBA's) performance against its mandates, given the economic conditions prevailing in the banking sector in the European Union. The review was carried out as part of the 2012 Financial Sector Assessment Program assessment of the European Union, and was based on the regulatory framework in place, the supervisory practices employed, and other conditions as they existed as of December 12, 2012.

BACKGROUND

Banks are a key contributor to the EU financial and professional services industry. EU credit institutions (including banks) account for 3.6 times the European Union's GDP and €900 billion in revenues, that is, 7 percent of the European GDP.[1] The sector employs more than three million people in Europe, 1.5 percent of the European Union's workforce. At end-October 2012, there were 7,913 credit institutions licensed in the European Union, of which 75 percent were in the euro area[2] (European Central Bank, ECB/FBE). European financial integration has also resulted in a sharp increase in cross-border banking groups, with 87 EU cross-border banking groups as of June 2012. As integration has progressed, crises involving a bank have increasingly had significant cross-border implications.

The recent financial crisis has demonstrated that both the quality and the size of the global banking system's capital and liquidity base were insufficient to withstand severe economic shocks. Over the September 2008–December 2011 period, EU member states committed a total of nearly €4.5 trillion, that is, 37 percent of the European Union GDP, for backstopping their financial sector. The ECB also provided enhanced liquidity support by broadening the scope of eligible assets for central bank funding and extending the maturity of central bank

---

[1] European Banking Federation, 2010.
[2] European Central Bank, ECB/FBE.

funding through the Long-Term Refinancing Operations, up to €1.2 trillion in October 2012. The EU supervisory framework has been reshuffled as well, with the setup of European supervisory authorities (ESAs).

Three ESAs were created on January 1, 2011: the EBA, the European Securities and Markets Authority (ESMA), and the European Insurance and Occupational Pensions Authority (EIOPA). Their creation aims at enhancing the mechanisms to coordinate cross-border supervision, facilitate cooperation between supervisors, promote convergence of supervisory practices, and monitor implementation of the so-called single rulebook, a single set of rules across the European Union. The ESAs are regulatory agencies of the European Commission accountable to the European Parliament and the Council of the European Union. They have legal personality as well as administrative and financial autonomy.

A new European supervisory mechanism will complete the framework. In September 2012, the European Commission came with a proposal for the Single Supervisory Mechanism (SSM) that would assign broad supervisory tasks to the ECB, with defined objectives and powers to supervise all euro area banks. This legislative package followed the Euro area summit on June 29, 2012, which called on the commission to present proposals for setting up an SSM as a precondition for a possible direct recapitalization of banks by the European Stability Mechanism (ESM). Unanimous agreement on the commission's proposal was reached in the Economic and Financial Affairs Council on December 13, 2012. The co-legislators (European Parliament and the European Council) reached agreement on the package in April 2013. The SSM is envisaged to be in place one year after the entering into force of the agreed texts.

The EU regulation has also been reviewed to implement new Basel III capital rules, through the Fourth Capital Requirements Directive and Capital Requirements Regulation. The text of this new regulation was published in the Official Journal on June 26, 2013, for an implementation scheduled on January 1, 2014.

REGULATORY FRAMEWORK FOR EUROPEAN UNION BANKING

The Basel Committee on Banking Supervision (BCBS) is the international standard setter for banking regulation. Originally composed of G-10 countries, after the 2008 financial crisis it was expanded and now has 27 members, of which nine are also European Union members.[3] The European Commission, the ECB, and EBA are observers.

In September 2010, the BCBS published new international standards for the capital adequacy and liquidity framework for internationally active banks

---

[3] The BCBS members are: Argentina, Australia, Belgium, Brazil, Canada, China, France, Germany, Hong Kong SAR, India, Indonesia, Italy, Japan, Korea, Luxembourg, Mexico, the Netherlands, Russia, Saudi Arabia, Singapore, South Africa, Spain, Sweden, Switzerland, Turkey, the United Kingdom, and the United States.

(know as the "Basel III package"). BCBS members agreed to implement Basel III gradually, starting from January 1, 2013, according to transitional and phase-in arrangements by which full implementation will be achieved by January 2019. Basel III complements and modifies the 2004 Basel II framework, introducing a new definition of regulatory capital (and higher requirements for better-quality capital), increased risk coverage, a leverage ratio as a backstop to the risk-based requirement, additional capital buffers that can be drawn down in periods of stress, and two liquidity standards.

BCBS standards need to be transposed into national regulations; in the case of the European Union, the Capital Requirements Directive (CRD) had introduced the regulatory framework. Member states transposed, and banks had to apply, the CRD implementing Basel II, from January 1, 2007. Since then, the CRD has been revised twice. On September 2009, the CRD II amended the regime for large exposures, supervisory colleges, hybrid capital, liquidity risk management, and securitization. Adopted on September 16, 2009 by the European Council and the European Parliament, the directive was transposed into national law by October 31, 2010. CRD III, agreed in the summer 2010, reformed the trading book, resecuritization, and remuneration, and entered into force in December 2011. In the European Union, CRD rules are applicable not only to internationally active banks but to all the European Union's 8,300 credit institutions.

The CRD IV/Capital Requirements Regulation will implement Basel III in EU laws. The new EU legislation consists of two instruments: a regulation that applies directly in every member state and a directive that will have to be transposed into the national laws of each member state. The Capital Requirements Regulation lays down prudential requirements for capital, liquidity, and credit risk for all investment firms and credit institutions in EU member states. It will impose a single set of rules across the European Union—the single rulebook[4]— leaving no scope for arbitrary interpretation and ensuring certainty about the law for all EU single-market players. By contrast, the CRD will cover rules on bankers' remuneration and bonuses, prudential supervision, corporate governance, and capital buffers. It will allow member states to require their home banks to hold more capital under certain conditions (as part of a supervisory process or as a macroprudential tool within the European Union harmonized framework[5]).

There are discrepancies with Basel standards, however. In 2012, the BCBS conducted a peer review exercise in the United States, the European Union, and

---

[4] The single rulebook derives from the idea that technical rules should be defined at the European Union level and adopted through EU regulations. That would ensure their direct applicability to all banks, eliminating the additional layer of local rules. Such measures would reduce costs of compliance, limit the scope for regulatory arbitrage, and prevent loss of competitiveness of EU-wide groups.
[5] National options and discretion would be the exception, although flexibility is envisaged for financial stability risks that differ across jurisdictions and institutions. National authorities may impose systemic risk buffers, without the European Commission's preapproval, up to a limit, and with preapproval above the limit. They may temporarily impose stricter requirements, e.g., in relation to risk weights for certain sectors, large exposure limits, and liquidity requirements. They also retain the flexibility to impose stricter requirements on individual institutions through Pillar 2 reviews.

Japan, with the objectives of identifying domestic regulations and provisions that were not consistent with the standards and assessing their impact on financial stability and the international level playing field. The BCBS reviewed the May 2012 draft version of the CRD IV, and the results of the assessment were published in October. Several discrepancies were detected, and some of them were considered material: "the proposed EU approach falls substantially short of the Basel framework in two areas: Definition of capital and the Internal Ratings-based (IRB) approach for credit risk." Specifically, the BCBS pointed out that

- the CRD definition of capital did not specify that common equity capital requirements should be met only with common shares,

- the criteria for accepting other tier 1 capital instruments were not consistent with the Basel III criteria,

- the treatment for recognition of minority interests was less stringent than the Basel III criteria, as was the derecognition from capital of unrealized gains and losses from changes in fair value liabilities, and

- the Capital Requirements Regulation definition of "indirect holdings" to minimize double gearing and the consolidation of insurance investments (instead of deductions) were considered potentially material discrepancies.

The concern about the implementation of the internal-ratings-based approach mostly derived from the European Union's application of partial exemptions for material exposure portfolios.

The BCBS Level 2 assessment will be updated based on the recently finalized rules, but it seems that at least some of the inconsistencies found may remain. The EU authorities have stated that the differences are derived from the wider scope of application of the CRD, which includes non-internationally active banks, and were also needed to accommodate certain legal constraints arising from local legislation. While the framework does build in some safeguards, including a role for EBA regarding supervisory enforcement practices and monitoring, the differences regarding the definition of capital (for example, not imposing common shares for listed banks) may give rise to financial engineering, impairing the quality of capital.

There are also some concerns about the timeliness of implementation. For instance, the BCBS has already introduced a gradual phase-in of the implementation of the liquidity coverage ratio,[6] which establishes a minimum level of high-quality liquid assets to withstand an acute stress scenario lasting one month. However, according to the European Union text, the European Commission may be able to delay the introduction of the requirement, scheduled for 2018, if justified by international developments. Similarly, the leverage ratio will be introduced by way of an observation period, through standard reporting formats to be

---

[6] Because of concerns that too-rapid implementation of the original liquidity coverage ratio could have a detrimental impact on the real economy, the text published by the BCBS on January 7, 2013 proposed a phasing-in of the liquidity coverage ratio similar to the capital requirements, starting with 60 percent of the ratio in 2015, rising progressively to reach 100 percent in 2019.

developed by the EBA. On the basis of these reports, the EBA will prepare reports for submission to the European Commission. The commission will have a delegated power to specify the detailed liquidity coverage requirement for implementation in 2015.

THE EUROPEAN BANKING AUTHORITY
Institutional Arrangements and Accountability

The EBA is governed by a Board of Supervisors (hereafter, the EBA Board). Like the other ESAs, the EBA Board is composed of the heads of the 27 national supervisory authorities (NSAs), with observers from the European Commission, European Systemic Risk Board (ESRB), ECB, ESMA, and EIOPA. Only the heads of the NSAs (or in their absence, their alternates) have the right to vote. The EBA chairman is responsible for preparing the work of the EBA Board and participates in its meetings but has no voting right. During 2012, the EBA Board met seven times and had four conference calls (in 2011, it met six times and had 10 calls). Only one EBA Board member attended only one physical meeting, infringing Article 40 of the EBA regulation that requests a minimum of two attendances.

The assignment of one vote per member and a decision-making process requiring a majority—either simple or qualified[7]—have facilitated decision making, but national interests may still influence decisions. The EBA Regulation explicitly cites (in Article 42) that the voting members of the EBA Board shall act independently and objectively in the sole interest of the European Union. However, some alliances or concerted decisions may take place. A voting member cannot vote on a matter where he or she has a material personal conflict, but that does not prevent him or her from voting on a matter concerning his or her own jurisdiction or country.

Within the banking union, new issues may arise. Countries that will not participate in the SSM may fear that the current decision-making process at the EBA Board will allow the SSM members' position to always prevail. There will be safeguards for non-euro zone member states by means of double-majority voting requirements for EBA decisions on mediation and on technical standards. This should ensure that decisions are backed by a majority of both the SSM-participating and the nonparticipating member states, but it could also make the decision-making process more complex.

It would be desirable to confirm in practice the EBA's independence from the European Commission. The procedure for the adoption of technical standards gives room for objections by the commission on certain grounds (which have to be based on EU-wide interests and provided within three months). When the commission does not endorse a draft regulatory technical standard, it sends it back to the EBA, explaining why it does not endorse it and explaining the reasons

---

[7] Adoption of technical standards requires a qualified majority.

for its amendments. The EBA has six weeks to amend the draft and resubmit it in the form of a formal opinion to the commission. If the new draft is not amended "in a way consistent with the Commission's proposed amendments," the commission can make its own amendments and adopt it. While the period under review remains too short to draw conclusions, there has been no example of undue interference on the substance of technical standards by the European Commission.

The EBA also has a management board that focuses on executive aspects such as the development of the annual work program, the budget, and resources. The management board is composed of six members selected from the EBA Board. It is chaired by the EBA's chairman. Decisions of the management board are adopted on the basis of a majority of the members present, each having one vote. In the event of a tie, the EBA chairman has a casting vote. The quorum is reached once at least two-thirds of the members with the right to vote are present. The EBA executive director and a representative from the European Commission participate in the meetings of the management board, with no voting rights.

The EBA's chairman and executive director are appointed by the EBA Board, following an open selection procedure. Both are appointed for five-year terms with the possibility of reappointment to a second five-year term. Before the EBA chairman takes up his or her duties, the European Parliament may object to the designation. The chairman may be removed from office only by the European Parliament following a decision by the EBA Board. The executive director is appointed by the EBA Board after confirmation by the parliament. The executive director may be removed only by decision of the EBA Board.

The EBA is accountable to the European Parliament and the European Council. In accordance with Article 43, the EBA Board reports its work program to the European Parliament, European Council, and European Commission each year as well as submitting an annual report on its activities and on the performance of the chairman's duties. Article 50 of the EBA Regulation provides for EBA's chairman to be invited to the European Parliament and Council to make a statement and to answer questions put by members. It also provides for the chairman to report in writing on EBA's main activities when requested.

The Banking Stakeholder Group facilitates consultation with stakeholders in areas relevant to the EBA's tasks. The Banking Stakeholder Group is composed of 30 members appointed to represent in balanced proportions the credit and investment institutions operating in the Union and their employees' representatives as well as consumers and other users of financial services, such as small- and medium-sized enterprises. This group is consulted on actions concerning regulatory technical standards and implementing technical standards, guidelines and recommendations, to the extent that these do not concern individual financial institutions.

Governance arrangements should be reviewed with the aim of promoting a more supranational orientation in decision making. Providing voting rights to the chairs of the ESAs, moving fully to a full-time board, and delegating more decisions to the management board should be considered. In order to mitigate national interests, representatives of some other EU institutions (except the

European Commission) and possibly the EBA chairman could have a vote on the EBA Board as well.

Data Issues

The regulation establishing the creation of the ESAs contains provisions indicating that the ESAs should be able to access, through European and national counterparties, all the information necessary to conduct their activities. Where information is not available or is not made available by the NSAs, the EBA can address a duly justified and reasoned request to other institutions or to the financial institutions themselves, but always through the respective NSAs. This provision has not been used in practice. In at least one case, seeking to assess the NSAs' handling with regard to the financial conglomerate directive, the EBA has only received partial answers from NSAs and has not used its powers of data collection further.

This lack of direct, easy access to institution-specific data has in practice posed reputational risks. Since the EBA needs to go through NSAs to obtain detailed supervisory data, delays are incurred, and this negatively affects most EBA oversight activities (e.g., stress tests and risk assessments). In particular, requiring a vote from the EBA Board to provide data for particular studies that the EBA wants to implement might hinder its ability to be timely in its work. Furthermore, as the EBA does not have powers to collect data directly from the financial institutions, it has to rely on the NSAs, which perform the first-level data control and ensure the quality of the data transmitted. However, if NSAs' data quality control is deficient, the EBA incurs considerable reputational risk while using and publishing the inaccurate information.

EBA Staff and Budget

The last two years were crucial in setting up and extending the EBA's human resources team. EBA's staff increased from 58 to 95 between May 2011 and December 2012, according to the initial plan presented during the previous IMF mission (Table 16.1). Currently the chairman and chief executive officer are supported by three directors and seven heads of units. EBA staff are composed of 15 contractual (permanent) staff, 68 temporary staff, and 12 secondees. Staff were trained during 2011, on average, for one day per staff member, and in 2012 for 1.5 days per staff member.

TABLE 16.1

European Banking Authority Staffing Levels, 2011, 2012, and 2013			
	2011	December 2012	2013 Planned
Staff temporary	46	68	93
Secondees	8	12	15
Contractual	4	15	15
Total	58	95	123

Source: European Banking Authority.

Endowing the EBA with adequate resources, on a flexible basis, is crucial for it to achieve its ambitious objectives and meet its increasing responsibilities. Currently, the EBA's budget is part of the European Commission's overall budget. Forty percent of the EBA's revenue comes from the European Commission Section of the General Budget of the European Union, and 60 percent comes from obligatory contributions from the NSAs.

This budget process raises some concerns. Indeed, the salaries and levels of seniority are dictated by European Commission rules and the budget is determined by the European Commission to a great level of granularity. New tasks are not automatically covered by immediate additional staff resources. While tasks added from new regulations should in theory come with immediate additional budget, the European Commission budget rules allocate new staff only when a new regulation is published in the official journal. For instance, the new tasks addressing resolution powers (recovery plans) will require 16 new staff, according to the EBA. However, the resourcing will need to await the final publication of the directive, although in theory the technical standards should be mostly ready for consultation and validation by that time. Staff and other expenses are not fungible, making budget planning very rigid. EBA cannot use free budgetary resources from other projects to meet these immediate needs.

The participation of NSA staff in technical working groups is helpful and desirable in the current decentralized setting, but the EBA should not rely too much on such resources. Standing and technical committees—staffed by NSAs—are significant and desirable complementary resources. There are currently four standing committees (Standing Committee on Regulation and Policy; Standing Committee on Oversight and Practices; Standing Committee on Accounting and Auditing; Standing Committee on Financial Innovation) and 16 subcommittees. NSAs are also seconding staff for defined periods of time, sometimes for very short thematic projects. Since the NSAs have more abundant resources than the EBA, the resulting work may potentially reflect this national-based membership. In addition, work continuity may become overly dependent on the availability of NSAs.

Like the other ESAs, the EBA advocates for more flexibility in staffing. Given the current stage of the process of implementing Basel III, a critical mass of staff is necessary to ensure proper drafting and implementation of the technical standards across the European Union. To help this process, more flexibility in the budget should be considered. One option could be a separate and specific budget line in the overall EU budget, outside the European Commission's funding. The EU agency in charge of data protection (the European Data Protection Supervisor) is funded on the general budget of the European Union. An alternative that might be envisaged is to explore additional sources of funding, such as fees on financial institutions. The planning for staff also needs to take a medium-term view, particularly considering the establishment of the SSM. Since the ECB will be given a supervisory role for euro area member states, the EBA mandate should provide for the necessary adjustments to the range of its activities and may have to refocus on specific core tasks.

REGULATORY AND SUPERVISORY ACTIONS

Developing a European Regulatory Framework

The EBA is a regulatory agency of the European Commission, but it has no direct Level 1 regulatory powers. The directives and regulations for the banking sector are adopted by EU legislators based on the proposals of the European Commission. The EBA has been empowered to draft technical standards (Level 2), although these only have binding effect once endorsed by the commission, and to draft guidelines (Level 3). The EBA participates in the Level 1 process, giving opinions on the European Commission's rule-making proposals, but such opinions are not binding nor do they require a response.

EBA will develop the single rulebook, by imposing uniform regulatory technical standards (RTS) that will be binding, once approved by the European Commission. The draft RTS developed so far are mostly focused on CRDIV, on own funds, credit risk; and market risk but will eventually cover all the Level 1 regulation of the Capital Requirements Regulation.

ENHANCING SUPERVISORY CONVERGENCE

As part of its mandate, the EBA should promote the convergence of supervisory practices to a high standard across member states, so that regulatory and supervisory rules are implemented equally on the ground. This mandate serves both financial stability and the single market. There is a range of tools available to strengthen supervisory convergence, including training programs, harmonizing reporting, data sharing and disclosure, participation in colleges, and conducting peer reviews.

Several EBA subgroups are in charge of enhancing convergence, but besides issuing guidelines little has been accomplished so far. Member countries exchange practices through the ongoing work of the EBA Standing Committee on Oversight and Practices. Its subgroup on Home-host and Colleges is directly involved in the work on the colleges, in particular in their operational functioning (see Box 16.1), joint decision making on approval of advanced models, and joint decision making on institution-specific prudential requirements. Another relatively new standing subcommittee is focused on supervisory practices, in which convergence and harmonization of practices should be a core objective.

Guidelines for supervisory and reporting convergence issues include both recommendations on the implementation of EU regulations and best practices on issues covered exclusively by national legislation. Regarding the first, there are guidelines to harmonize processes concerning supervisory approval of changes in advanced measurement approach models for operational risk; guidelines on stressed value-at-risk (stressed VaR) and on the incremental default and migration risk charge modeling approaches employed by credit institutions using the internal model approach; and guidelines on the data collection exercise on high earners and remuneration benchmarking. On the other hand, the

Box 16.1 The European Banking Authority and Its Role in Supervisory Colleges

The EU banking regulation requires colleges of supervisors to be established for all cross-border banking groups in Europe. Capital Requirements Directive 2 (applicable from December 31, 2010) requires the establishment of colleges of supervisors to improve the supervision of cross-border banking groups and facilitate home-host dialogue, particularly in the context of the joint decision on capital (Pillar 2 capital add-on). The colleges should also help prepare and handle emergency situations. The Financial Stability Board has also promoted the establishment of supervisory colleges for all major financial institutions at the global level, as an immediate response to the financial crisis. European Banking Authority (EBA) colleges were set up for 87 cross-border banks in 2012 (of which 40 were in full-fledged colleges*). Core colleges need to be set up where a full college would be unwieldy for decision making; not all of the 40 full-fledged colleges have set up core colleges.

The EBA staff has participated in the colleges, yet with mixed success. According to EBA regulation (Article 21), in its 'facilitator' role the EBA will contribute to promoting and monitoring the efficient, effective and consistent functioning of the colleges of supervisors and foster the coherence of the application of EU law among the colleges of supervisors. Staff should encourage supervisory best practices to converge, and the EBA may develop technical standards with regard to the operational functioning of colleges. The EBA may collect and share all relevant information in cooperation with the national supervisory authorities while establishing a central system to make such information accessible to all college members. It may evaluate the risks to which financial institutions are or might be exposed under the supervisory review process or in stress situations. There seems to be considerable variety as to how this 'facilitator' role is performed in practice, depending on the group's structure, type of college, and EBA representative.

At the level of the colleges, joint assessment and decisions remain heterogeneous. The colleges, under the coordination of the consolidating supervisor, should lead to a joint risk assessment and reach joint decisions on the adequacy of capital at the group and entity level. According to an EBA staff note, most colleges have developed uniform approaches but with different levels of granularity and consistency. Joint decisions sometimes are only one page long, simply listing the individual capital requirements and without adequate evidence and analysis. In some cases, the EBA said it was not convinced that a joint decision had been reached, particularly where domestic authorities imposed higher capital requirements on entities that were the most profitable of the entire group. Use could have been made of formal mediation, where no joint decisions had been reached.

Cooperation from third-country supervisors is work in progress. EBA staff have been invited to participate in a few colleges that are set up for the European Economic Area parts of a banking group with a parent undertaking in a third country. For the time being, however, these appear to remain exceptional cases, and some third-country authorities have not granted full access to the EBA representative. Some authorities still object to granular data sharing, particularly at the level of the general colleges. Some third-country supervisors are reluctant to attend crisis management colleges.

The EBA should strengthen its leading role in cross-border supervisory colleges, but the arrival of the SSM will raise new challenges. The EBA should ensure that its guidelines are observed and implemented in practice. It should use its soft powers ("name and shame") to foster effective and regular multilateral exchanges of information, ensure genuine joint decisions, push for mediation when no joint decision can be reached, and seek to ensure that colleges reach action-oriented, forward-looking conclusions. Under the Single Supervisory Mechanism, the design of colleges will change. The European Central Bank will become the home supervisor, and in some cases the euro area home and host countries will participate in colleges as observers only.

---

*Committee of European Banking Supervisors/EBA released (nonbinding) guidelines for operational functioning of colleges distinguish between 'fully fledged' colleges for banks with presence through significant branch or subsidiary in two or more host countries, and 'non-fully fledged' colleges with smaller cross-border presence.

guidelines on "assessment of the suitability of members of the management body and key function holders" enter the realm of national legislation, since no harmonized EU legislation exists. The guidelines include criteria and minimum requirements for fit and proper assessments, and are aimed to be used by both banks and by local supervisors in assessing banks' practices.

Regarding peer reviews, the EBA adopted in May 2011 the decision to establish a review panel, but conducting peer reviews has been given relatively low priority. The decision establishes that peer reviews would assess the degree of convergence reached by members in the implementation of supervisory provisions set in legislation or by the EBA, and that they would monitor convergence in supervisory practices. It is interesting to note that reviews are also to cover the adequacy of supervisory resources and the governance arrangements of supervisory authorities.

The establishment of the ECB as a single supervisory authority for the euro area countries has triggered a renewed discussion on EBA's mandate on supervisory convergence. It is clear that the ECB will need to implement supervisory manuals and procedures that are consistent across participating countries and with their NSAs exercising delegated powers, and that might front-run or overlap with the EBA's mandate. In response, EBA's management has expressed the intention of producing a supervisory handbook. According to EBA's work plan for 2013, such a handbook would seek to unify supervisory methodologies and would be composed of papers summarizing best practices and guidelines. The focus of such a handbook should not be on detailed procedures, but rather on the interpretation of existing standards and regulations, and with an orientation to how supervisors can substantiate their assessments of banks risks.

The ECB and EBA will need to cooperate strongly so that the ECB, as a new supervisor, can build its procedures based on best practices. The ECB should align its procedures with the proposed supervisory handbook to be drafted by the EBA. Like any other supervisor in the European Union, the ECB will need to adjust its practices as guidelines and standards are updated.

ASSESSING SYSTEMIC RISK

EU-Wide Stress Tests and the Risk Dashboard[8]

The EBA has been strengthening bank stress-testing procedures and their application. Following the poor reception of the 2010 exercise, the 2011 solvency stress testing and recapitalization exercises were marked by extensive consistency checks and more transparency about methodology and data. The EBA 2011 stress and recapitalization exercises helped identify weak banks and increase capital buffers. The recapitalization exercises recommended the achievement of 9 percent core Tier 1 capital by end-June 2012, after establishing a sovereign buffer against

---

[8] A separate report on stress tests was produced by the IMF during the Financial Sector Assessment Program, so this chapter will not detail the issue.

banks' holdings of government securities based on a market-implied valuation of those holdings. The exercise led to an additional €200 billion in capital generation or release by June 2012, and government backstops were provided to the weakest banks. A few banks under restructuring and recapitalization programs did not achieve the target on time.

EU risk dashboard and assessment. The EBA is producing a risk dashboard (which is not public) to identify and measure systemic risk, and it also publishes a regular risk assessment. The dashboard is based on key risk indicators, which are a set of 53 ratios reported on a quarterly basis by EU national authorities and covering 57 EU banks from 20 European Economic Area countries. The definition of those variables is homogeneous and consistent with the supervisory and financial common EU reporting forms, known as the Common Reporting (COREP) and the Financial Reporting (FINREP). In terms of coverage, the banks in the sample cover at least 50 percent of each national banking sector. However, the time series are not complete, since they have been collected on a best-effort basis, and their quality still depends on national authorities, even though the EBA carries out automatic consistency checks to clean the data. The EBA provides the European Parliament, the European Council, the European Commission, and the ESRB with regular risk assessments of trends and potential risks and vulnerabilities in the EU banking sector.

Contribution to the Work of the European Systemic Risk Board

The EBA is a member of the ESRB. It participates in all decision-making bodies and in expert groups under the ESRB's Advisory Technical Committee, and in two permanent working groups: the Working Group on Analysis Tools and the Working Group on Instruments. The objective is that its input on microprudential issues is reflected in the ESRB's systemic risk measures. In expert groups under the ESRB's Advisory Technical Committee, the EBA has assumed the role of collecting bank-specific information, such as data on asset encumbrance and innovative funding and on interbank lending in the European Union. The EBA also provides the ESRB with its own bottom-up assessments of risks and vulnerabilities affecting the EU banking system.

The EBA is following up on ESRB recommendations. With regard to the recommendation on lending in foreign currency, by end-2013 the EBA must adopt guidelines to NSAs on capital measures relating to foreign exchange lending supervisory practices (those guidelines have been drafted and were open for public consultation in May 2013). The ESRB recommendation on dollar-denominated funding includes regular data collection on funding positions, which the ESRB collects from NSAs in its follow-up. The recommendation states that NSAs may report in aggregate through the EBA, which already has received such a notification and wants to establish its own account in this data collection. It is engaging with the ESRB Secretariat and NSAs to receive further notifications of the data collections.

Role in Fostering Transparency

The EBA has been acting to promote the harmonization of financial and supervisory reporting. It is currently finalizing a draft technical standard on supervisory reporting, which will cover all EU credit institutions and investment firms. The technical standard will harmonize the reporting framework in the European Union and will include reporting of own funds and own-funds requirements in COREP and FINREP, large exposures, liquidity, and leverage ratios. Banks will report the data to their national supervisory authorities, which will then forward data on an individual basis to the EBA. The EBA plans in the near future to collect comprehensive sets of regulatory and accounting data from the banks and hopes to be a hub of bank-specific data. Regarding COREP, FINREP, and large exposures, the EBA reporting will cover 100 to 200 banks in the first phase, but leverage and liquidity ratio reporting will cover all banks. This effort will not only facilitate stability analysis, but will also reduce the regulatory burden by harmonizing reporting requirements. The EBA is in the process of preparing a Regulatory Technical Standards specifying the new requirements contained in Basel III on own-funds disclosures, including a template for own-funds. It has not yet made a decision on public dissemination of the bank-specific data that will be collected through the new reporting framework.

The 2011 stress test exercise showed the value brought by disclosure of detailed information. The EBA has published the results of the EU-wide stress tests in 2010 and 2011 on its website. In 2011, a user-friendly tool was provided to access the disclosure of more than 3,000 data points for each bank disclosed.

However, quality assurance is key, more so even than the stress tests themselves. The EBA should strive to (1) enhance the quality assurance process; (2) promote the disclosure of granular asset quality information (including collateral and risk-weighted assets calculations); and (3) expand the depth and coverage of data audits. In addition, the EBA should raise supervisors' awareness of issues related to asset quality and the need for accurate and timely reporting, in particular by issuing guidelines for supervisors on best practices for conducting asset quality reviews. It should work with national authorities and coordinate the provision of technical expertise where needed.

The EBA should push for enhancing the comparability and granularity of Pillar 3 reports. While it has been working on assessing Pillar 3 reports for some time, this has not always been followed up with strong actions. The EBA (and Committee of European Banking Supervisors) assessments have led to the publication of yearly reports, containing findings and suggested best practices. Linked to the work on asset quality, Pillar 3 reports should also be adapted to provide the markets with more granular and comparable information.

BINDING POWERS

In very few cases, the EBA can issue recommendations or binding decisions directly to national authorities. This applies to cases where a national authority is incorrectly applying EU law (breach of EU law, Article 17); where there is a disagreement between national authorities (mediation, at the initiative of the NSAs, Articles 19 and 20); and in emergency situations declared by the Council (Article 18). In those cases, the EBA can take decisions directly applicable to financial institutions as a last resort only if the national supervisor has failed to comply and only when EU law applies directly to a financial institution (as a regulation and not a directive).

No formal case of this type has materialized so far. The EBA has been involved in a number of soft reconciliation measures, consisting of differences between home and several host supervisors and differences between home and individual supervisors. However, it has recently brought to its EBA Board two requests for investigation of breaches of EU law that could lead to a formal mediation process.

In 2012, several actions were taken on crisis management preparations. The EBA issued a crisis management manual outlining the role of colleges of supervisors in emergency situations, as well as an EBA internal crisis management procedure guide. It also began to attend the crisis management groups of a number of the major cross-border banking groups. In May 2012, it also published a discussion document containing a template for a standard recovery plan.

The EBA's coordination role in this area of activity will significantly expand when the Bank Resolution and Recovery Directive is adopted. In the forthcoming resolution directive, the EBA will have a strong role in coordinating and designing resolution plans for cross-border group entities in procedures for emergency situations.[9]

CONSUMER PROTECTION AND FINANCIAL INNOVATION

Consumer protection is one of the core functions laid down in the EBA regulation, which states that

> EBA shall take a leading role in promoting transparency, simplicity and fairness in the market for consumer financial products or services across the internal market, including by: (i) collecting, analyzing and reporting on consumer trends; (ii) reviewing and coordinating financial literacy and education initiatives by the competent authorities; (iii) developing training standards for the industry; and (iv) contributing to the development of common disclosure rules.

The EBA also has a monitoring role on new and existing financial activities.

Only in February 2012 was a unit established to deal with consumer protection issues, and the EBA has so far mostly relied on work done by its standing committees. The Standing Committee on Financial Innovation, mentioned

---

[9] Article 25 of the EBA regulation.

earlier, was established in May 2011 together with its two subgroups: the Subgroup on Consumer Protection and the Subgroup on Innovative Products.[10]

Focus has been on risk management and financial stability. Under the Standing Committee on Investor Protection, workstreams are focusing on different topics, such as exchange traded funds (ETFs). This workstream performed an in-depth analysis of risks from ETFs for banks, interviewing several smaller ETFs providers. The EBA Board has tasked this workstream with producing a note on good risk management practices related to ETFs directed toward banks; it has also tasked it with producing a paper on the key risks posed by ETFs as well as good risk management practices, directed toward national supervisory authorities. Another workstream conducted an in-depth analysis and held conference calls with the three largest providers of European Contracts for Differences (CfDs) providers (IG Markets; Saxo Bank; and the Royal Bank of Scotland, RBS) to discuss the nature of CfD structures, key risks associated with providers of CfDs, and CfD risk management. Finally, regarding structured products, a workstream is interviewing banks to receive a mostly qualitative overview on the European structured product market. Guidelines on handling borrowers in payment difficulties and on responsible lending in the area of mortgages were published as EBA Opinions in June 2013.

In the area of consumer protection, more staff and knowledge building are needed. The consumer protection unit seems to be too lightly staffed: it is composed of only one person and reports directly to the EBA's executive director. Support from the other ESAs may be sought, since some have been more proactive, issuing guidelines, reports on good practices, and consumer trends in this area. Work on financial innovation should be given a focus on consumer protection and not just on financial stability, and care needs to be taken to avoid duplication of the work conducted in the securities arena (e.g., work on ETF carried out by ESMA or by the Financial Stability Board).

CROSS-SECTORAL ISSUES

Cross-sectoral work is carried out by the Joint Committee of ESAs. The Joint Committee is a forum of cooperation on cross-sectoral issues for three ESAs. Established on January 1, 2011 (Article 54 to 57 of the ESAs), it succeeded the former Joint Committee on Financial Conglomerates (Article 54 to 57 of the ESAs). The Joint Committee of ESAs should ensure cross-sectoral consistency of work and should reach joint positions "where appropriate," in particular regarding the areas of (1) supervision of financial conglomerates (e.g., guidelines for colleges of financial conglomerates, which will be drafted by end-2014); (2) accounting and auditing (e.g., assessing and providing consistent cross-sector inputs and exchanges of views in order to ensure cross-sector consistency in their application); (3) microprudential analyses of cross-sectoral developments;

---

[10] The Standing Committee on Financial Innovation was recently renamed the Standing Committee on Consumer Protection and Financial Innovation.

(4) risks and vulnerabilities for financial stability; (5) retail investment products; (6) measures combating money laundering; and (7) information exchange with the ESRB and development of the relationship between the ESRB and the ESAs.

Its chairmanship of the Joint Committee of ESAs rotates between the three authorities. The chairman is the second vice-chairman of the ESRB. The members are the chairmen of the EBA, EIOPA, and ESMA, and the chairmen of each sub-committee of the Joint Committee; additionally, functioning as observers are the executive directors of EBA, EIOPA and ESMA, a representative of the European Commission, and a representative of the ESRB. The Joint Committee has a dedicated staff provided by the ESAs (one full-time employee in 2011 and two full-time employees in 2012). It meets at least every two months at the premises of the ESA that is chairing. The chairman may also convene a meeting when he or she deems it necessary, including in the case of adverse developments that may seriously jeopardize the functioning and integrity of financial markets or financial stability.

The Joint Committee of ESAs conducts risk assessment on cross-sectoral issues that also deserve close coordination with ESRB. It monitors and assesses the systemic risk work performed by the ESAs. It also assists in the development of cooperation between the ESAs and the ESRB. It produces policy-focused risk reports for the European Financial Committee–Financial Stability Table meetings in March and September each calendar year. These reports include preliminary policy conclusions and provide a cross-sectoral assessment that is to be fed into each of the ESA's sectoral systemic-risk assessment work.

SUMMARY OF RECOMMENDATIONS

Governance

- Representatives of some other EU institutions (except the European Commission), and possibly the respective EBA chairmen, could have a vote on the EBA Supervisory Board.

- The powers of the EBA Management Board could be further strengthened with more delegated powers from the Board; or a permanent Executive Board composed of independent representative could be formed.

- Members who do not comply with article 40 of the EBA regulation should see their votes suspended. To incentivize the right representation, a mechanism of written procedure should be introduced.

- More resources need to be allocated to the EBA, and more flexibility in the budget should be considered.

Regulatory and Supervisory Actions

- Supervisors' awareness of asset quality issues should be raised, in particular by issuing guidelines (nonbinding) for supervisors on best practices for conducting asset quality reviews, perhaps addressing some specific sectors and urgently pushing for the enhancement of comparability and complete-ness in Pillar 3 reports.

- Convergence on Pillar 2 practices (common methodologies for risk assess-ment) should be accelerated. A good example of activity that should receive priority is the current work on the consistency of treatment of risk weighted assets. This work should be harmonized with BCBS Level 3 exercises and followed up with the issuance of guidelines (and perhaps RTS) to ensure consistency.

- Cooperation should be fostered by encouraging joint on-site supervision by member countries, and resuming the performance of thematic peer reviews.

- Peer reviews should be implemented covering the adequacy of supervisory resources and the governance arrangements of supervisory authorities.

- The EBA should play more of a leading role in cross-border supervisory colleges and should be able to participate in the core colleges of EU banking groups that have activities abroad.

- The EBA should ensure that its guidelines are observed and implemented in practice. It should use its soft powers ("name and shame") to foster effec-tive and regular multilateral exchanges of information, to ensure genuine joint decisions, and to push for mediation when no joint decision can be reached.

- The EBA should work closely with the ECB as a new supervisor, so that the SSM can build its procedures based on the best available guidelines from the EBA and its handbook.

Oversight

- Strengthening the transparency and reliability of data should be given prior-ity. EBA should strive to (1) enhance the quality assurance process; (2) promote the disclosure of granular asset quality information; and (3) expand the depth and coverage of the 2012 audits.

- Pillar 3 reports should be enhanced and harmonized.

Consumer Protection and Cross-Sectoral Issues

- In the area of consumer protection, EBA should be organized to fulfill its mandate. More staff and knowledge building are needed. Support from the other ESAs may be sought, as some have already been more proactive in this area (issuing guidelines, reports on good practices, and reports on consumer trends).

- Work on financial innovation should be given a focus on consumer protec-tion, and overlaps with work conducted in the securities arena (for instance, work on ETF by ESMA or by the Financial Stability Board) should be avoided.

CHAPTER 17

Stress Testing European Banks

Daniel C. Hardy and Heiko Hesse

The European authorities have used, and will continue to use, stress testing as a very prominent tool in crisis management, the analysis of banking sector stability, and the development of financial sector policy. Starting with the 2010 test led by the Committee of European Banking Supervisors and reinforced by the 2011 test and the bank recapitalization exercise led by the European Banking Authority (EBA), the output of EU-wide stress tests has been viewed as essential information on the health of the system.[1] Moreover, the reliability of the results and the efficiency with which they were generated (especially the recapitalization exercise) have influenced the credibility of the European and national authorities involved. This prominence demands that future stress-testing exercises be very carefully designed and executed.

This chapter focuses on bank stress testing led by the EBA, and in particular on how to respond to changing circumstances and priorities going forward. The national supervisory authorities (NSAs), European Central Bank (ECB), and the European Systemic Risk Board (ESRB) conduct their own tests for various purposes, and this chapter will discuss those that have more or less Europe-wide relevance. Moreover, consideration will be given to both the solvency and the liquidity aspects of stress testing and how priorities are likely to evolve in the post-crisis environment, especially with the introduction of the Single Supervisory Mechanism (SSM). While the coordinated stress testing of nonbank financial institutions, specifically of insurance undertakings and pension funds, faces largely analogous issues, it will not be addressed directly in this chapter.

The chapter closely links to the wider discussion in the book on EU-wide crisis management and financial stability as well as the SSM. At the current juncture, repairing the balance sheets of European banks and smoothing the

---

[1] The 2010 exercise was relatively poorly received: the stress scenario was regarded as too mild in the circumstances, and there was little assurance that banks had not been able to incorporate an optimistic bias into the results. Limited information disclosure did little to relieve the intense uncertainty prevalent at that time. The 2011 solvency stress testing and recapitalization exercises, which were led by then-new EBA, were better received. Those efforts were marked by extensive consistency checks, more transparency about methodology and data (for example, regarding sovereign exposures), and higher "hurdle rates"—that is, minimum capitalization levels expected of banks. Even though the final estimated capital shortfall was modest, that result was largely the product of many banks—especially those with relatively weak capital buffers—preemptively increasing their capitalization, and of what with hindsight appears to be unduly optimistic baseline and stress scenarios, including with regard to the treatment of sovereign risk.

implementation of their strengthened prudential requirements and crisis management mechanisms are key. Stress-testing exercises can help toward these ends. Transparency and disclosure will be crucial not only regarding asset quality, but also regarding asset encumbrance, and the EBA will play an important role in promoting data quality and comparability (see Chapter 15 on EBA). Selective asset quality reviews (AQRs), coordinated at the European Union level, would also aid the ECB in the assessment of legacy assets for the SSM (see Chapter 3). Furthermore, with the continuing challenges on fragmentation and bank funding, especially in the periphery, the chapter argues for incorporating liquidity and structural elements in the design of postcrisis EU-wide stress tests.

FORTHCOMING STRESS-TESTING EXERCISES

The European authorities are expected to establish a regular cycle of coordinated bank solvency stress-testing exercises, with more emphasis on supervisory issues than in past exercises. One of the main supervisory issues in coming years will be the assessment of the realism, consistency, and robustness of banks' capital plans to meet the phased-in capital requirements under the Fourth Capital Requirement Directive (CRD IV). The use of stress tests for crisis management purposes—generating pass/fail results and immediate recapitalization needs—is expected to diminish, especially with European banks already boosting their capital for the Basel III phase-in period given market and regulatory pressures.

Lessons from past stress-testing exercises will have to be incorporated into the design and execution of the forthcoming exercises, but modified as needed in light of current conditions and the exercise's objectives. The improvements in efficiency and effectiveness seen since the 2010 Committee of European Banking Supervisors exercise should be extended, and in particular, the 2011 stress testing and recapitalization exercises offer additional lessons. Nonetheless, adjustments need to be made to allow for the fact that the situation of European banks is more diverse (also due to ongoing fragmentation, asset quality pressures, and funding strains) and also less uncertain than in 2010 or 2011. Some banks operate in program countries and others operate in a comparatively benign macroeconomic environment; some are heavily dependent on central bank refinancing and others have ample and excess liquidity, often deposited back at the ECB. Moreover, the tests need to be geared toward generating output and recommendations that are relevant for supervisory purposes, rather than those that are needed in an acute crisis situation. This section concentrates on identifying ways to reconcile these features in various aspects of the design of the exercise.

PUBLICATION AND TRANSPARENCY

The publication of detailed data on major European banks in the context of the 2011 stress testing and recapitalization exercises contributed to reducing uncertainty markedly and to the credibility of those exercises. The authorities were praised for providing enough information (more than 3,000 series, notably on sovereign exposures) that market analysts could check and with which they could run their own projections based on alternative scenarios and assumptions on banks' treatment of their sovereign exposures. It is inevitable that analysts will want to assess the situation of banks assuming the immediate full implementation of CRD IV (already under way), and banks may be basing their own planning on this assumption. Had relevant data not been provided, the market would look on the exercise with increased skepticism.

The authorities will have to publish data from forthcoming exercises in at least as much bank-by-bank detail and also covering the initial situation of individual banks at the reference date, if not necessarily all projections. To do otherwise would, at least, miss an opportunity to reduce the uncertainty that has contributed to the fragmentation of funding markets, and could lead to suspicions that the authorities have bad news to hide. There should be a presumption that test results would be published in detail as well. Even if the authorities do not highlight certain series, such as the projected evolution of banks' profitability, the information is valuable in the context of structural pressures on the sector. For instance, the 2011 stress test did not publish bank-specific data on the banks' starting positions that were as comprehensive as the projections from the adverse scenarios. However, there may be scope to keep some details confidential. For example, publication of results from sensitivity analysis may be more confusing than reassuring, in part because the market could regard those results as benchmark results and penalize banks that do poorly in the sensitivity stress tests.

Confidentiality will have to be maintained over certain aspects of the supervisory recommendations. Some recommendations may relate to a bank's confidential business planning, its detailed funding plans, or supervisors' own policies. But a possible negative market impact should not in itself be grounds for nonpublication, since such market discipline is desirable. Consistent treatment across banks would be essential, not least to maintain a level playing field for competition.

In this connection, it is worth stressing that full disclosure of banks' sovereign exposures (including those in the banking book) will be essential and that the tests will need to fully recognize the attendant risks. Given that the 2011 EBA recapitalization exercise involved marking to market banks' sovereign securities' exposure in the banking book (available for sale, AFS, and held to maturity), the market could be critical of a reversal. Admittedly, the Basel III rules envisage that just the trading and AFS books would be marked to market with a gradual phase-in period, while the held-to-maturity book would not be subject to marking to market. While authorities will have to trade off disclosure with the marking-to-market approach taken, relevant data should be published at a minimum. Nonetheless, if current market conditions persist, for most banks sovereign exposures are likely to be a smaller source of losses (or could contribute positively) in the baseline of the 2014 exercise. A relapse at least to recent peak sovereign spreads would be seen as constituting a plausible but not very extreme scenario. Hence, a conservative approach would probably not be disruptive. In any case, based on the disclosed detailed banking data, analysts would be able to calculate each bank's estimated haircut on its total sovereign securities portfolio.

Consistency and Quality Control Mechanisms

The authorities are making strong and commendable efforts to improve quality control mechanisms. For example, reporting templates are being developed to incorporate various consistency checks, and there is expected to be ongoing contact between the authorities and banks to ensure that the methodology, benchmarks, and reporting forms are well understood. The 2011 experience suggests that the ECB top-down macro stress test need to be prepared and used as a cross-check at an earlier stage, but to this end "clean-up" data needs to be provided to the EBA earlier on.[2] In particular, NSAs need to make a quick but thorough check of data as soon as it is received.

As part of this process, the authorities need to continue to build up time series of statistical benchmarks for probability of defaults, loss given defaults, and default rates by granular counterparties, countries, and sectors, as well as ensure consistent application by banks of point-in-time estimates of probability of defaults and loss given defaults. Those benchmarks should be cross-checked with the ECB's estimated probability of defaults and loss given defaults that are also being used to challenge banks and are adopted by banks under the standardized approach. Banks should use their point-in-time probability of defaults and loss-given defaults parameters for the bottom-up stress test and not through-the-cycle equivalents. The use of point-in-time parameters is important because results need to be sensitive to the scenarios, and the point-in-time probability of defaults is relatively forward looking. Stress tests are meant to say something about the ability of banks to survive bad points in time, so through-the-cycle parameters are not fully relevant to assessing resilience to conjunctural shocks.[3]

Reviewing Input Data

The banking systems of most program countries have been subject to detailed AQRs, and the question therefore arises of how to ensure consistency of input data. Elaborate and expensive "deep dive" AQRs have been carried out in individual banking systems in Europe and have formed a solid base upon which to conduct crisis stress tests. The IMF-European Commission-ECB "Troika" very much supported these efforts. Yet data from some of the non-program countries could conceivably contain important flaws, and a mere lack of consistency would make results difficult to interpret and could interfere with the internal market.

---

[2] In the 2011 EBA stress test, the ECB contributed the adverse scenario and top-down stress test, besides participating in the stress testing and quality assurance task forces.

[3] It is possible that, if probability of default and loss given defaults are not sufficiently sensitive to the scenario, and risk-weighted assets decline over the scenario due to losses, the positive impact on capital (from lowering the risk-weighted asset—the denominator) may offset the limited impact of losses on capital (the numerator).

In addition, some of the AQRs could be somewhat outdated if economic and financial sector developments have deteriorated more than initially forecast.

Inconsistencies may arise despite the (almost) universal application of International Financial Accounting Standards and a system of internal and external audits with supervisory oversight. First, the accounting standards allow some room for local differences in definition—for example, of a nonperforming loan or renegotiated/restructured loan. Second, interpretation of common definitions may differ across countries or banks. Third, interpretations may differ over time. In current circumstances, a bank may more readily choose to roll over a problem loan and make modest provisions, partly to help its borrower and partly to make its own results look better. It should be noted here, however, that consistency does not imply uniformity, as accounting differences may reflect underlying differences; probability-of-default and loss-given-default rates may genuinely differ, for example, because of large differences in bankruptcy laws and loan work-out arrangements.

Yet undertaking a full-blown AQR across the European Union would be very expensive, time consuming, and possibly counterproductive. Besides the practical difficulties and expense, announcing a comprehensive AQR would cast doubt on the integrity of past stress-testing exercises, national authorities, bank management, and the accounting and audit professions. Furthermore, consideration would also have to be given to undertaking an AQR for the assets of European banks outside the European Union, an enterprise that would add greatly to the complexity and cost.

In these circumstances, the authorities, coordinated by the EBA, need to give priority to unifying definitions of nonperforming loans and provisioning criteria. Efforts in this direction have been underway for some time, but now there should be momentum behind the project. Full implementation of all aspects might take place after the 2014 stress-testing exercise, especially for the SSM and the new supervisory role of the ECB, but that would not be a great drawback. There would need to be guidance offered to national authorities and the accounting and audit professions. While details for a comprehensive AQR as part of the SSM have yet to be decided, it seems likely to involve the ECB and the EBA as well as the NSAs. Overall, providing consistent and comparable banking sector data is among the responsibilities the (national) supervisors are accountable for.

Nonetheless, when a pressing need becomes apparent, it would be worthwhile to conduct limited reviews of input data, especially on asset quality. The focus would be on the most problematic sectors, and the stress-testing exercises would not be greatly impeded. Issues of special concern for such reviews are likely to include lender forbearance; impairment deficiencies; risk weighting and risk-weighted asset calculations by banks;[4] collateral valuations and credit-risk mitigation techniques; and treatment of restructured loans. The main concern

---

[4] For instance, the recent Bank of England Financial Stability Report (November 2012) shows that banks' risk-weighted asset calculations for the same hypothetical portfolio can differ vastly, with the most prudent banks calculating over twice the needed capital than the most aggressive banks.

should be to make the reference period data as reliable as possible, as judged by the situation at that time; the baseline projection is meant to capture the evolution of impairments going forward.

Public explanation of the effort will need to be handled with care and measures taken to ensure that the exercise is recognized as rigorous but limited.[5] In the publication stage, the EBA could promote the disclosure of granular asset quality information to enhance transparency and reduce market uncertainty about banks' asset quality. However, there is a risk that investors could come to expect the revelation of additional losses in banks' portfolios.[6] Should the AQR reveal bank losses, questions will arise about recapitalization backstops at the national level (given that the ESM would not be able to provide capital prior to the SSM) and the inherent budgetary implications. Some data may be highly market-sensitive; rules of engagement in such case should be worked out in advance, especially if the ECB is involved in the context of the SSM. Also, evidence of underprovisioning that is unquestionably consistent with International Financial Accounting Standards might prompt tougher guidance in the stress-testing methodology on the future evolution of losses, rather than being reflected in published stock data at the reference date. The experiences of data disclosure from the external AQRs already conducted could be useful here. The credibility of the exercise would be increased by the involvement of outside evaluators, or at least peer reviewers, to limit the potential national bias.

Achieving Supervisory Orientation

Future stress-testing exercises are meant to be mainly for supervisory purposes, as opposed to the past emphasis on crisis management and the assessment of bank capitalization. Translating this intention into the design and practice of the stress test and transcending the market's perception of past tests will require careful preparation. Market participants and analysts are likely to compare results across banks and try to quantify capitalization needs. If the capital needs are not "enough," analysts may question the rigor of the tests. The tests need to be designed to meet supervisory purposes, which may demand that they be quite complex, but they also need to communicate credible messages, to which end the main tests need to be suitably calibrated.[7]

---

[5] Using a term other than "asset quality review" might be one element of the communication strategy that distinguishes this effort from the more comprehensive AQRs undertaken in program countries. "Asset quality data exercise" or "input data review" might be suitable titles.

[6] It is possible that the exercise will reveal a sizable "hole" in the capitalization of some banks, even before any projections are made. The authorities will need to consider in advance how they would handle such a situation, for example, through immediate remedial supervisory action and exclusion of the affected banks from the regular stress test.

[7] Insofar as the effects of risk factors are linear, calibration of shock magnitudes is not important for understanding how the system works.

To achieve the supervisory purposes, the tests should yield recommendations for supervisors as bank managers and generate relevant indicators. Some of these recommendations, which may have to remain confidential, might include indications of the areas on which supervisors should focus their attention during the coming period (e.g., lending practices in especially vulnerable sectors or the sustainability of funding). To this end, it may be useful to generate relatively detailed projections, for example, for loan quality by sector and by country, capitalization by country, and profitability measures. Supervisory colleges could then discuss the implementation of these recommendations.

The authorities intend in particular to use the exercises to evaluate banks' plans to comply with the evolving capitalization requirements under CRD IV. Each exercise is likely to follow a certain procedure: each bank will provide its dynamic capital plan, which will also include related planned adjustments among its assets and liabilities (e.g., a shift-out of assets with high capital weights or out of short-term market funding). Each bank will also provide data on its balance sheet positions at the reference period (e.g., end-2012), and projections of its profit and loss under the provided baseline and stress scenarios and satellite model guidance, but with a static balance sheet.[8] A three-year projection period is typical. After checking plausibility and consistency, the authorities will substitute the projected losses and other elements from the two scenarios (baseline and adverse) into the bank's capital plan. The authorities will then assess whether the bank's capitalization level falls below, or close to, the CRD IV minimum requirements, such as on the definition of capital and risk-weighted assets, which are progressively tighter over the projection period due to the gradual phase-in period of CRD IV. If a bank's plan looks precarious or is based on implausible assumptions, the relevant supervisor will demand a revision.

The use of a static balance sheet over three years may be justified mainly on the grounds of tractability and the desire to facilitate comparability. The stress-testing exercises are already highly complex, and allowing balance sheets to change would greatly add to the complexity: the methodology and consistency checks would need to be more complex, because they would need to cover the capital plans. Also, peer reviews would be less informative.

Yet the static balance sheet approach has distinct risks and other drawbacks if the aim is primarily supervisory. First, precisely because static balance sheets facilitate comparisons (more so than dynamic balance sheets), market analysts will be better able to interpret the results as a "beauty contest" among banks, as they seek out those that look comparatively or absolutely undercapitalized. Second, there is an inconsistency between the treatment of the considerable number of banks under restructuring plans agreed in the context of EU state aid rules, which will be assumed (as in the 2011 exercise) to implement those plans, and

---

[8] The balance sheet is "static" in that it is not managed by the bank, but it will change as loan quality varies and capital is accumulated or depleted. Furthermore, the authorities envisage incorporation of the ending of the ECB's long-term refinancing operations and the replacement of this financing with more expensive market financing.

the treatment of the other banks. Third, there is an inconsistency between the macro projections, where monetary and financial aggregates change over the envisaged three-year stress-testing horizon, and the assumption of static balance sheets of monetary financial institutions. Fourth, there may be instances where a static balance sheet is inconsistent with other regulatory changes, such as those prompted by ESRB recommendations on foreign currency lending and the ending of long-term refinancing operations. Furthermore, market analysts also facilitate such a balance sheet adjustment by focusing not on the gradual CRD IV regulatory thresholds but on the fully phased-in ones.

The possibility of incorporating more dynamic elements into the balance sheet projections should therefore be kept under review, while comparability of the CRD IV definition should be ensured.[9] It may be reasonably easy to provide banks with guidance on the evolution of major balance sheet components that are consistent with the macroeconomic scenario (for example, aggregate growth in deposits and credit by country or use of loan-to-deposit limits) and indicate that they should avoid strategies that rely on "deus ex machina" (such as the sale of an unprofitable business at a handsome price). Such a differentiation would also allow for the ongoing process of financial fragmentation and de-integration. As in the case of the 2011 recapitalization exercise, banks should not be allowed to optimize their risk-weighted assets. Adherence to such guidance would reduce the need to subject plans to preliminary evaluation before the stress test is performed.[10] To ensure comparability across banks and jurisdictions, the stress-testing of CRD IV definitions and hurdle rates during the phase-in period should allow for no national discretion.

More effort in assessing the robustness of results, including the assumption of static balance sheets, would contribute to the results' usefulness to supervisors and to their overall credibility. For example, sensitivity tests might involve re-running top-down tests with slight variations in the macro scenario or the satellite models, to see the extent to which results vary (possibly in a nonlinear manner). Top-down analysis could be used to quantify the effects of changing balance sheet size and competition to reflect projected aggregate changes (e.g., money supply and credit stock evolution), banks' own plans, and the consistency of these elements. It may also be worthwhile to run tests for sensitivity to variations in input data.

Sensitivity to macroeconomic assumptions and projections needs to be assessed. Macroeconomic assumptions in the baseline and adverse scenarios play a crucial role in solvency stress tests, and can be key drivers for banks' loan losses.[11] It might be useful to use the ECB/ESRB top-down stress test for a country-specific

---

[9] Note that the external banking stress test conducted for Spain was based on a dynamic balance sheet assumption and banks' capital plans.

[10] In any case, assumptions need to be made consistent. For example, if the balance sheet is static, a well-capitalized bank cannot be expected to retain any dividends.

[11] For the 2011 EBA stress test, the European Commission provided the baseline scenario, while the adverse scenario was given by the ECB/ESRB. EBA identified the microprudential risk factors and the ESRB, and the ECB then mapped them into the macroeconomic scenarios.

sensitivity analysis of the adverse macroeconomic scenario. This could provide a sensitivity measure of banks' resilience to the severity (or lack of severity) of the adverse macroeconomic scenario, especially since a common scenario might affect banks in specific jurisdictions in very diverse ways.

LONG-TERM PRIORITIES

Refinement of Satellite Models

The authorities have collected data and undertaken analyses that allow the plausible projection of many variables of interest onto both a baseline and an adverse scenario, but certain important series have proven to be especially difficult to model and deserve more research attention. In past stress-testing exercises, the projections of some series differed greatly across banks for reasons that were at best unintuitive, and these peculiarities may have weakened confidence in the overall results. Such inconsistencies—which are found even across banks from one country—can undermine stress-testing credibility and usefulness. The following series are important but have proven difficult to forecast (including in national stress-testing exercises):

- *Noninterest, nontrading income*, which is of increasing importance to many banks and which may be disproportionately sensitive to a severe downturn. Banks' projections of their fee income could be subject to some guidance by EBA, especially for the adverse scenario, to avoid banks using fee projections to compensate for loan impairments;

- *Trading income,* which depends on banks' own-account trading activity of both on- and off-balance-sheet items. Financial instruments in bank portfolios could be revalued at the prices prevailing in the scenario, rather than through the use of satellite models, which might not adequately capture banks' trading income;

- *Funding costs,* which depend both on exogenous or macroeconomic conditions, such as the sovereign's credit rating, and on the bank's own situation. As seen during the financial crisis, the banks' cost of funding is linked to their capital buffers. Banks with lower solvency levels have seen either their funding costs sharply increase or their market funding channels closed entirely; and

- *Risk-weighted assets,* which may be affected by shifts in risk weights and write-offs, even if the overall balance sheet is static.

Solvency and Structural Issues

As the situation of the banking sector changes and supervisory institutions evolve, it is worth considering where best to allocate limited stress-testing resources. There are already a great many stress testing and simulations done not only by the EBA but also by the NSAs, for their own stability analysis and supervisory purposes, and by financial institutions themselves for risk management generally, internal capital adequacy assessment process (ICAAP), and recovery planning/living will purposes. Some streamlining would be welcome. EBA could also have some enhanced role on giving guidance to banks on their recovery plan/living will stress testing.

Over the medium term, EBA could shift efforts to running tests on hitherto relatively neglected topics, such as structural issues and funding vulnerabilities. In this connection, competing EBA, ECB/SSM, and ESRB stress tests are to be avoided. Under the new SSM architecture, EBA should continue to closely coordinate the EU-wide stress tests with ECB and NSAs and ensure quality control; the ECB should run supervisory stress tests for the banks in the SSM; while ESRB should focus its contributions on macroprudential issues, such as the identification and calibration of systemic risk factors and the use of stress test results in formulating policy advise.

The EBA regulation gives the ECB a mandate to oversee stress testing. The ECB's comparative advantages lie in such areas as (1) providing benchmarks and satellite models, especially for host-country operations;[12] (2) ensuring that NSAs benefit from the latest techniques and apply them with full rigor;[13] and (3) exercising its mandate to ensure that best use is made of stress testing by NSAs, for example in setting supervisory priorities and in evaluating banks' recovery plans. Consistency in scenario building may sometimes be desirable but may be of lesser importance for supervisory purposes for many banks. In this light, the EBA may wish to focus in 2014–15 on improving liquidity stress testing and its integration with solvency tests, which is a relatively new area, rather than devoting so much of its limited resources to another comprehensive solvency test during this period (see below). Also, the EBA may have occasion to assess the use of stress testing by NSAs as part of its peer review process.

It would be valuable to run stress tests and related simulations designed to incorporate more long-term factors and generate lessons that relate more to structural issues. As emphasized above, the European banking system faces a prolonged period of low interest rates, possibly low growth, increased regulatory burden such as Basel III and CRD IV, and demographic change—developments that will put pressure on profitability, the supply of savings, and competition, among other challenges. Hence, the stress test scenarios need to encompass a longer time horizon; incorporate structural shifts (e.g., ongoing deleveraging and changes of bank funding profiles) affecting the balance sheet and income; and emphasize other metrics, such as profitability and changes in risk-weighted assets. It should be noted that stress tests and simulations are only one instrument in the toolkit to examine the structural challenges faced by banks and complement other quantitative and qualitative approaches. The ESRB would be the leader for efforts in these areas—in addition to its analysis of more conjunctural issues and nonbank sectors—which

---

[12] The EBA is well placed to provide common benchmarks for the hosted operations of the banks that come from several home countries.

[13] The EBA is already active in this area, as evidenced by its guidance on ICAAP evaluations and review of practices.

Box 17.1 Principles for Macro-Financial Stress Testing

A recent IMF document (IMF, 2012c) has brought together principles that summarize good practices and strategies for macro-financial stress testing. They may be summarized as follows:

- Define appropriately the institutional perimeter for the tests.
- Identify all relevant channels of risk propagation.
- Include all material risks and buffers.
- Make use of the investors' viewpoint in the design of stress tests.
- Focus on tail risks.
- When communicating stress test results, speak smarter, not just louder.
- Beware of the "black swan."

---

would be guided by the emerging consensus on best practice in macro-financial stress testing (Box 17.1).

Stress tests that make full use of market data (such as those based on contingent claims analysis) need to be developed further and used to complement balance-sheet-based tests, at least where such data are available.[14] These methods, which are already deployed and being further developed by the ECB and some national central banks, are especially suited to capturing cross-sectoral and funding issues, for example by treating banks, nonbank financial institutions, and nonfinancial corporations on a consistent and integrated basis, and by linking sovereign and bank balance sheets. Furthermore, these models are intrinsically nonlinear and thus differentiate between behavior and pricing both in "normal" times and under stress conditions.

Stress tests might also be used to investigate the stability effects of the growth in "shadow banks." The shadow banking sector is diverse, and some parts of it might be of much greater systemic importance than others (for example, due to linkages to banks or to effects on aggregate credit supply). Even simple stress tests might shed light on how important it might be to tighten the regulatory and supervisory framework for this sector. In particular, the implementation of structural reforms in the banking sector (e.g., the Volcker rule or the Liikanen and Vickers proposals), with the potential migration of some banking activities to the shadow banking sector, will over time further increase the importance of stress testing and examining the systemic implications of these shadow banking actors.

Liquidity Stress Testing

The financial crisis has highlighted the need to better integrate solvency and liquidity stress testing. A sharp rise in their euro and U.S. dollar funding costs, or quantitative rationing, was often the trigger for the failure of banks during the

---

[14] See Gray and Jobst (2011) and Gray, Merton, and Bodie (2007) for details on the contingent claims analysis approach.

crisis and for the difficulties that many European banks continue to face. The EBA in its 2011 stress test introduced a cost-of-funding shock which, among others, was linked to the sovereign debt spread. The EBA in 2011 also conducted a less formal liquidity risk assessment, which indirectly captured fire sales through collateral haircuts.[15] Elsewhere, the ECB in its recent Financial Stability Report has incorporated an explicit funding volume shock and deleveraging path into its macro stress-testing framework.[16] The IMF (2012a and 2012d) has also been incorporating a dynamic deleveraging path in its analysis.

In the medium term, the EBA could intensify its work on liquidity stress test-ing, especially in the context of the phasing in of detailed common reporting templates on maturity mismatches, cost of funding, and asset encumbrance, as part of CRD IV.[17] The EBA already has experience with liquidity stress testing, especially from its 2011 cash flow-based assessment of European banks. Such a liquidity risk assessment would test the resilience of European banks to various funding shocks (deposits, wholesale, and off balance sheet). It would also con-sider the banks' behavior in response to more limited liquidity support such as, for instance, the tightening of central banks' collateral requirements. The output could also feed into ESRB's work stream on systemic risk assessments. The start-ing point for the EBA could be lessons learned from the 2011 internal EBA cash-flow-based liquidity risk assessment. The EBA could provide guidance on liquidity stress-testing issues and ensure some consistency of approaches by NSAs. It would likely need to boost its staff resources as well as adjust its medium-term work plan to incorporate such additional work on liquidity stress testing. It should also ensure the disclosure and transparency of the reporting templates and the overall liquidity stress-testing approach, while safeguarding sensitive results.

A cash-flow-based liquidity stress test, such as that used by EBA in 2011, offers certain advantages (see Schmieder and others, 2012). A cash-flow-based module along the lines of the 2011 internal EBA liquidity risk assessment or the forthcom-ing EBA cash-flow-based maturity mismatch template allows running detailed liquidity analysis, and hence it is well suited to capture a bank's funding resilience and its liquidity risk bearing capacity. Cash-flow-based liquidity stress testing allows for detailed maturity buckets and can also be adapted to different currencies.

---

[15] The exercise was generally well designed, and some of its features will be useful in preparation for the introduction of the liquidity coverage ratio. Granular cash flow data, including by currencies and maturity buckets, for a broad sample of European banks (54), was compiled and checked. Multiple scenarios capturing the banks' main liquidity risks and counterbalancing capacities were analyzed. On this basis, recommendations were conveyed to banks through the NSAs.

[16] The ECB has not conducted stand-alone liquidity stress tests of Euro area banks. It does incorporate funding and liquidity stress indirectly via its contribution to the EBA solvency stress tests, where a funding cost shock is assumed. Furthermore, in the June 2012 ECB Financial Stability Report, an explicit funding volume shock is incorporated into the ECB macro stress-testing framework. The ECB approach does not, though, take into consideration its collateral and haircut policies or banks' heterogeneous asset encumbrance levels.

[17] Recent contributions on liquidity stress testing include Van den End (2008), Wong and Hui (2009), Aikman and others (2009), Barnhill and Schumacher (2011), and Jobst (2012).

Liquidity risk exposure (net funding gap, cumulated net funding gap) and liquidity risk-bearing capacity are clearly separated in the cash flow template. The template incorporates securities flows and ensures consistency between them and cash flows. This is especially important given the role that unsecured and secured wholesale funding play for many large banks. Off-balance-sheet activities such as foreign exchange swaps or credit and liquidity lines can be easily incorporated as well. Finally, the approach can incorporate the importance of banks' asset encumbrance.[18]

Weaknesses of the cash flow approach include the high data intensity as well as initial set-up costs. While banks typically use a cash-flow-based approach for internal liquidity monitoring and liquidity stress testing, regulatory liquidity ratios are often based on stock accounting data, often with less data granularity than the cash-flow-based templates. The phase-in of EBA cash-flow-based maturity mismatch templates will provide regulators and banks with standardized templates that would need to be regularly filled out and reported. As with the EBA solvency stress tests, it is suggested that EBA staff have access to banks with NSA colleagues for a consulting/feedback process, and that they have direct interaction with banks' liquidity risk managers so as to facilitate the rollout of such cash flow templates.

CONCLUSIONS

Stress testing has become an essential and very prominent tool in the analysis of financial sector stability and the development of financial sector policy, but in itself it can have only a limited impact unless it is tied to action. Stress testing and related simulations can serve various functions, such as the calibration of the relative importance of various risk factors and the assessment of banks' capital needs when they are already under stress (e.g., Borio, Drehmann, and Tsatsaronis, 2012; IMF, 2012c; and Gray and Jobst, 2011). The publication of stress test results with enough supporting material (including on the initial condition of banks) can be helpful in reducing uncertainty (see also Jobst, Ong, and Schmieder, 2013); even banks that are revealed to be relatively weak may benefit if the market paralysis engendered by great uncertainty is relieved. But stress tests are of value mainly when they are followed up by concrete and swift actions by the authorities (supervisory and others) and by bank managers that improve the condition of banks and of banks' clients.

The purpose of Europe-wide coordinated stress testing is changing, and therefore so should the design of these exercises change. The apex of the crisis in interbank markets and generalized worries over bank capitalization seem to be past (though pockets of weak banks remain). But European banks and the authorities responsible for financial sector policies face a drawn-out period of

---

[18] Asset encumbrance lowers the resilience of a bank to further funding shocks by constraining its access to funding backed by suitable collateral; regarding liquidity risk, a bank that has encumbered much of its assets is in a similar position to one with few liquid assets. Either situation may undermine investor confidence.

regulatory reform in a possibly unfriendly environment. The Europe-wide stress tests therefore need to be adapted in a way that ensures that they continue to yield extra value added, as compared to the stress tests conducted by banks themselves and by national authorities.

The planned 2014 exercise aims to generate analysis relevant to the assessment of banks' capital plans during the gradual transition to the CRD IV requirements, rather than pass/fail results based on a single metric. Much effort has been and will be put into ensuring that methodologies are consistently applied, while reducing costs to participating banks as far as possible.

There remain a number of controversial issues, but experience suggests that the benefits of a bold approach outweigh the risks. A high degree of transparency, including on reference date data and on sensitivity to differences in definitions of input data, strengthens rather than weakens confidence and market functioning. The market would likely be critical if a wide range of detailed information on participating banks, and especially on their reference period conditions and (sovereign) exposures, were not published. Furthermore, uncertainty would be reduced by openness about data issues. Criteria for loan classifications and provisioning requirements differ across countries and, especially in current difficult conditions, banks may engage in some forms of forbearance: a bank may more readily choose to roll over a problem loan and make modest provisions, partly to help its borrower and partly to make its own results look better (see also IMF, 2013c).

To allay the most intense concerns, authorities should undertake selective AQRs, coordinated at the European Union level. Maximizing data consistency and quality will take time, and national supervisory authorities have the primary responsibility for the provision of consistent and interpretable banking sector data, but the EBA has an important role in coordinating and driving forward activities. Nonetheless, the Europe-wide exercise should acknowledge the caveat that data quality is probably uneven.

If the 2014 exercise is to focus on supervisory issues such as an assessment of banks' plans to implement the solvency elements of CRD IV, then it should be designed and presented for this purpose; otherwise, markets are likely to follow past form and be fixated solely on capital shortfalls and relative weaknesses. To this end, the 2014 stress-testing exercise needs to generate operational recommendations and supporting indicators for supervisors. In this connection, it will be necessary to include the effects of the phase-out of the Long-Term Refinancing Operations provided by the ECB. Further efforts could be made to assess the sensitivity of results to likely changes in balance sheet composition, rather than assuming that balance sheets stay static. Otherwise, the results may not be very relevant for evaluating banks' plans that involve significant balance sheet adjustment.

As the acuteness of the crisis diminishes, the identification of other vulnerabilities and issues, such as funding risks and structural weaknesses, will gain in relative importance (see also Kodres and Narain, 2010). Most major banks now seem comparatively well capitalized, but funding remains problematic for some, while the sector faces deep structural challenges relating to low profitability and growth and the longer-term impact of regulatory changes.

In the medium term, the European authorities and specifically the EBA could intensify their work on liquidity and funding stress testing, especially in the context of the phasing-in of detailed common reporting templates on maturity mismatches, cost of funding, and asset encumbrance, as part of CRD IV. Such a liquidity risk assessment would test the resilience of European banks to various funding shocks (deposits, wholesale, and off balance sheet). It would also consider the banks' behavior when faced with more limited liquidity support (for instance, due to the tightening of central banks' collateral requirements), and include risks from asset encumbrance (see also ESRB, 2013). The EBA could provide guidance on liquidity stress-testing issues and ensure some consistency in the approaches taken by NSAs. The EBA could also ensure the disclosure and transparency of the reporting templates and the overall liquidity stress-testing approach, while safeguarding sensitive results (see, for example, EBA, 2013).

It would be valuable to run European stress tests and related simulations designed to incorporate more long-term factors and generate lessons that relate more to structural issues. As emphasized above, the European banking system faces a prolonged period of low interest rates, possibly low growth, increased regulatory burden under Basel III and CRD IV, and demographic change. These developments will put pressure on profitability, the supply of savings, and competition, among other things. Hence, the stress test scenarios need to encompass a longer time horizon; incorporate structural shifts affecting the balance sheet and income (e.g., ongoing deleveraging and changes of bank funding profiles); and emphasize additional metrics, such as profitability. It should be noted that stress tests are only one instrument in the toolkit to examine the structural challenges faced by banks.

Efficiency and the need to avoid conflicting signals demand full coordination between the EBA, the SSM, and ESRB stress-testing exercises. For the 2014 exercise, the ECB could play a very active role, not only in making macro projections and top-down stress testing, but also, for example, in the review of input asset quality data. However, competing EBA, ECB/SSM, and ESRB stress tests are to be avoided. The EBA will still have a mandate to coordinate the EU-wide stress tests under the new SSM, working with the ECB and NSAs, and to ensure quality control. It should run supervisory stress tests for the banks in the SSM, while the ESRB should focus its contributions on macroprudential issues, such as the identification and calibration of systemic risk factors and the use of stress test results in formulating policy advice.

REFERENCES

Aikman, David, Piergiorgio Alessandri, Bruno Eklund, Prasanna Gai, Sujit Kapadia, Elizabeth Martin, Nada Mora, Gabriel Sterne, and Matthew Willison, 2009, "Funding Liquidity Risk in a Quantitative Model of Systemic Liquidity," Working Paper No. 372 (London: Bank of England).

Barnhill, Theodore, and Liliana Schumacher, 2011, "Modeling Correlated Systemic Liquidity and Solvency Risks in a Financial Environment with Incomplete Information," IMF Working Paper No. 11/263 (Washington: International Monetary Fund).

Borio, Claudio, Mathias Drehmann, and Kostas Tsatsaronis, 2012, "Stress-Testing Macro Stress Testing: Does It Live up to Expectations?" BIS Working Paper No. 369, January 2012 (Basel: Bank for International Settlements).

European Banking Authority, 2012, "Results of the Basel III Monitoring Exercise Based on Data as of December 31, 2011" (London).

———, 2013, "Consultation Paper on Draft Implementing Technical Standards on Asset Encumbrance Reporting Under article 95a of the Draft Capital Requirements Regulation (CRR)" (London).

European Systemic Risk Board, 2013, "Recommendation of the ESRB of 20 December 2012 on funding of credit institutions (ESRB/2012/2)," (Frankfurt).

Gray, Dale F., and Andreas Jobst, 2011, "Modeling Systemic Financial Sector and Sovereign Risk," *Sveriges Riksbank Economic Review*, September.

Gray, Dale F., Robert C. Merton, and Zvi Bodie, 2007, "Contingent Claims Approach to Measuring and Managing Sovereign Credit Risk," *Journal of Investment Management*, Vol. 5, No. 4, pp. 5–28.

International Monetary Fund, 2012a, *Global Financial Stability Report: The Quest for Lasting Stability*. World Economic and Financial Surveys (Washington, April).

———, 2012b, "Macro-financial Stress Testing—Principles and Practices," Policy Paper, August (Washington).

———, 2012c, *Global Financial Stability Report*, October (Washington).

———, 2013, "European FSAP: Technical Note on Progress with Bank Restructuring and Resolution in Europe" (Washington).

Jobst, Andreas A., 2012, "Measuring Systemic Risk-Adjusted Liquidity (SRL)—A Model Approach," IMF Working Paper No. 12/209 (Washington: International Monetary Fund).

Jobst, Andreas A., Li Lian Ong, and Christian Schmieder, 2013, "An IMF Framework for Macroprudential Bank Solvency Stress Testing: Application to S-25 and Other G-20 Country FSAPs," IMF Working Paper 13/68 (Washington: International Monetary Fund).

Kodres, Laura, and Aditya Narain, 2010, "Redesigning the Contours of the Future Financial System," IMF Staff Discussion Note No. 2010/10 (Washington: International Monetary Fund).

Schmieder, Christian, Heiko Hesse, Benjamin Neudorfer, Claus Puhr, and Stefan W. Schmitz, 2012, "Next Generation System-Wide Liquidity Stress Testing," IMF Working Paper No. 12/03 (Washington: International Monetary Fund).

Van den End, Jan Willem, 2008, "Liquidity Stress Tester: A Macro Model for Stress-Testing Banks' Liquidity Risk," Working Paper No. 175 (Amsterdam: Dutch National Bank) May.

Wong, Eric, and Cho-Hoi Hui, 2009, "A Liquidity Risk Stress-Testing Framework With Interaction between Market and Credit Risks," Working Paper No. 06/2009 (Hong Kong: Hong Kong Monetary Authority).

CHAPTER 18

An Assessment of Markets and Credit Rating Agency Regulation

ANA FIORELLA CARVAJAL

Within its resource envelope, the European Securities and Markets Authority (ESMA) has performed well during its first two years of operation, especially in connection with the single rulebook and credit rating agency (CRA) supervision. A significant number of technical standards, advice to the European Commission, and opinions were developed. ESMA has also been able to build its expertise in connection with CRAs and has worked on the development of a risk framework to anchor its supervisory program. Results are more modest in connection with other functions. To a large extent, this prioritization was driven by the financial sector regulatory agenda, which imposed regulatory obligations on ESMA under tight deadlines and required it to assume the supervision of CRAs, which until then had not been supervised in Europe.

As it has acknowledged, ESMA needs to step up its role in other areas and in particular on supervisory convergence. The institution has set up strategic directions for each area and in many cases has developed concrete actions to take these priorities forward.

- *Supervisory convergence.* Work on reengineering and strengthening peer reviews is essential to achieve convergence, since the direct breach of laws and mediation procedures would be appropriate for only a few cases. The objectives of the reengineering should be: (1) making reviews more rigorous by relying more on on-site work; and (2) sharpening the review outcomes by linking the reports to the development of best practices and/or guidelines, the implementation of which can be monitored and followed up. If necessary, stronger actions (such as a breach of law) could then be taken. These changes might also require a stronger role for ESMA in the peer review groups and in the review panel. It is important that the National Competent Authorities (NCAs) take the steps necessary to ensure the enforceability of ESMA's opinions and guidelines in their respective jurisdictions.

- *Risk identification and crisis management.* Projects under way will allow ESMA to make a qualitative jump in its contribution to financial stability and crisis management. However, it is critical that ESMA have access to data with the granularity and timeliness necessary to conduct in-depth analysis, including stress testing in connection with entities that could pose systemic risk. In this regard, requiring a vote from the ESMA Board of Supervisors to provide data for particular studies that ESMA wants to undertake may hinder ESMA's ability to be timely in its work. In addition, the ESMA Board of Supervisors should take a more active responsibility in this area. Thus, risk identification should remain a recurrent point in the board's agenda, and not only in times of crisis. In the second case, in addition to developing a framework for each scenario identified, ESMA should coordinate simulation exercises.

- *Investor protection*. The emphasis on product monitoring is warranted, and the consumer trends data project would be key to making a qualitative jump in this area. Effective monitoring of financial innovation should also have a positive effect on financial stability. The granting of product intervention powers to ESMA is welcome, but such powers should be exercised cautiously since ESMA is not a direct supervisor.

Having sufficient expert resources will be key to delivering results. The approved additional staff for 2013 will not be large enough to ensure that these other functions are sufficiently covered. Furthermore, the European Market Infrastructure Regulation will assign additional functions to ESMA for which resources will be critical. Expanded functions will also arise from other initiatives to be implemented in the upcoming years, such as the third reform of the CRA regulation (CRA3) and Markets in Financial Instruments Directive (MiFID) 2.

Finally, reviewing governance arrangements to strengthen ESMA's independence in relation to the NCAs is advised. Current governance arrangements might negatively affect ESMA's performance of its functions, in particular supervisory convergence. In addition, ESMA staff should continue to play a stronger role in the standing committees.

ESMA INSTITUTIONAL ARRANGEMENTS

Mandate and Powers

ESMA was created in 2011[1] as part of the new European System of Financial Supervision. This system consists of the European Systemic Risk Board (ESRB) and the three European Supervisory Authorities (ESAs), based in Paris; the European Banking Authority (EBA) based in London; and the European Insurance and Occupational Pensions Authority (EIOPA) based in Frankfurt. While new in its current structure and nature, it builds on the work of the Committee of European Securities Regulators.

ESMA's mission is to enhance the protection of investors and reinforce stable and well-functioning financial markets in the European Union (EU). To achieve

---

[1] Regulation 1095/2010 of the European Parliament and of the Council of November 24, 2010, establishing a European Supervisory Authority (European Securities and Markets Authority).

these objectives, several tasks are allocated to it, along with the powers to undertake them. Such tasks and powers can be grouped in the following themes:

- **Regulatory work.** ESMA has a key role in contributing to the development of a single rulebook by (1) the development of technical standards, (2) the development of guidelines, and (3) the provision of advice to the European Commission on secondary legislation.

- **Supervisory convergence.** ESMA has a role in supporting the convergence of supervisory culture and practices, mainly by (1) issuing opinions, (2) conducting peer reviews, and, as a last resort (3) making use of powers to investigate and remedy breaches of European Union laws. By regulation ESMA may develop new instruments to foster convergence.

- **Financial stability and crisis management.** ESMA's obligations include contributing to the assessment of risk and financial stability. To this end, it (1) carries out its own analysis, (2) contributes to the work of the Joint Committee, and (3) cooperates with the ESRB. Regarding crisis management, ESMA's role is fundamentally one of coordination except in connection with short selling, where direct powers were given to it.

- **Investor protection.** ESMA contributes to strengthening the framework of investor protection through different tools, including (1) the issuance of guidelines, and (2) the power to issue warnings in the event that a financial activity poses a threat to investors.

- **Supervision.** Since July 2011, ESMA has been responsible for the registration and supervision of CRAs in the European Union.

ESMA Governance

Governance arrangements have involved several bodies, all of them under the direction of the Board of Supervisors.

- *The ESMA Board of Supervisors* is the decision-making body of ESMA. It is composed of the heads of the 27 NCAs for the supervision of financial markets in each member state.[2] The regulation requires board members to act independently and objectively and in the sole interest of the European Union as a whole, and therefore they should not take instructions from any European body or domestic authority. Decisions are taken by a majority of votes, each member having one vote. However, the adoption of technical standards and guidelines requires a qualified majority whereby voting rights are weighted by population to ensure demographic representativeness.

- *Standing committees,* made up of staff from the NCAs, do the preparatory work. There are currently 11 standing committees. Ad hoc task forces can also be constituted. NCAs lead the work of the standing committees, that

---

[2] In addition, there are observers from the European Commission, ESRB, EBA, and EIOPA. Norway, Iceland, and Liechtenstein also attend as permanent observers.

is, they chair them and in some cases "hold the pen," while ESMA staff act as *rapporteurs.*

- *An ESMA Management Board,* composed of six members selected from the ESMA Board of Supervisors by its members, focuses on management aspects of ESMA's work, such as the development of the annual work program, the budget, and resources.

- *ESMA's chair and the executive director,* respectively, prepare the work of the ESMA Board of Supervisors and the ESMA Management Board. They are appointed by the ESMA Board of Supervisors, following an open selection procedure based on merits. Both are required to act independently and are prohibited from taking instructions from any European body or domestic authority. Both are appointed for five-year terms with the possibility of reappointment for one more term. ESMA regulation does not require the existence of "due cause" for their early removal.

- *There is one Appeals Board for the three ESAs,* composed of two experts from each sector (and their alternates). Decisions of the Appeals Board can be appealed to the European Court of Justice.

- *A Securities and Markets Stakeholder Group* facilitates consultation with stakeholders. It has 30 members appointed by ESMA for a period of two and a half years following an open call for candidates. In practice, this group is active and has its own work program. The group has periodic meetings with the ESMA Board of Supervisors, for which an agenda is set up in advance.

Independence is a key source of concern. Thus, in the context of the upcoming review to be conducted by the European Commission,[3] governance arrangements should be evaluated and if necessary further enhanced. Stakeholders interviewed concurred that work by majority represents a fundamental change from the Committee of European Securities Regulators' way of operating, since its decisions were taken by consensus, which in some cases meant agreeing to the lowest denominator. Furthermore, most of the stakeholders indicated that the presence of the board chair in the discussions of the ESMA Board of Supervisors ensures that ESMA's positions are heard. Thus, there is agreement that ESMA represents a significant evolution from its predecessor, not only from a legal perspective, but also from an operational perspective.

However, the conversations with stakeholders and examples given by them lead to the conclusion that decisions are still dominated by "domestic" views. Furthermore, ESMA's governance structure as a college of "peers" could be particularly troublesome in the context of supervisory convergence. The fact that there does not appear to be strong follow-up on the conclusions of peer reviews might be in part explained by the current composition of the ESMA Board of

---

[3] Article 81 of ESMA Regulation requires the European Commission to conduct a review of the performance of the ESMA by January 2, 2014 and every three years thereafter. The same obligation exists in connection with EBA and EIOPA.

Supervisors. Therefore, this issue should be further analyzed during the review of the ESAs, with a view to enhancing ESMA's independence in relation to the NCAs, while keeping a framework of high accountability to the European authorities. Different alternatives could be considered: from adding more independent members to the board, to moving to a full-time and fully independent board, to delegating more functions to the ESMA Management Board. In addition, the rules for removal of the chair and the executive director should be strengthened by requiring removal only with due cause.

It is important that ESMA staff continue to play a stronger role in the standing committees. There was consensus among the stakeholders interviewed that over time ESMA staff are becoming more active in the discussions at the standing committee level. ESMA staff highlighted that when consensus on a topic has not been reached, reports explicitly state ESMA's position, in addition to highlighting the different alternatives, more often now than previously. In addition, at the ESMA Board of Supervisors meetings, the chair presents the position of the institution.

From a transparency perspective, more engagement with the stakeholder group in connection with the work plan could be explored. ESMA already operates under a robust framework of accountability and transparency. Accountability has been made operational in two ways: (1) through an annual joint hearing at the European Parliament for the three ESAs, and (2) through ad hoc hearings of a more technical nature with the European Parliament and Council. Concerning transparency, a significant amount of information can be found on ESMA's website, including the minutes of the meetings of the ESMA Board of Supervisors; ESMA's annual work program, its budget, and its annual report; the reports of the different standing committees; and the proposals for technical standards and guidelines. One aspect where more engagement may be advisable is in relation to the development of the work plan. ESMA could engage with the Stakeholders Group early on in the process to get their views on priorities.

Funding and Budget Issues

ESMA has three sources of funding: a subsidy from the European Commission, a contribution from the NCAs, and a fee levied on registered firms under its direct supervision. Currently, only CRAs are subject to this levy, but with the approval of European Market Infrastructure Regulation, trade repositories would also have to contribute. For 2013, ESMA's budget will amount to €28.3 million, of which the European Commission's contribution would represent roughly 46 percent, the NCAs' contribution 30 percent, the CRAs' contribution 20 percent, and the trade repositories' contribution 4 percent. It was indicated that the contribution of the largest NCAs does not represent a significant proportion of ESMA's budget. Operationally, the European Commission decides on the budget proposal to be sent to the European Parliament. The European Commission can make changes to ESMA's proposal, and the European Parliament and Council in turn can make changes to the European Commission proposal.

The upcoming review should look at alternative funding structures, since in the medium term the current structure could become a problem. First, this funding structure could create conflicts of interest in relation to the NCAs—as in some cases there might be a bias against letting ESMA grow in light of views about the centralization of functions. Second, as ESMA grows, the contribution from the NCAs could become a heavy burden for the smaller jurisdictions and a risk of nonpayment could arise. Thus, as stated by the Committee on Economic and Monetary Affairs of the European Parliament,[4] additional funding models should be explored, including industry fees; in fact, part of ESMA's budget is already funded this way. However, it may be difficult in the short term to expand this type of funding mechanism beyond the CRAs. On the one hand, there would be resistance from market participants to a system of "double" charging (to fund the domestic authority and to fund ESMA), while on the other hand a system where the levy that was charged domestically would be offset to compensate for a levy charged at the ESMA level could negatively impact the operation of the domestic regulator. From a strictly technical perspective, the functions assigned to ESMA are not identical to those of the NCAs; furthermore, in many ways they benefit market participants, including for example by ensuring the existence of a level playing field across the European Union. Thus, a system of dual charging could very well be implemented. In addition, given the large number of regulated participants in the European Union, the levy on each could be relatively small. An alternative would be to be funded entirely by the European Union or to increase its share of funding.

It would also be important to review the current role of the European Commission in the approval of the ESAs' budget. While until now the European Commission has not made changes to ESMA's proposals, the experience of the other ESAs—whose budget proposals have been cut—leads one to conclude that in times of austerity the European Commission could be under pressure to reduce their budgets, using a mechanistic reduction scheme across the board, without any differentiation for the ESAs in relation to other public agencies (see note 4). It is worth exploring whether ESMA should present and justify its budget directly to the European Parliament and Council.

Organizational Structure and Resources

During ESMA's two years of existence, its management has worked on the development of its organizational structure and procedures for operation. It currently has three divisions (Markets; Investment and Reporting; and Operations) and three units (Credit Rating Agencies Unit; Economic Research and Financial Stability Unit; and Legal Cooperation and Convergence Unit). It is bound by the

---

[4] Committee on Economic and Monetary Affairs, European Parliament, "Opinion, for the Committee on Budgets, on the General Budget of the European Union for the financial year 2013—all sections, 2012/2092."

same administrative rules that apply to other public agencies of the European Union for purposes of recruitment and procurement.

ESMA's human resources are growing. It started with 35 staff from the Committee of European Securities Regulators. As of November 2012, it had 85 professionals, who were a mix of roughly 75 percent staff and 25 percent secondees from NCAs and contractors. Staff are hired under a three-year contract, with the possibility of renewal for another three years, after which they can be offered an "indefinite" position. ESMA's officials indicated that salaries have not hindered recruitment of qualified experts, since European Commission salaries, which also apply to ESMA, are reasonably high—although hiring experts from "the North" is more challenging, since their salaries are relatively higher.

However, ESMA needs more resources to carry out all its functions effectively. Its budget envelope for 2013 would not be enough to allow for the implementation of the different initiatives mentioned in this chapter, which are critical for ESMA to take a more active role in functions beyond the single rulebook and the supervision of CRAs. Furthermore, initiatives in the pipeline—such as European Market Infrastructure Regulation, CRA3, and Markets in Financial Instruments Directive 2—will create new responsibilities for it or expand existing ones.

Recruitment policies should be monitored to determine whether they pose any risk to ESMA's ability to attract and retain qualified staff. At this stage, recruitment policies, in particular the six-year term to provide an indefinite position to staff, might work to ESMA's advantage. However, at the outset, the six-year policy does not seem conducive to the stability of the organization, which should be a long-term objective of recruitment policies. Finally, it is important that a high ratio of permanent staff to secondees be kept in order to consolidate institutional knowledge.

ESMA'S REGULATORY AND SUPERVISORY CONVERGENCE WORK

Single Rulebook

During its first two years of operation, ESMA has dedicated a significant amount of resources to the single rulebook. Several pieces of legislation require ESMA to either develop technical standards or provide advice to the European Commission for it to develop secondary legislation (level 2). The following is a summary of the policy work conducted by ESMA:

- Forty technical standards were developed for the implementation of European Market Infrastructure Regulation;
- Four technical standards were developed for the new CRA supervisory regime;
- Seven technical standards were developed for the new short-selling and credit defaults swap regime;

- Five pieces of advice were provided to the European Commission on secondary legislation in areas such as prospectuses, undertakings for collective investment in transferable securities, alternative investment funds, and short-selling; and

- Six sets of detailed guidance and recommendations were developed in areas such as automated trading, alternative investment fund managers, exchange-traded funds, suitability of advice, and the investment firm compliance function.

In the future, it is important that ESMA be given sufficient time to deliver on its regulatory obligations, since tight deadlines can result in significant reputational risk and can also have a negative impact on the market. ESMA has had to deliver some of the technical standards under very tight deadlines. As a result, in some cases consultation processes have been squeezed. Many stakeholders have expressed concern about such a situation, since market participants did not have the time to conduct a thorough analysis of the proposals, nor ESMA to actively engage with them to discuss their concerns. As a result, neither industry nor ESMA had a comprehensive view of the costs and impact of the proposals.

Finally, the framework of transparency, including in connection with the European Commission role, remains critical. ESMA is required to conduct a public consultation process, as well as to consult the Securities and Markets Stakeholders Group. Technical standards must be endorsed by the European Commission. ESMA's officials have stated that so far, the European Commission has not made changes to the standards it has proposed. Because ESMA is the technical authority, it is critical that any intervention from the European Commission through its endorsement process be motivated by and grounded in technical reasons. The process devised in the regulation ensures that cases where the European Commission deviates from ESMA's proposal are visible.

Supervisory Convergence

Peer reviews have been the main tool used for supervisory convergence. Peer reviews are conducted by the review panel, which is a standing committee established for the purposes of fostering supervisory convergence. Currently this unit has two staff directly dedicated to convergence work and three more lawyers that support all of ESMA's work, including the standing committees' work. In addition, all the standing committees play a role, since in many cases they conduct mapping exercises and develop opinions and guidelines in connection with sectoral legislation within their remits.

- *Peer reviews.* The Committee of European Securities Regulators conducted several peer reviews. Since 2011, ESMA has conducted four peer reviews, and two of them—the review of sanctions under the Market Abuse Directive and the review of prospectus approval—have already been finalized. Three more reviews are planned for 2013. In the past, reviews focused on mapping rather than on assessments. When assessments were done, they were desk-based, which did not allow for thorough contestation of the responses provided by the NCAs. Thus, most countries were usually rated as fully compliant. Even when countries were found to be partially compliant, there was no systematic follow-up nor was any action attached to such noncompliance beyond the publication of the report. ESMA's chair has highlighted the intention to revamp peer reviews to make them more rigorous and their outcomes sharper. The committee also intends to conduct more peer reviews.

- *Opinions.* Two important cases are (1) an opinion on the treatment of sovereign debt under International Financial Reporting Standards, and (2) opinions on consistency with the Markets in Financial Instruments Directive for a large number of pre-trade transparency waivers.

- *Mediation and breach of laws procedures.* ESMA has not made used of its powers in connection with mediation and breach of laws procedures. In the first case, no case has been filed by an NCA, which is a requirement of the regulation. As to the latter, part of the reason is that there is no culture of filing complaints by firms or by the NCAs. However, ESMA acknowledged that it could start a procedure at its own initiative, and it stated that its involvement with the stakeholders group as well as having more staff will allow it to take a more proactive stance. There has only been one case brought by an NCA, and it concerned the application of one provision in the Undertakings for Collective Investment in Transferable Securities framework. In this case, the ESMA Board of Supervisors opted to issue an opinion on how such a provision should be interpreted.

As acknowledged by ESMA, supervisory convergence needs to be given priority in the future. Within the ideal of a single market, ensuring consistent transposition of laws—in which the European Commission plays a role—and convergence in supervisory practices is critical to minimize the risk of regulatory arbitrage and an unlevel playing field. The experience from the Financial Sector Assessment Programs, as well as conversations held with different stakeholders during these programs, lead one to the conclusion that the risk of regulatory arbitrage arising from inconsistent supervisory practices and/or interpretations of current regulations must not be overlooked.

To this end, reengineering and strengthening peer reviews would be essential to step up work on supervisory convergence. Breaches of laws and mediation procedures only would be fit for a limited set of cases. This leaves peer reviews as a key mechanism to foster convergence. The main two objectives of the reengineering should be: (1) making reviews more rigorous by, for example, relying more on on-site work; and (2) sharpening their outcomes, by linking the reports to the development of best practices and/or guidelines. Implementation of such guidelines could later be monitored and followed up in a systematic manner, and if necessary, stronger actions (such as a breach of law) could then be taken. Achieving these objectives might also require a stronger role for ESMA in the peer review groups as well as in the review panels. ESMA should draw a comprehensive strategy in this area. As supervisory convergence cuts across the whole organization, the development of the annual plan of peer reviews should consider input from all the standing committees.

As a principle, it is also important that NCAs take the necessary steps to ensure that ESMA's opinions and guidelines are enforceable in their respective jurisdictions. Some stakeholders have expressed concerns that in some countries the opinions and guidelines of ESMA are not being incorporated into the national framework, which creates uncertainty for them. This is an issue that needs to be addressed, if necessary by changes to the domestic legal frameworks, as appropriate.

ESMA'S ROLE IN FINANCIAL STABILITY

Direct Supervision of CRAs

Since July 2011, all registration and supervisory responsibilities concerning CRAs were transferred from the NCAs to ESMA. ESMA has a dedicated unit for the supervision of CRAs. Currently this unit has 16 staff (15 officers and the head of unit), with a mix of policy, market, and supervisory experience. There is also a Technical Committee chaired by the executive director, composed of NCAs and observers of the European Commission, EBA, and EIOPA, which provide advice to the unit on its policy work and international cooperation.

Since its operation, the CRA Unit has conducted significant supervisory work. This work included:

- *Registration and certification*. The unit provided advice and assistance to NCAs with the application process. Since July 2011, it has taken charge of the assessment of new applications, with one new CRA being registered upon application received directly by ESMA. There are currently 18 registered CRAs and one certified CRA. There are five applications pending.

- *Perimeter*. ESMA contacted roughly 30 companies whose activities could be considered to fall under the CRA Regulation and requested explanations. It is currently preparing guidance on the scope of the CRA Regulation.

- *Ongoing supervision*. ESMA is taking a multidimensional approach, which includes desk reviews and on-site inspections, both horizontal (thematic) and vertical (on individual entities). Last year, it conducted on-site inspections of three global CRAs. As a result of these inspections, ESMA (1) sent individual reports to each CRA with a request for changes and a plan for implementation, and (2) published a report summarizing its main findings, which is available on its website. Based on the findings from these inspections, it is currently conducting a review of banking rating methodologies. In addition, based on its risk analysis, it has decided to conduct a vertical, individual on-site inspection on the internal controls of another CRA. Following the CRA Regulation, the CRA Unit must conduct inspections on all CRAs by 2014.

- *Development of a central repository.* This is a data repository that makes available information on the past performance of ratings (with a six-month lag) through the ESMA web page. CRA3 will require such data to be available in real time. Another information technology tool, the Supervision of Credit Rating Agencies Tool, will facilitate the processing of ratings data in a standardized and automatic manner to support ESMA's supervisory activities.

- *Coordination with non-European Union regulators.* ESMA has finalized memorandums of understanding (MoUs) with a number of jurisdictions. In addition, it has been actively involved in the International Organization of Securities Commissions' consultation on the establishment of a global "college" for CRAs.

Over the next couple of years, ESMA needs to finalize the implementation of its risk-based supervisory approach for CRAs. The CRA Unit has made significant progress in the development of a CRA Risk Assessment Framework to anchor its supervisory program. It is estimated that roughly 70 percent of the supervisory resources would be spent on the large CRAs; however, the approach of the unit is to ensure some minimum engagement with all CRAs, even the small ones. Thus, each CRA has been assigned a relationship manager who is in charge of continuously monitoring it. Feedback from the relationship managers would be one of the inputs for the risk assessment framework. Such minimum engagement would include also annual meetings with the compliance officers of the CRAs.

Once the inspections on all CRAs are concluded, it is estimated that on an ongoing basis the unit will conduct two thematic reviews and two vertical reviews a year, in addition to other supervisory work (registrations, handling of complaints, etc). It would be important, however, that after the initial on-site inspections required by regulation for all CRAs, small CRAs are at least included from time to time in the samples for thematic on-site inspections. In addition, meetings with senior management of the CRAs should be considered. A key challenge in supervision would continue to be striking a right balance between the need to supervise the methodologies used by the CRAs to ensure that they are "rigorous, systematic, continuous and subject to validation" and the need to not interfere with their content, as required by the regulation.

It is also important that ESMA keeps close coordination with the NCAs. Due to their functions—in particular concerning market surveillance and the monitoring of issuers—the NCAs could provide valuable information to feed ESMA's risk-based approach.

Oversight mechanisms should continue to strike the right balance in the role that the ESMA Board of Supervisors should play in connection with CRA supervision. CRAs represent the first case where an ESA has direct supervisory powers. Therefore, it is critical that the exercise of this role is structured well from the start. Furthermore, since ESMA will get supervisory powers in connection with trade repositories, current oversight arrangements for CRAs should also serve as a blueprint. In this regard, as currently developed, the monitoring of specific and supervisory work should remain at the level of the ESMA Management Board, while the role of the ESMA Board of Supervisors should be one of oversight. This oversight should be exercised through the discussion and approval of the work plan and the risk-based supervisory approach that the CRA unit is developing, as well as through periodic reporting on the accomplishment of the work plan, as currently appears to be the case. Engagement in connection with individual supervisory work (for example, conduct of individual on-site inspections) should remain at management level.

Finally, as part of the review of the ESAs, the enforcement framework for CRAs should be reviewed. Recently, through secondary legislation, the European Commission established the amount of the fines that can be imposed.[5] The framework requires disclosure of the sanctions after their imposition by the ESMA Board of Supervisors. However, the sanctions that ESMA can actually impose appear to be rigid, since the approach seems very mechanistic. Moreover, depending on the size of the CRA, in practice the sanctions could be too low to have a deterrent effect—although it is early to predict whether the publication of the sanction would suffice to alter behavior.

Identification and Monitoring of Risks

Risk identification and monitoring is the responsibility of the Economic Research and Stability Unit. As of November of 2012, this unit was composed of six staff. In addition, there is a standing Committee for Economics and Market Analysis.

Projects underway will allow ESMA to make a qualitative jump in its contribution to financial stability and crisis management. Projects include work in four areas:

- *Periodic reports*. Risk identification is mainly based on the continuous monitoring of a set of indicators. This then feeds into two periodic reports[6] that must be approved by the ESMA Board of Supervisors. Currently this analysis is done based on publicly available data. The two reports are:
  - *A quarterly risk dashboard.* ESMA has produced seven risk dashboards. This publication is a market trends analysis divided into four categories: liquidity risk, market risk, contagion risk, and credit risk. The content of these reports is similar to that in reports produced by central banks. ESMA acknowledges that a key challenge is to adjust the categories/indicators in the risk dashboards to securities markets. A recent improvement, for example, was the inclusion in the most recent report (2012:Q2) of an indicator of stress in securities markets. A second challenge is to develop a set of early warning indicators, based on risks that originate in securities markets.

---

[5] Infringements are grouped in categories, and a minimum and maximum fine is assigned to each category. For example, the "lowest" category contemplates sanctions ranging from €10,000 to €50,000 and the "highest" category from €500,000 to €750,000. Aggravating and mitigating factors trigger increases or decreases, respectively, whose amounts are also specifically prescribed in the regulation.

[6] There is also a weekly *Financial Monitor*.

- *Biannual report of trends, risks, and vulnerabilities.* ESMA produced its first such report last year. The first section aims at providing a systematic analysis of markets; the second is a replica of the dashboard(s), and the third contains a thematic analysis of risks that deserve attention. ESMA acknowledges the need to further improve this report by having a more systemic analysis of the markets within its remit, which also requires improvements in the indicators to be followed, as discussed above.

- *Thematic work.* Two reports have been completed, on the risks associated with the current industry trends toward structured and complex retail products and an assessment of the size of shadow banking. Ongoing thematic work includes the following analyses: (1) the credit default swaps market, (2) the contribution of the hedge fund sector to systemic risk, (3) high frequency trading in European equity markets, and (4) bank funding issues and securities financing transactions.

- *Techniques for stress testing securities firms.* ESMA is focusing on three types of firms: trading venues, hedge funds, and central counterparties. However, at least in the first case, its informal request for data from the NCAs met with opposition, and the NCAs requested a strategic discussion at the level of the ESMA Board of Supervisors on ESMA's stress-testing strategy.

- *Building a full set of relevant data.* A data warehouse would incorporate publicly available data as well as the incoming regulatory data. In addition to the operational challenges described above, there are areas where data is not collected at the NCA level, and these gaps will need to be filled.

However, it is critical that ESMA have access to data with the granularity necessary to conduct in-depth analysis, including stress testing. ESMA Regulation provides it with the power to request information from the NCAs as long as such information is necessary to fulfill its mandate.[7] However, the recent experience of ESMA indicates the existence of practical challenges. In this regard, requiring a vote from the ESMA Board of Supervisors to provide data to ESMA might hinder its ability to be timely in its work.

It is important that the ESMA Board of Supervisors take a more active responsibility in risk identification and monitoring. The board has had discussions on risk in the context of the current crisis. What is key is that risk identification remain a recurrent agenda item for all meetings of the board and that input from those discussions be given to the corresponding unit (Economic Research and Financial Stability Unit). The same applies to the Committee for Economics and Market Analysis.

---

[7] Only when the information is not made available in a timely fashion and after following certain steps can ESMA request it directly from market participants.

Crisis Management

ESMA's role and its powers in crisis management generally focus on coordination. Pursuant to its regulation, it only has direct powers where sectoral legislation provides it with such power—which is the case in the short-selling regulation—or when an emergency has been declared by the European Council.

The short-selling regulation provides ESMA with direct but exceptional intervention powers. This regulation grants temporary intervention powers to NCAs. Measures available include (1) increased transparency requirements; (2) prohibiting or restricting natural and legal persons from engaging in short sales on a trading venue or otherwise limiting transactions on a specific financial instrument in such a trading venue for a maximum of three days in certain circumstances; (3) an outright prohibition on short-selling for a period of time; and (4) imposition of conditions on a short sale or transactions that indirectly create short positions. If an NCA intervenes, it is required to notify ESMA, which has to issue an opinion within 24 hours on whether it considers the measure necessary to address the exceptional circumstance faced by the NCA. If ESMA considers that there is a threat to financial stability that is not adequately addressed by the NCA's actions, it has the power to take any of the measures available to NCAs.

The use of these powers is a source of concern, although ESMA itself has not made use of them. In November 2012, two NCAs issued bans on short selling. There were concerns in the market that the bans were not identical, creating challenges for their implementation. ESMA did not use its direct intervention powers in this case, but it was required to issue an opinion on the measures of the NCAs.[8] While it could be argued that in the short term a restriction on short selling can slow down a downward spiral, in the medium term restrictions on short selling affect liquidity and price formation. Second, if such measures are to be used by NCAs, it is critical that NCAs aim at implementing nonconflicting and preferably identical measures, unless differences in domestic market structures do warrant the differences.

The development of a framework to deal with crisis management is a welcome priority. ESMA has recently started work on crisis management, with the goal of identifying the potential crisis scenarios where it would need to be involved and establish a framework to deal with such events. The starting point was the development of a definition of "crisis" for securities markets (i.e., one that seriously affects orderly trading or financial stability, with cross-border implications and an urgency element). Such a definition led to the identification of six types of events that would fit into it: (1) an EU-wide trading suspension; (2) an EU-wide ban on short selling; (3) EU-wide suspensions of redemptions of units in Undertakings for Collective Investment in Transferable Securities; (4) if a settlement fails on a pan-European basis; (5) EU-wide product intervention measures; and (6) failure of clearing members and central counterparties.

---

[8] Recently, the United Kingdom brought a suit against the European Parliament and the Council of the European Union for granting such powers to ESMA. The suit is pending (C-270/12).

A first output from such work is a protocol for exchanging information in connection with central counterparties that (1) identifies the potential emergency situations faced by central counterparties; (2) establishes principles for the exchange of information; (3) sets mechanisms for such exchange; and (4) identifies the information to be exchanged. It would be important that in addition to developing a framework for each type of crisis identified, ESMA coordinates simulation exercises.

Investor Protection

Investor protection issues are within the remit of the Investment and Reporting Unit. This unit currently has 17 staff, but it covers a wide array of issues in addition to investor protection. In addition, the Financial Innovation Standing Committee was recently established to assist ESMA in fulfilling its investor protection responsibilities. Its main function is to identify risks to investor protection and to financial stability in the financial innovation area and then to produce a risk mitigation strategy. There is also an Investor Protection and Financial Intermediaries Standing Committee.

Although it is still at an early stage, the emphasis on product monitoring is a very positive development. The objective is to monitor products sold to retail investors mainly to determine whether appropriate disclosure exists. Effective monitoring of financial innovation should also have a positive effect on financial stability. Currently, the main tools for monitoring are market intelligence, received through a network of regulators as well as industry participants, and data from private vendors. Through the Joint Committee, the ESAs have embarked on a project to determine the type of information that is critical for the authorities to have in order to make risk assessments (including, for example, complaints and information on products sold), as well as the format for that information. Other areas of emphasis are investor education and guidelines on information distribution and suitability obligations.

Granting product intervention powers to ESMA would strengthen its role. Currently, the main tools at its disposal to address risks to investor protection are warnings. It is expected that the second Markets in Financial Instruments Directive will give it product intervention powers, which is a good development. However, it is critical that such powers be exercised cautiously, since ESMA is not a direct supervisor, and that a clear and transparent protocol for their exercise be developed. On the other hand, the proposal to provide it with preapproval powers should be carefully evaluated, since the proposal seems to pose more risks than benefits. Such risks include slowing down innovation and the potential moral hazard brought by a supervisory body's giving early approval.

Cross-Sectoral Arrangements

According to the ESMA Regulation, the Joint Committee serves as a forum for cooperation and exchange of information among the ESAs, as well as for fostering cross-sectoral consistency. The chairs of the three ESAs sit on the committee. In addition, the executive directors, a representative from the European Commission and the ESRB, and the chairs of any of the subcommittees of the Joint Committee all participate as observers. The Joint Committee does not have a permanent secretariat, but each ESA has committed one staff person to it (these are the *rapporteurs*). The chairperson rotates on an annual basis. Each year the *rapporteur* from the ESA that is chairing the Joint Committee takes the lead on producing the committee's different documents, as well as setting the agenda for the meetings. The agenda for the Joint Committee meetings is set up taking into consideration requests from the three ESAs. A work plan is developed on an annual basis, based on feedback from the three ESAs. The bulk of the technical work is conducted by subcommittees, composed of the staff of the ESAs, who then report to the Joint Committee. There are currently four subcommittees.

The Joint Committee needs to adapt to the changing role of the different ESAs. As the authorities acknowledge, the Joint Committee had a slow start, since the first year was devoted to setting up the rules of engagement. However, the subcommittees have started to work on important projects, following their 2012 plan, such as their work on packaged retail investment products and on the harmonization of data on consumer trends. Thus the authorities should continue to commit resources for this cross-sectoral work. The establishment of a single website for the Joint Committee should add transparency to its work.

Cross-sectoral work on risk assessment has proven challenging. To some extent this is reasonable, since risk identification is a new focus for some of the ESAs (including ESMA). It is key that this work be closely coordinated with the ESRB to avoid overlap.

LOOKING AHEAD

It is important that the authorities develop a framework for ECB cooperation with ESMA in the context of the proposed Banking Union and the ECB's new supervisory role. The banking union will primarily affect the authorities involved in the prudential supervision of banks, but it will also have an influence on ESMA's work. National banking supervisors and securities supervisors presently cooperate extensively on a day-to-day basis regarding the supervision of specific banks. An important question is how day-to-day coordination will be arranged when the prudential supervision of banks moves to the ECB. The current proposal already includes the duty of the ECB to cooperate with the ESAs, but the scope of such operations would need to be defined.

In the short term, it is not desirable to assign additional direct supervisory functions to ESMA beyond those already in the European Market Infrastructure Regulation. The institution needs first to acquire certain stability in connection with its current mandate and deliver in the areas mentioned above. In particular, in connection with the central counterparties, ESMA will benefit from the experience of the other ESAs regarding its own role and the work of colleges of supervisors.

In the medium term, it would be worth exploring whether further centralization of supervisory functions in ESMA is desirable. There are a few areas where such centralization would be desirable, as listed below. However, it should be acknowledged that in many of the cases listed there are challenges (fiscal, legal, and/or operational) that would need to be addressed first.

- *Facilitating cooperation in connection with third-country regimes.* Given the global nature of financial services, global regulatory convergence is key. Regulatory convergence does not necessarily mean that all countries should have the same regulation, but rather that the trend is to move more and more toward mutual reliance. In this context, ESMA could play a role in helping to set up these systems of mutual reliance—for example, through a determination as to whether the frameworks are "equivalent" enough or to facilitate the execution of MoUs.

- *Direct supervisory activities where "domestic" presence is not critical, and/or where synergies and expertise would benefit from a centralized approach.* This category could include (1) supervisory responsibilities in connection with issuers' information, from the approval of the prospectus to the review of all the periodic and ongoing information that issuers are required to submit; and (2) market surveillance.

- *Direct supervisory responsibilities in connection with firms with pan-European reach or where a home regulator is not clear.* The list here could include (1) central counterparties (for which European Market Infrastructure Regulation already provides ESMA with some role), (2) trading venues, and, potentially, (3) auditors.

CHAPTER 19

European Insurance and Occupational Pensions Authority

Rodolfo Wehrhahn

The European insurance industry writes more than a third of insurance premiums globally. The €1,074 billion in premiums written by more than 5,500 European insurers in 2011 accounted for about 36 percent of the global insurance market. More than 91 percent of European premiums are written in the European Union (EU), highlighting the leading role of the EU for the global insurance industry (Figures 19.1 and 19.2). During 2011, insurers paid about €1,000 billion in claims: life claims, benefits, and annuities amounted to €615 billion; €100 billion for motor claims; €85 billion for health claims; and more than €55 billion for property claims.

Insurance penetration is among the largest in the world, although important differences between member countries exist. Notwithstanding the 5.9 percent drop in premiums in real terms experienced in the region in 2011, insurance consumption remains high. The average expenditure per capita in 2011 on insurance of €2,767 remains one of the highest in the world. Furthermore, with penetration of about 7.89 percent, the EU shows a penetration level close to that of the G7 (8.7 percent) but remains behind Japan's 11.3 percent. However, important differences in the consumption of insurance are present among member countries, for instance, the Netherlands reported insurance penetration of 13.3 percent in 2011 as compared with Bulgaria's level of about 2 percent. Also, the spread in written premiums is large, varying from more than €200 billion in the United Kingdom to about €300 million in several smaller country members (Figure 19.2).

The size of the top insurance corporations and occupational pension funds appears to be correlated with the GDP of the home country, but there are important outliers. The size of the top insurers in a country increases with the GDP of the given country, as depicted in Figures 19.3 and 19.4 showing a coefficient of determination of 0.415. However, the data show important exceptions of insurers that are three to four times larger than the expected average size corresponding to the correlation slope. With one exception, occupational pension funds follow the correlation slope of the home country much more closely. The presence of large insurers in relation to the GDP of the home country could pose a challenge to proper supervision, particularly if insufficient resources are available to be deployed for the required level of scrutiny based on the relevance of such insurers to the financial sector.

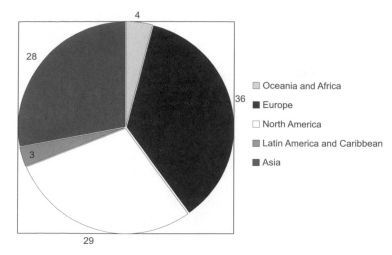

Figure 19.1 Insurance Industry Global Market Share, 2011 *(In percent)*

Source: Swiss Re, "Sigma 3/2012, World Insurance in 2011."

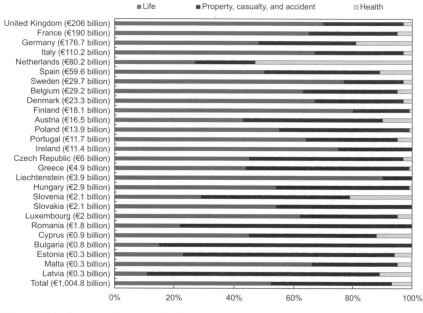

Figure 19.2 Insurance Premiums by Country, 2011

Source: Insurance Europe, 2012, "European Insurance: Key Facts."

Insurance investments have been increasing since 2008, and in 2010 reached their precrisis level. After the significant drop in value in 2007 from €7,300 billion to €6,600 billion, in 2011 the insurance industry invested about €7,500 billion or 60 percent of the EU's GDP, as indicated in Figure 19.5. Life insurers' investments have traditionally accounted for more than 80 percent of total insurers' invest-

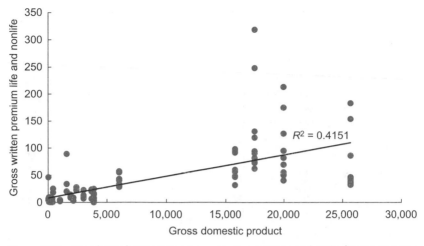

Figure 19.3 Correlation between Top Insurance Corporations and GDP of Home Country, 2011 *(In billions of euro)*

Source: European Insurance and Occupational Pensions Authority; and IMF staff calculations.

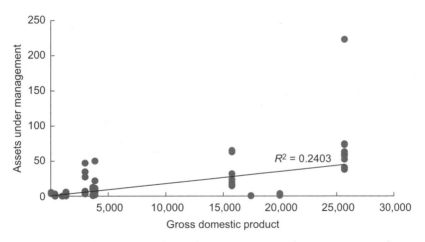

Figure 19.4 Euro Area: Correlation between Assets under Management of Top Occupational Pension Funds and GDP of Home Country, 2011 *(In billions of euro)*

Source: European Insurance and Occupational Pensions Authority; and IMF staff calculations.

ments. The United Kingdom, France, and Germany together accounted for more than 60 percent of all European life insurers' investments.

The last impact study, using 2009 data, confirmed that the industry overall remained well capitalized under the draft provisions of the Solvency II Directive[1] and options tested. However, balance sheets have deteriorated since 2009.

---

[1] See the European Insurance and Occupational Pensions Authority (EIOPA) web page for details on QIS 5 results.

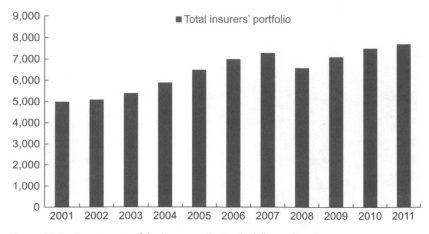

Figure 19.5 Investments of the Insurance Sector *(In billions of euro)*

Source: Insurance Europe, 2012, "European Insurance: Key Facts."

Between 2005 and 2010, the Committee of European Insurance and Occupational Pensions Supervisors conducted five pan-European quantitative impact studies (QISs) at the request of the European Commission. These studies analyzed the impact on the insurance sector of the proposed Solvency II requirements. In March 2011, the European Insurance and Occupational Pensions Authority (EIOPA) delivered to the European Commission a report on the results of the fifth QIS, which covered more than 2,500 individual undertakings and 160 groups from the 30 members of the European Economic Area (EEA). On a global level, the surplus under QIS5 was roughly 12 percent lower than the 2011 surplus of about €400 billion. However, deterioration of the balance sheets since 2009 could have worsened this situation, and the introduction of Solvency II could call for additional capitalization.

Protracted slow economic growth and the continuing low interest rate environment is putting pressure on the insurance sector. Profits during 2011 were in the 3 percent range or negative.[2] Solvency levels have been decreasing as a result of the poor investment climate, and the stagnating economy has resulted in lower production and higher claims in several member states. The high exposure to sovereign debt presents an additional vulnerability to the sector, in particular to the life industry. The long-lasting low interest rate environment prevailing in certain states (see Figure 19.6) coincides in most cases with insurance business models that provide long-term guarantees and that currently use solvency regimes that are less sensitive to market interest rates. The change to a market-consistent valuation in these countries is expected to have significant impacts on the liabilities of insurers and pension funds.

In addition to adverse market conditions, impending regulation adds uncertainty to the future of the industry. Besides Solvency II, initiatives such as the

---

[2] Insurance Europe, 2012, "European Insurance: Key Facts."

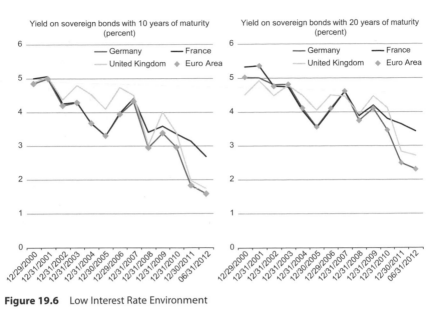

Figure 19.6 Low Interest Rate Environment

Source: Bloomberg, L.P.

Common Regulatory Framework for Internationally Active Insurance Groups (ComFrame) and the Second Insurance Mediation Directive (IMD2) will affect investment preferences, legal structures, and distribution channels as well as the insurance business models, thus creating a high level of uncertainty about the future of the sector. These negative aspects are likely reflected in the share prices and credit default swap spreads observed across the industry (Figure 19.7).

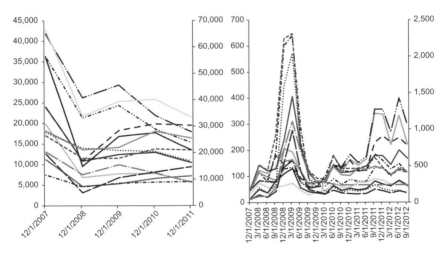

Figure 19.7 Market Cap (*billions of euro*) and Credit Default Swap Spreads (*basis points*) of Top European Insurers, 2007–12

Source: Bloomberg, L.P.

INSTITUTIONAL STRUCTURE

EIOPA has been assigned oversight, monitoring, and implementation roles in the insurance and occupational pension sectors. EIOPA's stated objective is to protect public interests by contributing to the short-, medium-, and long-term stability and effectiveness of the financial system, for the EU's economy, its citizens, and businesses, acting within the scope of various directives covering insurance and reinsurance undertakings, institutions for occupational retirement provision, and insurance intermediaries, as well as related issues not directly covered by these directives. EIOPA participates in the two joint bodies of the three European supervisory authorities: (1) the Joint Committee, which has the goal of strengthening cooperation between the European supervisory authorities, and (2) the Board of Appeal, which is independent of the European supervisory authorities' administrative and regulatory structures and gives parties the right to appeal decisions of the European supervisory authorities.

A high level of transparency characterizes the EIOPA's actions. EIOPA's commitment to transparency and public consultation has been achieved by instituting stakeholder groups that include representatives of the industry, consumers, and beneficiaries, as well as academics. EIOPA has established the Insurance & Reinsurance Stakeholder Group and the Occupational Pensions Stakeholder Group, each comprising 30 members. There are five scheduled meetings per year. During 2012, EIOPA published 13 detailed opinions and feedback documents from the stakeholder groups. A review of the effectiveness of the stakeholder groups is currently been carried out.

Operational independence could be enhanced by removing possible sources of interference. The legal status of EIOPA is that of an independent advisory body accountable to the European Parliament and the Council of the European Union. However, its financing structure could hinder effective independence. National authorities contribute 60 percent of the budget, and the national authorities are the voting members of the Board of Supervisors. Thus, members of the Board of Supervisors may face conflicts of interest in agreeing on the implementation of EIOPA's tasks and powers that affect their own powers and responsibilities as national supervisors. This conflict could be more important in crisis management or breach of union law situations. The remaining 40 percent of the budget is also not free from possible conflicts of interest, given that it is a subsidy from the EU embodied in the Directorate General Market Operations budget; but this directorate approves the standards drafted by EIOPA. This situation may make the dispositions in the EIOPA Regulation (EReg) on the adoption of regulatory technical standards less effective.

EIOPA applies an annual zero-based budgeting approach requiring each item of proposed expenditure to be justified with no automatic budget rollover. The rules and process steps for EIOPA's budget planning are included in the EReg, the Financial Regulation applicable to the general budget of the European Commission, and the individual Financial Regulation of EIOPA Title III, Chapter 1. EIOPA's budget planning is guided by Title II of the EIOPA Financial

Regulation regarding budgetary principles in a context of sound financial management. This budgetary approach aims to ensure that EIOPA receives the appropriate annual amount to meet its annual operational objectives and that EIOPA optimizes its level of budgetary usage.

A two-year advance budget planning process complements the zero-based budgeting approach. The Executive Director submits the draft statement of estimates of revenue and expenditure for year N+2 to the Management Board and to the Board of Supervisors at the beginning of year N+1. This draft statement is built to cover the business needs and activities as expressed in the annual work program for year N+2. In parallel to the draft estimate, a staff establishment plan for EIOPA is drafted and submitted to the same boards. The Board of Supervisors, in turn, transmits the statement of estimates of revenue and expenditure for N+2 to the European Commission, together with the draft establishment plan as per Art 63 of EReg. After a consultation process, the budgetary authority (European Parliament, Council) adopts in November the establishment plan for EIOPA and authorizes the appropriations for the subsidy to EIOPA. The budget is finalized at the final adoption of the general EU budget. During the process, budget cuts can and have occurred, requiring a change in the priorities of the agency.

EIOPA has been able to attract qualified professionals. The number of employees is expected to rise from 57 in 2011 to 114 for 2013. Currently, the Chairman and Executive Director are supported by the Director of Regulations and the Director of Oversight and Operations, who lead a team of 64 staff members, 10 secondees, and 13 contract agents. The number of staff dropped by 10 percent in one year, but these employees were replaced by an increased number of secondees and contract agents. It appears that work continuity and institutional knowledge did not suffer from this attrition, considered natural in the current dynamic stage of development faced by EIOPA. Staff received an average of 0.58 days training in 2011 and 2.11 days in 2012.

Significant changes in the regulatory environment affecting insurance and occupational pensions are expected in the coming years. Solvency II is scheduled to be implemented in 2014, and revised legislation for occupational pensions should be in force. These major changes will affect the work required from EIOPA. A shift from developing technical standards, issuing guidelines and recommendations, and providing opinions toward monitoring, implementing, and enforcing will be necessary. EIOPA's human resources framework, as well as its operational processes, will need to be realigned to the new challenges.

Budgetary framework flexibility supporting Solvency II implementation should be considered. Given the current stage of the European insurance framework, which is in the process of implementing Solvency II, special skills and expertise are required for the initial development of adequate tools to properly monitor harmonized implementation, including internal models for approval processes, reporting tools, and the like. Investing in this initial phase will require temporary access to special expertise that may not be within the payment framework that currently applies to EIOPA. Flexibility on a temporary basis in the salary scales and swift access to external consultants will allow the necessary high-level expertise to be gained for the creation of solid supervisory tools, especially in the modeling, information technology, and actuarial areas. Furthermore, should direct supervisory mandates be assigned to EIOPA, budgetary treatment similar to that which applies to the European Central Bank should be considered.

Powers and Mandates

The multiyear business plan for 2012–14 and the annual plan for 2013 focus on key deliverables that are aligned with EIOPA's mandates. The tasks include the completion and monitoring of the implementation of Solvency II, the further development of supervisory colleges, and consumer protection issues as well as financial stability and crisis management actions. The plans also focus on adapting and further growing the internal organization to cope with the changing and growing assignments. The need for a centralized, efficient, information technology platform to allow for confidential information exchange with national authorities is recognized, and its development is accordingly planned. Some of the specific actions required to meet the new challenges are mentioned in EIOPA's working plan document for 2012–14:

- Establishment of the operational tasks required of EIOPA under Solvency II;
- Enhancement of convergence in supervision by greater use of tools, for example, supervisory review processes, Q&A; and
- Use of EIOPA's existing tools for assessing the effects of regulatory changes, that is, regulatory impact assessments.

Powers granted to EIOPA appear sufficient to accomplish the current tasks. During the introductory and construction phase of Solvency II, the powers residing in the agency—including the development of draft regulatory and implementation technical standards and the issuance of guidelines and recommendations that need to be adopted or explained—have proved to be sufficient, albeit there were some delays and certain inefficiencies with respect to the initial implementation plan of Solvency II. In the area of contributing to a common supervisory culture, a soft approach based on peer reviews, training, and frequent engagement in the colleges of supervisors supported by the use of guidelines has been effectively taken.

The new challenges ahead for EIOPA will require revisiting its current powers. The implementation and monitoring of Solvency II will require more intrusive tools to prevent undue delays that could result in regulatory arbitrage and thus threaten to defeat the purpose of a harmonized supervisory regime in the EU. The power to collect the necessary information about financial institutions as provided for in Article 35 of the EReg has been challenged with respect to the level of detail. Considerable granularity in data collection appears to be fundamental to accomplishing tasks related to financial stability surveillance and emergency situations. The data collection powers need to allow for the necessary level of information gathering.

In the area of promoting effective colleges of supervisors, stronger powers would help accelerate the process; conflicting views among the participant supervisors will emerge that will require strong leadership for their efficient resolution. These additional powers could even go so far as to enhance the supervisory responsibility of the group, including the power to impose sanctions. The supervisory powers should, at a minimum, cover important large groups. However, such a change might require changes in numerous laws.

Systemic Risk and Stress Testing

EIOPA's mandate includes working with the European Systemic Risk Board on identification of, measurement of, and response to systemic risk. EIOPA's role is defined as a supporting role to the European Systemic Risk Board, as stated in Article 23(1) and Article 17 of Regulation (EU) No. 1092/2010.2. Due consideration of international approaches, including those established by the Financial Stability Board, the International Monetary Fund, the International Association of Insurance Supervisors (IAIS), and the Bank for International Settlements, is required. EIOPA's work in this area includes the development and coordination of effective and consistent recovery and resolution plans, procedures for emergency situations. and preventive measures to minimize the systemic impact of any failure of insurers or occupational pension funds.

A framework for EIOPA's action in a crisis situation has been developed. In mid-2011, a task force on crisis management was created to develop EIOPA's institutional structures to discharge its crisis management responsibilities under Article 18 of EReg. The Board of Supervisors adopted a core crisis-management framework in December 2011. This framework sets out clear procedures for EIOPA's action in the event of adverse developments as defined in Article 18 or of a declaration of an emergency situation by the council.

EIOPA has been engaged in a process of regular, structured dialogue with national supervisory authorities (NSAs) throughout the global financial crisis. EIOPA's internal monitoring group is a key element supporting EIOPA in fulfilling its crisis prevention and management duties. The internal monitoring group comprises selected members from national supervisors and meets several times a year. It is at this venue that information and analysis can result in supervisory or other action by EIOPA and its members. The internal monitoring group, by drawing together analytical and other information from other EIOPA working groups, assesses whether responses are needed or prepares proposals for action that are put to the EIOPA Board of Supervisors for decision. Among the key activities carried out by the group during 2012 was the introduction of a bimonthly qualitative survey on significant balance sheet changes and exposures to sovereign and bank risk, liquidity risk, and cash flow risk, among other themes.

Further work is required in the area of crisis management to allow for efficient, swift actions by EIOPA. With the framework on crisis management, EIOPA has met an important operational requirement. However, relevant elements still need to be put in place, such as the missing sectoral legislation for consumer protection during emergency situations. An important gap relates to the requirement for a declaration of emergency by the European Council that would allow the agency to take decisive, effective action to combat matters affecting the orderly functioning and integrity of financial markets or the stability of the whole or a part of the financial system in the Union, or in those situations concerning directly applicable Union law. The possibility of allowing EIOPA to act in a decisive manner without an explicit declaration of an emergency should be evaluated.

Access to information and the use of such information for monitoring, analyzing trends, and preventing systemic risk need to improve. Financial stability data are collected from the 30 biggest cross-border insurance groups, including three Swiss groups and some of the solo institutions above a certain threshold of gross written premium. EIOPA, however, does not receive the data on an identifiable individual group level that would be necessary for performing the authority's tasks. Furthermore, EIOPA does not have direct access to any national supervisory data, although data are submitted to EIOPA upon request (for example, data related to financial stability and crisis prevention). EIOPA should be granted the power to request supervisory data for any institution on a timely basis.

Stress testing is one of the explicitly indicated tools to be used by EIOPA for crisis prevention. In accordance with Article 32 of EReg, EIOPA uses stress testing as a tool to assess the resilience of financial institutions Union-wide. In particular, the systemic risk posed by financial institutions is evaluated under theoretical adverse market developments. Also, consistent use of stress testing across the NSAs is part of its mandate. For the 2011 exercise, covering 50 percent of all national markets measured by gross written premium, almost all risk drivers were included in the stress scenarios, and stress levels were determined based on a historic distribution analysis. The stress levels were approved by EIOPA's Board of Supervisors. Results of the individual industry submissions were validated by the NSAs first and then again by a central validation team made up of NSA and EIOPA experts. The final report was approved by the Board of Supervisors. Disclosure of the results occurred on an aggregated basis.

EIOPA's stress tests under the Solvency II regime should focus on EU-wide systemic vulnerabilities. EIOPA currently uses stress tests to analyze the effect of shocks adversely affecting the traditional areas of insurance vulnerability, such as mortality, lapse, and market exposures. A strong emphasis has been put on supporting the development of Solvency II through a series of qualitative impact assessments. Once the new solvency regime is in place, EIOPA's stress test should move to enhance and harmonize the national stress-testing activity with a special focus on identifying cross-border systemic risk. This move will require consideration of single and multiple shocks affecting the relevant variables in the areas of financial market structure, interactions, and regulation and supervision responsible for the fallacies of composition, that is, situations in which the sum of the individuals does not describe the behavior of the whole group. Such stress tests should incorporate systemic feedback effects under macroeconomic scenarios, as well as allow for contagious shocks to spread rapidly through the whole financial sector.

Harmonizing Supervisory Practices

From March 2010 to April 2010, EIOPA's predecessor, the Committee of European Insurance and Occupational Pensions Supervisors, carried out a survey of the level of preparedness of insurance supervisors with reference to the implementation of Solvency II. From the 27 supervisory authorities that answered the questionnaire, 11 are small supervisory authorities (with fewer than 40 employees dealing with insurance), 11 are medium-sized supervisory authorities (with 40–100 employees dealing with insurance), and 5 are larger supervisors (with more than 100 employees dealing with insurance). The number of staff varies widely, from 25 to more than 3,300, and depends on market size as well as the level of integration of the financial sector supervisory authorities. As to the number of supervised insurance and reinsurance undertakings subject to Solvency II in each country, the range is also wide: from 10 up to 625.

The evaluation of NSAs' ability to implement the forthcoming solvency regime should take priority. The difference in resources among the NSAs presents an important challenge to EIOPA's supervision harmonization efforts. Along with the review of capacity to implement Solvency II, a peer review of stress test practices is recommended.

To monitor and enhance supervisory convergence within the EEA, the Board of Supervisors established a review panel. The panel is a permanent group comprising representatives of the NSAs with the necessary independence, objectivity, seniority, knowledge of the community legislation and EIOPA measures, and expertise in supervisory practices to guarantee the credibility and the effectiveness of the peer review mechanism. The last peer review (so far, the only one completed) dates back to 2009 and comprised the application of the provisions of information exchange and supervisory cooperation in the context of the General Protocol, the Budapest Protocol, and the Helsinki Protocol. The peer review activity has recently been revived. EIOPA has started peer reviews in the areas of internal model application and supervision of branches, and for a few articles of the occupational pension directive.

Harmonization of supervision through the peer review exercise should be enhanced by having EIOPA in a role to challenge the outputs. The peer review panel issues best practices that need to be adopted or explained by each NSA; EIOPA's independence and strong European view should add value to this process. EIOPA will accelerate supervisory harmonization by playing a role that goes beyond that played by the secretariat under current practice and by owning the process.

Supervisory Colleges and Group Supervision

In the area of group supervision, EIOPA's tasks go beyond pure regulatory work. Following Article 242 of Directive 2009/138/EC, EIOPA is required to contribute to the proper functioning of colleges of supervisors; to make an assessment of the benefit of enhancing group supervision and capital management within a group of insurance or reinsurance undertakings, including possible measures to enhance sound cross-border management of insurance groups, in particular in respect of risks and asset management. In addition, EIOPA may report on any new developments and progress concerning practices in centralized group risk management and functioning of group internal models, including stress testing, intragroup transactions, and risk concentrations; a harmonized framework for asset transferability, insolvency, and winding-up procedures that eliminate the relevant national company or corporate law barriers to asset transferability; and an equivalent level of protection of policy holders and beneficiaries of the undertakings of the same group, particularly in crisis situations.

During 2011, 89 insurance groups with cross-border undertakings were registered in the EEA. Some 69 colleges of supervisors had at least one meeting or teleconference. A total of 14 national supervisory authorities acted as group supervisors to organize the events. During the setup phase in the first year after its establishment, EIOPA staff attended supervisory college meetings or teleconferences held by 55 groups. Important issues like crisis preparedness were introduced and some aspects were tested, confidentiality agreement templates were developed, and best practices on group supervision were presented.

EIOPA's engagement in its oversight role of supervisory colleges has been intense, but much work remains to be done. A harmonized level of group supervision in the EU remains to be achieved for when the Level 3 legislation (implementation measures) comes into force. EIOPA's engagement in colleges should go beyond the EU and encompass the larger international groups active in Europe. For financial stability purposes, consideration should be given to assigning EIOPA a supervisory role for the largest important groups.

Consumer Protection

EIOPA has been proactive in the area of consumer protection. Promoting transparency, simplicity, and fairness in the market for consumer financial products or services across the EU is a stated objective of EIOPA. The first guidelines applicable to NSAs under the "comply or explain" scheme have been issued on Complaints-Handling by Insurance Undertakings. In addition, a report on Good Practices for Disclosure and Selling of Variable Annuities as a tool to promote common supervisory approaches and practices has been published. A consumer strategy day takes place annually, when consumers, industry, and the NSAs discuss current issues under EIOPA's leadership.

An initial report on consumer trends was published in June 2012. EIOPA does not yet collect statistics on the number or type of insurance complaints received from NSAs of member states; however, based on information collected from the NSAs, it has presented its first initial consumer trends overview. Three main trends were identified:

- Consumer protection issues around payment protection insurance,
- Development of unit-linked life insurance, and
- Increased use of comparison websites by consumers.

In addition, EIOPA's intention is to publish regular reports on consumer trends using a recently adopted enhanced methodology based on quantitative and qualitative data collection, including number and type of insurance complaints received.

EIOPA is engaged in the revision of the IMD2. The proposal provides that "all information, including marketing communications, addressed by insurance intermediaries and undertakings to customers or potential customers should be fair, clear and not misleading." The IMD2 proposal also sets the expectation that EIOPA will periodically develop guidelines for the assessment and supervision of practices of tying an insurance product to an ancillary service or bundling an insurance product together with an ancillary service. Under the current text of the legislative proposals on packaged Retail Investment Products and the IMD2, EIOPA is expected to work on delegated acts ensuring that information about products is adequately disclosed and products are sold in a fair way to consumers, for example, to ensure suitability of the product to the customer and to mitigate conflicts of interest. EIOPA is in a position to highlight the particular aspects of insurance products and insurance distribution practices when cross-sectoral discussions take place.

EIOPA's powers to restrict or ban certain products are limited. Warnings on, as well as prohibitions and restrictions of, certain financial activities can be issued by EIOPA should such activities pose a serious threat to the stability and effectiveness of the financial system. This power, however, can only be used if cross-sector legislation is enacted, setting out the specific cases and conditions under which EIOPA would be able to issue such temporary prohibitions and restrictions. A permanent prohibition or restriction of certain financial activities would require the European Commission's authorization. A framework for the effective monitoring of products with the potential to impact financial stability and to severely affect consumers should be established as a first step toward justifying any prohibitions.

EIOPA's initial findings on existing guarantee schemes show an urgent need for harmonization. EIOPA's task force on insurance guarantee schemes has published two reports, the "Report on the Cross-Border Cooperation Mechanisms between Insurance Guarantee Schemes in the EU" in 2011, followed by the "Report on the Role of Insurance Guarantee Schemes in the Winding-Up Procedures of Insolvent Undertakings in the EU/EEA" in 2012. The first report is a mapping exercise of existing cross-border cooperation mechanisms and it resulted in five recommendations. The findings of the second report highlight the lack of harmonization in areas such as the ability to transfer portfolios, the lack of prewarning systems for when insurance undertakings are in difficulty, and the role of the supervisory authority when insurance undertakings become insolvent.

Occupational Pensions

EIOPA's response to the call for opinions on the proposed new directive on occupational pension funds highlights the need for transparency in the level of protection and modernization of the existing regimes. EIOPA's response evaluates the advantages of enhancing transparency through improved harmonization of reporting, stricter requirements on governance and risk management similar to the second pillar of Solvency II, and the use of a holistic balance sheet approach for measuring the solvency position of the different institutions for occupational retirement provision (IORPs). A QIS of IORPs using a holistic balance sheet valuation method was undertaken and the results were published in July 2013. The report shows wide dispersion in impacts using the holistic balance sheet method, ranging from surpluses in some member states to large shortfalls in other member states. The results underscore the need for further work toward guaranteeing the sustainability of pension funds and the protection of current as well future generations' pensions.

The initial purpose of the new IORP directive—to remove impediments to the creation of a single market—has been relinquished in favor of creating more comparability in the solvency and resilience of the different IORPs. The lack of demand for cross-border activity—only a handful of IORPs currently provide cross-border pensions—as well as the fact that important aspects of cross-border activity, such as labor, social, and tax laws, remain within the national purview, has shifted the focus of the new IORP directive toward enhancing transparency of the level of resilience of the different IORPs. Greater transparency and a holistic balance sheet approach that takes into account both implicit and explicit guarantees of the sponsors will allow comparison of the various IORPs throughout the EU. This comparison is recognized as an important step toward the creation of a single market. Given the complexity of the current solvency regimes in the different jurisdictions, the results of the QIS exercise can only be seen as a first step before a final sound valuation methodology can be introduced.

Solvency II

The more than 75 percent of supervised insurers that produce about 85 percent of the EU's gross written premiums will need to comply with Solvency II. Based on the last QIS exercise, of the 4,753 supervised entities, 3,680 are expected to be covered by the Solvency II directive, that is, they write premiums larger than €5 million or they have technical reserves in excess of €50 million. These entities are responsible for more than 95 percent of the aggregate technical reserves. The fact that several EU members have delegated most of the necessary updating of their existing national solvency regime to the efforts undertaken by EIOPA has increased the relevance of the proper and timely implementation of the new solvency regime for Europe.

The impact study highlighted the areas in which further work was needed: definition of contract boundaries in the valuation of technical provisions; the need to reduce complexity in certain areas; developments in the calibration of catastrophic risk; and the treatment of long-term guarantees in the context of Solvency II. This work has been initiated by EIOPA.

EIOPA is currently developing draft standards and guidelines in the following areas:

- Solvency capital requirements for the standard formula as well as for internal model users; own funds; valuation of technical provisions; valuation of assets and liabilities;
- Group supervision;
- Supervisory transparency and accountability, reporting and disclosure, external audit;
- Governance and own risk solvency assessment; and
- Supervisory review process; capital add-ons; extension of recovery period (Pillar 2 dampener[3]); finite reinsurance; special purpose vehicles.

The implementation of Solvency II is now scheduled to take place in January 2014. The Solvency II Directive text is under revision as part of the Omnibus II Directive revision, which is still at the time of writing under discussion among the council, parliament, and the commission. The Omnibus II trialogue provisionally scheduled for October 1, 2012, did not take place. The main disagreement centers on extending the long-term guarantees package (especially the matching adjustment) to a wider range of products. A directive (2012/23/EU) was published as an interim measure to specifically revise the date of transposition and entry into force of the Solvency II Directive to June 30, 2013, and January 1, 2014, respectively. However, although the Omnibus II Directive remains a matter for discussion, the implementing measures (or delegated acts) remain in draft form with the commission.

In July 2012, the trialogue parties requested that EIOPA conduct an impact assessment on the long-term guarantee aspects of the Solvency II package. EIOPA was asked to run a technical assessment to collect both qualitative and quantitative information from insurance and reinsurance undertakings and supervisory authorities on the effects of the long-term guarantees package. EIOPA was to launch the exercise on October 15, 2012. Insurance and reinsurance undertakings would have eight weeks to provide the information requested to their NSAs. The final report was scheduled to be provided to the colegislators by March 31, 2013, by the commission based on the findings of EIOPA's technical assessment. However, the terms of reference were only agreed upon by the trialogue parties at the end of 2012. The results of the technical assessment were published on June 14, 2013. Discussions of the final measures for addressing short-term volatility and ultimately properly regulating long-term guarantees were to happen in the subsequent months.

Important discussions on the final form of Solvency II are taking place, with a main focus on the proper treatment of long-term liabilities. A market-consistent valuation of liabilities, as required by Solvency II, in a low rate environment will require the use of a low interest rate discount curve. This will have a negative

---

[3] Pillar 2 dampeners are any technical elements that allow deviations from market consistent valuation of the capital requirements.

impact on the solvency position of insurers under Solvency II, and asset-liability matching needs must be developed to avoid distortionary or noncredible effects. However, adjustments to the discount curve for asset-liability matching must to be carried out without reducing the market-consistency principle of the new solvency framework. Adopting rules for the valuation of long-term liabilities that exaggerate solvency positions of insurers under current adverse market conditions will weaken the credibility of Solvency II as a market-consistent solvency regime.

Preparation for the implementation of Solvency II is the central task for EIOPA. Although EIOPA's involvement is required in other areas, and resources have been dedicated to these areas, the lion's share of the authority's activities focuses on readiness for the implementation of Solvency II. Fundamental changes are needed in the supervisory methodology, tools, and procedures in all areas of insurance supervision—quantitative requirements (Pillar I), qualitative requirements (Pillar II), supervisory reporting and public disclosure, and group supervision—in nearly all NSAs.

Weaknesses in insurance supervision in several EU member states will remain in the absence of Solvency II. The implementation of Solvency II is critical because important aspects of prudential supervision, such as valuation, disclosure, and risk management, in several EU member states will remain out of compliance with IAIS principles (as reviewed in recent Financial Sector Assessment Program reports) in its absence. Consideration should be given to early implementation of as much as possible of Solvency II to allow more supervisors to raise their standards.

The approval of internal models is a crucial step in determining capital adequacy to ensure a solvent industry. The level of expertise and amount of work required is severely straining the NSAs. EIOPA agreed on a workflow process to be followed by the NSAs and insurers for both pre-application and approval. EIOPA has been holding monthly meetings, open to operational supervisors from all member states, to discuss particular issues related to pre-application and the review of internal models. EIOPA has also held meetings with the main external stakeholders concerned with internal models, including undertakings, consultations, and external providers. Following these discussions with external stakeholders, in May 2012 EIOPA issued an opinion on the use of external models. Finally, consideration should be given to introducing a centralized oversight mechanism for the approval of internal models that would make efficient use of highly qualified resources and would guarantee a consistent, elevated level of technical proficiency.

Solvency II Equivalence and International Representation

EIOPA's work on Solvency II equivalence certification is intense and relevant. The Solvency II Directive gives the European Commission the authority to decide on the equivalence of a third country's solvency and prudential regime. EIOPA provides advice to the European Commission on this matter. Such work promotes open international insurance markets and reduces regulatory burdens while simultaneously ensuring that policyholders are adequately protected globally. EIOPA equivalence assessments include desk and on-site work and have been carried out for the Swiss and the Bermudian supervisory systems under Article 172 (reinsurance supervision), Article 227 (inclusion of related third country insurance and reinsurance undertakings in group solvency calculation), and Article 260 (group supervision); and for the Japanese reinsurance supervisory system under Article 172. Although EIOPA's assessments have concluded, it will need to revisit its advice once the final Level 2 implementing measures, including the equivalence criteria, are published.

Transitional equivalence measures for several countries are also being evaluated. If a third country's solvency and prudential regime is currently not able to satisfy the equivalence criteria in full, but will be in a position to do so once the relevant changes to the regime have been made, transitional equivalence measures are in place. Transitional equivalence measures for professional secrecy and a gap analysis against the Solvency II framework for supervisory regimes in the following countries are currently been developed: Chile, China, Hong Kong SAR, Israel, Mexico, Singapore, and South Africa.

The mutual recognition work with the United States supervisory regime is under way. In early 2012, the European Commission, EIOPA, the National Association of Insurance Commissioners, and the Federal Insurance Office of the U.S. Department of the Treasury agreed to participate in a dialogue and a related project to contribute to an increased mutual understanding and enhanced cooperation between the EU and the United States to promote business opportunity, consumer protection, and effective supervision. The steering committee agreed on seven fundamentally important topics:

- Professional secrecy and confidentiality;
- Group supervision;
- Solvency and capital requirements;
- Reinsurance and collateral requirements;
- Supervisory reporting, data collection and analysis;
- Supervisory peer reviews; and
- Independent third-party review and supervisory on-site inspections.

Seven technical committee reports were jointly drafted. Following the end-September 2012 public release of the reports for interested party analysis and comments, conclusions were reached by the steering committee on each of the seven topics, and it published an agreed-upon "Way Forward" document that defines common objectives and initiatives. The shared objectives expressed in the document are expected to lead to improved convergence and regulatory compatibility between the EU and the United States. Work streams will continue through 2017.

EIOPA has been engaged in creating a common EU voice for insurance and pension matters. Achieving a common EU view on selected international agenda topics such as the development of a Common Regulatory Framework for Internationally Active Insurance Groups (ComFrame) and the designation of global systemically important insurers was initiated through the establishment and functioning of an internal network with representatives from NSAs. EIOPA became a member of the executive committee of the IAIS in 2011 and is active in its financial stability committee. EIOPA has also submitted its application to become an IOPS governing member in 2012.

EIOPA's representation role in international forums should increase. The actions taken in promoting a common European voice at the IAIS on key topics has been helpful in supporting the international agenda of achieving convergence of solvency and supervisory practices, as well as for designing a cross-border resolution framework. EIOPA should be allowed access to important documents of the Financial Stability Board and other international bodies to facilitate performing its assigned international role The participation on the IOPS governing board should have a strong priority.

EIOPA has an important role in representing the insurance sector in standards-setting bodies in the fields of accounting and auditing. EIOPA is an official observer and active participant at the European Financial Reporting Advisory Group meetings as well as at the Accounting Regulatory Committee meetings. EIOPA is involved on an ongoing basis in exchanges of views and interacts with the Federation of European Accountants and the International Accounting Standards Board. EIOPA also follows discussions within the accounting experts group at IAIS and maintains contacts with the U.K. Financial Reporting Council, the German Deutsches Rechnungslegungs Standards Committee, the U.S. Financial Accounting Standards Board, and the International Federation of Accountants. In addition, coordination among the accounting and financial reporting areas of the other European supervisory authorities takes place through the Joint Committee. Also, discussions are ongoing with the European Commission's Directorate General Internal Markets Unit F3: Accounting and financial reporting and Unit F4: Audit.

Current accounting treatment of assets and liabilities in the EU varies. Comparison of the financial positions of insurers in different jurisdictions is severely affected by the different supervisory accounting regimes. This problem is particular relevant when assessing the financial position of active cross-border insurance groups. The implementation of Solvency II will address this issue for EU operating groups. However, for internationally active insurers, comparison of solvency regimes will remain difficult because liabilities valuation under Solvency II and under International Financial Reporting Standards currently exhibit important differences. EIOPA's representation in the standards-setting bodies in the fields of accounting and auditing should be leveraged to gain convergence or at least higher transparency in the treatment of liabilities.

CHAPTER 20

Macroprudential Oversight and the Role of the European Systemic Risk Board

THIERRY TRESSEL AND JIANPING ZHOU

The role of macroprudential policy is to identify and reduce risks to financial stability that arise along both a time dimension and a cross-sectional dimension. Macroprudential policy relies on prudential instruments to (1) limit the buildup of financial imbalances, (2) address the market failures related to risk externalities and interconnectedness between financial institutions, and (3) dampen the procyclicality of the financial system.

Currently, national authorities in the European Union (EU) are responsible for macroprudential oversight of each national financial system, but adequate frameworks are still lacking in many EU countries. Coordination and internalization of cross-border spillovers is achieved at the EU level by the European Systemic Risk Board (ESRB) through a (nonbinding) "act or explain" mechanism. In December 2011, the ESRB issued recommendations on the macroprudential mandates of national authorities. Subsequently, guidance for establishing common macroprudential toolkits was issued in June 2012.

Macroprudential policies at a national level need to be effective and efficient as well as aligned with the overall objectives of the internal market while protecting financial stability. This approach suggests that the set of available instruments should be comprehensive enough to address multifaceted macroprudential concerns at the national and EU levels, but efficient coordination is also needed to limit possible negative externalities or unintended effects, including on the integrity of the single market.

Coordination of national macroprudential policies is especially important in the EU, given its highly integrated economic and financial markets. Such coordination would help identify correlated risk exposures of major EU financial institutions. Coordination is also important for minimizing negative spillover effects of national policies, reducing the possibility of regulatory arbitrage, and fostering policy effectiveness. But the ESRB still lacks formal modalities to coordinate macroprudential policy at the EU level.

The implementation of the Single Supervisory Mechanism (SSM) will have important implications for the institutional setting of macroprudential oversight in Europe. Within the Economic and Monetary Union, it is advantageous to assign macroprudential policy to both the European Central Bank (ECB) and national authorities, because strong monetary policy and macroprudential policy frameworks can be mutually reinforcing, and the ECB will internalize cross-border effects within the banking union. The established independence of the ECB would help build up a strong institutional framework for macroprudential policy and capacity to implement macroprudential instruments without undue political interference. National authorities should be provided a similar degree of operational independence and powers. The ECB and national authorities should be responsible for a wider range of macroprudential instruments, going beyond those included in the Capital Requirements Regulation (CRR) and Capital Requirements Directive IV (CRD IV) (collectively, CRR/CRD IV).

Methods for coordination between the ESRB as the EU macroprudential oversight body and the SSM among the participating countries need to be devised. The ESRB would need to have legal powers and sufficient resources to be effective. Whereas the SSM will comprise the euro area and any opt-in countries, the ESRB encompasses the entire EU. Within the countries of the SSM, the ECB will appropriately have macroprudential powers and will closely coordinate with national macroprudential authorities. The ESRB should interact with the ECB on macroprudential toolkits when it takes on macroprudential responsibilities, as it will continue to do with national supervisors. The ESRB should be able to exercise its powers and issue recommendations to the ECB as it does to national authorities. To be effective, the ESRB would also need to improve its capacity for effective identification, analysis, and monitoring of EU-wide systemic risks, supported by timely access to information on financial markets as well as on individual financial institutions. The coordinating role of the ESRB should be further enhanced through closer cooperation with the European Supervisory Authorities (ESAs) because the ESRB's scope goes beyond the banking sector to cover the entire financial system, including all financial institutions (such as insurance and pension funds, market infrastructure, and so forth) and financial markets and products.

INTRODUCTION TO THE EUROPEAN SYSTEMIC RISK BOARD

EU context. The ESRB was set up in January 2011 following the 2009 de Larosiere report, which resulted in the establishment of the European System of Financial Supervision, a network of national supervisors working in tandem with the new European Supervisory Authorities (ESAs) and the ESRB. The reorganization of the European financial architecture was a response to the weaknesses in the EU financial supervisory framework that was exposed by the 2008 financial crisis, particularly with respect to the supervision of cross-border banks. Despite the highly integrated and interconnected financial systems and the importance of cross-border financial activities in the EU, supervisory and regulatory frameworks had remained fragmented along national lines. Moreover, there was little or no emphasis on macroprudential oversight and on a more integrated approach to financial stability, as each national central bank (and the ECB) produced its financial stability analysis independently.

Systemic crisis in the euro area. The ESRB began operations shortly before the euro area was engulfed by a systemic crisis arising from bank and sovereign risks interacting with architectural weaknesses. Uncoordinated actions resulted in a deep fragmentation of the EU financial system. Against this backdrop, the ESRB had to balance and prioritize activities between systemic risk warnings and policy recommendations on regulations and to correct medium-term risks while developing a macroprudential toolkit for the EU—an important task for the EU macroprudential oversight body. Given the deeply interconnected nature of the EU financial system, the ESRB has a role to play in promoting a more integrated approach to systemic risk and macroprudential policies, although the creation of the banking union will require a well-designed division of labor between the ESRB and the SSM.

The ESRB operates under a set of constraints that may hamper its effectiveness. Constraints originate from the supranational dimension of the ESRB, resulting in a complex decision-making process, and its lack of binding powers. Resources are provided by the ECB and national authorities to support the activities of the ESRB. The ESRB has access to disaggregated data through the ECB and the ESAs, but no direct access to supervisory data. This may adversely affect its ability to assess systemic risks that may arise from large cross-border and interconnected financial institutions.

The chapter is organized as follows. The next section is devoted to a description of ESRB activities and an assessment of its effectiveness. The third section explores the choice of macroprudential toolkits for EU countries. The fourth section explains how the macroprudential institutional landscape should be organized, including by giving a strong role to the ESRB in coordinating the use of macroprudential instruments across the EU and sectors of the financial system. It also discusses the respective roles of and interactions between the ESRB and the SSM when the latter starts operating.

A REVIEW OF THE ESRB

The Role of the ESRB: Mandate, Tasks, and Organization

Role of the ESRB. As recommended by the de Larosiere report, the ESRB is responsible for macroprudential oversight of the financial systems and institutions within the EU to prevent or mitigate systemic risks, to avoid episodes of widespread financial distress, to contribute to the smooth functioning of the internal market, and to ensure a sustainable contribution of the financial sector to economic growth.[1] Given the highly integrated and interconnected nature of the EU financial system, the ESRB also has a natural role in ensuring

---

[1] Regulation (EU) No. 1092/2010 of the European Parliament and of the Council of November 24, 2010.

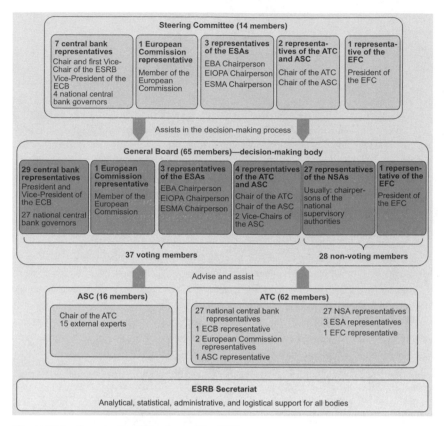

Figure 20.1 Organizational Structure of the ESRB

Source: Bundesbank Monthly Report, April 2012.
Note: ASC = Advisory Scientific Committee of the ESRB; ATC = Advisory Technical Committee of the ESRB; EBA = European Banking Authority; ECB = European Central Bank; EFC = Economic and Financial Committee; EIOPA = European Insurance and Occupational Pensions Authority; ESA = European Supervisory Authority; ESMA = European Securities and Markets Authority; ESRB = European Systemic Risk Board; NSA = National Supervisory Authority.

effectiveness, convergence, and coordination of macroprudential policies to protect the integrity of the single market and to protect financial stability at the national and supranational levels.

Mandate, tasks, structure, and policy instruments of the ESRB. The ESRB is performing its mandate under a set of institutional constraints set out in EU regulation. The ESRB has a complex organizational structure that results from the need to ensure high-level policy representation of 27 member states (Figure 20.1). The ESRB has no legal personality and is dependent on the ECB, which provides administrative, logistical, statistical, and analytical support to the ESRB. The powers of the ESRB are nonbinding and the impact of its policy instruments depends on the effectiveness of an "act or explain" mechanism. The ESRB is accountable to the European Parliament, as stated in its regulation.

Approach of the ESRB to Monitoring and Assessing Systemic Risk

Short-term risks. In addition to the risk dashboard (described below), various inputs are used for systemic risk analysis, including documents such as ECB risk surveillance notes, risk analysis reports, the ECB white book, market intelligence reports by the ECB and the Bank of England, European Commission staff reports on systemic risks, the ESA's dashboards, the Joint Committee of the European Supervisory Authorities' report on risks, and notes by the ESRB Secretariat with bottom-up questionnaires for identifying risks.

Medium-term risks and activities. Once identified, medium-term and long-term risks result in the setting up of working groups involving staff from the ECB, the European Commission, ESAs, national authorities, and academics. The working groups provide analytical papers to prepare policy recommendations on medium-term risks. In 2011 and 2012, attention was focused on risks arising from bank funding and asset encumbrance, U.S. dollar–denominated bank funding, lending in foreign currencies, loan forbearance, regulatory treatment of sovereign exposures, interconnectedness of credit swap and interbank markets, stress testing, securities financing transactions, money market funds, high-frequency trading, and the treatment of long-term guarantees in insurance.

Data exchange with national and EU institutions. Data exchange between the ESRB and other national and EU supervisory authorities is guided by the EU regulation, which allows the ESRB to receive aggregate and disaggregated data from the ESAs, the European System of Central Banks (ESCB), the European Commission, and NSAs, and for them to receive necessary information on relevant risks from the ESRB. Unlike the ESAs, ESRB's access to data on an individual systemic institution is limited and usually requires justification. This restriction may hamper systemic risk analysis, which often needs to be based on real-time supervisory data.

Main Outputs of the ESRB

When significant risks to the EU financial system are identified, the policy instruments available to the ESRB to avert or mitigate them are *warnings* or *recommendations* (which could be confidential or made public) issued to the EU, EU member states, the European Commission, the ESAs, or the NSAs. The implementation of these warnings and recommendations is essential for the credibility and the policy relevance of the ESRB.

Risk Warnings

The ESRB delivered confidential messages to governments during 2011, in response to the deterioration of market conditions. The ESRB Chair, Jean-Claude Trichet, made public reference to concerns addressed in his communication to governments, without revealing their format, frequency, and contents. Press releases published after the General Board meetings, however, regularly hinted at the substance of the ESRB assessment and contained substantial warning elements. The launch of Long-Term Refinancing Operations in late 2011 and early 2012, the announcement of steps to establish an SSM at the ECB in June 2012, and an Outright Monetary Transactions program in September of the same year contributed to reducing tail risks of exit from the euro area and associated redenomination risks. The ESRB did not issue statements referring to risks in relation to the banking union, but positions were taken publicly by the Advisory Scientific Committee of the ESRB (ASC) in reports (July 2012 report on "forbearance, resolution and deposit insurance" and September 2012 report on the EC proposal for a banking union).

Recommendations by the Board of the ESRB

The ESRB has publicly issued six recommendations:

- *Recommendation on lending in foreign currencies (issued September 2011; published November 2011; deadlines June and December 2012 and December 2013).* The recommendation focused on improving the resilience of national financial systems to currency risks, reducing asymmetric information between borrowers and lenders, and taking policy actions to contain foreign currency lending in a countercyclical manner and improve incentives and risk pricing, including through supervisory actions.

- *Recommendation on U.S. dollar denominated funding of credit institutions (issued December 2011; published January 2012; deadline June 2012).* Noting that a number of EU credit institutions have significant U.S. dollar funding needs and maturity mismatches, creating strains in the financial system, the ESRB recommended that steps be taken to mitigate risks of tensions in U.S. dollar funding, and improve monitoring and data collection.[2]

- *Recommendation on the macroprudential mandate of national authorities (issued December 2011; published January 2012; deadline June 2013).* The ESRB noted that the effectiveness of EU macroprudential oversight also necessitates national macroprudential frameworks to be in place to ensure effective follow-up on ESRB warnings and recommendations. The text provided guiding principles for core elements, including requiring clear objectives, tasks, and powers to overcome bias toward inaction, and recommended giving a leading role to central banks.[3]

- *Recommendation on funding of credit institutions (issued December 2012; published February 2013; specific timeline between December 2013 and December 2016).* This recommendation addresses the issue of asset encumbrance with a comprehensive approach, based on enhancement of institutions' risk management and supervisory monitoring. The ESRB is still deliberating on a proposal for market transparency of asset encumbrance.

---

[2] A nonpublic recommendation on U.S. dollar funding was also issued.
[3] The Selected Issues Paper to the IMF 2011 euro area Article IV consultation developed a similar argument on the importance of having effective macroprudential frameworks in place at the national level (Nier and Tressel, 2011).

The recommendation also touches upon funding risks and feasibility, on an aggregated basis, of funding plans in the near future, and on the identification of best practices for covered bonds.

- *Recommendation on money market funds (issued December 2012; published February 2013; deadline June 2014).* In light of the upcoming European Commission review of the Undertakings for Collective Investment in Transferable Securities framework, the ESRB recommends that money market funds move from the constant to the variable net asset value model. Moreover, explicit liquidity requirements, as well as enhanced public disclosure and reporting by money market funds, should be introduced. Finally, better information sharing between authorities on money market funds is recommended.

- *Recommendation on intermediate objectives and instruments of macroprudential policy (issued April 2013; published June 2013; deadlines December* 2014 *and December 2015).* The ESRB specified the intermediate policy objectives, proposed an indicative list of macroprudential instruments to achieve these objectives, and made recommendations on policy strategy for national macroprudential authorities, and periodic evaluations of intermediate objectives and instruments. The ESRB recommended that countries set up appropriate legal frameworks that permit macroprudential authorities to hold direct control or recommendation powers over the macroprudential instruments.[4] It also recommended that macroprudential authorities be involved in the resolution of financial institutions, more specifically, in the design and national implementation of (1) recovery and resolution regimes for banking and nonbanking financial institutions and (2) deposit guarantee schemes. Last, it recommended that the European Commission ensure, in its legislation, efficient interaction among member states and sufficient flexibility for the activation of macroprudential instruments.

Other Activities of the ESRB

ESRB risk dashboard (first publication, September 2012).

- As requested by the regulation establishing the ESRB, a risk dashboard has been produced and a set of quantitative and qualitative indicators published on the ESRB website. The set of indicators is one of the inputs for the Board's discussions on risks and vulnerabilities. The dashboard will be updated and revised on a quarterly basis.

ASC reports and other publications and advice on regulatory reforms.

- Various reports have been published on the ESRB website, including ASC reports on the European Commission proposal for a banking union (September 2012); and on forbearance, resolution, and deposit insurance (July 2012). Other publications include an occasional paper on money

---

[4] www.esrb.europa.eu/news/pr/2012/html/pr120116_1.en.html.

market funds in Europe and financial stability (June 2012); commentaries on the ESRB institutional setup (February 2012); on the macroprudential mandate of national authorities (March 2012); on systemic risk resulting from "retailization" (July 2012); and on lending in foreign currencies (December 2012); a letter from the Chair to EU legislators on macroprudential tools in the CRR/CRD IV (April 2012); and two advisory notes to the European Securities and Markets Authority in the context of the European Market Infrastructure Regulation on eligible collateral for central counterparties and the use of over-the-counter derivatives by nonfinancial corporations.[5]

Were the Various Instruments of the ESRB Effective and the Framework Credible?

Criteria. Assessing the effectiveness of the ESRB framework and instruments is a complex task, given that no established international best practices are available for assessing macroprudential authorities. Moreover, it is important to keep in mind that the supranational dimension of the ESRB is, by its nature, a political constraint that national macroprudential bodies would not have to deal with. Against this background, several indicators can provide a useful gauge of the effectiveness of the ESRB instrument and framework:

- Prioritization and quality of risk warnings and recommendations;
- Policy relevance, including through the publication of risk warnings;
- Publication and implementation of recommendations by addressees; and
- Capacity to communicate its analysis of systemic risks.

Risk warnings and recommendations of the ESRB were relevant and adequately prioritized. The ESRB's risk warnings appeared to be timely given that they were issued when the crisis became systemic for the EU financial system. They correctly identified the emerging systemic risks and called for policy implementation, readiness to take action, and the need for coordinated supervisory actions, including recourse to backstop facilities. Policy recommendations also correctly identified medium-term risks to the EU financial system and called for adequate policies to mitigate these risks. In retrospect, the recommendation on U.S. dollar funding of EU financial institutions also appeared to pinpoint a key vulnerability that contributed to the seizure of wholesale funding markets at the end of 2011.

The ESRB managed to partly communicate its warnings publicly, although it is not clear how influential or timely they were. The press release of the September 21, 2011, ESRB Board meeting explicitly referenced this warning, for example, the systemic nature of the crisis, the need for coordinated supervisory action, and suggested recourse to "the possibility for the European Financial

---

[5] Policy advice on the CRR/CRD IV was provided in three stages: two nonpublic letters to EU institutions in 2011 and a public letter in March 2012. Policy advice to the European Securities and Markets Authority on the European Market Infrastructure Regulation was published in August 2012.

Stability Facility to lend to governments in order to recapitalize banks, including in non-program countries." It is, however, difficult to assess the extent to which these public statements (let alone the private warnings) were influential. At the time that the European Banking Authority recapitalization exercise was being debated and concerns about disorderly deleveraging were being raised, the ESRB took a public position, but only at a late stage, through the introductory statement of Sir Mervyn King at the press conference of the General Board meeting of December 22, 2011. At that time, the parameters of the recapitalization exercise had been decided on and it was already clear that there would not be any common guarantee schemes and backstops established at the EU level, and the deleveraging of EU banks was already proceeding in an uncoordinated fashion.

Implementation of ESRB recommendations has been satisfying so far. All six recommendations were published within two months of their issuance, demonstrating broad consensus among member states on the importance and relevance of these policy recommendations. So far, implementation of the first five recommendations has been satisfactory:

- On foreign exchange lending, all EU member states, Norway, and Iceland have responded on the self-assessment part, but some member states with fixed exchange rate regimes pointed out that measures should be applied only with respect to lending in foreign currencies other than their reserve currency.

- On U.S. dollar funding, implementation has also been very good, while further follow-up may be needed in some specific areas.[6] The recommendation has also helped raise important issues requiring further consideration. Implementation of the nonpublic part has been linked to adoption of the CRR/CRD IV legislative proposals.

- The recommendation on national macroprudential mandates received extremely high responsiveness (all EU countries, plus Norway), highlighting the positive reception of the ESRB recommendations. The high level of compliance in the first follow-up phase is a positive signal for the role of the ESRB in coordinating future uses of macroprudential tools at the EU level.

The ESRB should further develop its capacity to communicate its systemic risk analysis. Publication of the risk dashboard is an initial step in setting up a regular analytical tool to analyze systemic risks. This tool is complemented by surveillance notes produced by the ECB. However, as noted in the ESRB regulation, publication of the risk dashboard should be associated with publication of an analysis of systemic risks. This coordinated publication would help enhance the capacity of the ESRB to communicate its systemic risk analysis and warnings.

The effectiveness of the ESRB framework may need to be strengthened. Future effectiveness of the ESRB hinges on its "will to act," the enforceability of its recommendations, and the policy impact of its warnings. Its capacity to act will depend on a decision-making process that will need to be flexible enough to facilitate timely

---

[6] Some member states referred to a proportionality rule as a reason not to implement the recommendation.

decisions on the communication of emerging risks and policy recommendations. To promote a "bottom-up" approach to risk identification, the ESRB staff could propose the work program and systemic risk analysis to the Steering Committee, while the Advisory Technical Committee could play a more technical role. The ESRB was designed to operate without legally binding powers; the key is to assess whether this constraint could impede its future effectiveness. With respect to recommendations, the "act or explain" mechanism seems to have operated relatively well so far, but follow-up on risk warnings has been less evident. Another area that may require attention is the frequency of the General Board meetings. As experienced in 2011, quarterly may not be adequate to ensure timely communication of risk warnings in the midst of a financial crisis. It could be useful to consider a simplified, more focused, decision-making structure in an emergency situation.

Should the ESRB Play a Role in Crisis Management?

Although it was established during a systemic crisis, the ESRB has produced outputs broadly balanced between medium-term and short-term risks. Although recommendations were more focused on medium-term risks, two timely risk warnings were issued, and various publications and communications were highly relevant in the context of the ongoing financial crisis. The ESRB Board did not take explicit positions or issue risk warnings in relation to the proposal for a banking union, partly limited by its mandate.[7] The ESRB is supportive of the banking union, as clarified, for instance, in the ASC report on the European Commission proposal, but discussions seem to have demonstrated a diversity of opinions among member institutions. This example demonstrates that the constraints of the ESRB framework may become binding on policy issues that are highly political and on which Board members hold diverse views.

The ESRB has a clear mandate to issue risk warnings during systemic crises, but it is excluded from playing a role in crisis management. Although the ESRB should play a role in the use of macroprudential tools across EU countries (more on this below), the application of macroprudential tools is likely to remain asymmetric, and tools for systemic crisis management (including exceptional liquidity provision) will remain in the hands of central banks and other institutions. However, the ESRB should bring a macroprudential perspective to stress tests, in collaboration with the ECB and the European Banking Authority, including when they are used for crisis management purposes.

MACROPRUDENTIAL TOOLKIT FOR EU COUNTRIES

The macroprudential toolkit should include a carefully selected set of instruments that would be sufficient to address the most foreseeable sources of systemic risks. Macroprudential risks are multidimensional and arise through various institutions,

---

[7] The ESRB's role in influencing legislation is limited once negotiations between the legislative bodies and the EU have started.

> ## Box 20.1 Lessons from Macroprudential Policies in Emerging Europe
>
> During the past decade, many countries in central and eastern Europe relied on a rich set of macroprudential instruments to respond to capital inflows and credit booms (Ötker-Robe and others, 2007). Credit and housing booms across the region were commonly fueled by foreign-exchange-denominated or indexed loans. Instruments included reserve or liquidity requirements, capital requirements, loan classification and provisioning rules, as well as specific measures to limit foreign currency lending or restrict credit eligibility. When policymakers took action, they did so through different instruments, at different times, and with different levels of intensity. Many of the governments joining the EU in 2004 preferred to strengthen supervisory and monitoring measures and limited their use of administrative and prudential measures. In some cases, policies were tightened at a late stage, while in others, policies were relaxed during the expansion. There are cases in which prudential requirements were set very high; for example, reserve requirements on short-term and foreign currency deposits reached, at their peak, 30 percent in Romania and 45 percent in Serbia.
>
> Studies typically found modest impacts of macroprudential measures on overall credit growth and temporary effects on capital flows (Kraft and Galac, 2011; Vandenbussche, Vogel, and Detragiache, 2012; Bakker and Klingen, 2012). A reason for the limited effectiveness in limiting credit booms is that some of the prudential measures were circumvented through cross-border lending or lending by nonbanks. In a number of cases, subsidiaries in emerging Europe simply booked some loans with the parent institution or a nonbank subsidiary (leasing company) instead of with the local banking affiliate to avoid restrictions on lending imposed by host country authorities. Some studies found that domestic credit growth was significantly affected by macroprudential measures; others also find a dampening effect on house price appreciation. Measures taken during the upturn, however, helped build buffers that became valuable during the downturn.

markets, and sectors. One instrument may address more than one dimension of systemic risk, but there are uncertainties about the effectiveness of instruments. An effective toolkit should be able to mitigate amplification channels for systemic risks. It should have built-in flexibility to address the changing nature of systemic risks. Some instruments would have a broad range of action whereas others may be more focused on specific markets or sectors. Some instruments may be more effective at constraining the buildup of systemic risks or at mitigating the impact of shocks, whereas others may be more efficient and create fewer distortions. It is also important to select instruments that provide the ability to determine the appropriate timing for their activation or deactivation. Some instruments may have a broad scope, affecting both the time dimension and cross-sectional dimension of systemic risk, while other instruments (perhaps of a more structural nature) would be more appropriate for addressing the only cross-sectional dimension or only the time dimension. Given the size, interconnectedness, and complexity of European global systemically important banks, ensuring a specific focus on structural elements of the toolkit has merit. Last, instruments should duly consider the diversity of countries and circumstances within the EU. For example, the experience of emerging European countries may have been more similar to that of other emerging markets than to the experience of advanced EU countries (Box 20.1).

The Basel III countercyclical capital buffer (CCB; the only macroprudential instrument adopted by the Basel Committee on Banking Supervision) is a necessary but not sufficient element of the toolbox; it should be complemented by more targeted instruments to address the cross-sectional and time dimensions of systemic risks (Box 20.2).

- *Although broad in scope, the CCB has limitations.* There will be long lags (up to a year) between the announcement of capital add-ons by supervisors and implementation by banks, although under the draft capital requirement directive (CRD), a shorter lag may be possible under extraordinary circumstances. During downturns, the decision to release the buffer by the *macroprudential* supervisor may be inconsistent with the *microprudential principle* under which banks should not deplete capital when nonperforming assets are building up. The CCB may be a blunt tool: the buildup of imbalances concentrated in particular sectors could lead to a crisis well before the buffer is triggered by aggregate developments.[8]

- *Limits on loan-to-value ratios (LTV) and debt-to-income ratios (DTI) are examples of the possible instruments that could usefully complement the CCB.* Contingent upper bounds on LTV, potentially complemented by an upper limit on the DTI to ensure ability to repay, would be useful instruments to complement the CCB, and can be adapted to specific real estate developments. Implementation could be challenging because of the risks of regulatory arbitrage and political economy considerations, but evidence from emerging markets suggests these ratios may be effective instruments for mitigating house price appreciation, at least temporarily. Empirical evidence from euro area countries' lending standards tends to confirm the same view. The benefits of ratios may differ across countries, according to the characteristics of their mortgage markets (including, for example, whether mortgages are full recourse). Relaxing the LTV limit in a downturn may also create conflicts between the macroprudential and the microprudential perspectives.[9]

A set of principles should be adopted to ensure the willingness to act and trigger the use of macroprudential instruments during upswings. The ability to identify and measure systemic risks and vulnerabilities is a key factor for successful implementation of macroprudential tools, and there must be clear criteria for activation (BIS, 2012). The decision to trigger activation is likely to be complex because there is no easy measurement of systemic risk as a result of its multidimensional nature. Assessing success is also difficult because the counterfactual may not be known. Costs of mistimed activation could be asymmetric—delayed action may be more costly than too-early intervention. Delayed

---

[8] The impact on credit supply will depend on the speed at which the buffer is built up. A fast buildup will presumably be more effective in constraining credit supply, in particular if banks have to resort to costly issuance of equity.

[9] See also evidence reported in Lim and others (2011).

Box 20.2 Effectiveness of Macroprudential Instruments in Advanced EU Countries and Lessons from Euro Area Bank Lending Standards

Most advanced economies have no or little experience with macroprudential policies; as a result, there is little empirical evidence of the effectiveness of macroprudential instruments in mitigating systemic risk in these economies. Model simulations of the impact of Basel III instruments, such as the countercyclical capital buffer, imply, however, that the impact on credit growth or house prices would most likely be modest. For example, according to results reported in the Macroeconomic Assessment Group's interim report of August 2010, the long-term impact on credit of a 2.5 percent increase in capital requirements phased in over two years is estimated to be between 2 and 9 percent (Table 20.2.1). Although non-negligible, these effects remain modest in comparison to the amplitude of recent housing booms in the euro area (Table 20.2.2).[1]

TABLE 20.2.1

Impact of a 2.5 Percent Increase in Capital Requirement on Credit (in percent) Phased in Over Two Years		
Horizon	4.5 Years	8 Years
Median	−3.5	−4.8
Minimum	−1.8	−2.0
Maximum	−9.0	−9.0

Source: MAG Interim Report August 2010; based on "satellite model."

TABLE 20.2.2

Euro Area Housing Booms (in percent, Cumulative 2000–07)		
	Spain	Ireland[1]
House price appreciation	140	104
Household mortgage credit growth	158	145

Source: Authors' calculations.
[1] End 2006.

Although macroprudential instruments have rarely been used in the Economic and Monetary Union, banks in the euro area typically rely on nonprice measures to contain credit supply or to screen borrowers. The ECB Bank Lending Survey provides very useful information on price and nonprice measures used to tighten credit supply and on the contribution of various factors affecting the supply of credit. Among the former, the Bank Lending Survey reports the net proportion of banks that reported a net tightening of the loan-to-value ratio (LTV). Among the latter, the survey also provides the net proportion of banks reporting that the cost of capital contributed to the tightening (or loosening) of lending standards. Such indicators provide, indirectly, very useful information that would help gauge the potential impact that macroprudential measures could have on credit growth and house price appreciation in the euro area.

An econometric analysis using panel data suggests that limits on LTVs would have an economically significant impact on credit growth and house prices in Economic and Monetary Union countries (Tressel and Zhang, forthcoming). A panel data analysis was performed to assess the impact of net changes in LTVs on credit growth and house price appreciation. An instrumental variables approach was designed and appropriate control variables were included to correct for the endogeneity of lending standards. The analysis suggests that the impact of net changes in LTVs on credit growth or house prices would be very large, and significantly larger than the impact of price margins. As an illustration, a figure reports that the estimated net tightening of lending standards would reduce

---

[1] Spain relied on dynamic provisioning as a measure to build capital buffers, but the measures were weakened after 2004.

Box 20.2 Effectiveness of Macroprudential Instruments in Advanced EU Countries and Lessons from Euro Area Bank Lending Standards (*Concluded*)

mortgage credit growth or house price appreciation by 10 percentage points. The analysis implies that the required net tightening of LTV to reduce mortgage credit growth and house price appreciation would be 8 percent and 25 percent, respectively. As a benchmark, the net tightening of lending standards in the euro area in the year following the collapse of Lehman Brothers was a net 117 percent.

While quantitative conclusions from survey responses should be arrived at cautiously, the comparison with the post-Lehman period does suggest that changes in limits on LTVs may have relatively strong effects on mortgage credit and house prices (Figure 20.2.1).

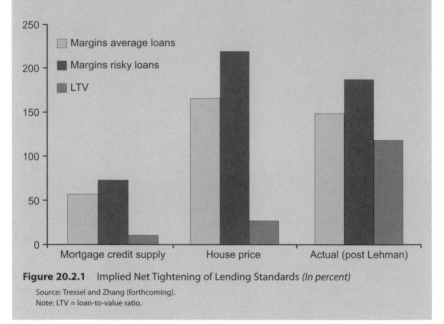

Figure 20.2.1   Implied Net Tightening of Lending Standards *(In percent)*

Source: Tressel and Zhang (forthcoming).
Note: LTV = loan-to-value ratio.

activation might suggest that the instruments are not as effective as believed because there may not be enough time for the instruments to have an impact, but too early activation may lead to unnecessary side effects. Having rules in place is important to reduce uncertainty and to anchor expectations, but, given the limited experience with macroprudential policies, a large element of discretion and judgment is likely to be necessary to determine the timing and extent of tightening (Borio, 2009).

Finding a set of early warning indicators to trigger the use and release of instruments is key to the successful implementation of macroprudential policies. The indictors could include (1) the credit-to-GDP ratio or its deviation from a trend level (the gap measures), at an aggregated or a sectoral level; (2) indicators of market volatility (e.g., credit default swap spreads) or other price-based measures of default or distress; and (3) indicators measuring bank vulnerability and potential funding stress, such as noncore bank liabilities. Sectoral measures (such as measures of household or corporate indebtedness) would more easily identify the buildup of sectoral vulnerabilities that may not be well captured by the private-credit-to-GDP ratio. The rules-based triggers should be transparent, thus preventing surprises to markets. They would help constrain the incentives for risk taking, and prevent forbearance. The triggers based on market prices need to be carefully designed to minimize the risk of touching off a downward spiral, which could undermine financial stability.[10]

The set of EU principles for macroprudential policies should provide guidance on their interaction with monetary policy. On one hand, conventional monetary policy instruments are not well suited to mitigating systemic risks, and on the other hand, maintaining price stability may not always coincide with the financial stability objective. The experience of the recent crisis has demonstrated that relaxed monetary policy can, however, help fuel the upturn of the credit and asset price cycle, including by affecting risk-taking behaviors. It also plays a role in financial downturns by supplying liquidity to financial intermediaries and markets. In the EU, several key considerations should be taken into account to ensure that monetary policy tools and macroprudential instruments enhance rather than reduce the effectiveness of each policy.[11]

- *Interactions between monetary and macroprudential policies.* The two policies share several transmission channels, including bank lending channels, and therefore will interact—and perhaps conflict—with each other even if they have, in theory, different objectives. Monetary policy may have to respond to the buildup of systemic risks, especially when macroprudential instruments are constrained. In a downturn, monetary policy decisions (including unconventional ones) may have to internalize financial stability considerations. Uncertainty about the effectiveness and side effects of specific macroprudential instruments adds a motivation to consider possible complementarities and synergies between these instruments and instruments of monetary policy.

- *Principles guiding the use of macroprudential instruments in a monetary union.* Where monetary policy is constrained, such as in the euro area, macroprudential instruments become relatively more important policy instruments, particularly if financial cycles are not synchronized across countries and if price stability is more likely to conflict with financial stability. Although macroprudential policies should not substitute for macroeconomic policies, they should be well placed, in the absence of alternative policy instruments, to play a prominent role in helping mitigate the

---

[10] See also IMF (2011).
[11] General considerations are discussed in IMF (2013).

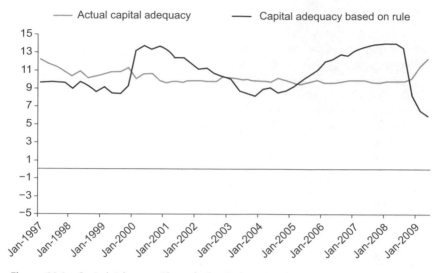

Figure 20.2 Capital Adequacy Through the Cycle in Sweden *(In percent of risk-weighted assets)*

Source: Ingves, 2011.

buildup of systemic risks when monetary policy cannot be relied upon to "lean against the wind" and when fiscal policies are constrained and cannot be relied upon to react in real time to asset price developments. In the euro area, macroprudential instruments could play an even more important role given the lack of a fiscal union that could provide transfers to help cushion the impact of a crisis and smooth the necessary rebalancing at the national level.

The macroprudential toolkit should also be complemented by guidance on macroprudential actions that would be needed to mitigate adverse effects during an economic downturn. Many instruments are conceptually more suited for the upturn than for the downturn. In a downturn, a fundamental tension arises between microprudential and macroprudential objectives, and market pressures may prevent policymakers from being able to release capital buffers or relax limits on other macroprudential tools (Figure 20.2).[12] While liquidity provision by the central bank and unconventional measures may be essential tools for stabilizing markets during systemic crises, there may also be merit in considering the potential role of structural or cyclical macroprudential instruments in correcting fire sale externalities and dampening other contagion effects.

---

[12] During a crisis, market pressures may become the binding constraint. See, for example, the discussion at the Bank of England Financial Policy Committee at the time of the wholesale funding market pressures in September 2011: http://www.bankofengland.co.uk/financialstability/Pages/fpc/meetings/default.aspx.

Proposal for the Minimum Set of Macroprudential Instruments

The minimum set of instruments, in addition to the CCB and limits on LTV and DTI that all EU countries should have in place, could be enriched by an additional set of indicative instruments that would play a complementary role. Among others, such instruments could include the following:

- *Time-varying exposures to specific sectors.* Time and sectoral contingent risk weights would usefully complement the CCB for two reasons. First, they would target more specifically the sectors in which systemic risk is developing, thus allowing a cross-sectoral differentiation of risks. Second, because of their targeted nature, they could more effectively tame financial imbalances without adversely affecting the supply of credit to other segments of the economy. Examples of such measures include contingent risk weights on interbank lending and lending to sovereigns, corporates, or households.[13]

- *Funding of financial intermediaries.* Balance sheet expansions during the boom leading up to the global financial crisis were financed by relying on wholesale funding, often of a short-term nature. A possible instrument complementing the two quantitative liquidity constraints of Basel III would aim at limiting the use of noncore funding instruments and could help address both the time dimension and the cross-sectional dimension of systemic risk.

- *Collateralized lending markets.* A possible instrument would be contingent margins or valuation haircuts on existing securities used as collateral in the securitized lending markets (such as for repos). This instrument would be used to regulate the supply of secured funding, which would help reduce the risk of fire sales. It would also counteract the shadow banking system's contribution to procyclicality by affecting the system's funding conditions in wholesale markets. Ideally, strong margining should be extended to OTC markets to provide an incentive for the move to central clearing of derivatives.

EFFECTIVE MACROPRUDENTIAL OVERSIGHT FOR THE EU

Because EU financial systems are integrated, a supranational approach to macroprudential oversight is necessary. Decisions to act on macroprudential risks must have an EU dimension to overcome cross-country externalities, leakages, and ring-fencing tendencies and minimize the risks of regulatory capture at the

---

[13] Optimal risk weights may differ from a microprudential perspective as compared with a macroprudential one. For example, collateralized short-term assets (such as reverse repo transactions) may appear safe from a microprudential perspective, and therefore attract low capital requirements. But they could be systemically important because a decision not to roll over the transaction may trigger fire sales of assets by the counterparty, which may amplify a financial crisis (Morris and Shin, 2008).

national level. Strong coordination of policy actions at the EU level is needed to avoid regulatory arbitrage by financial institutions that are located outside of the country setting macroprudential policies. The establishment of the SSM, which gives the ECB macroprudential powers, will require designing systems for coordination between the ECB and the ESRB.

Role of the ESRB

The ESRB has a role to play in ensuring effective macroprudential oversight for the EU financial system as a whole, in close cooperation with the ECB. The ESRB should continue providing guidance on the macroprudential policy framework (including mandate, institutional arrangement, and instruments) to ensure that macroprudential policy is operational in all member states. Notwithstanding resource constraints, the ESRB may also play a role in the calibration of individual macroprudential instruments across all EU countries, while collaborating closely with the ECB for SSM countries. The calibration should ensure the identified risk is adequately addressed, and allow for flexibility at the national level while also ensuring convergence of practices across countries. In particular, the instrument should be calibrated in a way that mitigates risks effectively—without imposing undue costs on the financial sector—and all national macroprudential authorities should be encouraged to adopt similar quantitative responses to systemic risks.

The ESRB should play a forceful role in cross-border coordination, particularly in ensuring reciprocity across EU countries and in harmonization of national macroprudential frameworks. National authorities may not have jurisdiction over all lending within their territories, including by foreign bank branches. To avoid regulatory arbitrage and negative spillover effects, and to ensure the effectiveness of macroprudential action across the highly interconnected EU financial systems, a mechanism is needed whereby home country authorities reciprocate the macroprudential measures put in place by host countries, based on the exposures of the consolidated national financial institutions to the asset class of the host country under consideration.[14] Ensuring policy effectiveness is particularly relevant for emerging economies with high degrees of cross-border banking activities and direct cross-border lending. Thus, the use of macroprudential instruments over a particular activity could be referred by national authorities to the ESRB for approval so that all EU banks, regardless of origin, are covered. Even though reciprocity is not required by the legislation, the ESRB should, if it is satisfied that the macroprudential action taken by the host authority is justified, issue a recommendation to other macroprudential authorities to reciprocate the measures taken by the host authority, when home and host countries are not part of the SSM (see below). The ESRB has already announced its intention to establish coordination procedures when appropriate.

---

[14] For example, an asset class would be defined as sovereign bonds of country A or mortgages on properties of country B.

The ESRB could validate the decisions of member states to set or modify macroprudential instruments when these decisions interact with EU standards. For example, under CRR/CRD IV,[15] member states will have the flexibility to vary risk weights and sectoral buffers at the national level for macroprudential purposes. A potential solution to prevent arbitrage, leakages, and negative externalities may be for the use of risk weights to be based on asset classes that could apply to all financial institutions irrespective of their location.

Interaction with Other EU Bodies and the SSM

The ESRB will need to continue to work closely with the ESAs. Continued interaction between the ESRB and the ESAs will be important to ensure a proper meshing of macroprudential and microprudential instruments and risk assessments. Strong cooperation is needed also in the exchange of data and information. As noted in the European Financial Stability Framework Exercise report, the current regulations stipulate that requests for detailed data from the ESAs will have to be ad hoc and motivated, and the ESRB (or the European Banking Authority) has no direct access to data. This constraint may continue to hamper the effectiveness of the ESRB.

The ESRB depends on the ECB for analytical, statistical, logistical, and administrative support. Close collaboration between the two institutions may remain important in the future. Because the ESRB is an EU institution covering non–euro area countries and nonbanks, there may be a future need to strengthen its analytical resources, independently of the analytical contribution of the ECB. The creation of the SSM may further require that the ESRB develop its own resources and acquire some measure of independent analytical capacity.

The ESRB will need to continue work closely with the European Commission. In particular, the ESRB needs to issue a warning when the commission's legislative action unduly constrains macroprudential policy action. In addition, the ESRB should recommend that the commission take positive legislative action to ensure that common macroprudential toolkits are available to policymakers across the EU, potentially beyond the instruments included in the CRR/CRD IV.

The creation of a banking union covering at least the euro area countries will likely have a profound impact on the ESRB:

- *The ECB will appropriately have macroprudential power over banks under the SSM.* The Draft Council Regulation (2012/0242) concerning the establishment of the SSM assigns to the ECB macroprudential powers over banks under the SSM. However, the ECB will not have macroprudential powers over other financial institutions. The ECB's macroprudential powers will facilitate early identification and action on systemic risks, and enhance

---

[15] After Parliament's vote, the council needs to formally approve the rules. The Regulation and the Directive will then be published in the Official Journal (OJ) and enter into force. The new rules will apply beginning January 1, 2014, if published in the OJ by June 30, 2013; otherwise, they will apply beginning July 1, 2014.

information sharing, home-host coordination, and internalization of cross-border externalities within the SSM. The ECB is appropriately given binding powers to be able to use macroprudential instruments that are in the CRR/CRD IV if deemed necessary, but its toolkit should include macroprudential instruments that are not included in the CRD IV (such as limits on DTI and LTV) when a common macroprudential framework for the SSM countries is in place. The established independence and financial stability expertise of the ECB would help build a strong institutional framework among SSM countries and provide capacity to implement macroprudential instruments against national political pressure while taking into account interactions with monetary policy. However, the ECB could be subject to political pressures and disagreements with national authorities, which would add rigidities to the system, but the ECB should be able to have a final say and be able to act if needed.

- *Interaction between national authorities and the ECB within the SSM.* National authorities will be allowed to retain macroprudential powers under the SSM—providing flexibility to tailor solutions to local conditions—but in close cooperation with the ECB. Either party that takes such a step needs to inform and consult with the other party ahead of time, using methods described in the European Council draft regulation for the SSM. In practice, cooperation will be critical to ensuring the flexibility to manage macrofinancial developments in particular countries or asset markets, and the coherence and effectiveness of measures. Mechanisms would also need to be in place to ensure effective decision making and willingness to act. However, accountability lines between the ECB and national authorities will need to be clarified to prevent accountability gaps from arising. Mechanisms to resolve conflicts of interest between national authorities and the ECB and to overcome inaction bias must also be designed. Governance mechanisms must also protect the independence of the ECB.

- *The role of the ESRB will be complemented and enhanced by the SSM.* The methods for coordination between the ECB and the ESRB in the area of macroprudential policies will need to be clearly spelled out. Although some overlap is inevitable between the tasks of the ESRB and of the ECB in the area of banking and coverage of euro area countries, this overlap should be seen as reinforcing the macroprudential oversight of the EU financial system. The ESRB will continue to coordinate macroprudential oversight between countries participating in the SSM and those remaining outside. Furthermore, the ESRB could continue to be tasked with the development of the macroprudential toolkit as outlined previously. Ensuring macroprudential oversight at the EU level will also remain important for nonbanks and markets, which will not be covered by the SSM. The ECB should coordinate closely with the ESRB, and implement warnings and recommendations issued by the ESRB in close cooperation with national authorities.

RECOMMENDATION AND CONCLUSION

The macroprudential policy toolkit should be applicable not only to the upturns but also to the downturns of economic cycles. During the upturns, instruments need to prevent the buildup of aggregate or correlated risks over time, such as aggregate or sectoral credit imbalances; during the downturns, instruments need to mitigate the amplification and contagion effects arising from interconnectedness and the procyclicality of financial markets, most importantly, to prevent fire sales of bank assets.

Within the banking union, the ECB should have macroprudential powers, because strong monetary policy and macroprudential policy frameworks can be mutually reinforcing, and the ECB is well placed to have an integrated approach to systemic risk identification. One key challenge for macroprudential supervision is to design and calibrate macroprudential instruments and implement them against political interference. The established independence of the ECB would help build up a strong institutional framework for macroprudential policy, but accountability and governance mechanisms must be in place to limit conflicts of interest and protect the ECB's monetary policy objective. For this reason, the ECB should be responsible for a wider range of macroprudential instruments, going beyond those included in the CRR/CRD IV, as envisaged under the European Commission proposal for SSM.

The ESRB should remain responsible for macroprudential oversight at the EU level and must have a clear mandate and legal powers to be effective. Cross-border externalities and EU-wide financial stability concerns provide the rationale for a supranational macroprudential supervisor at the EU level—these concerns cannot be effectively addressed without a coordination mechanism. The ESRB is also the EU body responsible for the macroprudential oversight of nonbanks. The establishment of the ESRB in January 2011 was a crucial step in providing greater traction for macroprudential oversight at the EU level. However, as for all EU institutions, its mandate and legal powers are limited and it has been subject to a set of institutional constraints—a complex decision-making process at the Board (with 27 member states and EU and euro area institutions being involved), no direct access to supervisory data, and no binding powers. Future consideration may be given to granting the ESRB binding powers and providing it with more resources independent of the ECB.

The coordinating role of the ESRB should be further enhanced through closer cooperation with the ESAs and the ECB as the single supervisor for the banking union. Continued interaction between the ESRB and the ESAs will be important to ensuring a proper meshing of macroprudential and microprudential instruments and risk assessments. The ESRB should interact with the ECB on macroprudential toolkits when the ECB takes on macroprudential responsibilities. In particular, the ECB should implement warnings and recommendations issued by the ESRB, or require national authorities to "act or explain" when the ESRB issues a warning directed to them. The ECB should continue to provide support to the ESRB.

The use of macroprudential instruments at the national level would need to be consistent with the overall objective of the internal market (more specifically, the free movement of services and capital) while protecting financial stability. This approach suggests that although the available set of instruments should be comprehensive enough to address multifaceted macroprudential concerns at a national level, efficient coordination would be needed to limit possible negative externalities or unintended effects on financial stability and the sustainability of the single market.

REFERENCES

Bakker, B., and C. Klingen, 2012, *How Emerging Europe Came Through the 2008/09 Crisis: An Account by the Staff of the IMF's European Department* (Washington: International Monetary Fund).

Bank for International Settlements (BIS), 2012, "Operationalising the Selection and Application of Macroprudential Instruments," CGFS Paper No. 48 (Basel: Committee on the Global Financial System, Bank for International Settlements).

Borio, C., 2009, "Implementing the Macroprudential Approach to Financial Regulation and Supervision," Banque de France, *Financial Stability Review 13, The Future of Financial Regulation*, September.

Ingves, Stefan, 2011, "Challenges for the Design and Conduct of Macroprudential Policies," BIS Paper No. 60 (Basel: Bank for International Settlements).

International Monetary Fund (IMF), 2011, "Toward Operationalizing Macroprudential Policies: When to Act?" Chapter 3 in *Global Financial Stability Report: Grappling with Crisis Legacies*. World Economic and Financial Surveys (Washington, September).

———, 2013, "The Interaction of Monetary and Macroprudential Policies," IMF Board Paper (Washington).

Kraft, E., and T. Galac, 2011, "Macroprudential Regulation of Credit Booms and Busts —The Case of Croatia," World Bank Policy Research Working Paper No. 5772 (Washington: World Bank).

Lim, C.H., F. Columba, A. Costa, P. Kongsamut, A. Otani, M. Saiyid, T. Wezel, and X. Wu, 2011, "Macroprudential Policy: What Instruments and How to Use Them?" IMF Working Paper 11/238 (Washington: International Monetary Fund).

Morris, Stephen, and Hyun Song Shin, 2008, "Financial Regulation in a System Context," Brookings Paper on Economic Activity, Vol. 39, No. 2 (Washington: The Brookings Institution), pages 229–74.

Nier, E., and T. Tressel, 2011, "The European Systemic Risk Board: Effectiveness of Macroprudential Oversight in Europe," in *Euro Area Policies: Selected Issues*, Country Report No. 11/186 (Washington: International Monetary Fund).

Ötker-Robe, Inci, Zbigniew Polanski, Barry Topf, and David Vávra, 2007, "Coping with Capital Inflows: Experiences of Selected European Countries," IMF Working Paper 07/190 (Washington: International Monetary Fund).

Tressel, T., and S. Zhang, forthcoming, "Macroprudential Policies in the Euro Area: Evidence from Lending Standards," IMF Working Paper (Washington: International Monetary Fund).

Vandenbussche, J., U. Vogel, and E. Detragiache, 2012, "Macroprudential Policies and Housing Prices—A New Database and Empirical Evidence for Central, Eastern, and Southeastern Europe," IMF Working Paper 12/303 (Washington: International Monetary Fund).

CHAPTER 21

Addressing Cross-Border Aspects of Securities Clearing and Settlement Systems in the European Union

FROUKELIEN WENDT

This chapter focuses on the effectiveness of the regulatory, supervisory, and over-sight frameworks for central counterparties (CCPs) and central securities depositories (CSDs) in the European Union (EU). CCPs and CSDs are essential in promoting and maintaining financial stability.[1] CCPs and CSDs can vastly improve the efficiency, transparency, and safety of financial systems but also concentrate systemic risk. If not properly managed, they can be sources of financial shocks, such as liquidity dislocations and credit losses, or a major channel through which shocks are transmitted across domestic and international financial markets. The systemic importance of CCPs will increase with the implementation of the Group of Twenty (G20) reforms comprising the mandatory clearing of all standardized over-the-counter (OTC) derivatives. Therefore, the appropriate regulation, supervision, and oversight of CCPs and CSDs are essential to reducing systemic risk.

Cooperation between authorities within and outside the EU is a critical component of the regulatory, supervisory, and oversight framework because it may reduce risks related to the cross-border nature of clearing and settlement within the EU. CCPs and CSDs are regulated, supervised, and overseen by their national authorities. Given the increased interconnectedness between countries, a lack of efficient and effective communication and consultation may result in various risks and inefficiencies, such as regulatory arbitrage and competition on risk management. Protection of national markets may result in an unlevel playing field between CCPs in various member states and between CSDs in various member states. This is risky and inefficient and impedes the creation of a single market for securities and derivatives clearing and settlement.

---

[1] The analysis is based on the concepts described in the relevant international standards, which are the Committee on Payment and Settlement Systems–International Organization of Securities Commissions' *Principles for Financial Market Infrastructures* (PFMI), published in April 2012 (http://www.bis.org/publ/cpss101a.pdf).

Crisis management arrangements between EU authorities are critically important so that authorities can adequately fulfill their various responsibilities in relation to CCPs and CSDs in crisis situations. Therefore, this chapter also analyzes the existing crisis management frameworks, taking into account the lessons learned during the recent defaults of, for example, Lehman Brothers and MF Global.

DESCRIPTION OF CCPS AND CSDS IN THE EU

Overview of Securities and Derivatives Clearing and Settlement

There are currently more than 20 CCPs in Europe, clearing a wide range of markets and products. Appendix 21A contains a description of the main CCPs. CCPs in the EU clear one or more asset classes, varying from financial and commodity derivatives to cash equities and bonds or repos. The instruments cleared can be traded on organized trading platforms as well as over the counter. In many cases, such as in France, Germany, and the United Kingdom, CCPs for securities have been developed from established CCPs for derivatives. Some CCPs are exchange owned, for example, in Germany and Italy, whereas others are independent (e.g., LCH.Clearnet Group) or combined with CSDs, as until recently in Eastern Europe. Some CCPs only service their domestic market, whereas other CCPs provide clearing services for a range of EU markets.

The EU hosts various OTC derivative CCPs. The largest global CCP for interest rate swaps is the London-based SwapClear. SwapClear was launched by LCH. Clearnet Limited in September 1999 and started clearing interest rate swaps in four major currencies. ICE Clear Europe, also based in London, has a global leading position in clearing credit default swaps. Following the agreement reached at the G20 Pittsburgh Summit stating that all standard OTC derivative contracts should be centrally cleared, other CCPs have developed or extended their OTC derivatives offering, for example, in France, Germany, and Sweden.

There are more than 30 CSDs in the EU. Appendix 21A contains a description of the main CSDs. Historically, CSDs have been separately developed for equity markets and for government bond markets. For the past 20 years, many central banks in the EU have shifted their CSD activity for government securities to the private sector, creating one CSD per country that handles all types of securities. Currently, some CSDs are exchange owned as in Germany, Italy, Poland, and Spain. Some CSDs are owned by the private sector, whereas some are owned by the public sector, as in Hungary. Some are listed companies or belong to listed companies, whereas others are user owned. Some CSDs service their domestic markets; others are cooperating across borders, either by the merger of national CSDs (Euroclear) or by optimizing link arrangements (Link Up Markets).

Two international central securities depositories (ICSDs) are located in the EU offering global settlement, custody, and collateral services. The ICSDs (Euroclear Bank and Clearstream Banking Luxembourg) were created in the 1970s to settle Eurobonds. Over the years, ICSDs have extended their scope to all types of internationally traded financial instruments, including equities and investment funds. Under their respective banking licenses, the ICSDs provide cash accounts and credit lines to their participants to facilitate settlement. The ICSDs compete with each other as well as with global custodians. Several global custodians are currently considering applying for CSD licenses to increase their services to include securities settlement in addition to their asset services. Bank of New York Mellon was the first to apply in early 2013.

The EU's focus on financial stability and the reduction of risk has increased since the global financial crisis, whereas more emphasis was placed on efficiency before the crisis. Beginning in 2006, changes in the EU legal and regulatory framework, such as the Markets in Financial Instruments Directive and the Code of Conduct for Clearing and Settlement, led to increased competition between cash-trading platforms and clearing and settlement institutions. The Markets in Financial Instruments Directive abolished concentration rules and encouraged the proliferation of alternative execution venues, primarily multilateral trading facilities. To serve the multilateral trading facilities, new CCPs entered the market, such as the European Multilateral Clearing Facility and EuroCCP.

Competition in the cash market led to significant cuts in trading and clearing fees and ultimately to an interoperability arrangement between four CCPs for the clearing of securities transactions at various trading platforms. Interoperability between the CCPs European Multilateral Clearing Facility, EuroCCP, LCH.Clearnet Limited, and SIX x-clear allows access to various trading platforms via one CCP. Positions are netted across trading platforms and clearing members no longer need to deposit collateral at more than one institution.

A recent trend is the reverticalization of infrastructure, where exchanges hold the CCP as a subsidiary rather than conduct business with a CCP as a separate company. In the United Kingdom, the derivatives exchange New York Stock Exchange–London International Financial Futures and Options Exchange (NYSE-Liffe) is developing its own CCP to provide the services that had been delivered by LCH.Clearnet. Similar decisions were made earlier by Intercontinental Exchange (ICE) Clear and the London Metal Exchange. The London Stock Exchange awaits the decision of the U.K. Office of Fair Trading to buy a majority stake in LCH.Clearnet.

Overview of the Regulatory, Supervisory, and Oversight Framework

The objectives of the EU are to ensure the smooth functioning of the internal market for CCP and CSD services by increasing safety, ensuring a high level of investor protection, creating a level playing field, and improving the efficiency of clearing and settlement in general.[2] In line with these objectives, the European Commission (EC) has drafted regulations covering CCPs and CSDs.

---

[2] As described in the introductory parts of the European Market Infrastructure Regulation and the draft CSD Regulation of March 2012.

The European Market Infrastructure Regulation (EMIR) provides for the regulatory and supervisory framework for CCPs. EMIR's text came into force on August 16, 2012. In September 2012, the European Securities and Markets Authority (ESMA) delivered its draft technical standards to the EC for endorsement. The technical standards came into force on March 15, 2013. EMIR is also the relevant EU legislation for trade repositories and OTC derivative markets because it provides the framework for implementing the G20's mandatory clearing agreement. EMIR includes (1) common rules for CCPs; (2) the introduction of a passport for CCP services; (3) a clearing obligation for eligible OTC derivatives with measures to reduce counterparty credit risk and operational risk for bilaterally cleared OTC derivatives; (4) a reporting obligation for derivatives to trade repositories; and (5) rules on the establishment of interoperability between CCPs clearing cash markets. EMIR allows third countries to provide clearing and trade repository services in the EU, provided the legal and supervisory regime in the third country provides for an effective equivalent system for the recognition of CCPs under foreign legal regimes.

It is the EC's intention that the draft CSD Regulation will provide the regulatory and supervisory framework for CSDs. In March 2012, a draft proposal for CSD regulation was passed to the European Parliament and the Council of the European Union for negotiation and adoption under the co-decision procedure. The proposal introduces common standards across the EU for securities settlement and CSDs as well as a passport regime. The regulation also aims to harmonize the differences between settlement practices in the EU and increase settlement efficiency.

Under the new EU regulations, the national authorities remain the competent authorities for CCPs and CSDs, with new roles for ESMA and the European System of Central Banks (ESCB). Table 21.1 outlines the responsibilities as envisaged under the new regulations. Each member state is to designate a competent authority that is responsible for the authorization and supervision of a CCP or CSD established in its territory.[3] ESMA's responsibilities increase under EMIR and the draft CSD Regulation. ESMA's new competences include the development of binding technical standards and a coordinating role among competent authorities and across CCP colleges. The increased role for the ESCB includes participation in the CCP colleges as overseer and central bank of issue. The ESCB is also involved in the drafting of technical standards, guidelines, and recommendations, with ESMA having the final responsibility.

Other relevant directives in relation to CCPs and CSDs in the EU are the Settlement Finality Directive (SFD) and the Financial Collateral Arrangements Directive. The SFD contains provisions to reduce the risk linked to the insolvency of a participant in financial market infrastructures (FMIs). The SFD has been adapted to include lessons from the 2008 financial crisis, including provisions to

---

[3] The members of the ESCB and other national or public bodies are exempted from the authorization and supervision requirements. Central banks are to immediately inform ESMA of any CSD that they operate.

TABLE 21.1

European Union: Supervision and Oversight under EMIR and the Draft CSD Regulation		
	Authorization, Supervision, and Regulation	Oversight
CCPs	A CCP is authorized by the competent authority of the member state in which the CCP is established, having obtained the opinion from the college for that CCP. Supervision is conducted by the competent authority of the member state in which the CCP is established, in cooperation with the college for that CCP, which includes ESMA in a nonvoting capacity. ESMA has authority to develop binding technical standards under EMIR, which have to be adopted by the EC.	Typically the national central bank in which the CCP is established, either as competent authority of the CCP or as member of the college. The central banks of issue of the most relevant EU currencies of the financial instruments cleared will also be members of the college.
CSDs/SSS (proposed CSD Regulation of July 3, 2012)	A CSD is authorized and supervised by the competent authority of the member state where it is established, in close cooperation with other relevant authorities, including relevant members of the ESCB. Before granting authorization, the competent authority has to consult with competent authorities of other member states if the CSD is a subsidiary of or belongs to the same group as a CSD authorized in another member state. ESMA has the authority to draft, in consultation with the members of the ESCB, binding technical standards under the CSD regulations, which have to be adopted by the EC.	Typically the national central bank of the state in which the CSD is established, either as competent authority of the CSD or as one of the relevant authorities that have to be consulted.

Sources: EMIR; draft CSD Regulation; and Eurosystem Oversight Annual Report 2011.
Note: CCP = central counterparty; CSD = central securities depository; EC = European Commission; EMIR = European Market
    Infrastructure Regulation; ESCB = European System of Central Banks; ESMA = European Securities and Markets
    Authority; EU = European Union; SSS = Securities Settlement System.

ensure consistency with regard to the moment of entry of a transfer order into a system and irrevocability for interconnected systems. The Financial Collateral Arrangements Directive contains provisions related to the enforceability of collateral arrangements to limit contagion effects in the event of default by a participant in the FMI.

Recent Reforms and Reforms Scheduled for the Near Future

TARGET2-Securities (T2S) is a project of the Eurosystem aiming to centralize settlement operations for central bank funds on a single pan-European platform, thereby further integrating the posttrade market in the EU. The T2S project was initiated in 2006 and is currently under development. Based on the latest announcements, it is scheduled to go live in 2015. T2S will be a single information technology (IT) platform for securities settlement in Europe, accommodating both the market participant's securities accounts, held at either one CSD or at multiple CSDs, and its central bank cash accounts in the TARGET2 payment system. The main objective is to reduce cross-border settlement fees, which are, on average, higher than domestic fees, through a single IT platform and standardized communication protocols. The IT platform will be built, owned, and operated by the ECB and the 17 national central banks in the euro area (Eurosystem). So far, 24 national CSDs have signed up to join T2S; however, the central banks in the Czech Republic, Sweden, and the United Kingdom have announced they will not participate.

Foreseen legislative initiatives of the EC related to CCPs and CSDs are the following:

- Securities Law Legislation, which aims to ensure that investors have full control over their securities and gives lenders confidence in their claims to securities collateral. This legislation will focus on addressing the question of "who owns what" to address threats that have been identified to financial stability and investor protection. It looks at the legal, operational, and economic challenges involved in holding, buying, selling, and lending securities. The initiative will also consider how to improve the exercise of rights flowing from securities for investors.

- Consultation on a possible recovery and resolution framework for financial institutions other than banks, which was issued by the EC in October 2012 and includes recovery and resolution issues for CCPs and CSDs.

MAIN ISSUES AND RECOMMENDATIONS

Effectiveness of the Supervision and Oversight of CCPs and CSDs[4]

The EU regulations for the authorization, regulation, and supervision of CCPs and CSDs are expected to significantly improve the safety and efficiency of, as well as level the playing field in, the EU posttrade market because they provide common standards across the EU. Early adoption of the CSD Regulation is recommended. Box 21.1 provides a summary of this and other recommendations on supervision and oversight of CCPs and CSDs. EMIR and the CSD Regulation are expected to mitigate the risks and inefficiencies resulting from the diversity of national rules and supervisory frameworks. Without such common standards, conflicts of law may result in legal risks. Inconsistencies in the financial risk management of cross-border clearing may cause credit and liquidity risks. Differences in operational procedures may threaten cross-border operational reliability, and contagion between cross-border operating systems may entail systemic risk. The regulations also support cooperation between supervisors, which is essential during crises to react swiftly and accurately, as became apparent during the Lehman Brothers collapse and other defaults of participants

---

[4] Based on Responsibilities A through D for authorities of FMIs in the PFMI (see pp. 126–32 of http://www.bis.org/publ/cpss101a.pdf).

Box 21.1 Summary Recommendations on Regulation, Supervision, and Oversight of Financial Market Infrastructures

- Early adoption of the CSD Regulation is recommended to provide national authorities, ESMA, and the ESCB with the legal basis for raising the bar for CSDs.
- It is critically import that regulators from the EU, the United States, and other relevant countries continue bilateral and multilateral coordination to reduce gaps and inconsistencies between legal and regulatory frameworks for OTC derivatives clearing.
- The EC is encouraged to develop legislation for the recovery and resolution of CCPs and CSDs.
- ESMA's resources need to be significantly increased to enable ESMA to adequately accomplish its extended duties.
- The ESCB overseers should improve their information sharing regarding CCPs and CSDs and aim for the development of a comprehensive macro view on the financial stability of CCPs and CSDs in the EU.
- The ESCB should be sufficiently staffed to fulfill its coordination and information-sharing tasks with regard to CCPs and CSDs and to ensure efficiency in the representation of the Eurosystem in supervisory colleges.
- ESMA is encouraged to improve the accessibility of its website.

Note: CCP = central counterparty; CSD = central securities depository; EC = European Commission; ESCB = European System of Central Banks; EU = European Union; OTC = over the counter.

---

of FMIs. In the absence of a European passport, CCPs and CSDs based in one member state must comply with the diverse requirements of the different national supervisors in other states, which may paralyze cross-border clearing and settlement and entail significant costs.

The new EU regulations are based on the Committee on Payment and Settlement Systems-International Organization of Securities Commissions (CPSS-IOSCO) *Principles for Financial Market Infrastructures* (PFMI). The provisions of the new regulations, including the technical standards, follow the existing recommendations developed by CPSS-IOSCO and ESCB-Committee of European Securities Regulators (CESR). While EMIR was drafted in parallel to the PFMI, the draft CSD Regulation benefits from the finalized international standards.

Although EMIR and the draft CSD Regulation improve consistency within the EU, inconsistencies do exist between the legal and regulatory frameworks in the EU, the United States, and elsewhere regarding OTC derivatives clearing, threatening the safety and efficiency of the process. Following the G20 agreement for mandatory clearing of all standardized OTC derivatives, the EU, the United States, and other relevant authorities have developed requirements for clearing in parallel.[5] Despite regular communication and coordination between the United States and EU authorities, relevant differences remain, for example, in relation to the segregation and portability requirements and requirements for the calculation

---

[5] As included in EMIR for the EU and the Dodd-Frank Act for the United States.

of margin. Other differences relate to extraterritoriality and recognition of CCPs located outside their own territory. It is critically important that regulators from the EU, the United States, and other relevant countries continue bilateral and multilateral coordination to reduce these inconsistencies, and develop mechanisms based on the mutual recognition of their respective regulations to limit, as much as possible, conflicts, inconsistencies, and duplication of rules.

To further improve the regulatory framework in the EU, the EC is encouraged to develop legislation for the recovery and resolution of CCPs and CSDs because such legislation is expected to further contribute to safe and efficient CCPs and CSDs. Legislation will provide an EU framework for recovery and resolution, enhancing consistency across countries. It is of particular importance that recovery and resolution plans work across borders if there were to be large market disruptions, as described in the recovery and resolution plans of CCPs and CSDs.

Under the new regulations, the competent authorities will receive legal powers to obtain timely information and induce change. The competent authorities are able to apply administrative sanctions and measures to CCPs and CSDs, designated credit institutions, the members of their management bodies, and any other persons who effectively control their business, as well as to anybody who is held responsible for a breach. The competent authorities have the power to impose at least the following administrative sanctions and measures: public statements, withdrawal of the authorizations, dismissal of the members of the management bodies of the institutions responsible for a breach, and administrative pecuniary sanctions.

ESMA will have sufficient legal powers to fulfill its duties. ESMA may, at any time, request information of the competent authority about the compliance of the CCP or CSD with the conditions under which the authorization is granted. ESMA participates in CCP colleges, which enables ESMA to ensure consistency in supervisory practices. ESMA will have no voting rights on the opinions of the college, but in case of disagreement, one competent authority is needed to escalate the issue to ESMA and ESMA's opinion will be binding. ESMA can issue level 3 guidelines addressed to authorities on various matters. ESMA has made a head start by drafting several protocols regarding the functioning of the colleges, a risk assessment framework, and the exchange of information and crisis management procedures. ESMA also has the power to withdraw the recognition of a third-country CCP or CSD.

ESMA's current resources are not sufficient to carry out these responsibilities and need to be increased.[6] ESMA's role is important to safeguarding the stability of the financial sector and of high political priority; therefore, the institution should be adequately resourced. In practice, current resources are insufficient to adequately develop and execute all new tasks. The national competent authorities and ESMA should ensure that skilled resources are available to enable the ade-

---

[6] Reported in the Financial System Stability Assessment (IMF, 2013). At the time of the assessment, ESMA's staff responsible for posttrading issues consisted of five full-time employees.

quate validation of the complex risk models of CCPs, as part of their role in the validation process for these models.[7]

The new and explicit legal basis for the ESCB members' involvement in the supervision of CSDs is important: central banks have an intrinsic interest in the safe and efficient functioning of securities settlement systems because of their relevance to financial stability. Securities are used to carry out monetary policy through open market operations. Difficulties in securities settlement systems could disrupt the ability of the central bank to implement monetary policy effectively. Securities settlement systems are essential for the timely delivery of collateral for payments and other purposes.

Central banks are in a unique position for developing a macro view of the stability of CCPs and CSDs in the EU, with their ability to take into account monetary policy interests and collateral issues. Information sharing could be improved between central banks, including with the ECB. The development of a macro view by the ESCB adds to the supervisory activities of national competent authorities and ESMA. In doing so, the ESCB could take into account the relevance of CCPs and CSDs for monetary policy operations and related collateral issues. The ESCB is encouraged to implement plans for information sharing between national central banks and the ECB by establishing a dedicated information-sharing group for ESCB representatives that participate in colleges for CCPs and eventually CSDs. This is necessary to complement the current decentralized organization of oversight[8] with proactive, comprehensive, and consistent analysis. The ESCB's resources need to be increased to facilitate the new coordination tasks as well as the increased duties to represent the Eurosystem as central bank of issue in supervisory colleges. The ECB Governing Council is encouraged to evaluate the effectiveness of information sharing within the ESCB.

Laws, regulations, and standards for CCPs and CSDs are publicly disclosed, in line with Responsibility C of the PFMI; however, the presentation of information on the ESMA website could be improved. EMIR and the draft technical standards are available on the Internet, as is the draft CSD Regulation. ESMA will be a center for relevant information on EU supervision of CCPs and CSDs. Regulations require ESMA to publish a range of lists and registers on its website, such as lists of competent authorities and authorized and recognized CCPs and CSDs, including services, products, branches, and links. ESMA also must publish its opinions on its website. In practice, ESMA's website is not very accessible—it assumes the user has a high level of knowledge on clearing and settlement topics, and information is not presented clearly. The Eurosystem discloses its oversight policies on its website. Annual oversight reports provide a description of oversight

---

[7] EMIR article 49 specifies that a CCP shall obtain an independent validation of its models and parameters and inform its competent authority and ESMA of the results of the tests performed and shall obtain their validation before adopting any significant change to the models and parameters.

[8] Oversight on securities and derivatives clearing and settlement systems is typically conducted by national central banks with a limited role for the ECB as standard setter.

Box 21.2 Members of Supervisory College for a CCP

A college for CCP authorization and supervision should consist of

- ESMA.
- The CCP's national competent authority.
- The competent authorities responsible for the supervision of the clearing members of the CCP that are established in the three member states with the largest contributions to the default fund of the CCP on an aggregate basis over a one-year period.
- The competent authorities responsible for the supervision of trading venues served by the CCP.
- The competent authorities supervising CCPs with which interoperability arrangements have been established.
- The competent authorities supervising CSDs to which the CCP is linked.
- The relevant members of the ESCB responsible for the oversight of the CCP and the relevant members of the ESCB responsible for the oversight of the CCPs with which interoperability arrangements have been established.
- The central banks of issue of the most relevant European Union currencies of the financial instruments cleared.

Source: EMIR Article 18.
Note: CCP = central counterparty; CSD = central securities depository; ESCB = European System of Central Banks; ESMA = European Securities and Markets Authority.

activities. The Eurosystem has clarified its oversight role in a policy statement called "Eurosystem Oversight Policy Framework," which is regularly updated.

Cooperation among Authorities[9]

Cooperation among authorities of CCPs will receive legal underpinning in EMIR. Today, several supervisory colleges for CCPs are in place to coordinate cross-border supervision and oversight.[10] The colleges are governed by memoranda of understanding. The current pile of memoranda of understanding between authorities of cross-border-operating CCPs will be replaced by EMIR, which requires the competent authority to establish, manage, and chair a college for the authorization and supervision of CCPs. The college should be involved in risk management model validation and interoperability arrangements with other CCPs and related risk management measures. The establishment and functioning of the college should be based on a written agreement between all of its members. EMIR provides college members with the power to determine the college's decision-making procedures, including detailed rules on voting procedures. Box 21.2 outlines the EMIR prescriptions for the composition of the CCP colleges. EMIR prescribes that the college should vote in accordance with the general principle

---

[9] Based on Responsibility E for authorities of FMIs in the PFMI (see pp. 133–37 of http://www.bis.org/publ/cpss101a.pdf).
[10] Colleges exist for LCH.Clearnet, LCH.Clearnet Group Limited, and the European Multilateral Clearing Facility.

> ## Box 21.3 Summary Recommendations on Cooperation between Authorities
>
> - The CSD Regulation should require the establishment of colleges or other comprehensive cooperation frameworks for supervisors of CSDs.
> - The ICSDs should be among the first institutions taken into SSM supervision. SSM supervision should relate to banking activities, and ESMA and national supervisors under the envisaged CSD Regulation should supervise CSD activities.
> - The ECB, ESMA, and supervisory authorities should develop a cooperation framework for CSDs that are subject to banking supervision under the SSM in addition to supervision under the CSD Regulation.
> - Securities accounts within a CSD that also provides banking services should be ring fenced to protect settlement operations in case of a crisis, although additional measures are needed to ensure continued settlement operations.
> - It is essential that authorities cooperate in the event of a potential major downgrade of one of the member states, to optimize the protection of CCPs and ICSDs in the EU through collateral.
> - The EC should pay particular attention to the drafting of access rights for CCPs and CSDs in the Markets in Financial Instruments Regulation and CSD Regulation. Access criteria should be nondiscriminatory and risk based (excluding business risk), contributing to a level playing field for the offering of CCP and CSD services.
>
> ---
>
> Note: CCP = central counterparty; CSD = central securities depository; EC = European Commission; ECB = European Central Bank; ESMA = European Securities and Markets Authority; EU = European Union; ICSD = international central securities depository; SSM = Single Supervisory Mechanism.

whereby each member has one vote, irrespective of the number of functions the member performs.

Box 21.3 summarizes the recommendations for cooperation among authorities in the EU. The EMIR colleges are expected to represent EU interests effectively, while ESMA is expected to contribute significantly to supervisory consistency and oversight. EMIR sufficiently underpins the role of the colleges and of ESMA to justify the expectation that the colleges will ensure consistent authorization, supervision, and oversight of CCPs within the EU. This will contribute to ensuring that the CCPs comply with the requirements of EMIR and subsequently to financial stability. Whether the combination of the decentralized supervisory structure for CSDs and CCPs and the coordination function of colleges and ESMA results in efficient supervision will have to be assessed in the future. A more centralized structure would be the alternative.

It is recommended that a similar cooperation framework for national supervisors of CSDs be established in the upcoming CSD Regulation, building on the example of CCP colleges. The draft CSD Regulation does not prescribe a supervisory college or other comprehensive cooperation framework among national supervisors of CSDs.[11] Colleges or other frameworks would oblige national

---

[11] Although the competent authority is required to cooperate closely with ESMA and various other authorities in certain cases.

supervisors to cooperate on a broader range of topics than currently requested under the draft CSD Regulation. Colleges provide authorities with more ways to influence decision making or refer to ESMA, which is important in the supervision of CSDs that provide cross-border settlement services. With the drafting of the Securities Law Legislation, more CSDs will potentially be of interest to authorities from other member states.

The supervision of the two ICSDs, and any systemically important CSD providing banking services, may benefit from centralized banking supervision under the SSM. The ICSDs should be among the first institutions taken into SSM supervision, because the current regulatory and supervisory structure is insufficient to ensure financial stability.[12] The SSM may contribute to the stability of these CSDs if the relevant national fiscal authorities have insufficient resources to facilitate an eventual bailout. Centralized banking supervision should reduce the chance that competitive pressures will result in competition on risk measures. It may contribute to a level playing field and ensure enhancements to the ICSDs' credit and liquidity risk management frameworks. Because the ICSDs will be supervised by different authorities for their banking and CSD activities, a cooperation framework should be established to coordinate among these different authorities, that is, among the ECB as banking supervisor, and ESMA, the ESCB, and the national competent authorities responsible for the supervision and oversight of CSD activities.

Cooperation among authorities is also necessary to support the establishment of a backup arrangement for settlement operations in case a CSD with a banking license goes bankrupt. Ring fencing of settlement accounts from any ancillary risk-taking services will be beneficial from a systemic risk point of view and is in line with the PFMI, for example, Principle 3 regarding plans for recovery and orderly winding down of operations. A CSD that holds a banking license is exposed to credit and liquidity risks and may be subject to bankruptcy procedures. In that case, the CSD could have a backup arrangement in place with another provider of cash accounts to allow for swift continuation of settlement operations. Such a backup provider of cash accounts should also have a limited risk profile. The current requirement in the draft CSD Regulation, to place cash accounts in a separate legal entity, could be a solution for securing the protection of settlement operations, but the backup provider of cash accounts should not have a risk profile that increases risks for the securities account holders. The requirement to hold cash accounts in a separate legal entity may discourage a CSD currently without a banking license from requesting one under the new regulation.

Cooperation between authorities is crucial in the event of a default or downgrade of one or more countries in the EU and will help prevent measures in one member state from disrupting markets, CCPs, or CSDs in other member states. The default or downgrade of a country may heavily affect the value of specific government securities held as collateral by CCPs and ICSDs and subsequently

---

[12] See the detailed assessment reports of Euroclear Bank (IMF, 2013) and Clearstream Banking Luxembourg (IMF, 2011).

> ### Box 21.4 Summary Recommendations on Crisis Management
>
> - The SFD notification regime should be reviewed, standardized, and enhanced, with the inclusion of all relevant authorities, including the ECB as overseer of T2S and EURO1.
> - Crisis management arrangements between ESMA and the ESCB should be further developed and tested.
>
> ---
>
> Note: ECB = European Central Bank; ESCB = European System of Central Banks; ESMA = European Securities and Markets Authority; SFD = Settlement Finality Directive; T2S = TARGET2-Securities.

leave the FMIs with insufficient coverage. Wrong-way risk should be mitigated because clearing participants holding the securities may default and cause losses to the CCP or ICSD. In addition, procyclicality should be limited by seeking a careful balance between protecting the CCP and avoiding the exacerbation of financial problems of participants and markets. Authorities should monitor and analyze such a situation in a cooperative way and pursue the interests of the EU as a whole.

With the reverticalization of infrastructures, the rights of CCPs and CSDs to access other markets and infrastructures should gain particular attention to further level the playing field. Interoperability between cash CCPs can be a useful tool for enhancing the efficiency of the clearing market, but may also threaten the market share of incumbent CCPs. A trading platform that also owns a CCP can refuse access of other CCPs, and eventually CSDs, to the platform. CSDs should also gain nondiscriminatory access to CCPs. Restrictions to access rights as prescribed in EMIR, and potentially the Markets in Financial Instruments Regulation and the CSD Regulation, should be exclusively risk based (excluding business risk) and publicly disclosed. Competitive distortions should be avoided.[13]

CRISIS MANAGEMENT[14]

EU legislation recognizes the need for crisis management arrangements for authorities of CCPs and CSDs. Information sharing among authorities is covered in several EU Directives. EMIR, the draft CSD Regulation, and the SFD specify ESMA's role in times of crisis. Other information-sharing requirements are set forth in the Banks Winding-Up Directive, the Market Abuse Directive, and the Capital Requirements Directive. The framework prescribes information sharing with known creditors and the sharing of information between designated competent authorities in the EU.

Box 21.4 summarizes the recommendations on crisis management arrangements for authorities. The SFD notification scheme did not work properly during recent defaults of major participants and should be reviewed. Market participants

---

[13] See PFMI Principle 18 (pp. 101–104 of http://www.bis.org/publ/cpss101a.pdf).
[14] Based on Responsibility E for authorities of FMIs and Principles 13 and 17 in the PFMI (see pp. 133–37, 78–81, and 94–100 of http://www.bis.org/publ/cpss101a.pdf).

and public authorities alike perceived that information sharing on a defaulting market participant was not always timely and comprehensive.[15] It is recommended that the awareness of designated authorities under the SFD be raised regarding their obligations in case of a crisis, and that tests be conducted to familiarize authorities with their obligations. ESMA should play a leading role in this regard together with the ESCB. The SFD notification scheme should include all relevant authorities, including the ECB in its role as lead overseer of T2S and EURO1.[16]

Colleges (chaired by respective competent authorities), ESMA, and the ESCB are encouraged to continue the development of a crisis management framework to deal with the potential failure of a CCP, CSD, or other relevant FMI. The benefit of this crisis management framework in addition to the SFD is that information sharing can precede the actual default and that all EU competent authorities and central banks would be involved. The plan should be regularly tested and updated.

REFERENCES

European Central Bank (ECB), 2010, *Report on the Lessons Learned from the Financial Crisis with Regard to the Functioning of European Financial Market Infrastructures* (Frankfurt).

International Monetary Fund (IMF), 2013, "European Union: Financial System Stability Assessment," IMF Country Report No. 13/75 (Washington).

————, 2011, "Luxembourg: Financial System Stability Assessment—Update," IMF Country Report No. 11/148 (Washington).

---

[15] See, for example, ECB (2010).

[16] EURO1 is a private-sector-owned large-value payment system for interbank payments in euro.

APPENDIX 21A. MAIN CENTRAL COUNTERPARTIES AND CENTRAL SECURITIES DEPOSITORIES IN THE EU

System	Description	Value of delivery instructions, 2011
Main CSDs		
Clearstream	Clearstream: An international central securities depository (ICSD) and CSDs of Germany and Luxembourg.	CBL: €74 trillion CBF: €80 trillion
Euroclear S.A.	Euroclear Bank: ICSD for Eurobonds and other international securities.	€367 trillion
	ESES CSD: The Belgian, Dutch, and French CSDs operate one common platform	Euroclear Belgium: €0.6 trillion Euroclear Nederland: €5 trillion Euroclear France: €146 trillion
	Euroclear United Kingdom & Ireland: CSD for United Kingdom and Ireland	€150 trillion
	Euroclear Sweden: CSD for Sweden	€11 trillion
	Euroclear Finland: CSD for Finland	€ 0.5 trillion
Monte Titoli	CSD for trades executed on the Italian trading platforms. Part of LSE Group.	€72 trillion
Iberclear	Spanish CSD for trades executed on the Spanish stock exchanges, Latibex, and for debt transactions.	€88 trillion
Main CCPs—Cash Markets[1]		
CC&G	CCP clearing for the Italian markets.	€3 trillion
CCP Austria	CCP for Austrian cash and derivative markets.	€0.08 trillion (in 2010)
EUREX Clearing	CCP incorporated in Germany, offering clearing services for derivatives and equities traded on German markets.	€3 trillion
LCH.Clearnet Limited	Part of the LCH.Clearnet Group. Clears equities and derivatives for various platforms, including the London Stock Exchange. SwapClear is part of LCH.Clearnet Limited and is the largest CCP for interest rate swaps globally.	€4 trillion (in 2009)
LCH.Clearnet SA	Part of the LCH.Clearnet Group. Clears equities and derivatives for the Euronext markets in Belgium, France, the Netherlands, and Portugal; government bonds for MTS Italy; equity for Bourse de Luxembourg and several electronic trading platforms	€6 trillion
EuroCCP	CCP incorporated in the United Kingdom; clearing for 17 markets in Europe and the United States.	n.a.
European Multilateral Clearing Facility	CCP incorporated in the Netherlands; clearing for 19 European markets through nine different exchanges and trading platforms.	€6 trillion
KELER CCP	CCP for Hungarian market	n.a.

Source: European Central Bank.

Note: CBF = Clearstream Banking Frankfurt; CBL = Clearstream Banking Luxembourg; CCP = central counterparty; CSD = central securities depository; ESES = Euroclear Settlement for Euronext-zone Securities; ICSD = international central securities depository; n.a. = not available; OTC = over the counter.

[1] No consistent statistics are available on cleared values of exchange traded or OTC traded derivatives per CCP. CC&G, Eurex Clearing, LCH.Clearnet Limited, LCH.Clearnet SA, and MEFF clear substantial amounts of derivatives transactions. LCH.Clearnet Limited and the United Kingdom's ICE Clear Europe clear substantial amounts of OTC derivatives.

CHAPTER 22

Mortgage Markets and Foreclosure Processes in Europe and the United States

MICHAEL MOORE, MARTA RODRÍGUEZ-VIVES, AND NOLVIA N. SACA-SACA

Home mortgage defaults and foreclosures in Europe increased during the crisis, but remain well below those in the United States during the peak years of its mortgage crisis in 2009 and 2010. Stricter foreclosure processes in some European countries, as well as lenders' having full recourse to borrower assets, seem to have kept defaults and foreclosures to lower levels than in the United States. Research on the U.S. crisis has shown that although the duration of foreclosure processes (which average about one year) and the fact that deficiency judgments are not generally pursued in the event of negative equity have been factors in higher overall default and foreclosure rates, they nevertheless have also contained the length of the mortgage crisis and the severity of its impact on the economy.

Foreclosure is a process that allows a lender to recover the amount owed on a defaulted mortgage by selling or taking ownership of the property securing the loan. This process is also known as repossession, particularly in Europe. There are two basic methods of foreclosure: *judicial foreclosure* requires the lender to go to court and receive a judge's approval to foreclose a property; under *nonjudicial foreclosure*, the lender may sell the collateral (the property) or repossesses it without a judge's approval.

There is increasing research on mortgage markets and the effects of home foreclosure processes across the United States, for which legal frameworks vary by state. The research is aided by detailed data on foreclosures by states and by zip codes (RealtyTrac and CoreLogic databases). The European Mortgage Federation (EMF) publishes an annual statistical study, Hypostat, but comparisons between housing and mortgage markets in Europe and the United States are difficult.

The authors would like to thank the Legal Departments of the IMF and the European Central Bank (ECB) for guidance in the national mortgage law and foreclosure processes. They also thank Ad van Riet (ECB) and Alvaro Piris (IMF) for valuable comments. Remaining errors in the chapter are the sole responsibility of the authors.

By contrast with the United States, the research and information for European countries is limited, especially data on repossessions, which are not systematically compiled and published. To the best of the authors' knowledge, the only Europe-wide exercises were conducted by the European Commission (2011) on mortgage default rates from 2007 to 2009, and a monographic study on nonperforming loans (NPLs) in the EU by the European Mortgage Federation (2011).

Early research compared housing finance developments (ECB, 2009) and dealt with the similarities and differences of housing markets and institutions across countries (Bardhan, Edelstein, and Kroll, 2011; Lea, 2010; EMF, 2007). This chapter seeks to (1) provide a comparative review of foreclosure processes for a selected sample of European countries and the United States;[1] and (2) highlight that differences in mortgage laws and practices in a representative sample of mort-gage markets may lead to different outcomes for mortgage default and foreclo-sures, and for the speed of resolving the mortgage crisis and reviving the housing market.

MORTGAGE MARKETS AND HOUSE PRICE DYNAMIC

Housing markets are critical for any economy, but their role in the United States and in some European economies (e.g., Ireland and Spain) is significant. Several factors account for this importance, including the size of the sector, its contribu-tion to economic growth, and its linkage to other sectors (banking, investors, and the government).[2]

Growing home prices in the United States, and in some countries in Europe in the early 2000s, prompted by high demand and liquidity, masked the unsoundness of many mortgages, specifically subprime mortgages in the United States, and loans given to real estate developers in Ireland and Spain. Foreclosure rates were very low during that period because borrowers who could afford the debt service would not walk away from the appreciated assets, while those who could not honor their debts would find it easy to sell their homes at a profit. This led banks to relax even further their lending standards, increasing mortgage finance and demand for housing and pushing home prices even higher.

---

[1] The selected sample includes Cyprus, Denmark, Germany, Greece, Ireland, the Netherlands, Por-tugal, Spain, the United Kingdom, and the United States. Other countries (France and Italy) are included in a few figures and tables for comparison with the main sample.

[2] In Ireland and Spain, for example, government finances were overreliant on property. In Ireland, tax revenues increased by 10 percent per year from 2002 to the end of the housing boom in 2007; as a consequence, the tax structure shifted toward a cyclical source of revenues, most of which was real estate related. In 2006, Ireland reported a budget surplus of 3 percent and a government-debt-to-GDP ratio of 25 percent. Both figures were the second highest in the euro area (Addison-Smyth and McQuinn, 2009). In Spain, the contribution of property transactions to tax revenues during 1999–2007 amounted to about 1.5 percent of GDP, of which about 0.4 percent of GDP related to increases of value-added tax receipts and 0.8 percent of GDP related to increases in property transfer and stamp duty taxes (Morris and others, 2009).

TABLE 22.1

Housing Price Dynamics for Selected Countries *(percentage change)*		
Country	Accumulated change, 2000–07 (unless otherwise indicated)	Accumulated change, 2007–12 (unless otherwise indicated)
Cyprus[1]	22.1 (2006–07)	−0.2
Denmark	84.2	−23.2
Germany	−3.3	13.2
Greece	86.9	−28.3
Ireland	105.0	−97.7
The Netherlands	44.7	−12.2
Portugal	14.2	3.6
Spain	135.7	−38.9
United Kingdom[2]	130.4	−21.7
United States	57.0	−20.7

Sources: European Central Bank (ECB) Statistical Data Warehouse (based on national data) except for the United States. Data for European countries are the annual residential property price index statistics, with base year 2007. Back data for Spain and Ireland are ECB estimates. Data for the United States are the composite home price, with 2000:Q1 = 100, from the Economic Research Division of the Federal Reserve Bank of St. Louis. For the United States, housing prices started to recover during 2012; through 2011, the accumulated decline in housing prices was 26.11 percent.

[1] For Cyprus, house prices started to fall in 2009, after a sharp increase of 17 percent in 2007–08. Other data sources (Haver Analytics) show an accumulated change of −12.5 percent for 2007–12.

[2] For the United Kingdom, the *Economist* ("Searching for solid ground," August 18, 2012) estimated a more moderate drop in prices, −10.2 for 2007–12, because the housing market in Britain is heavily reliant on London and the southeast.

Before the crisis, the number of homeowners in the United States increased steadily by about 1 million per year as a result of active policies, introduced in the mid-1980s and 1990s, favoring property ownership over renting; and Federal Reserve Board policies of cheap credit that began in the early 2000s. Home ownership rates thus increased from roughly 65 percent in the early 1990s to more than 69 percent by 2004. As house prices began to fall from their record peaks in mid-2006, and mortgage delinquencies and foreclosures started to climb, the conditions in the housing market become progressively worse with serious negative effects, incidence of default, and prevalence of negative equity. As a result, the home ownership rate declined to its long-term level of 65 percent.

By contrast, in Europe, the tenure status (owning versus renting) differs across the region, partly for historical and cultural reasons, but more significantly, because of varying tax treatment of ownership, different mortgage interest rates, and differences in disposable income across the region. On the one hand, in countries like Germany, the home ownership rate is 43 percent because homeowners have not benefited from subsidies provided in other European countries, for example, the Netherlands and Spain. Instead, housing policy in Germany is largely oriented toward the rental social housing sector, with lower emphasis on home ownership (Bardhan, Edelstein, and Kroll, 2011). Moreover, the underlying capital for mortgages is tied to covered bonds that include strict requirements for loan-to-value (LTV) ratios, interest rates may vary only within fixed limits, and loans are full recourse. German house prices remained stable for a long period before the crisis, and during the crisis house prices increased (see Table 22.1). On the other hand, Cyprus, Greece, Ireland, Italy, Portugal, and Spain have home

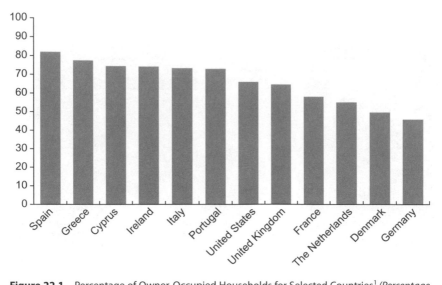

Figure 22.1 Percentage of Owner-Occupied Households for Selected Countries[1] *(Percentage of total end-2010, unless otherwise stated)*

Source: European Central Bank Statistical Data Warehouse (based on national data).
[1] Data for Cypress (2010), Ireland (2010), and the United States (2011) are from the European Mortgage Association. Data for Germany, the Netherlands, Portugal, and the United Kingdom refer to 2011; and Denmark to 2012.

ownership rates of more than 70 percent, followed by moderate rates in the United States and the United Kingdom of about 66 percent (Figure 22.1).

Developments in housing markets have been shown to play an important role in episodes of financial instability. The link between housing bubbles and the emergence of financial crisis has become an important topic in the literature and for policymakers. The global financial crisis started with U.S. subprime mortgage market crisis in 2008, which in turn put an end to the housing prices appreciation in many countries in Europe.[3] House prices started to decline in 2008, particularly, in Ireland, Spain, and the United States.

ORIGIN AND END OF TWO BUBBLES

The precrash bubble saw households borrowing excessively in the United States, but also in some European countries. Figure 22.2 displays at the aggregate level the evolution of stocks of debt relative to GDP for different sectors (see also Cour-Thimann and Winkler, 2012), and reveals a different picture for the euro area than for the United States regarding the indebtedness of households in relation to other economic sectors. In the United States, the household sector

---

[3] An exception is Germany where housing prices continue rising strongly.

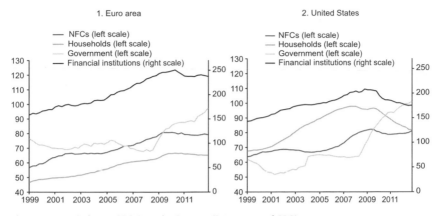

1. Euro area

2. United States

— NFCs (left scale)
— Households (left scale)
— Government (left scale)
— Financial institutions (right scale)

Figure 22.2   Debt-to-GDP Ratio by Sectors *(Percentage of GDP)*

Sources: Euro Area Accounts (European Central Bank and Eurostat); National Economic Accounts (U.S. Department of Commerce, Bureau of Economic Analysis); and U.S. flow of funds accounts (U.S. Federal Reserve).

Note: NFC = nonfinancial corporation. Debt is defined as loans, debt securities, and insurance reserves, net of loans granted within the same sector at market value. Government debt reported in the figure is thus different from the Maastricht definition of government debt. Latest observation: 2012:Q4.

accumulated a higher stock of debt relative to other sectors before the crisis, which contrasts with the euro area experience, with its relatively less indebted household sector, despite an increase of about 15 percentage points since 2000.

Because the indebtedness of households is highly dominated by the evolution of the housing market, published figures show a significant heterogeneity at the country level. Figure 22.3, panel 1, shows a group of countries that substantially increased their debt levels, starting from relatively low ratios of residential mortgage to GDP (about 30 percent) in the early 2000s, particularly Ireland (to over 90 percent), and Spain and Portugal (to about 65 percent) in 2009; and Cyprus from about 6 percent in 2000 to 71 percent in 2011. Other countries with traditionally high residential-mortgage-debt-to-GDP ratios also increased their mortgage debt substantially, with their peaks ranging from 85 percent of GDP in the United States in 2007 to more than 100 percent in Denmark and the Netherlands in 2009.

A second group of countries (Figure 22.3, panel 2), such as Greece and Italy, show relatively low indebtedness levels in 2011 despite the high homeownership ratios in those countries. The residential mortgage ratio has grown at a more moderate pace over the past decade, reaching values of less than 50 percent of GDP. Households in Germany reduced their residential mortgage debt levels as a share of GDP by about 8 percentage points between 2001 and 2011, despite an increase in homeownership rates from 40.3 in 1998 to 43.2 in 2011 (EMF, 2011), but these levels are still the second lowest in Europe, after Switzerland.

In the United States, an unprecedented rise in house price and sales transactions began in the late 1990s. This steady appreciation of home values, the main asset held by households, was seen as a basis for increasing consumption, the driving force of the U.S. economy. As Bardhan (2009) notes, this period saw the emergence of a number of facilitating conditions for supporting the housing

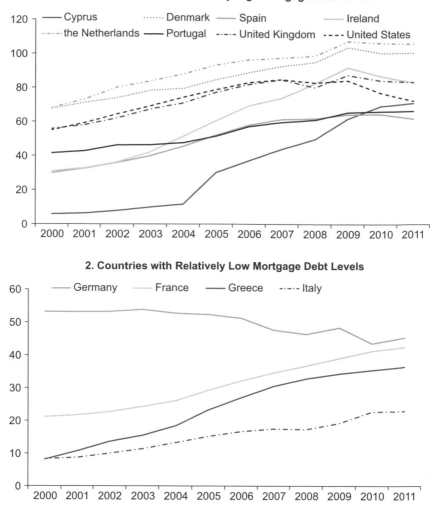

Figure 22.3 Residential Mortgage Debt in Selected Countries *(percentage of GDP)*

Sources: For the U.S. data, Board of Governors of the Federal Reserve System, Economic Research & Data; and European Mortgage Federation Statistics.
Note: CY = Cyprus; DE = Germany; DK = Denmark; ES = Spain; FR = France; GR = Greece; IE = Ireland; IT = Italy; NL = the Netherlands; PT= Portugal; US = United States; UK = United Kingdom.

bubble. First, historically low interest rates created a conducive financial environment for borrowing, while lax lending standards set up an accommodating institutional setting for subprime mortgages and other loans, involving little or no documentation and zero down payment requirements. Second, low interest rates, growing house prices, and expectations of growing appreciation of home values increased the appetite for investment in this sector (Bardhan, 2009). Similar facilitating conditions also emerged in Europe. Table 22.2 presents information

TABLE 22.2

Comparative Information on Housing Market Policies

	Loan-to-value ratio (percent)	Mortgage deductibility	Government guarantee or mortgage insurance	Variable or fixed rates	Mortgage securitization or capital market role
Cyprus	70–80		No	Both	Less developed
Denmark	65 Maximum is 80 by law.	Yes	No	Variable	Covered bonds
Germany	74 Maximum is 80	No	No	Variable with fixed limits	Covered bonds
Greece	67	No	No	Both	Less developed
Ireland	100 +	Yes (5 years)	No	Variable	Some, mortgage-backed bonds and securitization
The Netherlands	80 + Maximum is 106[1]	Yes, for new mortgages only if they are fully amortized in 30 years or less.	Yes, government loan guarantees and assets backing debt	Fixed	Less developed, and typically trade over the counter
Portugal	80–90	No	No	Variable	Some, covered bonds (14.5%) and securitization (27.3%)
Spain	70–80 Maximum is 100	Only for low-income borrowers	No	Variable	Covered bonds (64%) and securitization (36%)
United Kingdom	71 for home movers and 81 for first-time home buyers. Maximum is 110	No[2]	Insurance available for mortgagors	Short-term fixed then variable	Covered bonds and securitization
United States	80–90 Maximum is 100	Yes[2]	Multiple agencies involved	Both	Highly developed

Sources: Exhibit 1 in Bardhan, Edelstein, and Kroll, 2011; European Mortgage Federation; IMF staff calculations; and Lea, 2010. The country-specific information provided by Constant Verkoren, Dermot Monaghan, Joaquin Gutierrez, and Uffe Mikkelsen for this table is gratefully acknowledged.
[1] The policy in the Netherlands is to reduce the loan-to-value (LTV) ratio by 1 percentage point each year until the maximum LTV reaches 100 percent.
[2] Capital gains tax limited.

on government policies for the sample of countries to explain that the strong increase in mortgage debt has been partly fueled by government policies and cheap credit in the United States and in some European countries, particularly the Netherlands, and to some extent, Spain, leading to high LTV ratios.[4]

---

[4] There are other reasons for the increase in mortgages, including increases in disposable income and growth in residential property prices and house transactions, combined with demographic factors. Additionally, there have been supply-side factors, such as high increases in construction in some countries, like the remarkable case of Spain. The number of housing starts in absolute value in Spain during the period 1999–2008 was 6 million, which contrasts, for example, with France, which started

In Ireland and Spain, mortgage markets experienced credit-fueled construction booms. The Spanish housing market boom and house price increase began in the mid-1990s, stimulated by an expanding economy that benefited from the EU membership. But other factors also played a part, including an increase in the risk appetite of lenders who provided financing for much riskier loans on real estate development and construction of apartments and second homes, building up high borrower indebtedness. As prices began to turn in 2008, the conditions of the real estate market deteriorated substantially, leading to a significant overhang of properties. Because real estate development was a significant part of the economic boom, the distress in the real estate market significantly affected the economy, particularly employment and the financial sector.

Similarly, in Ireland, the economic transformation of the economy that began in the mid-1990s led to economic growth based on an increase in competitiveness and real exports. By 2000, Ireland's income per capita had reached the level of Western Europe, but the economy continued to grow at high rates, despite losses in competitiveness caused by a domestic price increase, driven by a second boom based on credit and construction (2000–07). With the rapid expansion of bank lending, house prices increased. Ireland's housing prices rose substantially during both booms;[5] but with the end of the building boom, the construction industry and the banking system were clearly in trouble. Accumulative housing prices declined by 49.5 percent between 2007 and end-2012.[6]

The situation has changed in recent years as a result of the burst of the housing bubble in many European countries, especially regarding the price of real estate developments. As shown in Table 22.1, prices in most of the selected countries are adjusting downward since their highest levels in 2007, with the notable exception of Germany and, to a lesser extent, Portugal, where prices are steadily increasing (in line with trends in large cities generally[7] and also because of renewed interest in real estate as an investment option in times of crisis). The strongest corrections in nominal housing prices since 2007 are found in Ireland (a drop of about 50 percent); Spain (–28 percent); Greece (–22 percent); Denmark (–8.8 percent); the United Kingdom (–17.8 percent); and the Netherlands (–10.9 percent). This drop in real estate prices is mainly explained by lower national demand for acquisition of housing (attributable to a decrease in disposable income as a consequence of the economic slowdown) and an oversupply combined with less favorable fiscal incentives to homeowners and higher transaction costs (e.g., value-added taxes) in some cases.

3.9 million houses during the same period. However, when looking at 2008–11, Spain had adjusted its supply more than other countries, with 0.6 million house starts, as compared with the 1.1 million houses started in France for the same period.

[5] From 1994 to 2006:Q3, house prices in Dublin increased by 580 percent, from an average of €80,000 to €550,000 (Stevenson, 2011).

[6] Similar to the estimate in the *Economist*, "Searching for Solid Ground," August 18, 2012.

[7] Housing prices in big cities like London, New York, and Paris respond to global market conditions and are still rising.

The correction in house prices damaged the economic conditions of many countries[8] and put pressure on their banking systems, particularly on banks that were highly exposed to the real estate market (e.g., Ireland, Spain, and the United States). House price drops, combined with lower real disposable incomes and higher unemployment rates, led to an increase in the number of loans in arrears, deteriorating the quality of banks' loan portfolios and weakening their balance sheets to the extent that they faced potential failure and needed to be recapitalized.

In the United States, the delinquent mortgage loan rate increased from 1.31 percent in the fourth quarter of 2006 to 8.75 percent in the same quarter in 2009 (see Figure 22.4, panel 1). In addition, the foreclosure rate increased from about 1 percent in 2006 to more than 4.5 percent in 2009, and then started to decline (see Figure 22.4, panel 2).

In Europe, mortgage default rates and foreclosure data are not readily available for all the countries in the selected sample, but the European Commission (2011) collected default rates for the period 2007–09 (Table 22.3). In addition, EMF (2011) contains data on repossessions for some of the sample countries— Denmark, Spain, Ireland, and the United Kingdom—but with different periodicities and forms of presentation (ratios and numbers of repossessed properties), which are not comparable. These data constitute the only published cross-country data at the European level.

Default rate methodologies generally use data on NPLs and unemployment rates as the main components of default rate predictions. However, according to some national statistics and the narrative in the newspapers, the rate of foreclosures in Europe has been much lower than in the United States, despite the high ratio of NPLs and unemployment in some European countries (see Appendix 22A). Some observers, as discussed below, have argued that different foreclosure

TABLE 22.3

Evolution of Default Rates, 2007–09 (percentage)			
Country	Default rate as of Dec. 31, 2007	Default rate as of Dec. 31, 2008	Default rate as of Dec. 31, 2009	Accumulated increase 2007–09
Cyprus	3.24	3.90	6.90	Yes
Denmark	0.12	0.26	0.55	Yes
Germany	n.a.	n.a.	n.a	n.a.
Greece	3.60	5.30	6.40	Yes
Ireland	1.21	1.44	3.60	Yes
Netherlands	n.a.	n.a.	n.a.	n.a.
Portugal	1.30	1.50	1.70	Yes
Spain	0.72	2.38	2.88	Yes
United Kingdom	2.30	3.40	3.30	Yes

Sources: European Commission, 2011, except for the United Kingdom. Data for the United Kingdom are from the U.K. Financial Services Authority.

Note: n.a. = not available. Default rates refer to the volume of outstanding residential mortgage loans in default to the total volume of outstanding mortgage loans. Data provided as of September 2010.

---

[8] For example, in Spain at the peak of the cycle (2006–07), residential investment accounted for 9.3 percent of GDP, and 13.5 percent of the workforce was employed in the construction sector.

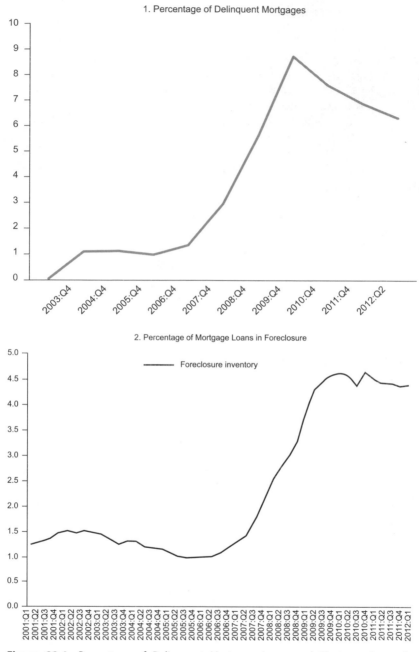

1. Percentage of Delinquent Mortgages

2. Percentage of Mortgage Loans in Foreclosure

Figure 22.4 Percentage of Delinquent Mortgage Loans and Mortgage Loans in Foreclosure in the United States *(Not seasonally adjusted)*

Sources: Federal Reserve Bank of New York (panel 1); Mortgage Bankers Association National Delinquency Survey (panel 2).

outcomes are explained partly by variation in the mortgage legal framework across countries, as well as by other interventions that block lenders from starting foreclosure proceedings.

DIFFERENCES IN MORTGAGE LAWS AND FORECLOSURE PROCESSES: AN OVERVIEW OF SELECTED EUROPEAN COUNTRIES AND THE UNITED STATES

In practice, the mechanisms for the enforcement of mortgages differ significantly among countries, and international best practice has yet to emerge in this area.

Foreclosure Methods: Judicial and Nonjudicial

When a borrower becomes delinquent on a mortgage, three main factors in the country's mortgage legal framework affect the probability and the speed of foreclosure or repossession of collateral against defaulted borrowers.

The first factor affecting the probability and timing of foreclosure is the method of foreclosure that is used. Some countries require the lender to go to court and receive a judge's approval to foreclose on a property. This is known as *judicial foreclosure*. In a judicial foreclosure, the lender initiates legal action against the debtor in the courts. The court notifies the debtor with demand for repayment by a specific date to avoid foreclosure. If there is no payment, a judgment will be entered in favor of the lender, who will request that the property be auctioned off or repossessed by the bank. In other countries, the lender may sell the property without a judge's approval if the mortgage contains a *power-of-sale* clause. This method is known as *nonjudicial foreclosure*. A judicial foreclosure, in general, takes longer because of the need for court hearings. Nonjudicial countries allow for private parties to divest the debtor of the title after appropriate notice and an opportunity to cure any arrears. The lender may use a notary or trustee to schedule the foreclosure auction.

The second main factor that affects the probability and speed with which a lender can foreclose on a property is *redemption rights*. A redemption right is the right of the borrower to redeem the property by paying off the entire balance of the mortgage. A redemption period is a period during which a borrower has redemption rights. If the redemption period precedes the foreclosure process, the right of the borrower to redeem during that time is known as an *equitable redemption right*. Such right might take the form of requiring the lender to wait, say, six months after the first serious delinquency before it can initiate the foreclosure process.

The third factor is the possibility of *recourse* or allowing lenders to pursue deficiency judgments. The EMF (2007) study on the efficiency of mortgage collateral found that borrowers remain liable for deficiencies in Belgium, France, Germany, Greece, Ireland, the Netherlands, Portugal, Spain, and the United Kingdom. The duration of the debtor liability was without limit in Belgium, Germany, Greece, and the Netherlands (EMF, 2007). In Germany, since 2008, borrowers may consider a petition for personal insolvency and, in that case, ultimately be discharged from paying the deficiency in full. Ireland introduced reforms in 2012–13 that would allow borrowers to seek relief for deficiencies as well.

Research in the United States has shown that recourse decreases the probability of default, and that this is an important factor that lowers the default rate in some countries, for example, in Europe, where mortgage recourse acts as a strong disincentive to default, even in cases of negative equity. As Feldstein (2008) noted, the creditors' "ability to go beyond the house to other assets or even future salary is a deterrent in Europe."

Foreclosure Processes in Selected European Countries

For Europe, the majority of countries follow a judicial foreclosure process. The exception is the Netherlands, which follows an expedient nonjudicial foreclosure process primarily handled by a notary. Countries in which the collateral deed must be made enforceable through a judicial decision include Denmark, Germany, Greece, Ireland, and the United Kingdom, as well as other countries not included in the sample, such as Austria, Finland, Hungary, Poland, and Sweden. Countries that use a notary deed allow private parties to divest the debtor of title after appropriate notice. In many countries, there is some judicial oversight of this process, such as through valuation and hearings; thus, the system is mixed. In Spain, for example, both judicial and nonjudicial methods exist. The nonjudicial process was simplified in 2012 through a legislative change.

In most European countries, lenders adopt a range of measures aimed at helping the borrower before resorting to foreclosure. These measures range from a compulsory official summons to a more detailed conciliatory procedure. Countries in which the legal obligation is limited to a summons include Denmark; Greece (3 days); Italy; and Spain (10 days). However, the usual practice in Europe is that the borrower is granted a number of supplementary warnings, and months elapse before the enforcement procedure is started. For example, in Greece, in practice, six to nine months pass before foreclosure is started (EMF, 2007). Law 3869/2010 on Debt Arrangements for Over-Indebted Individuals and Other Rules, as amended and currently in force, provides for a precourt settlement process between creditors and debtors with permanent inability to pay back debts, followed by a judicial validation of the settlement within two months of filing the petition, then by a judicial hearing within six months of filing the petition. Throughout this process, the debtor is protected from any foreclosure measures, while, in any case, the court is obligated to decide on reasonable installments to be paid by the debtor. Moreover, Greek law also provides that the primary residence of any debtor is protected against any foreclosure measures. This provision was initially enacted in 2011 and has been extended until December 31, 2013.[9]

---

[9] The comments on Greece, provided by Anna Damaskou and Asimina Koutsoukou from the Legal Department of the ECB, are gratefully acknowledged.

In other countries (Germany, Ireland, and the United Kingdom), lenders must follow more detailed procedures. In Germany, the procedure includes the following steps:[10] First, a lender may initiate foreclosure proceedings if the debtor is in arrears for at least two consecutive loan installments (arrears of at least 2.5 percent of the nominal loan amount). Second, since 2008, changes in the law concerning land charges (*Grundschuld*) lengthened the foreclosure process for new mortgages by barring contractual waivers of a preexisting, mandatory six-month waiting period before initiation of foreclosure proceedings. When the lender has an enforceable title, the lender can initiate a court-administered enforcement process.

In the Netherlands, a nonjudicial country, the lender has the obligation, based on a code of conduct, to grant the consumer a number of months before the enforced procedure is started (EMF, 2007).

According to Table 22.4, the duration of the foreclosure process varies across the sample countries, from about one year in the Netherlands, the United Kingdom, and the United States; to 16 months in Spain and Portugal; to 42 months in Ireland; finally to about 135 months in Cyprus.[11]

In Europe, Ireland and Spain deserve more exhaustive analysis because housing markets were critically important in both of these economies in the precrisis period, and their financial systems were seriously affected by the collapse in the housing market. The two countries have very different foreclosure frameworks. Ireland has one of the most borrower-friendly foreclosure legal frameworks, particularly since the introduction of the Land and Conveyancing Reform Act of 2009, while Spain has one of the most stringent in Europe. Boxes 22.1 and 22.2 present the foreclosure frameworks of Ireland and Spain, respectively.

Ready access to credit in Ireland fueled a housing boom that led to very high levels of mortgage debt by households, increasing LTV ratios to more than 100 percent. Mortgages were the largest household liability by far, and a significant component of Irish bank lending (68 percent of Irish household debt). From 2000 to 2008, residential mortgage debt increased from 30 to more than 90 percent of the GDP (Figure 22.3, panel 1). After reaching a peak in early 2007, house prices fell by more than 50 percent at end-2012, with more than 200,000 borrowers holding debts exceeding the value of their homes. Partly the result of high unemployment (15 percent), about 144,000 mortgages were in arrears at end-2012, of which 94,000 were in arrears by more than 90 days, and a further 40,000 mortgages were restructured (Goodbody, 2012).

Despite the high level of mortgage loans in arrears,[12] the number of foreclosures was very low—only about 0.25 percent. Reasons for this include the following:

---

[10] The information on Germany, provided by Maike Luedersen of the Legal Department of the IMF, is gratefully acknowledged.

[11] An ECB (2009) study finds that the average duration of foreclosure procedures in Europe is 24 months, although it varies significantly across countries, ranging from a minimum of 2 months (Finland) to a maximum of between 56 months (Italy) and 132 months (Cyprus). In Italy, however, according to the Ministry of Justice, the average length of the legal procedure leading to repossession was about three years in 2011.

[12] About 25 percent of total mortgage were either in arrears or restructured at the end of 2012 (Goodbody, 2013).

TABLE 22.4

Methods and Timeframes of the Foreclosure Processes in Selected Countries

Country	Method of foreclosure or repossession	Redemption period: measures taken before starting the enforcement procedure (limited to a summons or detailed procedure) and time frame	Time frame of the foreclosure process	Recourse or nonrecourse
Cyprus	Judicial	Detailed procedures	135 months[1]	Recourse
Denmark	Judicial	Summons; 3 days	6 months	Recourse; 20 years
Ireland	Judicial	Detailed procedures	42 months	Recourse
Germany	Judicial	Detailed procedure; 6 months	18–46 months	Fully recourse
Greece	Judicial[2]	Legal obligation is limited to summons (3 days)[3]	12–36 months depending on the parties' objection or nonobjection before the court.	Recourse; 20 years
Spain	Judicial and nonjudicial (by auction conducted by a notary public)	Summons (demand for payment)	16 to 24 months, depending on the courts[4]	Recourse
The Netherlands	Nonjudicial	Notification[5]	12 months	Recourse
Portugal	Judicial	Summons	On average, 16 months	Recourse
United Kingdom	Judicial	Detailed procedures;[3] to 6 months	8–12 months	Recourse; 6–12 years
United States	Mix of judicial and nonjudicial depending on the state	Redemption period; typically 6 months	Average period in judicial states is 400 days; average in nonjudicial is 270 days, including the redemption period.	Many states are de jure recourse; but de facto, the U.S. states are nonrecourse

Sources: Authors' compilation from consultations with the IMF and ECB Legal Departments; EMF, 2007; Lea, 2010; national mortgage laws; and RealtyTrac website.

[1] Lea (2010) and confirmed by the Memorandum of Understanding. It follows from the Cypriot Memorandum of Understanding that adjustments are necessary to Cypriot legislation in connection with the seizure and sale of collateral, to ensure that, at least for primary residences, the process can be completed within 2.5 years of the initiation of relevant legal proceedings.

[2] However, the Greek Code of Civil Procedure (Article 904 par. 2(d) & Article 918 par. 2(c)) also provides for the possibility of basing the foreclosure on a document issued by a public notary.

[3] However, Law 3869/2010 on Debt Arrangements for Over-Indebted Individuals and Other Rules, as amended and currently in force, provides for a precourt settlement process between creditors and debtors with permanent inability to pay back debts, which may extend the redemption period to six months.

[4] According to Banco Novagalicia, the repossession process is getting longer, from 12 months in 2009 to 16 months in 2012.

[5] If the borrower fails to meet the monthly mortgage payment, the bank automatically obtains the right to repossess the home. After notifying the mortgagee, the bank can evict the borrower from the home within two months and organize a public sale of the property (Brounen, 2011).

Box 22.1 Does Ireland's Foreclosure Framework Need Further Reforms to Address Mortgage Market Distress?

The introduction of the Land and Conveyancing Reform Act of 2009, and subsequent rules, restricted the ability of lenders to repossess collateral against defaulted borrowers who took out mortgages before December 2009. Lenders were required to first obtain a Well-Charging Order and Order of Sale before obtaining an order of repossession. The lender must then apply to the High Court or the Circuit Court (Order for Sale Execution) to arrange for the sale by public auction. These factors led Fitch to increase their estimate of the time of foreclosure to 81 months from 42 months.

In February 2010, Ireland's central bank instituted further procedural measures that resulted in additional delays. The regulator required that all banks, buildings societies, and financial institutions refrain from repossession proceedings for at least a year from the date of the borrower's first payment arrears. The central bank's Code of Conduct on Mortgage Arrears (CCMA)[1] set out the framework that lenders must use when dealing with borrowers in mortgage arrears or in pre-arrears. The CCMA requires lenders to handle all such cases sympathetically and positively, with the objective at all times of helping people to meet their mortgage obligations. Under the CCMA, lenders must operate a Mortgage Arrears Resolution Process (MARP) when dealing with arrears and pre-arrears customers. The five steps of the MARP are communication, financial information, assessment, resolution, and appeals. If these five steps have been exhausted and the lender intends to repossess a home, they must then adhere to the MARP rules governing repossession proceedings.

Additionally, the 2009 act created a gap in the legislation for repossession of the collateral. In July 2011, a High Court Judge found that if a loan went into default, but demand for full payment was not made until after December 1, 2009, the lender could not apply for repossession.

Lenders may bring cases of repossession to the Circuit Court or to the Higher Court, but the court proceeding takes a number of years as the result of adjournments and subsequent appeals, with significantly high costs for the lender. Prolonged and costly foreclosure on mortgage collateral gives rise to moral hazard and tends to be associated with a slower recovery in the property markets (Frantantoni and Moore, 2013).

At this writing, a 2013 bill amending the Land and Conveyancing Law Reform Act 2009 is pending that should restore the availability of summary repossession proceedings for mortgages created before December 2009 (except for cases already pending in court).

Source: Mortgage Arrears Resolution Process (MARP) and Land and Conveyancing Reform Act of 2009.
[1] Code of Conduct on Mortgage Arrears (www.centralbank.ie/publicinformation/Documents/2013%20 CCMA.pdf).

First, legal and regulatory restrictions hampered the ability of lenders to collect on defaulted mortgage loans.[13] Second, although loans are full recourse, borrowers had limited capacity to make up any deficiency between the value of the loan and the collateral; therefore, lenders sought to restructure loans, which, in the near

---

[13] The lender must not apply to the courts to commence legal action for repossession of collateral until every reasonable effort has been made to agree on an alternative arrangement. If the borrower is cooperating with the lender, the lender must wait at least 12 months from the date the arrears were classified as a MARP case (31 days after the first missed repayment) before applying to the courts.

Box 22.2 The Spanish Mortgage Law

Under Spanish mortgage law, among the most stringent in Europe, borrowers in default are liable, with all their present and future assets, for the debt. The creditor retains the right over assets, including principal residence, and the debtor's future income (notwithstanding certain exceptions) until the debt is settled.

The banks normally have the possibility of accelerating the maturity of the loan. Mortgage loans usually include a clause providing for the early termination of the mortgage contract based on, among others, nonpayment of a single installment.

Insolvency proceedings are not widespread in Spain for cultural reasons and institutional inefficiencies. Spain has traditionally had one of the world's lowest business bankruptcy rates (Garcia-Posada, 2013). In 2012, a protection scheme for main residence mortgagors was adopted, which included a code of good practices to which financial institutions may voluntarily adhere, and more flexible foreclosure proceedings; the scheme also allows for the transfer of the principal residence in lieu of payment (*dación en pago*), cancelling the secured debt in full on certain conditions (see Banco de España, 2012, for further details).

The Spanish legal framework for housing foreclosures and evictions was changed, in part, as a follow-up to a ruling of the European Union Court of Justice (March 14, 2013). The court considered that the Spanish legal framework does not comply with EU consumer protection rules because it restricts a judge's ability to suspend foreclosure proceedings while deciding whether the terms of a loan are abusive.

A new law (Law 1/2013) amending the Spanish legal framework was approved May 14, 2013. The law includes a prohibition on initiating foreclosure proceedings before three loan installments are unpaid, a suspension of foreclosure proceedings if such proceedings are based on abusive clauses in the secured loan contracts, and a two-year moratorium on evictions "vulnerable" families from their main residences in case of foreclosure.

In contrast to the United States, most Spanish mortgage contracts do not include the possibility of cancelling the remaining debt after applying the funds from the auction of the collateral property in the foreclosure procedures. This situation leaves many mortgagors highly indebted even after they have been divested of their property. The new amendment to the Spanish foreclosure framework does not change this in general terms, but it is aimed at moderating the burden of the foreclosure proceedings by (1) limiting default interest expenses and costs; (2) cancelling all remaining debt if the sale of the collateral does not cover the debt, but the debtor has no other assets but manages to pay 65 percent of the remaining debt in 5 years or 80 percent in 10 years; (3) introducing the transfer of the principal residence in lieu of payment (dación en pago) for certain extreme cases, as explained above; (4) stopping repossession if the judge determines that there is an abusive clause until another court determines whether this is the case; and (5) establishing new requirements to ensure the independence of appraisal companies.

Vulnerable households have to meet the following criteria, among others: (1) total household income must be less than three to five times the IPREM (Indicador Publico de Renta de Efectos Multiples), depending on other circumstances (based on the current indicator, three times the IPREM is €1,596 a month); (2) there has been a significant alteration in the household's economic circumstances in the previous four years (defined as debt service as a percentage of income having increased 1.5 times); (3) debt servicing is more than 50 percent of the family unit's income; and (4) the secured loan was granted to purchase the mortgaged main and only residence.

Note: The comments on Box 22.2 from Ignacio Sánchez-Román and Luis Tovar French of the Legal Department of the ECB are gratefully acknowledged.

term, results in lower loss recognition, but defers the associated problems of high mortgage debt and poor asset quality for banks.

This contrasts with the regulatory treatment for a nonperforming mortgage in the United States, where loss recognition occurs much earlier. Banks are legislatively required to suspend any accrual of interest income after the mortgage is 90 days in arrears and must charge off principal down to the realizable value of collateral after 180 days in arrears.[14] The result has been that the absolute level of NPLs peaked much earlier and at a lower level in the credit cycle (see Fratantoni and Moore, forthcoming, for more details).

The weaker options available to lenders in Ireland to collect on defaulted mortgages have led to increasing levels of strategic default, that is, default by borrowers who have a greater capacity to pay but choose not to. Strategic default increasingly reflects the ability, conferred by the long delays in the foreclose process, of the borrower to live in the house for extended periods without payment. Based on averages, this time in Ireland is more than double the time in Spain and Portugal and four to five times longer than in Denmark, the Netherlands, the United Kingdom, and the United States.

By contrast, Spain has one of the most stringent repossession laws in Europe, and strategic default occurs much more infrequently. About 450,000 properties were foreclosed between the bursting of the property bubble in 2008 and end-2012. Repossession as a consequence for default on mortgages helps to explain why the rate of default on mortgages has remained considerably lower (less than 4 percent of mortgage loans are more than 90 days in arrears; IMF, 2013). However, the May 2013 amendments to the Spanish mortgage law (see Box 22.2) aim to mitigate the perceived bias toward the lender in the use of repossessions.

Foreclosure Processes in the United States

For the United States, the foreclosure framework is set out in state law.[15] About 24 states require that lenders pursue defaulting borrowers through a judicial proceeding involving the courts, and many states stipulate a nonjudicial process. In a few states, both means are available, and lenders often choose foreclosure through a nonjudicial process, also known as a foreclosure by "power of sale," which allows the bank to initiate a foreclosure sale of the collateral (the property) without court approval. The average period for completing a foreclosure was 414 days at end-2012, up from 348 days at end-2011. The shortest period was observed in Texas (90–113 days) in a nonjudicial process, excluding the

---

[14] The "charge off" is only on the bank's financial accounts and does not result in debt forgiveness to the borrower; the bank is still expected to pursue all avenues to collect the loan, including through repossession of the collateral.

[15] According to RealtyTrac, the foreclosure process varies somewhat from state to state and depends primarily on whether the state uses mortgages or deeds of trust for the purchase of real property. Generally, states that use mortgages conduct judicial foreclosures, using the court system to execute the foreclosure; states that use deeds of trust conduct nonjudicial foreclosures using an out-of-court procedure defined by state law.

redemption period, which is typically 180 days; comparably short periods were also observed in two judicial states—Delaware (145 days) and Virginia (146 days). The longest periods were all in judicial states (New York at 1,089 days, New Jersey at 987 days, and Florida at 853 days, according to RealtyTrac).

By reputation, home mortgage debt in the United States is nonrecourse—if the borrower defaults, the lender gets the home as collateral but cannot pursue the borrower for any deficiency between the home's value and the remaining debt. However, lenders do have the ability to pursue deficiency judgments in 41 of the 50 states. But in practice, lenders do not pursue deficiency judgments because the added recovery of value beyond the value of the collateral does not support the effort to collect (Ghent and Kudlyak, 2009).

Measures to Prevent or Delay Foreclosure Processes

The recent financial and economic crisis has brought about, on both sides of the Atlantic, a proliferation of measures implemented to protect households from the risks of foreclosure repossessions because their ability to make payments has been reduced considerably since 2007–08. In theory, debtors and creditors have incentives to prevent foreclosure.

Loss-Mitigation Tools

Loan modification is by far the main foreclosure prevention measure. Loan modification involves changing the terms of the mortgage contract so as to lower the borrower's monthly payment and, in some cases, to also lower the principal owed. This is typically implemented by creditors when payment difficulties are deemed temporary and the loan is viable in the long term.

European Commission (2011) lists the different possibilities of loan modifications at the country level for Europe. Without being exhaustive, the guiding principle is to foster the restructuring of the mortgage debt by courts under certain conditions, especially the circumstances of the debtor, such as unemployment. Alternatives to *loan modification* have been used recently (European Commission, 2011). Among the measures that allow households to stay in their properties are the following:

- Under *reconciliation procedures*, based on the good faith principle, creditors should explore acceptable solutions for debtors shortly after arrears occur and before starting any foreclosure process. A partial repayment strategy is the usual form.

- When the debtor's financial difficulties are more severe, but still short-term, there is the possibility of *forbearance*, which allows a grace period during which the creditor agrees not to foreclose and the debtor agrees to a mortgage repayment plan to fulfill its obligations by the end of the forbearance period (Gerardi and Li, 2010).

- Another possible alternative to foreclosure is a *mediation* or arbitration process, which is a neutral setting in which the parties, creditors and debtors, negotiate and identify cost-effective solutions.

There are other alternatives, but these oblige the household to abandon the property:

- One possibility is the *short sale*, in which the debtor is allowed to sell the property, and any outstanding amount due after the sale is either forgiven or renegotiated by the creditor.
- The other possibility is the *donation* of the property in payment (lieu of payment). In this case, the creditor is obliged to accept delivery of the guarantee of the mortgage by the debtor to settle the debt.

Government Intervention

Active public policies to avoid foreclosures in the United States and Europe since the surge of foreclosures in 2007–08 differ by country. In the United States, the government, in cooperation with the industry and related associations, has sponsored several programs to modify the conditions of loans. These programs provided incentives in the form of subsidies to debtors, creditors, and intermediaries for loan modification in the Making Home Affordable framework (see Fratantoni and Moore, 2013, for more details). European Commission (2011) provides a good overview of practices by European policymakers regarding public rescue schemes. The experiences differ across countries and comply with the state aid rules to avoid distortions in an economic union. The policy responses include granting public loan guarantees, the possibility to sell the home to a publicly sponsored association or other fund, financial relief for unemployed homeowners, and temporary tax relief. All of these are typical mitigating actions recently implemented in several European countries as protection schemes for debtors.

For instance, Ireland and Portugal[16] illustrate the logic of these programs. The CCMA and MARP in Ireland and the recent law in Portugal (Law No. 58/2012, of November 9, 2012) created protection schemes for residential mortgage loan debtors in special economic need, valid in principle until December 31, 2015. The programs provide options for the restructuring of debts, including grace periods, extension of payment deadlines, spread reductions, and the granting of additional loans. It is also possible to transfer the mortgaged asset to the credit institution or to a real estate home leasing investment fund (Fundo de Investimento Imobiliário para Arrendamento Habitacional) as a means of paying the entire debt, in which case the borrower may become entitled to lease (mortgage to rent) and, later on, to repurchase, the mortgaged asset or exchange it for a less valuable real estate asset (trade-down mortgages).

How Does Recent Literature Evaluate the Different Foreclosure Processes and the Policies to Delay Them?

Empirical research for the United States shows a very strong negative correlation between actual foreclosure and whether the state requires judicial foreclosure.

---

[16] This information was provided by Gustavo Botelho Maria da Graça Peres of the Legal Department of the ECB.

States that require judicial foreclosure had a rate of foreclosure per owner during 2008 and 2009 that was 3 percentage points lower than states without judicial foreclosure (Mian, Sufi, and Trebbi, 2011). The authors also estimated the causal effect of differences in foreclosure state laws on foreclosure rates and other economic outcomes. They found that states with nonjudicial foreclosure laws are twice as likely to foreclose on delinquent homes and those foreclosures negatively affect house prices and real activity. By contrast, another line of research argues that judicial foreclosure results in high costs from delaying foreclosure; and Gerardi, Lambie-Hanson, and Willen (2013) find that judicial foreclosure alters the timing but not the number of foreclosures. The conclusion is that anti-foreclosure laws are not actually fixing the underlying problem, but instead are delaying the inevitable in many situations (Gerardi, Lambie-Hanson, and Willen, 2013).

In general, judicial foreclosures take longer than nonjudicial foreclosures. This fact, and the many policies put into effect in 2008 to prevent homeowners from being evicted from their homes, generated extensive literature on the unintended effects of these laws and policies, which were meant to help homeowners, but, according to this research, they may actually be actively hurting housing markets. This research has shown that foreclosure prevention efforts are neither necessary nor a sufficient condition for keeping people in their homes. This research found that the likelihood of a delinquent homeowner averting foreclosure is remarkably small, making programs that attempt to prevent foreclosure mostly futile (Adelino, Gerardi, and Willen, 2009).

According to this research, there is room for moral hazard, because borrowers do live rent free during the period in which a loan is in foreclosure, and delays in the foreclosure process promote this behavior. Zhu and Pace (2011) investigated the influence of foreclosure delays on borrowers' default behavior and concluded that the longer the delay, the higher the benefit one could obtain from default, given that during the duration of the foreclosure the defaulting borrower could legally remain in the property without making payments. Rational borrowers make their default decisions based on the expected value of default. Everything else being equal, the longer the expected period of foreclosure, the higher the expected benefit from default, and the more valuable the default option becomes.

LESSONS AND CONCLUSIONS

The elements that have contributed to the different default and foreclosure rates, and the severity and length of the mortgage crisis, are related to lack of diversification, or excessive reliance on the housing markets in the United States and in some European countries, particularly in Ireland and Spain, but they are also related to the legal framework and foreclosure practices in each country.

The experiences of Ireland and Spain confirm the argument discussed in the literature on the U.S. foreclosure process. Specific mortgage laws and practices may lead to different outcomes in mortgage default and foreclosures, and the speed of resolving the mortgage crisis and recovery of the housing market. Delays in the foreclosure process create moral hazard that leads to increases in default rates because borrowers obtain free rent during the period the lender forbears on collection or that a loan is in the foreclosure process.

In Europe, mortgage defaults and home foreclosures seem to be more related to borrower credit quality than to the value of the collateral property, given that in all the countries in the sample, the mortgages are recourse, and in some of the countries (Spain and the Netherlands) foreclosure processes are very much tilted against the interests of the borrowers. Thus, households have very strong incentives to avoid foreclosure. By contrast, in the United States, given that mortgages are both de jure and de facto nonrecourse, the value of the collateral plays an important role in the decision to foreclose. Borrowers in the United States have stronger incentives to default when they have negative equity. Nevertheless, U.S. lenders' limited prospects for collecting anything beyond the value of the collateral promotes earlier loss recognition, which has led to a quicker recovery of credit markets.

APPENDIX 22A

TABLE 22A.1

Nonperforming Loans as Percentage of Gross Loans[1]						
Country	2007	2008	2009	2010	2011	2012
Cyprus	3.4	3.6	4.5	5.6	9.6	10.7
Denmark	0.3	1.2	3.3	4.1	3.7	4.2
Germany	2.7	2.9	3.3	3.2	3.0	
Greece	4.6	5	7.7	10.4	14.4	17.2
Ireland	0.6	2.6	9	10.8	19.6	24.8
Netherlands	n.a.	1.7	3.2	2.8	2.7	3.1
Portugal	2.8	3.6	4.8	5.2	7.5	9.8
Spain[2]	0.9	3.4	5.1	5.8	7.6	7.1
United Kingdom [3]	0.9	1.6	3.5	4.0	4.0	4.0
United States	1.4	3	5.4	4.9	4.1	3.9

Sources: Data for Ireland for 2010–12 are from the Central Bank of Ireland. World Bank and IMF.

Note: n.a. = not available.

[1] Nonperforming loan definitions and measurements differ across countries, making data comparability difficult.

[2] Data as of June 2012.

[3] Figures for the United Kingdom are based on the consolidated global operations of domestically controlled banks reporting in the United Kingdom, so may not be representative of the financial soundness of the subgroup of banks that account for the bulk of retail activity in the United Kingdom. Other sources (Bloomberg, L.P.) report much higher figures for major U.K. banks.

TABLE 22A.2

Rate of Unemployment in Selected Countries							
Country	2006	2007	2008	2009	2010	2011	2012
Cyprus	4.7	4.0	3.8	5.6	6.4	7.9	12.1
Denmark	3.9	3.8	3.5	6.1	7.5	7.6	7.6
Germany	10.2	8.8	7.6	7.7	7.1	6.0	5.5
Greece	8.9	8.3	7.7	9.4	12.5	17.5	24.2
Ireland	4.5	4.7	6.4	12.0	13.9	14.6	14.7
Netherlands	4.4	3.6	3.1	3.7	4.5	4.4	5.3
Portugal	7.7	8.0	7.6	9.5	10.8	12.7	15.7
Spain	8.5	8.3	11.3	18.0	20.1	21.7	25.0
United Kingdom	5.4	5.4	5.6	7.5	7.9	8.0	8.0
United States	4.6	4.6	5.8	9.3	9.6	8.9	8.1

Source: IMF, World Economic Outlook database.

REFERENCES

Addison-Smyth, D., and K. McQuinn, 2009, "Quantifying Revenue Windfalls from Irish Housing Market," Research Technical Paper 10/RT/09 (Dublin: Central Bank and Financial Services Authority of Ireland).

Adelino, Manuel, Kristopher Gerardi, and Paul Willen, 2009, "Why Don't Lenders Renegotiate More Home Mortgages? Re-defaults, Self-Cures, and Securitization," Public Policy Discussion Paper No. 09-4, Federal Reserve Bank of Boston.

Banco de España, 2012, *Financial Regulation Economic Bulletin* Q1, April, pp. 147–52.

Bardhan, Ashok, 2009, "Housing and the Financial Crisis in the US: Cause or Symptom?" *Vikalpa, The Journal for Decision Makers*, Vol. 34, No. 3, p. 1.

Bardhan, Ashok, Robert H. Edelstein, and Cynthia A. Kroll, 2011, "The Financial Crisis and Housing Markets, Worldwide," in *Global Housing Markets: Crises, Policies, and Institutions*, ed. by Ashok Bardhan, Robert H. Edelstein, and Cynthia A. Kroll (Hoboken, New Jersey: John Wiley & Sons).

Brounen, Dirk, 2011, "House Prices and Market Institutions, the Dutch Experience," in *Global Housing Markets: Crises, Policies, and Institutions*, ed. by Ashok Bardhan, Robert H. Edelstein, and Cynthia A. Kroll (Hoboken, New Jersey: John Wiley & Sons).

Calomiris, C., and E. Higgins, 2011, "Policy Briefing: Are Delays to the Foreclosure Process a Good Thing?" Shadow Open Market Committee, Economic Policy for the 21st Century, March.

Central Bank of Ireland, 2012, "Residential Mortgage Arrears and Repossessions Statistics (2012–2013)."

Cour-Thimann, P., and B. Winkler, 2012, "The ECB's Non-Standard Monetary Policy Measures: The Role of Institutional Factors and Financial Structure," *Oxford Review of Economic Policy*, Vol. 28, No. 4, pp. 765–803.

Ellis, Luci, 2008, "The Housing Meltdown: Why Did It Happen in the United States?" BIS Working Papers No. 259 (Basel: Bank for International Settlements).

European Central Bank (ECB), 2009, "Housing Finance in the Euro Area," Occasional Paper No. 101 (Frankfurt).

European Commission, 2011, "National Measures and Practices to Avoid Foreclosure Procedures for Residential Mortgage Loans. Accompanying Document to the Proposal for a Directive of the European Parliament," Working Paper No. 357 (Brussels).

European Mortgage Federation, 2007, *Study on the Efficiency of Mortgage Collateral in the European Union* (Brussels).

———, 2011, *Study on Non-Performing Loans in the EU* (Brussels).

Feldstein, Martin, 2008, "How to Help People Whose Home Values Are Underwater—The Economic Spiral Will Get Worse unless We Do Something about Negative Equity," *Wall Street Journal*, November 18.

Foote, C.L., K.S, Gerardi, L. Goette, and P.S.Willen, 2009, "Reducing Foreclosures," Public Policy Discussion Papers, No. 09-2, Federal Reserve Bank of Boston.

Frame, Scott, 2010, "Estimating the Effect of Mortgage Foreclosures on Nearby Property Values: A Critical Review of the Literature," Economic Review, Federal Reserve Bank of Atlanta.

Fratantoni, Michael, and Michael Moore, forthcoming, "The U.S. Mortgage Crisis—Are There Lessons for Policymakers?" IMF Working Paper (Washington: International Monetary Fund).

Garcia-Posada, M., 2013, "Insolvency Institutions and Efficiency: The Spanish Case," Banco de España Working Paper No. 1302, February 8.

Gerardi, K.S., L. Lambie-Hanson, and Paul Willen, 2013, "Do Borrower Rights Improve Borrower Outcomes? Evidence from the Foreclosure Process," *Journal of Urban Economics,* Vol. 73, pp. 1–17.

Gerardi, K.S., and W. Li, 2010, "Mortgage Foreclosure Prevention Efforts," Federal Reserve of Atlanta, *Economic Review* No. 2/2010 (Atlanta, Georgia).

Ghent, Andra C., 2012, *The Historical Origins of America's Mortgage Laws*, Special Report, Research Institute for Housing America, October. http://www.housingamerica.org/RIHA/ RIHA/Publications/82406_11922_RIHA_Origins_Report.pdf.

Ghent, Andra C., and Marianna Kudlyak, 2009, "Recourse and Residential Mortgage Default: Theory and Evidence from U.S. States," Federal Reserve Bank of Richmond Working Paper No. 09-10, July 7 (Richmond, Virginia).

Goodbody, 2012, *Irish Economics & Financials: Household Debt, the Housing and Mortgage Markets*, November.

Goodbody, 2013, *Economic First Glance,* June 21.

Goodman, 2010, "Dimensioning the Housing Crisis," *Financial Analysts Journal*, Vol. 66, No. 3, pp. 26–37.

International Monetary Fund (IMF), 2013, "Spain: Financial Sector Reform—Second Progress Report," IMF Country Report 13/54 (Washington).

Herkenhoff, K., and L. Ohanian, 2012, "Foreclosure Delay and U.S. Unemployment," Federal Reserve Bank of St. Louis, Working Paper 2012-017A, June.

Kobie T.F., and S. Lee, 2011, "The Spatial-Temporal Impact of Residential Foreclosures on Single-Family Residential Property Values," *Urban Affairs Review* Vol. 47, No. 1, pp. 3–30.

Kimball, Z., and Paul Willen, 2012, "US Mortgage and Foreclosure Law," *The New Palgrave Dictionary of Economics*, edited by Steven Durlauf and Lawrence E. Blume, Online edition.

Kiff, John, and Vladimir Klyuev, 2009, "Foreclosure Mitigation Efforts in the United States: Approaches and Challenges," IMF Staff Position Note No. 09/02 (Washington: International Monetary Fund).

Lea, Michael, 2010, *International Comparison of Mortgage Product Offerings*, Research Institute for Housing America (Washington: Mortgage Bankers Association).

Mian, Atif, Amir Sufi, and Francesco Trebbi, 2011, "Foreclosure, House Prices, and Real Economy," NBER Working Paper No. 16685 (Cambridge, Massachusetts: National Bureau of Economic Research). http://www.nber.org/papers/w16685.

Morris, R., C. Rodrigues Braz, F. de Castro, S. Jonk, J. Kremer, S. Linehan, M. R. Marino, C. Schalck, and O. Tkacevs, 2009, "Explaining Government Revenue Windfalls and Shortfalls: An Analysis for Selected EU Countries," ECB Working Paper No. 1114 (Frankfurt: European Central Bank).

Stevenson, S., 2011, "The Dynamics of the Irish Housing Market," in *Global Housing Markets: Crises, Policies, and Institutions*, ed. by Ashok Bardhan, Robert H. Edelstein, and Cynthia A. Kroll (Hoboken, New Jersey: John Wiley & Sons).

Zhu, S., and Kelley Pace, 2011, "The Influence of Foreclosure Delays on Borrower's Default Behavior," paper presented at the 46th Annual American Real Estate and Urban Economics Association Conference, Denver, Colorado, January 7–9.

CHAPTER 23

Resolving Systemically Important Financial Institutions: Mandatory Recapitalization of Financial Institutions Using "Bail-Ins"

Jianping Zhou, Virginia Rutledge, Wouter Bossu, Marc Dobler, Nadege Jassaud, and Michael Moore

Large-scale government support of the financial institutions deemed too big or too important to fail during the recent crisis has been costly and has potentially increased moral hazard. To protect taxpayers from exposure to bank losses and to reduce the risks posed by too-big-to-fail, various reform initiatives have been undertaken at both national and international levels, including expanding resolution powers and tools.

One example is *bail-in*, which is defined in this chapter as a statutory power of a resolution authority (as opposed to contractual arrangements, such as contingent capital requirements) to restructure the liabilities of a distressed financial institution by writing down its unsecured debt and/or converting it to equity. The statutory bail-in power is intended to achieve a prompt recapitalization and restructuring of the distressed institution. This chapter studies its effectiveness in restoring the viability of distressed institutions, discusses potential risks when a bail-in power is activated, and proposes design features to mitigate these risks. The main conclusions are:

- As a going-concern form of resolution, bail-in could mitigate the systemic risks associated with disorderly liquidations, reduce deleveraging pressures, and preserve asset values that might otherwise be lost in a liquidation. With a credible threat of stock elimination or dilution by debt conversion and assumption of management by resolution authorities, financial institutions may be incentivized to raise capital or restructure debt voluntarily *before* the triggering of the bail-in power.

- However, if the use of a bail-in power is perceived by the market as a sign of the concerned institution's insolvency, it could trigger a run by short-term creditors and aggravate the institution's liquidity problem. Ideally, therefore, bail-in should be activated when a capital infusion is expected to restore a distressed financial institution to viability, with official liquidity support as a backstop until the bank is stabilized.

An earlier version of this chapter was published as an IMF Staff Discussion Note (Zhou and others, 2012).

- Bail-in is not a panacea and should be considered as one element of a comprehensive solution to the too-big-to-fail problem. It should supplement, not replace, other resolution tools that would allow for an orderly closure of a failed institution.

Most importantly, the bail-in framework needs to be carefully designed to ensure its effective implementation. More specifically,

- The *triggers* for bail-in power should be consistent with those used for other resolution tools. They should be set at the point when a firm would have breached the regulatory minima but before it became balance-sheet insolvent. To make bail-in a transparent tool, its scope should be limited to (1) elimination of existing equity shares as a precondition for a bail-in, and (2) conversion and haircut to subordinated and unsecured senior debt. Debt restructuring under a bail-in should take into account the order of priorities applicable in a liquidation.

- A *clear and coherent legal framework* for bail-in is essential. The legal framework needs to be designed to establish an appropriate balance between the rights of private stakeholders and the public policy interest in preserving financial stability. Debt restructuring ideally would not be subject to creditor consent, but a "no creditor worse off" test may be introduced to safeguard creditors' and shareholders' interests. The framework also needs to provide mechanisms for addressing issues associated with the bail-in of debt issued by an entity of a larger banking group and with the cross-border operations of that entity or banking group.

- The *contribution of new capital* will come from debt conversion and/or an issuance of new equity, with an elimination or significant dilution of the pre-bail-in shareholders.

- Bail-in will need to be accompanied by mechanisms to ensure the suitability of new shareholders. Some measures (for example, a floor price for debt/equity conversion) might be necessary to reduce the risk of a "death spiral" in share prices.

- It may be necessary to impose minimum requirements on banks for issuing unsecured debt or to set limits on the encumbrance of assets. Such limits have been introduced by many advanced countries. This would help reassure the market that a bail-in would be sufficient to recapitalize the distressed institution, thus forestalling potential runs by short-term creditors and avert a downward share price spiral. The framework should also include measures to mitigate contagion risks to other systemic financial institutions, for example, by limiting their cross-holding of unsecured senior debt.

OVERVIEW

The recent financial crisis demonstrated that the distress of a systemically important financial institution (SIFI) and its subsequent disorderly liquidation can create risks to overall financial stability. A failing SIFI can endanger financial stability in three ways:

- Through direct *counterparty risks* when the failing institution fails to meet its financial obligations (Gorton and Metrick, 2012) or high demand for collateral (or "margin").
- Through *liquidity risks* and fire-sale effects in asset markets, when the distressed institution is forced into asset sales to obtain liquidity, which further depresses asset prices (and thus raises demand for higher "margin") and causes credit crunches (Brunnermeier, 2009; Acharya, Shin, and Yorulmazer, 2011).
- Through *contagion risks* when the panic caused by the failure of one institution spreads to other financial institutions (Duffie, 2010; and FDIC, 2011).

Government-funded rescues of SIFIs to preserve financial stability have been costly, and, as a result, the potential risks to financial stability posed by SIFIs have increased. In some countries, government bailouts have contributed to unsustainable public finances that are threatening the solvency of the banks with heavy exposure to sovereign debt. The government-assisted mergers and acquisitions have resulted in further consolidation of financial institutions in the United States and across Europe. Consequently, the top financial institutions of today have become *larger* and the European and U.S. financial sectors have become even *more* concentrated than before, aggravating the too-big-to-fail problem (Bernanke, 2013; Tarullo, 2013). At the same time, the "shadow" banking system, which played a crucial role in generating and spreading systemic risks, remains underregulated, despite various reform efforts (Duffie, 2010; and Metrick and Gorton, 2010).

Solving the too-big-to-fail problem requires a comprehensive approach. An adequate policy framework would need to include (1) more stringent capital and liquidity requirements to limit contribution to systemic risk, (2) intensive supervision consistent with the complexity and riskiness of the institutions, (3) enhanced transparency and disclosure requirements to capture emerging risks in the broader financial system; and (4) effective resolution regimes at national and global levels to make orderly resolution a credible option, with resolution plans and tools that lead creditors to share losses (see Ötker-Robe and others, 2011).

An effective and *credible* resolution framework for distressed SIFIs is one important element of a comprehensive solution to minimize potential costs to taxpayers of future bank failures, and to break the adverse feedback loop between sovereign debt and bank debt. In the absence of such a framework, policymakers will continue to face the dilemma of whether to let a financial institution fail with a potential risk to financial stability or to bail it out at taxpayer cost, and with serious moral hazard consequences. Any credible and effective resolution framework for SIFIs must therefore be able to:

- Reduce the likelihood of government bail-out by ensuring that shareholders and creditors bear losses, thereby limiting moral-hazard risk and improving market discipline.
- Minimize systemic risks by quickly restoring confidence, thereby reducing the need for fire sales or disorderly liquidations of financial contracts, and preserving the going-concern value of the distressed institutions.
- Achieve effective cross-border resolutions.

Some European countries are considering adding bail-in mechanisms to their resolution toolkits to improve crisis management. For instance, the recent European Commission's proposed bank recovery and resolution directive laid out detailed bail-in proposals (European Commission, 2012). The concept, scope, and design features of bail-ins are also the subject of various ongoing and sometimes confused discussions at the national or international levels. The confusion stems from the fact that bail-in can take many forms, and after the recent Cyprus bail-in that involved a write-down of customer deposits, countries were forced to clarify their national bail-in proposals to prevent the potential loss of depositor confidence.

The current debate also concerns the legal basis and financial stability implications of bail-in tools. In particular, a clear and coherent legal framework is essential to underpin the use of the statutory bail-in power. The legal framework would need to balance private rights and the public interest in preserving financial stability to ensure that statutory bail-in can be exercised without conflicting with any applicable constitutional provisions on the protection of property or contract rights. The design of bail-in power also needs to take into account the possibility that the decision to trigger bail-in power to a distressed SIFI could send negative signals to the market about its solvency and thus increase the risk of a run prior to the triggering of the bail-in power. The potential impact on financial institutions' funding costs and liability structures should be carefully studied as well.

This chapter studies the usefulness of statutory bail-in power as a resolution tool for SIFIs. While bail-in would be a useful tool with respect to a broad range of financial institutions, the discussion of the legal framework to support bail-in will focus on a special resolution regime for banks.[1] The chapter addresses the following issues:

- *Relative advantages and disadvantages.* Under what circumstances would bail-in be preferred to other resolution tools, including liquidation and powers to transfer assets and liabilities to other legal entities, such as bridge banks?

- *Design features.* What are the design features (triggers, scope, ability to remove management, creditor seniority, and so on) that ensure a credible, transparent, and effective bail-in regime while mitigating the risk that the power itself could trigger instability?

- *Cross-border effect.* What are the cross-border challenges and possible solutions to ensure the regime's effectiveness in all relevant jurisdictions?

- *Market impact.* What will be the potential impact on banks' funding cost and funding structure? What are the implications for financial stability?

---

[1] Though this chapter discusses the concept of bail-in as a resolution tool for systemically important banks and nonbanks alike, the structure and design details of resolution regimes for systemically important nonbanks can differ from those applicable to banks.

STATUTORY BAIL-IN: CONCEPT AND ECONOMIC RATIONALE

What Is Bail-In?

Bail-in has been defined differently in various bail-in proposals. The discussion essentially takes one of the following two approaches: (1) a contractual approach to write down and convert nonequity liabilities, which could refer to contingent capital instruments or to a broader set of contractual "bail-inable" debt instruments that could include other unsecured liabilities (for example, unsecured senior debt); and (2) a statutory approach to debt write-down, often accompanied by a debt-equity conversion, commonly referred to as statutory bail-in power. The objectives of various bail-in proposals also differ, from restoring a failing institution's viability through recapitalization to increasing its loss-absorbing capacity and improving its resolvability.

In this chapter, we analyze bail-in as a statutory power to recapitalize a distressed SIFI by converting and/or writing down its unsecured debt while maintaining its legal entity.[2] The idea is to recapitalize an ailing financial institution by restructuring its liabilities, without having to involve public funds (with liquidity support as a backstop). The restructuring of liabilities would need to be able to restore capital to meet regulatory requirements and provide additional capital to ensure the financial institution's viability, including under stressed assumptions. This will be achieved either through conversion of debt-to-equity or through capital brought in by new shareholders, or a combination of the two. The aim is to have a private sector solution as an alternative to government-funded rescues of SIFIs.

We also differentiate the statuary bail-in mechanism from contractual contingent capital instruments or any other contractual instruments with write-off or conversion features. Both involve creditor-financed recapitalization of SIFIs and spreading losses between creditors and shareholders, and they could form a complementary approach, with contingent capital as the first line of defense and bail-in kicking in to deal with the SIFIs that are nearly insolvent even after the conversion of contingent capital.[3] In this case, the contractual instruments would have been written off or converted before bail-in power is enacted.

The following example is a simple illustration of how bail-in might work and what its effect on a bank's balance sheet might be (Table 23.1). Suppose there is a bank with total assets of US$100 billion, financed by deposits (US$50 billion), repos, and other short-term funding (US$20 billion), and long-term unsecured senior debt (US$20 billion). Hence, the bank's equity position is US$10 billion. Assume that its capital is eliminated due to a large loss (US$10 billion) in its long-term assets. A mandatory recapitalization under a bail-in power would restore the equity position to US$10 billion by converting

---

[2] Specifically refers to keeping the legal entity of the concerned financial institution unchanged.
[3] For a detailed discussion on contingent capital, see Pazarbasioglu and others (2011).

TABLE 23.1

Effects of Bail-in on Banks' Balance Sheets: A Simple Example *(in billions of U.S. dollars)*			
Bank balance sheet at the starting point			
Asset	100	Liability	90
Cash and other fixed assets	5	Deposits	50
Securities and short-term investment	45	Repos and other short-term borrowing	20
Loans and other long-term investment	50	Long-term unsecured debt	20
		Equity	10
Bank balance sheet after a write-down of $10 billion in long-term assets			
Asset	90	Liability	90
Cash and other fixed assets	5	Deposits	50
Securities and short-term investment	45	Repos and other short-term borrowing	20
Loans and other long-term investment	40	Long-term unsecured debt	20
		Equity	0
Bank balance sheet after recapitalization under the bail-in power			
Asset	90	Liability	80
Cash and other fixed assets	5	Deposits	50
Securities and short-term investment	45	Repos and other short-term borrowing	20
Loans and other long-term investment	40	Long-term unsecured debt	10
		Equity	10

50 percent of unsecured senior debt into equity, without the bank having to resort to asset sales. In this example, pre-restructuring shares are completely written off, but deposits, repos, and other short-term funding are not affected by the bail-in power, while restructured senior debt holders are now shareholders (with downside as well as upside potential).

The bail-in capital could be seen as a form of insurance (provided by creditors) against bank insolvency and, hence, bank runs, especially runs on repos and other short-term funding. Consider the example given above and assume there is no bail-in power in place. Runs on repos and other short-term funding now become a high risk as the bank's capital is eroded by losses. But if a part of the bank's debt can be converted into equity under a bail-in power (the bail-in capital) to absorb losses, the risk of runs on short-term funding could be significantly lowered (though rollover risk of long-term debt could increase as a result). The crucial point is that investors need to be convinced that a recapitalization under a bail-in will provide *sufficient* time to restore the bank's capital strength and, hence, the bank's long-term viability. Otherwise, the triggering of the bail-in power could be seen as signaling a bank's nonviability, causing a run instead of preventing it.

Why Do We Need Bail-In?

The recent crisis has demonstrated the need to expand resolution powers available for SIFIs. During the crisis, a lack of robust bank resolution tools meant that many countries had to rescue failing SIFIs with bail-outs or rely on general corporate insolvency proceedings to deal with the failures, with mixed results. For example, Commercial Investment Trust (CIT) Group was restructured successfully after filing for bankruptcy under Chapter 11 of the Bankruptcy Code in the United States.[4] Lehman Brothers' filing for bankruptcy protection, however, resulted in a disorderly liquidation that destroyed asset value and destabilized financial markets (FDIC, 2011). This experience, as well as experience in other countries, clearly demonstrated the need to expand resolution tools, so that SIFIs could undergo resolution in a way that preserved asset values and systemic business functions and minimized contagion.

General corporate insolvency proceedings do not provide sufficient tools to manage the risks to financial stability that can arise from the failure of a SIFI.[5] Many SIFIs are holding companies with a mix of retail banks, broker-dealers, asset management funds, money market funds, corporations, and insurance companies. The bankruptcy proceedings for these financial companies can be very complex, lengthy, and costly.[6] Under highly volatile and uncertain market conditions, a lengthy and uncertain wind-down could undermine market confidence and risk destabilizing the financial system (Metrick and Gorton, 2010; and Shleifer and Vishny, 2011).

Because SIFIs typically hold large positions in financial derivatives, insolvency can trigger a disorderly unwinding of these financial contracts, causing significant disruption to financial markets. For example, in the United States, financial contracts are not subject to the automatic stay that generally applies in bankruptcy, nor are they subject to a general stay in bank insolvencies. As some have argued, the disorderly liquidation of financial contracts was a key contributing factor to the recent financial crisis (FDIC, 2011; and Gorton and Metrick, 2012). In the case of Lehman Brothers, the bankruptcy filing of its holding company constituted a default that terminated swaps and other derivative trades activated emergency clearing-house rules that allowed the liquidation of all its positions, and led to serious disruption in its settlement and transfer operations.

In response to the crisis, some countries have adopted or extended special resolution regimes for the orderly resolution of ailing financial institutions on a closed (gone-concern) basis. Under these frameworks, an institution may cease to exist as a legal entity, although parts or all of the institution's businesses and operations may continue through another legal entity, such as a purchasing institution or a bridge bank. The objective is to ensure an orderly closing of the original legal entity while selling off the valuable parts. In the United States, the Orderly Liquidation Authority under the Dodd-Frank Act grants the Federal Deposit Insurance Corporation (FDIC) the powers and authority to resolve

---

[4] CIT Group filed for Chapter 11 bankruptcy protection on November 1, 2009, with US$71 billion in assets and support from its creditors. It emerged from its bankruptcy proceedings 38 days later, after its creditors reached an agreement on a voluntary debt restructuring plan.

[5] The systemic nature of a financial institution would also depend on the market conditions. At a volatile time, the failure of a relatively small institution could also have a destabilizing impact on the financial system.

[6] For example, Lehman's bankruptcy has involved five bodies of laws applicable to its various corporate entities, including over 80 jurisdictions' insolvency laws applied to its non-U.S. entities (Summe, 2011), with legal costs exceeding US$1 billion and still rising.

failed systemically important nonbank financial companies through receivership, mainly using the procedures and tools already available to resolve failed FDIC-insured banks (FDIC, 2011).[7] In the United Kingdom, the Banking Act of 2009 introduced a special resolution regime for deposit-taking financial institutions only.

Bail-in powers would offer an additional and complementary tool for the resolution of an ailing SIFI on an open (going-concern) basis. This tool involves recapitalization through relatively straightforward liability adjustments. Though the bank is not closed, the management responsible for the loss of capital would be removed as part of the resolution, and existing shareholders would be substantially diluted or fully eliminated. Unlike the gone-concern resolution tools discussed earlier, the objective of bail-in powers is to restore the viability of the distressed institution, allowing it to continue as an open and operating legal entity, thus mitigating the systemic risks associated with insolvency-induced disorderly liquidation. More importantly, by eliminating insolvency risks, the pressure on distressed financial institutions to post more collateral against their repo contracts could be significantly reduced, thereby minimizing liquidity risks and preventing runs on repos or other contracts. Equally important is that bail-in would reduce the need for assisted mergers and, therefore, provide an alternative to even larger SIFIs.

The bail-in proposal and its variations have been included in reform agendas at both national and international levels. Prior to the crisis, some countries already had some form of debt restructuring mechanism applicable to banks. More recently, the Financial Stability Board (FSB) has included bail-in as one of the key attributes of effective resolution regimes (FSB, 2011a and 2011b).[8] Most of the post-crisis reforms have not yet incorporated statutory powers to restructure bank debt as a means of resolving a bank without closure, but various bail-in proposals have been put forward at the national and international levels, including in the United Kingdom (Independent Commission on Banking, 2011) and at the European Commission (EC, 2011).

---

[7] The FDIC has used three basic resolution methods for failing institutions: purchase and assumption transactions (most commonly used), deposit payoffs, and open bank assistance transactions (which are no longer commonly used). The Orderly Liquidation Authority specifically focuses on mitigating the systemic risk of disorderly liquidation of financial positions by granting the FDIC the authority to suspend the termination rights in "qualified financial contracts" as defined in the Federal Deposit Insurance Act by one business day and allowing the FDIC a short period of time (up to three days if a resolution commences on a Friday) in which it may transfer the qualified financial contracts to a solvent third party or to a bridge company. If a transfer occurs, the counterparties would continue to be prohibited from terminating their contracts and liquidating and netting out their positions solely on the basis of the appointment of a receiver.

[8] Further work on the design of mandatory debt restructuring will be carried forward through the FSB, its Resolution Steering Group, and Legal Advisory Panel; the last is providing more detailed legal analysis and recommendations on implementing the recommendations of the FSB with respect to resolutions.

A PROPOSED FRAMEWORK FOR BAIL-IN

A well-designed and comprehensive framework is essential to ensure the effective implementation of a bail-in regime. First and most importantly, bail-in must be based on a robust legal framework, as with all resolution tools that affect the rights of stakeholders. As a resolution tool, bail-in would be one of an array of techniques available to the resolution authority under a well-designed special resolution regime. Such a regime would include a going-concern form for proceeding, such as "official administration," which would give the authorities extraordinary power to take control of a bank by virtue of its having crossed some legally defined threshold of financial weakness or other serious difficulty.[9] An administrator would be appointed and empowered by bank supervisory or resolution authorities to design and implement a restructuring plan for the bank and, if restructuring were not an option, to prepare the bank for orderly liquidation.[10] Second, the design of a bail-in framework should take into consideration its potential impact on short-term creditors as well as on other financial institutions, and include mitigating measures, such as a government liquidity backstop and a limit on the encumbrance of assets.

Procedural Elements

A well-designed resolution regime will typically contain a number of different thresholds, both qualitative and quantitative, for triggering resolution proceedings. An overall goal of a well-designed resolution framework is to empower the resolution authority. This includes providing a flexible toolkit that enables the authorities to determine when a bank meets the legal thresholds for initiating resolution proceedings and how best to resolve the bank, taking all of the facts and circumstances into account.

The triggers for bail-in power should be consistent with those used for other resolution tools. Moreover, the determination of what should trigger bail-in needs to strike a balance between legal certainty and early interventions to maximize the likelihood of restoring a distressed financial institution's viability.

- *Insolvency-related triggers.* Under this approach, bail-in power would be triggered at a stage when a financial institution is close to being either balance-sheet or cash-flow insolvent. The principal argument in support of this

---

[9] One question raised was whether bail-in could form part of the general framework for enforcement measures and remedial actions, which would apply before reaching a stage of deterioration or difficulty requiring formal resolution (for example, prompt corrective action). Our view is that the triggers for taking enforcement actions, usually along the lines of violations of law or regulations or unsafe or unsound practices, are not necessarily sufficient to justify the direct effect on third-party rights (both creditors and shareholders) that are entailed in statutory bail-ins.

[10] Many jurisdictions have some form of such a regime, though it may be called by other names such as temporary administration, interim administration, statutory management, conservatorship, or other similar terms.

approach is that bail-in implies such a substantial interference with the rights of stakeholders that it should only be possible when the bank is insolvent and in danger of liquidation. However, a key disadvantage is that stage may be too late for the bail-in to achieve its intended purpose of restoring the bank to viability.

- *Pre-insolvency triggers.* Bail-in could be implemented at an earlier stage than that described above—for example, when the official administration may itself be initiated. Official administration is generally triggered by either qualitative (e.g., repeated breach of regulatory standards) or quantitative triggers, such as capital adequacy ratios falling below a certain level (for example, below 50 percent or 75 percent of the norm). In some countries, a "public interest" finding may also be required.[11] Pre-insolvency triggers would generally allow for a prompt and effective response to a bank's difficulties. The disadvantage is that, in some legal systems, the pre-insolvency triggers could raise legal questions as to the position of senior creditors relative to other stakeholders (including shareholders), official interference with contractual rights, and nondiscrimination, which may, as with other resolution tools, require compensation to debt holders that are adversely affected.[12]

Weighing these issues, it may be appropriate for the trigger for the bail-in power to apply at a point that is close to but before the institution is balance-sheet insolvent. The trigger could be based on a combination of quantitative and qualitative assessments, such as a combination of a breach of regulatory minima (for example, minimum capital adequacy ratio) and concerns about the distressed institution's liquidity problems. The triggers, although discretionary, should not be seen as arbitrary, which means that the resolution authority should be able to decide to initiate the process of bail-in only when the trigger criteria are met.

It is important to minimize the uncertainty generated by discretionary use of bail-in power and to avoid surprising market participants by making the intervention criteria as transparent and predictable as possible. To the extent consistent with maintaining orderly market conditions, disclosure concerning remedial measures against a troubled institution (up until the point of intervention) may enhance certainty.

The role of the judiciary is another important procedural design issue. While the resolution framework invariably depends on the specific legal tradition and constitutional framework in a country, there are compelling arguments in favor of an approach that minimizes the role of the courts. Given the need to act

---

[11] Such public-interest tests could include references to whether the intervention would likely maximize the value of the institution, minimize its losses to creditors and other stakeholders, preserve its going-concern value for the benefit of creditors and other stakeholders, and avoid or mitigate any severe disruption in the stability of the financial system.

[12] Basically, pre-insolvency shareholders should not inappropriately benefit from haircuts on creditors. Therefore, in case of early pre-insolvency triggers where losses may not be large enough to eliminate shareholders completely, senior creditors should not be subject to outright haircuts but only to debt-to-equity conversion, so that the pre-insolvency shareholders are diluted.

quickly and to vest restructuring decisions in the hands of officials with the necessary technical expertise, it would appear more appropriate for these decisions to be taken by the banking authorities. As an example, decisions could be made by the official administrator, subject to prior approval of the supervisory or resolution agencies and follow-up judicial review.[13] Follow-up judicial review should not be able to reverse the resolution; rather, it should be limited to review of the legality of the action and the awarding of damages as a remedy.[14]

The need for quick and decisive action in the interest of financial stability pleads against incorporating a procedure for creditor approval in the bail-in framework, even though such approval is typical when debt restructurings are implemented in the context of corporate insolvency. However, care should be taken to ensure that eliminating creditor consent will survive legal challenge in the relevant jurisdiction and will not undermine the ability to achieve cross-border recognition of bail-in as an appropriate insolvency or reorganization proceeding.[15]

Another consideration is whether an additional test should be met before implementing a bail-in power. For example, the authorities might only be permitted to proceed with the bail-in if they (or another competent authority) were assured that bail-in was mostly likely to restore a distressed bank to viability.[16] In addition, bail-in might also be subject to a "no creditor worse off" test. Where restructuring is not subject to creditor consent, the introduction of such a requirement would provide important safeguards for the interests of creditors and the protection of stakeholders' rights, such that they would be made no worse off than in the counterfactual of insolvency.

Bail-in should be applied to existing debt as well as debt issued after the bail-in power is enacted. In general, amendments to insolvency laws apply to existing debt and other contracts, though the approach may differ from jurisdiction to jurisdiction. Because bail-in power would be a resolution tool that could be employed in proceedings analogous to bankruptcy reorganizations, the same principle should apply.

Substantive Design Elements

Determining the trigger for opening restructuring proceedings will raise the question of whether bail-in is legally considered an "insolvency proceeding" in the relevant jurisdictions. The characterization of bail-in by official administrations as

---

[13] This is the case in Japan, where the Japanese Financial Services Agency may apply to the court to open proceedings.

[14] As suggested by the Japanese bank-debt-restructuring framework, the centralization of procedures in certain (specialized) courts may also be useful.

[15] In Italy, the creditors do not have a say in the haircuts imposed upon banks.

[16] If the pre-insolvency triggers were too early, for example, prior to a breach of regulatory minimum, the determination of the test for proceeding with the restructuring would be more complicated, since creditors could argue that alternative recovery action (recapitalization, asset disposals) might avoid imposing haircuts.

an insolvency proceeding should help justify the interference with stakeholder rights and improve the ability to achieve cross-border effectiveness. However, some jurisdictions may experience tension between keeping banks open as going concerns and insolvency.[17] More specifically, the question arises whether various insolvency rules aimed at ensuring equality among creditors have a place in any form of going-concern resolution, such as bail-in. For example, most insolvency proceedings include "claw-back rules," which authorize undoing certain transactions that occurred before the initiation of insolvency.

A related question would be whether termination and close-out netting rights against the bank should be enforceable. As will be discussed below, legislative amendments should limit the possibility for counterparties to *close out*, or terminate, agreements on the grounds of debt restructuring.

The legal framework will need to clearly specify which bank liabilities may be restructured under the bail-in power. To improve transparency and avoid uncertainty, only subordinated and senior unsecured debt should be subject to bail-in. Insured/guaranteed deposits, secured debt (including covered bonds), and repurchase agreements should be excluded from restructuring. A different but related question is whether, with respect to senior unsecured debt, it may be appropriate to carve out some types of senior unsecured debt from the restructuring process, including interbank deposits, payments, clearing and securities settlement system obligations and, arguably, also some trade-finance obligations. These liabilities may be of systemic or strategic importance and might justify a differential treatment from other senior debt, even if they rank equally in a liquidation context.[18] Any legal concerns might be addressed either by creating different classes for unsecured creditors or by providing compensation to creditors who are made worse off than they would have been by liquidation.[19]

To avoid the possibility that pre-restructuring shareholders and junior creditors could benefit from haircuts imposed upon senior creditors, the debt restructuring under a bail-in should reflect the order of priority applicable to liquidation. Thus, before haircuts are imposed on creditors, a balance sheet offering a fair and true view of the financial situation of the bank should be established. Any losses should first be attributed to pre-restructuring equity (including postconversion contingent capital). Subordinated debt outstanding at the time of the debt restructuring should be the next in line to absorb the outstanding losses before imposing haircuts on unsecured senior creditors.

Given that the equity will be reduced before the debt is restructured, new capital will be needed to make the bank viable again. The contribution of new capital would come from converting part of the haircut-adjusted debt into equity

---

[17] But this would not be the case for those jurisdictions whose insolvency framework includes forced debt restructuring mechanisms.

[18] A further question that may affect the legal analysis would be whether the differential treatment should be automatic or discretionary for the resolution authorities.

[19] On the creation of such different classes on the basis of different economic interests: see Hagan (1999), pp. 66–67.

and/or an issuance of new equity. In both instances, this would lead to significant dilution of the pre-restructuring shareholders, if they were not already written off. To make this effective, it will be imperative that company law rules do not prevent such recapitalization, for instance through excessively rigid preemption rights or procedural requirements related to authorizing and issuing any necessary additional shares. Furthermore, the legal framework will need to specify a process for determining when and how the bank is restored to private control once bail-in is completed and the bank's capital position is restored.

Bail-in needs to ensure that new shareholders pass the required supervisory scrutiny for suitability. This can be addressed by early regulatory action to write down the equity stake within a timeframe that avoids forced sales. Moreover, certain institutional investors (such as hedge funds) could be prohibited from owning equity stakes, and alternative ownership structures could be considered (for example, through trust funds). Addressing these issues after the fact is important for avoiding a fire sale of shares, especially when unsuitable investors are forced to sell in an illiquid market.

Bail-in, in and of itself, should not trigger a termination of the bank's transactions and agreements. More specifically, legislation should prohibit contractual counterparties of a bank from terminating or walking away from agreements for the sole reason that bail-in powers have been invoked against a bank. (The termination of contracts for actual default should, however, not be prohibited.) In designing rules for such prohibition, close attention should be paid to the issue of cross-default clauses in standard financial contracts to avoid situations where the debt restructuring of the bank triggers the close-out of contracts with other components of a banking group.

Bail-in may need to be coupled with adequate official liquidity assistance. Official guarantees for some debt may also be necessary to stem outflows. In this case, government financing provided during the debt restructuring should receive priority treatment if the bank were to subsequently fail.[20]

GROUP ISSUES AND CROSS-BORDER CHALLENGES

Given that most SIFIs have international operations, the effectiveness of a statutory bail-in will depend crucially on the extent to which all relevant jurisdictions will give effect to its terms. Otherwise, the balance sheet adjustment pursued by the debt restructuring will fail. A statutory bail-in framework needs to address:

- Issues associated with the bail-in of debt issued by entities that form part of a larger banking group; and
- Issues associated with the bail-in of debt of a bank or banking group that operates in multiple jurisdictions.

---

[20] This would be similar to "debtor-in-possession" rules in the United States Chapter 11 framework.

This section will examine the principal group and cross-border issues that could arise in a statutory bail-in and offer some possible solutions.

The analysis outlined below assumes that a restructuring would be implemented on the basis of the following principles and applied on a legal-entity-specific basis:[21]

- The *home-country authorities* would initiate, approve, and implement the restructuring process.[22]

- The statutory bail-in powers could, in principle, apply to all liabilities of the ailing bank, including liabilities "held" abroad[23] and claims governed by foreign laws (foreign *lex contractus*).

- The process of debt restructuring would be governed by the law of the home country (*lex fori concursus*). However, as noted below, this process could be undermined by separate proceedings in third countries, including concurrent territorial insolvency procedures of jurisdictions hosting branches.

Generally, insolvency or reorganization proceedings for banks and other types of corporations are carried out on a legal-entity-specific basis, and the triggers and powers of resolution are entity-specific. In the context of bail-in, such an approach would mean that the authorities could only apply the bail-in power to the debt of a banking group member if that member itself had crossed the relevant threshold for bail-in. This approach would have a number of implications:

- If the relevant bank was a subsidiary, a bail-in of its debt could result in the "de-grouping" of the bank by wiping out the parent company's equity in the bank. This could destabilize the parent and the group, although that may be unavoidable if the subsidiary was no longer viable and liquidation was the only other alternative.

- If the relevant SIFI obtained its funding by borrowing from another entity in the group that itself issued debt in the market, an entity-specific bail-in regime would permit the restructuring of the debt of the SIFI held by the other entity, but not the debt that the entity had issued in the market to fund the SIFI. Such an approach might not address economic reality (whereby the other entity may have served as a conduit through which the relevant bank raised debt in the markets) and could destabilize the other entity to the point where it could not repay its own creditors. Additional difficulties might arise

---

[21] Some have raised the question of whether resolution frameworks in general and bail-in in particular could be applied on a group-wide basis. However, there is very little support among policymakers for collapsing the estates of the components of a banking group into one single insolvency estate.

[22] This assumption is made to streamline the discussion of cross-border issues rather than to take a specific position on which jurisdiction should take the lead in resolving a problem bank. What will be important is that there is agreement in advance regarding which jurisdiction should control the resolution process. This same jurisdiction will likely need to be the one that provides any necessary liquidity until the bank is stabilized.

[23] While some liabilities of a bank may be booked with a foreign branch, ultimately they represent claims on the entire legal entity and should be included in the overall balance sheet of the bank.

if the other entity was a nonbank not subject to a bank-specific bail-in or insolvency regime (for example, a passive, off-balance-sheet vehicle), or if its debt were guaranteed by the relevant bank or by another entity within the group.

There is no clear consensus on solutions to these problems. As a conceptual matter, it would appear necessary to design the bail-in regime in a manner that allows the resolution authority to restructure not only the balance sheet of the entity subject to bail-in, but also the balance sheets of other entities within the group; for example:

- By allowing the resolution authority to convert claims held against the subsidiary subject to bail-in into the parent's equity in the subsidiary; or
- By restructuring the debt of related entities that provide funding to a bank that is itself subject to bail-in.

However, any such approach would represent a significant departure from traditional entity-specific approaches and would raise a significant number of legal and policy issues.

Whether or not the statutory bail-in is applied directly to a single legal entity or to more than one member of the group, the effectiveness of the statutory bail-in will depend crucially on the extent to which all relevant jurisdictions will give effect to its terms. In practice, significant legal obstacles may prevent the debt restructuring from taking full cross-border effect. These obstacles may arise in two separate contexts, depending on whether the bank under restructuring has, or does not have, branches in jurisdictions outside of its home country.

With respect to the debt restructuring for a single bank and its branches, there are legal mechanisms under which the restructuring might be given effect in relevant jurisdictions other than the home jurisdiction of the bank, though their effectiveness in a given case is unpredictable. These mechanisms include choice-of-law rules, general principles of "comity" that have been recognized by the courts of many countries, and specific statutory frameworks for recognition that countries have put in place in connection with international law instruments, such as the United Nations Commission on International Trade Law model law on cross-border insolvency or the European Union (EU) Winding-up Directive.[24] However, the exercise of statutory bail-in powers is more likely to be effective in other jurisdictions if the resolution proceeding under which statutory bail-in is carried out is an insolvency or insolvency-related reorganization regime.[25] Moreover, a host jurisdiction may be less likely to recognize statutory bail-in

---

[24] Where the host jurisdiction is the jurisdiction of the choice-of-law provision in a debt contract, recognition of an insolvency proceeding will mean that the insolvency proceeding takes precedence over the terms of the debt contract.

[25] Whether the proceeding would be considered an insolvency or insolvency-related reorganization regime may depend on, among other things, the protections the regime provides for the various stakeholders. In the context of bank resolutions, what constitutes an acceptable level of protection will need to be balanced against the reality of the need to act quickly in the interest of preventing contagion and preserving financial stability.

actions taken by the home jurisdiction if insolvency proceedings have been initiated against a branch in the host jurisdiction where ring-fencing is applied.

Furthermore, cross-border effectiveness becomes far more complicated in the case of a restructuring of the debt within a banking group, where the intragroup issues identified above would have to be addressed across jurisdictions. For example, the balance sheet of an entity in one jurisdiction could be restructured as part of the bail-in of a related entity in another jurisdiction. The establishment of such a regime would require significant legislative change in the relevant jurisdictions that would abandon the traditional entity-specific approach to resolution, and resolution authorities would be given the power to take extraordinary action as part of a resolution that was initiated and applied to related entities in other jurisdictions.

There are essentially two approaches to increasing the likelihood of the cross-border recognition of bail-in power:

- One approach would be for policymakers in each jurisdiction to ensure that debt instruments issued by banks in their jurisdictions include provisions that give effect to any restructuring the home authorities might impose. A strengthening element to this approach might be for the home jurisdiction specifically to identify those host jurisdictions whose laws could be chosen as the *lex contractus* based on whether that jurisdiction would give effect to the debt restructuring.[26] This approach would add a consensual element to an otherwise involuntary process—which could make it easier to give effect to the restructuring in some jurisdictions. However, by definition, such an approach could be applied only to newly issued debt instruments. Also, it may prove difficult to determine beforehand which debt would likely be subject to restructuring and would thus require the inclusion of provisions of this type (if at all possible).[27] Notwithstanding these difficulties, the addition of a contractual clause could be implemented relatively quickly and may be a particularly viable option for the short term.

- An alternative approach would be to ensure that relevant jurisdictions put in place legislation that recognizes bail-in powers that are implemented by the authorities in other jurisdictions. One way to do this would be through the direct recognition of orders made by the competent authority in the home jurisdiction (for example, the home regulator) in other relevant jurisdictions. An alternative would be for the competent authority in the host jurisdiction to issue parallel or protective measures consistent with those taken by the home jurisdiction. In either case, countries may be reluctant to introduce such a framework, given the loss of national sovereignty that it would entail in some cases, unless they believed it would provide them with certain safeguards.

---

[26] The identification of permissible jurisdictions could affirmatively identify acceptable jurisdictions or, in the alternative, the authorities may establish a list of unacceptable jurisdictions.

[27] For instance, loans from parent banks to subsidiaries would typically not be incorporated in debt securities, but could well be subject to restructuring.

The IMF has proposed a framework for enhanced coordination for the resolution of cross-border banks (IMF, 2010). The IMF approach encourages countries to recognize bank-resolution measures implemented in another country, provided they are satisfied that the framework in that country meets certain "core coordination standards," including a minimum level of harmonization of national resolution tools and sufficiently effective levels of prudential supervision. Where these coordination standards are met, jurisdictions could then be encouraged to enact any necessary legislation to clear the way for cross-border effectiveness of bank resolution measures, including bail-in.[28]

COMPARISONS WITH OTHER RESOLUTION TOOLS

Compared with other key resolution mechanisms, bail-in may offer a more appropriate resolution tool for distressed SIFIs, whose primary problem is inadequate capital. Hence, replenishing an institution's capital account is likely to be sufficient to restore the viability of the institution. While the objective of gone-concern tools, such as purchase and assumption (P&A) transactions and bridge-bank powers, is to ensure an orderly closure of a failed financial institution (including selling off the parts with going-concern values), the objective of bail-in is primarily to restore the viability of a distressed financial institution and prevent insolvency-related runs on the institution. Both approaches share the goal of protecting financial stability by preserving systemic business functions while imposing losses on some creditors to reduce moral-hazard risks. Both have advantages and disadvantages in practice, and it is therefore important to view bail-in as complementary to other resolution tools and not as their substitute.

The key distinctions between bail-in, P&A, and bridge bank powers are set out below. Some arise from the nature of the proceedings within which the transactions occur (for example, receivership vs. official administration) and some arise from the nature of the transactions themselves. Bail-in does not involve finding purchasers for a distressed SIFI, which could be difficult due to its size or time constraints. This makes bail-in a potentially more useful tool to avoid the value destruction associated with a fire sale of assets. In addition, when P&A powers are used to transfer a business to multiple purchasers, as with a large firm, then intensive due diligence will be required to ensure that the associated transfer of assets and liabilities does not undermine creditors' rights, such as set-off, netting, and rights to collateral. The alternative of a bridge-bank approach, while it does not immediately involve purchasers, provides a temporary rather than permanent solution, since, ultimately, private sector purchasers or investors will need to be found.

Bail-in may entail lower execution risks. First, there are likely to be more contracts governed by foreign law that are transferred under a P&A than are treated

---

[28] Given that the assets of the most important global institutions may be clustered in a few jurisdictions, agreement among a few key financial centers could make forced bank-debt restructuring a viable resolution technique for financial institutions that are globally systemically significant.

to a haircut under a bail-in. As a result, the probability of defaults arising across borders could be higher under a P&A than under a bail-in. Second, because bail-in does not involve a transfer of business operations, it will not require the legal due diligence by the resolution authority prior to the resolution, which is necessary in a P&A to assess the practical and legal effects of the transfer on critical contracts and business functions. It will be especially important to consider whether a transfer creates problems with respect to contractual rights involving other entities in the same financial group of the failing institution or with respect to contractual provisions relating to off-balance-sheet vehicles. Finally, since issued debt will likely be governed by the laws of relatively few jurisdictions, it may be more straightforward to achieve cross-border effectiveness through the use of bail-in than through a P&A, because the latter would require achieving legal effect in all of the countries with jurisdiction over the tangible and intangible property of the failing SIFI.[29]

However, bail-in by design does not directly address the issues related to problem assets and loss-making business lines. In a P&A transaction, problem assets can be left behind in the receivership. Bail-in may thus fall short in restoring investor confidence because of the unknown level of asset impairment on the balance sheet of a distressed bank. Therefore, to improve client and creditor confidence, it would be desirable to establish an expectation that a bail-in will over-capitalize the bank to ensure that hard-to-predict losses from impaired assets will be covered. Moreover, if the bank's operations are fundamentally unsound and need to be restructured, then bail-in capital could simply delay the inevitable failure. The resolution authority to change management and revise the business strategy would thus be necessary.

Finally, contingent liabilities, including off-balance-sheet liabilities and litigation, can also be left behind in the receivership in a P&A, and to the extent that they can be proven they are claims against the receivership estate. In a bail-in, because the entity remains open, these liabilities may need to be paid in the ordinary course of business. Transition arrangements are needed to allow for regulatory approval of the new shareholders (the haircut creditors or third-party new investors) and to allow for the orderly divestiture or placement into trust of shareholder interests for creditors who do not subsequently secure approval.

POTENTIAL MARKET RISKS AND MITIGATING MEASURES

Ultimately, the effectiveness of bail-in will depend on the ability of the resolution authority to exercise its power in a manner that enhances financial stability. Individual banks and the banking system are vulnerable to bank runs and banking

---

[29] Though work is being done at the international level to develop mechanisms for efficient and effective cross-border recognition, under the current state of affairs achieving recognition may involve court-based processes that can take time. Furthermore, the complexity of various legal doctrines that may achieve recognition makes it difficult to predict the outcome in any given case.

panics, which can be caused by weak fundamentals or self-fulfilling shifts in market sentiment (Diamond and Dybvig, 1983).[30] If the market believes the viability of a distressed SIFI would be restored with the recapitalization under a bail-in power, investor confidence will be enhanced, and this will have a positive reinforcing effect on financial stability. However, if the use of a bail-in power is perceived negatively by the market as a sign of insolvency, bail-in could trigger a run by various creditors and lead to financial instability and contagion. This section discusses potential market risks and mitigating measures to safeguard financial stability, especially measures to reduce counterparty, liquidity, and contagion risks.

Potential Impact on Funding Costs

To the extent that bail-in reduces or even eliminates the implicit too-big-to-fail subsidy to SIFIs, it would, by design, have an impact on banks' funding costs. Banks' ratings have had a strong degree of public support built into them.[31] Banks' senior ratings are expected to be adjusted downwards to reflect the loss of government guarantees. The removal of the ratings' uplift may result in an average downgrade of senior, unsecured debt. For instance, in Europe, JP Morgan estimates the percentage of EU banks shifting to non-investment grade would increase from 2 percent to 33 percent (Henriques, 2011).

The removal of the too-big-to-fail premium will help restore market discipline by aligning bank funding costs more closely with risks. This will also help differentiate banks on the basis of their risk-taking activities and reintroduce a level playing field between SIFIs and non-SIFIs. Therefore, by bringing funding more in line with risks, the least viable parts of the banking systems may be ultimately consolidated or simply eliminated, with positive implications for financial stability. On the other hand, once bail-in succeeds in restoring the viability of a distressed financial institution, it could create value by providing creditors with higher returns, since the loss given default under bail-in is likely to be smaller than under disorderly liquidation.

Moreover, bail-in could break the observed negative feedback loops between sovereign risks and bank funding costs. The current pressure on sovereigns has exacerbated pricing pressures on bank senior debt, since bail-out can be seen as a government put. Since bail-in implies the termination of such a put option, the correlation between senior bank and government spreads would be reduced.

---

[30] This vulnerability arises from the inherent risk due to a fundamental mismatch between the long-term illiquidity of physical investments (bank assets), households'/creditors' desire for liquidity (bank liability), and banks' function as providers of intermediation between creditors and producers. With the financial innovations (for example, securitization), the intermediation chain has become longer and more unstable and bank runs have extended to wholesale funding, causing a systemic banking crisis. For example, some have seen the recent financial crisis as "a run on repos" (Gorton and Metrick, 2012).

[31] In Europe, for instance, the support factor for the banking sector contributed up to five notches to the long-term ratings from Fitch for 31 out of the 58 EU banks rated by the credit rating agency at the end of 2010.

However, the introduction of bail-in needs to be carried out in such a way that it ensures financial institutions can adequately adjust to this new regime. The general trend of increased funding costs could weigh on banking systems currently under pressure. For instance, at the end of 2010, 10 out of 33 of the largest international banks were refinancing themselves as if they were rated at speculative levels.[32] Higher cost of funding over a long period of time could prompt bank managers to seek riskier assets or simply deleverage. A systemwide bank deleverage could hinder economic recovery.

Effects on Bank Liability Structure

Higher funding costs for unsecured debt could result in changes in banks' liability structures. Banks' capital structures tend to be determined by the tradeoff between the marginal costs of debt (for example, bankruptcy costs) and the marginal benefits of debt (for example, tax incentives, cash flow incentives). To the extent that bail-in increases the marginal cost of debt, its share in total liabilities could fall. Banks might just increase their total capital to lower the cost on senior debt—this is reflected in the renewed interest in contingent capital securities, and would be a desirable outcome. However, banks could also shift toward short-term and secured borrowing (for example, covered bonds) to lower funding costs and possibly to circumvent bail-in. In the case of covered bonds, while they bring benefits to banks (lower costs) and investors (protection),[33] they have a potentially undesirable impact on issuer balance sheets and on the efficacy of bank resolution frameworks (including bail-in) and deposit insurance schemes.

Consideration could therefore be given to imposing minimum requirements upfront on banks for issuing unsecured debt (as percent of total liability) or setting limits on the encumbrance of assets. This would help reassure the market that bail-in would be sufficient to recapitalize the distressed institution and restore its viability. Independent of bail-in proposals, the increasing popularity of covered bonds has already raised questions as to whether there should be limits to protect against the structural subordination of unsecured creditors (ECBC, 2011). In a large number of countries, explicit issuance limits on covered bonds are already in force. Since 2009, many countries have updated or adopted covered bond laws and several advanced countries (Australia, Italy, the Netherlands, the United Kingdom, and the United States) have introduced asset encumbrance limits. For most banks, their current liability structure suggests that new issuance of unsecured debt may not be needed, although this could change with regulatory

---

[32] Moody's has indicated that a seven-notch gap between an entity's credit rating and the corresponding credit default swap–based, market-implied rating results in the probability of the credit rating being downgraded, increasing by 40 percent over a one-year horizon.

[33] They are cheaper because investors are protected by collateral. A covered bond typically provides a preferential claim on segregated assets and entails a degree of over-collateralization to improve its credit rating, thus undermining the position of senior unsecured creditors by encumbering the highest quality assets.

reforms.[34] A minimum requirement on unsecured senior debt might be more effective and easier to monitor and implement than a limit on asset encumbrance, because the market could work around encumbrance limits through securitization. The difference between those two benchmarks, though, might not be as significant as expected in the presence of liquidity requirements.

Potential Contagion Risks

Another design issue is to ensure that systemic risk is not simply being shifted to other parts of the financial sector. This would argue for regulating investment in unsecured senior debt issued by SIFIs. A large share of debt instruments, including senior debt, is purchased by other financial institutions, although their share has steadily declined from close to 20 percent (on average) in 2007 to 17 percent in 2010 for the euro area banks and from 15 percent to 12.5 percent during the same interval for U.S. banks. Therefore, before applying the bail-in power, regulators should have a preliminary assessment of its potential effects on the balance sheets of other banks. Insurance companies are also major investors, with bank bonds accounting for 20–30 percent of their investment portfolios and up to three times their capital, although, with the introduction of Solvency II, they may shift their senior unsecured exposure to other long-term assets.

Bail-in is untested in a systemic crisis and should ideally be used if it is likely to restore a distressed financial institution to viability. As discussed above, the risk of contagion could be mitigated by a range of carefully designed measures, including restrictions or quantitative limits on the cross-holdings of bail-in instruments with timely monitoring by authorities, convergence of supervisory criteria, triggers for bail-in across jurisdictions, frequent and transparent disclosure, communication by SIFIs and authorities, and effective resolution planning. Statutory bail-in needs to be considered in the context of a comprehensive framework that includes effective supervision to prevent bank failure and an effective overall resolution framework. That framework must allow for an orderly resolution of a failing or failed institution with minimum market disruptions, facilitated by up-to-date recovery and resolution plans.

CONCLUSIONS

Bail-in power needs to be considered as an additional and complementary tool for the resolution of SIFIs. Bail-in is a statutory power of a resolution authority, as opposed to contractual arrangements, such as contingent capital requirements. It involves recapitalization through relatively straightforward mandatory debt restructuring and could therefore avoid some of the operational and legal complexities that arise when using other tools (such as P&A transactions), which

---

[34] For example, under the Solvency II framework for European insurance companies, senior unsecured bonds are treated less favorably than covered bonds.

require transferring assets and liabilities between different legal entities and across borders. By restoring the viability of a distressed SIFI, the pressure on the institution to post more collateral, for example against their repo contracts, could be significantly reduced, thereby minimizing liquidity risks and preventing runs by short-term creditors.

The design and implementation of a bail-in power, however, need to take into careful consideration its potential market impact and its implications for financial stability. It is especially important that the triggering of a bail-in power is not perceived by the market as a sign of the concerned institution's nonviability, a perception that could trigger a run by short-term creditors and aggravate the institution's liquidity problem. An effective bail-in framework generally includes the following key design elements:

- The *scope* of the *statutory power* should be limited to (1) eliminating or diluting existing shareholders; and (2) writing down or converting, in the following order, any contractual contingent capital instruments, subordinated debt, and unsecured senior debt, accompanied by the power of the resolution authority to change bank management.

- The *triggers* for bail-in power should be consistent with those used for other resolution tools and set at the point when an institution would have breached the regulatory minima but before it became balance-sheet insolvent, to allow for a prompt response to an SIFI's financial distress. The intervention criteria (a combination of quantitative and qualitative assessments) need to be as transparent and predictable as possible to avoid market uncertainty.

- It may be necessary to require banks or bank holding companies to maintain a minimum amount of unsecured liabilities (as a percentage of total assets) beforehand, which could be subject to bail-in afterwards. This would help reassure the market that bail-in is sufficient to recapitalize the distressed institution and restore its viability, and thus reduce the risk of runs by short-term creditors.

- To fund potential liquidity outflows—given the probable temporary loss of market access—bail-in may need to be coupled with adequate official liquidity assistance.

- Bail-in needs to be considered as one element of a comprehensive framework that includes effective supervision to reduce the likelihood of bank failures and an effective overall resolution framework that allows for an orderly resolution of a failed SIFI, facilitated by up-to-date recovery and resolution plans. In general, statutory bail-in should be used in instances where a capital infusion is likely to restore a distressed financial institution to viability, possibly because, other than a lack of capital, the institution is viable and has a decent business model and good risk-management systems. Otherwise, bail-in capital could simply delay the inevitable failure.

REFERENCES

Acharya, Viral, T. Cooley, M. Richardson, and I. Walter, 2010, *Regulating Wall Street: The Dodd-Frank Act and the New Architecture of Global Finance* (Hoboken, NJ: John Wiley & Sons).

Acharya, Viral, Hyun S. Shin, and Tanju Yorulmazer, 2011, "Crisis Resolution and Bank Liquidity," *Review of Financial Studies*, Vol. 24, No. 6, pp. 2166–2205.

Adrian, Tobias, and H. Shin, 2010, "The Changing Nature of Financial Intermediation and the Financial Crisis of 2007–2009," *Annual Review of Economics,* No. 2, pp. 603–18.

Basel Committee on Banking Supervision (BCBS), 2010a, "Basel III: A Global Regulatory Framework for More Resilient Banks and Banking Systems," (Basel: Bank for International Settlements, December).

_____, 2010b, "Proposal to Ensure the Loss Absorbency of Regulatory Capital at the Point of Nonviability," BCBS Consultative Document, (Basel: Bank for International Settlements, August).

Bernanke, S. Ben, 2013, "Monitoring the Financial System," Remarks given at the 49th Annual Conference on Bank Structure and Competition sponsored by the Federal Reserve Bank of Chicago, May 10 (Chicago).

Brunnermeier, Markus, 2009, "Deciphering the Liquidity and Credit Crunch 2007–08," *Journal of Economic Perspectives*, Vol. 23, No. 1, pp. 77–100.

Calomiris, Charles, 2011, "An Incentive-Robust Program for Financial Reform" February, independently published on the web and available at www.hertig.ethz.ch/Calomiris_Analytical_2011.pdf.

Chance, Clifford, 2011, "Legal Aspects of Bank Bail-ins," unpublished briefing note for clients, April.

Council of the European Union, 2013, "Proposal for a Directive of the European Parliament and of the Council Establishing a Framework for the Recovery and Resolution of Credit Institutions and Investment Firms and Amending Council Directives," June 28 (Brussels).

Diamond, Douglas, and Philip Dybvig, 1983, "Bank Runs, Deposit Insurance, and Liquidity," *Journal of Political Economy*, Vol. 91, No. 5, pp. 401–19.

Duffie, Darrell, 2010, *How Big Banks Fail and What to Do About It?* (Princeton, New Jersey: Princeton University Press).

European Commission, 2011, "Technical Details of a Possible EU Framework for Bank Recovery and Resolution," DG Internal Market and Services Working Document, January 6 (Luxembourg).

European Covered Bond Council (ECBC), 2011, *European Covered Bond Fact Book* (Brussels).

Federal Deposit Insurance Corporation (FDIC), 2011, "The Orderly Liquidation of Lehman Brothers Holding Inc. under the Dodd-Frank Act," *FDIC Quarterly*, Vol. 5, No. 2.

Financial Stability Board (FSB), 2011a, "Effective Resolution of Systemically Important Financial Institutions: Recommendations and Timelines," FSB Consultative Document, July 19 (Basel, Switzerland: Bank for International Settlements).

_____, 2011b, "Key Attributes of Effective Resolution Regimes for Financial Institutions," FSB Consultative Document, October (Basel, Switzerland: Bank for International Settlements).

Gorton, Gary, and Andrew Metrick, 2012, "Securitized Banking and the Run on Repo," *Journal of Financial Economics,* Vol. 104, No. 3, pp. 425–51.

Hagan, S., 1999, *Orderly and Effective Insolvency Procedures* (Washington: International Monetary Fund).

Henriques, Roberto, 2011, "The Great Bank Downgrade: What Bail-In Regimes Mean for Senior Ratings?" JP Morgan Chase *Europe Credit Research*, January 7.

Huertas, Thomas, 2011, "Barriers to Resolution," draft for discussion, London School of Economics Workshop on Bail-ins, March.

Independent Commission on Banking (U.K.), 2011, *Final Report and Recommendations*, September (London).

International Monetary Fund, 2010, "Resolution of Cross-Border Banks—A Proposed Framework for Enhanced Coordination," June (Washington: International Monetary Fund).

Metrick, Andrew, and Gary Gorton, 2010, "Regulating the Shadow Banking System," *Brookings Papers on Economic Activity* (Washington: Brookings Institution, Fall).

Ötker-Robe, Inci, Aditya Narain, Anna Ilyina, and Jay Surti, 2011, "The Too-Important-to-Fail Conundrum: Impossible to Ignore and Difficult to Resolve," IMF Staff Discussion Note No. 11/02 (Washington: International Monetary Fund).

Pazarbasioglu, Ceyla, J. Zhou, V. Le Lesle, and M. Moore, 2011, "Contingent Capital: Economic Rationale and Design Features," IMF Staff Discussion Note No. 11/01 (Washington: International Monetary Fund), January.

Rawcliffe, Gerry, and D. Weinfurter, 2010, "Resolution Regimes and the Future of Bank Support," Fitch Ratings, *Global Special Report* (London, December).

Shleifer, Andrei, and R. Vishny, 2011 (winter), "Fire Sales in Finance and Macroeconomics," *Journal of Economic Perspectives,* Vol. 25, No. 1, pp. 29–48.

Summe, Kimberly, 2011, "An Examination of Lehman Brothers' Derivative Portfolio Post-Bankruptcy and Whether Dodd-Frank Would Have Made any Difference," unpublished (Palo Alto, California: Hoover Institution, Stanford University).

Tarullo, Daniel, 2013, "Evaluating Progress in Regulatory Reforms to Promote Financial Stability," Remarks given at the Peterson Institute for International Economics, May 3 (Washington: Peterson Institute for International Economics).

Tirole, Jean, 2006, *Theory of Corporate Finance* (Princeton and Oxford: Princeton University Press).

Viñals, José, J. Fiechter, C. Pazarbasioglu, L. Kodres, A. Narain, and M. Moretti, 2010, "Shaping the New Financial System," IMF Staff Position Note No. 10/15 (Washington: International Monetary Fund), October.

Zhou, J., V. Rutledge, W. Bossu, M. Dobler, N. Jassaud, and M. Moore, 2012, "From Bail-Out to Bail-In: Mandatory Debt Restructuring of Systemic Financial Institutions," IMF Staff Discussion Note No. 12/03 (Washington: International Monetary Fund).

PART III

Beyond the Crisis

CHAPTER 24

Structural Measures for the New European Architecture

CHARLES ENOCH

As noted in other chapters in this volume, much has been accomplished in strengthening banks in Europe, and actions are in train to identify and address remaining gaps.

Nevertheless, there is a view—both in the United States and Europe—that measures taken so far are not enough. One response is to propose a qualitative jump in the prudential requirements imposed on banks. In the United States, much of the focus is on leverage ratios: while the average leverage ratio in the United States presently is around 3 percent, there are Congressional proposals to raise it up to 15 percent. In the United Kingdom, requirements up to 10 percent have been suggested. Meanwhile, the head of the Scientific Committee of the European Systemic Risk Board has argued that capital requirements of perhaps 30 percent might be needed to make the banking system safe.

Prospects for enactment of increases of such magnitude are at the moment not realistic. Banks lobby heavily against them; and, at a time of concern about lack of credit growth, policymakers listen to arguments that such imposts would be heavily burdensome and would serve to depress lending and economic activity. In any case, there is far from consensus that such levels would be appropriate and not counterproductive. More limited, albeit still ambitious, measures may well be enacted. For example, on July 9 joint proposals by the U.S. Federal Reserve Board, the Federal Deposit Insurance Corporation (FDIC), and the Office of the Comptroller of the Currency were published for a 5–6 percent leverage ratio for the eight largest banks by 2018.

Absent full protection of the banks, there is recognition that one day banks will fail again. Indeed, a regulatory regime that did not permit failure would be too tight for banks to properly undertake their activities.[1] Thus, attention needs also to be on resolvability in case a bank does fail. In that connection, the Financial Stability Board has been working on developing the "Key Attributes" for a resolution regime, under which authorities would be able to resolve even the most complex banks should this become necessary. Within Europe, the prospective

---

[1] That said, a number of policy innovations also serve to reduce the risk of crisis. See, for instance, Chapter 20 of this book on developments in the design and implementation of macroprudential policies.

Recovery and Resolution Directive and its associated regulations will mark a fundamental step for enhancing the resolvability of banks.

Again, while progress in this regard has been impressive, the challenges ahead remain daunting. Resolving large cross-border institutions will be highly complicated. In addition, given the wide consensus that such resolution should in the future not be simply a public sector bail-out, significant policy and institutional change may be necessary. Work on increasing resolvability is proceeding on many fronts.

In this regard, policymakers are looking at bifurcating the institutional and regulatory regimes. The emerging legal and regulatory infrastructure may well be able to cover the great majority of bank failures, particularly in normal times. For the largest banks, more may be needed.[2]

As regards these largest banks, both within Europe and outside there is focus on the dual nature of banks, between "traditional" banking that provides essential deposit and payment services to the public, and investment banking that is deemed more risky and which is not as directly connected to basic financial infrastructure. Having the two activities linked within a single entity may lead to spillovers because the riskiness of investment banking may also deplete the financial soundness of the traditional banking part. Since it will be widely assumed that the traditional banking part may not be allowed to fail, there also will be an implicit subsidy on the risky part that will reduce its costs and allow it to undertake more activities than if it had to finance itself on a standalone basis. Moreover, if the joint entity does fail, the necessity of keeping the basic infrastructure operating will constrain the authorities in how they deal with the entity, potentially making it irresolvable except through the traditional public sector bail-out.

A separate argument for the toxicity of having both types of activity within a single organization draws attention to the respective cultures of the two types of institutions. Within the traditional bank, the emphasis may be on soundness and safety, and remuneration is relatively modest, while on the investment side short-term profit maximization is overriding, and remuneration for successful traders is a high multiple of that of their traditional-side colleagues. The resulting tendency for those who make their marks in the investment side of the banks to run the organization as a whole may lead to policies that jeopardize the traditional emphasis on soundness in the commercial banking side.[3]

In response to similar concerns in the 1930s, the Glass-Steagall Act in the United States required that commercial banking activity be undertaken by separate entities from those involved in investment banking. Notwithstanding that there had been extensive seepages across the boundaries, Glass-Steagall was not repealed until 1996. Although its repeal was followed by the major accumulation of banking sector risks that ultimately contributed to the financial crisis, there is

---

[2] The Financial Stability Board has identified 28 globally systemically important financial institutions, for which additional capital buffers are proposed. As noted below, the European Commission (EC) is considering the thresholds above which banks should become subject to a special regulatory regime.

[3] This argument is put forward most strongly by Paul Volcker, former Chairman of the Federal Reserve, as well as by John Reed, who oversaw the merger of Citibank with Travelers to create Citigroup.

no support for a full return to Glass-Steagall. Banking business nowadays is far more complicated and interrelated than in the 1930s, and the prospect of full separation of activities would be much more complicated and disruptive.

In the United Kingdom, following proposals by a commission headed by John Vickers, legislation is in train to require banks to separate their domestic retail banking from their other activities.[4] Unlike the "Volcker Rule" incorporated in the Dodd-Frank Act in the United States, under which banks have to divest proprietary trading, such activities can remain within the same banking group under Vickers, albeit separately capitalized. The aim is to ensure "super resolvability" of the domestic retail bank. Only U.K. business is separated out. Thus, cross-border resolvability issues do not come into play.

Meanwhile, Michel Barnier, European Commissioner for Internal Markets and Services, established a high-level committee under Finnish central bank governor Erkki Liikanen to consider whether the various measures put in place to strengthen the banking system were sufficient or more would be needed. The Liikanen group offered a number of recommendations, the most far reaching of which is to require that banks above a particular size divide their activities between their commercial banking and their trading and investment banking functions into separately capitalized units (see Liikanen and others, 2012). Like Vickers, Liikanen would allow both types of activity to remain within the same banking group. Unlike Vickers, the Liikanen proposals cover cross-border as well as domestic operations, so issues of cross-border consistency come into play. Liikanen allows underwriting and trading business to remain with the retail business, while Vickers does not. Liikanen considered whether to make the proposal apply just to banks that had certain characteristics but determined that it should be mandatory for all banks in the EU, subject only to a minimum size threshold.

Given the perceived urgency of moving forward and political pressures to be seen to act, a number of European Union (EU) members, including France and Germany, have moved ahead to introduce proposals at a national level, even before the EC has prepared a common EU position. French President François Hollande had included in his election manifesto a commitment to segregate investment banking activities. In the end the French proposal—similar to Liikanen—avoided full separation of investment banks and preserved the so-called "universal banking model." It is lighter than Liikanen, however, as it would permit banks to retain within the commercial banking side those commercial banking activities that are considered linked to the real economy, such as market-making, investment and financing services to clients, hedging, and asset management activities.[5] The German proposal (recently passed into law by parliament) has been closely coordinated with that of France and is along similar lines, although again allowing limited extra activity to remain within the commercial

---

[4] Work is also in train in the United Kingdom, as part of the banking bill, to "change the culture of banking" through instituting more individual accountability for the heads of failing institutions.
[5] Under Liikanen, the provision of hedging services to clients would also remain part of the retail banking arm.

banking side of the institution. Both the French and German governments have indicated that, if necessary, they will modify their proposals to be fully in line with EU requirements.

There is some support among policymakers and observers for moving in this direction, as part of a "belt and braces" approach for enhancing the soundness of the EU financial system. Even so, the proposals have also drawn criticism, including from the banks.[6] The first priority in any case is that such measures should not be seen as substitutes for stronger capital and other buffers, but rather as complements and serving a somewhat different purpose. The second priority is that any transition be managed carefully, so as not to disrupt banking business in the meantime and not expose the bank to additional risk. A recent IMF paper argues for a full cost benefit analysis, including on cross-border costs of introducing Liikanen-type policies.[7] The EC has undertaken that it will include an impact study when it presents its proposals in late 2013.

Three further issues remain. First are the various aspects of the cross-border impact of such separation. With differences in structures likely among EU members (not to mention also U.S. banks), there would be scope for regulatory arbitrage: if some activity is permitted within the commercial banking part in one jurisdiction and not another, and if that is deemed to give it a financial advantage, then such activity may gravitate to jurisdictions where such activities are permitted. This would not be consistent with the single market and could be an added element toward fragmentation. The actual impact cannot be determined before the EC proposals are presented, including the degree to which harmonization will be required within the EU and the extent to which existing proposals will be modified in line with these. The more the EC proposals are merely an umbrella under which various national proposals can be accommodated, the greater the scope for arbitrage. On the other side, the more the EC proposals accommodate national preferences for including particular activities within the commercial bank side of the operations, the less the need for banks to arbitrage, but also the lower the impact of the measure. In principle, it seems that the EC could determine a set of measures that are fully consistent with those proposed by the various national authorities, although in sum they would require banks to set up quite complex structures to meet all national requirements. An example would be if the tighter separation envisaged by Vickers only for U.K. domestic activities were to be applied on cross-border banking activities, as advocated in Liikanen.

There may be cross-border impact also from the application of a minimum size threshold as the requirement for a bank to segregate its business. A single minimum size affecting only the large banks would have a markedly diverse impact across Europe. A country such as France, with a small number of very large banks dominating the sector, would be heavily affected; Germany, with both

---

[6] A Bank for International Settlements study looked at the implication of Liikanen-type proposals for banks' business models (see Gambacorta and Van Rixtel, 2013).

[7] Viñals and others (2013) provide a decision tree framework that can be followed to determine whether to adopt structural measures such as those under consideration in the first place.

large and small banks, less so; and countries with no large banks (particularly if a single metric is used across Europe) probably not at all. A single minimum size based on trading volume or market share, by contrast, would have even more impact across countries since, within the major banks' universe, it would not affect smaller capital players.

The second issue relates to the possibility that segregating "risky" business from commercial banking activity may serve to push the former into the shadow bank sector. If, as argued by Liikanen, risky activities benefit from their cross-subsidization with commercial banking activities, then once this possibility is removed there will be less incentive to retail within an overall banking group, and such activities may be spun off. In answer to this, policymakers have stressed that the investment banking activities themselves will require a banking license, so spinning off out of the regulated banking sector will not be an easy option. In addition, if indeed there is spin-off into shadow banking, the response cannot be to seek to prevent this by restoring the cross-subsidization. Rather, it would be necessary to expand the perimeter of regulation and supervision so that soundness is maintained in the shadow banking sector, too.

Finally, there is the question as to whether all the disruption that would be involved in enforcing Liikanen-type proposals actually would enhance resolvability.[8] Much of recent bank distress has emerged from the core of commercial banking, as banks overinvested in local real estate lending or in government bonds. On the other side, where authorities have been prepared to close an institution that had no commercial banking function, in particular Lehman Brothers, this was in hindsight a significant contributor to setting off the global financial crisis.[9]

There is no single answer, and no quick solution. Liikanen-type proposals do not of themselves ensure resolvability, let alone bank soundness. The problem of excessive lending for real estate needs to be handled at a prior level. The legacy issue of bank purchases of bonds of governments they previously considered safe needs to be resolved by fiscal adjustment so that government finances are restored to soundness, as well as, in time, possible mutualization of debt obligations, so that bank holdings are of institutions whose soundness is not in doubt.

There is also the issue that, even when segmented, resolving a large cross-border bank will be complicated and difficult. In this connection, the recent agreement between the FDIC and the Bank of England may show a way forward for the large banks in the EU. Under this agreement, banks would be required to establish holding companies with the banks as subsidiaries under them. In the event of resolution, the authorities would work on a "Single Point of Entry" basis on the holding company, allowing the bank subsidiary to continue to function

---

[8] There are differences among bankers as to how far Liikanen-type proposals would actually disrupt existing banking structures, with some banks claiming that they already have quasi-Liikanen segregation in place.

[9] For empirical evidence on the link between trading activities and banks' vulnerability, see for instance, Chow and Surti (2011).

while eliminating shareholders and others subject to "bail in" at a holding company level. If the triggers are set at a sufficiently high level, if intervention is mandatory, and supervision is strong enough to identify the deterioration in the bank's position at an early enough stage, then resolvability will be more assured. But such an approach requires that banks are organized nationally as subsidiaries of holding companies, and that all the group's borrowings are conducted at the level of the holding company. This proposal clearly has merits, but it implies a cross-border structure for the banks that does not cover all affected banks at the moment and may not be the best suited for all types of cross-border banking.

In short, although full cross-border analysis of the costs and benefits of enforcing structural measures in line with those proposed by Governor Liikanen is still awaited, there may be a case for such measures as an added instrument in the "toolkit" for establishing and managing a sound financial system. Cross-country consistency will need to be assured, and introduction of such structural measures should not be at the expense of ongoing work to strengthen banks' soundness and increase resolvability. Many of these qualifications, however, are short-term and operational in nature. In the longer term, if the structural changes can be implemented in Europe in a way that ensures consistency without just, in effect, validating a patchwork of disparate initiatives, there could be merit in a European approach in this area to reduce the riskiness and enhance of resolvability of the Union's largest banks.

REFERENCES

Chow, J., and J. Surti, 2011, "Making Banks Safer: Can Volcker and Vickers Do It?" IMF Working Paper No. 11/236 (Washington: International Monetary Fund).

Gambacorta, Leonardo, and Adrian Van Rixtel, 2013, "Structural Bank Regulation Initiatives: Approaches and Implications" (Basel: Bank for International Settlements, April).

Liikanen, Erkki, and others, 2012, "Report of the High-Level Expert Group on Reforming the Structure of the EU Banking Sector," (Brussels: European Union, October). Available at: http://ec.europa.eu/internal_market/bank/docs/high-level_expert_group/report_en.pdf.

Viñals, José, Ceyla Pazarbasioglu, Jay Surti, Aditya Narain, Michaela Erbenova, and Julian Chow, 2013, "Creating a Safer Financial System: Will the Volcker, Vickers, and Liikanen Structural Measures Help?" IMF Staff Discussion Note No. 13/4 (Washington: International Monetary Fund).

CHAPTER 25

Some Wider Challenges

CHARLES ENOCH

As discussed in Chapter 1 and subsequent chapters, there are multiple immediate challenges to bringing the European financial system out of crisis and establishing a sound financial system that will underpin and foster economic growth for the future. Establishing the Single Supervisory Mechanism (SSM) at the European Central Bank (ECB) as a step toward a Banking Union, while necessary, carries within it a number of risks. Strengthening the nascent European Union (EU) supervisory authorities also will be critical. In addition, cross-border resolution arrangements need to be put in place and be seen to be robust in order for the recent fragmentation of the European Union single market in financial services to be curtailed and reversed. Macroprudential instruments have become an important addition to the toolkit for managing the financial system, with the European Systemic Risk Board established to monitor macroprudential conditions, develop instruments to address macroprudential risks, and warn of incipient problems. Structural measures aiming to segment banks' riskiest activities also are being considered to eliminate cross-subsidization across activities and increase resolvability.

Underlying and going beyond the issues discussed above, a number of wider challenges come into play.

LOW GROWTH

Sustained low growth in the EU will make emergence from the financial crisis and the construction of a framework for financial sector management much more difficult. Past financial crises have been resolved to a considerable extent by the resumption of strong growth, often external, that drove down debt ratios and enabled affected countries to emerge from austerity programs before austerity fatigue had set in too heavily. Thus, 1984 was an *annus mirabilis* as the "Reagan boom" and parallel growth elsewhere started lifting Latin American economies out of their crisis-level indebtedness, although the debt reductions of the Brady Plan in 1989 were still needed to properly resolve it. In addition, the widespread growth spurt of the early years of this century enabled Asian countries, which had recently been in deep financial crisis, to grow at rates of 6 percent or more; this growth rapidly brought down high debt ratios and enabled the countries to wind down their emergency infrastructures and arrangements. They were able within a few years to close their restructuring agencies and decline follow-on IMF programs, and in some cases even prepay their IMF borrowing.

Growth prospects for Europe were in early 2013 being revised downward, with many of the countries most affected by the crisis showing significant declines in output for several years ahead, and even the stronger economies not providing a powerful enough engine to lift the region as a whole. Outside Europe, too, growth has not returned to precrisis levels, and in some areas there are signs of renewed slowdown.

While policymakers debate the merits of breaking from ongoing austerity policies, what is clear is that the trade-off among policy choices has worsened. Debates about relaxing debt ratio targets take place against a backdrop of uncomfortably high fiscal deficits. Fiscal austerity over the past several years has generally failed to reverse the rapid rise of debt ratios, and the negative impact on growth was higher than earlier projected. Nevertheless, the use of fiscal resources to help resolve legacy assets and avert a credit crunch is problematic when fiscal space in many countries is exhausted well beyond levels that until recently would have been considered at the limits of riskiness.

The present environment makes even stronger the case for a number of the policies put forward earlier in this volume. First, it reinforces the message about the need to *reverse fragmentation and resume economic and financial integration*. National economic retrenchment was a pervasive result of, and contributor to, the depression of the 1930s. Fortunately, the general commitment among global policymakers to maintaining open markets has served so far to mitigate the impact of the recent global financial crisis. Nevertheless, there has been increasing financial fragmentation within Europe, under which banks have run down their cross-border activities. In addition, national authorities have sought to protect their domestic economies and national taxpayers by ring-fencing banks' capital and liquidity positions to protect them from cross-border developments and the actions of cross-border authorities. Given where we are, only a secure and credible EU financial management architecture can be expected to reverse this fragmentation and to provide for a resumption of Europe's progress toward creating a genuine single market. The proposals for establishing the SSM at the ECB, as discussed in Chapter 1 and in subsequent chapters, will represent a critical step toward financial management integration. This in turn can contribute toward stimulating growth both in the region and in the wider global economy.

The second theme is the need for *greater transparency*. If there is to be a reversal from fragmentation, and cooperative efforts at integration, policymakers and the wider public need to have confidence in each other. Banks need to be forthcoming in disclosing their financial positions and prospects. Data in a particular country need to be consistent and comparable with those in each other country, and there needs to be general oversight to ensure that this is indeed the case. Thus, the proposed asset quality review is important, as well as that the results, and the details of the methodologies, are published. The SSM will rightly undertake such a review as it takes on its role, and it will have powers heretofore not available to ensure cross-country consistency, as well as to enhance disclosure. As is increasingly recognized, it will be important to have a framework for resolution or recapitalization of the banks fully in place by the time of the review, so that any problems that emerge can be promptly addressed.

There needs also to be transparency over how much is not known. Especially in a crisis, outcomes are uncertain. Precision may be desirable, but spurious, and optimistic targets may be confused with central projections and thus lead to disappointment if not realized. Start dates for the SSM, and dates for countries under stress to recover market access, are examples where subsequent postponements have risked leading to disappointments and loss of credibility more generally. Even worse, overoptimistic targets risk inducing policymakers to go ahead with policies prematurely to avoid market reaction; the ECB has rightly been adamant that it will not succumb to any such pressures and will not declare the SSM effective before it is confident that the necessary requirements are in place.

The third theme is that of the need to *establish and maintain strong banks*. Capital buffers are the first line of defense against a bank's losses. Deficiencies in early Basel agreements have been among the factors blamed for bank failures in the global financial crisis, and a new Basel agreement has been put in place to combat such deficiencies. The Basel III agreement prescribes a significant strengthening in banks' capital; further increases in the levels of minimum capital have been proposed by the Financial Stability Board for systemically important banks and incorporated in the EU's Capital Requirements Directive (CRD IV), with some countries indicating that they will require levels even above those being mandated under Basel and the prospective EU directive.

Against that, banks argue that tougher capital standards impede their ability to lend, and thus dampen economic growth. Although their argument is exaggerated,[1] low economic growth and policymakers' keenness to stimulate without using fiscal resources have given arguments more weight at this time than might otherwise be the case. Most importantly, such arguments may influence regulators, supervisors, and policymakers as they implement CRD IV. In the low-growth environment, when banks are most fragile, the requirements put upon them are likely to be less strong, and over a more extended period, than would otherwise be the case. A number of the Basel proposals have been adapted for CRD IV, arguably thereby weakening it. Extending the transition period, as has occurred, would be a valid response to the conjunctural weakness, but setting lower standards for the end of the period would not help establish and maintain a strong European banking sector for the future. Responding to subregional cyclical differences in economic and financial conditions may well become the role of macroprudential policies.

Taking forward the reform agenda set out in this book is urgent and critical for resolving the crisis. It cannot wait until the conjectural environment has improved. Indeed, as argued here, the environment may well not improve until the reform agenda is in place. Reversing the fragmentation in EU financial markets, enhancing disclosure of financial statements, and increasing transparency

---

[1] See Oliveira and Elliott (2012).

more generally, as well as building strong banks, are necessary and interrelated conditions for taking forward the agenda to establish the new architecture for European financial oversight.

PARADIGM SHIFTS

The new architecture is being established against two emerging paradigm shifts: first, that financial sector oversight in the EU can no longer be predominantly national; and second, that concern for financial sector stability will no longer be an argument justifying that the public sector (the "taxpayer") will come first to pick up the pieces when things go wrong. The new paradigms themselves are not fully evolved, but nevertheless they provide a framework under which policymakers now operate. The growing perception that the EU's financial sector problems are likely to be resolved through action at a Union (or euro area) rather than national level, and that it is bank creditors rather than taxpayers that have to be bailed in first, is very different from that held for instance during the Nordic banking crises of the 1990s.

The introduction of the euro transformed the economic environment, not only of those economies already in the Euro but also those seen to be aspiring to membership. Interest rates were lower, and borrowing and inward investment higher, in the "peripheral" economies in southern Europe and the emerging economies of central and Eastern Europe than if those economies were seen as fully self-standing.[2] When the global financial crisis emerged, although it did not originate within Europe, it spread to Europe quickly. The economies at the periphery were among those most affected and were where remedial measures were most out of line with domestic capacity. Their net foreign liabilities were already much higher than those, for instance, in the Asian countries at the time of the crisis there. Substantial policy and institutional innovation has been needed at the regional level and has kept the situation in check. Arguably, however, the limits to this innovation have so far kept the situation fragile, and full recovery not yet assured.

In this context, it is worth stressing that the increased impact of a Union framework in addressing the consequences of the crisis has not been limited to the more visible examples of the countries under "troika" (EU/ECB/IMF) adjustment programs, or even those of the euro area. The establishment of the EU's single market in financial services means that the European financial landscape has been dramatically changed throughout the EU, in particular through the mandate of the Directorate-General for Competition of the European Commission (DG COMP). The major banks in, for instance, Netherlands and the United Kingdom that have received state aid have been required by DG COMP to downsize substantially, in principle providing space for new financial groups to emerge and

---

[2] See, for instance, Enoch and Ötker-Robe (2007).

other groups to operate on a "level playing field."[3] There has been much criticism of the specifics and the timing of DG COMP's interventions, as well as whether the linkage within DG COMP of the competition and financial stability mandates makes sense. However, there has been no questioning of the general principle that competition policy is a legitimate Union concern—one of most integral elements of the single market—and that safeguarding competition is an issue to be addressed at the Union level.

The planned introduction of the SSM as an element toward a full banking union for euro area countries and any other EU members that wish to join is a fundamental step toward increasing decision making at a supernational, if not full Union, level. The implications of the SSM, and the further steps toward a banking union, are discussed in Chapter 1 and subsequent chapters of this volume. Overall, the establishment of the SSM will involve a marked shift in policy responsibilities toward the ECB. A number of important challenges as this shift occurs are enumerated in Chapter 9. In the future, the decision to establish the SSM may be seen as the "tipping point" beyond which a country's economic prospects (at least for all except possibly the few largest) is seen as dependent more upon decisions at the regional level rather than in individual member states.[4]

All this said, the EU works on the principle of subsidiarity, and national authorities are keen to safeguard their involvement in policymaking and in the financial sector infrastructure where this remains effective. For instance, the operation of the payments systems, the heart of the financial sector plumbing, remains under national responsibility. Where a function moves to the Union (or euro area) level, Union (or euro area) decision making involves many participants, ensuring democratic accountability is maintained. This process, however, can give the appearance of dithering and ineffectiveness at times when demonstrations of more rapid and forceful interventions may be critical.

As important, the oversight architecture being put in place is designed under a paradigm that seeks to eliminate, or at any rate to minimize, bailout-related public sector expenditures. The announcement in 2009 by the Irish government of a blanket guarantee on all deposits in Irish banks was fully in line with governments' handling of past financial crises, but it drove up the cost to the public sector of resolving the bank problems beyond the level at which the Irish government was able to pay. So as to avoid deposits flooding to Ireland to take advantage of this guarantee, other EU countries followed suit, offering similar guarantees,

---

[3] This process is in train, for instance in the United Kingdom, although elsewhere—for instance in the Netherlands—such restrictions seem to have largely served to increase the dominance of the unaffected existing banking groups.

[4] The IMF has for some years been conducting Article IV consultations for the euro area, as a complement to the traditional Article IV consultations for individual member states. With the establishment of the SSM further areas of policy are likely to be covered in the euro area consultation; similarly, future EU Financial Sector Assessment Programs may be expanded to assess compliance with the Basel Core Principles at the euro area level, leaving national assessment programs to cover these principles only for those countries that have not joined the SSM.

driving up the potential cost of bank resolution across the region, and reducing the options of how to achieve resolution.

Several interrelated factors have driven the consensus away from using taxpayer money as a first resort for resolving banking problems. The first is that most EU countries feel they have exhausted their fiscal space, and that protecting their banks would not be their greatest priority. In the early stages of the crisis, many countries (including Germany, the Netherlands, and the United Kingdom) spent large amounts to capitalize their banks, while others (such as France) faced large fiscal shortfalls as a direct result of deteriorating economic conditions. As important, the protracted economic slowdown has led to a major deterioration in countries' fiscal positions, with fiscal recovery projected for the periods ahead to be slow and uncertain. In a number of countries, the sovereign has already suffered contamination from its banks. For the sovereign to take on large additional commitments might worsen its position further and, in some extreme cases, not be credible.

Moral hazard is the second factor leading to a change in paradigm. Public sector support is seen as a "bail out" of the banks, which in turn implies that the private sector does not incur the costs of its own actions and may therefore not be deterred from undertaking such actions again. While the recent financial crisis was geographically and quantitatively different from earlier crises, some of the largest banks in the crisis (particularly in the United States) were playing a repeat role, having been involved in other crises in other places. There is an increasing view that, with bail-outs, lessons may not be fully learned, and that behavior leading to crisis may rapidly resume.

The third factor is the feeling that managing banks during restructurings is complicated, and that up-front nationalization with taxpayer money may lead to a deterioration in the quality of the assets, and thereby lower ultimate recoveries. There is evidence in some past cases of a deterioration in the quality of such assets, leaving the state with higher costs than anticipated, for instance in Indonesia,[5] there have been cases where the state has managed its assets well, and substantially recovered its earlier outlays—for instance in Sweden in the Nordic crisis and more recently the takeover of AIG.

Perhaps most fundamentally, there is popular revulsion against using scarce taxpayer resources upfront to bail out banks' risky activities, especially at a time of cuts in many other areas. Widespread stories about bankers' bonuses and pension payoffs have only served to increase this feeling.

There is the empirical question as to how far private sector bail-ins can fully compensate for the withdrawals of public support. This is a work in progress. As discussed earlier in this book, new instruments are being developed that can be used to absorb losses in a bank: contingent capital instruments can add to a bank's capital base.[6] In addition, liabilities of the bank can be subjected to haircuts to

---

[5] In some cases, the shortfall could be attributed to deficiencies in the valuation of the assets at the time of the takeover. Also, direct public sector involvement through nationalization may facilitate control over the institution, avoids having to make excessive concessions to satisfy groups such as potential investors, and enables the taxpayers to benefit on the upside.

[6] See Pazarbasioglu and others (2011).

reduce any remaining hole; minimum levels of bail-inable capital are being defined, so that larger holes can be filled. Also, a significant share of liabilities can be insured, through a deposit guarantee fund, with such a fund preferably financed ex ante by the banking sector but in any case under an authority with powers to levy funds from the banks ex post.

These measures that bear on a bank's balance sheet are to be complemented by three sets of more structural measures. First, as shown in Chapter 14, in some countries there are moves to improve the legal position of creditors, thus enhancing banks' ability to take action against nonperforming debtors, and thereby increase their ability quickly to take control of any nonperforming assets. Second, as shown in Chapter 23, there are plans that large banks involved in "more risky" business have the risky business separately capitalized, in part so that it can be resolved separately without spillover on to the more traditional banking business. Finally, the prospective EU Resolution and Recovery Directive should have clear rules for early intervention, so that a failing bank can be resolved before its losses have grown beyond the capacity for resolution through its own balance sheet and the funds that provide backing.

Even with all these elements in place, bank resolution may continue to need public involvement, albeit at lower levels than hitherto. However, a number of these elements are not certain, and most will take some time. For instance, even when a deposit guarantee scheme is established, it will take time in most countries for levies to produce sufficient funds ex ante that could cover the insured liabilities of a large bank failure. Also, even with all elements in place, there will not be assurance that these will be sufficient. There thus remains a need for public sector backstopping. Arguably, as with liquidity support, the greater the potential availability of such support and the credibility of assurances that it will be provided, the less likely that it will actually be needed.

The new paradigm in Europe therefore focuses on strengthening the banks themselves, and then increasing the share of the bank's balance sheets that is either insured by industry-financed funds or available for bail-in. National fiscal backstopping is needed behind this. Then for those countries without fiscal capacity, there needs to be a regional backstop. It has been agreed that the European Stabilization Mechanism (ESM) can under certain conditions directly recapitalize banks. Although its resources are limited, given that it is to be the backstop to the backstop, they may be sufficient—and experience of recent years has shown that if more is needed there can quickly be agreement that more will be provided. It is strongly urged that agreement on the modalities of accessing the ESM be finalized quickly.[7]

---

[7] The recent experience of Cyprus demonstrates the risks of not having the full oversight infrastructure in place. With banks that were deeply insolvent and had not been resolved at an early stage, with a fiscal authority lacking resources to resolve the banks, and with the ESM and other potential regional backstops not yet operational, extreme measures on the bank's balance sheets were proposed that would have severely undermined confidence if they were to have been applied in a country less perceived as a one-off special case.

VARIABLE GEOMETRY

In moving forward on creating the architecture for financial sector oversight, the EU reaches a new stage. Up to now, there has been a single aspiration to which the "European project" has been heading. Thus, the single currency was designed for the EU as a whole, albeit with two countries having "opt outs" that at least notionally were temporary, and with other member states waiting to meet specified economic criteria before they were admitted. There are other areas where opt outs have been granted to meet specific national concerns: for instance, Denmark has the right to discriminate against foreigners buying certain residential property. Such waivers have not, however, had any systemic impact on the overall perception of an EU heading toward a common goal.

The establishment of the SSM, mandatory for all members of the euro area and open to all others, changes this.[8] Sweden and the United Kingdom have indicated that they do not wish to join the SSM at this time, and other member states may also do so. This is no longer even a "two-speed Europe" since some of the outs have indicated that they do not wish to go at any speed in the direction in which countries of the EA are heading. Meanwhile, the SSM is being followed by important further institutional development, in particular the single resolution mechanism, for SSM countries. The envisaged recapitalization agency, the ESM is only for the countries in the euro area, raising questions as how non-euro area countries that join the SSM will obtain support. Over the next few years, therefore, financial oversight and management across the SSM countries will become increasingly integrated. But as this develops there is a risk that there will be increased fragmentation in the EU outside the SSM area.

The single market is one of the main achievements of the EU, even though it is still a work in progress and has suffered serious setbacks since the onset of the global financial crisis. Moves toward further integration over the past several decades were prompted in part by the vision of an ever-closer union, and also because of perceived instabilities in the halfway house to integration. Thus, a single market without currency union was perceived from the experience of the exchange rate mechanism to be unstable, leading to work that culminated in the introduction of the euro. And now the single currency is seen as unstable, leading to pressures for a banking union as well as a fiscal union. Work is fully in train at least on the first of these.

This raises the question as to whether financial stability in the EU, or even in the SSM member states, can be assured when parts of the EU participate in the single market and yet not in the new elements of the financial oversight infrastructure. After all, every major bank that operates inside the euro area also operates in countries in the EU outside the euro area. Also, one of the key elements of the single market in banking is the single passport: hence the SSM authorities have no power to deny access to the SSM area to a bank that is licensed elsewhere in the EU. Given that the establishment of the SSM is seen

---

[8] Issues concerning the banking union and SSM more generally are covered in Chapters 9 to 11.

as a necessary concomitant to the single market in banking, it may be unclear as to how the establishment of the SSM in only a part of the EU is sufficient to create the conditions to retain the single passport and other elements of the single market in the rest of the EU.

One answer may be that ring-fencing will continue. Unless "out" countries participate in the SSM and the prospective single resolution mechanism, incentives for national action will likely remain as before. While separate capitalization, for instance, may be eliminated within the SSM area, it may persist in the "out" countries, and indeed within the SSM area as a whole vis-à-vis the out countries. This hardly would reflect the necessary re-integration of the EU financial system.

To combat this risk, the establishment of the SSM and the single resolution mechanism for the countries in the SSM cannot be the end of the story. Intensive work also is needed to ensure common supervisory practices across the EU, as well as common arrangements for resolution. Arguably, this can be handled by the SSM bilaterally with the individual "out" authorities. Consistently with past institutional development, however, the European Banking Authority (EBA) would be a natural body to take on this role, consequent on the completion of its "single market rulebook." Consistent application of the single rulebook across the EU is needed to give assurances in both directions: first that the "out" countries are not free-riding by seeking, for instance, to attract banking activity through having a lighter supervisory touch, and on the other hand that the countries of the SSM are not seeking to obtain an unfair advantage through using their dominant position within the EU to turn the rules in their direction. Careful attention will need to be given to ensure that the EBA is able to deliver in this area. It will need to devote resources to explaining this particular aspect of its work, researching and making clear to the wider community the benefits of maintaining the single market in banking, the threats that could undermine the single market, and the losses to the Union as a whole if it were to fall apart. At the moment the ECB has insufficient resources even for its current responsibilities.[9] Also, there has so far been no recourse to its powers for mandatory mediation, which might be considered a precursor to the role that is envisaged here. Urgent consideration should therefore be given to a model of partnership, wherein the EBA works with the EU supervisors—the SSM and the "out" authorities—to ensure the level playing field across the EU. The agreement of December 2012 for a "double majority" of the SSM countries and the "out" countries will have been a helpful step to bring this about if all member countries accept the concept of the variable geometry within the opportunities and constraints of the single market.

As important will be the need to find a way to ensure ex ante arrangements for resolution across the EU that can generate sufficient confidence to foster the dismantling of intra-EU ring fencing and the continued acceptance of the single European passport for banking. Much work has been undertaken by the Financial

---

[9] Priorities for, and constraints on, the EBA are covered in Chapter 16.

Stability Board on the Key Attributes of resolution (see Chapter 7). Also, the United Kingdom has recently announced an agreement with the U.S. Federal Deposit Insurance Corporation on a Single Point of Entry approach for large banks, under which national authorities defer to the home country authority for the resolution of the whole bank, and that the home country tries to achieve this by working first on the holding company above the bank while in principle allowing the banking subsidiary to continue operating. While these proposals are primarily intended for systemically important banks, and serious questions remain as to how easily the Single Point of Entry can be applied, they could have applicability for other cross-border banks in the EU.

In this connection, as cross-border financing of bank resolution develops—through single country resolution funds, the ESM, or possible successor agencies—clarity will be needed as to how the "out" countries interact with those in the SSM. For example, the United Kingdom has contributed to the multiparty financing package for Ireland but declined involvement elsewhere. Correspondingly, it is understood that the United Kingdom would continue to follow the practice it has adopted so far during the crisis and resolve any U.K. bank where needed entirely through its own resources. Insofar as there are banks that operate in the EU, both in SSM and non-SSM countries, cross-border issues are likely to be resolved in line with the Key Attributes for resolution developed by the Financial Stability Board, and with the EU's Resolution and Recovery Directive. And where state aid is concerned, under existing rules, DG COMP will seek to ensure comparability across the Union.

In short, it should be possible to progressively eliminate fragmentation in EU banking within a framework of variable geometry in the EU, given the overarching EU framework on regulations, resolution, state aid, and associated issues. This is possible as long as all member states, including those not participating in the SSM, cooperate in ensuring a level playing field for supervision and resolution, and demonstrate their ability and commitment to resolve any emerging banking problems within these emerging frameworks. The EU has shown resilience in other areas of the agenda where "one size does not fit all." This may be a further area for meeting such challenges.

FINANCIAL CENTERS

In the United States, particular states have emerged as the dominant location for particular types of activity. Similarly in Europe, a number of countries have developed particular specialties or attractions that have led them to attract a disproportionate share of a segment of the EU's financial business (see Chapter 8). Most importantly, London is the host for a large part of the EU's banking activity, while Luxembourg is dominant in particular segments. Among countries in the periphery, before the crisis Ireland attracted much business, aided at least in part by its low corporate tax rates, while banks in Cyprus held volumes many times the size of the country's gross domestic product in large deposits from outside the EU.

While the activities of some of these centers have caused irritation and concern elsewhere in the EU, particularly when they fell into difficulty, the enduring nature of the major financial centers indicates that they are seen as benefitting both the centers themselves and the EU as a whole. Although the EU is a large market, much of its banking activity relates to the rest of the world, and the infrastructure requirements for global activity may be different from those that are employed for activity within the EU. All major EU banks divide their activities between those conducted locally and those in London (as well as cross-border in the EU and sometimes in other financial centers, too). Analogously, in the United States international business is conducted from New York; also, 75 percent of non-U.S. business of U.S. banks is reportedly conducted through London.

One risk to the EU of having financial centers within the Union area is that a country seeking to attract such business may distort the level playing field by offering fiscal or other financial incentives, or by being less intrusive in its prudential oversight. The "soft touch" approach to supervision indeed seems to have been one of the selling points of putative financial centers before the crisis. That model has now been discredited. Indeed, with depositors and investors nervous about the safety of their deposits or investments, the picture has reversed, and centers seem to be seeking business on the basis of how tough their supervisory regime now is. This has led, for instance, to accusations that prudential requirements above regulatory minima may reflect "gold plating," and that regulatory requirements should therefore also represent levels of "maximum harmonization." While there may be something to this argument, in the present environment it is not tenable to deny individual countries scope to raise requirements above minimal levels if they consider this necessary on prudential grounds. It is therefore recognized that capital requirements on banks will vary somewhat from country to country, but it is not clear whether those in financial centers will be higher or lower than elsewhere.

The other main risk is that a country is so successful in attracting business that a level of activity results that the country itself could not handle if its banks fell into difficulty. A difference with New York is that the State of New York would not have to handle problems that arise from activity on Wall Street. In the EU, countries participating in the SSM will progressively benefit from the resolution infrastructure being established for the SSM members. Other countries would likely be much more on their own. Given the integration within the EU, and the intensity of spillover effects in the event of difficulty in a major member state of the EU, there is clearly a common interest in securing full assurances that each member state has capacity to resolve any banks in its jurisdiction that fall into difficulty. As noted above, this will require, among other things, intensive work between the SRM and the authorities in the various "out" countries.

In short, especially after the Cyprus experience, countries may be leery about seeking to establish themselves as financial centers. Moreover, in an environment of nervousness and fragility, they may not be very successful if they try to do so through measures that reduce the soundness of activities in their jurisdictions.

Asset quality reviews and enhanced oversight, particularly within the SSM area, are likely to further reduce the scope for developing a financial center through unsound practices, and assessment of resolution capacity should mitigate the risks if such centers do develop. Possibly the security of the single currency, and the progressive integration of the financial sector oversight framework more generally, will lead business to move toward the SSM area. If so, the synergies inherent in close geographic proximity may lead to the emergence of a financial center within the SSM area, possibly in the location of the SSM headquarters itself. On the other hand, measures such as a transaction tax, if applied through part of the Union, could lead business to redomicile to parts where the tax is not levied. In any case, market-distorting restrictions intended to attract centers are likely to be counterproductive. In an EU with a healthy financial sector, properly supervised financial centers—which may be general or seek a specific market niche—will make a positive contribution to the EU economy as a whole.

BEYOND THE CONSTRAINTS: A TREATY FOR FINANCIAL STABILITY

Views differ as to how far one can take the development of the financial oversight infrastructure without seeking a change in the present EU Treaty. The various steps envisaged in the near term for establishing an SSM and a single resolution mechanism can be achieved without treaty change, although working with the present treaty means working around certain constraints. Meanwhile, partly because of limitations as to what can be done under the existing treaty, certain elements of establishing a comprehensive architecture are being left to a later stage. Correspondingly, key elements of the infrastructure now being introduced could be made more robust at a later stage if they were also incorporated into a new Treaty. In the long term, a Treaty for Financial Stability—when the time is right—would give prominence to financial stability as a central area for EU oversight and be a culmination of the process of building the infrastructure that has been going on since before the start of the crisis. It should be stressed again, however, that the fact that the ultimate Banking Union may well involve treaty change is not an argument for delaying the establishment of the SSM and single resolution mechanism as quickly as it is possible safely to do.

Regarding the first of the factors listed above, one key element that a Treaty could address is the emergence of the SSM and its complementary institutions as key elements of financial sector oversight within the EU. Under the present Treaty, all ECB decisions must formally be taken by the Governing Council, and only member states using the single currency can participate on the council. This becomes problematic insofar as the SSM includes countries that have not adopted the single currency. The ECB has worked around this, with a separate body taking decisions on supervisory matters, with the Governing Council limited to a ratifying role, but a separate decision-making body for supervisory matters would accord better with the reality. Perhaps more problematically, decisions by the Council of the EU require the votes of all EU members, with unanimity required for some decisions and qualified majorities for others. There would seem to be scope for some decisions regarding supervision and related matters affecting only those member states participating in the SSM to be decided just by those member states.

Much can be done without a change in the Treaty and should not be delayed because Treaty change may be useful for some later stages of the reform program. Beyond that, however, the establishment of a Single Resolution Authority may also be facilitated by Treaty change insofar as it involves potential commitments of the funds of a member state to another member state. While, as discussed above, the prospective single resolution mechanism, together with the innovative approach to bail-ins, may limit the need for cross-country backstopping, its potential availability could serve to reassure markets and could provide incentives for member countries in the SSM to exercise effective oversight of the banking systems in the SSM area as a whole.

There has been a thoroughgoing restructuring of the EU's financial oversight infrastructure over the past few years. It would be helpful to codify these, and therein identify possible inconsistencies and gaps. The result would also be legally more robust and therefore deter opportunistic challenges that might emerge with the present regulatory backing. Although such challenges might be frivolous with little chance of success, they could be distinctly unhelpful at a time of fragility.

Finally, financial stability could be specified as an area of EU competence, alongside competition policy, agriculture, and others. It could give an overarching framework both for the SSM and its complementary mechanisms, as well as the further integration envisaged by the participating countries. At the same time it could codify the arrangements regarding countries in the EU (or more broadly in the European Economic Area) so as to avoid segmentation from the SSM participants, safeguard financial stability across the region, and ensure the prospective reestablishment and development of the single market for the wider membership. Even if at the moment only an aspiration for the medium term, this would be a fundamental achievement for the EU, and would make a significant contribution to fostering strong and sustainable growth for the foreseeable future.

REFERENCES

Enoch, Charles, and İnci Ötker-Robe, eds., 2007, *Rapid Credit Growth in Central and Eastern Europe: Endless Boom or Early Warning* (New York: Palgrave Macmillan).

Oliveira, André, and Douglas Elliott, 2012, "Estimating the Costs of Financial Regulation," IMF Staff Discussion Note No. 12/11 (Washington: International Monetary Fund).

Pazarbasioglu, Ceyla, Jianping Zhou, Vanessa Le lisle, and Michael Moore, 2011, "Contingent Capital: Economic Rationale and Design Features," IMF Staff Discussion Note No. 11/01 (Washington: International Monetary Fund).

Contributors

Nikita Aggarwal is a consulting counsel in the IMF's Legal Department, advising primarily on legal frameworks for financial sector supervision, crisis resolution, and sovereign debt management. Prior to joining the IMF, Ms. Aggarwal worked as a lawyer in the London, Singapore, and Beijing offices of Clifford Chance LLP, specializing in EU financial regulation and sovereign debt restructuring. Ms. Aggarwal holds an LLB from the London School of Economics and Political Science, and is a qualified solicitor of England and Wales.

Wouter Bossu is deputy to the assistant general counsel of the Financial and Fiscal Law Unit of the IMF's Legal Department, providing advice on legal frameworks for financial systems of advanced, emerging market, and developing countries. Previously, he was the head of the financial law unit in the National Bank of Belgium and also worked at the European Central Bank. He was educated in law and business administration at Leuven University.

Ana Fiorella Carvajal is a senior financial sector expert in the IMF's Monetary and Capital Markets Department, where she focuses on regulation and supervision of securities markets and shadow banking. She has conducted assessments of the regulatory framework for securities markets in both industrialized and emerging market jurisdictions, and provided technical advice to a wide range of emerging market countries. Ms. Carvajal holds a law degree and a master's degree in public administration.

Jorge Chan-Lau is a senior fellow at the Fletcher School, Tufts University, a senior economist at the IMF, and the author of the comprehensive how-to manual, *Systemic Risk Assessment and Oversight* (Risk Books, 2013). At the IMF, he leads analytical and policy work on stress testing and systemic risk and has been a regular contributor to the IMF's *Global Financial Stability Report*. His published research work covers capital markets, risk analysis, financial regulation, macroprudential policy, and asset allocation. He has also served as an advisor on systemic risk to the central banks of Canada, Chile, and Malaysia, and managed a pilot frontier markets local currency portfolio at the International Finance Corporation in 2007–08. He has PhD and MPhil degrees from the Graduate School of Business, Columbia University, and a BS in Civil Engineering from Pontificia Universidad Católica del Perú.

Marc Dobler is a senior financial sector expert in the IMF's Monetary and Capital Markets Department.

Charles Enoch is a deputy director of the Monetary and Capital Markets Department of the IMF. In 2012, he led the IMF's first Financial Sector Assessment Program exercise for the European Union. He has contributed to a number of published volumes and edited several books, including *Rapid Credit Growth in Central and Eastern Europe: Endless Boom or Early Warning?* (Palgrave Macmillan, 2007). He led teams conducting the IMF's financial sector work during the Asian and Central/East European crises. He holds a PhD from Princeton University and an MA from Cambridge University.

Luc Everaert is an assistant director in the Monetary and Capital Markets Department of the IMF, focusing on sovereign risk, sovereign asset and liability management, nonbank financial intermediation, and financial stability. Previously he worked at the IMF on the euro area. He holds a PhD in International Economics from the Graduate Institute of International Studies in Geneva.

Dale Gray is a senior risk expert in the Financial Sector Assessments and Policies Division of the Monetary and Capital Markets Department of the IMF. He has developed risk and finance tools for balance sheet risk analysis in economies and linkage to macroeconomic models. He is coauthor of the book *Macrofinancial Risk Analysis* (Wiley, 2008), and has published forty-four papers and articles. He regularly teaches and gives presentations to central banks and at risk conferences. He previously worked on Wall Street, at the World Bank, and as advisor to various governments. He has developed macro-financial risk and valuation models for systemic risk, sovereign bank risk, network models, and integrating the financial sector into dynamic stochastic general equilibrium/macro models. He has a PhD from the Massachusetts Institute of Technology, a master's degree from Stanford University, and is a Certified Financial Risk Manager.

Alessandro Gullo is a counsel for the IMF's Legal Department, advising on supervision and resolution regimes of financial institutions, crisis management, and public financial management. Prior to joining the IMF in 2008, Mr. Gullo worked for international law firms. He Gullo received an LLM with distinction in International Legal Studies from Georgetown University and a law degree from the University of Rome "La Sapienza." He is admitted to the bar in New York and Italy.

Daniel C. Hardy is an advisor at the IMF. In the course of his career, he has worked on a wide range of industrialized, emerging market, and developing countries. He has contributed to macroeconomic surveillance, financial sector surveillance, and, in particular, Financial Sector Assessment Programs, as well as the design and implementation of IMF-supported programs, policy development, and technical assistance. His recent research has centered on bank behavior, stability analysis, and political economy issues.

Heiko Hesse is an economist in the Monetary and Capital Markets Department at the IMF, where he works on financial crisis issues and most recently on the European Union financial sector assessment. Before that he worked on the Turkish financial sector. He also covers the banking sector in the Romania program. Previous IMF assignments include a number of Middle East countries, and he has been a contributor to the *Global Financial Stability Report*. Prior to joining the IMF, he worked for the World Bank, on the Commission on Growth and Development. He holds a PhD in Economics from the University of Oxford and was a Visiting Scholar at Yale.

Barend Jansen is assistant general counsel in the Legal Department of the IMF, where he heads the Financial and Fiscal Law Unit. Prior to the IMF he worked for eighteen years at the central bank of the Netherlands, where he was involved in the preparation of the third stage of the European Monetary Union. At the IMF Mr. Jansen's expertise spans financial sector law reform and policy issues in the areas of central banking, banking, bank restructuring and resolution, and nontax fiscal matters.

Nadege Jassaud is a senior economist in the Monetary and Capital Markets Department (Financial Crisis Division) at the IMF. She was recently involved in the bank restructuring of the Greek program, as part of the Troika in 2011–12. She has also coauthored an IMF Staff Discussion Note on bail-in and contributed to an IMF board paper on macroprudential policies. Prior to the IMF, she was deputy head of the Financial Stability Division at Bank of France. Nadege obtained a master's degree in political finance from Sciences Po Paris, and in financial markets from Universite de Louvain La Neuve. She is a lecturer in finance at the University Paris Dauphine.

Luc Laeven is deputy division chief in the IMF's Research Department and Chaired Professor of Finance at Tilburg University. Prior to this, he was a senior economist at the World Bank. His research focuses on banking and international finance issues, and has been published in top academic journals, including the *American Economic Review*, *Journal of Finance*, *Journal of Financial Economics*, and *Review of Financial Studies*. He is the coauthor of *Completing the Eurozone Rescue: What More Needs to Be Done?* (voxEU.org, 2010), and coeditor of *Systemic Financial Crises: Containment and Resolution* (Cambridge University Press, 2012), *Deposit Insurance around the World: Issues of Design and Implementation* (MIT Press, 2008), and *A Reader in International Corporate Finance* (World Bank, 2006). He is a Research Fellow at the Centre for Economic Policy Research (CEPR) in London and a Research Associate at the European Corporate Governance Institute (ECGI). He studied economics and finance at Tilburg University, the University of Amsterdam, and the London School of Economics.

Fabiana Melo is a senior financial expert in the Financial Regulation and Supervision Division of the IMF's Monetary and Capital Markets Department. Since joining the IMF in 2009, she has been involved in Basel III/G20-related policy work, including the revision of the Core Principles for Effective Supervision, as well as several Financial Sector Assessment Programs and surveillance. Before joining the IMF, she worked at the Banco Central do Brasil, where she was involved in the development of prudential regulation and implementation of international regulatory standards, in particular, the Basel

Core Principles for Effective Banking Supervision, and regulatory convergence within Mercosur. She was responsible for the Basel II implementation project in Brazil until 2009, and participated in several international working groups with the Basel Committee, including the Core Principles Liaison Group and the Capital Working Group. Mrs. Melo studied international relations and has an MSc in Economics from the University of Brasilia.

Michael Moore is the deputy division chief of the Financial Sector Oversight Division, which is part of the Monetary and Capital Markets Department at the IMF. His primary responsibilities in this role are to develop IMF policy and operational positions on financial sector supervision and regulation. Prior to this he held the position of deputy division chief of the Financial Market Integrity Division, where he was responsible for the development of the IMF's policy and operation positions for financial integrity. Prior to joining the IMF, Mr. Moore worked as a senior analyst and bank supervisor for the U.S. Federal Reserve.

Marta Rodríguez-Vives is currently a senior economist in the Fiscal Policies Division at the European Central Bank. Her research interests include government debt and fiscal sustainability risks, the balance-sheet approach to the correction of macroeconomic imbalances, and the linkages between the government sector and the financial system. She holds a PhD in Business Administration and a Postgraduate Diploma in Economic Policy.

Scott Roger joined the IMF in 1998, working in the Asia and Pacific Department and then the Monetary and Capital Markets Department. There he focused primarily on monetary policy issues, including inflation targeting and macroprudential policies, drawing on his previous experience as a central banker at both the Bank of Canada and the Reserve Bank of New Zealand. More recently, Mr. Roger served at the IMF European Office, liaising with the Organization for Economic Co-operation and Development and the Bank for International Settlements. He is now serving as the coordinator of the IMF's Pacific Financial Technical Assistance Centre in Suva, Fiji.

Virginia Rutledge was formerly a senior counsel in the IMF's Legal Department.

Nolvia N. Saca-Saca is currently a senior economist in the Monetary and Capital Market Department of the IMF, where she works on the area of crisis management and bank resolution. She participated in a secondment program to Pacific Investment Management Company, where she worked on economic analysis and research on emerging market countries. Prior to joining the IMF, she held a variety of positions in public and academic institutions in El Salvador, including eight years as economic advisor of the Central Bank of El Salvador. She holds a PhD in Economics from the University of Kiel, a Postgraduate Diploma in International Economics from the Graduate Institute for International Studies in Geneva, and an Advanced Studies Certificate in Economic Policy Research from the Kiel Institute of World Economics.

Thierry Tressel is a senior economist in the European Department of the IMF, covering euro area and European Union policies. Previously he worked in the Research and Asian Departments of the IMF on macroeconomic issues, development and finance, and on emerging markets. He joined the IMF in 2002, and previously worked at the Organization for Economic Co-operation and Development and the World Bank. He has published in books and academic journals, including the *Journal of Finance*, *Journal of International Economics*, *Journal of Financial Intermediation*, *Journal of Economic Growth*, *Journal of the European Economic Association*, and volumes by the National Bureau of Economic Research. He holds a PhD in Economics from the Ecole des Hautes Etudes en Sciences Sociales and an engineering degree from the Ecole Polytechnique in Paris.

Rodolfo Wehrhahn is a senior financial sector expert in the IMF's Monetary and Capital Markets Department, currently responsible for advice on insurance and pensions. He was formerly a senior insurance specialist at the World Bank. Since 2008, working at the World Bank and the IMF, he has provided advice on and evaluated the performance of the supervision and regulation of insurance and pensions in advanced and developing economies, including the United Kingdom, Spain, the European Union, Japan, Italy, Mexico, Brazil, Israel, Russia, Mozambique, Nigeria, and Indonesia. He has carried out full assessments of the International Association of Insurance Supervisors principles, and appraised the stability of the insurance and pension sectors, and also worked in multiple technical assistance projects globally in insurance and pension supervision, development, and Microinsurance. He has also worked in the private sector and as a lecturer and researcher in mathematics and physics at the University of Hamburg. He holds PhD and master's degrees in mathematics, as well as a master's degree in physics from the University of Hamburg, Germany.

Froukelien Wendt is a senior financial sector expert at the IMF, with a specialization in financial market infrastructures. She is responsible for policy development and has participated in various Financial Sector Assessment Programs, with a focus on central counterparties and central securities depositories. She also participated actively in the development of the new international principles for financial market infrastructures. Before joining the IMF she worked at the World Bank, De Nederlandsche Bank, and NYSE Euronext.

Jianping Zhou is a Senior Economist in the IMF's Monetary and Capital Markets Department, focusing on financial sector assessment in the European countries. Previously she worked with the IMF's European and Asian Departments, covering euro area and emerging economies, including China and Korea. She has published on macroeconomic adjustment, policies for too-big-to-fail institutions, and crisis management and resolution in Europe. She holds a BS in mathematics from Zhejiang University and a PhD in economic from Georgetown University.

Index

Note: Boxes are denoted by b; figures by f; notes by n; and tables by t.